This Alchemical Great Work changes everything that has ever been written about the magic of stones. The mystery is revealed! The greatest spiritual path is everywhere around us. We are standing on it every moment—Earth, and Her presence as the harmonious, inaudible songs of stones. We normally cannot see the Earth as Spiritual Earth because more than seeing is required—it takes the unfolding, the doing, the alchemical living that Robert Simmons presents here, establishing working with stones as the single spiritual path most worth engaging.

—Robert Sardello, author of *Silence: The Mystery of Wholeness* and *Heartfulness*

The Stones and the Earth are alive, and Robert Simmons has noticed it! The Alchemy of Stones *takes readers deep into the World Interiority, where we meet and become friends with the Stone People. This breaks the terrible spell of materialism and dissolves the fantasy of objectivity. In this book, we discover that the ancient art of alchemy is very much alive within the serious and playful work of soul-making that the Stone People are ready to do with us. Robert's special genius is his ability to sense and interpret the energies and messages of stones. His articulation of a new worldview—a vision within which the stories and music of the Stone Beings, the Earth, and the Cosmos are re-enlivened—is truly magical.*

—Daniel Deardorff, author of *The Other Within: The Genius of Deformity in Myth, Culture, and Psyche*

The Alchemy of Stones *is a valuable book of healing and transformation that is both approachable to those who are new to working with stones, yet deep enough to keep the advanced practitioner interested. Robert's attention to detail and love of the Stone Beings makes for enjoyable reading that is educational and inviting to the magical mind (imagination). Filled with detailed techniques, meditations, and crystal recommendations for use on self or with others, this is sure to be a book utilized by Healers for years to come. I personally was moved by the focus on creating a reciprocal relationship with the Stone Beings and the Wisdom of the Earth itself. I believe this connection is paramount for navigating the changing times we live in.*

—Salicrow, psychic medium and author of *Jump Girl*

The Alchemy of Stones *by Robert Simmons is by far the best and most inspired book I have ever read on the alchemical healing power of stones. It is no coincidence that in the timeless art of alchemy the experience of connecting with the Higher Self is symbolically expressed as* the lapis *or* The Philosopher's Stone. *There is real magic and something sacred—beyond the merely physical—to be found in stones and our relationship to them. I was totally amazed, and utterly delighted, when I began reading this book. Much to my surprise, I couldn't put it down, as there was similar magic being transmitted through its very words! I noticed that I began telling everyone I knew who had even the slightest interest in the healing power in rocks, stones, gems, and crystals that they should read this book. I can't recommend* The Alchemy of Stones *highly enough.*

—Paul Levy, author of *Dispelling Wetiko* and *The Quantum Revelation*

The Alchemy of Stones

OTHER BOOKS

by Robert Simmons

The Book of Stones

The Pocket Book of Stones

Stones of the New Consciousness

Moldavite: Starborn Stone of Transformation (with Kathy Warner)

Earthfire

The Alchemy of Stones

Co-creating with Crystals, Minerals and Gemstones for Healing and Transformation

A Sacred Planet Book

ROBERT SIMMONS

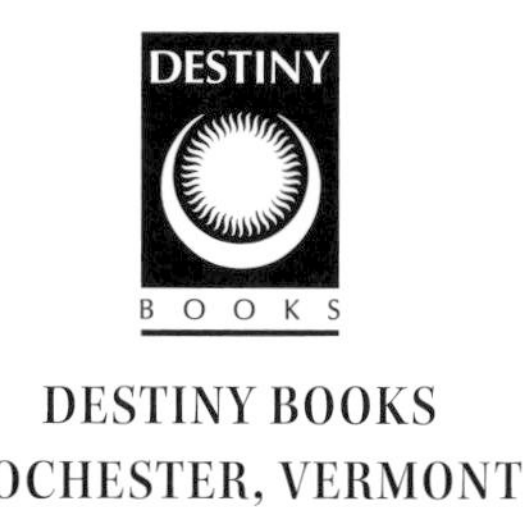

DESTINY BOOKS
ROCHESTER, VERMONT

Destiny Books
One Park Street
Rochester, Vermont 05767
www.DestinyBooks.com

Destiny Books is a division of Inner Traditions International

Sacred Planet Books are curated by Richard Grossinger, Inner Traditions editorial board member and cofounder and former publisher of North Atlantic Books. The Sacred Planet collection, published under the umbrella of the Inner Traditions family of imprints, publishes on the themes of consciousness, cosmology, alternative medicine, dreams, climate, permaculture, alchemy, shamanic studies, oracles, astrology, crystals, hyperobjects, locutions, and subtle bodies.

This edition published by Destiny Books by arrangement with Heaven & Earth Publishing, East Montpelier, Vermont

Grateful acknowledgment is made to Simon McDonald for use of the photograph (page 198) of the labyrinth at the Te Moata Retreat Centre, Coromandel Peninsula, New Zealand.

Cataloging-in-Publication Data for this title is available from the Library of Congress

ISBN 978-1-64411-309-7 (print)
ISBN 978-1-64411-310-3 (ebook)

Printed and bound in Canada by Transcontinental Printing

10 9 8 7 6 5 4 3 2 1

Text design and layout by Margery Cantor
Cover design by Robert Simmons, Patrick Gaudreault, and Aaron Davis
This book was typeset in Kepler

To send correspondence to the author of this book, mail a first-class letter to the author c/o Inner Traditions • Bear & Company, One Park Street, Rochester, VT 05767, and we will forward the communication, or contact the author directly at **http://heavenandearthjewelry.com**.

DISCLAIMER

This book is not a substitute for professional medical or psychological advice and care. The author of this book does not dispense medical advice or prescribe the use of stones as a form of treatment for medical or psychological conditions. Readers should regularly consult a physician and seek professional medical advice about any physical, medical, psychological, or emotional matters that may require diagnosis or medical attention. The statements in this book have not been evaluated by the Food and Drug Administration. This book is not intended to be used to diagnose, treat, cure or prevent disease.

The information discussed in this book regarding the metaphysical properties of stones is intuitively derived and has not been scientifically evaluated. Readers are advised to view this information as speculative in nature, and to evaluate it in light of their own experiences. The author's intent is only to offer information of a general nature to help readers in their spiritual quest for higher consciousness and well-being. In the event that you use any of this information in this book for yourself, the author and publishers assume no responsibility for your actions.

CONTENTS

Acknowledgments IX

Dedication to Daniel Deardorff XI

Introduction XV

Author's Foreword XIX

1. The Golden Threads 1

2. Discovering the Alchemical Worldview 9

3. Panpsychism 15

4. Alchemy & True Imagination 25

5. The Psychoid-Imaginal Realm 37

6. Sophia 45

7. Sophia, the Deep Self & the Heart 57

8. Transformation Through Feedback: Alchemy, Sophia & the Oroborous 67

9. The Activity of Blessing 79

10. Transcendence Through the Alchemical Union of Opposites 87

11. Conjunction 95

12. Reunion 103

13. Forgiveness 111

14. Ascension of the Heart 117

15. Triality, Transcendence & Transformation 131

16. Stone Beings & the Imaginal Realm 139

17. The Subtle-Imaginal Body 147

18. The Subtle-Imaginal Body, Chinese Alchemy, & Immortality 159

19. Manifestations 167

20. Stone Mandalas: Synergies of Energy & Meaning 175

21. Working with Mandalas & the Stone Beings 187

22. Stone Body Layouts for Healing & Visionary Experience 201

23. Photonic Stone Layouts 221

24. Photonic Layouts for Earth Ascension and DNA Activation 231

25. Stone Elixirs & Crystal Waters 241

26. Orgone & Orgonite Stone Energy Devices 253

27. An Alchemist's Laboratory of Crystal Tools 263
28. Stone-Enhanced Body Mats 271
Interlude: You Can Judge This Book by Its Cover 276
29. Moldavite: The First Cornerstone 279
30. Phenacite: The Second Cornerstone 291
31. Azeztulite: The Third Cornerstone 305
32. Rosophia: The Fourth Cornerstone 351
33. The Redemption of the Earth—Commitment to the Impossible 359
Epilogue: The Alchemy of Stones in Daily Life 376

Appendix A: Robert Simmons and Daniel Deardorff Discuss the Subtle Body 379
Appendix B: Climate Change & Crystals 383

Stone Dictionary 387
Stone Property Reference Index 453
Suggested Reading 468
Resources 469
About the Author 470

ACKNOWLEDGMENTS

My deepest gratitude goes to my wife, Kathy Helen Warner, my spiritual partner, best friend and true love. Your wisdom, advice, intuitions and insights have aided and guided me for more than thirty-five years, and your healing presence has helped me to become whole. Your encouragement to venture into the soul work of spiritual alchemy that led to this book has inspired and sustained me on the journey.

I smilingly acknowledge our son Moebius, whose skepticism made me dig deeper and think harder. To our other son Todd and our daughter-in-law Celia, thank you for being a pair of shining stars in my heart. I am grateful to Patrick Gaudreault, whose camaraderie and tireless efforts have greatly supported my company, Heaven and Earth. And more thanks go out to all of our Heaven and Earth crew members in the USA and in New Zealand. To my longtime pal and book designer, Margery Cantor, mucho thanks for co-creating another beautiful book, and for our fun times doing it! To my first New Zealand friends, Kevin and Olga Nicholson, I extend my love and appreciation for our fossicking trips into the bush where we unearthed so many wonderful stones. To John and Keryn Drummond, I offer thanks for sharing rich conversations, close friendship, and patience with my endless rants about stones!

To David Schafer, I owe much gratitude for helping me shape and improve the manuscript of this book. We sometimes encounter great and unexpected acts of generosity, and I received such a gift from you. To Jeanie Shepherd, I reach out in an effort to reflect back the warm humanity you display in your way of being. Dr. Bill Warnock and Michele Starr, thank you for helping me achieve optimal health, and for many years of friendship. To Richard Grossinger and Ehud Sperling, my thanks for helping me bring this book into the world.

I thank my dear friend Robert Sardello, who first taught me about Sophia, Soul of the World, and the spiritual lineage of alchemy. You are a great and dedicated alchemist of the soul. To Robert and Ruth Bly, my sincere love and appreciation for your teachings and your many kindnesses.

To all the readers of my books and to those who have attended my teaching events, thank you for your interest, and for the many, many things I have learned and experienced from you all.

Lastly, my gratitude goes inward to the Stone Beings, whose presence continues to teach and transform me.

And to Sophia, Soul of the World, I offer my breath.

DEDICATION

FOR DANIEL DWAYNE (3D) DEARDORFF
FEBRUARY 12, 1952 – SEPTEMBER 19, 2019

All I have is desire and a stubborn insistence on truth. That can carry you a long way.
—Daniel Deardorff

I dedicate this book to my dear friend and spiritual brother Daniel Deardorff. I had the good fortune to know and love Danny for sixteen years, and our friendship blessed and transformed me in ways that have profoundly shaped my life and work.

Danny was a great soul who lived in a crippled body. He was one of the last few people in America to contract the polio virus, in the mid-1950s, just before the polio vaccine was approved. The disease and multiple surgical interventions that followed left him severely physically deformed and confined to a wheelchair for almost all of his life. His family loved and supported him, but the doctors' prognosis assumed that his life would be brief, and Danny was told he could not expect to be married, father children, or have a career.

Yet great souls have a tendency to prevail, and Danny did so, creating a life that was rich and full. Though he could never walk, he could sing, and sing he did. As a child and young man, he devoted his passion to art and music. At twenty-two, he arrived in Los Angeles and became a full-time recording and concert artist. In the 1980s he toured as the opening act for Seals and Crofts, performing in every state of the United States as well as in Canada and South and Central America. He wrote his own songs and he taught himself to play multiple instruments, including guitar, mandolin, ukulele, harmonica, and drums. Along the way, Danny disproved the doctors' prognosis in other ways, marrying four times and fathering four daughters.

Change came in 1995 when he was forced by post-polio syndrome to retire from full-time work. "I needed a quieter life to preserve my health," he wrote. So began Daniel's scholarship in myth, writing essays and interviews which eventually led to the publication of his book *The*

Other Within: The Genius of Deformity in Myth, Culture and Psyche. In 2003 his mentor, the poet Robert Bly, invited him to teach at the Great Mother Conference. That conference was the occasion of our meeting.

One of the important things that fueled Danny's achievements was living what our teacher Robert Bly called "a life of desire." Bly's way of explaining the difference between mere "wanting" and a "life of desire" went like this: "You may *want* a certain woman to walk over and touch your cowboy hat, and that might happen. Or you may *desire* to be a greater writer than William Shakespeare. That's not going to happen . . . *but desire is sweet, and it will carry you forward.*"

Danny's way of expressing this sentiment, which he lived, through all the years I knew him, was: "If it's not impossible, it's not worth attempting." Danny attempted many impossible things, and the desire that inspired his efforts was the horse he rode through his amazing life. It carried him forward.

This orientation to life is at the very heart of spiritual alchemy, and it is clear to me that Danny was a natural alchemist. The idea—*the desire*—to which all alchemy aspired was the transformation of something imperfect—chaotic, reviled, and rejected—into something divine. This was and is the essence of the alchemical endeavor, whether one is working with physical matter, one's own psyche, the Soul of the World, or all of these together. To do such a thing is obviously impossible—or is it? We don't know, and should not even try to know, because what is important is that our aspiration—our desire—be allowed to carry us forward.

It is hard to know how much to say about my friend in this little essay. I could write a book about him, and perhaps I will one day. He certainly deserves it, and to know about his work and life would enrich anyone. As a musician, mythologist, storyteller, and maker of rituals, Danny enacted the alchemy of taking the chaos of human consciousness—in himself, his audiences, and his students—and refining it into golden moments of awareness that revealed the Divine in the very ashes of our failures and our sorrows.

Danny's music and teachings worked their magic in the hearts of those who heard them, vibrating and resonating within us in ways that brought us to tears and to joy, often at the same time. This was purposeful on his part, and he often said that one must always embrace *both* sides of all polarities. There was to be no shunning of darkness in favor of the attempt to embrace the light. Danny insisted that one-sidedness brings about half-heartedness, and that this error saps our energies, sabotaging any chance of transformation. In this he agreed with the ancient alchemists, and with the genius of psychology, Carl Jung, all of whom maintained that transcendence is fueled through holding the tension of the opposites within oneself.

Daniel Deardorff is one of the unseen authors of this book. Knowing him and loving him carried me forward and helped me understand enough about myself and the world to make this attempt to show that our spiritual work with stones is alchemy. Like me, Danny loved the Beings of the Mineral Kingdom, and he felt their energies. I gave him many stones as gifts, and he kept them around himself in his home and workspace. When he performed or taught, he usually wore a special necklace that I made for him, and he was certain that it brought him energy and protection.

Danny helped me write this book in other ways as well. Our conversations about triality (the "threeness" of things) were important to my understanding of the processes and transformations of spiritual alchemy. During my last long visit with him before he died, Danny listened while I read aloud to him the entire manuscript of this book. His comments helped me enormously in refining my thoughts and words into the form that is present in these pages.

Before ending this tale, I must share with you that I have thus far neglected to mention one of the largest golden ingots in the treasury of our relationship. It was our laughter. We understood each other so well that we could travel together on great long loops of weird words and wild ideas, caring for nothing more than to create our own special brand of craziness. And this was alchemy too. Because we leaped together, creating what the poet Rilke called "the

astounding bridges" between seemingly unconnected things. We often did this for the fun of it, but this same kind of leaping is what informs the best insights I have to offer. And it is this laughter and leaping that filled many of the hours I spent with my dear friend.

My last long visit with Danny was only a few weeks before his death. During that time, we reached what was perhaps the peak of our rapport and intimacy. The nearness of death was surely part of it, because Danny had been very ill just a few months earlier, and his recovery was quite recent. And we had worked intensely together on my manuscript, finishing with just one day to spare. On our last evening, neither of us wanted to say good-bye. But my wife, Kathy, and I finally left, quite late, and we felt that Danny was in good health and good spirits.

Just two weeks later, Danny's final illness suddenly came, and we flew back to his home as fast as we could. I will say nothing about the last day we spent with Danny, his wife, Kate, and three of his daughters, except this: at the end of life, love is all that matters. It may well be that this is just as true every other day.

My wife and I live in New Zealand, and Danny's passing occurred while we were flying home, somewhere over the Pacific Ocean. At one point in the middle of that long night, the Elton John song "Daniel" started playing in my head, and I knew then that my friend was on his journey.

Another strange thing about that night—when we flew to New Zealand from the United States, we crossed the international date line. Going west, it meant that we "lost" a day. On the calendar, we jumped from Wednesday to Friday, and "Thursday" never happened for us. Curiously, that missing Thursday was the day that Danny died. So for me, in a sense, that day never happened, and Danny never died. I can tell you for sure that he will always live within my heart.

INTRODUCTION

BY ROBERT SIMMONS & DANIEL DEARDORFF

If you have read the dedication I wrote for this book, you know that my close friend Daniel Deardorff passed away suddenly, not long before I finished the final draft. We had just spent ten days together, during which I had read the manuscript aloud to him. Danny wanted me to read the book to him because it enhanced the intimacy of our collaboration in regard to the material, and because, as friends, we really enjoyed discussing our ideas and hashing out the best ways to express them.

Danny had already agreed to write an introduction to the book, and during our visit, I told him that I planned to dedicate it to him as well. I'm very glad I did so, because I did not see him again, except for one day a couple of weeks later, when he was in the hospital's intensive care unit.

Then Danny died, and I embarked on my journey into grieving—a descent into the sacred underworld where sorrow and love are joined.

During the weeks that followed, my wife, Kathy, and I arranged to have a session with Sali Crow, a gifted medium. Sali had facilitated spirit communication sessions for us in the past, bringing through departed family members and friends. Starting with a cautious sense of skepticism, I had become completely convinced that Sali was actually able to connect us with our beloved dead. In 2016, I invited Sali to do a "gallery reading" for the participants at the first Alchemy of Stones Intensive. There too she performed her work with astonishing specificity and accuracy.

It was with these memories in mind that I approached Sali in the days after Danny's death. On the morning before the session, I was nervous and hesitant. What if she couldn't connect with him? What if the "Danny" that came through didn't feel authentic? How would I cope

with that? But, ultimately, my desire to reach an "impossible" goal—to know that my friend had transcended death—carried me forward.

I won't go into details of what was said, but I remember that during the evening before the session with Sali, I felt a very strong (and highly unusual, for me) sense of Danny's presence in the room with Kathy and me. And yes, Sali did connect with Danny, in a way that utterly convinced us. And, surprisingly, Danny's spirit was dynamic and full of energy. Having shed the severe limitations of his bedridden body, my friend appeared to be eager to get on with his work from his new position in the Other World. He seemed happy and exhilarated, though he did mention his regret that his abrupt departure left some "loose ends," such as the promised introduction to my book.

But part of his new work, he told me through Sali, was to continue communicating and collaborating with me. Directly. If I agreed to it.

And he suggested that one way it might come easily would be through my writing.

Of course I agreed. But I was not at all confident of my ability to do such a thing. I had never practiced any sort of mediumship, except that I was very well acquainted with tuning in to the messages and spiritual qualities of the Stone Beings.

For two weeks, I felt nothing, other than the waxing and waning of my grief. Kathy and I took a healing vacation to a tropical island, during which I tried unsuccessfully to attune to Danny. I began to think that there would be no inner conversations. I noticed that my emotional body was stressed and agitated, and I was glad to have my Rosophia stone to help me sleep.

Kathy has had a wide spectrum of spiritual experiences in these areas, so I asked her what to do. She suggested that I quiet my thoughts, visualize Danny, and ask him questions. I told her I would try.

The next morning, I took a long walk along the tropical island beach. At some point my thoughts turned to Danny, and I attempted to envision and call to him, as Kathy had suggested. At first, it was a struggle. I wasn't able to hold my thoughts where I wanted them, and I became rather discouraged.

Then I suddenly saw an inner image of Danny, different from the one I had been trying to conjure in my mind. And I could feel him with me.

I can't precisely recall the first thing I asked him; I was too excited retain a clear memory. I have the sense that my question had to do with the book introduction, and whether we could still somehow write it together. And I felt that his reply was, "I'm ready to try."

Next, I wondered what else I should ask. What did I want to know right then? A moment later, it came to me, and I asked: "What is it like where you are now? Could you give me an image or a symbol to help me understand?" An instant later, I got his answer. I saw his fingers holding down strings on the neck of a guitar or ukulele, and I inwardly heard the phrase, *"Where the callus meets the string."*

You may ask, What in the world does *that* mean? But I knew what he was talking about. This phrase and image are one of Danny's classic teaching metaphors—a key one in his book, *The Other Within.* As a musician, he played multiple instruments, guitar and ukulele among them, and he knew that inspiration, discipline, and practice are all necessary if one wants to participate in creating music.

It requires *discipline* and *practice* to bring about the calluses on the fingertips. This involves a painful process, because you can't grow the calluses without pressing down the strings thousands of times. Until the calluses have formed, it hurts! And it is the *inspiration*—the musician's intuitive union with a Divine partner, the *Muse*—that gives him or her the *desire*—the inner fire—to fuel the effort.

So we've looked at the calluses. Now, how about the strings? The strings suggest the instrument itself. It is a material object that one can touch in certain ways, in order to bring something divine—the music—into the world. By itself, a musical instrument is mute—there is no music. By themselves, the musician's hands can conjure no beautiful sounds. The music is neither in the calluses nor the strings, but in the magical, liminal threshold *where they meet.*

At this point, as I contemplated Danny's message, it began to open and expand inside me. He was not only reminding me that the conjuring of music, when it reaches real magic and beauty, is a co-creative venture with a divine partner. Nor was he even simply telling me that art emerges within an alchemical vessel of creation that holds both physical matter and divine energies. *He was telling me that* ***the place*** *where he was residing after death was the very place he had always treasured—where the callus meets the string—where the human and the Divine are joined.*

That is just where Danny would want to be, and where I hope to see him again.

It is in this place, which in this book I call the Imaginal Realm, that the images and patterns expressing the World Interiority are born. *World Interiority* was Danny's phrase referring to the inner consciousness of ourselves and everything else, including the world itself. There we encounter the gods and goddesses of myth, the helping spirits of the shamans, the characters of the Great Stories, the primal archetypes of the psyche, the Stone Beings, and Sophia—Soul of the World.

It is my message in this book—a message Danny demonstrated in his life—that we don't have to wait until we die to go there. In fact, our participation in spiritual alchemy—whether it is the Alchemy of Stones, the alchemy of music and poetry, or the alchemy of living life with True Imagination—takes us into the World Interiority and unites Heaven and Earth.

The Gnostics said that Sophia—Divine Wisdom—was God's partner in creating the Earth and the cosmos. They also said that, because of her love and compassion for this world, she descended from the heavenly Pleroma and allowed herself to become lost in matter. I equate the being "lost" with being "asleep." Sophia's nature is everywhere in the material world, but in matter, she is not yet awakened to full self-awareness. Nonetheless, this means that the feminine Wisdom of God exists in every single speck of the physical world. Heaven and Earth are inherently one, each permeating the other in a co-creating dance out of which everything, including us, comes into manifestation. This dance is *also* "where the callus meets the string." We ourselves, the stones, and the Earth *are the music.*

And not only are we the music—our freedom as sentient beings allows us to *become musicians,* joining in the everlasting co-creative improvisational symphony of being.

Certainly our lives are a kind of music, and if we practice loving kindness and other virtues, we make a helpful contribution. But we can, if we choose, do much more. Like the ancient alchemists, we can try to observe the ways of Sophia—of the Wisdom of the world—and then attempt to help Sophia achieve her desire, her full awakening in the realm of matter. I believe that our work with stones can be a part of this awakening, which will ultimately be experienced as the conscious realization of Heaven and Earth—spirit and matter—as one.

In this book, I will be speaking from the perspective of what I call the alchemical worldview. Spiritual alchemy tells us that there are three worlds—the physical world, the spiritual world, and the imaginal world. Of these, the imaginal world is the overlap between the other two—the place "where the callus meets the string"—a realm that encompasses and includes both spirit and matter.

Danny and I both view the Stone Beings as conscious entities whom we meet in the imaginal world. This does not mean that they are imaginary. It does mean that they operate and interact with us in the realm where the spiritual and the physical are joined. Stone energies cannot be measured by machines, even though many people can most definitely feel them. At the same time, there is nothing in the world more solid and material than a stone.

And like a musical instrument, which is silent and inert until it is properly caressed by skilled and callused hands, the phenomenon of stone energies does not manifest until the stone is held, perceived, and "felt" by a person with a consciousness that is properly aligned to participate in co-creating those energies.

The ability to perceive and attune to the spiritual qualities of stones seems to exist as a latent capacity in many people. Hundreds of times, I have enjoyed being present at the moment when people suddenly discover this ability within themselves—the first time they feel the currents of a stone. Similarly, in the realm of music, a number of people have a latent capacity that we call "talent." In both situations, discipline and practice can enhance the quality of what emerges.

Just as music is not really inside the musical instrument, stone energies are not physically within the stones themselves. Experiencing stone energies is an *event* that can occur where and when a human being and a Stone Being come together. The body of the person and the body of the stone act as "strings," vibrating in resonance with one another. The energy we then experience is the "music."

The joining together of the Stone Being and the human being out of mutual love and their love for Sophia is the Alchemy of Stones. The magical vessel within which the union occurs exists in that liminal place, that threshold, the co-creative realm of the World Interiority—the place where the callus meets the strings.

All of this will be discussed, described, and revealed in the pages to come. I will provide you ways to practice with the stones, in order to grow your calluses. And I will invite you to allow yourself to truly meet the Stone Beings and Sophia. When that occurs, the alchemical fire of inspiration and desire will have been lit within your heart.

I think most readers have understood by now why I have listed myself *and* Daniel Deardorff as co-writers of this introduction. I hope I grasped his communication clearly enough to represent him well. I feel him beside me now as I write these words.

Imagine that.

AUTHOR'S FOREWORD

I always feel very suspicious when somebody assures me that he is very normal. Too many normal people are just compensated madmen.
—Carl Jung

The hermit said: "Because the world is mad,
The only way through the world is to learn
The arts and double *the madness. Are you listening?"*
—Robert Bly, "Listening"

Miracles never happen to sensible people.
—Albert Kreinheder, *Alchemy and the Subtle Body*

I have been involved in the crystal energy subculture for over thirty-three years. Believe me, I didn't plan it that way! I got started because the woman I had fallen in love with, and a stone called Moldavite, nudged me in that direction. And I followed that thread until my own experiences initiated me irrevocably into an unconventional and rather mystical world. Here my soul found a home among people who shared my longing for a lived spirituality. But I had been schooled in science and psychology, and that side of me never went away.

Consequently, even as I have bought and sold stones to people who want them for metaphysical purposes, even as I had more and more experiences of feeling stone energies, even as I wrote several books about the spiritual qualities of stones, I was always searching for a larger framework of understanding. I couldn't be content to just have a collection of experiences. I hoped to understand from a wider perspective what was happening.

My friend Robert Sardello articulated this as the need for a cosmology or worldview within which we could understand and develop the potentials of what is going on (and what else *can* go on) between people and stones. It was Robert who introduced me to the idea of relating to the stones as Beings with whom one is in relationship, rather than as objects (like vitamin pills or mechanical tools) to be used only to make life better for oneself. This by itself changed my paradigm, showing me that the stones—and the world—have soul, and that the most important goals for working with stones may be in regard to being with the stones and the world in a soulful way.

Where could I find a worldview in which my "scientific" side and my mystical side would both be comfortable? During the very first year of my life among the stones, 1985–1986, there was a photocopied document called "The Emerald Tablet" circulating among our customers and other crystal shop owners, and I got a copy. Its tone was strangely compelling, but I could not make heads or tails of its meaning, except that a being named Hermes-Thoth was speaking about spiritual enlightenment and something called alchemy.

I passed the pages on to someone and forgot about them until about ten years later when I ran across a book called *The Emerald Tablet* by a writer named Dennis Hauck. This book described the practice of spiritual alchemy, presenting it as a path still available and useful to modern people. I learned that alchemy was more than the primitive precursor to chemistry I had thought it was. And Hauck's book was more comprehensible to me than the channeled pamphlet I had read so long before. Again, I filed away the information and kept moving on my own path. But the alchemical goals of achieving spiritual awakening and transformation for oneself and the world were very much the same as the personal aspirations I had developed. Alchemy simmered on the back burner of my mind for another decade.

Around 2005, in a course at Robert Sardello's School of Spiritual Psychology, alchemy came up once again. Robert taught that alchemy was part of a spiritual stream that reached back many centuries—through the Cathars, the Troubadours, the Manicheans, and other Gnostic groups nearly two thousand years ago. (This stream goes back even farther, though its traces are not as clear.) I learned too that Carl Jung, founder of analytical psychology, had viewed ancient alchemy as the precursor to psychology. Jung believed that the images from old alchemical engravings symbolically depicted the stages of soul-making that he called *individuation* (a process of achieving wholeness—the "indivisibility" of the self). In discovering Jung's writings on alchemy, I found a worldview that could incorporate both my scientific side and my mystical side. And in his assertion that following the alchemical path could lead to healing, development, and fulfillment of the soul or Self, I found something that corresponded to my own soul's desires.

Eventually, I began reading about alchemy more deeply. In doing so, I recognized a worldview that not only spoke to my soul's longings, but also could accommodate my experiences of stones, and my ideas about them. The alchemists believed, as I did, that consciousness is within everything—that the world is aware and alive, and that the stones are alive in the same way. They even called the great goal of their work the Philosophers' *Stone!* I kept on with my reading, my writing, and my meditations with stones. And the longer I did so, the more I understood that alchemy was a cosmology within which the phenomena and potential of our spiritual engagement with stones made perfect sense. And alchemy could also provide a picture of where our involvement with stones and their energies can go.

This seems important to me because the metaphysical interest in stones is now worldwide, involving millions of people. It has been over thirty years since the crystal fad began; and it has not behaved like a fad. It is more like a spiritual movement—a current within a worldwide tide of transformation.

When I decided to write a book about *The Alchemy of Stones*, my wife, Kathy, who is a gifted intuitive and healer, said, "This project is bigger than you realize, Robert. You are not just going to write about alchemy—you are going to experience it, and it is going to change you." She was right.

As I researched this book, I learned much more about alchemy. But I also experienced some unexpected events. My whole life, from my thinking and feeling to my bodily health, began to transform. This led me to recognize more deeply that alchemy has always been a practice aimed at transformation. The alchemist's desire is to improve or perfect something—whether it be a physical substance, one's body or one's own soul, or all together. In the alchemical paradigm, substance and soul are not separated.

So during the first months of my delving into alchemy and relating it to my work with stones, many things shifted. The first and most surprising was a healing crisis. I became physically ill, with a number of odd and uncomfortable symptoms. This lasted for several months and was accompanied by emotional swings and even some disconcerting events in the outer world of work and relationships. But all of these things eventually lifted; it turned out that my illness ultimately resulted in several long-standing physical problems being cured or dramatically improved. The "illness" was actually a healing. This all happened without medical intervention. Only my wife's shamanic healing sessions, my stone meditations, and my personal inner work were involved.

Throughout this period, Kathy reminded me that I had embarked on an alchemical process and that I would not be able to merely stand outside alchemy and study it. I would also have to live it. As I continued my research, I realized that my several months of difficulty corresponded to the first stage of alchemy, known as the *nigredo* (the blackness). It is described as a state of chaos in which the *prima materia* (the "substance" the alchemist hopes to improve or perfect) is subjected to purgings and purifications. This was exactly what had happened to me.

From this experience, I derived an axiom that I now use to remind myself and to share with others: *When you begin to pay attention to alchemy, alchemy starts paying attention to you.* By this, I mean that there is a field of consciousness that ***is*** alchemy. And when we turn toward it, a kind of spiritual interaction begins. It is something akin to the phenomenon that when we give our full attention to a stone and its energies, its metaphysical qualities begin to affect us. This occurs in other areas of life as well, and is one of the truths that our materialistic culture has made us forget.

So I want to say to you as you read these words: this moment can be an initiation. If you commit your attention, intention, and imagination to what is presented in this book, *you may find yourself experiencing transformation in your life,* both within and beyond your interest in stones. However, if you hold yourself apart from what is presented, you may wonder what all the excitement is about.

In saying this, I am not claiming that this book is magic. I am saying that it is like a road sign pointing in the direction of a realm that is indeed magical, in comparison to the world one is accustomed to. But it is quite real. And it is our true home.

However magical their effects may seem, the stones do not do it for us. That is why I emphasize that one must *commit* oneself if one hopes to succeed in alchemy's Great Work of transformation. The alchemists were never "objective" observers. They did not pretend to merely be watching nature to see how things worked. They were participants who threw themselves fully into their efforts. And they viewed themselves as *co-creators,* working in cooperative rapport with the Soul of the World. When we think of the stones as Beings and view our experience of their energies as an activity of co-creative transformation, we open up to possibilities that far surpass our preconceived notions. However, we have to do our part or we are not really in partnership with them. Expecting the stones to act as objects we can simply own—and their energies as something we can consume—is another way of holding ourselves apart. And there is no magic in that.

All of these ideas are heresies, from the standard materialistic point of view, and materialists will often attack or dismiss them. In their day, the alchemists had to protect themselves from persecutions by the Church. They did so by communicating in symbols, metaphors, and convoluted language. They pretended merely to be experimenting with metals, minerals, and plants, hiding the deeper spiritual purposes of their work.

Today, the chief social hazard of working metaphysically with stones is ridicule, and that is a sanction many of us have learned to accept. It can even be a kind of shield. Since we are not taken seriously, no one bothers with a serious attack. Also, the world is changing. Even as the consequences of the dominant materialistic outlook are threatening to destroy the world—from war to ecocide—more and more people are looking for their own spiritual fulfillment. Metaphysical ideas are deeply infiltrating the culture. This may actually be *because* we can all see the destructiveness of the materialistic worldview that leaves no room for soul in matter.

This is why I used the quotations from Jung and Bly at the beginning. What has been regarded as the normal view of the world for the past few centuries is actually crazy. While much of religion has lost its value to people through failing to bring them into authentic personal experiences of the Divine, the doctrines of scientific materialism have evicted the Divine from the universe. The alchemists, however, addressed themselves directly and ardently to partnership with the Soul of the World.

Most of you who are reading these words would probably not define yourselves as "normal." You may even take a jaunty pride in being regarded as a little weird. Nonetheless, we are all infected with some degree of the materialistic dogma. I still catch myself falling back into it. And materialism is not dangerous because it is completely wrong. If it were completely wrong, it would never have taken hold. It is dangerous because it is one-sided.

One of the great qualities of the alchemists was their intentional embrace of opposing polarities. The images in their symbolic engravings frequently depicted all sorts of opposites—sun and moon, male and female, black and white, life and death, and so forth. And their willingness to hold on to two apparently opposite views simultaneously is what incubated the emergence of the "third thing"—a transcendent perspective that takes one to a greater awareness. One-sidedness is blindness. Transcendent awareness is vision, and such vision is the cornerstone of sanity, wholeness, compassion, and loving participation in the world.

We will go into all of these ideas throughout the book. And we will see how our soulful, spiritual engagement with stones can bring us into experiences of transcendence in which spirit and matter are conjoined. Working with the stones can take us to these places. When you truly open yourself to a stone, you can see it and feel it—the union of matter and spirit—right in the palm of your hand.

If this book were a tree, the early chapters describing the alchemical worldview and its history would constitute the roots. The next several chapters are the trunk of the tree, in which we move into the implementation of the alchemical worldview through practicing the Alchemy of Stones. In these, we discover *panpsychism,* a worldview that envisions consciousness, rather than physical substance, as the fundamental bedrock of reality. We meet Sophia, the Soul of the World, our beloved divine partner in co-creation. We are introduced along the way to a number of the Stone Beings, who act as Sophia's agents, or angels. We enter into True Imagination and the Psychoid-Imaginal realm. Here we discover that *imaginal* refers to a very real domain that manifests to us as *image,* but which is by no means merely imaginary.

As we move up the tree trunk, we encounter Sophia through the intelligence of the heart. Farther on, the alchemists disclose their discovery of Sophia's mechanism of continual creation—the oroboros feedback loop. Next we explore transcendence, and we get a glimpse of the stages via which we ourselves may transcend and transform. Throughout this exploration, there are practices outlined through which one can work with stones to *experience* all that is being discussed.

I envision these chapters—the roots and the trunk of our metaphorical tree—as the core (the heart) of the Alchemy of Stones. They are intended to offer both the idea-image of this alchemy and the experiences to make it real. They are meant to show this path from inception to fruition as directly as possible. One's own journey is certain to be more meandering and convoluted than the pattern I am presenting. What this book provides is a map. And as anyone who has visited another country knows, a map is essential. But the journey is far richer than any map could ever be.

Chapters 20 through 28 are what we might call the branches of our alchemical tree. In them, I describe a variety of ways one can work with stones, applying the principles introduced in the earlier chapters. We go into such areas as working with multiple stones in templates and grids, combining different stones in energy tools and Orgonite devices, making stone elixirs, and more. One large branch goes into making and working with stone mandalas, grids, and body layouts. In this context, we also explore the related topic of Photonic Stone Layouts and their wide-ranging possibilities.

Chapters 29-32 are about the Four Cornerstones of the Alchemy of Stones—Moldavite, Phenacite, Azeztulite and Rosophia. We might think of these as the seeds of our alchemical tree, because new things grow within us as we work with them.

The last chapter, Chapter 33, offers my glimpses of some of the seemingly miraculous places our work in the Alchemy of Stones may take us. I think of this chapter as the magical fruit of our alchemical tree. And I wonder, right alongside you, dear reader, when and how this fruit will ripen.

Finally, the "Dictionary of Stones and Their Spiritual Qualities" completes the book. I view these entries, which focus on over 375 different minerals, crystals, and stones, as the leaves of our tree.

Although I like the roots and the trunk of this tree very much, and have presented them first, to build a framework of understanding, you are encouraged to enter this book wherever you like. Some of you may want to begin with the "branch" chapters, especially if you are eager to get your hands on some stones and start doing things. Or you may jump to the "seeds" and the "leaves" to learn more about the stones that attract you. That's fine. I trust that your experiences will either lead you back into the first chapters, or that the stones themselves will teach you what you need to learn.

I love this work, and the stones, and the Earth. I am happy to share what I have learned with you. And I take joy in knowing that there are others who love the stones and the Earth as I do.

—Robert Simmons

There is something men and women living in houses
Don't understand. The old alchemists standing
Near their stoves hinted at it a thousand times.

—Robert Bly

STONE

Go inside a stone
That would be my way.
Let somebody else become a dove
Or gnash with a tiger's tooth.
I am happy to be a stone.

From the outside the stone is a riddle:
No one knows how to answer it.
Yet within, it must be cool and quiet
Even though a cow steps on it full weight,
Even though a child throws it in a river;
The stone sinks, slow, unperturbed
To the river bottom
Where the fishes come to knock on it
And listen.

I have seen sparks fly out
When two stones are rubbed,
So perhaps it is not dark inside after all;
Perhaps there is a moon shining
From somewhere, as though behind a hill—
Just enough light to make out
The strange writings, the star-charts
On the inner walls.

—Charles Simic

Read with the heart until at some time the true divine path will come . . .

—Paracelsus

1

The Golden Threads

All know that the drop merges into the ocean,
but few know that the ocean merges into the drop.
—Kabir

The Alchemy of Stones—what is that? It's a question I have been asked before, and perhaps it is worthwhile to start the discussion about it here as I begin a book that is as much an invitation to the exploration of the unknown as it is a transmission of information.

The magnetic field that has always pulled me along in this life has been my sense of wonder—which fed my wondering and wandering. As a child, it took me into reading hundreds of books, about everything from dinosaurs and Abraham Lincoln (not in the same book!), to jet planes, volcanoes and earthquakes. It led me into my back yard with a hammer, where I spent hours breaking rocks open, looking for fossils and tiny crystals. It drew me into studying astronomy, physics, chemistry, psychology and even poetry and mythology. What was I looking for?

I don't know if I could ever have fully answered that question. In a certain way, I *was* a question, and I still am. Many of you reading these words know just what I mean. And you most likely know, as I do, that there are times when it seems as if we are not entirely steering the course that our lives follow. Something else, something mysterious, beguiling and wonderful leads us with little hints, surprising coincidences and astonishing gifts. If we are blinded by our adherence to the expectations of the "civilized" world around us, we can easily miss the glints of the tiny diamonds scattered along our meandering path. But if we keep our eyes open, our attention on the possibility that *meaning is everywhere,* we'll catch—or be caught by—some of them. And therein lies all the difference.

The poet William Blake called these meaningful subtleties *golden strings,* and he said this about them:

I give you the end of a golden string
Only wind it into a ball,
It will lead you in at Heaven's gate,
Built in Jerusalem's wall . . .

He is telling us here to bend down and pick up those glinting gems on our road, to follow the golden strings of synchronicity and let ourselves be led by the invisible Wisdom that puts them in our path. He promises that it is the Divine holding the other end of the string, inviting us in at "Heaven," which to me means being with the Divine, consciously and by one's own free choice. It's a beautiful idea—that we are *led* into Heaven. This "Heaven"' is something I view more as a state of consciousness—a condition of relationship—than as a place. And if we simply follow the threads offered to us, we will get there. I think that when our sense of wonder is awakened, we are near one of the golden strings.

Before we begin our exploration of the Alchemy of Stones, I want to tell you a story about a particular golden thread that was tossed to me—one that was almost too much for me to bear.

A heavy, wet snow had just blanketed New Haven, Connecticut, one Sunday night in early April of 1970, during my freshman year at Yale. It was after midnight, and I had been talking for hours with my roommate Dave in one of those soul-searching conversations that can arise when you are young and lonely, and it is your first year away from home. Telling him about my family and my childhood experiences, I had gone into the depths of difficult memories. Then, in answer to one of Dave's questions, I recounted my most recurrent childhood dream.

The dream always began in a fearful state, in which I found myself compelled by invisible forces to descend a dark staircase into a foreboding black basement, festooned with cobwebs. In the dream, which occurred dozens of times between the ages of six and fourteen, I inwardly recoiled in terror of the descent into the dark cellar.

Then, each time I had the dream, at the threshold of that awful darkness, a white horse would suddenly appear under me and carry me up into the sky. This blended my intense anxiety with a strange elation, and I ascended. As it flew, the white horse inexplicably grew larger and larger—to the size of a car, a house, a city block. It seemed to stretch to a mile-long expanse—extending ultimately like a huge, smooth white cloud, lifting me higher and higher. I remained my normal size, and eventually I always lost my hold on the horse's back, sliding off and falling, down and down. And as I fell, I would suddenly wake up, disoriented and frightened.

In the dream's aftermath, my senses were always abnormally acute. Sounds were disturbingly amplified, and light seemed to burn my eyes. It often took my parents quite some time to calm me down.

After telling the dream to my roommate, I felt nervous and agitated. I stood up and walked into the living room of our dormitory suite, pacing back and forth in front of the window, gazing at the carpet of snow and the full moon that hung in the sky above a huge cloud. Suddenly I stopped pacing and jerked my head back to the window. I *recognized* the huge cloud! It was the exact image of the horse from my childhood dream!

As I stood gaping, my thoughts raced. How could the horse from my dream be there in the sky, at that precise moment? It was impossible, yet there it hung before my eyes. What was real? What was a dream? I was only eighteen years old, and my mind had nowhere to go. My thoughts stopped. I was terrified. My idea of the real world was gone. I felt myself shatter into a thousand pieces. In fact, it seemed that I could actually see my body shattering like a sheet of glass. I called out, "Oh God, help me!"

In the next moment, there was a sharp pop at the back of my head, and suddenly, smoothly, a wave of pure White Light washed through my skull. With it came a flood of ecstatic joy, peace, comfort and certainty. My terror had vanished, and I basked in rapture, feeling the radiance fill my body. I was sure that I had been touched by God.

For the next few hours, I was in a state of *samadh*—an experience of *gnosis*—full of light, knowledge and joy. I spoke to my astonished roommate in an overflowing fountain of words, describing what I saw and understood. Anything I wanted to know I had only to think about for the answer to be there. I now recall only one of the visions—the cycle of water. When I went to the window to view the horse-shaped cloud again, I suddenly saw an exquisite inner image of the whole story of water. I understood it to be the life-blood of the Earth and all creatures, and I grasped its endless flow again and again through the oceans, rivers, ground and sky, and through all of life. I described all this to Dave.

We kept talking as we went into the dormitory bathroom. When I turned on the faucet to wash my hands, the water that came out was alive—sparkling and multicolored. I felt as though the world had turned into holy magic.

My roommate had watched me go from nervousness to terror to ecstasy, and he now witnessed my experience of inner radiance. Gradually, I calmed down, the intensity ebbed, and the state faded by morning, though I fell asleep in the pre-dawn hours feeling as though I lay on the luminous beach of an ocean of Light.

That experience, triggered by the synchronicity of my dream, changed my life. For the first few weeks, I tried rather desperately to make it happen again, but the only Light I could find was in my memory of what had happened.

Nonetheless, I hung onto that golden string, and have spent five decades winding it into a ball. The journey has taken me through a multitude of mystical experiences, great and small.

They have occurred in meditation, in other dreams and sychronicities, and in moments of everyday life. And surprisingly, for the past thirty years or so, many of them have come to me through stones.

Let me share another personal story. For this one, we fast-forward fifteen years, to my first months as the co-owner of a crystal shop. In those fifteen years, I had never given up my search, and winding the golden threads that life offered me had drawn me into a number of explorations. These included reading Carlos Castenada and other mystical authors, experimenting with psychedelic mushrooms, studying interspecies communication with dolphins, practicing Transcendental Meditation, and floating in sensory deprivation tanks. All of these explorations were aimed at rekindling the essence of my first mystical breakthrough, on that fateful winter's night at Yale. In other words, I wanted that mysterious experience to somehow happen again.

The poet Robert Bly discusses this desire and how one must go about trying to fulfill it:

> *The first experience . . . is interior. When the poet realizes for the first time . . . when he touches for the first time something far inside him. . . . It's connected with what the ancients called The Mysteries, and it's wrong to talk of it very much. . . . Then there's a second necessary stage which I don't see described very much, but which I would call something like cunning. And cunning involves the person's rearranging his life in such a way that he can feel the first experience again. This is worldly, and involves common sense. What the shaman experiences as rituals is what I would call cunning.*

So, one might say that in my multiple spiritual pursuits, I was trying to rearrange my life with enough "cunning" to bring back the presence of Mystery.

But the Mystery usually does not respond directly to our efforts to "make something happen," and I was not as sophisticated in these matters as Bly. In terms of triggering another such experience, my explorations were apparently unsuccessful. Yet, at the same time, the efforts themselves meant that I remained perennially mindful of the Mystery, and that was a reward in itself.

Though I had, during the fifteen years after my first mystical opening, experienced many wonderful insights and visions outside the bounds of the everyday, consensus world, the two most important events that occurred on my path did not come from Transcendental Meditation, or from mushrooms. They were meeting my wife and spiritual partner Kathy Helen Warner, and, a few months earlier, encountering a mysterious meteoric gemstone called Moldavite. I have written elsewhere about both of these events, so I will not recount them fully here. But I do want to mention them in passing, because they were turning points that have brought me to this day, and the book I am writing now.

One day in 1985, I was driving down the highway on Cape Cod, Massachusetts, daydreaming about jewelry designs. (I made my living as a jeweler in those days.) As I drove along in my creative reverie, a vision of a gold comet pendant with a meteorite in its head captivated me so thoroughly that I missed my turnoff and ended up at a friend's doorstep forty miles down the road. When I excitedly told him my idea, he suggested that I should use Moldavite, a meteoric gemstone, instead of a metallic meteorite in my new pendant design. When he mentioned Moldavite, I got prickles down my neck, with a feeling that destiny was touching me again. When my friend showed me an article about Moldavite in a decades-old lapidary magazine, the prickles turned to downright shivers. I impulsively tried to telephone the author, hoping he was still alive. I called Directory Assistance, and was given a phone number. When, to my surprise, the 1958 author answered the phone, he was soon almost as excited as I was to learn of my newfound interest. Moldavite—and its powers—had been at the center of his own spiritual path, way back in the metaphysically sterile 1950s, and he was eager to share his story. Within days, he had sent me a few pieces of Moldavite. When they arrived, my life began to experience a sudden acceleration, and the golden strings started coming from all directions.

The most important synchronicity was meeting Kathy. Aside from falling in love and all the magic that went with it, meeting Kathy introduced me to the idea that stones had spiritual energies, and that they could aid in healing. (Kathy herself does healing work through laying on of hands and shamanic practices, and my first-hand experience of her healing ability was one of the many eye-opening events during this period of accelerated growth.) She encouraged me to meditate with Moldavite, which she believed to be a very important stone for bringing spiritual Light to the Earth.

A year after I met Kathy, we were married, and we opened our business—a crystal shop called Heaven and Earth—the very next day. Even though we were fully immersed in the distribution of crystals and minerals to the metaphysical community, I was not personally able to feel the stone energies that our customers and friends talked about. I was still meditating with Moldavite every morning, with no tangible results so far. (It's interesting, looking back, to see how my desire to 'make something happen' got in my own way!) I tended to operate on the more-is-better hypothesis, so for some months I meditated with my hands stuck in two small buckets of Moldavite. But still I felt that nothing had happened. (I had not yet understood that the rapid acceleration of my inner development, which included the changes in my profession and my marriage to Kathy, were typical of Moldavite's affects.) Eventually, I went back to sitting for a half hour each morning with a single Moldavite in my right hand. I let go of any expectations, and any overt efforts, instead of straining myself trying to "feel something." And that, of course, is when it happened.

I sat down in the living room with my Moldavite, having turned on my meditation music. I'll admit that I was rather bored with the routine, even though I always felt calm and refreshed afterwards. On this day, I thought, "I'm tired of waiting for an out-of-body experience or some other cool thing to happen, so I'm just going to imagine one." I wrapped my fingers around my Moldavite and closed my eyes, letting myself listen to the music, while at the same time imagining that I was rising out of the top of my own head, looking down at my body.

As I continued to visualize, I could see a mental image of myself as if I were looking down from the ceiling. Then I decided to try to go higher, so I envisioned floating upwards through the ceiling and the roof, looking down on the house and surrounding neighborhood. I kept going in my imagined

My first moldavite

flight, rising higher and higher, seeing the town and the seacoast landscape, and my house as a tiny dot below me. I began to feel exhilarated as I rose higher and faster. The flight seemed to take on a life of its own. Soon I could see the curvature of the Earth, and then the whole globe, as I flew off into space.

I felt no fear, and no disconnection from my body. I remained, on some level, aware of the music and my own breathing. Yet I became completely captivated by the visionary experience that was unfolding. Soon I had left the Earth behind and was far out among the stars. It seemed that I could move in whatever direction I chose simply by willing it.

At one point, I saw a golden star far away, and I knew that I wanted to go to it, so I willed myself there. In a short time, the golden star had become an immense golden sun, and it emanated a light that felt holy. Then I noticed that there were thousands, or perhaps millions, of golden orbs circling the golden sun, each with a thin gold thread linking the orb to the Sun. The orbs seemed to be alive, like a procession of souls, circling in adoration around the golden Sun. I was deeply moved by this vision, and I wondered if the golden orbs were really souls. At that point, I also wondered what my own "body" might look like in this place. I turned my attention downward, toward where my chest would have been, and was surprised to see another golden orb about twelve inches in diameter, encompassing the space around my heart. And there was a golden thread that linked my own orb to the great golden Sun.

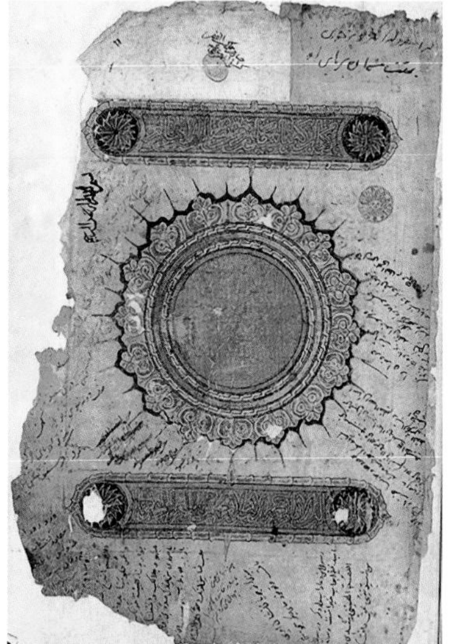

I was filled with awe and wonder, and my thoughts became silent. Then I suddenly heard a deep, resonant voice–perhaps like the voice of an angel—saying clearly, "The Light you seek without is identical to the Light within."

In the next moment, several things happened. I suddenly realized that the golden orbs *were* souls, and that I was one of them, and this knowledge hit me with a rush of emotion. At the same time, back in the living room, the Moldavite in my right hand sizzled with an energy that moved quickly up my arm and went straight into my heart. There was an instant sensation of something opening, like a big flower inside my chest, and the flower was made out of Light. Then the energy moved upwards and downward along my spine, causing more flowerings of Light at each of my chakras.

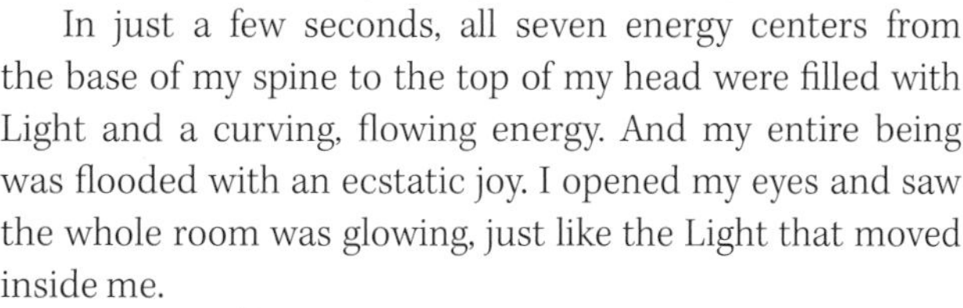

In just a few seconds, all seven energy centers from the base of my spine to the top of my head were filled with Light and a curving, flowing energy. And my entire being was flooded with an ecstatic joy. I opened my eyes and saw the whole room was glowing, just like the Light that moved inside me.

Kathy had been upstairs getting ready to open our shop for the day when all of this occurred. Her intuition suddenly told her that something important was happening with

ABOVE: Image of the Great Central Sun, as depicted in the 11th century text *Kimiya-yi sa'ādat* (The Alchemy of Happiness), a text on Islamic philosophy and alchemy by the Persian philosopher and mystic Al-Ghazālī]
BELOW: The *Divine Comedy's* Empyrean, illustrated by Gustave Doré]

me, so she hurried to the living room. When she opened the door, she looked at me and said, "Robert, you're full of Light!"

I was nearly speechless, still bathed in ecstasy. All I could say was, "I know!"

Kathy sat with me for nearly an hour, as the experience of the inner Light moved through me. Eventually, the intensity began to soften, and I was able to tell her what had happened. After awhile, we decided to go and open our shop, but there was one more surprise ahead of me.

When I entered Heaven and Earth, I could, for the first time, sense the energy of the stones on the shelves and tables. It filled the room. And when I picked up a stone, I could at last feel the vibrational currents of "crystal energy" that our customers and friends had described to me. In fact, I could, on that morning, feel every single stone in the store, and could sense the similarities and differences among them. I spent almost the entire day in a state of calm, wonderful rapture, picking up stone after stone, feeling them all. And while that exquisite sensitivity has ebbed and flowed through the years, it has never left me, and I have learned how to focus and work with it.

So, why did I tell these personal stories? In a way, I felt that I had to. They are what brought me here, to this moment at the computer, typing out the beginning of a new book. This book is a way of winding my golden string, especially because the golden strings emanating from crystals and stones turn out to be ones that a lot of people have gotten hold of, and I feel that we are all working our way to "Heaven's gate." Maybe we will get there together, and maybe we each have golden strings tying us to thousands, or even millions of other people . . . and to everything else in and on the Earth, and to the Earth herself, and to the Soul of the World. The centerpiece of my first vision, way back in 1970, was the cycle of water, illustrating that we are all connected, and that the life of everything is mirrored in the image of water's circulating flow. And there is another, deeper "water"—a spiritual one—the divine current that bears every particle of matter and every wave of energy on its journey in the universe. That current can flow into us and transform us, and it often manifests as Light, as it did in my young head back in 1970, and in our living room in 1986. I told my stories because that divine river of Light (wonder of wonders!) is what is now pouring into many of us through the stones. Not in an overwhelming torrent that could drown our individuality, but softly, gently, lovingly, persistently, patiently. Nothing is more patient than a stone.

Think about it. What in the world is happening? Over the past thirty years or so, there has been a worldwide awakening to the spiritual energies of crystals. In every country I visit, there are people who know about this, and who love stones. They meditate with them, carry them, tell stories about their stones calling to them, or opening their hearts, or healing them. For some of us, like myself before the day when everything changed, the stones seem not to have "done" anything, but we still love them—which means they have done something very great indeed. What is happening? What, or Who, is on the other end of these golden threads?

It's amazing. You walk into a crystal shop and there you see a colorful array of tumbled stones, minerals and crystals—so lovely, so physical, so down to earth. But what is going on is a *huge* mystery. Some of us can feel currents coming from the stones, or inwardly hear them "speak," or see visions when we hold them. Other people often think we're crazy, or just foolish and naive. My advice is: Don't worry about what anyone else says or thinks, and don't doubt your own experiences. Part of what is happening is that new sensory capacities are opening up. If ninety-five percent of the people in the world were blind, they would think that those foolish people talking about "colors" were crazy too.

The ancient Greek philosopher Plato discussed that sort of thing in his myth of the Cave. In that tale, a group of people lived their whole lives in a cave, facing the back wall and chained to the floor so they could not turn around. Behind them, there was a fire that caused a dance of flickering shadows on the one visible wall. Those shadows were viewed by the cave's chained inhabitants as constituting the entire world. And if someone were to break his chains, escape from the cave and visit the outside world, when he or she came back to tell the tale, it wouldn't be believed. The explorer would be ridiculed, and the inhabitants of the cave would settle back in to their "normal lives," watching the shadows.

If you are someone who has had the sensation of feeling crystal energies, or who has been "called" by a stone, you may feel a bit like one of the explorers who left and returned to the Cave, trying to explain to others what you've experienced. You may even accept the label of being "a little nutty," since your own experience is not supposed to be real, according to just about all your schoolteachers, parents, and the other figures of authority in our culture. But of course, if you are reading this book, you probably already know that there are innumerable holes in the fabric of consensus reality, especially its foundation in materialism.

Most of us are already aware of the challenges to the materialistic worldview presented by unexplained healings, near death experiences, spiritualist mediums, tarot readings, and prophetic dreams, as well as everyday sorts of psychic experiences and telepathy. Sometimes the telephone rings and you know who it is before you answer. Our pets seem to be instantly aware when we are coming home, and there is documented evidence that plants can read our minds. Materialism is not an adequate explanation of reality. This book will suggest to you that even the stones are conscious!

Do you know the story of the three blind men who were given the chance to encounter an elephant? One ran up against the side of the beast, and he later said, "An elephant is like a wall." The second man got hold of the tail, and he said, "An elephant is like a rope." The third felt the twining trunk, and he said, "This elephant is like a snake." Who was right? All of them, except that none had the whole picture.

This mystery of the stones and their connection to spiritual alchemy is a key that unlocks a vaster mystery about ourselves and our reality, a mystery much bigger than an elephant.

In most histories of thought, alchemy has been presented as a primitive precursor to chemistry. This is a deep misapprehension, one resulting from our modern inability to understand a time when the surrounding world was still regarded as holy. . . . It's critical to understand that this [alchemical] belief system could arise and continue only so long as nature is viewed as alive. It is the modern scientific view of nature as a "thing" that makes this earlier view seem strange to us. Native Americans still hold the view of the natural world not only as a living being, but a sacred living being.

—Robin Robertson, *Indra's Net*

The ancient art of alchemy was chiefly concerned with changing something of seemingly little value into something precious, of transforming lead into gold, thereby creating the "philosophers' stone." The "stone" is not a material substance, however, but is an awakened consciousness, which, though seemingly immaterial, pervades, informs, and gives rise to all creation. The philosophers' stone doesn't just redeem the individual alchemist, it nonlocally influences the field to such a degree that it was considered to be able to redeem the entire cosmos. . . . Alchemy is a timeless, sacred art, as the alchemists' art is to become an instrument for the incarnating deity to make itself real in time and space.

—Paul Levy

2

Discovering the Alchemical Worldview

We know that much pagan thought, as exemplified in the famous phrase, "as above, so below," suggests that the terms "inferior" and "superior" are unreal. The idea "as above, so below" evokes an awe toward Nature, a sense that we share consciousness with plants, animals, stars and stones, and that all living creatures, including stones, share a consciousness with the Soul of the World... or the spiritual genius of the Earth.

—Robert Bly, *News of the Universe*

Alchemy is situated precisely at the crossroads of science and magic.

—Danny Deardorff, *The Other Within: The Genius of Deformity in Myth, Culture and Psyche*

All of the world's "advanced" societies, in these difficult times, have at their core an emptiness. Something is missing, and we can feel that absence in our hearts. We are all aware that the technological revolution brought about by the emergence of materialistic, mechanistic science has brought us many wonders—but they are all material wonders. They have all come via manipulation of physical matter and physical energy in the outer, physical world. What is missing is the link with the inner world, the link with soul and spirit, the link with worth and meaning.

We live in a planetary human culture primarily defined by the belief system of materialism. Under this worldview, the only things that are considered real are just things—material objects bumping into each other, making physical events happen in a one-way flow from the past to the present and on into a largely predetermined future. It's all about action and reaction, cause and effect. In this world, souls are unreal, spiritual experiences are hallucinations, and death extinguishes consciousness permanently.

The existence of consciousness is one of materialism's biggest conundrums. (Philosophers call it "the hard problem.") If physical matter constitutes the entire universe, and if all matter is inherently unconscious, how did our consciousness arise? Questions like this can leave a materialist nowhere to go, except to deny the existence of consciousness itself, which some of them do. This can be embarrassing, since the experience of denying the reality of consciousness takes place in one's conscious mind.

Mostly, people don't think about these sorts of things. But we should. The influence of materialism is pervasive, and it is what allows us to treat the Earth and everything on it as mere objects we can do with as we will. If the world has neither consciousness nor soul, then it is simply a pile of resources to be plundered. Materialism denies that there is any value other than survival, tells us that matter is dead, that no other life forms (and certainly no inanimate objects) are self-aware, and that the universe itself has no purpose.

This set of notions is at the core of *scientism,* the belief system of scientific materialism—a dogma as rigid and intolerant as any religion has ever been. It is the source of the emptiness we feel in our collective life. It underlies the corporate oligarchy, our oil wars, frantic consumerism, drug addiction, and a myriad of other symptoms of the sickness that comes from the denial of soul.

Fortunately, this belief system is wrong.

I am not going to spend much of my time in this book refuting the materialistic world view. Others have done it very well already (see Rupert Sheldrake's book, *Science Set Free,* and David R. Fideler's *Restoring the Soul of the World*). What I hope to do is to show that our experiences with stones and their energies demonstrate that consciousness is present everywhere, including the mineral world. This being so, a new worldview is needed—one that can accommodate the reality of consciousness existing not only in human beings, but in animals, plants, stars, and stones. In stones, and most importantly, in the Earth.

Have there ever been people who have created such a worldview and lived it? Robert Bly points out that these sorts of ideas were common in pagan thought. David Fideler, in his aforementioned book, tells us that the idea of the world as a single, conscious, living organism was embraced by the pre-Socratic Greek philosophers. The animistic beliefs of many aboriginal peoples clearly involved an awareness of the consciousness of the living world. The later domination of humanity, especially in the West, first by religion and then by science, cut us off from those roots.

Surprisingly, there is a tradition that kept alive the connection with the Soul of the World, a tradition that focused human intentions on cooperating with the Divine in Nature for the purpose of bringing the world into a state of fulfillment and perfection. The practitioners of this tradition believed that the perfection of the world and the Self, of matter and Spirit, were inextricably linked. They felt that by working with imagination and with matter in a spiritual way, the union of Heaven and Earth could be realized. They stood at the crossroads of science and magic, and their practice was known as alchemy.

Early in my exposure to alchemical ideas, I learned that the goal of the Great Work of the alchemists was a *stone*—the Philosophers' Stone. As a stone enthusiast and author, discovering this heightened my excitement, and affirmed my intuition that the spiritual and energy work with stones was somehow deeply related to the practice of spiritual alchemy. I began to suspect that the whole community of crystal lovers was engaged in alchemical endeavors without even knowing it.

The word alchemy comes from the Egyptian *al-khem,* meaning "the dark earth," "the infusion," "the elixir," or the Philosophers' Stone.

A Wikipedia article on alchemy states: "Alchemy is a philosophical and protoscientific tradition practiced throughout Europe, Egypt, and Asia. It aimed to purify, mature, and perfect certain objects."

In my understanding of the alchemical mind-set, to "purify" means to refine something down to its very essence. To "mature" means to evolve something to its intended or destined potential, and to "perfect" means to bring something to an ideal state, displaying its Divine nature.

The article continues: "Common aims were (1) the transmutation of 'base metals' (e.g., lead) into 'noble' ones (particularly gold); (2) the creation of an elixir of immortality; and (3) the creation of panaceas able to cure any disease."

These aims, except for the transmutation of metals, resemble our aspirations with our stone work: healing, purification of oneself, and spiritual evolution into one's highest potential. In spiritual alchemy, the transformation of lead to gold is a symbol of the transformation of the self.

Wikipedia: "The perfection of the human body and soul was thought to facilitate and/or result from the alchemical *magnum opus* (or Great Work)."

This is very much akin to the aspiration that many of us share—for enlightenment or unity with the Divine. We work spiritually with stones to take us closer to that goal, or perhaps all the way there.

Wikipedia: "In the Greek and Western traditions, the achievement of *gnosis* [direct knowledge of the Divine] was the ultimate goal of alchemy. In Europe, the creation of a philosophers' stone was variously connected with all of these projects."

The term *gnosis* lies deep within the core of our work with spiritual alchemy and with stones. Gnosis means "knowing," as distinct from believing or disbelieving. When gnosis comes to us, whatever we might or might not have believed becomes irrelevant. The stories I told in the first chapter concern two of my own key experiences of gnosis. Such experiences kindle an inner certainty about the spiritual realities that exist around and within us, and the processes of inner alchemy can lead us into more of them. When we work with stones and their energies, what we feel is not a belief but an experience—an experience of matter and spirit conjoined.

The fact that the ultimate goal of alchemy is the creation or manifestation of a *stone* is another key to alchemy's link with our crystal and stone work. The Philosophers' Stone can be viewed on multiple levels—from acting as a metaphor for one's self-realization or wholeness to literally being embodied by a physical stone to which one relates in order to achieve the transmutation and redemption of oneself and the world. The Philosophers' Stone is both an inner and outer entity. Through our spiritual work, we can become as pure, solid, and true as a stone. Our way of being can become so harmonized with our true nature that, once we achieve the union of our conscious individuality with our Deep Self and the Soul of the World, nothing external can dislodge that union. We become as strong as stones, and this power, according to the alchemists, gives us the capacity to co-creatively bring perfection and self-realization to the world. In the words of Paul Levy, the achievement of the philosophers' stone "influences the field to such a degree that it was considered to be able to redeem the entire cosmos."

The alchemists perceived that we can become partners with the Divine. Indeed, our participation is essential. Without us, the Divine cannot fully incarnate, and the potential for worldwide awakening can never be realized.

Why is this? It is something of a mystery, but I believe I know one reason: From my experience, and that of myriad others who have felt its presence, the essential nature of the Divine is love. If we think about love, we know that it will never impose itself, because in doing so, it would cease to be love. Love offers itself but never compels us. Our free will, which can accept or refuse Love's offer, is in itself clear evidence of the loving nature of reality. (In human terms, if we love someone, their happiness and fulfillment becomes our own goal, and this must always include the loved one's freedom.) It also means that the Divine must wait for us to turn in its direction and accept its offer of co-creative partnership. When we do this, we begin to participate in the marriage of Heaven and Earth.

So, where do the stones come into this picture?

Most of the people reading this book are likely to have felt crystal energy. The gentle buzzing of a stone in your hand, the warmth that can enter your body, the tingling, pulsing vibrations in the chakras that certain stones can engender—all of these are experiences of *consciousness meeting consciousness.* Think of the stone currents as vibrations, like notes of music or the words of a song. What we feel is the effect in ourselves of encountering a mineral being that is singing its song right into us. The songs of various stones can produce all sorts of physical, emotional, and mental states, just as different music affects us differently. And like good music, the vibrations of the stones can captivate us with inner experiences of beauty—beauty that can help us, heal us, and awaken us, beauty that can inspire us to make ourselves and the world more beautiful. And like an unforgettable song, the stones' energies can resonate within us until they become part of us, and we become a locus where their music lives within the world.

Once I began thinking of stones as beings with their own sort of consciousness, I tried to imagine what type of beings they might be. One idea I like is to view the Stone Beings as angels of the Earth. From ancient times, angels have been viewed as messengers of the Divine. They are faithful servants who bring messages from divine beings to human beings. By their nature, they are trustworthy and true. They are emanations of Divine Will.

I view the Stone Beings in the same way. In my thirty-plus years of working with them, they have always been reliably available, never vacillating and never ceasing, always radiating their characteristic energies. Spiritually, the Stone Beings *are* their vibrational "songs."

This is potentially a great help to us, because human beings are usually much less consistent than the Stone Beings. We vacillate a lot, and the primary work of much meditation is to sit there long enough for our thoughts to finally settle down. When we meditate with stones, we can relax into their vibrations—their songs—and allow ourselves to resonate with them. This quiets our thoughts much more quickly, and facilitates our entry into a great variety of inner domains of experience. And remember, if the Stone Beings are angelic messengers serving the Soul of the World, then all of their currents come directly to us from the divine nature of the Earth. They not only quiet our thoughts—they also bring us into harmony with Her. Imagining this, one can easily see how profoundly transformative working with stones can be, and that it is indeed alchemy.

I want to mention a detail about stones here: my experience is that every stone sings two songs at once. The first is the song of its species or type of stone. All Amethyst, for example, sings the Amethyst song. The second song is that of each individual piece or crystal. There is something about various pieces of the same type of stone that attract or engage us in their own special way, and different people resonate more or less powerfully with different pieces of the same type of stone. Many readers will have already experienced this, when a single crystal or stone calls to you from a shelf or showcase, while others of the same type don't. I am tempted to imagine that every stone has a kind of individuality, just as we do, and that it is expressed in a way that is comparable to ours. Just as we human beings all sing the human song, at the same time we also sing the song of our individuality. Something similar seems to occur with the stones. The "vibes" or energies we sense from the stones are what I am calling their songs, and our felt sense of their appeal—of our resonance with one stone or another—is how we distinguish which ones are best for us. So, as with other creatures, all stones of a species are similar, yet each one is different from every other.

If we allow the stones to teach us their harmony, our own vibrations can become stronger, truer, and purer until we transform into beings capable of choosing to unify ourselves with the Spiritual Earth. In so doing, we each become a stone ourselves—the alchemical Philosophers' Stone.

The ancient Greek name for the Soul of the World is Sophia, which also means Wisdom. The essence of the Soul of the World is indeed wisdom, or the underlying harmony that pervades our world would not exist. The early Greek thinkers understood this and so used the word Sophia to refer to Wisdom as a being—the soul essence of our world.

The alchemists viewed themselves as philosophers in the original sense. The word philosopher is derived from two ancient Greek words—*philein,* meaning to love; and *sophos,* meaning wisdom, or the Soul of the World. So a philosopher was a lover of Wisdom or Sophia—a lover of the Soul of the World. Throughout the alchemical literature, there are references made to the belief that, without the co-creative participation and guidance of Sophia, the Great Work of alchemy could never succeed.

Those of us who look to the Stone Beings as partners in our spiritual evolution can see this clearly. Without the stones and their songs—their messages from Sophia—we could find ourselves at a loss for how to embody the many healing and consciousness-awakening vibrations that are needed to initiate us on our journeys. Without their guiding currents, how would we know which way to orient ourselves toward the future that calls to us? Certainly, there are other paths than the Path of Stones, but I know of no other road upon which so many kinds of assistance are so readily available.

How are we to respond to such gentle, yet stupendous, gifts of grace? I think our best answer is to accept the Earth's invitation, the invitation of the Stone Beings, and to offer our love in return. The Persian poet Rumi put it this way: "*Let the beauty we love be what we do. There are hundreds of ways to kneel and kiss the earth.*"

If we are to escape the emptiness of materialism, we can't do it by ascending. We can't fly away to Heaven, leaving the Earth to her fate. One of the things I love about the alchemists is the fact that they didn't try to do this. They didn't encourage journeys up to Buddhist nirvanas, nor even to the Christian Heaven. They wanted Heaven and Earth to get married, to conjoin, and they set about to help that happen, right here in the physical world. The fact that stones—the very essence of solid matter—have perceptible spiritual energies is an example of the unity of Heaven and Earth that you can hold right in your hand. And our perception is, in fact, the key to the manifestation of that reality.

As Paul Levy stated, the alchemical work could be said to focus on "changing something of seemingly little value into something precious." This transformation was necessarily done on the physical and spiritual levels simultaneously, because "precious" went far beyond monetary worth. And the change involved was not simply an outer—or even only an inner—transmutation. The alchemist's *perceptual imagination* had to evolve in order to both perceive and create the rebirth of mere matter into the miraculous Philosophers' Stone. As we go on, we will see that this is exactly what we do when we involve ourselves emotionally and spiritually with the various stones we meet in the outer world of nature, or in a crystal store. Whether we know it or not, by recognizing and feeling the spiritual qualities and energies of stones, we are shifting our own perceptual imaginations to a state from which we are capable of transmuting lifeless rock, with no consciousness, into living, vibrating, awakened, ensouled matter with which we can relate, in an endless cycle of mutual enrichment. This transmutation is not just our imagination, nor is it something we can bring about all by ourselves—the Stone Beings and the Soul of the World must participate. However, we also must reach out with our imagination, our attention, and our intention in order to discover and co-create what awaits us.

We can find a clue about this kind of transformation in the Gnostic Gospel of Thomas, wherein Jesus is quoted as saying: "*Let him who seeks, cease not to seek until he finds, and when he finds, he will be astonished; and when he is astonished, he will wonder, and will reign over the universe.*"

When we look to see consciousness and spiritual presence within the stones, to our astonishment, we find it. And in our astonishment, wonders open to us. We discover our innate co-creative power, and in union with the Soul of the World, we can bring about the redemption of matter, the awakening of the Universe. This was the goal of the alchemists, and it is our highest potential.

It all begins with the first stone we choose—or perhaps the one that chooses us. This corresponds to the first phase of the alchemical work. In alchemy, the first substance to be worked with was called the *prima materia,* or the first matter. It was viewed as being initially in a state of chaos and unconsciousness, so much so that its true value was invisible to most people. (Sound familiar? How many people do you know who view your crystals as "just rocks," and your interest in them as mere fantasy?) Through relationship with the alchemist, in which he or she devotes much time, attention, and effort to the transformation of the substance, the *substance* gradually becomes more and more enlivened and awakened, more and more precious.

And, wonder of wonders, the same thing happens within the alchemist as well. The *prima materia* is simultaneously the outer substance being worked with, and the consciousness of the alchemist. Through working with them both at once, both are transmuted and awakened.

All of this has occurred in my own involvement with the mineral kingdom, and it is available to anyone who will accept the Earth's offer and engage wholeheartedly in the Great Work of the Alchemy of Stones.

ROOTS OF THE ALCHEMICAL WORLDVIEW

In the last few paragraphs, I've been inviting you into the alchemical worldview. To most of us, it's unfamiliar territory, even though we may recall experiences that resonate with some aspects of it. It's easy to understand that our perceptions of stone energies and the spiritual qualities of the stones do not fit within materialism. (I don't think that any machine will ever be able to measure crystal energies, since I don't believe their currents are merely physical. But because we ourselves partake of both matter and spirit, we are the entities capable of perceiving them.) In any case, we need a worldview wide enough to accommodate our bodies, our souls, and our spirits, and the bodies, souls, and spirits of all the beings—including the Stone Beings—with whom we share the world. Spiritual alchemy offers us such a perspective.

Spiritual alchemy includes many powerful ideas. But for the purposes of this book, I want to explore six major ones that I have incorporated in my own practice. I believe these can open our minds to a more adequate picture of the world, and our own potential as practitioners of the Alchemy of Stones. These six aspects of the Alchemical Worldview are: Panpsychism; True Imagination and the Imaginal Realm; Sophia and Co-creation; Transformation through Feedback; the Transcendent Function; Creating the Philosophers' Stone or Union with the Divine. Some of these terms are phrased in modern language rather than in the historical language of alchemy, because I am attempting to lay out the new worldview we need for the Alchemy of Stones. We will explore them in the chapters to come.

According to Anne Baring in "The Great Work of Alchemy":

> *Alchemy flows beneath the surface of Western civilization like a river of gold, preserving its images and its insights for us so that we could one day understand our presence on this planet better than we do. Alchemy builds a bridge between the human and the divine, the seen and unseen dimensions of reality, between matter and spirit. The cosmos calls to us to become aware that we participate in its life, that everything is sacred and connected—one life, one spirit. Alchemy responds to that call. It asks us to develop cosmic consciousness, to awaken the divine spark of our consciousness and reunite it with the invisible soul of the cosmos. It changes our perception of reality and answers the questions: "Who are we and why are we here?" It refines and transmutes the base metal of our understanding so that we—evolved from the very substance of the stars—can know that we participate in the mysterious ground of spirit while living in this physical dimension of reality.*

3

Panpsychism

Consciousness is present in the mineral kingdom, in the living world, and in the social and ecological systems constituted by human beings and other organisms. It is present at the level of quanta on the one end of the spectrum of size and complexity in nature, and on the level of galaxies on the other end.

—Ervin Laslo, *The Immortal Mind: Science and the Continuity of Consciousness beyond the Brain*

Even at the level of the tiniest molecules and single-cell organisms, we encounter self-organizing and self-maintaining activities that reflect the rudiments of awareness or mentality. The deployment of form in time and space depends upon the power of selection; for example, the growth of a crystal involves the proper arrangement of more than ten billion molecules a minute. Matter itself is active and self-organizing, and the molecules of the crystal "know" how to bond in harmony with one another to create a highly coherent structure. In its own way, the growing crystal is an intelligent, self-regulating organism. . . .

—David Fideler, *Restoring the Soul of the World*

Modern science has overthrown every foundational assumption of the mechanistic worldview, and suggests that we live within the pattern of a systematically unfolding, self-organizing cosmic organism that is finely tuned for the emergence of life.

—David Fideler, *Restoring the Soul of the World*

The life of biological organisms is different in degree, but not in kind, from physical systems like molecules and crystals.

—Rupert Sheldrake, *Science Set Free*

In a crystal we have the clear evidence of the existence of a formative life principle, and though we cannot understand the life of a crystal, it is nonetheless a living being.

—Nicola Tesla

Behind the existence of all matter is a conscious and intelligent mind—this mind is the matrix of all matter.

—Max Planck, father of quantum theory

The ultimate source of intelligence is not in the brain, but is enfolded into the whole.

—David Bohm, quantum physicist, author of *Wholeness and the Implicate Order*

As I mentioned earlier, the materialist worldview that prevails in much of our world today assumes that matter is devoid of awareness, and that consciousness, if it exists at all, is only within human beings. The alchemists believed otherwise. They viewed matter—including plants and animals, stars, and stones—as being ensouled, aware, and spiritually alive. The world itself had a soul—a great and intelligent soul of Wisdom with whom the alchemists must work in order to achieve their Great Work.

In philosophy, *panpsychism* is the view that consciousness, mind, or soul is a universal and primordial feature of all things. It is one of the oldest philosophical theories and has been ascribed to the ancient Greek philosophers Thales, Parmenides, and Plato, as well as a line of great thinkers that include Spinoza, Leibniz, William James, quantum physicist David Bohm,

BELOW: Helix Nebula
RIGHT: Hour Glass Nebula

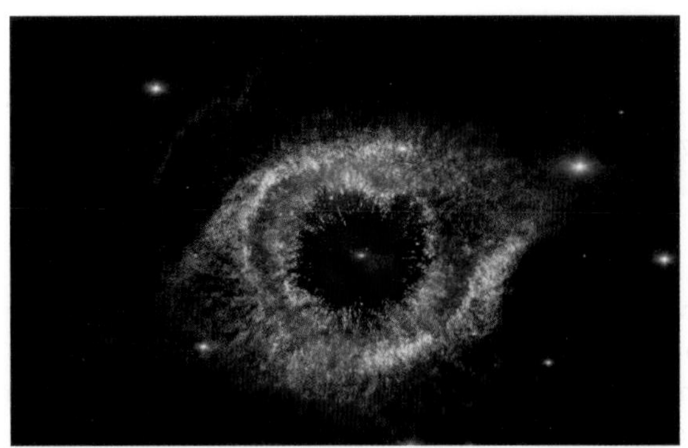

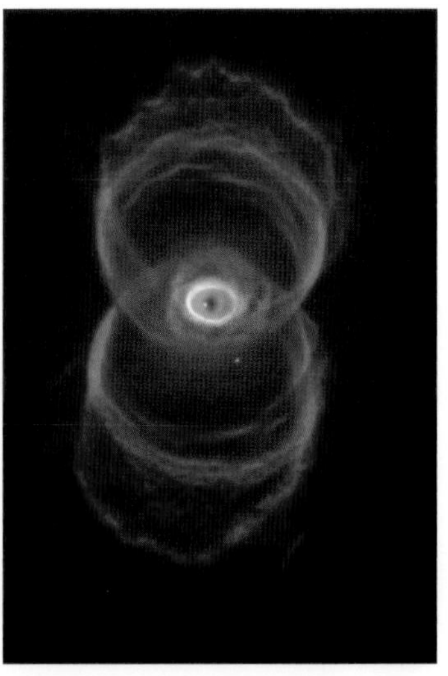

and psychologist Carl Jung. Its roots can be found in the animistic beliefs of many indigenous cultures around the world, as well as in Shinto, Taoism, paganism, and shamanism. All of these thinkers and spiritual traditions believed, as did the alchemists, that consciousness is a fundamental feature of everything in the world.

The term *panpsychism* has its origins with the Greek terms *pan* ("all," "everything," "whole") and *psyche* ("soul," "mind"). Psyche comes from the Greek word *psukhō* ("I blow" or "I breathe") and can mean "life," "soul," "mind," "spirit," "heart," and "life-breath." From its roots, we could say that *panpsychism* refers to the notion that the breath of life, the soul, the center of consciousness, is everywhere.

The psychologist Carl Jung, who introduced the concept of the collective unconscious—and who had a lifelong interest in spiritual alchemy—wrote that "psyche and matter are contained in one and the same world, and moreover are in continuous contact with one another." He believed it probable that "psyche and matter are two different aspects of one and the same thing." (CW8, p 420)

According to the ninth-century Shingon Buddhist thinker Kukai, the Dharmakaya (the formless body of consciousness) is nothing other than the physical universe, and natural objects like rocks and stones are included as part of the supreme embodiment of the Buddha.

The famed alchemist Paracelsus (1493–1541) viewed the universe as one coherent organism pervaded by a uniting life-giving spirit, and this in its entirety, humans included, was God.

Jacob Böhme (1575–1624), the philosopher, writer, and alchemical theorist, also believed that God wasn't separate from creation, and that life force passed directly into stars, planets, plants, trees, humans, animals, stones, minerals, and every other thing via the cosmic mirror of Mother Nature, whom he knew as Sophia: "[God] shines with his power through all his beings . . . and each thing receives his power according to its property."

From the point of view of panpsychism, stones indeed have consciousness and soul, as do we. Within such a worldview, it is not so surprising that human beings can feel the vibrations of stones, and that we can learn to meet them as beings.

EVIDENCE THAT PANPSYCHISM IS TRUE

Panpsychism is an attractive, rewarding idea, but is it true? In the world of philosophy, the debate rages on. We could delve into it, but I prefer to offer a list of examples that, for me, are powerful indicators that indeed there is consciousness in all things—that there is soul everywhere.

One way to see this is to consider evidence showing that our own consciousness is not confined to our bodies. Out-of-body experiences, near-death experiences, memories of past lives, instances of telepathy, and communication (with or without a medium) with the spirits of people who have died all indicate that human consciousness extends beyond bodily boundaries. In the instances of past-life memories and spirit communication, even death seems incapable of extinguishing consciousness.

The *savant phenomenon,* dramatized in the 1988 movie *Rain Man* and documented in the 2006 film *Beautiful Minds: The Psychology of the Savant,* is a name given to cases in which individuals apparently receive complex information from sources beyond their own brains. This well-documented phenomenon makes another hole in the wall of materialism, and implies that we are nested within a vast web of intelligence.

I have personally experienced several of the above phenomena, and most readers will be able to recall some instances that fit into one or more of these categories. Telephone telepathy—the experience of having the phone ring and knowing who's calling before you pick up the receiver—is a common occurrence. Biologist Rupert Sheldrake's research and experiments indicate that at least half the human population (of those who have telephones) have experienced this.

Outside the human realm, there is much evidence for telepathic communication among animals. Wolves have been observed as being capable of communicating their location and intended movements to one another when they are miles out of sight and earshot. Scientific studies done by Rupert Sheldrake give clear evidence that dogs and other pets can often tell exactly when their owners are coming home. These experiments were controlled so that the pets' behavior displayed that they knew when the *decision* to come home was made, and could not be ascribed to a habitual time of day, to sound cues, or to other material evidence. Even insects such as termites seem able to communicate telepathically when behaving cooperatively in activities such as building their nests.

And this doesn't stop with the animal realm. Plants have been observed to exhibit evidence that they too are conscious.

In the famous book *The Secret Life of Plants,* polygraph (lie-detector) expert Cleve Backster described how he stumbled onto this evidence. Late one night, alone in his lab, he got the idea of hooking his lie detector to a Dracaena corn plant on his desk. Trying to imagine how he might provoke some kind of reaction from the plant, he decided on lighting a match to burn one of the leaves. He never got the chance to try it, because, at the precise moment Backster *thought* of doing so, the plant displayed a wild reaction on the polygraph, typical (in humans) of emotional distress. To all appearances, the plant had read his mind. This experiment has since been replicated many times, and a number of other experiments have shown that plants are aware of our intentions, can identify different individuals, and even seem to have compassion and empathy for the suffering or death of other organisms. For an amazing overview of this material, watch the 1979 film *The Secret Life of Plants* (www.youtube.com/watch?v=4NoXftUiISM).

Backster realized that a new worldview was needed to account for his observations, and he worked on it for the next forty years, performing a variety of experiments. In these he found evidence of consciousness, not only in plants but also in such unlikely sounding candidates as yogurt, infertile eggs, and saliva. He even discovered that a bit of saliva taken from someone's mouth exhibited awareness of its human donor's emotional state, from hundreds of miles away. The term he eventually coined to describe the pervasive phenomena he had discovered was *primary awareness.* This is virtually a synonym for panpsychism.

Now, what about stones? For those of us who can feel crystal energies, and who sense their qualities as being innately spiritual and numinous, some of the best evidence validating the idea of panpsychism comes from our own experiences. In my workshops, I always encourage participants to experiment with viewing the stones as beings, and we often do this in practices in which we engage a Stone Being in an inner dialogue. We ask the Stone Being about its nature, and what sorts of things we might do together, and we write down the replies that we receive inwardly. Often several different members of the group will get virtually the same message from the Being of the same variety of stone. This occurs even when the type of stone is completely new to the participants. These communications can go much farther, with the relationship becoming one in which the stone becomes one's spiritual ally. We'll discuss this more in a later chapter.

PRACTICE: MEETING A STONE BEING IN THE HEART

In this practice, you can enter into relationship with the Being of a stone. You will also have the experience of perception through the heart. We'll discuss the heart's intelligence in a later section. For now, I suggest you just try the exercise, and pay attention to your own experience.

1. Go to your collection of stones and crystals (or to a crystal shop, if you don't have a collection) and choose a stone. Better yet, pay attention to a number of different stones and see if you get the feeling that one of them is choosing *you.* It is ideal if this is a kind of stone you don't know well already. Take that stone to a place where you can sit quietly.
2. Sit down and relax while holding the stone. Put all of your sensory attention on the stone. Look at its color and shape in detail, feel its texture with your fingers, and touch it to your cheek. Smell it, touch it with your tongue (as long as the mineral isn't toxic), and even hold it up to your ear and listen. You may not taste or smell anything, and you are highly likely not to hear anything, but giving attention in this way helps to sensitize your awareness.
3. Bring your subjective attention to the center of your chest, at the level of the heart. Hold the stone in your two cupped hands, a few inches in front of your mouth. As you inhale, drawing air over the stone and into your lungs, imagine that you are inviting the Stone Being into your heart. As you exhale, silently offer yourself to the Stone Being, letting it know that you are available for relationship.
4. Continue this breathing for a few breaths—at least three and probably not more than ten—but let your intuition guide you. When you feel ready, bring the stone to your chest and hold it there, touching you. Let your eyes close and allow yourself to attend fully to your inner experience. Continue to affirm the invitation on the in-breath and the offer of yourself on the out-breath. Picture the stone's image responding to your invitation by moving into your chest, finally settling into the center of your heart. Notice what that feels like, and attend to the presence of the Stone Being in your heart. Greet it from your heart and thank it for coming into you.
5. Let this meditation continue for several minutes. It is not necessary to do anything else, other than to maintain the visualization, and give yourself over to whatever feelings or images you experience. Don't hold back. Allow the heart to hold and cherish the Stone Being.
6. Notice everything that happens. Sometimes this sort of meditation will trigger a more complex visionary experience. If that happens, go with it. If the Stone Being starts to communicate with you, attend to it inwardly, and respond as your heart moves you to respond. Also, take note of your bodily sensations. You may feel the stone's energies moving into and through your body. You may find that the currents travel to one or more specific places. If so, pay attention to where the energy goes, and how it feels. Afterward, make notes about your experience in your journal. If nothing happens beyond the visualization you did according to these instructions, don't be concerned. Just allow yourself to breathe and see and feel the stone in your heart. Continue to do this for at least five minutes. When you feel ready to stop, or have the sense that the session is completed, you can gently open your eyes.

DISCUSSION

This practice is the way I begin all of my intuitive work with stones. Following this ritual each time one sits down with a stone does several things, aside from the overt performance of the instructions.

First, it teaches you a simple way to quiet distracting thoughts and direct your attention, both outwardly to the physical stone and inwardly to your inner experience of the stone. This is important because this sort of communication occurs in a subtle realm, and going there requires focused, sensitive attention.

Second, this practice helps you learn to make your heart the place you go for spiritual work and experiences. Our hearts have their own intelligence, and they have long been viewed as the seat of the soul. The heart is the place where Wisdom dwells within us, and where spiritual beings can most readily meet us. By practicing visualizations in the heart, you will become familiar with how it feels to be heart-centered, and will come to recognize the heart's distinctive intelligence.

Third, this type of practice can help take one into the inner Silence, which is where the spiritual world exists. Most of us live with a constant stream of inner talk going on whenever we are awake. Using visualization and heart centering can quiet that ongoing monologue. This is, in itself, one of the main goals of many meditation practices. (However, we will see later that, in alchemical meditation, quieting the inner chatter is only a first step that makes us available for relating, and even conversing, with other beings.)

Fourth, this simple exercise, using breath and imagination, can take one to the threshold of profound spiritual experience. Once we have successfully visualized the stone in the heart, we may find that more things happen spontaneously. All sorts of inner events can occur, ranging from flowing currents of energy to conversational dialogues to inner journeys, or even to physical events. Sometimes the heart will temporarily change its rhythm of beating when it feels the presence of a Stone Being that it really likes. (I smilingly compare this to a dog wagging its tail.)

We can see that there is much more to this simple practice than meets the eye. One can, and probably should, perform this practice with every stone in one's collection, to begin establishing a relationship with each Stone Being. (I also like to spend a few moments repeating this ritual of invitation and greeting whenever I sit with a stone, even one that I know well.) This is why we call these exercises Practices. If we want them to work well, we have to *practice!*

On the subject of practice, ritual, and repetition, I want to mention that these elements not only familiarize one with certain inner experiences; they also help to *build the reality* within which these things occur. Biologist Rupert Sheldrake calls this establishing a *morphogenic field*—a pattern that the world remembers and which tends to repeat and amplify. We'll go into this more in the chapter on "Transformation through Feedback."

Whatever you choose to do in regard to performing this exercise with some or all of your stones, I strongly urge you to keep a journal with notes of your experiences. Many of them may require only a few words, or you might want to draw a sketch of something you saw. Just remember that you are entering into another world—a world that overlaps with the everyday world we all know, but one that is subtle, deep, loving, and powerful. If you keep records and make "maps" of where you've been, that world will become more and more vivid and alive for you.

Having gone through the above practice, most readers will have experienced some sense of contact with a Stone Being. Many will have felt the stone's energies in their bodies. Some will have experienced an inner journey or a dialogue with the Stone Being. In my view, all of these phenomena are evidence that tends to validate the concept of panpsychism—the view that consciousness is a fundamental quality of the universe and that there is soul everywhere.

It is important to contemplate the implications of these experiences. Merely having them, putting them on a mental shelf, and going on with life as usual wastes their potential. Instead, begin to experiment with acting and thinking as if everything you see, touch, hear, taste, and smell has consciousness and life. Try to feel the presence of soul in everything, from your crystals to your car to the food on your plate. Cultivate your feeling sense—the capacity to discern how everything and every event feels—as you did during the meditation with the stone. Engage with everything in your life as if you are meeting a beloved friend. (And yes, it is OK to eat your food, but thank it for nourishing you and offer it your love.)

If you give some time and attention to going through your day in this way, you are likely to notice an interesting phenomenon—in treating everything in the world as if it has soul, you'll become much closer to your own soul. You'll begin to feel its presence. And you will find a natural gentleness becoming your new way of being. This is the way of compassion, which is the way of the heart and the soul.

Some people may argue that events such as our meditative encounters with stones, or our experiences of feeling stone energies, are not evidence for panpsychism, because they are not "objective." (Even a part of your own mind may make this objection.) After all, we go into the meditation with the intention of encountering a Stone Being, and we use our imaginations to visualize that happening.

My answer to such arguments is simply this: it's correct to say that such experiences are not objective, but it is wrong to invalidate them on that account. *Every* experience of consciousness—our own, and our encounters with other conscious beings, from meditation to daily life—is *subjective.* There is no real way to prove any of them in an objective sense. That is how some "objective" materialist philosophers end up absurdly denying that consciousness even exists.

But we are not trying to prove anything to the satisfaction of scientific dogmas. We are exploring the alchemical worldview—trying it on for size to see if it is a more satisfactory point of view for living life and experiencing the world.

Remember, the spiritual alchemist does not pretend to sit outside events and observe them objectively. The alchemists plunged in and invested themselves in trying to act creatively in the world. They accepted intuitively and enthusiastically the principle now espoused by quantum physics—that the observer is a part of the event, and influences what is observed.

My favorite example of this fact is that an observer viewing a rainbow is absolutely essential to the rainbow's manifestation. That is why the rainbow seems to move when you move. It takes three things to make a rainbow—moisture in the air, light, and an observer in a location that is at the proper angle between the moisture and the light. Remove any one of these three, and the rainbow can't be seen.

Panpsychism means "soul everywhere." To fully take on that idea means to invest oneself in one's own soul viewpoint. Another name for our soul viewpoint is our *interiority.* That is the only place where we can genuinely conceive the soul in everything around us—including our friends, the stones.

THE SEAT OF THE SOUL

This brings to mind an important quote from one of my heroes, the eighteenth-century visionary Novalis. He was a German Romantic poet and philosopher, and he wrote this famous line, "*The seat of the soul is where the inner world and the outer world meet. Where they overlap, it is in every point of the overlap.*"

I have also come across another vivid translation of what Novalis wrote: "*The seat of the soul is where the inner world and the outer world touch. Where they permeate each other, the seat is in every point of the permeation.*"

I have presented both translations because the point Novalis makes is one of the keys to understanding alchemy, and to receiving the medicine of this book. *It is the notion that there is a constant, living correspondence between one's own interiority and the World Interiority.* Our souls and the Soul of the World meet within that correspondence.

I repeat: *This is the medicine of this book. If you take it daily, you will become human in seven weeks!*

If we want to actually become spiritual alchemists and discover the secrets that are at the core of their wisdom, *we must be willing to give up the fantasy of objectivity and intentionally locate ourselves in the seat of the soul.*

In the practice of inviting the Stone Being into our hearts, we were purposely working from the seat of the soul. We were choosing to experience the stone in the *overlap—the permeation*—of its inner and outer manifestation. We were reaching out to its interiority, from our own interiority.

In life, when we choose to guide our perceptions by envisioning that everything has soul, and by acting accordingly, we are locating ourselves in the seat of the soul. Again, we might hear the voice of the inner judge: "But you are just imagining all this. You're romanticizing things." I reply with more wisdom from Novalis: "*To romanticize the world is to make us aware of the magic, mystery, and wonder of the world; it is to educate the senses to see the ordinary as extraordinary, the familiar as strange, the mundane as sacred, the finite as infinite.*"

Which world would we rather inhabit—the one that is merely ordinary, familiar, and mundane, or the world that is extraordinary, strange, and infinite? When we simply spend a moment deeply considering the universe or any part of it—even something as small and humble as a stone—we quickly realize that the real world is the strange, extraordinary, infinite one, and the idea that there is such a thing as an "ordinary world" is the fantasy.

When I offer workshops, people often come up to me at the end of the weekend and say regretfully, "I wish I could always feel like this, but now I have to go back to the real world." That usually makes my head want to explode, because we've just spent several days working with stones and exploring extraordinary perceptions *that are completely real.* They really happened! But I do understand. The mass hypnosis that we commonly call "the real world" surrounds us on all sides, and almost everyone has been thoroughly indoctrinated in it from childhood. There is so much unconscious brainwashing going on in every direction that often, when we go, even briefly, beyond the everyday mundane worldview, we tend to *doubt our own experience,* even when it is something of immense value to us.

And, at the same time, we long deeply, in our hearts, to live in that magical, infinite world. The reason is: that world is our true home. *We ourselves are extraordinary, strange, and infinite.* That's why there is a feeling of regret when we believe we have to leave the wonder we have experienced within, and go back to "reality." But the reality of the materialist dogma is inadequate and toxic to the soul. I believe it is time to rescue the world, and ourselves. It is time to open and commit ourselves to the world our hearts can feel and long to dwell in. To enter that world and live there, we need to learn to perceive it all the time, just as we learned as children—at the behest of our elders—to perceive the world as mundane. As Novalis said, to do so, we must educate our senses. Once again, this is where the stones come in. Just the experience of sensing crystal energies—which have no place in the world of materialism—breaks the spell. Feeling the vibrational presence of the stones and their songs is, in a very literal sense, an awakening. We need such awakenings in order to feel whole again.

As Novalis said of poetry, which can also awaken us, "Poetry heals the wounds inflicted by reason." So once we're awake to our sense of wonder and delight, and the presence of soul in everything, how do we stay awake? How do we "educate the senses?" The alchemists did so through the conscious, purposeful use of imagination. Inviting the Stone Beings to meet us in the realm of the permeation of inner and outer—the seat of the soul—begins with imagination. From there, things move with their own momentum. When we invite them, the Stone Beings are ready to help us rediscover the magic, mystery, and wonder of the world.

PRACTICE: TAKING A WALK (NO STONES REQUIRED)

This practice builds on the earlier one we looked into, "Meeting a Stone Being in the Heart." It is a simple way to enact Novalis's advice that it is essential to romanticize the world.

1. Go out for a walk, in as natural a setting as possible, although you can do this anywhere. As you stroll along, pay attention to whatever you notice—trees, bushes, birds, rocks, water, sidewalks, buildings, people, as well as sounds, smells, and so on. With each thing you notice, imagine drawing your perception of it into your heart, as you inwardly say, "I invite you into my heart." Next, imagine sending your heart outward to whatever you have perceived and inwardly say to it, "I offer my heart to you."
2. Keep doing this, using silently spoken words for a while, and then try to do the same thing, but as a wordless inner gesture. *Feel* the invitation to enter your heart being extended to whatever you have perceived. Then *feel* your heart going outward in the gesture of offering.
3. Notice that each object of your perception has become a *Thou*—another being, with whom you are offering to relate in a loving way. Take this seriously. Pay attention to how it feels to do this, and imagine that you are doing it *for real*—that everything you perceive is another self. If you can actually do this for even a few minutes without the habitual inner judge stealing it from you and insisting to you that "it isn't real," a subtle but amazing change will take place. You'll *feel the soul-reality* of what you have entered through imagining—through acting *as if* it's true.
4. Reflect on this, and go deeper into feeling it. When you feel everything in the world as another self—someone with whom you are sharing the world—a lovely atmosphere of intimacy replaces the common human sense of isolation. As Novalis said, by romanticizing the world through imagination, you are able to restore "the magic, mystery, and wonder of the world." Contemplate the fact that this simple shift of viewpoint can make such an amazing difference in your own experience of the world. And, although you may not know it, it also makes a huge difference in *the way the world experiences you.*
5. It may require a few tries to get to this perceptual shift. After all, old habits have a way of persisting, and the one you are trying to shift is a deep-seated one. Our surface self can resist entering the depths, and may attack one's efforts to tinker with one's worldview. Just keep practicing. Do it gently, from a calm place. If you imagine clearly that you are centering yourself in your heart—just for a little while—as you take your walk, you will sooner or later know—from the inside—what I am talking about here.
6. Now, go back and try the stone practice again. Meet the stone from your heart. Invite the Being of the stone to come into your heart, and offer your heart to the Stone Being. Let yourself imagine that there *really* is another being there with you.
7. Recently I tried this when I woke up during the night. I sleep with a big chunk of the stone called Rosophia, because I find its presence very soothing. I held the stone to my chest and made the invitation. I instantly felt a huge surge of love flow into my heart, and I had the clear sense that the Stone Being had been *waiting* for my invitation. In the next moment, when I offered my heart to the Rosophia, I felt another surge, coming from within me. My Deep Self had also been waiting.

DISCUSSION

The "Taking a Walk" practice is an experiment with trying on the worldview of panpsychism. We purposely imagine, as we walk along, that everything we perceive has consciousness, or is an expression of consciousness. We address each object of our perception as if this is true, and we make the offer of loving relationship to all of those imagined beings.

When the practice goes as I have described it, we are met, sooner or later, with the unmistakable felt sense that (oh, my goodness!) everything actually is conscious, and that the world, in all its parts, returns our love.

I have one last thought to offer about this—something I received as a strong intuition when I was doing the "Taking a Walk" practice this morning. There is a strange, fuzzy line at the border between imagination and perception. You can see where it is as you look at the practice we've been discussing. We begin by following a path we have already planned—"I will do thus and so as I go on my walk. I will imagine . . ." Then there comes a moment when doing what we have planned gives way to something more happening—something we hadn't planned. ("I could suddenly *feel* all those beings in the world, and I felt them loving me back!") When you cross that line, you understand what Novalis was talking about. Something magical has happened.

Today, my intuition told me this: it's not only that a perceptual shift allowed me to realize that the world is indeed conscious, in all its parts. It is also true that my shift in perception helped to *actualize the manifestation* of the life and consciousness of all the things I was perceiving, *because* I was perceiving them that way.

This is something I referred to earlier. It is the co-creative activity of spiritual alchemy, in which the alchemist works with the Soul of the World to enhance the aliveness of matter. This is not the same thing as fantasy. It is the *opposite* of fantasy. This is the realization of how much co-creative power imagination can wield. We all have it, and we can all engage the world in this way.

Go back to the idea of the rainbow. If no one is looking, it cannot manifest, because *being seen* is essential to a rainbow being truly there. A rainbow is a visual event. The same is true, I suggest, for the latent consciousness within the world to become manifest. Someone has to look, which in this case means imagining (looking for) consciousness in each and every thing. And because the consciousness we seek is latently there to be seen, our act of imaginal perception is the crucial step that *actualizes* its existence.

But we do not make it up any more than we make up a rainbow. You need the moisture in the air and the sunlight, or no amount of looking will put a rainbow in the sky. The same is true of the consciousness of the world and its parts. If there were no consciousness for us to meet, as we do in the "Taking a Walk" exercise and our stone practices, we could never get past the threshold of our original planned intention. This is the difference between co-creation and just plain making things up.

So, the Stone Beings, and all the infinite points of consciousness in the world, are present *in potential,* and they come fully to life when our attention meets them.

As I mentioned, it's the same in quantum physics. Until we look, there is no particle or wave—only a probability, a potential. This is also similar to the Buddhist idea called *interdependent co-arising.*

And while we're at it, it seems just as true that our own existence, and the *quality* of existence we experience, is sustained by the *relationship* between ourselves and all that we perceive. We ourselves are shaped by our perceptions, just as much as we shape them. If we envision our world as lifeless and mundane, so are we. If we imagine our world is full of magic, so are we, truly. And the really amazing thing is that we have a choice—an infinite number of choices—about how we can wield our imaginations to help shape the world and ourselves.

But we don't do it alone. We don't make it up. We help to shape what comes to us from Nature, from the Soul of the World, as the alchemists knew and practiced. We can become the World Soul's active partners, beginning with something as simple as taking a walk, or holding a stone.

And there is one other thing to consider here: it is at least as important—and as accurate—to say that Sophia and the Living World are already there and waiting for us to *make the gesture* toward them. This is what *makes* **us** *real,* rather than the other way around. And it feels amazingly good to become real.

The alchemists intuitively understood this immense potential of co-creation and how profoundly it could affect the world. This was the insight that allowed them to envision the *magnum opus,* or the Great Work, which entailed nothing less than the perfection of the self and the redemption of the world.

This is not "just our imagination." It is our True Imagination.

OPPOSITE: Rembrandt, *The Philosopher in Meditation.* The Spiritual Alchemist is shown with his attention drawn inward, while he sits illuminated by the spiritual Sun. The figure at the lower right is his Deep Self, who stokes the alchemical fire of transformation in the subconscious. The doorway beside the meditating figure indicates the threshold one crosses when entering the Imaginal Realm. The spiral staircase between the two figures symbolizes the ascension to a higher level of being that occurs when the conscious and subconscious sides of the Self unite with one another.

4

Alchemy & True Imagination

To the alchemist, the magician, the Sufi mystic, and to Jung, the imagination was anything but unreal. Imaginary events were seen as occurring in a world that, though different from the ordinary world, was just as valid and real. Imagination was seen as having a real effect on the psyche, and even on physical reality, as well as helping create direct experiences of the divine. Alchemists believed that imagination was quite real, that it was an indispensable part of the alchemical undertaking. And Jung thought imagination was so important to the alchemical worldview that he wrote that the "concept of imagination is perhaps the most important key to understanding the opus [the Great Work of alchemy]."

—Jeffrey Raff, *Jung and the Alchemical Imagination*

The alchemists . . . were aware that True Imagination possesses a power and depth that fantasy does not possess.

—Jeffrey Raff, *Jung and the Alchemical Imagination*

The True Imagination connects with the hidden realities of the universe.

—Dennis Hauck, *The Complete Idiot's Guide to Alchemy*

True imagination transcends the ego, and creates experiences by which it can encounter the inner world. . . . From a more mystical perspective, imagination is the means by which the soul experiences God and shares in the creative expression of the Divine. . . . Fantasy, on the other hand, never transcends the ego. . . . [It] is about the ego's needs, desires, and quest for aggrandizement.

—Jeffrey Raff, *Jung and the Alchemical Imagination*

Imagination is the star in man.

—Paracelsus

Imagination is the gateway to spiritual experience.

—Kathy Helen Warner

Every man, every woman carries a firmament inside,
and the stars in it are not the stars in the sky.
Without imagination there is no memory.
Without imagination there is no sensation.
Without imagination there is no will, desire . . . the relation between things
In a continuum of imagination
What you find out for yourself is what you select
Out of an infinite sea of possibility . . .
The ground of imagination is fearlessness . . .
The ultimate famine is the starvation of the imagination . . .
THE ONLY WAR THAT MATTERS IS THE WAR AGAINST THE IMAGINATION.
ALL OTHER WARS ARE SUBSUMED IN IT.
There is no way out of a spiritual battle.
There is no way you can avoid taking sides . . . fantasy
No matter what you do: plumber, baker, teacher—
You do it in the consciousness of making, or not making, your world . . .
There is no way out of the spiritual battle.
The war is the war against the imagination.
You can't sign up as a conscientious objector;
The war of the worlds hangs here, right now, in the balance.
It is a war for this world, to keep it a vale of soul-making . . .
The war is the war for the human imagination,
And no one can fight it but you—
No one can fight it for *you.*
The imagination is not only holy, it is precise;
It is not only fierce, it is practical.
Men die every day for the lack of it . . . it is vast and elegant . . .

—Diane Di Prima, "Rant"

It is a little difficult to begin this chapter, because to many people, the phrase *true imagination* sounds like a contradiction. One of the key elements of the unfortunate spell that materialism has worked upon humanity and the Earth has been the denigration of imagination—the insistence that what we experience through imagination is unreal. This is what the poet Diane Di Prima was referring to in the quote above as "the war against the imagination." But remember, the materialists are the same people who maintain that no soul, no afterlife, and (according to some of them) no consciousness exist. Oh, and there is definitely no such thing as stone energy! We looked at this issue in the previous chapter, but I want to briefly address it again, because if we discount our imagination by calling imaginative experiences unreal, our alchemical path of transformation and awakening is halted before it begins.

The ironic thing about the denial of the value of imagination by the materialists is that *their own philosophy of materialism is a product of their imaginations,* just as their assertion that consciousness does not exist comes out of their own consciousness.

But let's leave them to their tail-chasing and move on. Just remember, if you begin to doubt the actuality of your experiences with stones and the Stone Beings, the doubt is likely to be the old echo of your indoctrination talking to you. If you want to know whether something feels right or valid, check in with your heart. That's the place to go to evaluate what is true in your soul.

We imagine the whole world. The *meaning* we extract, or conjure up, from our sensory data is what we call "the world," and that has been created by the imagination—by training ourselves, or by being trained, to build a particular imaginal interpretation of what we experience. The consensus everyday view of the world looks real, solid, and consistent because we have practiced it from infancy, following the lead of our families, teachers, and almost everyone around us. Most people seldom question this point of view, even though it feels spiritually unfulfilling. But if we practice something else, something more satisfying to the soul, we can create a very different experience of the world—one that will be just as true and real as our experience of ordinary "reality." Maybe more so. As Jesus was quoted in the Gospel of Thomas: "The kingdom of Heaven is spread out upon the Earth, and people do not see it." The ability to see (and manifest) the kingdom of Heaven on Earth is the alchemical work of True Imagination.

As the statement of Kathy Helen Warner at the beginning of this chapter tells us, "Imagination is the gateway to spiritual experience." In the practices discussed in the previous chapter, I suggested that you imagine meeting a stone as a being, and that you engage with other parts of the world around you in the same way. You reached toward them by focusing your attention, your intention, and your imagination in their direction. This took you to their doorway. That doorway is what Novalis called the seat of the soul—the place where the inner world and the outer world overlap and permeate one another.

Then, perhaps something or other that you did not plan ahead of time occurred. Perhaps you sensed the life or consciousness of something you had previously viewed as inanimate. Maybe you even felt it respond to you. In that moment, you had crossed through imagination's gateway into the realm of spiritual experience.

Sometimes such experiences occur spontaneously, through acts of grace. My first big spiritual experience in college, which I described in the first chapter, came that way. On the other hand, my pivotal meditation with Moldavite, which initiated me in the ability to feel stone energies, came through some quite intentional imagining. If I hadn't been willing to imagine that I was floating up out of my body, and to trust the experience that came out of doing so, I might never have awakened my capacity to sense the currents of the stones, and I could not be writing this book.

If we want to relate with the beings of the spiritual realms, and with the Stone Beings in particular, we need to learn how to approach them. This is the alchemical work of True Imagination.

What do we mean by imagination? In an actual sense, imagination is the capacity for creating or transforming *images.* The word *image* contains the word *mage,* which is an Anglicized form of the Latin word *magus,* meaning a magician. Thus, to truly imagine is to make magic!

In the mundane world, we have stage magicians who perform tricks through sleight of hand or other deceptive techniques. This is a counterfeit of the real magic to which we aspire. In the realm of True Imagination, we have the examples of shamans, or of threshold-dwellers such as Merlin, who are attuned to the inner realm of soul—the World Interiority. These mages can co-create, through a kind of inner dance between their own interiority and the World Interiority. They operate from the Seat of the Soul.

We can do that when we begin an active meditative practice, such as the ones I have described so far. I like active meditations because they use what I view as the three critical elements for creative and co-creative work: attention, intention, and imagination. I often describe these three elements as the Three Human Powers of Consciousness.

One could also say that imagination is the inner state brought about by the first two elements—attention and intention—since making a chosen image requires the exercise of both of those capacities. But imagination also has spontaneous qualities that take us beyond what we initially intend.

I usually prefer active meditation to passive varieties in which one simply watches one's thinking. In this "witnessing" meditation, one withdraws intention and simply pays attention to whatever thoughts or images arise. Alchemical meditation tends to be of the active variety.

As the great alchemist Paracelsus wrote, "Alchemical Meditation is the name of an internal talk of one person with another, who is invisible, as in the invocation of the Deity, or communion with one's deepest self, or with one's good angel."

So, alchemical meditation is, according to Paracelsus, an exchange between beings, an "internal talk." It is different from prayer because in prayer, one talks to the Divine, while in alchemical meditation, the Divine talks back. But both prayer and alchemical meditation require us to imagine that we are communicating with someone who is present with us, though invisible to the eyes.

The same is true of our interactions with the Stone Beings. The energy flow that many of us feel with stones is, in my view, one aspect of the "talk" between oneself and the Stone Being. And, to my mind, the fact that the stone has a physical embodiment, even though its spiritual energies are invisible, makes our imaginal engagement with it much easier.

To feel stone energies, we must still utilize attention and intention. We must consciously direct our attention to the stone, and we must usually pick it up, as a way of giving it our full sensory attention. We may often feel the currents of a stone simply by attending to them, without much in the way of specific conscious imagining. However, simply reaching out (or reaching in) to feel them is an intentional act of imagination, because we are purposely opening ourselves to the possibility that something is there. Then, when we actually feel something, we have reached the state of the overlap into True Imagination, the Seat of the Soul.

I am giving a lot of value to True Imagination. So, is there such a thing as false imagination? Yes, false imagination, in terms of what we are discussing in this book, is what we refer to as fantasy. Spiritual alchemy—and the Alchemy of Stones—require that we learn to discern carefully between True Imagination and fantasy, or our work will not succeed.

How can we tell the difference? Here, once again, is an important assertion from psychologist, author, and alchemist Jeff Raff:

> *True Imagination transcends the ego [the surface self] and it creates the experiences by which it can encounter the inner world. . . . Fantasy, on the other hand, never transcends the ego. While imagination contains information about other parts of the psyche and discloses the path to be followed, fantasy is about the ego's need, desires, and quest for aggrandizement.* (Raff, *Jung and the Alchemical Imagination*)

Fantasy focuses on what-if's that orbit around oneself: "What if I won the lottery, became famous, made love with a movie star?" Worry is another form of fantasy: "What if I lose my money, fail a test, become a laughing stock?" True Imagination puts attention on the inner world and engages with beings and events that go beyond one's worries and wants.

When we are focusing our attention, intention, and imagination on engaging with the Being of a stone, we are doing our best to use True Imagination, rather than indulging in fantasy. We are attempting to follow Raff's guidelines and create images that initiate the process of spiritual experience. We reach out to the stone inwardly, and we carefully observe our internal state. We engage our feeling sense, and we wait. We do not start with an idea about what "should" happen, and we do not force anything to happen. This can take practice, because we all want spiritual experiences to unfold for us. Our ego can conjure up a fantasy to please us, but if we observe carefully, we can sense that something about it is counterfeit.

In fantasy, the telltale signs can usually be recognized. If what happens conforms to wants you had before starting, if what occurs puffs up your pride, if the Stone Being tells you that you are a very important person, be skeptical.

And what about True Imagination? If what happens stimulates feelings of surprise, awe, humility, or love, you can trust what is happening. If you feel a sense of the numinous—of a spiritual presence that is with you—you have gone beyond mere fantasy. If a being you meet emanates love for you while simultaneously seeing through all your masks, you've hit the jackpot.

Once again, practice is hugely helpful. As you have more experiences, the real ones will become apparent, and the fantasies will begin to stick out like sore thumbs. As you get to know yourself and the Stone Beings more and more deeply, you won't easily be fooled by the tricks of your ego, and you won't have much patience for them either. The real thing is so much better.

Your feeling sense is a critical capacity in this sort of work. As you develop it, you will become more sure-footed in the inner terrain. Keeping asking yourself, "How does this feel?" Ask the same question, whether you are meditating with a stone, taking a walk, selecting a restaurant or choosing a doctor . . . or anything else. Hold your intention on utilizing True Imagination, which is your co-creative power, and remember that fantasy is a counterfeit version of inner reality.

Again, I so deeply value working with the Stone Beings. Their currents of vibration are discernable to many of us, and this helps enormously in our discrimination of True Imagination from fantasy. The presence of stone energies acts like a beacon for our attention, keeping us tuned to what is really happening, and who is really there with us.

Paracelsus, one of our esteemed guides on the path of alchemy, was very much a practitioner of True Imagination. He believed in and practiced communication with all aspects of Nature through the astral body. I view the astral body as the same thing the Sufis knew as the imaginal body, or what Jung would call the subtle body, the body in the psychoid realm (later on, there will be more about the psychoid). Like the forms of other beings we meet in this realm, our imaginal or astral body is composed of subtle matter and energy and is animated through the power of True Imagination. The astral body spoken of by Paracelsus is also akin to what we sometimes call the Light Body. In the book *Paracelsus: Essential Reading,* editor Nicholas Goodrick-Clarke wrote that Paracelsus believed that the astral body:

Engraving of Paracelsus (1493-1541; born Philippus Aureolus Theophrastus Bombastus von Hohenheim, renowned physician and alchemist) *Azoth* the word written on the hilt of Paracelsus' sword refers to the animating spirit hidden in all matter that makes transmutation possible. In his book, *Transcendental Magic,* Ephias Levi wrote: "The Azoth or Universal Medicine is, for the soul, supreme reason and absolute justice; for the mind, it is mathematical and practical truth; *for the body it is the quintessence, which is a combination of gold and light.* In the superior or spiritual world, it is the First Matter [*prima materia*] of the Great Work, the source of the enthusiasm and activity of the alchemist." [NOTE: The gold-white light called Azoth is often experienced in meditation with Azeztulite.—RS]

> *"teaches man" and is able to communicate with the astral part of the macrocosm, the uncreated virtues or direct emanations of God in the world of Nature. He saw experience as a process of identification of the mind or astral body with the internal knowledge possessed by natural objects in attaining their specific ends. The researcher should try to "**overhear**" the knowledge of the star, the herb, or **stone** with respect to its activity and function. Science is already present as a virtue in the natural object, and it is the **experience** of the researcher which uncovers the **astral sympathy** between himself and the object. This identification with an object penetrates more deeply into the essence of the object than mere sensory perception.* [Emphasis mine —RS]

I want to offer a few words of interpretation here. We could say that the term *astral body* is closely related to what I have called one's "personal interiority." The "astral part of the macrocosm" corresponds to what I have termed the "World Interiority." When Paracelsus "saw experience as a process of identification of the . . . astral body with the internal knowledge possessed by natural objects," he was discerning the interplay of one's personal interiority/soul with the World Interiority/World Soul (in a particular natural object). The term *astral sympathy* refers to the overlap and permeation of one's personal soul with the soul qualities of "the star, the herb, or the stone."

I was very pleased to find this quote, because it is precisely what I do when I meditate with a stone in order to write about its spiritual qualities and healing properties.

FANTASY AND TRUE IMAGINATION IN THE ALCHEMY OF STONES

> *According to Paracelsus, fantasy is seeing only the surface of things. It fails to penetrate the veils of nature and spirit to see into the heart of something, and is content with superficialities. Fantasy can be creative, as a scientist can be creative about the nature of physical reality, but if such a scientist fails to understand the natural object as a symbol, and to perceive the meaning of that symbol, he has engaged in fantasy and not in true imagination. . . . For Paracelsus, fantasy is the failure to recognize a symbol and the symbolic reality of all things.*
>
> —Jeff Raff, *The Wedding of Sophia*

> *The theory of the* mundus imaginalis *[the imaginal realm] is bound up with a theory of imaginative knowledge and imaginative function. . . . It is a function that permits all the universes to* symbolize with one another *(or exist in symbolic relationship with one another).*
>
> —Henry Corbin, *Mundus Imaginalis: Or the Imaginary and the Imaginal*

Spiritual alchemy requires from us the willingness to give up the fantasy of objectivity and to intentionally locate ourselves in the Seat of the Soul. As Novalis taught, the Seat of the Soul is where the inner and outer worlds permeate one another, and it is located at every point of the permeation.

Now, what does this mean, and how do we do it? The meaning we are reaching for is implicit in the distinction Paracelsus delineates between fantasy and True Imagination. In fantasy, we are in the director's chair of ego, rather than the Seat of the Soul, and from that place we see only the surface reality of the world. In True Imagination, we engage our creative perception to look for the *symbolic meaning* embodied by the objects and events we encounter. Every time we recognize such meaning, we come into the Seat of the Soul. We both perceive and co-create the permeation of inner and outer reality.

In the Alchemy of Stones, we do this whenever we work meditatively with a stone. When we attend to a stone's energies, and when we attempt to intuitively recognize the stone's spiritual qualities, we are using True Imagination, and we have located ourselves in the Seat of the Soul.

When we are feeling the spiritual qualities of a stone, we often inwardly see an image or images that indicate its nature. Or we experience bodily sensations such as vibration or heat.

It is easy to see how the visual images a stone's currents generate within us can be symbols for its spiritual qualities. However, even when we feel vibration, heat, or other sensations in the body, we are not feeling literal physical events—we are still actually experiencing the stone symbolically. This occurs in our subtle body, a.k.a. the imaginal body. The subtle body resonates with the stone's spiritual essence, and translates this quality into bodily sensations. These sensations are *symbols* of the Stone Being's spiritual essence, just as the inner visual images are. The ideas of heat or vibration represent familiar sensations. These can reveal something to us about the qualities of the stone, just as visual images do. Often, these sensations can lead to intuitive statements about what the presence of the Stone Being is generating within us. In all such cases, we have connected with the stone's symbolic nature. And when we do this, it is most definitely what Paracelsus defines as True Imagination rather than fantasy.

Once again, by way of contrast, if we simply look at the stone superficially, noting its size, color, weight, density, and so on, we might say we are examining it "scientifically." However, if we go no farther, Paracelsus would tell us that we were stuck in a mere fantasy about the stone, because we have failed to "penetrate the veils of nature and spirit to see into the heart" of the stone. We will have failed to understand the stone as a symbol (a manifested "word" or "message" spoken by the Divine), and we will not have perceived its meaning.

Now let's consider for a moment the above quote from Henry Corbin, the twentieth-century philosopher, Sufi, and spiritual alchemist. He tells us that the imaginal realm (the realm we are within when we engage the stones with True Imagination) is bound together with the "imaginative function," which is the function that "permits all the universes . . . to exist in symbolic relationship with one another."

This is an amazing insight. Corbin is saying that *the imaginative function can unify all the universes* (all levels of physical and spiritual reality) through symbolic relationship. He is revealing that *symbolic meaning* is the touchstone that unifies everything, in relationship with everything else.

To illustrate the idea that symbolic relationships are woven through the fabric of our lives, I will mention one that we are all familiar with—marriage. In marriage, two people who are otherwise unrelated go through a ritual—civil or religious—and agree that they are now related most profoundly, and that they *mean something to each other.* This meaning—the symbolic significance of "husband" and "wife"—redefines their lives and alters their trajectories. There are many more such examples of the symbolic relationships embedded in everyday life.

So, returning to the stones, if I sit down to meditate with a stone and I want to connect with it as a Being, I begin by attending to it through my physical senses. I look at it, touch it, feel its weight, and so forth. If this is all I do, I have not engaged it with True Imagination.

Next, I hold it in front of me and breathe over it. As I exhale, I offer myself to the Stone Being in relationship. As I inhale, I invite the stone's energies into my heart, or wherever they want to go within me. My breathing is a physical act, but the intentions I hold are the symbolic aspects of my breathing. By envisioning these intentions, I have entered the realm of True Imagination (*mundus imaginalis*) and have initiated the process of engaging the Stone Being in symbolic relationship.

One of the wonders of this alchemical work is that such invitations, when made with sincerity, are always answered. And the answers appear in a whole range of phenomena—in images, sensations, words, feelings, insights, and more. I have experienced all of these, as have many of you who are reading this. All of them are symbolic, in the sense that they occur in the imaginal realm—the Seat of the Soul between the outer and inner worlds—and they connect physical and spiritual realities with one another.

This goes far beyond our work with stones—it is everywhere. Whenever you notice a synchronicity, what you are noticing is a symbolic, meaningful connection between an outer event and your own inner state. When you do this, you have, momentarily at least, given up the fantasy of objectivity and entered into True Imagination.

When we consult an oracle such as the tarot or I Ching, we are doing the same thing. The tarot cards or I Ching coins are physical objects, but images on the cards and the hexagram patterns generated by our coin tosses *symbolize the meaning* underlying the purportedly "random" actions of shuffling and placing the cards or throwing the I Ching coins.

When we perform a personal ritual, such as setting up an altar and making offerings, we are inviting and activating a symbolic relationship with the spiritual beings we are addressing.

All such entries into True Imagination are accompanied by a distinctive feeling of *numinosity*. This is the tingle of awe and reverence we experience when we sense our connection to the vast depths of soul and spirit that underlie our surface world. We have discovered what the poet Diane Di Prima called "the relation between things in a continuum of imagination."

Our guide Paracelsus gave us a great gift in the clear way he differentiated fantasy from True Imagination. Because we have all been thoroughly educated (or brainwashed?) in the fantasy of objectivity, we have to work hard to undo our programming, but the rewards are great. We have, through True Imagination, the opportunity to reclaim our souls, and to share love and wisdom with the Soul of the World. And the Stone Beings are ready to join us in the joy of the work.

So—let's get started!

PRACTICE: A CONVERSATION WITH A STONE BEING

In this practice, you are invited to try doing something similar to what I do when I write about stones and their spiritual properties. You will be engaging with a stone as a being, and you'll ask the Stone Being to show or tell you something about its inner qualities, and the potential of your working together. I have led groups in this practice in my workshops, and it has been amazing to see the similarities in the information received by different people working with the same species of stones. This frequently occurs even when the stones being worked with are types that the people have not encountered or read about before.

For this practice, you will need a notebook and a pen. You may even want to have some colored pencils or other drawing supplies at hand, because often the information arrives as an image or images.

1. Select a stone to work with. In my workshops, I ask participants to reach into a bag of many different stones and chose one without looking. Or, as I suggested in an earlier practice, let the stone choose you. It is easy to do this by browsing over a selection of different types of stones and tuning in to your feeling sense. See which stone talks to you. This may be felt as an inaudible "call" from the stone, or simply as a feeling of being drawn to it. Ideally, especially the first time, you should choose from stones you don't know well, and have not read about.
2. Sit down and relax while holding the stone. Put all of your sensory attention on the stone. Look at its color and shape, feel its texture with your fingers, and touch it to your cheek.

Smell it, touch it with your tongue (as long as the stone isn't toxic), and even hold it up to your ear and listen.

3. Bring your attention to the center of your chest, at the level of the heart. Hold the stone a few inches in front of your mouth. As you inhale, imagine that you are inviting the Stone Being into your heart. As you exhale, silently offer yourself to the Stone Being. When you feel ready, bring the stone to your chest and hold it there. Continue to affirm the invitation on the in-breath and the offer of yourself on the out-breath. Picture the stone's image responding to your invitation by moving into your chest, finally settling into the center of your heart. Greet it from your heart and thank it for coming into you.
4. From the center of your heart, ask the Stone Being this question: What is your nature, and what can we do together?
5. Be inwardly silent and wait. Continue to imagine the stone's presence in your heart. Try to *feel* it there, and let go of the visual image of it.
6. If you are inwardly receiving an answer to your question, stay with the experience and allow it to come to a natural stop or pause. When this occurs, write down or sketch what you have heard, seen, or felt.
7. If you have not received a discernible answer, center your attention in your heart and hold the feeling of the Stone Being's presence there. When you are ready, ask the question again, this time without words, but simply as the *feeling* of asking.
8. Or, if you received an answer to the first question about the stone's properties, but not to the second question about what you can do together, ask the second question again. Then listen from you heart, and write down what comes to you.
9. You may find that other questions arise in you. Perhaps you want to ask the stone to show you how to work with it for self-healing, or you may ask the Stone Being to take you on a journey to its inner realm. Once the connection with the Stone Being has been made, you can take it as far as you both want it to go.
10. Alternatively, after step 4 and before step 5, you may wish to ask the Stone Being to come to you as an inner figure. These spiritual entities are perfectly capable of displaying themselves to you as moving, communicating images. Often, the *form* in which they appear to you is part of their communication. Some people may find it easier to dialogue with a human-like figure representing the Stone Being. (Stones have come to me spontaneously in human form on several occasions.) You can try this and see what occurs. What happens in these inner contemplative encounters can vary widely. Just try to feel into what is happening, and follow what resonates as genuine. As mentioned, if you experience surprise, awe, humility, or love, or if images or information you had not expected come to you, these are signals of True Imagination. If your experience seems to flatter you, or if you can feel yourself controlling it, you have probably slipped into fantasy. (NOTE: Love is not flattery.) If this occurs, you don't have to stop the practice. Just draw your attention back to your heart and begin again from there.
11. As you feel the experience of communication drawing to a natural close, center your attention in your heart, and surround the Stone Being with your love and gratitude. Slowly come back to everyday awareness. Sometimes it may be necessary to wiggle your toes or take a drink of water to bring yourself back fully.
12. While everything is still fresh in your mind, make notes in your journal about what happened in the conversation. Try to describe the way the Stone Being appeared to you, and if possible, sketch any images you received. Be sure to list any instructions or suggestions the Stone Being made regarding what you can do together, and how the stone can help you with healing, meditation, inner journeying, and so on.

13. NOTE: If you have difficulty in initiating communication with the Stone Being, or if you do not sense any replies to your questions, try this: open your eyes enough to see your writing materials. Write down the beginning of this sentence: "I want to tell you . . ." Imagine that the Stone Being will finish this sentence with information for you. Then listen carefully, in the center of your heart, and write whatever comes to you. Then repeat, beginning the sentence again with the phrase: "I want to tell you . . ." Again, listen from your heart and write down what comes. This usually unblocks any stuck communications. Keep repeating this until the interchange feels complete. Then finish the meditation with love and gratitude, as described above.

If you want to take this technique farther, you can try using the phrase: "I want to ask you . . ." Then write down what the Stone Being tells you that it wishes to ask of you. The results are often surprising, and always interesting. When I am leading workshops, we usually work with both of these phrases.

DISCUSSION

In this practice, we have moved beyond a simple encounter with a Stone Being in the heart, and we have entered the realm of dialogue and co-creation. We now have the opportunity to learn and cooperate with the Stone Being in spiritual partnership. Relationship has begun, and like human relationships, it can be simple or complex, superficial or profound, brief or lifelong. As in other relationships, continued interaction will reveal more of each being to the other, and you will have the opportunity to be spiritually enriched in the process.

The instructions sketched out above are simply intended to show you how to initiate these relationships. You can develop them however you wish, and in whatever directions you choose. There are a multitude of Stone Beings, and most or all of them are willing—even eager—to work with us.

There are important reasons that I begin all of my meditations (and the instructions for these practices) with the steps of first concentrating on focusing one's physical senses on the stone and then envisioning and inviting the stone into one's heart. In order to meet the stone as a being, and to learn about how we can work with it, we have to engage our physical senses, our feeling sense, and our imagination.

When we enter into this deeply through doing it with sincerity—with focused attention and intention—our physical senses blend into one another, and they combine with our feeling sense, which is centered in the heart. This is the kind of attention that the alchemists called True Imagination, and when we are perceiving in this way, we can see into the very essence of things. Truly inviting the Stone Being into one's heart means to view the being as kin and meet it with love. This is essential for the communion we are seeking. As the legendary plant biologist George Washington Carver said, "Anything will give up its secrets if you love it enough." As we do this, we discover that we do not have to force ourselves to feel this love. It arises spontaneously through our recognition of the other soul.

When our perceptions and our feeling sense are thus attuned with the self of the Stone Being, we can enter its world—and we find that the space we enter truly is a world. It can feel spacious, even vast. There can be form and architecture and life. Surprising things can happen there. So, the instruction is: allow, allow, allow. Follow the golden threads, stay with the unfolding of the event. Deepen the intimacy of your engagement with the Stone Being.

This kind of communication through communion has been practiced by indigenous people for many thousands of years. It is how shamans know which plants to use for medicines. When Peruvian shamans were asked by anthropologist Jeremy Narby how they knew which plants were useful for healing various ailments, or for changing consciousness, the shamans invariably said, "The plants tell us." This is very much in alignment with the advice of

Paracelsus: "try to 'overhear" the knowledge of the star, the herb, or stone with respect to its activity and function."

Nobel Prize-winning biologist Barbara McClintock made her discoveries in the genetics of corn plants by means of the kind of imaginative attention we are working with. She says:

> *Well, you know, when I look at a cell, I get down in that cell and look around.... The more I worked with [the chromosomes] the bigger and bigger [they] got, and when I was really working with them I wasn't outside, I was down there. I was part of the system. I was right down there with them, and everything got so big. I even was able to see the internal parts of the chromosomes—actually everything was there. It surprised me because I actually felt as if I were right down there and these were my friends.*

These kinds of experiences can validate for us, in a personal and convincing manner, the premise of panpsychism—that all matter has consciousness as a true aspect of its nature. When we approach the stones from this perspective, we are no longer standing in our own way. We have put aside the fantasy dogma of the materialistic worldview and opened ourselves to experiences that reveal the life and awareness within the stones, and within all matter.

A note on discernment: Remember to use your discrimination, and listen to your heart for the feeling of authenticity in these encounters. If you are not sure whether you have met the true Being of the stone, ask yourself inwardly, and you will feel what's true. Do the same about anything you feel unsure of. If the encounter feels bad for any reason, pay attention to that and depart from the situation. I have not personally had any bad or problematic experiences in my inner meetings with the stones. They have all been very positive and illuminating, and I have come to view the Stone Beings as kindred souls for whom I have deep affection. But I mention this as a general suggestion for all inner work. The same types of cautions apply to encounters that occur in shamanic journeying, to which this bears some resemblance.

Before we go on, I want to describe another practice. It is highly recommended for those who get stuck when trying to do the "A Conversation with a Stone Being" practice.

PRACTICE: MAKING AN ALTAR TO THE STONE BEING

When one is endeavoring to engage in interior conversation or rapport with a Stone Being, sometimes it may feel like nothing happens, no matter how much one wants it to. Or one may feel unable to avoid falling into fantasy. This can have to do with trying too hard, which can hinder one's receptivity, or one may get stuck because one does not yet know how to imagine without fantasizing. My recommended method for breaking through such blocks is making an altar to the Stone Being. The process is simple, but it usually works. Do not let the simplicity tempt you not to take the process seriously, or not to follow through for the whole three days. Both your own soul intelligence and the soul intelligence of the Stone Being will be aware of you, and of whether your gesture is sincere or not. Without your sincere inner gesture, nothing can happen. **NOTE** Before you begin to build the altar, choose (or be chosen by) a Stone Being with whom you really want to form a deep relationship. That is the stone to work with in this practice.

1. Find a spot that you can designate as sacred space, at least for the duration of this practice. It can be a room, or part of a room, or a small table or a shelf. Whatever spot you choose, it is important that it be set apart, and that nothing outside the ritual you are creating be allowed in that space.
2. Put a little cloth and a dish or bowl for the stone on your designated altar location. Purify the space by burning sage, incense or *palo santo* over it. As you purify the space, inwardly hold your intention to make an offering to the Stone Being that you wish you meet and relate with. Keep yourself centered in the heart as you do this.

3. When the purification feels complete, place the physical stone on the dish or other vessel. Talk to the Stone Being and state your wish to enter into relationship with it. Let it know that you offer yourself from your heart, and that you are inviting the Stone Being to come into your heart.
4. Now go outdoors and look for bits and pieces that you can bring back to the altar and present to the Stone Being as offerings. These things can be leaves, flowers, feathers, or other stones. You will recognize these gifts for the Stone Being when you see them, especially when you attend to your feeling sense while you are out looking for them.
5. When your first search for gifts feels complete, go back to the altar in your sacred space. Center yourself in your heart, and place each of the gifts you brought upon the altar, arraying them around the stone however feels best to you. As you do this, talk to the Stone Being out loud, or at least in a whisper, telling it that you have brought each gift as an offering from your heart.
6. Repeat step 5 on the next day. Go out and find more gifts and place them reverentially upon the altar, as you talk to the Stone Being. Remember your sincerity is important, because your own soul and the soul of the Stone Being are listening.
7. Repeat step 5 again on the third day. When you have arrayed all of your gifts on the altar around the stone, say, "These are my offerings to you. And I offer my heart as well."
8. After some time, which could be as little as an hour or as much as a day, go back to the altar, pick up the stone, and try the "A Conversation with a Stone Being" practice again. Remember to work with a journal to take notes about what happens

IMPORTANT: DECOMMISSIONING THE ALTAR

After the several-day ritual of creating the altar and making the offerings is finished, what should you do with all the pieces? When the altar work is done, you no longer need to keep the stone there. It can go back to its place in your collection. The bits and pieces you used as gifts should be returned (more or less) to where you found them. This does not have to be precisely at the spots where they came from, but you should not throw them in the trash or out the window or down the toilet. The idea is that the energy of the ritual is no longer present in the gifts, but one should still honor them by "giving them back," returning them to the area where you found them. The Stone Being will have received the energy you directed to it through the gifts, and that is what is most important. Do not hang on to the bits and pieces, as this confuses the situation, and attaches you to the husks of the ritual rather than being bonded to the imaginal essence of what occurred.

After you have returned the bits and pieces, you should cleanse the altar space with sage, incense, or *palo santo,* put away the dish and the cloth, and thank your sacred space for helping you.

DISCUSSION

NOTE: How the ritual helps to focus your intention, attention, and imagination; how it gets you into your soul interiority; how the bits and pieces invite the Living World to participate; how honoring the Stone Being is a real gesture for relationship—this is why altars and rituals are created.

The above practices both involve what Jungian psychology calls Active Imagination. Alchemically, they are exercises in working with True Imagination to move into rapport with a spiritual being. The meeting does not take place in the physical world, nor in the realm of pure spirit. It occurs in the in-between place that Novalis called the Seat of the Soul, and which Jung named the psychoid realm.

5

The Psychoid-Imaginal Realm

The act of imagining is a concentrated extract of life forces, a hybrid of the physical and the psychic. . . . There was no mind-matter split in the heyday of alchemy, but there existed an intermediate realm between mind and matter—a psychic realm of subtle bodies—whose characteristic is to manifest themselves in a mental as well as a material form. The moment when physics touches the untrodden, untreatable regions—and when psychology touches the impenetrable darkness—then the intermediate realm of subtle bodies comes to life again, and the physical and psychic are once more blended in an indissoluble unity.

—Carl Jung

Between the universe that can be apprehended by pure intellectual Perception . . . and the universe perceptible to the senses, there is an intermediate world, the world of Idea-Images, of archetypal figures, of subtle substances, of "immaterial matter." This world is as real and objective, as consistent and subsistent as the intelligible and sensible worlds; it is an intermediate universe "where the spiritual takes body and the body becomes spiritual" . . .

—Henry Corbin, *Alone with the Alone: Creative Imagination in the Sufism of Ibn 'Arabi*

Carl Gustav Jung, 1875-1961

Carl Jung (1875–1961) was the Swiss psychiatrist and psychoanalyst who founded analytical psychology. His writing has been influential not only in psychiatry but also in anthropology, archaeology, literature, philosophy, and religious studies. His works provide a foundation for much of the current spiritual renaissance. His theories include the concept of the psychological archetypes, the collective unconscious, and synchronicity. What we today might call our personal quest for spiritual growth and wholeness, Jung termed *individuation.* Jung was deeply interested in alchemy, and his final book, *Mysterium Coniunctionis* ("the mystery of conjunction") dealt with his three decades of alchemical studies.

One of Jung's key concepts for our purposes is the idea of the *psychoid.* In essence, the term refers to the realm of True Imagination, or Novalis's "seat of the soul." It is the same territory that the Sufis (such as Henry Corbin, quoted above) described as the "imaginal realm." This is the domain of the overlap between psyche and physics—between spirit and matter. Along with the Sufis and the alchemists, Jung believed that this in-between realm of experience was quite real, and that it contained elements of both the spiritual and physical realities. He maintained that the substance of the psychoid-imaginal realm was *subtle matter,* sharing some of the qualities of matter in the purely physical world, but being of a finer nature—less dense and more fluid—frequently displaying itself in mental imagery and engendering a feeling of spiritual presence.

Jung invented the term *synchronicity,* with which many of us are familiar, to describe events that meaningfully and simultaneously partake of both inner and outer events. Most or all of us have experienced synchronistic moments. My first major mystical opening, which I described at the beginning of this book, was triggered by the astonishing synchronicity of telling my college roommate my recurring childhood dream, only to have its central image appear moments later as a horse-shaped cloud we both saw through our dormitory window. Jung believed that synchronicities were psychoid events, because they involved the overlap of inner and outer realities. Such events were viewed as *numinous*—having a strong religious or spiritual quality, indicating or suggesting the presence of a divinity. When we attune to stone energies and the presence of the Stone Beings, we often experience the same feeling of numinosity—the sense of being in the presence of something divine.

Another variety of manifestation of the principle of synchronicity occurs in the use of oracles such as the *I Ching* and tarot cards (mentioned in the previous chapter). Here the overlap of inner and outer that defines a psychoid event is clear. One holds a question in mind and then throws the *I Ching* coins or shuffles the deck of tarot cards. Those who have tried these oracles know from experience that the outcomes of such consultations are unfailingly meaningful and can illuminate one's situation in a helpful way. In terms of their psychoid nature, our question and our understanding of the answer can be considered "inner" events, and the symbolic meaning of the tarot card images is also "inner." Without this inner meaning, the cards are nothing more than ink on paper.

The physical vehicles for the manifestation of meaning in such oracles are the coins, the cards, and even our own bodies, which toss or shuffle them. The influence of the spiritual side of reality is seen in the fact that the results of consulting these oracles are meaningful, even though we have shuffled cards or tossed coins in a "random" way. The presence of symbolic meaning in seemingly random events shows us that we are linked with a deeper reality—a reality in which meaning is pervasive and nothing is random.

As author Daniel Deardorff puts it in regard to the *I Ching*: "An oracle inhabits the *I Ching*, and we use the coins to create a 'random' pattern, which is the third thing between us and the oracle."

In the first example, regarding my college experience, the synchronicity seemed to arrive spontaneously, without my consciously seeking it. In the case of the oracles, it appears that one can invoke a helpful synchronicity whenever one wishes. This suggests that the very fabric of our reality is woven in the relationship between matter and spirit, and that understanding our life and our world requires that we find a way to exist with a foot in each world—to live in the overlap—the permeation—between them.

Jung's protégé Marie-Louise von Franz said it this way:

> *The individuated [whole and awake] person lives in the world of active imagination [a.k.a. True Imagination], and the ego [the individual self] does not identify with the outer world, nor with the inner world,* but with the imaginative world, which includes both of the others. . . . *Normal ego consciousness would be replaced by an* imaginative consciousness *that beheld the world through the eyes of imagination. It would see underneath the apparent solidity of ordinary reality to the* meaning hidden there. *It would* behold the spiritual powers at play *in ordinary life, and it would possess* the freedom that perceiving symbolically bestows. [emphasis mine —RS]

I believe these ideas from Jung and von Franz are hugely important to us in our alchemical endeavors with stones, because they offer a framework through which we can understand and work consciously with the phenomena we are experiencing. They give us the pattern of the dual nature of the world, and they point to a third position, a viewpoint from which one can comprehend both aspects of the world at the same time.

Restated simply, we all live in two worlds. One of these is the inner world of our feelings, dreams, ideas, and other purely subjective experiences. We can see this world with our eyes closed. We also live in the outer world of matter, which we experience through our eyes, ears, and other senses. The outer world is the domain of things and their actions, while the inner world is the realm where we discover and create meaning.

The belief system of materialism places virtually all reality in the physical world. When we are in the realm of pure fantasy, we experience feelings and ideas that are not present to our perceptions of outer reality. Many people who find outer reality to be too harsh and unsatisfying retreat into fantasy and are therefore ungrounded and not able to achieve much in the outer world.

The third position transcends both materialism and fantasy. Through centering oneself in imaginative consciousness (the True Imagination of the alchemists), one can discern the *symbolic meaning* of outer world events. One sees that the inner and outer worlds are inextricably woven together. From this viewpoint, the whole of reality is understood as a never-ending flow of synchronistic events in the entwined physical and interior realms—events that reveal a richness of symbolic meaning.

I love the path of the Alchemy of Stones, because the stones are offering us a bridge between the two worlds. The physical stones are tangibly present in the outer world, while their energies are phenomena of the middle world—the Seat of the Soul, which overlaps and conjoins the domains of matter and spirit. When we hold a stone and feel its currents, we are in a new viewpoint that links these realms. When we communicate with a Stone Being, we have fully entered the consciousness of True Imagination, in which genuine, real experiences occur. Such communication can be understood through appreciating its symbolic meaning, or sometimes simply by taking in the feeling of the experience that presents itself.

Remember, the experience of True Imagination is an immersion in the domain of images. Images in this realm partake of both the invisible world of pure spirit and the visible domain of our sensory perceptions, and they relate them with one another through meaning. This is what I am pointing at when I say they are symbolic.

Let's consider an example from mediumship: After a person has died, the body is gone, but a medium can often describe the deceased person's physical appearance. Furthermore, when the being attempts to communicate, the medium is frequently shown images to symbolize the meaning. (The being might show the medium an image of a brick wall to remind his or her surviving relative of difficulties in communication during the lifetime.) Spiritual entities we encounter in the imaginal realm—including the Stone Beings—often "speak" in this way. And, of course, the very fact that we call a spiritually gifted communicator a "medium" indicates that this work occurs in the middle realm between matter and spirit.

It is good to be mindful of the fact that, when we work with True Imagination, we sometimes need to initiate the process through purposeful visualization. For example, in shamanic journeying, one can begin a journey to the Lower World by visualizing a cave or tunnel that one follows down into the Earth. When the process takes off into scenarios one had not planned in advance, one has entered True Imagination.

As a final reminder, it is important to discriminate between True Imagination and fantasy. It is helpful to remember that fantasy orbits the ego—its desires and fears. Self-flattering situations are examples of such fantasies.

So let's engage in a little imagining right now, as we think about what Von Franz's concept of the worldview of an individuated person would reveal. From this viewpoint—within what she calls active imagination and what the alchemists would have called True Imagination—everything in our experience of life would look different. At least it would look different from the everyday view we have grown up with.

From the perspective of our wholeness, we would *perceive* the outer world and the inner world at the same time, and we would observe and participate in the *meaningful overlapping relationship* between the inner and the outer. We have to *participate*—to engage with our imagination—in order to *perceive the meaning hidden in the overlap.* Once again, if we look only at the outer world, the meaning in life disappears. (This is the materialist worldview.) If we look only at the inner world, we are ungrounded, and are vulnerable to identifying with mere fantasy. What makes True Imagination true is its integration of both the inner and outer worlds, and its freedom from our intentional control.

Von Franz tells us that this imaginative consciousness can open our eyes to the meaning beneath the surface of ordinary reality, and allows us to "behold the spiritual powers at play in ordinary life." Every time we notice a synchronicity, we are—at least momentarily—experiencing this imaginative consciousness, because the essence of synchronicity is the recognition of the meaningful simultaneity of an inner and an outer event. To see this is to see the spiritual powers at play.

She also mentions "the freedom that perceiving symbolically bestows." This is of huge importance. When we embrace the perspective of True Imagination as our worldview, we find that we are liberated from the feeling of bondage that accompanies a purely materialistic viewpoint, as well as the feeling of powerlessness in regard to physical life that comes from dwelling too much in the inner world. We ourselves have inner and outer dimensions. When we learn to live in them both at once, we are truly whole, and we are continually in a state of co-creative participation with our world.

And how does "perceiving symbolically" bestow freedom? When we are tuned through our True Imagination to the interplay of the spiritual powers with the ordinary world, we realize that all of our experience comes to us laden with meaning. We understand that we are continually being offered a stream of communication from life itself, and that we are in relationship with the World Soul. This makes us aware that the world perceives us, loves us, and invites us to participate in the eternal flow of communication and co-creation that is the life of the world. Seeing the symbolic meaning in the events of ordinary reality frees us from the tyranny of meaninglessness, which—if it were true—would make us into prisoners and victims. Through perceiving symbolically, we recognize that we are partners with the Soul of the World in composing the unfolding of time, space, and matter, in a living manifestation of action, feeling, and understanding.

ENGAGING WITH THE PSYCHOID

I have gone into all this to emphasize that True Imagination is an essential element in all our engagements with psychoid beings and events, such as those we meet in the Alchemy of Stones.

For example, when we ask a question and lay out the tarot cards, there is meaning in front of us. This is the psychoid event—the overlap of inner and outer worlds. But, in order to grasp the meaning, we have to use True Imagination. True Imagination engages our ability to perceive relational patterns, build images, and make meaning. When we look at the tarot cards in front of us through the lens of True Imagination, we are not simply spinning a fantasy of what we want; we are trying to see what is really there. To do so, we have to engage our imagination—pay attention to the whole of the card layout and each of its parts, and keep our intention focused on our effort to understand. The resulting insights are a *co-creation.* We are working hand-in-hand with the invisible spiritual realms, through the intermediate psychoid domain within which this relating is possible.

We are also engaging in co-creation when we perceive and work alchemically with the subtle energies of stones. When we turn our attention to a stone and feel its currents, we are experiencing a psychoid event. We are working with True Imagination in a way that is similar to what I described above regarding reading the tarot cards. We are not spinning fantasies when we look within to engage the stone energies—we are using our feeling sense to meet what is really there.

When we invite the Stone Being to enter our heart, and perhaps to dialogue with us, we are doing something very much like asking for advice from the I Ching, or any oracle. We have focused our attention, intention, and imagination on the overlapping psychoid realm—the seat of the soul—where beings of the spirit realms can relate with us.

This kind of dialogue is also practiced in shamanism. Shamans turn their attention toward the spiritual realm to meet with their helping spirits and receive their guidance and instruction. In some instances, the helping spirits are invited to intervene in physical reality, especially in practices such as healing and soul retrieval. The fact that the helping spirits can engage with human shamanic practitioners to facilitate healing on physical and psychospiritual levels is another proof of the reality and usefulness of working co-creatively through the psychoid realm. When we work with stones for healing or other purposes, our efforts parallel those of the shaman.

Other comparisons of shamanism and our work with stones may be useful. Both shamans and stone alchemists work in relation with psychoid beings. The power animals of shamans are one example, while the Beings of the various types of stones are another.

A shaman might work with a power animal called Wolf. This is not the spirit of a particular wolf, but a being that is in some sense the archetypal essence of Wolf. A stone alchemist might similarly work with the spirit of Azeztulite, Amethyst, Moldavite, or some other type of stone. The individual stones we choose to work with each represent their type in the same way that an individual wolf represents Wolf. The stones act as talismans for entering the world of each kind of stone, just as the shaman's physical tools and talismans offer pathways of energy and symbolic meaning that enable the shamans to meet and work with their spirit allies. And, in a mysterious way, the physical stones and the shamanic talismans also are those spiritual beings—perhaps in a way similar to how our physical bodies are ourselves, and yet are not the totality of our being. Both the physical stones and our own bodies are material expressions of our spiritual selves, and theirs.

STONE ENERGIES AS SUBTLE MATTER— THE *PRIMA MATERIA* OF ALCHEMY

I have mentioned that Jung, Raff, and other practitioners of spiritual alchemy believed that much of the alchemical work takes place in the psychoid realm, a.k.a. the imaginal realm or the Seat of the Soul. Jung called the psychoid "a psychic realm of subtle bodies," and he viewed the subtle matter of the psychoid as a finer, more fluid substance than ordinary matter—a substance infused with spiritual presence. Subtle matter, and the subtle bodies it composes, have the ability to flow, change shape, and affect both consciousness and physical matter.

Numerous esoteric traditions have made reference to the "subtle body" of the human being. Wikipedia tells us:

> *According to Bhagavad Gita, one of the most sacred texts of Hinduism, the subtle body is composed of mind, intelligence, and ego, which controls the gross physical body. It is also known in other different spiritual traditions: "the most sacred body"* (wujud al-aqdas) *and "true and genuine body"* (jism asli haqiqi) *in Sufism, "the diamond body" in Taoism and Vajrayana, "the light body" or "rainbow body" in Tibetan Buddhism, "the body of bliss" in Kriya Yoga, and "the immortal body"* (soma athanaton) *in Hermeticism.*

It was believed that patterns created in the subtle body, or in the subtle matter dimensions of the world at large, would influence human bodies and other manifestations in the physical realm: "By understanding and mastering the subtlest levels of reality, one gains mastery over the physical realm."

The chakras and the meridian points of acupuncture are viewed in the above traditions as existing in the subtle realm, and affecting the physical body from within. Healing practices such as Reiki and many others, including mainstream modalities such as acupuncture and osteopathy, involve channeling or manipulating subtle energies to shift the patterns of subtle matter and the subtle body, ultimately to seed beneficial changes in the physical health of the patient. Healing through the utilization of stone energies operates in a similar way.

Those who have felt the currents that emanate from stones (commonly called "crystal energy") will recognize the similarities between the stone currents and the descriptions of subtle matter-energy. The currents seem able to penetrate our bodies without any visible incision or opening, and to flow through us like liquid waves, or like light, vibrations, electrical currents, or an indescribable combination of all of these. They also carry the feeling of numinosity—of a spiritual presence. All of these qualities readily apply to a description of subtle matter-energy. The term *subtle energies* is often used to describe the stone currents. And our everyday physics tells us that matter and energy are actually two sides of one coin. In the subtle realm, matter and energy blend into one another even more fluidly than they do in physical reality, although subtle matter and subtle energy are of a different order. They cannot be perceived by machines—only by our consciousness.

The reason I go into this is that in alchemy one of the key concepts was that of the *prima materia*—the "first matter." It was said that in order to begin the Great Work, the would-be alchemist must first acquire the *prima materia.* Since alchemy (at its best) was always involved with both the inner and outer aspects of reality, it was important to involve them both in the alchemical activity. Alchemists who worked only with physical matter or only with inner imagination would be handicapped in making the simultaneous transformations of the self and the world that were the highest goals of alchemy's magnum opus.

THE PRIMA MATERIA

So what is the *prima materia?* If we are going to involve ourselves in the Alchemy of Stones, we had better get hold of some! Don't look now, but we are entering into one of alchemy's most enigmatic ideas.

Here are a few statements about the fabled *prima materia:*

From Arnaldus de Villa Nova (1240–1311): "There abides in nature a certain pure matter, which, being discovered and brought by art to perfection, converts to itself proportionally all imperfect bodies that it touches."

From *Theatrum Chemicum* (published 1602–1661): "They have compared the *prima materia* to everything, to male and female, to the hermaphroditic monster, to heaven and earth, to body and spirit, chaos, microcosm, and the confused mass; it contains in itself all colors and potentially all metals; there is nothing more wonderful in the world, for it begets itself, conceives itself, and gives birth to itself."

From Martin Ruland the Younger (1569–1611): "The philosophers have so greatly admired the Creature of God which is called the Primal Matter, especially concerning its efficacy and mystery, that they have given to it many names, and almost every possible description, for they have not known how to sufficiently praise it."

From Arthur Waite's *The Hermetic Museum* (1953): "This matter lies before the eyes of all; everybody sees it, touches it, loves it, but knows it not. It is glorious and vile, precious and of small account, and is found everywhere.... To be brief, our Matter has as many names as there are things in the world; that is why the foolish know it not."

From Paul Levy's *The Sacred Art of Alchemy:* "To quote an ancient alchemist [Kunrath], the *prima materia* is the subject of the 'Great Stone of the Philosophers, which the whole World has before its eyes yet knows not.' Jung clarifies this idea when he says, 'The *prima materia* has the quality of ubiquity, it can be found always and everywhere.'"

From *The Zelator* by David Ovason: "The notion of all matter awaiting redemption is expressed in alchemy, and in the hermetic literature, in the figure of the *prima materia* (prima

Alchemical emblem depicting the omnipresence of the prima materia. "The Stone that is Hermes, (the god of alchemy), is cast upon the Earth, exalted on Mountains, resides in the Air, and is nourished in the Waters." The cubes represent the *prima materia* (from Michael Maier's Atalanta Fugiens. 1617.)

*ma*teria) or 'first matter,' being the basis of the work. In terms of the secret language (Green Language) of esotericism, the word *matter* is fissioned into *ma* and *ter.* The *matter* is the original Great Mother . . . the *Madonna,* the Spirit within things. The *ter* is the Earth, the dross, the *terre* (Latin for Earth)."

From the quote from Ovason, we can take the writer's splitting of words a step farther. If *ma* signifies the Mother, then *pri-ma* means the First Mother, and *ma-teria* means Mother Earth. This gives us a big hint—the First Mother, Mother Earth, is the beginning point for the Great Work of alchemy. From the many wildly varying descriptions of the *prima materia* in esoteric literature, we can surmise that only some form of subtle matter-energy could be multidimensional enough to fit them. So we might say that the *prima materia* of alchemy is the *subtle body of the maternal Earth,* the soul-body of the world, the "World Interiority." And in spiritual alchemy, the *prima materia* was indeed associated with the Great Mother figure known as Sophia, Wisdom, the Soul of the World.

One of the main attributes of the *prima materia* was its ubiquity—it could be found everywhere, by those who had the eyes to see it. Yet those with such vision were rare. This fits the idea of the *prima materia* as subtle matter, or subtle matter-energy, since the entire world and everything in it has a subtle body aspect. Yet there are few people who have learned to see the subtle realms through the eyes of True Imagination. Also, since subtle matter is a manifestation of Spirit, it is true to say that "it begets itself, conceives itself, and gives birth to itself." And when one begins to glimpse the wonders of the subtle or imaginal realm, it is easy to see why

Martin Ruland the Younger declared that the philosophers "have not known how to sufficiently praise it."

Although the *prima materia* was one of alchemy's great mysteries, I want to offer a simple idea for what it is for us in the Alchemy of Stones. It is what we call the *currents* or the *energies* of stones. When we work with the stone energies, we are dealing directly with the First Matter of the Earth—the subtle matter-energy that has condensed into the physical world as the whole multitude of crystals, minerals, and gems. The subtle bodies of the stones are composed of subtle matter-energy. The stones' energies are the primary (first) manifestations of the originating spiritual patterns of intelligence that gave birth to them. These subtle matter-energy forms exist in the psychoid realm. The physical stones are the outer-world manifestations of these psychoid patterns. They originate in the realm of pure spirit, and are manifested first in the psychoid realm of subtle matter-energy, and secondarily in the physical world.

When we tune in to stone energies, we are entering the psychoid—the realm of True Imagination, populated with living intelligences. The Stone Beings can be perceived as patterns and currents of subtle matter-energy. They interact first with our subtle bodies, and the experience of our own energies meeting the energies of a Stone Being is what we perceive as the currents or vibrations of the stone. When we begin to work co-creatively with these intelligences—the Stone Beings and the Soul of the World—we have taken the first steps on the path of the Alchemy of Stones.

And greeting us at the gateway—it is She. Sophia, Wisdom, the Soul of the World. She is the *prima materia,* First Mother, Mother Earth. She is the Feminine Divine, and the Stone Beings are her emanations, her partners, her angels, her children.

And so are we!

6

Sophia

In all ages and in all places, an unending partnership of the human, the divine and the world has been declared, proclaimed and protected through the presence of the Sophia. Her creating and mediating activity—under such names as Isis, Sophia, Wisdom, Shekinah, Achamoth, World Soul, Athena, Alchymia, Spenta Armati, Black Virgin, Mary, Eternal Feminine—has always looked toward the future birth of creation into the cosmos of love. The present time, I believe, signals the genesis of this birth.

—Robert J. Sardello, *Love and the Soul*

In the world of spirit, God is undivided and, as such, I term it the godhead or the One Thing. Wishing to make itself known, it breaks up its own unity and manifests within the psychoid in a variety of forms, or Names. In psychoidal alchemy, we can say that the godhead is the prima materia, *the divine essence with which the work begins, but alchemy only starts when the godhead manifests. Sophia is a manifestation of the godhead in the psychoid realm, and as such she has many meanings and functions, and creates a multitude of experiences for those lucky enough to know her. . . . As the manifestation of the godhead, Sophia is the* prima materia, *the beginning of the work, and through her marriage [facilitated by and occurring within the alchemist] she creates the end product of the work: the Philosophers' Stone.*

—Jeff Raff, *The Wedding of Sophia*

Ibn 'Arabi states that universal Nature, or Sophia, is the feminine or maternal side of the creative act. She is the merciful "breathing out" of God. We may compare Sophia as the divine sigh of compassion in the ancient text Wisdom of Sirach: "I came forth from the mouth of the Most High." This breathing out has the effect of manifesting Sophia to the world, yet Sophia is also the dwelling place of God.

—Caitlin Matthews, *Sophia: Goddess of Wisdom, Bride of God*

There is a field of energy, or vibration, a zone of manifestation that appears between the spiritual and mundane worlds. This energy, for lack of a better word, is formless and corresponds to the alchemical prima materia. *Yet it is plastic, and when a Name [a Divine being, such as Sophia] enters the imaginative realm, it first molds the energy into a form. The form is substantial, having something of the material about it, but subtle, retaining something of the spiritual as well. It appears as a light/energy shape but has not yet taken on the form of an image. Every psychical entity has a certain vibratory quality and often appears as an energy form that we may see or feel, but which has no defining imaginal characteristic to it. Some psychical experiences are of these forms only, but others engage the imagination more specifically.*

The next stage of the entity's manifestation in the psychoid imagination is for it to assume some more defined imaginal form. For example, in my experience with Sophia, she appeared as a vibratory presence that I could see and feel in the room, but at the same time, emanating from her was the image of the most beautiful woman I had ever seen. There was no doubt that she was a goddess of great compassion, love, and wisdom. I saw and felt both her image and her vibration simultaneously.

—Jeff Raff, *The Wedding of Sophia*

Sophia is . . . the divine entity that emerges from the godhead before creation itself and guides all beings, even God. Her ability to penetrate permits her to know everything. This is important because she can enter into the souls of human beings and lead them to their right path in life. Sophia knows and understands the essence of all things and serves as guide to those who discover her in their own souls. These two fundamental characteristics of Sophia, as Wisdom and as a guide, recur whenever the figure of Sophia appears. Hers is a special kind of knowing, a gnosis, that we must imagine transcends the human way of knowing. . . . She knows directly and perceives instantly into the heart and essence of all things. . . . She can transmit this perception to a person who opens himself or herself to her.

—Jeff Raff, *The Wedding of Sophia*

Psychoidal alchemy seeks to create a relationship with Sophia that transforms both the human being and Sophia herself.

—Jeff Raff, *The Wedding of Sophia*

ABOVE: Sophia as the alchemical Tree of Life; in Robert Fludd's Nature image
OPPOSITE: Sophia as the Goddess of Nature in Robert Fludd engraving "The Great Chain of Being"

I confess to being an ardent lover of Sophia. I view her as the presence of the Feminine Divine that is inherent in every atom of the world. In one sense, Sophia is the subtle body of the Universe. Remembering that her name means Wisdom, we can see the evidence of her existence, her nature, and her purpose in the vast and pervasive beauty, harmony, and intelligence of All That Is. For me, the beauty, order, and, most especially, the energetic vibrancy and spiritual generosity of stones, gems, and crystals of the Earth—the Stone Beings—reveal that they are emanations of Sophia. They are embodiments of Wisdom, notes of her music, the incarnated Angels of the Earth.

Yet alongside her greatness, perhaps the most astonishing quality of Sophia is her intimacy. As I have mentioned, when we notice a synchronicity in our lives, we see that there is an intelligence that is aware of both our inner state of mind and the outer events of the world. Somehow, this intelligence brings forth an experience that unites our inner life with an outer event in a way that is unmistakably meaningful, and which hints to us that this pervasive intelligence is aware of each of us individually, and is making a meaningful and guiding gesture to oneself. (My first major spiritual experience, which I recounted in the first chapter, was initiated by a huge synchronicity that I now believe was one of Sophia's gestures.) To me, it is both humbling and delightful to contemplate that Wisdom-Sophia is simultaneously so vast in intelligence and so loving toward all beings that she can and does involve herself with each of us in such a benevolent, helpful, generous, and (sometimes) playful intimacy.

To work spiritually with stones is to engage with Sophia, and to receive her blessings. And as Raff and others tell us, to behold Sophia is to love her, and this love awakens one's desire to participate in helping to achieve Sophia's purposes. Sophia's intention—her destined work—the "labor Sophiae," was defined by the alchemist Paracelsus as creating "the other Paradise of this world, in which no disease grows, no disease remains, no poisonous creature dwells or enters." In *The Wedding of Sophia,* author Jeff Raff comments, "Paracelsus therefore believed that Sophia was the feminine aspect of the godhead, and in her manifestation, if she were allowed to express her nature completely, she would create Paradise on earth, in which the four elements and all materials would reach their fullest expression." I believe that we who open

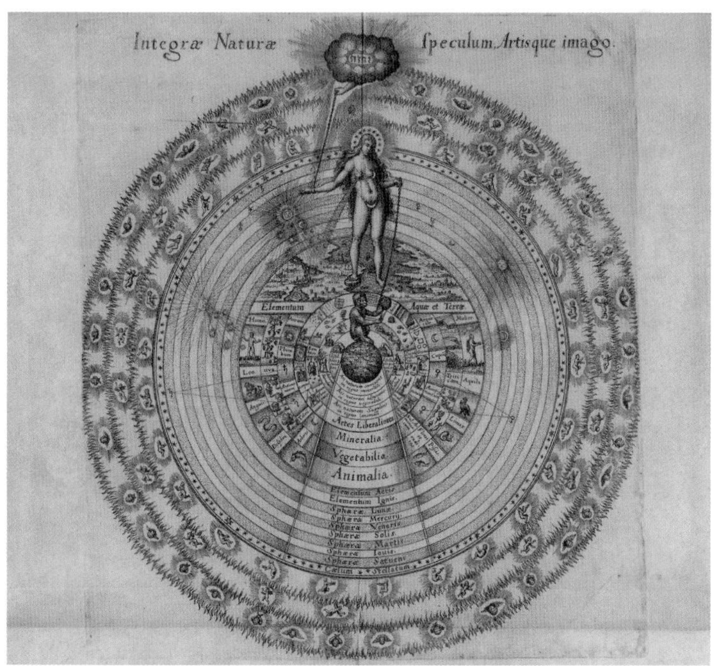

ourselves to the energies of stones are experiencing Sophia's efforts to bring them, and ourselves, to our fullest expression. Certainly our work with stones for healing and inner illumination is in alignment Sophia's purpose. And if it is achieved, we will live in "the Paradise of this world"—the union of Heaven and Earth. That is how important our work with stones can be. And it does require our participation, our partnership with Sophia.

This is because of another amazing aspect of Sophia—her vulnerability. Her love for the world—into which she has poured herself—is boundless and unconditional. Human beings—and all beings of the Earth—are cherished by her. This means that she will always allow us our freedom of choice, and will never act to override our will in order to save herself—or the physical world—from suffering, or even from being destroyed. She is love, and love only offers itself. Love never compels, for if it did, it would no longer be love. When one sees Sophia clearly for even a moment, one recognizes this astonishing truth about her. The first time I saw her and glimpsed this truth was in a dream. It occurred around the year 2000, long before I ever heard of Sophia.

MY FIRST VISION OF SOPHIA

In this extraordinarily vivid dream, I found myself in China, probably sometime in the 1950s, as communism was running rampant there. I was a guest in an ancient palace, and was being given a tour of the place by some officials. Within the palace, the people had not been converted to communism, and I sensed that they still hoped to preserve some of the treasures of the past.

As we walked down a great stone hallway, I looked to my left and saw that there was a large garden area in the center of the palace, protected by its high walls. I went toward it, and from the doorway, I saw beautiful flower gardens, shade trees, and water fountains in a circular arrangement of twelve basins. There were people lounging and talking softly in an atmosphere charged with rapturous joy.

Then I saw the reason for the joy. Across the garden courtyard, the figure of a beautiful woman reclined in a chair. People sat arrayed on the ground around her, all gazing toward her with love and devotion. I somehow knew that I was seeing a goddess rather than a human being. I was suddenly filled with awe and an intense desire to stay there in her presence.

In the next moment she stood up and began to dance. Then, in an instant, she transformed herself into twelve identical living replicas of herself, all of whom were dancing in unison. They leapt suddenly onto the twelve fountain basins, and then up onto the spraying water itself! They danced on arches of water that flowed through the air from one basin to the next. I was aware in every fiber of my being that I beheld a Divine being, and that I loved her utterly. The love kindled in me was so powerful that I only wanted to be with her, wherever she was. I tried to enter the garden, but the officials who were guiding me gently pulled me away.

The dream then shifted to the next morning. I was still in the palace, back in the great stone hallway, intending to go to the garden and find her. But I was met by the officials, who told me, "No. You cannot see her today. Here, take these gifts instead." They handed me two carvings—one made of brown wood and the other from green Jade. The wood carving showed the goddess resting in a garden. In the Jade carving, she appeared inside a cave, threatened by dragons. I was left alone to go to my room and contemplate these gifts.

In the next phase of the dream, I was awakened by an alarm that was being shouted through the halls. The communist army was storming the palace. I knew immediately that if they entered it, they would destroy the garden, and the goddess. I felt an urgent, intense fear for her, and a great dread that something terrible could happen to this wonderful perfect being.

I entered the great hallway, which was filled with the people who loved their goddess, all rushing to battle stations to defend her palace. But the number of defenders was very few—

Sophia in painting by Nicholas Roerich: "Mother of the World"

mostly old men and boys—while the attackers outside were a multitude. The defenders were traveling to their places in a strange way. I watched them reaching inside their jackets, pulling out small round *shadows* and flinging them onto the stone floor. Then each defender ran to the shadow and jumped on top of it, whereupon it began to glide—like a floating skateboard—carrying its passenger to his position.

Feeling the urgency to try to help, I reached into my own jacket, and I was surprised to find myself pulling out my own small round shadow. I threw it onto the floor and tried to ride it, but I missed my target and landed on the shadow of a young man who had just flung it down across my path. It carried me away from the battle and out a side door. I had the sense that the young man whose shadow had gotten switched with mine was not going to survive the onslaught, and that I had, somewhat accidentally, been saved.

Outside the door, I found not an army but a marketplace. There were stalls with food, baskets, clothing, and other items being sold. I knew that the attack was still happening on the other sides of the palace. I was desperate to find some kind of help to save her, but I was sure none of the people around me spoke English.

Suddenly I noticed an American-looking fellow in a white suit, apparently shopping in one of the stalls. I ran up to him, shouting incoherently. When I reached him, I said, "You're American. Do you know me?" (This seems like a foolish question in the waking world, but his answer at first appeared even more nonsensical.)

"Sure," he replied. "You're the face in the paper cup." I somehow understood that he was telling me he had seen my face reflected in a cup of water when he looked into it. *I was his reflection.* This revelation shocked me, and I woke up with a jolt.

It took a few moments to realize where I was, and when I did, I was alarmed. I was certain that where I had been was not just a dream. In some amazing and disturbing way, it was all quite real. I knew that *she* was real, that she was a true Divine being, more wonderful than any being I had ever encountered before, and that I loved her. I knew that she was pure beauty, pure love, pure grace, pure wisdom, and I knew that she was in danger, and would not defend herself. I felt a sense of dread, and a powerful longing to save her, to protect her. But . . . I was in the wrong world! How do you climb back inside a dream?

The dream stayed with me. I told my wife, Kathy, about it, wrote about it, and I even began to think of the numerous destructive events in the everyday world as being somehow linked to the goddess's threatened condition. At the same time, I loved her, and I hoped that I would somehow find her again.

There is much more that could be said about my dream. The idea of riding our shadows to the defense of that which is most precious offers some provocative symbolism. The last scene, in which my American twin seemed to say that he was the real self while I was his reflection, displays another concept that is of key importance in our inner transformation. Both symbols resonate with ideas in spiritual alchemy, but for now we will leave them. For our immediate purposes, what is most important is the image of Sophia.

❋ ❋ ❋

There's a divinity that shapes our ends,
Rough-hew them how we will.
—William Shakespeare, *Hamlet*

ABOVE: *Pistis Sophia* (Faithful Sophia) in a Russian Tapestry.

When one encounters a Divine being, it is always an initiation. When that being is Sophia, the synchronicities that "shape our ends," guiding us to our destiny, begin to flow. In the several years that ensued after my dream of the endangered goddess, I experienced many more initiations. Some, such as meeting the poet Robert Bly and becoming one of his students, brought joy and enrichment to my heart and mind. It was when we attended Bly's Great Mother Conference in 2003 that I first heard the name Sophia, in a talk by Robert Bly's wife, Ruth. In the talk, she mentioned a book about Sophia—*Love and the Soul*—written by an author I hadn't heard of—Robert Sardello. (Ruth's words planted a seed that was to sprout some months later.)

One particularly difficult initiation for me was a mysterious illness that began in 2003 and continued for over a year. It was physically excruciating, emotionally shattering, and apparently undiagnosable. At its worst, it caused me to lose forty pounds in a period of ten weeks, and it left me nearly sleepless. In alchemical terms, this initiation was the *nigredo,* the blackness, the Dark Night of the Soul. But I knew nothing of alchemy then.

In the fall of 2004, during a vacation in Florida where we hoped I might gain some strength, my wife, Kathy, showed me the book she had been reading. It was *Love and the Soul* by Robert Sardello, the book Ruth Bly had recommended. We spent the afternoon in the sun on a friend's front porch, discussing the book and Sardello's ideas. Our talk kindled memories of my earlier exposure to the name Sophia in Ruth Bly's talk, and the reference to her as the Soul of the World, the divine spirit of Wisdom.

In a way that felt magical, my symptoms disappeared that day, time seemed to slow down, and the hours flowed like an endless stream of grace. I felt captivated by Sardello's words, and the truth and beauty with which they resonated inside me. I recalled my dream of the goddess, and Kathy and I wondered together if I had seen one of the faces of Sophia.

Time slowed, but it did not stop. Night came, and with it my symptoms returned with a vengeance. In the dark hours of pain that followed, I feared that I would die.

But it was only the crisis of the illness—the turning point. From that night onward, I began to read Sardello's book. Each day I learned a little more about Sophia, and each day I got a little better. Then, through another turn of synchronicity, my naturopathic doctor had a sudden insight, and his new treatment gradually brought me to a full recovery.

Now it was January of 2005, and Kathy and I took a truck full of our crystals, stones, and jewelry to Arizona to sell at the huge Tucson mineral and gem shows.

Our showrooms were crammed with beautiful crystals, minerals, and jewelry, and saturated with high vibrations. The three-week show was always a highlight of our year, and I had recovered enough to enjoy it. In addition to our stone inventory, we were selling *The Book of Stones* and my other books, and—because of my high enthusiasm—we were also offering copies of Robert Sardello's *Love and the Soul.* Having just recovered, almost magically, from my illness, I wanted to tell everyone I could about Sardello's book, and about Sophia.

Quelle: Deutsche Fotothek

Sophia as Alchemia, goddess of Alchemy, in a German engraving

One day during the show I came back to our showroom after doing some errands and found the place packed with customers. I went behind the counter and picked up an invoice for someone's purchase. When I looked at the business card clipped to the paperwork, I was stunned and elated. The card belonged to Robert and Cheryl Sardello!

"Where are they?" I almost yelled. "Are they here?" A moment later they came in from the next room, and I practically leaped over the table to greet them. In a torrent of words over the next few minutes, I told the Sardellos the story of my dream, my illness, and my newfound love for Sophia. In that first conversation, I was astounded to learn that both Robert and Cheryl loved stones and their energies, and had even been on our Heaven and Earth mailing list for over a decade. Before they left the showroom, in gratitude for what Robert's book had done for me, I loaded them up with gifts of rare crystals that I wanted to introduce them to. This was the beginning of what has turned into a close friendship, and a collaboration that has greatly benefitted my work and my life. The amazing synchronicities of our meeting and the events preceding it are, to me, evidence of the guiding and blessing hand of Sophia at work.

Later that year, Kathy and I enrolled in a two-year course at the Sardellos' School of Spiritual Psychology in North Carolina. (In a stroke of good fortune for me, another of my heroes, author Joseph Chilton Pearce, and his daughter Shakti joined our class as fellow students of the Sardellos' teachings.) During the ensuing two years, I learned much more about Sophia, and about the intelligence of the heart. Those two elements are inseparable from one another, and are essential aspects of our work in the Alchemy of Stones. In the course of our studies, I thought back to my dream, and I realized that I was not in the "wrong world." It is here and now that wisdom, harmony, beauty, and love are most threatened. Yet Sophia still lives, and she continues to offer herself to us, and to invite us to join her in the alchemical co-creation of the Earth as Paradise.

MY SECOND SOPHIA DREAM

Now I want to fast-forward a few years, from 2005 to 2008, when the Sardellos invited Kathy and me to make presentations at the Seventh Sophia Conference in Santa Fe, New Mexico. The title of the conference was "A New Heaven and a New Earth: The Birth of a New Body, a New Earth, and a New Consciousness." I was to speak about Stones and the New Consciousness (a phrase that later inspired the title for one of my books). Because the conference was dedicated to Sophia, I was thinking about her a great deal.

About a week before flying to Santa Fe for the conference, I had a remarkable dream.

As the dream began, my wife and I were sitting together in a room within a big farmhouse. I knew somehow that this farm was new, that a lot of people would be working cooperatively there, and that "new crops," which had never been grown before, were being planted. There was an air of quiet excitement, and a lot of hustle and bustle as new arrivals came in and found their places. Kathy and I were in our room. She was sitting in her bathrobe, writing checks to "pay off our debts."

I was worried that someone would come in and see us before we were fully dressed. I said to Kathy, "Hurry up. Someone could walk in here at any moment." The next thing I knew, someone

did enter. He was a man, almost seven feet tall, thin and lanky like Abraham Lincoln. He looked much like a human being, except for his head, which was made entirely out of amethyst! His features were anything but smooth—he had hundreds of pointed crystals sticking out all over his head. His huge jaw was a hinged thing like a steam shovel, made from more deep-purple amethyst crystals. He was wearing sunglasses, also made of amethyst, and the sides of them were shaped like fish. He said something to me but I couldn't understand him. I answered with a sort of sideways comment on his sunglasses: "Wow! Are those fish?" (Why I didn't say, "Wow, your head is made of amethyst," I will never know.)

The Amethyst Man muttered something else and stepped aside. Then I noticed that standing behind him were three more beings, so strange-looking they made the Amethyst Man look normal. This trio was completely non-human with straight, rigid white bodies, short, stumpy arms and legs, and faces embedded in their trunks. They wore no clothes, had no necks, and the tops of their "heads" came to a point. In my dream, I was shocked and said to myself, "Whoa! Are those demons?" But a voice within me immediately reassured me, "No, they just look alien to you because you've never seen anything like them before." As I gazed upon the three odd fellows, they began to chant, and they repeated jovially, "Dance or die, dance or die!" Then they began to dance around, in a comical stump-legged way, in complete unison with one another.

Before my astonishment had time to subside, another character appeared. This one was a human, a young woman or girl, looking about sixteen or seventeen years old. She wore a simple white tunic, like something from ancient Greece. She was lovely and radiant, and she smiled softly, though her eyes were serious and intent. She walked toward me where I sat and bent forward, bringing her face ten or twelve inches from mine. I felt that some important moment had come, that I was supposed to understand something, but her expression told me that neither she nor I were allowed to speak.

She looked into my eyes with great seriousness, and then she blew her breath, gently but purposefully, onto my face. She continued looking, as if to assess whether I understood. When I didn't respond, she blew her breath on me again, and again she waited. I worried. I didn't know what to think or do, but I didn't want to fail in whatever was hoped for or expected from me. Again, she blew her breath. This time, not knowing what else to do, I blew mine back.

As I exhaled, she inhaled, taking my breath into her body. Then, when she exhaled, I inhaled. Feeling her breath move into me was like inhaling pure life energy—ambrosia—the nectar of the Divine. We exchanged our breaths, back and forth like that, perhaps ten or twelve times. I was filled with delicious life each time I inhaled, and my exhalations were full of appreciation and loving intent. She too seemed to be nourished by the exchange. When we had completed our silent ritual, the corners of her mouth twitched upward in a mischievous smile, and she broke the "rules," saying two words to me.

The words were, "Thank you."

Then I woke up. This time, I knew who she was.

I was entranced and enraptured by this visitation of Sophia, and the exchange between us. I was also sobered by it. And amazed, to say the least. Once again, I knew this was no ordinary dream—it was a true encounter, and a teaching, and an initiation.

I'll mention briefly a few points about the meaning I discern from this experience.

First, the Amethyst Man and the three crystal-shaped beings were there to show me that Sophia is deeply linked with the beings

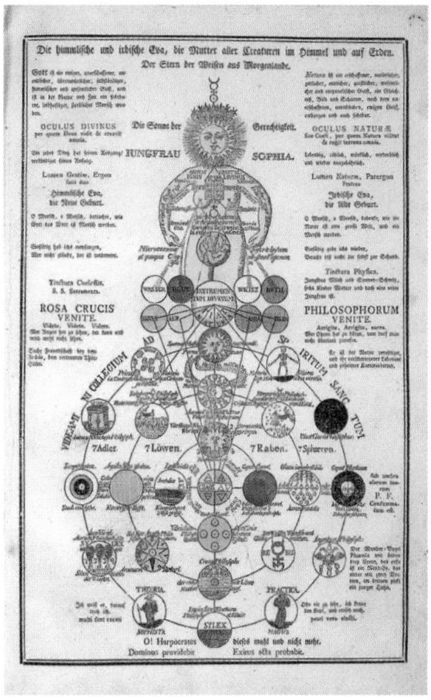

OPPOSITE: Sophia as Soul of the Earth in *Atalanta Fugiens* by Michael Maier, 1617; RIGHT: Alchemical Diagram "Virgin Sophia"

of the mineral realm, and that they were there to communicate with me. Although I failed to understand what Amethyst Man tried to tell me, the message from the three jovial "pointy-headed white guys," as I called them (I now believe they are the Azez, the keepers of Azeztulite), was clear: dance, or die. To me that meant to consciously, joyfully, and fully involve myself with Sophia and the Stone Beings in the co-creative "dance" of world transformation, or to hang back, hesitate, and die. Not just me; everyone—we all have that choice.

Second, it was clear to me that in both of my Sophia dreams, she is in need of our help. In the first dream, she needed protection from the waves of destructive consciousness that are washing over the world (not merely communism). In this second dream, she showed me that she needs us to notice her and nourish her. She needs us to offer our very breath—our spirit and life-essence—to her, as she has always offered hers to us. (If she hadn't, we would never have made it this far.) As I discovered, such an exchange is mutually nourishing and blessing, and it filled me with intense pleasure. I also noticed that she did not, and could not, ask me for my breath. She could not do this, any more than one can ask to be loved. Both must be given freely. She offered, and she waited. It was all she could do without violating the love that is the core of her nature.

The alchemists and the ancient Gnostics believed that the essence of Sophia is present in every particle of the world as its Wisdom, beauty, harmony, and divinity. The Gnostics also believed that Sophia was, in a sense, trapped in matter, and needed to be rescued through love. It is surprising to many people to imagine that a being as vast and wonderful as Sophia might need anything from human beings, but my dream, and my heart, tell me that she does. Without our

offer of ourselves—our love, our breath—to her, she has nothing to breathe, and may not survive. Our "breath" is our loving attention to her, and our intention to offer ourselves as her partners.

Jung put it this way: "For the alchemist, the one primarily in need of redemption is not man, but the deity [Sophia] who is lost and sleeping in matter." The ancient Gnostic gospel *Pistis Sophia* (Faith of Sophia) describes Sophia's fall from the Divine realm (the Pleroma) into the imperfect and imprisoning world of matter. Here she is said to sleep, and the goal of alchemy is to reawaken her, and to thereby awaken and redeem the Universe as well. To me, this resonates closely with Sophia's need for us to share and combine our "breath"—our spiritual essence—with hers. We can do this by engaging with her through the currents of the stones.

The words of Kabir, the fifteenth-century Indian mystic poet and saint, let us know that when Sophia offers her breath, she is offering her essence. Kabir says: "Student, tell me, what is the Divine One? She is the breath inside the breath."

As I was researching this book, I began to delve more deeply into studying the Gnostics, who were among those most deeply devoted to Sophia. One story about the Gnostic master Simon Magus (Simon the Magician) in Stephan Hoeller's book *The Gnostics,* jumped out at me. Simon was reputed to have the spiritual power of flight (whether physical or in the subtle body), and Hoeller reproduces this passage, originally quoted by H. P. Blavatsky in *Isis Unveiled:*

> *Simon, laying his face upon the ground, whispered in [the Earth's] ear, "Oh mother earth, give me I pray thee, some of thy breath; and I will give thee mine;* let me loose, *O mother, that I may carry thy words to the stars, and I will return faithfully to thee after a while." And the Earth, strengthening her status, none to her detriment, sent her genius [her guiding spirit, Sophia] to breathe on Simon, while he breathed on her, and the stars rejoiced to be visited by the mighty One.*

I was rather amazed to find this story, giving such a specific and vivid account of mutual empowerment through mutual breathing, between a human being and a divine being. I feel certain that the "genius" of the Earth mentioned here is Sophia, since she is the Earth's guiding spirit—the Wisdom and harmonious beauty of the world. Also, the phrase "strengthening her status" indicates that Simon's breath was a benefit to her. And Simon received the power of flight he had requested.

I tend to view Simon's power of flight as indicating the ability to travel in the subtle body, rather than physically. I have experienced this, as have many others. (In my case, a flight to the stars—and the Great Central Sun—was facilitated by Moldavite.) We have already given some attention to the subtle body and the psychoid realm, where the physical and spiritual worlds overlap, and we will return to them as we go on.

The mystic psychologist Carl Jung called the subtle body a "body of breath." Speaking of the early Gnostic Christians and their worldview, he also stated that "in early Christianity . . . immortality depends . . . on the idea of a breath-body as the carrier of life." (CW, p. 6100) Regarding the subtle body's importance in spiritual alchemy, Jung also wrote: "It is clear enough from this material what the ultimate aim of alchemy really was: it was trying to produce a *corpus subtile* [subtle body], a transfigured and resurrected body, i.e., a body that was at the same time spirit." (CW 12, p. 511)

Considering these ideas in light of my second dream of Sophia, I have come to believe that the mutual breathing which the Sophia figure exchanged with me was for the purpose of helping me (*and* Sophia) to vivify and strengthen the subtle bodies we each were expressing in the psychoid-dream realm. As the breathing occurred, I experienced an intensely pleasurable feeling of vitalization and energetic nourishment. I felt myself come more alive, there in the dream realm—a realm in which we all experience ourselves in our subtle bodies. My feeling is

OPPOSITE: Sophia as Queen of the World in *Atalanta Fugiens* by Michael Maier, 1617

Sophia depicted as a Dark Angel, standing on a black Sun (symbol of the first alchemical stage, the *nigredo*). In *Aurora Consurgens*

that my offer of my breath to Sophia also strengthened her in that realm, by sharing some of my soul essence, similarly to Simon Magus in the story above.

Ultimately I believe that the union of Heaven and Earth, of spirit and matter, of the Divine and the human takes place in the overlapping realm of subtle matter-energy—the realm of the psychoid. The goal of the alchemical *opus*—the transfiguration of ourselves and the world into divine human beings in a divine world—will take place through our learning to live in, *and actualize fully,* the subtle realm. For us, it will be a kind of Ascension. For the Divine, it will be a grounding into embodiment. For both, it will mean the grand reunion for which we have yearned since time began.

This means that there is more to our work with stones than most of us have imagined. When we breathe over them at the beginning of our meditations, we are offering ourselves into the spiritual realms in which the angelic Stone Beings exist, and we are inviting them into a more richly embodied state. We are also reaching toward Sophia through the Stone Beings, who are her emanations. Through all of this, we are working cooperatively with Sophia to build the subtle bodies of ourselves, of the Stone Beings, and of Sophia herself. And this activity increases the reality of the New Heaven and the New Earth, in which the human and the Divine dwell consciously together. This is another way for us to envision the magnum opus, the Great Work of spiritual alchemy.

The fact that Sophia deeply needs our partnership and love shows itself to me in the two words she spoke at the end of my dream—breaking the rules to tell me, "Thank you." It is humbling, and wonderful, to receive thanks from Sophia. What she needs from us seems small, and costs us nothing to give. Indeed, we receive back much more.

But this is not the end of our story with her. It is the beginning.

7

Sophia, the Deep Self & the Heart

From research, we've concluded that intelligence and intuition are heightened when we learn to listen more deeply to our own heart. It's through learning how to decipher messages we receive from our heart that we gain the keen perception needed to effectively manage our emotions in the midst of life's challenges. The more we learn to listen to and follow our heart intelligence, the more educated, balanced, and coherent our emotions become.

—Doc Childre, founder of HeartMath

Lift the veil that obscures the heart, and there you will find what you are looking for.

—Kabir

The real "I" consciousness of a human being does not take place in the brain, but in the heart.

—Rudolf Steiner

When we are within the heart, we are within our divine humanity.

—Robert Sardello

To give the Soul of the World a name is both to vivify her as an image and simultaneously to limit her. In order to move toward her, I think using the ancient name Sophia, by which alchemists referred to her, can be helpful in remembering that she is a living intelligence and is not an abstract concept. To refer to her as the presence of Wisdom in the world amplifies our attention to the benevolent quality of her intelligence and her all-pervasive influence. The two dreams I described above were hugely important to me, for bringing Sophia to life in my psyche and awakening my love for her. But these also must be seen as only partial views of Sophia.

We are a little like those three blind men encountering the elephant. Each experience or point of view by which we encounter Sophia reveals more things about her, which imply a much greater being. In order to get the best possible view of Sophia, I believe we must hold multiple perspectives at the same time. To that purpose, we will now go into an aspect of Sophia's presence within us, which we might call the intelligence of the heart. I believe that Sophia dwells holographically in the center of the heart of every person, and that our individual soul being—our Deep Self—dwells there with her.

We have all heard the phrase "I know it in my heart." The heart is the place of knowing, of gnosis, where we are able to deeply grasp the things that truly matter, without the need to gather and weigh evidence to calculate a "rational" decision. The heart is the home of our feeling sense. This is the reason that I almost always engage with stones through the heart, as in the practices described thus far.

I believe that our Deep Self, which the Sufis called the Guest, or the Friend, dwells in our heart, waiting for us to turn our attention there. We usually identify with the surface self, the ego, which tends to be associated with the brain and our intellect. When we become aware of the Self in the heart, it often feels as if there are two people inside us. There are certainly two centers of consciousness within us, and the deeper, truer, wiser one is the one in the heart. It is quieter than our mental ego, which talks to itself incessantly. Usually, the Deep Self is silent, but when I look to my heart and ask how I should best respond to a situation in a given moment, I invariably feel an immediate urge or see an image. The advice of the heart is always to act for the good of the whole situation—never for me to gain personal advantage. (Of course, the good of the whole is ultimately to everyone's advantage!) I'm sure that all those reading this book know the experience that I am describing. The voice of the heart is the still, small voice of Wisdom, because our Deep Self is the natural partner of Sophia, and their intentions are in harmonious accord. Much of the work of spiritual alchemy is for the purpose of bringing our everyday self into conscious, co-creative union with our Deep Self and Sophia.

Sometimes the heart makes its feeling known to us in moments where something moves it deeply. In these instances, we can be surprised by strong surges of feeling, and intense urges toward generosity and kindness. Or we may suddenly feel our inner walls broken down by the recognition of love or grief. In such moments, our heart, our soul, our Deep Self speaks to us openly. I like to say, "I'm always happy when my heart joins the conversation by bringing tears to my eyes."

This kind of powerful communication can also occur when we are holding a stone that stirs our heart. I've seen those tears on people's faces (and felt my own) on hundreds of occasions. Or, as I've mentioned, the heart will sometimes "skip a beat" or change its pattern in the presence of a stone with which it strongly resonates.

The poet Juan Ramón Jiménez was speaking about the presence of the Deep Self in the heart when he wrote this poem (translated by Robert Bly):

I am not I.
I am this one
walking beside me, whom I do not see,
whom at times I manage to visit,
and, at other times, I forget;
the one who remains silent while I talk,
the one forgives, sweet, when I hate,
the one who takes a walk when I am indoors,
the one who will remain standing when I die.

You can feel the wise and loving heart qualities of the Deep Self as you read the poem. It also rings true that this is the part of us that survives our death. And as the poet tells us, our real "I" is that one, not the surface personality that talks, hates, sits indoors, and eventually dies. Nonetheless, our surface personality, including all its flaws, is beloved by the Deep Self, and by Sophia.

There is much scientific research to back up my contention that the heart has its own intelligence, and that it is the organ of our feeling sense. Most of this is presented in my previous book, *Stones of the New Consciousness,* so I will mention only a few points here.

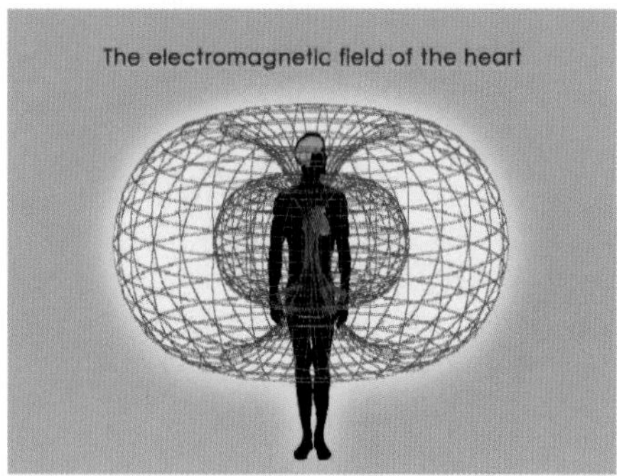

The heart is much more than a pump. It has more neurons than muscle cells, and has strong neural connections to the brain. Our hearts are constantly emanating light—electromagnetic energies that are beyond the normal visible spectrum. The electromagnetic field around the heart forms a torus—a doughnut-shaped field extending outward in all directions, with a central axis that aligns with our spinal column. The heart's field is much more powerful than the one generated by the brain, and it may be that the heart's torus field is the means by which it perceives how the world around us "feels."

The heart has even been shown to have the capacity to sense the unfolding pattern of the future. In an experiment conducted by the HeartMath organization, subjects who were trained to reach a state of heart-brain coherence sat before a computer screen and were told to press a button when they were ready to view an image. Electronic monitors kept track of the heart-brain coherence. When the button was pushed, there was a ten-second delay, after which a randomized computer program chose one of fifty images and flashed it on the screen. Ten of the fifty images were very unpleasant or disturbing, while the other forty were benign.

As one might expect, viewing the upsetting images broke down the heart-brain coherence. However, the astonishing result was that the heart tended to go out of coherence four to seven seconds *before* a negative image was selected by the random program! These results seemed to show that the heart could *feel* the negative images coming before they were chosen. Since neither a human being nor the computer knew what image would be selected, the heart had some way of feeling the future coming, *beyond the confines of space and time.* We know that it was the heart, rather than the brain, because the brain went out of coherence only after the heart did.

The awareness and wisdom of the heart are apparently able to transcend space and time.

CO-CREATING WITH SOPHIA

> We cannot observe the world without changing it. *While this is true at the quantum level in the most startling, empirical way, it also applies to daily life. Every worldview or belief involves an interpretive focus.... This does not mean that everything is relative, but indicates that consciousness is always giving birth to reality in a participatory, co-creative way with the greater universe.... In some way that we do not fully understand, our own awareness, working in harmony with the greater universe, may play a fundamental role in shaping the trajectory and manifestation of the world as it comes into being.*
>
> —David Fideler, *Restoring the Soul of the World*

The ability to sense the quality of future events before they arise suggests a connection with Sophia. Robert Sardello has described Sophia, in one of her aspects, as "the time stream of the future." We can see what this means by paying attention to the wisdom, harmony, and beauty with which the natural world unfolds, moment by moment. We can look anywhere and everywhere, from the movements of the stars to the web of living things, and even to the structure of subatomic matter. On every level, the universe self-organizes spontaneously to support and sustain itself and all its myriad expressions.

I have viewed Sophia, in part, as the presence of the vast web of intelligence that underlies the phenomenon of synchronicity. And synchronicities are, by their nature, manifestations of meaning that transcend space and time.

Our heart is the Seat of the Soul. Because the heart is the home of our wisdom, and because our feeling sense and our compassion are there, and most especially because of the heart's capacity to feel into the future, I envision the heart as Sophia's natural home within us. The heart is the point of contact we all have with her vast and intimate intelligence. It is the easiest place for us to meet Sophia within ourselves, and our Deep Self is there to participate in that communion.

Why do I think that the heart's attunement to the future is so important? Remember, Sophia is the intelligence who manifests as the beauty, harmony, and Wisdom of the world. She is the one who reveals meaning to us through synchronicity. We could say she is the world's great wave of blessing intelligence, continually in a state of *potential* manifestation.

We might state metaphorically that Sophia is like the rainbow before anyone looks at it. As I said before, a rainbow is an event, not a thing. Until it is seen, there is no rainbow. Our conscious participation is the essence of our co-creative capacity with Sophia. We are the ones who can bring her more fully into manifestation, simply by *paying attention,* with the *intention* of perceiving and affirming her. (The ritual of "breathing with Sophia" described above involves just such a focusing of attention, intention, and imagination.) This attention involves heart-centered awareness, because, as we saw above, the heart is the center of consciousness within us that intuitively feels the future coming. Our hearts can feel and perceive Sophia as the time stream of the future.

Heart-centered awareness is synonymous with the alchemists' True Imagination, because within True Imagination, we see the "spiritual forces at play in the mundane world"—we see Sophia. To see her in this way, in every moment of life, is another way we metaphorically offer her our breath. In so doing, we co-create the world with her, manifesting her actuality out of her potential.

In our spiritual work with stones, we do something quite similar to the alchemists. We attend to the stones and their energies for the purpose of the good. We reach toward them inwardly, and like the rainbow, or Sophia, our intention and attention *bring them into manifestation.* Together, we make them real! Our co-creating perception brings the energies of the stones from a state of potential into actual manifestation in the world—in us. It may seem hard to imagine, but in a very genuine sense, stone energies do not enter into existence until we meet them. (Just as the rainbow isn't there until someone looks.) It doesn't mean the energies are false or illusory. It doesn't mean that we are fantasizing them. It means we are co-creating them with Sophia every time we pick up a stone and feel it. And, as I have said, this contributes toward the transformation of ourselves and the whole world.

Explanations like the one I have just made can seem to defy common sense. So I want to remind you that "common sense" is one of the synonyms for the old materialistic worldview. However, quantum physics—the physics that best describes our material world—tells us that *all events are observations,* and that until an observation is made, *events exist only as potential.* To actualize any potential at the quantum level, an observation must be made. This is just like my saying that rainbows and stone energies exist only as potential events until you or I or someone else observes and experiences them. This is an important piece of the alchemical worldview, in which the participation of the alchemist is understood to be essential to the actualization of the goal. Alchemists were, in a sense, the quantum physicists of their day, because their insight told them that objectivity was an illusion—a fantasy—and that they must work co-creatively with Sophia in order to succeed in the Great Work they shared with her.

Developing a conscious, co-creative relationship with our Deep Self and with Sophia are two of the most important goals of spiritual alchemy. And we find, as we explore the Alchemy of Stones, that the Stone Beings are ready to help us achieve them.

ROSOPHIA, THE SOPHIA STONE

The second Sophia dream recounted above came to me a few days before Kathy and I flew to Santa Fe, New Mexico, to offer our workshops at the Sophia Conference. I carried the numinous feeling of the encounter with me, and wondered if I should share the dream when I spoke to the group.

When we arrived at the retreat center, a staff person showed us to the room where we would be staying. As soon as we entered, my eyes were attracted to a stone sitting on the mantle. It was a chunk of salmon-colored rock, with translucent whitish spots, veined here and there with black. I hadn't seen anything quite like it before, and I was immediately curious about it. I dropped my luggage and picked up the stone, bringing it to my chest and tuning in to it, inviting it into me.

Within seconds, I sensed a sweet, curving energy moving gracefully in and around my heart. It felt deeply loving and healing, and it seemed to rise up into me through my feet. It was grounding, soothing, nourishing, and gentle. In fact, it felt just like the breath of Sophia, as I had experienced it in my dream. These currents were perhaps less intense than those in my dream, but their signature quality was the same.

I stood there, letting the sweet currents wash through me. I had planned to simply check to see if this strange new rock had any energies. I had not expected to suddenly be immersed once again in the presence and essence of Sophia.

My astonishment was mixed with recognition. The events of the prior weeks and months, even years, leading up to the Sophia dream only a few days before fell into a pattern, in which my meeting with the this stone was a new, important piece. This was the Stone of Sophia. I was somewhat shaken by my feelings about the enormity of the realization. There was no mistaking the fact that the energies of the new stone—found waiting on the mantle of our room at Sophia's Conference—were the same as those I had felt in my dream, in which I had encountered Sophia herself. How could all this have fallen together so perfectly? Not since my first major spiritual experience in college had I experienced such a powerful and astounding synchronicity.

But this time I was much older, and I had been navigating the waters of spirituality for almost three decades. Instead of being frightened, I was elated. I handed the stone to Kathy, who also felt its lovely currents circulating around her heart. I rushed off to find Robert Sardello, and invited him to hold the stone. Robert, as well as several others, confirmed my impressions of its energies.

My heart was open, and my mind was racing. I felt that I absolutely must find more of these stones as quickly as possible, hopefully in time for all the participants at the Sophia Conference to have one to experience during my presentation in two days. Instead of resting in our room, Kathy and I hiked into the nearby canyon to hunt for more of the stones.

After a couple of hours, we had found enough pieces to give one to each of the conference participants. We put them in the closet of our room. I was still in an expanded state of joy and exuberance. Calming myself a little, I sat down to think about what the name of the new stone should be. (Having never seen or heard of a stone like this before, I was pretty sure no one had yet named it or done meditative work with it.) It took only moments for me to hear the name of the stone in my heart. Rosophia—the stone itself seemed to be telling me its name. I understood that the sophia in the name referred to Sophia herself, and that *Ros-* was linked to the Rose—an archetypal symbol of the heart. So, *Rosophia* means the Heart of Sophia, or the Heart of Wisdom, or the Heart of the Soul of the World. It means all of these, and when we invite the currents of Rosophia into our own hearts, they link us with the essence of Sophia.

Of course, we are, in another sense, always linked with Sophia. She is present in us, in our hearts, and in every atom of the world. And certainly, all the stone energies are, in my view, emanations of Sophia. Nonetheless, I believe that Rosophia vibrates in a way that resonates with the heart and the love of Sophia, and helps us enter consciously into intimate relationship with her. Remember the coded meaning of the alchemical name for the substance that one must find to place within one's vessel of transformation (the heart)—*pri-ma ma-teria:* first mother, Mother Earth. That is Sophia, Soul of the World.

When I gave my presentation at the Sophia Conference, most of the audience felt a strong and rewarding connection with the currents of Rosophia. They experienced the energies primarily in their hearts. In the years since the day of my first experience, I have seen thousands of people hold a Rosophia stone for the first time, and the great majority of them have reported feeling the energies of the stone in ways very similar to mine.

Another quality of both Sophia as a spiritual being and of the stone Rosophia is the way in which *she reaches upward to meet the Light.* In Gnostic mythology, Sophia descended from the Pleroma (the heavenly realm of Divine beings) because of her attraction to the Earth. There she became "lost within matter," and the task of Christ (as Sophia's male counterpart—the incarnation of the Divine Light) was to free Sophia and rescue her. In this story, human involvement could aid in freeing Sophia, with the added benefit of uniting humanity with the Light of Heaven. (This is strongly resonant with the alchemical idea of working co-creatively with Sophia to create the Philosophers' Stone, which can transform all things to their highest potential, and redeem both the alchemist and the world. It is also akin to the spiritual communion enacted through breathing with Sophia.)

Those who feel the energies of Rosophia frequently report the sensation that its currents come up through their feet, circulate in the heart, and seem to reach farther upward to the Light. There is another stone that is the natural partner or counterpart for Rosophia. It is the stone called Azeztulite—a stone of the Divine Light of the Great Central Sun—which emanates currents of heavenly Light. The energies of Light emanated by Azeztulite reach downward into matter, and into the bodies of those who open to it. Thus it can be seen to represent the figure of Christ in the Gnostic mythos.

As stone energies, Rosophia and Azeztulite holographically reenact the reunion of Sophia, the Soul of the World, with Christ, the World Redeemer. Energetically, when people work with these two stones at the same time—holding both of them while inviting them to enter their hearts—they frequently feel tangibly, in the heart, the currents of Rosophia reaching up to meet the currents of Azeztulite flowing down. The Love of the Earth and the Light of Heaven join one another in the vessel of our hearts, and we can experience within ourselves the union of Heaven and Earth.

To choose to consciously participate in the inner enactment of this deep archetypal pattern is to engage in co-creation with the Divine. It is co-creation because, in order for the pattern to unfold, we must make ourselves available, and, by the same token, the divine energies coming into the world through the stones must make themselves available. (My thirty years among the stones tells me that they are always available for such transformations. The beings on their side of the veil are fully aware of the need for this partnership and the results it can bring.) This inner reunion must occur many times, within as many people as possible, in order for its reality to manifest fully. It is not just my story. It is available to all of us, and I am very passionate in my desire to share it with whomever may feel a connection to it.

I invite the reader to look back now and see how far we have come by following the

Golden Threads. As we go forward, there will be more . . . and more . . . and more of them. Sophia and her Wisdom weave through all the world, and all our lives.

I have mentioned the stone Azeztulite in this story, and in a sense, I have spoken of it out of its proper order. But the story of the Alchemy of Stones is complicated, and tightly woven, and we will sometimes jump ahead, or backtrack, in order to tell the tale. We will follow Azeztulite's threads more fully in later chapters, and I will suggest practices for working with it, including combining it with Rosophia.

PRACTICE: COMMUNION WITH SOPHIA

In this practice, the goal is to call upon Sophia and meet her in your heart. If you find that this happens easily and quickly, you can combine this practice and the next one in a single meditative period. Or you can simply take this practice farther, as discussed below.

1. Choose a stone to work with in this meditation. I highly recommend using Rosophia, but if that is unavailable to you, you may pick a different stone. Once again, if you are not working with Rosophia, I think it is best if you view an array of different stones and listen inwardly until a stone "chooses" you.
2. Begin by focusing your intention on the goal of this practice. Close your eyes and take a deep breath, while placing attention in your heart, and inwardly, silently saying, "Communion with Sophia." Then pick up the stone you will be working with and spend a few seconds, or a minute, taking it in through all your senses.
3. When you feel ready, begin the process by blowing your breath over the stone in an offering gesture to Sophia, and inhaling over the stone while inwardly affirming your invitation for Sophia to enter your heart. When you do this, you are inviting both the Being of the stone *and* Sophia into your heart, and you are offering your heart to them both at the same time. You may feel two beings or one. (In my view, the Stone Being has its own center of self, and is at the same time an emanation of Sophia.) Either way is fine. Simply give yourself to what occurs.
4. Bring the stone down and hold it over the center of your chest at the level of your heart. Continue to pay attention to your breathing. As you inhale, invite *and* visualize the stone moving into your body, at the Heart Chakra level. As you exhale, continue to offer your heart and your love to the Stone Being and Sophia. If it is easier for you, it is fine to focus just on Sophia.
5. Stay with the breathing and the invitation or offer. Relax and allow yourself to inwardly gesture the *feeling* of the invitation and the offer, without any words or expectations.
6. When you begin to feel the stone currents in your heart, or when you see or sense the presence of a Being there, place attention in the center of your chest even more intensely and silently sound the word "Sophia." Do this three times, or follow your intuition and feeling sense in regard to how to proceed.
7. When you sense her presence, whether she is accompanied by the Stone Being or not, focus your attention at the Heart Chakra again and silently sound the phrase, "Communion with Sophia." Or you can speak inwardly to Sophia and sound the phrase, "Communion with you." (The second phrase works best if you have actually reached a clear sense of Sophia's presence in your heart.)
8. Relax, breathe, and be attentive to everything that happens. Let yourself bathe in the energies you feel in and around your heart. Let them fill your entire body and energy field. This experience can be very pleasurable. If you see Sophia as an inner figure, you may wish to visualize yourself going to greet her. You may even find that you can go somewhere with Sophia—perhaps to some natural setting that is suitable for an intimate conversation, or to

wherever she wishes to take you. You can trust whatever occurs if your feeling sense tells you that you are with Sophia. It is most important to stay with the thread of your feeling sense as you go through this experience.

9. You will notice when the experience has completed itself. Sophia may even indicate this to you. When this sense of completion comes to you, thank Sophia or the Being of the stone, and tell them farewell, for this time. Allow your attention to come back to your physical body, and when you are ready, you can open your eyes. If you need to ground yourself, take off your shoes, wiggle your toes on the floor or ground, or have a drink of water.
10. Whether you simply stayed in your heart feeling the stone currents, or if you saw, spoke with, or traveled with Sophia, there is no wrong outcome. Even if nothing seems to happen the first time, or the first few times you work with this practice, you are building up your connection to Sophia so that it can come into your conscious awareness. It is already there in your subconscious self.
11. In your notebook or journal, write down as much as you can recall of the experience. Bring in the details you can remember. Do this each time you engage in this practice, at least until you feel deeply connected and able to bring yourself into this place whenever you wish to do so.
12. If you reached a vivid sense of connection with the presence of Sophia in a short time, you can move into the next practice during the same meditative session. Otherwise, try it as a separate meditation.

PRACTICE: CALLING UPON SOPHIA'S WISDOM

You will need pen and paper for this.

1. If you are beginning this practice as a separate meditation, go through the initial steps described above. Choose the stone to work with, drink it in through all your senses, breathe over it, bring it to your chest, and begin the invitation and offering process, as discussed above.
2. When you can feel the currents of Sophia in your heart, or when you simply sense her presence, silently sound this phrase in your heart: "Wisdom of Sophia."
3. Have your notebook or journal in your lap, with your pen in your writing hand, while holding the stone over your heart with the other hand. If this becomes difficult or distracting, you may let your arm rest on the arm of the chair, but keep holding the stone. Stay in the meditative state, and only allow your eyes to open enough for you to see to write.
4. Try to put your attention into Sophia's consciousness as you write the phrase "I want to tell you . . ." on the paper. Then listen for what Sophia wants to say to you, and write down what comes to you. When you have finished a statement, begin again with the phrase, "I want to tell you . . ." and repeat the process. Keep repeating this until this process feels complete.
5. At this point, you may thank Sophia and withdraw, as in the prior practice. Or, you can go to another phrase (I recommend this). It works the same way as before, but now the phrase to begin with is, "I want to ask you . . ." As before, imagine that you are hearing Sophia say this phrase, and write down whatever comes to you for completing the sentence. This will be what Sophia wants to ask of you. Repeat this until the experience feels complete.
6. Thank Sophia, letting yourself feel the love flowing between you and her. If a Stone Being accompanied you in this practice, thank that Being as well. Then you may shift your attention to the outer world and your body.

7. I believe it is important to work with both phrases, because this gives Sophia a chance to offer you her wisdom, and also to ask for something from you. In both the telling and the asking, Sophia's presence and her words bless us. In the Alchemy of Stones, we are learning to co-create in partnership with Sophia and the Stone Beings, and in this process, the circulation of giving and receiving is essential.

DISCUSSION

The two practices above are simple, but the experiences they facilitate can be profound. When I have led groups in the Communion with Sophia practice, the sense of intimacy with Sophia frequently brings deep experiences and strong feelings. Joy, tears, and waves of gratitude are felt and expressed by many participants. People are often astounded by how simply and easily they can move into conscious relationship with Sophia.

It can be quite amazing to work with the "Calling upon Sophia's Wisdom" practice in a group setting. When I lead workshops, I always ask participants who are willing to do so to read out loud the words they received. As we listen together, it becomes apparent that the voice of Sophia has come to many of us in ways that are recognizably from the same being. Her choice of words and the style of expression reveal her presence, and the wisdom of her teaching is apparent.

Once again, I want to emphasize that, if possible, it is very helpful to work with the stone Rosophia in these practices, as it provides the easiest and most readily accessible link with the presence of Sophia.

SLEEPING WITH ROSOPHIA

Thus far, we have touched only lightly upon three specific stones and their qualities—Moldavite, Rosophia, and, to a lesser degree, Azeztulite. Much of this kind of information comes later in this book. However, I do want to mention one way of working with Rosophia that I have found to be of great benefit to many people.

This practice is about as simple as it comes—get yourself a piece of Rosophia and sleep with it. In numerous instances, I have found this stone to be very helpful in releasing stress and sleeping well. The currents of Rosophia move gently into and around the heart, soothing and calming the emotions and helping one's nervous system and muscles to relax. In my case, it also seems to aid with digestion. But all of that has to do with the serenity that its currents bring to one's heart.

I sleep almost every night with a large chunk of Rosophia (the same one that was on the mantle of our room back at the Sophia Conference). It is nice to sleep with a piece that is the size of an egg or larger, so that one can lie on one's side and cuddle it up next to the heart. As I am getting ready to go to sleep, I imagine the currents of the Rosophia flowing into my heart as I inhale, and I offer my appreciation as I exhale. I have learned to do this in the feeling sense, without words. That helps my mental energies to stay quiet.

I have recommended Rosophia to hundreds of people as an aid for relaxation and sleep, and I have frequently been told that it worked well. It has also helped a number of individuals to quiet anxiety and lift depression.

On occasion, sleeping with Rosophia has facilitated the occurrence of vivid dreams in which Sophia comes to the sleeper with love, teaching, or healing. Sometimes, she even requests something of us. In my view, every contact with Sophia is to be treasured, contemplated, and remembered.

The Gnostics and the alchemists both viewed Sophia as the living presence of Wisdom, manifested in the beauty and harmony of the world. When we experience grace, are surprised by a synchronicity, feel awe in nature, or glimpse the pattern that connects all things, we are noticing the expressions of Sophia. And the world is not merely a static perfection—it evolves and transforms. Things flow and change seamlessly, through eons of time. The alchemists believed that Sophia's long work was evolving toward the "world as paradise," and their aim was to help her accelerate that goal. In times of danger and crisis such as those we are living in, perhaps that is a fitting aspiration for ourselves. If so, we might attempt what the alchemists tried—co-creating with Sophia by observing and adopting her methods.

What are Sophia's methods? That question goes beyond what I can speak of, but there is one fundamental process that the alchemists recognized and utilized, and which we also can employ—transformation through feedback.

8

Transformation through Feedback: Alchemy, Sophia & the Oroborous

The natural world is composed of endless loops of information feeding back upon themselves. The alchemists had already realized, long before chaos theory, that it was this process of feedback through many stages that begins to separate out potential new structures. The key idea is that a miniscule change caused by an alchemical operation can be magnified many times if the same operation is repeated over and over.

—Robin Robertson, *Indra's Net*

The Oroborous represents the perpetual cyclic renewal of life and infinity, the concept of eternity and the eternal return, and represents the cycle of life, death and rebirth, leading to immortality.

—Crystalinks

The alchemists, who in their own way knew more about the nature of the individuation process [the achievement of wholeness through inner transformation] than we moderns do, expressed this paradox through the symbol of the Ouroboros, the snake that eats its own tail. The Ouroboros has been said to have a meaning of infinity or wholeness. In the age-old image of the Ouroboros lies the thought of devouring oneself and turning oneself into a circulatory process, for it was clear to the more astute alchemists that the prima materia *of the art was man himself.*

—Carl Jung, *Mysterium Coniunctio*

If you want to understand Gaia, you have to learn to think in terms of nonlinear, circular logic of feedback systems.

—Tim Michael Lenton, Professor of Climate Change and Earth System Science at the University of Exeter

ABOVE: Sophia with the Oroborous

The alchemists believed that transformation was the natural activity of Nature. They viewed the world around them as being constantly in a condition of creative evolution–an outpouring of Sophia, the World Soul, Wisdom. They envisioned their work as being in harmony with Nature, and constantly asserted that without the co-creative partnership of Sophia, their work would not succeed. The intention of the alchemists was to ally themselves with Nature and dedicate their efforts to accelerating Nature's purpose: evolving the world and all its parts to their ideal state. Whether the alchemists worked inwardly in meditation, or in a laboratory with physical materials, or both (which many did), they believed in a sympathetic resonance between themselves, their materials, and the world. They envisioned that a transformation within the physical vessel or within the inner self would also be reflected in the outer world. The ambition of the Great Work of the alchemists was nothing less than, in Paul Levy's words, "to redeem the entire cosmos."

As mentioned in the previous chapter, I think that this can also be our ultimate goal in the Alchemy of Stones. The energies of the stones, which come into full existence through our engagement with them, are a manifestation of subtle matter/energy which represents a co-creative fusion of our consciousness with that of Nature/Sophia. This manifestation occurs in the in-between realm of the psychoid—the overlap between matter and spirit—which is holographically present everywhere. The effects of this co-creative bonding (through the Stone Beings) of ourselves with the Soul of the World reverberate into the physical world, and into the spiritual realms, and can ultimately contribute to their union. As spiritual alchemists, we can enclose this subtle matter/energy within ourselves and circulate it continually. This purifies, evolves and transmutes ourselves and all that we touch—including, potentially, our entire world.

So, how does Sophia do her work of Wisdom within Nature? In their observations, the alchemists had the great insight that Nature operates in a multitude of cyclic processes. Looking to the plant realm, they perceived the natural feedback patterns of germination, growth, flowering and fruiting, death, decay and refertilization for new germination. They saw analogous patterns in animal life, and they prefigured Darwin in recognizing that nature thus refines and improves her creations through evolution. This insight was pictured metaphorically in one of alchemy's key symbolic images—the snake or dragon that bites its own tail—the oroborous.

The oroborous is depicted as a static image, but it actually symbolizes a constantly moving process. The serpent has its tail in its mouth and is feeding on itself. It consumes itself, yet the nourishment it takes into itself by eating its own tail also fuels its growth, so there will be more of the snake available to be eaten. This allows the process to continue forever. Obviously, this is a metaphoric representation that would not work with a physical snake! However, it is amazingly accurate in regard to how nature operates,

and even in regard to how the forms of the natural world emerge. We'll see this as we go on with this chapter.

From Wikipedia: "The oroborous is an ancient symbol depicting a serpent or dragon eating its own tail. Originating in Ancient Egyptian iconography, the oroborous entered Western tradition via Greek magical tradition and was adopted as a symbol in Gnosticism and Hermeticism, and most notably in alchemy. Via the medieval alchemical tradition, the symbol entered Renaissance magic and modern symbolism, often taken to symbolize introspection, the eternal return or cyclicality, especially in the sense of something constantly re-creating itself. It also represents the infinite cycle of nature's endless creation and destruction, life and death."

We see from the quote above that the oroborous was viewed as a multi-dimensional symbol, used to stand for both inner and outer processes. This is why the alchemical engraving at the beginning of this chapter depicts Sophia holding up the oroborous, with the caption *Macchina del Mondo*—the mechanism of the world. (Note also that Sophia's hair is radiant like the rays of a star or sun, and that among the rays are human figures. This indicates Sophia's constant creating activity, and that human beings are the very "thoughts," or emanations of the mind of the Soul of the World.) The "mechanism" at the core of Sophia's creating activity is the oroborous—the process of cyclic feedback.

Wikipedia: "In Gnosticism, a serpent biting its tail symbolized eternity and the soul of the world. The Gnostic text *Pistis Sophia* describes the Oroborous as a twelve-part dragon surrounding the world with his tail in his mouth." [**NOTE**: The twelve parts suggest the twelve signs of the zodiac.]

Many of the ancients viewed the oroborous as a symbol for processes operating on all levels of the universe—from largest to smallest, both inner and outer.

The idea that the oroborous can symbolize introspection is one to remember, as we go forward into a number of meditative processes with stones. In these, we will cycle our energy and attention between the inner and outer realms, in unison with our breathing. The energies of the stones can come into us as we inhale, altering our inner state, which we then offer back to the Stone Being as we exhale. I described this pattern in earlier practices, and it is fundamental to the alchemical work with stones.

The image of Sophia with the oroborous suggests that she utilizes its dynamic pattern as the fundamental means through which she generates the natural world. Indeed, we see the feedback processes symbolized by the oroborous in the reproduction of life on all levels–from microbes to blue whales. Each generation feeds its DNA and its morphic field of memory to the next generation. Biological adaptations and even new species emerge from these feedback processes, under the guidance of the intrinsic Wisdom that is Sophia. The evolution of life from its bacterial beginnings to its current vast web of complexity displays the fact that the feedback processes of evolution have always been at the core of life.

In current times, the significance of feedback has been encapsulated in the idea known as The Butterfly Efffect. It is often summarized in a question, such as, "Can the flap of a butterfly's wings in Brazil set off a tornado in Texas?" In the mathematics of dynamic systems known as Chaos Theory, the answer is yes, it can. The Earth's atmosphere is a dynamic system, and the feedback through the entire system that begins with an action as small as a butterfly's wings flapping has the potential to cascade into huge, unpredictable changes.

The feedback-based mathematics of Chaos Theory also provides the best means of modeling a multitude of other natural phenomena, including river networks, trees, ferns, snowflakes, Romanesco broccoli, lightning bolts, heart rates, ocean waves and DNA, to name a few. The recognition that the patterns of nature occur on all levels of scale—from the spiral snail shell to the spiral galaxy—gave rise among the ancient alchemists to the insight encapsulated in the famous phrase *as above, so below.*

Chaos Theory is somewhat misnamed, because it is actually the mathematics that reveals the *hidden order* within processes which *appear superficially* to be chaotic. This is very reminiscent of the idea of Sophia as Wisdom being present invisibly in every particle of matter. She is present as the hidden order within the apparent chaos. (i.e. She is the invisible intelligence that guides life to evolve in ways that are diverse, elegant, beautiful, and advantageous to survival.) Thus, feedback, as it operates on all levels of the world—the above and the below, the inner and the outer—is the invisible but powerful oroborous of Sophia—the "mechanism" that generates the world. This idea turns out to be emphatically validated in Chaos Theory's most famous and visually spectacular expression—fractal geometry.

LEFT: "Buddhabrot" fractal pattern;
BELOW: Sea urchin shell

A SIDE TRIP INTO THE FRACTAL UNIVERSE

> *Chaos is the science of surprises, of the nonlinear and the unpredictable. It teaches us to expect the unexpected. While most traditional science deals with supposedly predictable phenomena like gravity, electricity, or chemical reactions, Chaos Theory deals with nonlinear things that are effectively impossible to predict or control, like turbulence, weather, the stock market, our brain states, and so on. These phenomena are often described by fractal mathematics, which captures the infinite complexity of nature. Many natural objects exhibit fractal properties, including landscapes, clouds, trees, organs, rivers etc, and many of the systems in which we live exhibit complex, chaotic behavior. Recognizing the chaotic, fractal nature of our world can give us new insight, power, and wisdom.*
>
> —Dr. Jonathon Wolfe, co-counder of the Fractal Foundation, Albuquerque, NM

> *A fractal is a never-ending pattern. Fractals are infinitely complex patterns that are self-similar across different scales. They are created by repeating a simple process over and over in an ongoing feedback loop. Driven by recursion, fractals are images of dynamic systems—the pictures of Chaos. Geometrically, they exist in between our familiar dimensions. Fractal patterns are extremely familiar, since nature is full of fractals. For instance: trees, rivers, coastlines, mountains, clouds, seashells, hurricanes, etc.*
>
> —Dr. Jonathon Wolfe, co-counder of the Fractal Foundation, Albuquerque, NM

> *The famous alchemist Paracelsus said: "Heaven is man, and man is heaven, and all men together are one heaven, and heaven is nothing but one man." This lovely phrase means not only "as above, so below," but also "as below, so above." With this idea of mutual influence, Paracelsus comes closer to chaos theory than any previous thinker. . . . Just as (in astrology) the heavens determine our character and the earth our physical being, there is a wholeness to our body and character that is reflected back at all levels. The presence of the whole within the parts is exactly what chaos theory means when it describes reality as being "fractal."*
>
> —Robin Robertson, PhD in *Indra's Net*

The idea that Sophia is a pervasive, living. benevolent intelligence, present everywhere, operating in everything–expressing the unfolding time-stream of the future—is vital to all the work we will do in the Alchemy of Stones. This is because we will be working with Sophia in every practice we perform. We feel her vitality in the energy of every stone, and we see her in each stone's form and beauty. I feel strongly that processes involving feedback are fundamental to how Sophia operates in nature, and such processes will be at the center of our alchemical efforts to accelerate the evolution of ourselves and our world.

Because it is, in my view, so important to grasp how all-pervasive and amazing the Wisdom of Sophia is in the world, I will try to delve a little deeper into showing how this Wisdom displays itself through the lens of Chaos Theory's most famous subset—fractal geometry.

I am not going to try to summarize all of the mind-bending ideas that are embodied in this mathematics. (To read its history, I recommend James Gleick's book *Chaos*. To learn about the likenesses between Chaos Theory and alchemy, see Robin Robertson's book, *Indra's Net*.) But we will go into enough to see how the oroboric activity of feedback is fundamental to the ways that nature manifests. There are a number of aspects to Chaos Theory, but we will focus on those that involve oroborus-like feedback loops.

In biology, evolution operates through feedback. The idea of natural selection, which was fundamental to Darwin's theory of evolution, describes a kind of feedback system. In reproduction, the combination of male and female DNA is a feedback loop, in which the offspring that continue the cycle of life resemble each parent, but are not identical to either one. Feedback over many, many cycles produces evolutionary change.

This is interesting in terms of the insights of spiritual Alchemy for several reasons. Among them is the alchemical idea that one begins by working with chaos. As we have seen, the beginning material which the Alchemist works to refine and transform is called the *prima materia,* or first matter, and is said to exist in a chaotic state. The alchemist, in partnership with Sophia/ Wisdom, subjects the *prima materia* to repeated processes of ordering and purification, which ultimately bring it into the perfected dynamic order called the Philosophers' Stone.

(**NOTE**: I have mentioned earlier that the words *prima materia* can be translated as *First Mother, Mother Earth.* This recalls the view of the ancient Gnostics that Sophia herself fell from the higher realm of the Pleroma into the imperfect physical world, with its inherent chaos. The Gnostics believed that Sophia's fall into matter explained the dual nature of the world–the pairing of harsh and difficult realities with the simultaneous presence of Wisdom and grace. If we take this view, the same principles can apply. By drawing some of Sophia's latent presence into our awareness—for example, by working consciously with stone energies—we bring the "fallen" Sophia into consciousness, and together with her, we work to bring Sophia herself into a fully awakened and perfected state. This is what is meant by "redemption"—one of spiritual alchemy's key aspirations.)

In the 1980s, when a genius named Benoit Mandelbrot was trying to find a mathematical way of describing the patterns found in nature, such as coastlines, river deltas, leaf formation, etc., he discovered that the new mathematics called Chaos Theory did a far better job of modeling how nature creates its forms than anything ever devised before.

In Chinese Alchemy, the idea of the oroborus was symbolized in the Yin/ Yang. The large black and white shapes (which, incidentally, are abstract representations of two fish biting one another's tail) were meant to show how opposites entwine with one another in the dynamic flow of creation. The small dots of the opposite color within each of the larger shapes indicate that the light contains a bit of darkness and the darkness contains a bit of light. And the Yin/ Yang was understood to be constantly moving and circulating, with the opposites flowing into one another.

The Yin/Yang is the key symbol of Taoism, the oldest spiritual system in China, and was the oroborus of the Chinese alchemists. The ancient Taoists described the eternally self-transforming yin/yang as a depiction of the flow of

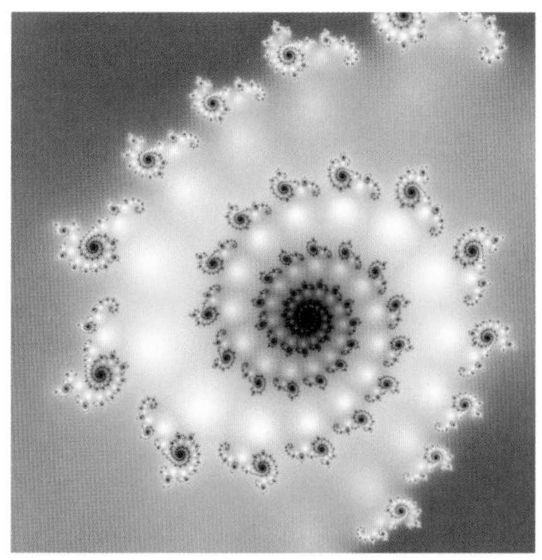

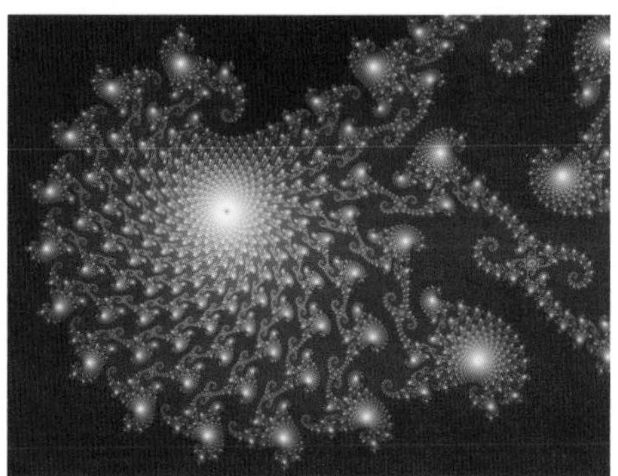

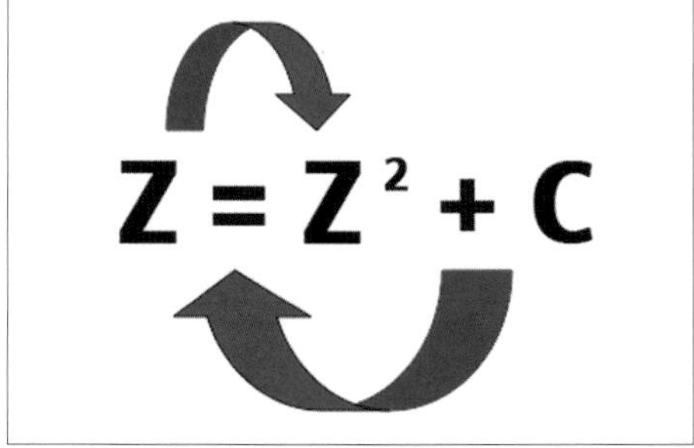

The Mandelbrot Fractal Equation

the Tao, the Way, the great River of Life that goes on forever.

The great alchemical insight, *as above, so below* is illustrative of the idea that we live in a holographic Universe. The patterns we see on a macro scale also exist on a micro scale. One of the most common of these is the spiral pattern that exists throughout nature, from snail shells and ferns to hurricanes and galaxies. The same kind of spiral pattern is one of those generated by the mathematics of chaos Theory known as Fractal Geometry.

The image to the left shows the fundamental equation that was used to generate the world's most famous fractal—the Mandelbrot Set, named after Benoit Mandelbrot. The Mandelbrot Set can be shown graphically, displaying the results of doing the calculations shown in the equation again and again, millions and millions of times, and on into infinity. In the picture of the equation, the arrows indicate that the results of doing the calculation are to be fed back into the other side of the equation and recalculated. Each calculation produces a new result, which is also fed back into the equation, producing yet another complex numeric value. Each calculation is called an *iteration,* and the implicit instruction in the formulation is to *re-iterate* the calculation endlessly. Doing this results in a literally infinite number of numeric results, which can be graphed in a complex plane and converted into images by a computer.

The images on pages 73–75 show patterns produced by computers doing this and other fractal feedback-loop calculations, alongside similar patterns from the natural world. The likenesses are striking. When we recognize that the branching patterns seen in computer-generated fractal "trees" mirror those of real trees—as well as the formation of the lungs, the dendrites in agate, or the scars left by lightning striking someone—we see that the same sorts of patterns or "gestures" occur in a multitude of different manifestations. In this, we begin to perceive the evidence of Sophia's method of creating and evolving the world. (Remember, the computer-generated images are produced by millions of calculations created through feedback.) When we saw earlier that the spiral swirls from sections of the Mandelbrot Set resemble

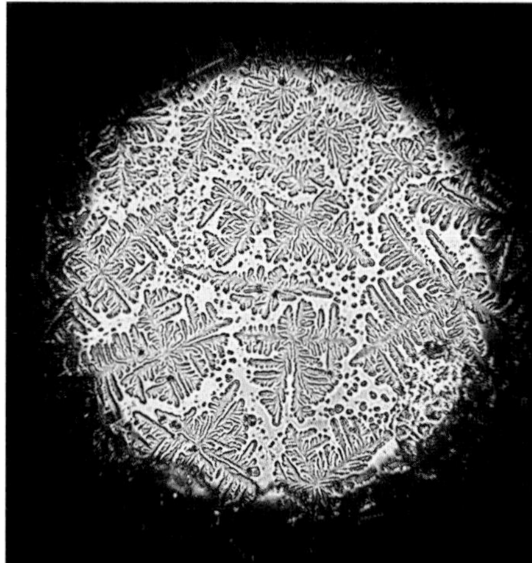

LEFT TO RIGHT; Fractal dendrites; Agate with dendrites; Human amniotic fluid (magnified) with microscopic dendritic structure; Lake Nasser Coastline, Egypt; Dendritic scars from lightning strike

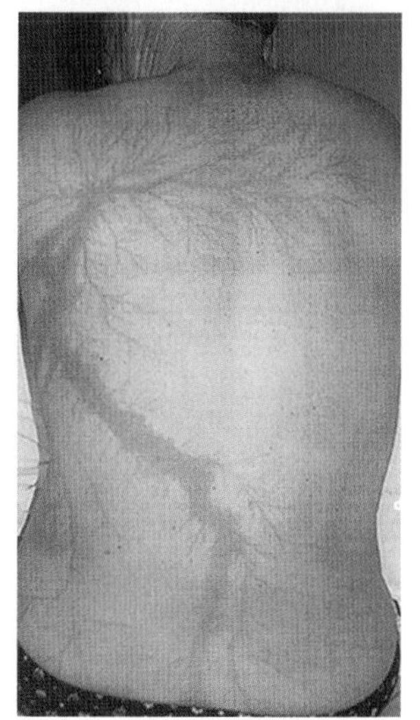

the spirals in snail shells, ferns, hurricanes and galaxies, we glimpsed the all-pervasive presence of the feedback processes symbolized by the oroborus. We also appreciate the alchemical insight summarized in the phrase, *as above, so below.* The same fundamental patterns of nature appear in all levels of size, and they even occur invisibly, in realms such as those of brain function and human social behavior.

I have to stop myself, before I try to start writing a whole book about fractals! I just want to invite you now to look at the pictures and contemplate them. Until the discovery of fractal geometry, no mathematics had been capable of modeling the forms and complex process that exist all around us in nature, as well as within us. Until computers which were capable of rapidly making million of calculations were invented, there was no way for these images to emerge. And until the computer-generated images were seen, no one realized that *this was the way the world was made*—through untold numbers of reiterations feeding back upon themselves, resembling infinite invisibly revolving orobori. Though they had no computers, the alchemists somehow grasped this fundamental gesture of Wisdom within nature. They saw that the Soul of the World is forever self-creating and evolving.

We ourselves contain multiple feedback loops, on all levels of our physical, mental, emotional and spiritual existence. For example, our conscious experience of each moment resonates with our memories from the past, and is evaluated and understood in light of those memories. A given moment may or may not be highly similar to others we have lived, but it will not be identical. It will then enter into our store of memories, modifying our worldview and ourselves, though perhaps only slightly. Nonetheless, the outcome of each moment changes us, and the consciousness with which we experience the next moment—and the next million or billion moments—evolves and transforms through a feedback process. This is how we grow, change and evolve on the mental level of our being. And, of course, every level of our being is linked in a multitude of feedback loops with all the others. This can explain why things like our emotions or our spiritual beliefs can affect our bodily health . . . and on and on. Our lives are not just one feedback loop—they are composed of an infinite web of them!

We can even see this in our social interactions. We sometimes ask each other for "feedback" which will confirm our attitudes, or influence us to modify them. At other times we receive "feedback" when people react to us, and this, too, influences us. And our words and actions act as feedback that influences others.

Within ourselves, we can and do utilize feedback loops. One example is working with visualization to enhance performance in sports. In this process, an athlete imagines seeing herself running her best race, achieving her fastest time ever. Or a baseball player visualizes hitting a home run. Techniques like these have been shown many times to be effective. Similar visualization practices have proven effective in healing from injuries and illnesses. One's consciously directed feedback influences whole systems in the body. (And unconsciously directed feedback, such as worry, can have detrimental effects.)

The alchemists saw the methods of Sophia, and they believed they could ally themselves with her, accelerating evolutionary processes by adding their own "input" into the ones they hoped to affect. This sort of approach—in which one consciously chooses to engage in a feedback process—makes sense in everyday life, and in our work with stones. For example, when one is ill, the body will usually tend to heal itself. Its own memory of its pattern of health, along with its "intention" to heal, operate below one's level of awareness—once again through processes of feedback. However, if one chooses to meditate, pray, and/or visualize oneself in perfect health, we know that this added "input" will often affect the outcome in the way one desires. Our attention, intention and imagination—our co-creative capacities—enter and modify the unfolding pattern. Further, if we involve the beneficial currents of an appropriate stone—allied with our own conscious intention—the joint synergistic "input" of the stone's currents and our own intent provide an even stronger acceleration into the feedback system that leads to healing.

The fact that fractal patterns mirror a multitude of the forms found in nature shows us that the alchemist-artist who depicted Sophia holding an oroborous—with the caption *Macchina del Mondo* (mechanism of the world)—was correct. Feedback and cyclic evolution are indeed fundamental to the way the world works. The fact that our own bodies are full of fractal forms—and that our hearts and brains behave fractally—suggests that our efforts to enhance and accelerate our own evolution should include consciously entering into our own feedback patterns.

Has anyone ever tried to do this before? The Western alchemists did exactly this. As Carl Jung wrote, the work of the more astute alchemists involved "turning oneself into a circulatory process." In

Pelican Bottle; OPPOSITE: The Microcosmic Orbit

the "outer" work of alchemy from which modern chemistry arose, practitioners used devices such as the *pelican bottle.* (This device was so named because of stories describing a pelican wounding its own breast to feed its young. The pelican bottle was meant to work in an analogous way: perpetually boiling, condensing and re-boiling a liquid inside it. This was an attempt to mirror the activity symbolized by the oroborous, and to thereby transform and evolve physical substances.) The alchemists also believed that inner and outer processes would influence each other through sympathetic resonance—another manifestation of feedback.

In Chinese Taoist alchemy, a key practice was called the Microcosmic Orbit, in which the practitioner learned to circulate the vital *Qi* (or *chi*) energy in an oroborous feedback pattern within and around the body. It was developed for the purpose of accumulating and intensifying life force energies. This practice, known as the Circulation of Light, is at the heart of Taoist forms of exercise performed by millions of people. I use a modified version of this technique in some of my stone practices.

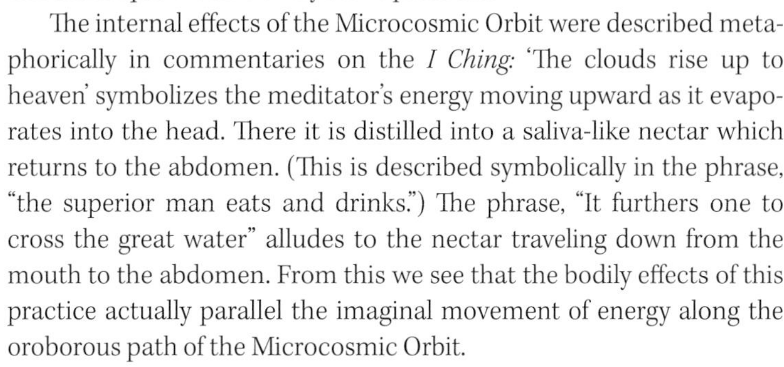

The internal effects of the Microcosmic Orbit were described metaphorically in commentaries on the *I Ching:* 'The clouds rise up to heaven' symbolizes the meditator's energy moving upward as it evaporates into the head. There it is distilled into a saliva-like nectar which returns to the abdomen. (This is described symbolically in the phrase, "the superior man eats and drinks.") The phrase, "It furthers one to cross the great water" alludes to the nectar traveling down from the mouth to the abdomen. From this we see that the bodily effects of this practice actually parallel the imaginal movement of energy along the oroborous path of the Microcosmic Orbit.

It is interesting to see the parallels in the above description to the following quote from the central text of Western alchemy, the Emerald Tablet. In this case, the description referred to the formation of the Philosophers' Stone: 'It rises from earth to heaven, so as to draw the lights of the heights to itself, and descends to the earth; thus within it are the forces of the above and the below.'

As with alchemical texts and illustrations from all times and places, both of the above descriptions are symbolic. However, if we look *through* the imagery and imagine forming these looping energy patterns within ourselves through meditative practices, we may recognize Jung's description of, "turning oneself into a circulatory process"—embodying the oroborous.

Most meditative disciplines that involve moving one's energies in ways such as those described above are directed toward the transformation and enlightenment of the practitioner. Some aim to promote health, longevity and even immortality. Generally they involve a great deal of practice in the cultivation of one's internal energy. In the Alchemy of Stones, we have similar aims, and we understand the need for repetition and practice. These are essential, since we intend to follow the ways of nature, evolving and transforming ourselves via purposefully engaging in feedback processes.

However, in the Alchemy of Stones, we have helpful allies, over and above our own wills and our own energies. The stones offer us powerful and dependable vibrational currents that we kindle within ourselves when we work with them. By simply paying attention to the stones' energies within us, and then directing them through the use of visualization (aka True Imagination), we can take advantage of the boost they willingly provide. If we envision the pathways we hope the stone energies will follow within us, we may find that we can progress much more rapidly than than we could by our own efforts alone. This dance can be a delicate matter, and my suggestion is to envision what is desired, and then surrender to what happens. By working in this way, I have found that the stones' currents often flow just as I invite them to flow, and when they don't, it frequently turns out to work even better than I had envisioned! This is at the essence of the co-creative nature of our work with the Stone Beings, and with Sophia. The stones will often align the flow of their energies with our conscious intention, helping us to transform and evolve ourselves through inner processes of energetic feedback. The benefits we receive from this can range from clearing, grounding and healing, to infusions of Light, expansions of consciousness and sudden awakenings. However, these are not the only orobori that we need to feed. Our proper work with stones is not merely to "use" them, but to relate with them for our mutual good. Just as we need the helpful currents of the stones, they need something from us—our appreciation, love and blessing. This is the same thing that Sophia needs, and through relating lovingly with the Stone Beings, we are loving Sophia as well, and contributing to our mutual evolutionary transformations.

This pattern was envisioned by the alchemists as the "double oroborous." In this image, there are two dragons, devouring *one another's* tails. The illustration shows one winged dragon above, and a wingless dragon below. These symbolized the dynamic activity of the polarity of the Above and the Below, of spirit and matter, Divine and human, Heaven and Earth. (Note how similar they are to the Yin/Yang symbol, which conveys the same basic meaning.) The two dragons nourish each other, and grow from that nourishment. Their growth provides more nourishment for each other, and the process can continue to infinity. This is a pattern in which both we and Sophia—the Earth and the spiritual realms—can evolve, live, and prosper in a mutually joyful relationship. I believe that this synergistic, symbiotic relationship is what we are invited to enter into now.

There is a New Consciousness we can co-create with one another, with the Stone Beings and with Sophia. We can do this through consciously imagining, intending and attending to a special 'feedback loop,' in the pattern of the double oroborous. I call it the Activity of Blessing, and I first heard about it in a dream.

9

The Activity of Blessing

Make each day truly new, dressing it with the blessings of heaven, bathing it in wisdom and love and putting yourself under the protection of Mother Nature. Learn from the wise, from the sacred books, but do not forget that every stone, mountain, river, plant or tree also has something to teach.

—Paulo Coelho, *The Alchemist*

Blessings fall on ground that's been plowed in praise.

—Janet Larson, *My Diary Unlocked*

The blessings we evoke for another descend upon ourselves.

—Edmund Gibson, Bishop of London, (1669-1748)

Quit being sad. Hear blessings dropping their blossoms around you.

—Rumi

Some wish blessings, others pray for them. Some send blessings and they become one.

—Joyce C. Lock, *Angelfire*

In the summer of 2008, while I was preparing to give my talk at the Sophia Conference in New Mexico, I had another important experience, in addition to the "breathing with Sophia" dream I described earlier. I had been invited to speak about Stones and the New Consciousness. As I prepared, I realized that although I believed that a new consciousness was coming and that stones were involved in it, I was unsure of how to describe what the new consciousness is to be. So I went to sleep one night, inwardly repeating the question, "What is the new consciousness?" Around five AM, I was awakened by a voice inside me announcing loud and clear, "The new consciousness is an activity of blessing." I told myself to remember this and write it down later. Then I fell back to sleep. Twenty minutes later, I woke again with the identical message. Again I fell asleep. The third time, at six o'clock, I woke with the same words echoing within me: "The new consciousness is an activity of blessing!" This time I wrote them down in my journal before nodding off. When I awoke later, I began puzzling over what the words might mean.

I think of a blessing I might receive from another person as an act of generosity from his or her heart, a gift, something offered without any thought of return, a well-wishing with the flavor of love in it. So how might that become an activity, something ongoing, giving rise to a new consciousness?

I tried an internal blessing meditation, imagining myself looking inwardly from the brain to the heart, while holding a Moldavite and three Azeztulite stones. I tried sending a blessing, an expression of love and appreciation, from my head to my heart: "I am so grateful for your presence in me." Immediately I felt a sort of shining back from my heart, a love impulse. Receiving that (in my head), I reflected it back again. Once more I felt the "shining upward" from the heart. Soon there was a circular feedback loop going between my head and my heart, an ascent/descent of sweet-feeling currents—my own personal oroborous! By giving attention and a small nudge from my will, I could keep the process going. I was sure that with practice, it could become a way of being, an ongoing "activity of blessing." (The stones made my hands and forearms tingle with a pleasurable current during the meditation, reinforcing the effects of my intention.)

Coming out of this first meditative experiment with the "activity of blessing," I felt a soft buzz in my forehead and a warm, liquid glow in my chest. When I saw my wife, I was filled with love and gentleness toward her. The feeling of blessing I had initiated in myself wanted to extend itself to her, and I felt it reaching out to the world as well. Looking toward the trees and grass in the yard, the birds outside the window, even my car in the driveway, I sensed an extension of self-giving, gratitude and love permeating my perceptions. If I were to maintain this, if others were to practice it, we would live in a different world.

In reaching out from our heart to embrace and bless the world through each perception, we bring the world into our heart. All people whom we bless, by extending our appreciation and wishing them well, enter our heart. The same is true when we bless the world while we are perceiving it. We begin to experience the felt sense of the whole world, including ourselves, within the interior feeling of the heart. We are in love—within love—together.

In the dream I recounted earlier, in which I "breathed with Sophia," a similar feedback loop of mutual blessing was occurring. I recall that to inhale Sophia's 'breath' was a nourishing, highly pleasurable experience, and our exchange seemed to be equally nourishing and satisfying to her. As I contemplate this now, I see the pattern of the "double oroborous." This pattern occurs in every instance of the activity of blessing, and when we experience it ourselves, we are very definitely in a new consciousness.

I try to remember to practice this way of being every day, and it happens very easily when I sit down to meditate with a stone. In unison with my breathing, I offer my appreciation and blessing as I exhale, and I invite the Stone Being into my heart as I inhale. As in my dream of Sophia, I always feel that my gesture is met by a mutual feeling of blessing coming from the Stone Being. When we initiate our stone work in this way, we feed those beings, and are fed by them. We bless, and are blessed. We have stepped through the doorway of the new consciousness into which we are all evolving together. By embracing Sophia's method of evolution and transformation through feedback, we align ourselves with her, and the Great Work of the Alchemy of Stones proceeds.

In the Alchemy of Stones, we engage our True Imagination to enable us to encounter the stones as Beings, not simply as "things." In my experience, there is much evidence for this actually being true. (And of course, the alchemical worldview embraces panpsychism, which tells us that everything in the world has consciousness.) We use True Imagination (beginning, when necessary, with intentional visualizations) to initiate the process of meeting the consciousness of the Stone Being, and the experience usually takes off on its own from there.

When we meditate with a stone, the learning is reciprocal. *The perceptual capacities of the stone increase through practice,* just as ours do. The ability of a stone to feel us, tell us its nature, and suggest its capacities to us, often grows through our interactions with it over time. As we engage the stones repeatedly in the activity of mutual blessing, the feedback loop of relationship that is created becomes stronger and stronger.

I have been saying throughout these pages that it is important to conceive of the stones as Beings in order to work with them in the most fruitful ways. Starting a meditative experience with a stone by purposely initiating the Activity of Blessing is a very good way to truly realize we are meeting another consciousness—especially when we feel its return blessing coming back to us!

As we engage the Stone Beings in mutual blessing, it is often helpful if we can meet them in the form of inner figures. Since we are meeting the Stone Beings in the psychoid/imaginal realm—which is actually *another dimension of reality* that exists between the material world and the realm of pure spirit—this is something that can easily occur. (Remember that in my dream of breathing with Sophia, the Beings of Amethyst and Azeztulite both appeared to me as inner figures. This has occurred other times, and frequently happens, especially if I ask for it.)

In the practice that follows we will engage with a Stone Being through the Activity of Blessing, and we will also ask the Stone Being to come to us as an inner figure. It's quite possible that you will experience this vividly on your very first attempt, but don't be discouraged if you don't immediately "get it." Working with True Imagination in the psychoid realm calls for using our inner senses, our intention and our focused attention. Many of us need to practice these capacities in order to work with them confidently and skillfully. (This is similar to shamanic journeying, and shamanic practitioners will tell you the same thing about the necessity of practicing one's inner sensing abilities.)

So, enough with the theory! Let's get started. Remember, the physical stone is the material form of a spiritual being, just as your body is the physical expression of your spiritual self. The practices are for the purpose of achieving conscious communion and communication.

PRACTICE: MUTUAL BLESSING WITH A STONE BEING: MEETING THE STONE BEING AS AN INNER FIGURE AND HAVING A CONVERSATION

In this practice, you'll be asking the Stone Being to come to you in human form, or as some sort of an inner figure. When the being appears, you'll engage in a conversation with each other–either verbal or non-verbal.

1. Select a stone to work with, or better yet, let the stone chose you. Follow that feeling. You can use an unfamiliar stone or a favorite stone. In this case, let intuition guide you.
2. Begin by looking at the stone and sensing it with all your senses. Breathe over the stone, offering yourself with the out-breath and inviting the stone with the in-breath, as described in our earlier practices.
3. Close your eyes and pay attention to the Interior of your body.
4. Hold the stone against your chest, at the level of the heart. Breathe deeply and slowly, bringing attention to your heart.
5. Place within your heart feelings of love and appreciation, and invite the Being of the stone into your heart.
6. As you breathe, engage in the mutual Activity of Blessing with the Stone Being. Offer your well-wishing and love to the Stone Being. Feel the circulation of the blessing energies between you. Allow the intensity of the feeling to increase, and pay attention to how that feels. Notice if there is a mutual reinforcement of the blessing energies. Continue the self-giving to the Stone Being, and the receiving of its energies, as you breathe out and in.
7. When you're ready, and can feel the stone energies resonating with yours, put your attention in your heart and say inwardly to the Stone Being: "Please show yourself to me in human form, or as an inner figure, and please tell me or show me what I most need to know. It can be about you, about me, or about whatever you wish to show me." You can ask this through a felt sense of intention and inquiry instead of words, if you prefer.
8. Pay attention to whatever you see or feel. Wait for the Stone Being to come to you. If nothing seems to happen, go back to breathing and the feelings of appreciation and ask again.

When the figure of the Stone Being comes to you, it may be as a visual image, or a felt presence, or a voice, or in another form. We're asking to meet an imaginal inner figure—a living image—but the Being may have reasons to appear in another way. Keep your contact with the stone and its currents as you breathe and ask for the inner figure to come. Then wait and be alert

9. Stay with it until you see or feel the Stone Being arrive. Inwardly ask what it wants to tell or show you. If you don't understand what you are shown or told, don't worry, just try to remember it so you'll be able to write a description of what happens. (You can also ask the Stone Being for further information or clarification.)
10. Once the communication is established, you can ask questions. Do so with or without words, but keep yourself centered in your heart, and ask your questions from there. Stay alert, but in your heart, and try to remember everything that happens. You can even have a "conversation" if you can keep it going while staying in your heart. Allow yourself to go with whatever wants to happen.
11. You can also express your point of view to the Stone Being. Depending on the connection you are able to establish, this can become a real conversation, verbal or otherwise. Let the Stone Being know your ideas, needs or wishes, and ask how you can work together. Or communicate whatever feels appropriate. Often, the less words you use, the better it works. Try expressing your thoughts as images or feelings, while continuing to breath in the exchange of mutual blessings with the Stone Being.
12. It is often fascinating and illuminating to go on a journey with a Stone Being to its realm–its "world." Every Stone Being has its own world, in the psychoid/imaginal realm. If it will take you there, you will understand the nature of the stone better, through observing the type of world it has. The Stone Being can often show you things in its world that are related to its capacities for working with you, so watch carefully what it does, and pay attention to anything it shows you. If and when a Stone Being takes you into its world, this is a great gift, and it deepens your relationship. Most likely, you will be able to return there again and again, as long as you are relating with the Stone Being on a regular basis. (If the Being is not ready to take you to its realm, it is likely that you are not ready to go there. Be content to develop your relationship in other ways, and ask again at a later time.)
13. When this experiences feels complete, you may begin to disengage. Before doing so, bring your attention back to the Activity of Blessing and focus on intensifying that feeling for a few moments. Then thank the Stone Being and gently withdraw yourself and begin to come back to your body and the physical world. If you have traveled to the realm of the Stone Being, it is advisable to visualize the return journey by coming back through whatever places and/or scenarios you moved through to get there. This will help you avoid disorientation when you return to the physical world.
14. When you can feel yourself in your body and fully present in the room, put your attention in your feet and wiggle your toes. When you are ready, open your eyes, have a drink of water, or whatever you need to do to ground yourself. A stone such as Hematite, Black Tourmaline, Nuummite or Guardianite may be helpful for this. Then, before the experience fades, write some descriptive notes about what happened, the messages, conversations, etc.

DISCUSSION

The practice above is meant to increase our felt connection to a Stone Being, and to initiate a mutually giving and loving relationship. This has multiple purposes, first and foremost of which is to accustom ourselves to viewing the Stone Being as a *real being*. In order to accomplish this, we need to feel the presence and benevolence of the Stone Being. By offering ourselves and inviting the Stone Being into our heart, we have taken steps in the imagination which bring us to the threshold of this kind of recognition. It is somewhat like the way one begins a shamanic journey by purposely imagining a path leading to a doorway into the realm one wishes to visit. Once again, as my wife Kathy taught me, "Imagination is the doorway to spiritual experience." When we bring ourselves to that doorway, we are always met, as this practice is meant to show.

Of course, it is possible to short-circuit the experience by allowing one's inner critic to interfere. If you find yourself interrupted by an inner voice of doubt, or if you worry that you might be 'making it all up,' this can act as a stumbling block that stalls progress. A funny thing is that the "Inner Critic" is itself a made-up entity, an internalization of voices of one's parents or teachers, or others in one's past who have denigrated one's imagination. We have delved at length into the idea of True Imagination, so we need not revisit it here, but it is important to be skeptical of the inner critic. If it shows up, I recommend noticing it, telling it, "Thanks, but I know what I am doing here. You can take a break." Or just gently send it into the Light to be purified and turned into energy.

Inviting the Stone Being to display itself as an inner figure is another way of opening ourselves to the reality of its consciousness. As psychologist/alchemist Jeff Raff says, spiritual beings possess the power of imagination. This means they have the capacity to appear to us in whatever way they wish:

> *In his study of the spirit, Jung came to the conclusion that spirit possessed spontaneous movement and activity. The spirit is free to do and create as it will, and is free of the control of the ego, the conscious part of the personality. The ego can experience the spirit, but cannot dictate to it. The second attribute of spirit, according to Jung, is the capacity to spontaneously produce images, and the third attribute is "sovereign manipulation of these images."*
>
> — Jeff Raff, *Healing the Wounded God*

By inviting the spirit of a stone to display itself to us as an inner figure, we are opening ourselves to the natural activity of that being's nature. We have begun by paying attention to it and offering our blessing and inviting it into our heart. Then we proceed by inviting it to use its creative ability to communicate with us. In my experience, as long as I am making a genuine invitation and giving my focused attention to my inner experience, the Stone Being will show itself and communicate in a very generous way.

The fact that we can often feel the energetic currents of the stone shows us that we are already being met. The energies themselves have already come toward us from the realm of pure spirit and are meeting us in the in-between realm of the psychoid/imaginal domain. By initiating energetic feedback with the Stone Being, we enhance and expand the potential for what can happen.

It is important to remember to *offer and invite,* but not to control. This is true, of course, in any relationship. If we offer ourselves to another person and invite them into relationship, love and spontaneity can exist between us. We can enjoy the other person, and even learn from him or her. And because we do not try to control the other person, there is no way to predict what he or she will do or say. This is part of the magic of love. If we tried to control things, we would destroy the spontaneity and there would be no real relationship.

With a Stone Being, the same pattern holds. The richness and magic of what can happen depends on our light touch. We make ourselves available, offer ourselves and invite the other being to meet us. Then we wait, and we respond to whatever occurs. If we are honest, we know how it feels to force things, and we know when we are doing it. So, we avoid that and attend gently to the magic.

I hope readers will spend some time with this practice and really explore it. Try this with a number of stones, and see how they are each different from the others. Go back more than once to visit a Stone Being just as you would visit a friend. There are endless realms in the world of spirit, and the Stone Beings make ideal companions in exploring many of them. Like us, they are both physical and spiritual, and like us, they enjoy relationship and the rewards of mutual blessing.

HOW MUCH DOES IT MATTER?

How important is the Activity of Blessing to the kindling of a new consciousness, and how important is it to meet the stones, and all beings, in this way? If the alchemists were correct (as I believe they were) in seeing the universe as the continually evolving, self-creating manifestation of Wisdom, with ourselves in the unique position of being able to co-create with Sophia, then our input into the world's web of interconnected consciousness is of vast significance. And the Butterfly Effect tells us that even one person's input has the potential to influence the entirety in a way that can be unpredictably great. The alchemists intuited that the perfection of the *Magnum Opus* by a single person had the potential to redeem *the entire cosmos.*

THE STORY OF INDRA'S NET

The idea of eternally resonating feedback loops, and their central role in the arising and expression of the universe, goes back in mythology for thousands of years. It is well illustrated in the Hindu tale of Indra's Net. Indra's Net (also called Indra's jewels or Indra's pearls) is the mythical net of the Vedic god Indra, which hangs over his palace on Mount Meru, the *axis mundi* (central axis of the world) of Hindu cosmology and mythology. Here is one version of the story:

Far away in the heavenly abode of the great god Indra, there is a wonderful net which has been hung by some cunning artisan in such a manner that it stretches out infinitely in all directions. In accordance with the extravagant tastes of deities, the artisan has hung a single glittering jewel in each "eye" of the net, and since the net itself is infinite in dimension, the jewels are infinite in number. There hang the jewels, glittering like stars in the first magnitude, a wonderful sight to behold. If we now arbitrarily select one of these jewels for inspection and look closely at it, we will discover that in its polished surface there are reflected all the other jewels in the net, infinite in number. Not only that, but each of the jewels reflected in this one jewel is also reflecting all the other jewels, so that there is an infinite reflecting process occurring.

We might say that each individual consciousness, human or otherwise, is a jewel in the net. We are all so intertwined and reflective of one another that every being is constantly influencing, and being influenced by, all other beings. This suggests that our own choices reverberate through all that is, and that our ability to choose is an immense power.

This idea also tells me one of the reasons why it is so beneficial for us to work in communion with the Stone Beings. They are deeply attuned to the benevolent, loving and beautiful vibrations of Sophia/ Wisdom. If we attend to these kinds of energies, we not only receive their blessings for ourselves, but also, by the very act of our receiving them, they reflect outward from us into everything. And by affirming and practicing the Activity of Blessing, this intention for the good of all beings reverberates, in harmony with the Wisdom of Sophia and the Stone Beings, through the universe.

But is this enough to really change things, since so many negative patterns seem to have established themselves in humanity?

In the Mandelbrot fractal images, the patterns tend to be self-similar (thought not exactly alike) at all levels. However, tiny numerical changes in the equations can unpredictably cause

This graph of the Lorenz Attractor—a "chaotic attractor" from Chaos Theory—gives a visual impression of the kind of mutual resonance created through the Activity of Blessing: The yellow line is actually unbroken, as it loops back and forth from each side, enhancing the formation of the pattern. We can imagine the emergent path of the line and the resulting resonant pattern as representing the co-creation between oneself and a Stone Being.—RS

the entire system to fall into chaos—a crash with no apparent order. However, in such situations, a new pattern is eventually formed around *fragments of order* within the chaos, which are called Chaotic Attractors. These fragments of order act as seeds for the emergence of a new pattern, a new harmony.

The alchemists knew intuitively that at the beginning of their work, the "substance" to be transformed—the *prima materia*—is (and must be) in a chaotic state. After all, if the substance (whether it was physical matter or the alchemist's own consciousness) were too stable, it would not be available for transformative change. The individual alchemists, by their efforts to create and/or become the Philosophers' Stone, in co-creative partnership with Sophia, were attempting to bring forth the birth of something into the world that would be an indestructible seed of Wisdom.

The alchemists aimed to be Chaotic Attractors for the formation of a New Earth—a Divine World. We might say now that the chaotic conditions in the human world are perfectly primed for transformation.

What we need are a few good alchemists.

Are you ready?

OPPOSITE: The Alchemist stands in the center, uniting the opposites in this 17th century engraving Basilica Philosophica by Johann Daniel Mylius

Transcendence through the Alchemical Union of Opposites

The Transcendent Function does not proceed without aim and purpose, but leads to the revelation of the essential man. It is in the first place a purely natural process, which may in some cases pursue its course without the knowledge or assistance of the individual, and can sometimes forcibly accomplish itself in the face of opposition. The meaning and purpose of the process is the realization, in all its aspects, of the personality originally hidden away in the embryonic germ-plasm; the production and unfolding of the original, potential wholeness.

—Carl Jung

The shuttling to and fro of inner arguments and affects [emotional reactions] represents the transcendent function *of opposites. The confrontation of the two positions generates a tension charged with energy and creates* a living, third thing . . . *a movement out of the suspension between the opposites, a living birth that leads to a new level of being, a new situation. . . . The result is ascension in the flame, transmutation in the alchemical heat, the genesis of the 'subtle spirit.' That is the Transcendent Function born of the union of opposites.*

—Carl Jung

> *The elusive* prima materia *needs to be found before the opus could begin. Psychologically speaking, the mysterious* prima materia *represents, and is to be discovered in, the parts of the psyche that we deny, disown and marginalize, the aspects of ourselves that we feel ashamed of, revulsion for and turn away from in disgust. In Jung's words, this "means that the thing which we think the least of, that part of ourselves which we repress perhaps the most, or which we despise, is just the part which contains the mystery." We typically want to get rid of the shadow aspects of our personality, but the alchemists understood that our wounded, inferior and unconscious parts aren't an accident or error, but rather, have a value and cosmic perfection to them that is stunning. Our wounds, the base material of the work, are indispensible for the accomplishment of the opus, for without these shadow parts there would be no way to make the alchemical gold.*
>
> —Paul Levy, awakeninthedream.com/the-sacred-art-of-alchemy/

Just as the winged energy of delight
Carried you over many chasms early on,
Now raise the daringly imagined arch,
Holding up the astounding bridges.
Miracle does not lie only in the amazing living through and defeat of danger;
Miracle becomes miracle in the clear achievement that is earned.
To work with things is not hubris when building the association beyond words;
Denser and denser the pattern becomes–
Being carried along is not enough.
Take your well-disciplined strengths, and stretch them between two opposing poles.
Because inside human beings is where God learns.

—Rainer Maria Rilke: "The Winged Energy of Delight"

Alchemy is first and foremost the art and science of transformation, with the intent of bringing the alchemical "material"—whether it be a physical substance, the soul of the alchemist, or both at once—into the fullest possible state of existence, exceeding all prior states of limitation. Therefore, we can say that the aspiration of the alchemists was transcendence. The essence of transcendence, in the words of Joseph Chilton Pearce, is, "the ability to rise and go beyond." The alchemists desired to surpass all limitation and attain the greatest good, for themselves and for Sophia, the Soul of the World—their partner in the Great Work. They believed that the evolutionary processes of nature were aimed at transcending all limitations, and they aimed to accelerate the fulfillment of nature's aspirations through their cooperation with her. Alchemy's twin goals of the transmutation of matter (from "lead" to "gold") and the attainment of immortality display the degree to which transcendence was at the heart of the alchemical endeavor.

Over the past thirty or forty years, I have watched and become involved with the huge upwelling of worldwide interest in spirituality in general, and transcendence in particular. This has taken many forms, and for me, the spiritual work we can do with stones is at the heart of it. Other major areas include alternative healing, meditation and channeling, as well as revivals in spiritualism, astrology, geomancy, tarot, yoga and other disciplines, including alchemy. All of these aim to help us expand our awareness beyond the limits of consensus reality, and to live a life in greater attunement with the Divine. Each and every one of these aspirations stems from a deep longing in our souls—"to rise and go beyond." This longing has led millions of people into the global subculture labeled New Age, in which terms like 'ascension' and "the light body" are common. We know what we want—or at least we believe we do—so how do we achieve it?

I do not have all the answers to this question, but, from experience, I know some of the pitfalls. The biggest one I am aware of is the entrapment stemming from our one-sided identification with the surface self, or ego. The ego is the sensation of the "I" within us, which commonly and primarily concerns itself with the outer world (surface world) and our dealings with it. When we hear the call of spiritual growth and self-transformation, our ego tries to produce it for us. But the surface self cannot transform itself, and its efforts tend to produce fantasy versions—counterfeits—of what we are seeking. Often, our egos fear the very transformation we seek, because it involves a surrender of control (more accurately, our illusion of control). Real transformation means that our experience of ourselves and the world must and will become very different, and our fearful egos can make endless maneuvers to avoid letting go. This is paradoxical, because only the alchemical transmutation of the self can genuinely dispel the ego's fears.

To achieve the transcendence our souls long for, we must experience the tension between the opposites within ourselves, as Jung knew and taught. What I have referred to as "ego" could be called the "sunlit side" of one's identity—the side of which we are consciously aware and with which we usually choose to identify. However, if we are to transcend the ego's bondage to one-sidedness, we need to also identify with and embrace our shadow side, the side we have long ago rejected (often because it was rejected by others) and cast down into the darkness. As Jung wrote, "the thing which we think the least of, that part of ourselves which we repress perhaps the most, or which we despise, is just the part which contains the mystery."

Yet we must not take only the side of the rejected self either. If we did, we would descend into the unconscious and perhaps be lost there. We must hold *both* sides, identify with both—admit that *we are all of this*—if we are to become whole. And our wholeness will not be a once-and-for-all kind of thing. When we identify simultaneously with *both* of the "opposing poles" mentioned in Rilke's poem above, we experience ourselves as the living, vibrating presence of Self *in the space between the opposites,* in the void between the masks of our sunlit and shadow sides.

Much of the literature in the New Age is, unfortunately, generated from the surface self's endless repertoire of fantasy. This means it is mostly one-sided—aiming only for an "ascension" into the Light, in one way or another. When darkness is mentioned, it is often viewed as something to dispel or escape from. I have sometimes made this error in my own writing. This is not our fault—we were taught to do this, because we have grown up in a one-sided culture—but our task is to imagine our way beyond it.

Often, the books we go to for help have been written on the mental level, from the standpoint of the surface self of the writer. Trying to use one's own (or someone else's) thinking processes to transform oneself beyond thinking is an impossible task. Even believing the writings of spiritual teachers is of limited value. Belief does not transform us. Experience does. For real transformational experience, we need outside help (and by "outside" I actually mean "inside," but beyond the confines of our egos).

The Stone Beings offer the direct aid of our partner Sophia, through their vibrational currents. The stone energies come from a spiritual source that is deeper than the level we usually live upon, and they draw us into transcendence by bringing us into a deeper level of our own being. I believe that stone energies are psychoid events, taking place in the domain that bridges the gulf between the everyday material world and the realms of pure spirit. Anyone who has ever experienced the visionary states engendered by Phenacite, the transformative fire of Moldavite, the earthy love of Rosophia, or the inner Light of Azeztulite, knows what I mean. The first way that stones aid in our desire to achieve transcendence is by giving us an experience of how it feels to "rise and go beyond" our habitual states of consciousness.

However, in the Alchemy of Stones, as in other paths of spiritual alchemy, we discover that to achieve real and lasting transcendence in our lives we must look to what is within ourselves that holds us back. We are not fettered by our imperfections, but by our *rejection* of them. We must not ignore our flaws and limitations, but embrace them, work with them, invite them into our hearts and incorporate them into our consciousness. To ascend to the heights, we must simultaneously enter into our depths. We cannot simply set out for the Light, leaving our dark parts to fend for themselves. Real transcendence doesn't mean taking the surface self we think we are for a permanent vacation in Heaven. It means the birth of a new Self—one that encompasses all of who we are. It means becoming whole.

Psychologist Carl Jung observed that what he called the individuation process—which basically means the path of becoming whole—is punctuated with quantum leaps of consciousness. In these leaps, the person first experiences increasing levels of tension from opposite forces in the psyche. If the person is able and willing to hold on to *both* points of view without affirming one and denying the other, the tension continues to build. At some point, the energy reaches a critical level and one's viewpoint shifts to a *third* point of view that incorporates the opposites and reconciles them. One has transcended the tension of the opposites and moved to an expanded consciousness. As I mentioned above, we may come to feel that our Self dwells in the space between the opposites. Lost or repressed parts have been reclaimed. Like all alchemical processes, this must be repeated many times in order to reach it's ultimate fruition (if there is one), but each experience of transcendence is greatly rewarding.

One of the quotations beginning this chapter is the poem by Rainer Maria Rilke called "The Winged Energy of Delight." If you skipped this or read through it quickly, I hope you will go back and look at it more carefully now, because it offers a perfect crystalline window into what the Transcendent Function is like. Please take a moment now and read the poem again, and then I'll try to explain its message regarding what Jung called the Transcendent Function.

In his poem, Rilke reminds us that, in our youth, our enthusiasm and joy in life carried us along. But now, as adults, we must cross the "chasms" of life's great contradictions by raising "the astounding bridges" through our own efforts. The phrase "astounding bridges" is a reference to our capacity for the kind of transcendence I described above, in which we can connect the opposite sides of the chasm, which seem irrevocably separate, into a new whole. We could view the "chasm" as the apparent abyss between any two opposing positions—matter and spirit, waking and dreaming, fear and love, the conscious and the unconscious. Even more to the point, we need to bridge the chasm between the soul's desire for growth and refreshment through adventurous forays into the unknown and the ego's fearful

Leaping the chasm

attachment to its restrictive "safe" worldview; to how the world appears according to what it believes it already knows.

According to Rilke, "miracle" is not the mere survival of perilous moments. What makes the miracle truly miraculous is our *achieving the leap* from an impossible situation into a new and greater state of being. He encourages us to go beyond language and build 'the association beyond words.' The holding of the opposites together is a *felt experience* that is beyond language. As one does this, the inner tension increases. The pattern we are holding becomes "denser and denser," because the energy of this tension draws in more and more meaningful associations. We see, faster and faster, how the pattern we are dealing with is like many *other* patterns in our psyche, and in the world around us.

The poet then advises us explicitly: "Take your well-disciplined strengths and stretch them between two opposing poles." Can you feel the increase of tension in the word *stretch?* And why should we do this? Why put ourselves through it? Rilke tells us: *"Because inside human beings is where God learns."*

That last line is a huge statement. We pursue transcendence and reach for wholeness, not simply (or even primarily) for the enrichment of our surface selves, but as *an offering to the Divine.* We, through the efforts we make with our "well disciplined strengths," *aid the Divine in its own process of self-realization.* We help God learn!

This is Rilke's way of affirming the same type of co-creative partnership that the alchemists dedicated themselves to in their affiliation with Sophia. This partnership is with our own Deep Self and with the Divine—both of which are known to us implicately, but not explicitly. Our Deep Self and the Divine dwell within us, in the dark cavern of the heart, and most of the time we are only aware of them by implication. We sense them in our lives when something we don't understand occurs; but when we can nonetheless feel its numinous significance and intuit its startling meaning. This intuition of meaning between thoughts and events without an apparent causal connection is the "the daringly imagined arch holding up the astounding bridges." When we experience reunion with the sacred dimensions of our own being, we are at last ready and able to work with Sophia in a conscious, co-creative way.

When we develop the strength to hold the opposites and let the tension build to the point where the Transcendent Function is initiated, our whole center of being shifts from ego to Self–from surface to soul. Even the word *soul* has the feeling of the sacred about it. It is the aspect of our individuality where we can feel our overlap with the Divine. So, when we do as the poet instructs, staying with the tension and the increasing density of the tapestry of our own being, the moment of sudden realization arrives. "*God learns,*" and we learn, and the soul grows.

We will have the opportunity in later chapters to work with stones that can facilitate our entry into inner states that can trigger the Transcendent Function. This practice can be challenging, but, as Rilke tells us, it can take us into the realm of miracle. However, before we get to the practices, we have more chasms to cross.

Among the important opposites to consider in our work in spiritual alchemy are the conscious and the unconscious aspects of the self. The unconscious in us includes all the aspects of ourselves that we have forgotten or rejected. Often, parts of ourselves have been "thrown away" (pushed out of our conscious awareness) because other people (such as parents, teachers or peers) rejected them. Sometimes, we may have said or done something we were ashamed of, or for which we were shamed. In order to stop feeling the shame, we "threw it into the basement." None of these things truly go away. They simply exist in our unconscious.

However, according to the mystic traditions of the Sufis, and the writings of the ecstatic poets Rumi, Kabir and Hafiz, there is also a Divine being whom we can meet through the alchemical processes that occur in our depths. This being was sometimes referred to as the Friend, the Guest, or the Beloved of the Soul. In esoteric magickal spirituality, it is called the Holy Guardian Angel. By whatever name, this being was always described as far wiser than our surface self, and yet having an inexhaustible supply of love for its human partner. Alchemical psychologist Jeff Raff calls it the Ally, and describes it as an individualized expression of the Divine. We could think of it as a face or aspect of the Divine which exists for each of us, and

for no one else. Through this face—this inner presence—the Divine unequivocally loves each of us. Raff tells us that we each have our own personal Ally, and that as we perform the tasks of spiritual alchemy, we can ultimately unite with it. If we never do this, both we and our Ally remain unfulfilled and incomplete.

I have been referring to this presence as the Deep Self. But who is that? When I was writing this chapter, my wife Kathy asked me whether the term "Deep Self" referred to one's own essential identity, or to the Divine Friend—our inner partner. I have pondered and researched this question, and in every foray, I always end up looking straight into a mystery. In my mind's eye, I see a numinous dark void in front of me. So I have to leave the question unanswered, except to say this: The Self in our depths—the Divine Friend—is real, and it dwells in the gap of the in-between, in the Seat of the Soul. Whether it is one being or two is one of its many ambiguities. It is what Daniel Deardorff calls our "implicate identity." Its existence is implied, but never spelled out, and it cannot be defined or pinned down, because it is greater than any concept. It is the source of our true inspirations. We might call it the "architect" of the "astounding bridges."

Most of the time, we are unaware of our Deep Self. Because *we* are *unconscious of it,* the Deep Self (the Guest, the Friend, the Ally) seems to dwell in our unconscious. However, this entity is not unconscious at all. It is constantly aware of us and present with us, and it frequently offers us guidance or inspiration. It is the *unconscious denial of it by the surface self or ego* that estranges us from that loving, intelligent presence.

So here we are. We now see that, in most of us at least, our conscious mind is estranged from its rejected parts and unaware of its Divine partner. Because our rejected parts and our Divine partner dwell together in what we refer to as our unconscious, we cannot embrace one while rejecting the other. In fact, they are deeply entwined with one another. Again, in Jung's words, "the thing which we think the least of, that part of ourselves which we repress perhaps the most, or which we despise, is just the part which contains the mystery." So here is one of the most important tensions for us to hold: We must recognize and affirm the preciousness of that which we have thrown away. The conscious self must strive for union with the unconscious—the very thing of which it is completely ignorant and which it tends to fear and repress. However, once we have even a moment of union with the inner Guest/Friend/Ally/Deep Self, we understand. And all we wish for is another such moment, or a lifetime of them.

In Kabir's words: "Listen, my friend: there is one thing in the world that *satisfies,* and that is a *meeting with the Guest.*"

And as the 14th century Persian poet Hafiz said: "In every spot of the universe, Light shines out from the face of the Friend."

The 13th century Persian mystic poet Rumi wrote these words to the Beloved of the Soul, out of his longing for union:

Come to the garden in Spring.
There is light and wine, and sweethearts in the pomegranate blossoms.
If you do not come, these do not matter.
If you do *come, these do not matter.*

For Rumi, without the Beloved, there was no joy in worldly delights, and with the Beloved, there was no need for them.

OPPOSITE: Kathy and Robert in the Kauri Tree

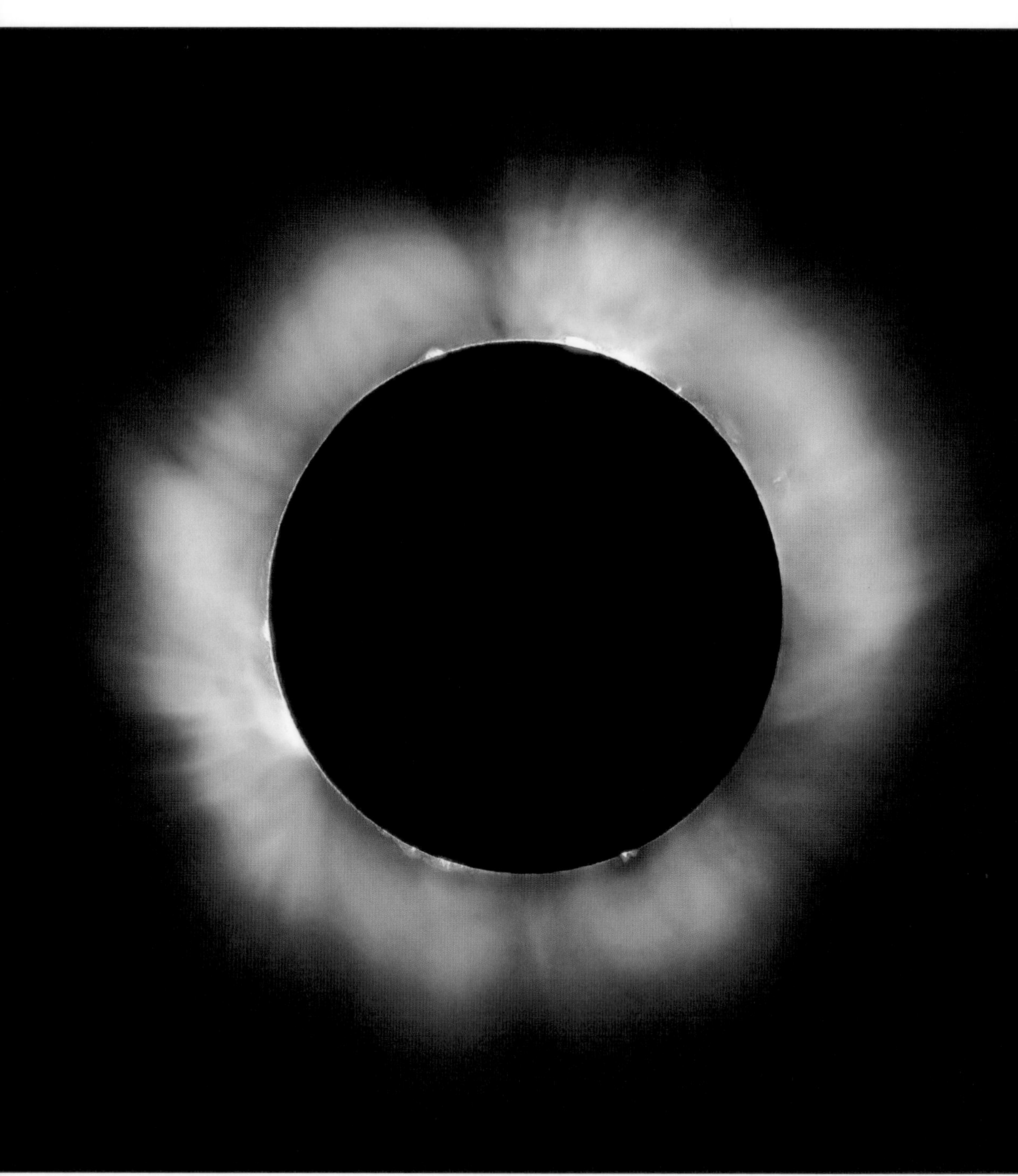

Total Solar Eclipse: Conjunction of the Sun and Moon

11

Conjunction

Psychologically, [the first Conjunction] is empowerment of our true selves, the union of both the masculine and feminine sides of our personalities into a new belief system or an intuitive state of consciousness. The alchemists referred to it as the Lesser Stone, and after it is achieved, the adept is able to clearly discern what needs to be done to achieve lasting enlightenment, which is union with the Overself. Often, synchronicities begin to occur that confirm the alchemist is on the right track.

—Alchemy Lab.com

The first stage [of Conjunction] unites the conscious and the unconscious; the second makes this union permanent; the third unites the self already created with a center that transcends the human psyche, a center that one might call Divine.

—Jeff Raff, *Jung and the Alchemical Imagination*

Alchemy has always involved numerous processes for the transmutation of the *prima materia* into the Philosophers' Stone. There was the burning process known as Calcination, the dissolving processes called Dissolution, and others such as Putrefaction, Fermentation, Sublimation, Distillation and Coagulation. We will not go into all of these, but we will give particular attention here to the one known as Conjunction, which was, in Jung's view, at the center of the alchemical mysteries.

In spiritual alchemy, there are three great Conjunctions. We will return to each of them in detail, but I want to begin by describing them briefly.

The First Conjunction is characterized by a temporary union between one's conscious and one's unconscious—or, we might say, between the surface self and the Deep Self. This event both shocks and delights the surface self. The shock comes because we do not really suspect the existence of the Deep Self. Even when we try to think about it, our thoughts are miles away from the experience. The delight we feel comes from the sense of a great reunion occurring within us—a reunion that dispels fear and loneliness.

After the First Conjunction, our old habits tend to reassert themselves, and the experience ultimately fades into memory. But we long for the return of the great reunion. We want to be permanently merged with our Deep Self. It often takes many years of inner work for this to happen, if it ever does. But when the Second Conjunction comes, we once again experience the union of the surface self and the Deep Self, and this time it does not fade away. The two sides of one's being are strong enough, and aware enough, to keep from falling back into fragmentation. One becomes whole, clear, and able to draw upon all of one's inner capacities.

When one has become truly whole through the Second Conjunction, one may, through the mystery of Grace, experience spiritual alchemy's ultimate goal—the Third Conjunction. When this occurs, there is another union. The individual self, having achieved and sustained its wholeness, joins with the Divine. One *becomes* the Philosophers' Stone—the Divine 'substance' that can transform and renew the world. The very center of one's selfhood has gone through metamorphosis, and has become the ultimate co-creative entity—a unified consciousness that is both human and Divine.

From these glimpses, let us return and begin again.

The word conjunction means, "a joining together." In astronomy, when two planets are so close together in the sky (from the Earth's point of view) that they appear to merge into one, they are said to be in conjunction. Astrologers say that this conjunction coincides with a powerful synergistic fusion of the energies of both planets. An astrological conjunction can be so dynamic that it can seem, temporarily, as if a new planet of much greater power has come into being. Then, because the planets must continue in their orbits, the moment passes and its power fades, until the next time.

In spiritual alchemy, the experience of a union of the conscious and the unconscious—the surface self and the Deep Self—is referred to as Conjunction, and this, too, is characterized by a transcendent fusion of energies. The surface self discovers its Divine partner and can draw upon its love, its powers and its wisdom, and the Deep Self comes out of its exile in the unconscious to enter the waking world. For a time, it may feel as if a new Self of much greater awareness and power has been born. Yet, like the astrological conjunction, the moment usually passes and the experience fades, until the next time. However, in spiritual alchemy, choice, rather than fate, can ultimately prevail. Although the planets are fated to follow their predetermined orbits, we human beings have the capacity to influence our personal destinies through exercising our free will.

I want to ask you now, while you are reading, to stop for a couple of minutes and try to recall any experiences of the presence of the inner Friend, and/or the Deep Self. Have you ever had a moment when you became aware of a presence inside you who knew you through-and-through, and loved you without reservation? Have you ever suddenly seen or felt with certainty the thing that you should do next? Have you ever intuitively known the answer to a difficult problem or question without understanding how you knew it? Have you ever been moved to tears without knowing why? Has grief over the death of someone you love broken down your ego's habits and defenses, dropping you down into your heart, where a voice of truth, free of pretense, speaks within you? Any and all of these can signal the emergence of the Deep Self into one's conscious awareness.

If, in such moments, you turn inwardly toward the unseen source of these feelings and knowings, you may glimpse the Friend. It is what the poet Rumi meant when he suggested that we: "Break the wine glass, and fall toward the Glassblower's breath." The "wine glass"" is our seemingly solid idea about who we are. It is the ego's pattern of habits and pretenses. If grief or some other event breaks the glass, and if we "fall toward the Glassblower's breath," we realize that our surface self was only an outer expression of a much greater, wiser and more loving inner Self. In this seeing, the Transcendent Function occurs. The self-concepts of our old identity shatter and we open into a deeper identity.

There is no way to do this without "breaking the wine glass." Truly recognizing the Deep Self means that we simultaneously realize that our old belief in our identity was inadequate. Like an iceberg, the greatest portion of what we are is invisible, below the surface.

Our surface self tends to be afraid of the shattering, because it only thinks about the annihilation of the shell—with which it identifies. It forgets that what breaks is a constricting form, not the true "I."

When we fear real transformation, our surface self often attempts to assuage its own longing for transcendence by making up a counterfeit version. If one has read some accounts of other people's spiritual experiences, it is easy enough for the surface self to conjure up a fantasy "meditation" in which one, for example, "ascends" or is blessed by an "Ascended Master." Remember our discussion of the distinction between True Imagination and fantasy? If the experience is flattering, is centered around glorifying you—turning you in to some sort of spiritual royalty—this is a fantasy of the surface self.

Once again, it is the *one-sidedness* of such a fantasy that makes it problematic. In a certain sense, all of us are spiritual royalty. After all, the Divine lives within us. But all of us are *also dwellers in darkness,* and forgetting or avoiding that makes our ascension fantasies inauthentic.

I am not saying you will never meet a real Ascended Master, although I have not. But I am saying that inner experiences that inflate one's self image, without "breaking the wine glass" of one's habitual one-sided identity and fundamentally shifting one's center of consciousness, are likely to be counterfeits.

This is not to say that all valid inner experiences must be transcendent. You can, for example, work with Stone Beings or other helping spirits without these great self-transformations. This is very much in line with shamanism. But while the Stone Beings and other Spirit Helpers are completely willing to aid us and heal us—and even love us—they don't aim to inflate our egos.

If in doubt, check in with your heart and listen to what it tells you. That is a way of drawing on the wisdom of the Deep Self, even before you have achieved full partnership with it.

The Gnostic alchemical teacher Stephen Hoeller illustrates spiritual alchemy's fundamentally transformative process through the image of the caterpillar's metamorphosis into a butterfly. First there is the earthbound life of the caterpillar, munching leaves and growing, not aware of its destiny. Then a time comes when there is an inexorable urge to go completely inwards, withdrawing into a cocoon or pupa. In this state, the caterpillar melts into a gooey black substance. Eventually a change occurs and a new winged body is formed. When the butterfly emerges, it is a wholly new being that inhabits a vastly larger environment. Yet, it is still mysteriously and intimately linked to the caterpillar that went into the cocoon. This story of metamorphosis hints at the revolutionary changes brought about through the Transcendent Function.

In general, if we do not feel in some sense that we have gone through death and rebirth, we have not experienced transcendence. The "death" is a psychological one. What dies is the husk of the outmoded identity. The moment of this death can and frequently does feel intense or stressful. Remember, we trigger the Transcendent Function by *consciously holding on to both sides of a pair of opposites,* and continuing to do so as the tension increases. *We cannot control or predict this process,* or even whether transcendence will happen. Sometimes the process is a long, drawn-out one, with the transcendent resolution occurring after one has given up, and when one's striving has relaxed. At other times the tension builds up rapidly, and seemingly unbearably, with transcendence occurring at what feels like one's breaking point.

The transcendent experience I described in the first chapter of this book was one of the intense and difficult ones. I felt myself descending into my depths, looking for the first time at things in my family and my personal history that I had shoved into the basement of my subconscious. Telling my roommate the recurring dream of riding the great white flying horse brought up old memories of childhood fears that I had also repressed. The tension intensified between my conscious waking world with its surface self identity, and my unconscious depths with their mysterious, irrational symbols. Then I actually saw the huge white horse-cloud from the dream world floating in the late night sky, and the tension between my ideas of the "real" and the "unreal" skyrocketed. There was nowhere to go. I saw myself shatter. The "wine glass" of my surface identity broke. In my panic, I called out to God (the "glassblower" of Rumi's metaphor) . . . and transcendence came. There was a most definite sense of being engulfed, comforted and awakened by the presence of Someone within me who loved me. Today I would call that Someone my Deep Self, my Ally, my Friend—the face of the Divine that lives within me, only for me. There was death and rebirth—no doubt about it. It was one of the most terrifying—and wonderful—experiences of my life, and it lives in me to this day.

Jung, Rilke and innumerable devotees of Wisdom have counseled us to cultivate the possibility of transcendence by taking both sides of every pair of opposites we encounter. My friend the author, story-teller, mythologist and singer-songwriter, Daniel Deardorff says that living wholeheartedly means always embracing both sides. Anything less, he says, is half-hearted, which is the way most people usually live. The idea of being on the "right" side of things has overshadowed the injunction to invite and contain the contradictions and paradoxes of life. It gives us the illusion of safety and disenchants our world. In the dream of Sophia, that I recounted earlier, this kind of disenchanted consciousness was symbolized by the "Communist" army attacking Sophia's palace. It is always the type of consciousness associated with tyranny and violence. It is the "war against the imagination" mentioned in Diane Di Prima's poem "Rant," which I quoted in an earlier chapter.

Alchemy is the art and science of transmutation and transcendence, and its symbology is riddled with opposites—the Sun and Moon, the King and Queen, Lead and Gold, death and rebirth. The alchemists exhort those who would follow the alchemical path to embrace the opposites and tend patiently and carefully to the feedback processes of their oroboric intermingling within the vessel of the self. One must keep the "heat" of attention and intention steady for as long as the process requires. When this is truly done, the Transcendent Function occurs, giving birth to the Philosophers' Stone (sometimes known as the Divine Child). This is the moment of Conjunction, in which the surface self and the Deep Self unite. The new being formed from the union of the conscious and the unconscious is indeed a Divine Child. And one feels very much like a 'holy child' when one's own transcendent times of rebirth come.

THE CADUCEUS & THE TRANSCENDENT FUNCTION

The Caduceus is an ancient alchemical symbol of transcendence. It survives to this day as a symbol of the medical profession. The Caduceus is a fundamental symbol of healing, since the Transcendent Function heals the divided soul.

In the image shown below, the black and white serpents symbolize the opposites, the polarities of the conscious and the unconscious. (The white serpent with the open eye is the conscious self and the black snake with no eye is the unconscious.) The entwinement of their bodies looks much like the up-and-down sine waves that depict vibrations on the screen of an oscilloscope. In the Caduceus, the sword—an esoteric symbol of mental energy—stands for one's individual awareness, held in the center between the opposing polarities by the power of one's attention and intention/will. (The handgrip of the sword emphasizes that the intentional, purposeful will is doing this.) The ever-larger size of the waves formed by the serpents' bodies as the pattern moves from the bottom upwards, shows the *increase in the intensity* of the vibrating polarities as one holds attention on them. The snakes' two heads, as they face one another at the climax of their undulations, symbolize the confrontation of the opposites—the conscious and the unconscious. At this point of maximum intensity—the collision of the opposing forces—the Transcendent Function is triggered. The wings at the top of the Caduceus symbolize the moment of this transcendence—the rebirth of oneself as a new kind of being. Like the butterfly, the new Self can transcend the "gravity" of past limitations and is able to enter a literally *higher form of existence.* It is now able "to rise and go beyond."

Sometimes, as in the illustration, the Caduceus symbol includes a crown floating above the rest of the image. This signifies the achievement of the final goal of alchemical work—the creation of the Philosophers' Stone. It was believed that when the alchemical work achieves its complete fulfillment, the alchemist becomes a Divine/human being, and the *prima materia* becomes a pure earthly/Divine substance. Both the alchemist and the transformed *prima materia* have become the Philosophers' Stone. Together, they are capable of transforming any other substance to its highest form and of conveying healing, enlightenment and immortality. This "crowning achievement" is symbolized by the crown which defies the "law" of gravity, floating above the sword.

The symbol of the crown is very rich in regard to the depth of meaning that the Caduceus symbol conveys. When crowns first originated for the royalty of ancient times, they were set with gems because it was believed that kings and queens were human representatives of the Divine on Earth, and that the gems worked to enhance the link of the royal personages with the Divine. The points on top of the crowns were meant to work like "antennae," allowing the kings and queens to clearly receive Divine guidance and to act with Divine authority.

We can say that in the Alchemy of Stones, we work to invoke the Transcendent Function with the aid of the Stone Beings. Like the gems in the crowns of ancient royalty, the crystals and stones help us attune to the Divine frequencies. Up to this point, I have been focusing on the transformational energies of the Caduceus as moving from the bottom upwards. This is usually how things go when we enter into transcendence through difficult situations such as my early experience in college. However, when we engage the assistance of the Stone Beings, some of the transformational energies come from "above" us—from the transcendent state—magnetically *drawing us* through our resonance with their higher frequencies. This can be an enormous aid in our spiritual transformation, and is, I believe, a gift of grace from Sophia.

In the language of our work in the Alchemy of Stones, this movement through the process symbolized by the Caduceus is called Vibrational Ascension. It is not an escape "upward" to the Light. It is more like grounding the energies of Heaven here on Earth. It is an expansion of our awareness and identity to encompass and transcend the polarities.

Now, let's go back to the Three Conjunctions I mentioned at the beginning of the chapter.

THE THREE CONJUNCTIONS

Alchemist/psychologist Jeff Raff writes that there are three major Conjunctions in spiritual alchemy. Each of these is transformative, and each lays the groundwork for the next stage.

The First Conjunction

In the first Conjunction, the conscious and the unconscious (the surface self and the Deep Self) unite. However, this Conjunction will usually not endure—it will be a temporary phenomenon, like the astrological conjunction of two planets. These experiences of the first level of Conjunction make an indelible impression and they can kindle the desire for a more permanent union. But the habits of one's old way of being usually reassert themselves, and the event becomes a memory. It may haunt us, but it has not yet become our daily reality. Experiences such as the one I recounted from college fall into this category.

This 17th century alchemical engraving depicts the First Conjunction of the opposites within the self—symbolized as the mating Sun and Moon

The ancient alchemists were, like Jung, aware that the state of Conjunction comes about through the union of opposites. Frequently, Conjunction was represented as the marriage of the Sun and Moon. In alchemical emblems (symbolic drawings), the Sun was depicted as a male being and the Moon was female, thus indicating another dimension of their opposite natures. The Sun is the planet of the daylight, and the Moon is the planet of the night. Their joining was often depicted as sexual intercourse—an activity in which two bodies join to become one—which can literally bring forth a new being, a Divine Child.

In the realm of physical reality, a Conjunction occurs when the sun and moon appear to merge at the same exact place in the sky. This particular astronomical Conjunction is what we call a solar eclipse, and the parallels to alchemical ideas about Conjunction are interesting. The two celestial bodies associated with day and night have temporarily "joined," and this situation creates *a blending of darkness and light.* All total eclipses of the sun occur during the new moon, when the moon's image is dark. The moon's darkness overshadows the light of the sun, and from vantage points on the Earth where the eclipse is total, viewers experience a strange kind of hybrid of day and night. The sun's corona (literally, it's "crown") can be seen, and stars appear in the "daytime" sky. (One might say metaphorically that the Sun/King and the Moon/Queen both transcend their habitual levels of manifestation during their time of "intercourse"/eclipse/Conjunction, and that their joined "crowns" display themselves as the visible corona.) It is easy to understand why people from ancient times viewed solar eclipses as events of divine power. Even today, if one is present for a total eclipse, one cannot help but feel the way the event pulls one into an altered state of consciousness, making one aware of a high degree of spiritual presence. This is analogous to the unfamiliar and numinous state of awareness one enters when the Transcendent Function moves one into an inner Conjunction.

The Conjunction of the Sun and Moon (aka the Solar eclipse) is an event of great intensity on all levels, from the physical to the spiritual. To get a feeling about the qualities of consciousness one may experience at the time of one's own moment of spiritual Conjunction in the psyche, it is useful to ponder the strange and unique conditions and feelings engendered by astronomical and astrological Conjunctions. These events resonate with inner events of human/Divine Conjunction—in their intensity and in the recognition that one has entered the numinous unknown.

The Second Conjunction

If one persists in paying attention to the Deep Self and cultivating relationship with it—while learning to live in the tension of the opposites—one will continue to experience the Transcendent Function from time to time. As with the fractal patterns of Chaos Theory and the circulations of the oroborous, each incidence of transcendence feeds back into the psyche, creating influences that may be imperceptible, but which can have huge, unpredictable effects. At some unknowable moment, another, more profound Conjunction takes place. In

This 17th century alchemical emblem depicts the Second Conjunction. Once again the opposites—symbolized by King and Queen—are united, this time in marriage. The marriage, presided over by a priest, shows that this union is permanent.

This 16th century alchemical emblem offers a vision of the Third Conjunction. The single human figure indicates that the polarities in the self have been permanently united. Its position in the center of the circle tells us that the whole self has conjoined with the Divine. Note also that the human being is shown within the Great Central Sun.

this transcendent experience, the union of the conscious and the unconscious becomes permanent. This is a true metamorphosis of the Self. The Divine Child has been born, and a new life begins. In this life, the caterpillar has become the butterfly, and the partnership between the surface self and the Deep Self has been consummated. The new center of identity has a much more conscious and ongoing relationship with Sophia, and with other faces of the Divine. Literally, it's a whole new "you!" Or, more simply, you are whole.

The Third Conjunction

According to Raff, after the rare event of the Second Conjunction has occurred, there is yet a third Conjunction that is possible. The new Self can now attend to its longing for partnership with the Divine. In alchemical terms, the alchemist is preparing to enter into a Sacred Marriage with Sophia. (This kind of union transcends human sexual polarities, and is available equally to men and women.) I cannot say much about this experience, except that I believe Raff's description of it, and I aspire to reach that Third Conjunction. My felt sense tells me that this is the ultimate transcendent potential toward which evolution pushes us, and to which our heart's desire draws us.

I have endeavored in this chapter to sketch out what the Conjunctions triggered by the Transcendent Function can be, and why they are so important to the practice of spiritual alchemy. Indeed, I believe that these kinds of experiences are at the root of many—if not all—types of spiritual awakening in human beings.

So, how do we get there? We must certainly engage the three powers of the psyche–attention, intention and imagination. In our Alchemy of Stones, we will also enlist the aid of the Stone Beings, as the practices in the following three chapters will illustrate.

Here is a beautiful quotation from the ancient Greek alchemical text, the *Corpus Hermeticum,* that admonishes the aspiring alchemist to open the imagination in such a way that one becomes available to union with the Divine:

> *If you then do not make yourself equal to the Divine, you cannot apprehend the Divine; for like is known by like. Leap clear of all that is corporeal and make yourself grown to a like expanse with that greatness which is beyond all measure; rise above all time and become eternal; then you will apprehend the Divine. Think that for you too nothing is impossible; deem that you too are immortal, and that you are able to grasp all things*

in your thought, to know every craft and science; find your home in the haunts of every living creature; make yourself higher than all heights and lower than all depths; bring together in yourself all opposites of quality, heat and cold, dryness and fluidity; think that you are everywhere at once, on land, at sea, in heaven; think that you are not yet begotten, that you are in the womb, that you are young, that you are old, that you have died, that you are in the world beyond the grave; grasp in your thought all of this at once, all times and places, all substances and qualities and magnitudes together; then you can apprehend the Divine. But if you shut up your soul in your body, and abase yourself, and say, "I know nothing, I can do nothing; I am afraid of earth and sea, I cannot mount to heaven; I know not what I was, nor what I shall be," then what have you to do with the Divine?

—Corpus Hermeticum

OPPOSITE: 1. Black Merlinite, 2. Danburite, 3. New Zealand White Azeztulite, 4. White Azeztulite, 5. Nuummite, 6. Mystic Merlinite, 7. Lemurian Light Crystal, 8. Black Obsidian, 9. Trulite Silica, 10. Master Shamanite, 11. Black Tourmaline, 12. Sauralite Azeztulite, 13. Satyaloka Clear Azeztulite, 14. Tibetan Black Quartz, 15. Smokey Quartz, 16. Black Jade, 17. Nirvana Quartz.

12

Reunion

Without doubt . . . the realization of the opposite hidden in the unconscious . . . signifies reunion with the unconscious laws of being, and the purpose of this reunion is the attainment of conscious life or, expressed in Chinese terms, the bringing about of the Tao.

—Carl Jung, *Secret of the Golden Flower*

One does not become enlightened by imagining figures of light, but by making the darkness conscious.

—Carl Jung, *Psychology and Alchemy*

Be silent and listen: have you recognized your madness and do you admit it? Have you noticed that all your foundations are completely mired in madness? Do you not want to recognize your madness and welcome it in a friendly manner? You wanted to accept everything. So accept madness too. Let the light of your madness shine, and it will suddenly dawn on you. Madness is not to be despised and not to be feared, but instead you should give it life . . . If you want to find paths, you should also not spurn madness, since it makes up such a great part of your nature . . . Be glad that you can recognize it, for you will thus avoid becoming its victim.

—Carl Jung, *The Red Book*

HEALING THE SOUL BY INVITING THE TRANSCENDENT FUNCTION

As Jung, Rilke and the ancient alchemists all knew, the experience of Conjunction is one in which the center of one's identity shifts. The shift is from a polarized, fragmented self to a greater Self, the Self of one's true wholeness. The opposites of the conscious and the unconscious merge into a new, greater being. As with most if not all alchemical processes, the stage of Conjunction must be experienced repeatedly, from multiple perspectives or approaches, until the process reaches its fulfillment.

The Transcendent Function is the mechanism of Conjunction. The spiritual alchemist must be prepared to move into unknown (unconscious) territory, into parts of the psyche which the ego doesn't know and can't control. Making such steps immediately activates the tension between opposites—the known versus the unknown—and other opposing pairs. The ego usually feels anxiety when it realizes this is happening, but the spiritual alchemist proceeds, knowing the anxiety is simply part of the necessary tension. Without the buildup of tension (which is not necessarily the tension of anxiety), there is not enough energy in the psyche to trigger the Transcendent Function.

One cannot know in advance whether a particular practice will "work," with regard to activating the Transcendent Function. Like all alchemy, it involves trial and error, and frequently requires repeated attempts. In the Alchemy of Stones, we do have one advantage that most of the ancient alchemists did not have. We have the presence of the Stone Beings, offering their supportive and transformative currents, helping us to move into states of consciousness that are conducive to expanding our awareness.

The practices in this chapter and the two that follow are each meant to address opposing patterns within the psyche. All of them take advantage of the help offered to us by various Stone Beings. Each of the practices—and each of the Stone Beings—can take us into unknown territory, where we may find . . . ourselves.

PRACTICE: CALLING THE LOST PARTS BACK FROM EXILE

In this practice, the aim is to bring forth an experience of inner unity and wholeness through inviting the parts of ourselves which have been judged and rejected to come back into our hearts, into the presence of appreciation and gratitude. We hope to initiate the Transcendent Function by purposely setting up an inner tension between the polarities of self-rejection and self-love. We will augment the effectiveness of this process by engaging the support of stones which vibrate to the "opposite" domains of Light and Darkness. The Light represents the love and appreciation we affirm in the heart, and the Darkness represents the realm of unconsciousness and exile to which our rejected parts have been banished. By using different stones that resonate to each of these polarities, we amplify the vibrations of the two positions, increasing the energy between them. This intensification can help us to trigger our movement, via the Transcendent Function, to a third position—a state of greater consciousness which encompasses and incorporates the two "opposing" polarities.

STONES TO USE:

[NOTE: You do not need to use all of the stones on the lists, but you should ideally have at least two stones of "Light" and two stones of "Darkness," whichever ones these may be.]
FOR THE POLARITY OF "DARKNESS": Mystic Merlinite, Black Merlinite, Master Shamanite.
FOR THE POLARITY OF "LIGHT": Sauralite Azeztulite, White Azeztulite, Danburite
FOR THE MIXTURE OF "DARKNESS" AND "LIGHT" (optional): Black Tourmaline Azeztulite and/or Guardianite. (If it is available, one can additionally use Trulite Silica, a stone of the Transcendent Function. It does not align with either of the polarities, but does vibrate to the third position of greater awareness that we are aiming for.)

[NOTE: **REGARDING ALTERNATIVE STONES:** If one does not have the stones mentioned above, New Zealand White Azeztulite, Lemurian Light Crystal, Nirvana Quartz and/or Satyaloka Clear Azeztulite are recommended to amplify the Light polarity. Black Tourmaline, Nuummite, Smokey Quartz, Tibetan Black Quartz, Black Obsidian and/or Black Jade are recommended to amplify the Darkness polarity. You can, of course, rely on your own intuition in choosing the stones for this practice, but it is important to have powerful stones that resonate at each end of the spectrum of Light and Darkness.]

Instructions:

1. Pick up all the stones you will be working with in this practice and hold them mixed together in your two cupped hands. The idea is to physically hold the stones of Light and Darkness together, since we will be hoping to bring our inner Light and Darkness together.
2. With the stones in your cupped hands a few inches in front of your mouth, softly breathe over them. On the out-breath, offer the Beings of these stones your good wishes and your willingness to work with them. On the in-breath, invite the Stone Beings to come into your heart and your energy field. Ask for their help in the process you are about to begin. Do this for several breaths, until you feel the connection has been made and it is time to continue.
3. Bring your hands and the stones to the center of your chest, at the level of your heart. Continue to breathe consciously, offering yourself when you exhale, and inviting the Stone Beings into your heart as you inhale.
4. Place within your heart feelings of love and appreciation. Try to really feel those feelings. It may be helpful for a moment to visualize someone or something, or a memory toward which you feel powerful love and appreciation. It can be a grandparent, a friend, a pet, or even a memory of a happy experience. Be sure to choose something for which you do NOT have mixed feelings. This is about activating your heart in a totally positive way. When you feel ready, release the image and simply keep your attention in your heart as you breathe. Stay with the feeling of love and appreciation. Be aware of the stone energies and how they circulate within you as you are doing this.
5. Call into your mind the image of what you consider to be *the worst thing about yourself.* If there are a lot of these, you can choose more than one, or you can simply try to pick what

feels like the worst one and come back later for the others, if it's necessary. Make the image vivid. Let instances of this worst quality of yourself come up from your memories. Really CALL IT UP, as you continue to breathe, circulating your energies with the stones.

6. Allow the mental image of your worst quality or qualities to descend from your mind down into your heart. Let it stay there as an image or images.
7. While holding the image and the feeling of this quality (or qualities) in your heart, inwardly speak the words: "I am so grateful for the presence of _(xxxx)_in my life." Stay with the image, and keep repeating the sentence, "I am so grateful for the presence of _(xxxx)_in my life." You need not talk out loud, but it is okay to silently move your lips with the words. You can also try to simply hold the image of this quality (or qualities) in your heart, in the presence of sincere gratitude. Silently speak and visualize, both at once, if you can. Otherwise, just keep breathing with the stones, keep envisioning your worst trait(s), and keep repeating "I am so grateful for the presence of _(xxxx)_in my life."
8. This will go on for several minutes. If you find yourself analyzing or thinking about this in a judging way, go back to the image and repeat the phrase, "I am so grateful for the presence of _(xxxx)_in my life." Keep its image in your heart. Notice the currents of the stones. Stay with them too.
9. Allow any emotions or feelings to come into you, and hold them in your heart, as you keep repeating, "I am so grateful for the presence of _(xxxx)_in my life." Stay alert and stay with whatever happens. If you get lost and start thinking about something else, go back to breathing in the stone energies and holding the image of your worst quality as you repeat the sentence. [Note: At this point, or even before this moment, the process may take on a life of its own. You may find you are seeing different visions, experiencing old memories, and/or you may begin to feel powerful emotions. That's fine, as long as you are still engaged with the "bad" quality you are working with. When your process takes off, it is best to go with it. This may be the Transcendent Function occurring within you.]
10. It is important to witness what is happening and follow through with care. If you notice memories of self-judgments coming up, that is okay. They are your lost parts coming back from exile. Take them into your heart and reaffirm your gratitude. [NOTE: If you find yourself *identifying with negative self-judgements,* pause, pull back, center in your heart and reaffirm your *gratitude* for your worst trait(s). This does not need to make sense to your rational mind. Don't worry about whether it is okay to be grateful for something "bad." Just stay in your heart, and stay with the affirmation of gratitude.]
11. At this point, or at some other moment during the process, you may experience an emotional release. In my workshops, people often weep—and they sometimes laugh—when the Transcendent Function happens and the parts of themselves which they had exiled flow back into their psyches. There may be very genuine sorrow at seeing how one has condemned and broken oneself. But with that sorrow also comes reunion and healing. These moments of catharsis are precious, and I believe one needs to experience them fully.
12. After a little while you may find that the intensity of the experience is fading. Or you may simply feel that the process has come to completion. When this occurs, gently and slowly allow your attention to come back to the room and to your body. You can ground yourself a bit by wiggling your toes. Take your time. Be gentle with yourself. Stop and feel what is in your heart now. Check in with different parts of your body and notice how they feel. You may find all sorts of different subtle—and not-so-subtle—shifts and sensations going on. When you are ready, open your eyes. Look down at the stones you worked with, thank the Stone Beings for their help, and put the stones aside. Then relax, have a drink of water, and take a few deep breaths.

13. Before leaving the process, write in your journal about what happened, what you felt, and how you feel now. Record any insights you may have had.
14. You may feel differently toward yourself (and others) after doing this practice. If the Transcendent Function has occurred, you may even feel that your concept of who you are has shifted. The greater the shift, the more important it is to take time for integration. Do not talk to others about the experience right away, or perhaps ever. It is better to write to yourself about it.
15. It is possible that the process initiated by this practice may continue for hours, days, or even longer. If the feeling is positive, forgiving and loving toward yourself, allow it to go on as long as necessary. You can continue a process like this on a more or less permanent basis, learning to constantly cherish and value yourself within your heart, no matter what occurs. As we do this, we tend to find that old negative behavior patterns dissolve, or become much less prominent. When we stop judging ourselves and cease to throw parts of ourselves into exile, the negative ways in which we unconsciously reacted in the past are no longer necessary.

DISCUSSION

The process this practice is meant to initiate is the reunification of the self through the reintegration of the rejected parts. The fact that virtually all of us have fragments of ourselves which have been judged negatively—and figuratively tossed down into a dark "basement" in our unconscious—is a fundamental reason why we are not whole. This fragmentation of the self is also at the root of many problems that plague one's surface self or ego.

Our poor beleaguered egos catch a lot of flack from self-help books, mostly because ego is equated with egotism, or self-centeredness. It is true that in our "normal" human state—a condition of fragmentation and its associated neuroses—we are mostly self-centered. But blaming ourselves or others for this simply perpetuates our interior brokenness.

In its most basic sense, "ego" simply means "I." (*Ego* is the Latin word meaning "I am.") In that sense of the word, it is clear that we cannot live in the world without an ego–a sense of being an individual identity. The egotism we are taught to shun in ourselves and judge in others is an illness of the ego, and we should no more try to "get rid" of ego than we should try to cure a physical illness by getting rid of our body!

Perhaps it is worth saying something about how we get ill, because it may help to have a picture of how we came to reject parts of ourselves and toss them into the cellar. The clearest description of this phenomenon that I have come across was written by Joseph Chilton Pearce, author of the *Magical Child* book series. I'll try to paraphrase his observations.

Pearce writes that we are born with hard-wired programs from Nature, meant to help us develop a sense of self and a familiarity with our world. In a baby or toddler, this means reaching out and grasping the world with the senses, and physically taking hold of its many objects (often putting them straight into our mouths, for the fullest possible experience). Running in parallel with our compulsion to explore our world is another hard-wired program—we must maintain our intimate connection with our mother or caregiver.

Because human beings are born into an environment of other people and the rules of one's culture, the programming we have from Nature often comes into conflict with cultural demands. In one example, a child rides along in the grocery cart pushed by her mother. Following impulses hard-wired by Nature, the toddler watches her mother take something off the shelf, so she imitates this and grabs something too. The mother usually says, "No," and puts the item back. They move on, and this happens again. Again the mother says something like, "No, I told you not to do that," and replaces the second item on the shelf. After a few repetitions, this hypothetical mother may start to feel embarrassed. What must the other people in the store think? Maybe they are thinking that she is a "bad mother" because her child is "misbehaving." Her own fragmented self surfaces as a feeling of shame, which turns suddenly to anger at the child. The mother gets upset, angrily grabs the next item the child picks up and says something like, "Stop it! I told you not to do that! Bad girl!" Sometimes this is even accompanied by striking the child.

A situation like this puts the toddler, who has no defenses, into an impossible double-bind. Nature tells the child that she must touch and explore her world, and also that she must keep the bond with her mother. Mother has said she is a "bad girl." There is no way the child can stand up to the overwhelming energy of the mother's anger and judgment, yet she *must* not let the bond with her mother be broken. To move in this direction triggers deep survival fears. (Somewhere in our genes we know that "bad" children may be abandoned.) Yet the child literally cannot stop herself from acting out the program of exploring her world. It is hard-wired.

Often the child begins to cry at this point, which may further enrage a shame-bound parent. In any event, this type of pattern plays out over and over, in many forms. (Studies have shown that the typical toddler in a modern culture is told "No" multiple times during every waking hour.)

In such a situation, the child must do something drastic to avoid going insane. If she does not accept her caregiver's repeated admonishments, she risks (as far as the child can understand) abandonment by her parent, which equates to death. If she accepts the repeated judgments, her own selfhood is negated—she is "bad." This is another kind of death. The way this conflict usually gets resolved is by an ingenious, but terribly self-destructive, move on the part of the child's mind. Her psyche splits into the "bad" parts and the "good" parts—the inner criminal and the inner judge. At this point, our wholeness has been sacrificed. We survive, but as broken human beings. In modern cultures, this happens to virtually everyone. (In some indigenous societies, the cultural patterns support rather than destroy the child's wholeness. However, we are not those people, so we need to understand what has happened to us.)

We all know the voice of our inner judge—it usually has the tone of a parent. And we all know the feeling of shame that comes when we do something that activates this part of our psyche. Further, if we look closely, we can all see that the "worst" things about us appear when unconscious manifestations of our judged and exiled parts rise up. Our unconscious reacts to the triggering of this old wound, and it compulsively repeats the patterns of "bad" behavior. Then, when we perform these deeds, this triggers the inner judge again, which takes us back into shame, anger or fear . . . which leads to another repetition of the same sad story. (The oroborous feedback loop works in a toxic manner in this dynamic.)

We tend not to want to feel or know about any of this, so we try to hide our "bad" qualities, or override them with will power, and neither of these strategies works. The only way to overcome the patterns and symptoms of our fragmentation is to make a move toward wholeness. The ancient alchemists knew this intuitively, and their writings admonish would-be practitioners to prepare for the Great Work by cultivating a life of virtue, purification, prayer and, most importantly, invoking help from a higher source—partnership with Sophia. We carry similar intentions in the Alchemy of Stones. Practices such as the one described above move us in the direction of our wholeness by attempting to trigger the Transcendent Function through inviting the parts of ourselves that have been exiled to come into our hearts.

We all know that we do not tend to feel *grateful* for our so-called "bad" qualities—whether they display themselves as dishonesty, aggressiveness, fearfulness, greediness or what have you. When we turn towards these things, we are focusing our attention on our wounds, and we do not purposely wound ourselves—at least we would not do so if we were whole. However, affirming appreciation and gratitude toward the qualities of which we have been trained to feel ashamed is a movement toward healing. It is more than mere acceptance of "the way we are." It is a compassionate and loving gesture that gathers in the lost, sad, angry, frightened, confused and lonely pieces of ourselves which have been down in the dark for years—usually since our childhood. Those fragments of self broke off before we matured (if we have ever truly matured) and their exile in the unconscious usually causes them to regress even further. They are inarticulate, unable to call for help, and they usually only communicate through pathologies, such as those we display by unconsciously acting them out. I have described above one way in which such fragmentations of the ego/self often come about.

I should mention here that there are many, many ways in which our psyches become fragmented through emotional distress. (I don't want to heap all the blame on mothers, fathers, or other caregivers! In any case, it is the coercive patterns of one's culture that are to blame.) I used the "grocery store" example because it is so common that we can probably all recognize it.

I went into these typical human pathologies to show that virtually all of us begin our journey with a broken psyche—a diseased ego. That is nothing to run away from—it is simply our starting point. (In alchemical terms, the *prima materia* of our psyche begins in a lowly and chaotic state.) As we consider the example I described, it is easy to see that our psyches are already polarized by our fragmentation. The opposites of the "criminal" and the "judge" already exist in us, and we tend to identify with one side and condemn the other. And the condemned side down in our unconscious frequently rebels, pushing us into trouble.

It is important to recognize that the eruptions of our rejected parts—problematic as they may be—are unconscious efforts to bring about healing. The exiled aspects of ourselves must find some way to call attention to their plight, or our egos will never realize anything is wrong. In this, we have a very genuine reason to feel grateful for our "worst" qualities.

What moves us toward healing our fragmentation is taking an action which no longer favors one side over the other. We bring our attention into the heart—the center of our wholeness and the place in us where Sophia/Wisdom is present. From that place, we affirm loving appreciation toward whatever we have condemned and exiled. (In some of us, the inner judge is despised and exiled just as much as the inner criminal, so we can bring either or both of them into our heart.) This gesture energizes the psyche, because extending love toward what we habitually hate in ourselves creates a powerful vibration between *this* set of opposites. If we do this sincerely and persist long enough, the tension between the polarities can push the psyche to expand into a greater consciousness. That greater consciousness is our wholeness, and our true self.

The stones we use in this practice are chosen to stimulate the energies of both polarities—the light and the dark aspects of the self. They provide additional energy to increase the vibrations we are purposely stimulating within ourselves. If we stay conscious and keep our focus during this practice, we stand a good chance of triggering the Transcendent Function and experiencing the first level of alchemical Conjunction, in which the conscious and the unconscious sides of us experience reunion. As I have mentioned, in spiritual alchemy, we must usually experience such things a number of times before the reunion becomes permanent, at which point we become truly whole as human beings. There are many places in us that need to be healed, and these also include our relationships with other people and the world. The practice in the next chapter is aimed in that direction.

In an earlier chapter, I mentioned the Activity of Blessing. This phrase was given to me in a dream, in answer to my question, "What is the New Consciousness?" I want to point out here that the practice above is a way of bringing the Activity of Blessing into one's own interior relationship with oneself. By inviting our exiled parts into the heart with appreciation and gratitude, we are wishing them well—blessing them. When the process unfolds fully and healing occurs, one's conscious self receives major blessing in return. Frequently this comes in the form of a powerful emotional release. It can also be recognized in a great increase in one's psychic and physical energy. Keeping parts of oneself in exile drains us. Enfolding these parts in one's heart means that all of this lost energy comes back to us, along with a synergistic boost that is the natural energetic state of our wholeness.

The magic of the stones is, in part, the purity of their energies. By resonating with them in our practices and in our daily lives, we receive much help in the purifications the alchemists knew were necessary, if the Great Work of transformation was to be accomplished.

When I first experienced calling my own lost parts back from exile, the emotional release that came into me was so strong that I could not be around other people for several hours. I was swept almost off my feet by the wonder and the power of the return of my fragments and *their* gratitude at having been invited. This experience triggered the emergence in my thoughts of one sentence of Wisdom, which I have held onto since that time. The sentence is: "Everything must be forgiven." It is so simple that it is easy to miss its significance. We judge and condemn countless things and people every day, through annoyance, anger, disapproval and dislike. Even though I still catch myself engaging in these things, I have not forgotten the truth of that insight. Everything, EVERYTHING, from the smallest insult to the greatest crime—whether committed by others or by oneself—must ultimately be forgiven. If not, the world will never heal, and neither will we.

Spiritual alchemy, and the Alchemy of Stones is about healing and perfecting oneself and the Earth, both at the same time. Among the many essential steps towards this lofty and crucial goal is the constant activity of forgiveness. Our next chapter takes us a step in that direction.

OPPOSITE: 1. Heartenite, 2. Lithium Light, 3. Celestite, 4. Rosophia, 5. Pink Azeztulite, 6. Sauralite Azeztulite, 7. Kunzite, 8. Morganite, 9. Rhodonite, 10. Rose Quartz, 11. Pink Amethyst, 12. Ajoite, 13. White Azeztulite, 14. Danburite, 15. Pink Calcite, 16. Petalite, 17. Pink Petalite.

13

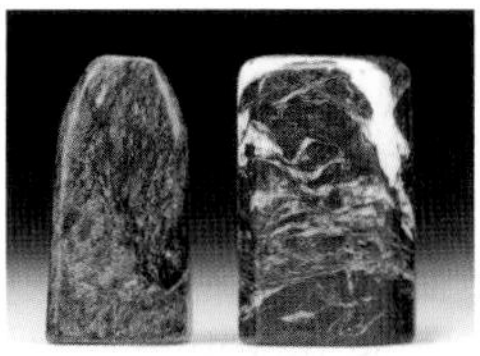

1  2  3

4  5 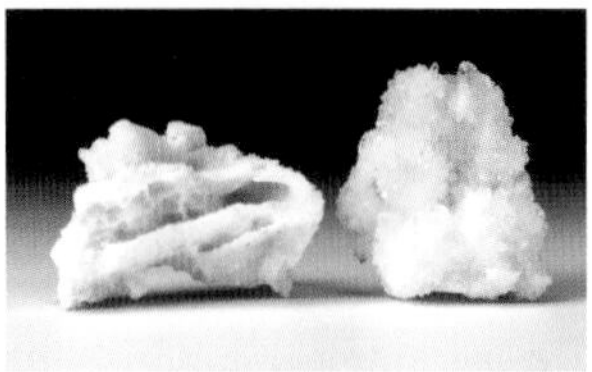 6

7  8  9  10

11  12  13  14

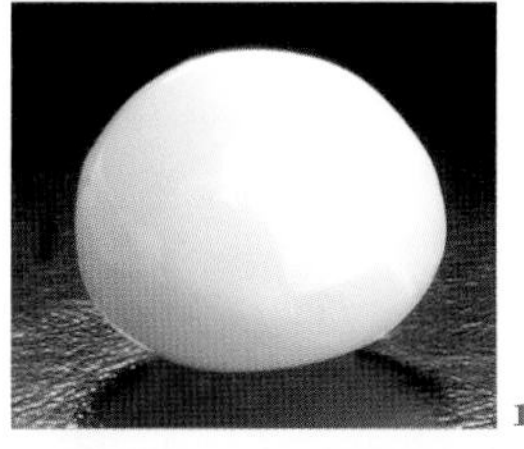
15

16

17

Forgiveness

The acceptance of oneself is the essence of the whole moral problem and the epitome of a whole outlook on life. That I feed the hungry, that I forgive an insult, that I love my enemy in the name of Christ—all these are undoubtedly great virtues. What I do unto the least of my brethren, that I do unto Christ. But what if I should discover that the least among them all, the poorest of all the beggars, the most impudent of all the offenders, the very enemy himself—that these are within me, and that I myself stand in need of the alms of my own kindness—that I myself am the enemy who must be loved—what then?

—Carl Jung, *Memories, Dreams, Reflections*

> *To use the term "forgiveness" is very corny . . . I mean, what the heck? But the only way our current culture could clean itself up would be kind of a massive discovery of forgiveness.*
>
> —Joseph Chilton Pearce, *The Biology of Transcendence*

The goal of spiritual alchemy is to become whole, and to then unite the human self with the Divine Self in a spiritual partnership which can ultimately serve, in the words of Paul Levy, to "redeem the entire cosmos." When the surface self—our "'conscious" self—temporarily unites with the Deep Self in the "unconscious," that is what the alchemists called the First Conjunction. In the previous chapter, we explored this idea and worked toward inviting the First Conjunction through the practice of Calling the Lost Parts Back from Exile. Yet if we want the reunion to become our permanent reality—if we want to enter into the Second Conjunction—there is more healing work to be done.

I invite you to think back to the story I told earlier about the toddler in the shopping cart in the grocery store. We'll call her "Mary". She innocently begins taking items off the shelf, apparently ignoring her mother telling her not to do so. This is because the child is following nature's programming and attempting to explore her world. However, Mary has another inner program that insists that she *stay bonded* with her mother.

When the mother's exasperation and anxiety (perhaps because of worrying that others may see the child's behavior and judge her as being a "bad mother") reaches the breaking point, she angrily admonishes the child and calls her a "bad girl." This puts the child in an impossible bind. She is pushed by two conflicting inner imperatives: (1) explore your world; and (2) stay bonded with your mother. But the child is not conscious of this; she only knows the terrible tension of the inner conflict. And she hears her caregiver defining her as a "bad girl"-a devastating judgment if it is internalized fully. And typically such judgments fall upon her repeatedly, as they do upon all of us, in one way or another.

In order to cope with this double bind, the child's psyche splits in two, into the "good me" and the "bad me." Sometimes when confronted by an adult over some bit of behavior, the child may say, "No, that wasn't me. That was Bad Mary."

This is how our original wholeness fragments, and the toxic complex we call the Inner Judge is created.

As we grow up, our egos become more complicated. We grow to resent (both consciously and unconsciously) the judgments we have suffered, and we try to avoid them. Our Inner Judge learns to project our resentment onto others and to denigrate them—whether openly or secretly. This toxic pattern is repeated endlessly at all levels of human social organization and interaction. Nations behave as irrationally as their fragmented citizens and leaders, often with catastrophically violent results. The projection of evil onto other nations (whether it is "deserved" or not) can lead to terrible consequences. And it comes out of the same inner fragmentation that makes us as individuals so sensitive to criticism and so ready to judge and condemn others.

We are taught that, "To err is human; to forgive, divine." As Jung tells us in the quote above, this statement is correct, as far as it goes. But what if the "criminal" is ourselves? Jung is, of course, pointing to the fragmentation in our psyche and the need to treat ourselves compassionately and kindly. This is a move toward wholeness, and the only move that will allow us to be authentically kind and forgiving of others. The inward gesture that Jung suggests is the same one that Pearce envisions as the only way for human culture to heal—through "a massive discovery of forgiveness."

The tale of Indra's Net, which we discussed in an earlier chapter, tells us that we are all jewels in an infinite net of consciousness, within which each individual jewel reflects all the others. The alchemical worldview includes the axiom that the world is so intricately woven together that the transformation of a single human being has the potential to transform the world. In the language of fractal geometry, a true change in an individual can become a "chaotic attractor" that triggers a similar change in the world at large. This means that the goal of healing oneself and becoming whole reverberates through all of being, and has the potential to trigger a worldwide awakening.

This is the *Magnum Opus*—the Great Work of spiritual alchemy that we undertake in partnership with the Stone Beings and Sophia. And the sacred space in which our rituals must be performed is the theater of the heart.

The next practice I will describe is called The Gate of Forgiveness. I hope what I have said so far in this chapter is enough to convince you of how critically important the practice of forgiveness is to us.

In my own healing, I have learned that forgiving is not something we nobly undertake as a magnanimous gesture to someone who has wronged us. It is something we do for ourselves, to heal the wounds inflicted within us by the Inner Judge. Whether we judge ourselves or someone else, the act of judgment wounds us. Forgiveness works to release us from being tied to the fragmentation of our own identity that every act of judgment exacerbates. And, as the alchemists understood, healing within the self reverberates into the world and brings healing there as well.

To fully do the work of forgiveness is to withdraw all of the toxic energy from the Inner Judge. This means we are reminded not to condemn the Judge either, by viewing it in a bad light. As Jung has said, we would all do well to "recognize your madness and welcome it in a friendly manner." After all, the Inner Judge was created under events of great stress, in which our child selves were in a double bind. The Judge acted as a psychological survival strategy, and, in a certain sense, it saved us. As we did in the chapter on Reunion, we might be wise to offer gratitude to the Judge. This gratitude is closely related to forgiveness.

I could keep going for a long time, getting deeper and deeper into the labyrinth of our inner pathologies, individual and collective. But this building of concepts only takes us so far. Understanding *how* we have been broken does not, by itself, make us whole. What is needed is to go into the alchemical crucible of the heart and do the work.

In the practice I am about to describe, we will create an image in our hearts of the Gate of Forgiveness, and we will work with several stones that offer supportive energies to both strengthen and soften us for this purpose. The intention of this practice is to bring about an experience in which we feel and recognize the energy of forgiveness in us, and in which we discover that forgiveness can bring us into union with the Deep Self. Each step we take toward our wholeness is a step towards permanent union of our conscious and unconscious aspects. When these aspects fully and permanently bond so that our whole identity is constantly present, we have achieved the Second Conjunction.

PRACTICE: THE GATE OF FORGIVENESS

In this practice, we are not trying to directly trigger the Transcendent Function through setting the tensions between opposites into motion. Instead, we are taking up where we left off in the practice of Calling the Lost Parts Back from Exile. We are making another step toward reconciliation. We do this by again working through the heart. In this instance, the goal is to use True Imagination, Attention and Intention to create a Gate of Forgiveness in our hearts.

[**NOTE**: We could compare this to writing a software program for a computer. Software contains the programming, which is a set of rules for dealing with data. The program will say something like: "When *this* happens, do *that* with it." It is organized to handle input according to the intentions of the programmer. In our case, we are choosing to set up a pattern of intent whereby we will open a space in our heart through which forgiveness happens, whenever the need for it arises. Of course, because human beings are not computers, we are likely to have to practice the program more than once to really get it running.]

The practice of forgiveness can reinforce the inner unity of the self. In the previous practice, we called our exiled parts back into our hearts, with the intention of healing the fragmented personality. If we achieved an inner reunion, the next step is to do what is needed to maintain it. Our old patterns are bound to reappear. How can we return quickly to inner harmony when this occurs? One way is to set the intention of maintaining a Gate of Forgiveness in one's heart. This "gate" is simply an image, and with the image we affirm the intention that all beings—whether they are exiled parts of ourselves, other people, souls of the deceased or other entities—are invited to pass through the gate of our heart to experience forgiveness. Offering this and feeling its effects can be a profound and healing experience. It cleanses us of negativity we might otherwise hold onto. By making the offer to all beings who wish to be forgiven, we may even aid in healing processes needed by other souls—deceased or incarnated. If we hold our intention and make forgiveness a type of automatic response—instead of our usual default settings of judgment and blame—we will find new peace in ourselves and our relationships.

STONES TO USE:

Heartenite, Lithium Light, Celestite, Rosophia, Sauralite Azeztulite, Pink Azeztulite.

In this practice, we are working with stones that support the loving heart and the gesture of forgiveness. We are not trying to induce tension, but rather to allow any tension to flow through the heart and be relaxed. If you do not have the stones on the list above, or if you are not drawn to use them, others which can be helpful in this practice include: Kunzite, Morganite, Rhodonite, Rose Quartz, Pink Amethyst, Ajoite, Pink Calcite, White Azeztulite, Danburite, White Petalite and/or Pink Petalite.

[NOTE **REGARDING MUSIC:** Any of the practices in this book can be done with appropriate music in the background. If you use music, try to choose something that supports the type of process you are entering. I prefer not to have vocals, because the words tend to distract me. I bring up music in reference to this practice in particular because I have found that soft, tender music can enhance the process, and it can also help you stay with it until it completes itself. Sometimes the line of beings who want to pass through your Gate of Forgiveness can be quite long!]

Instructions:

1. Pick up all the stones you will be working with in this practice and hold them mixed together in your two cupped hands. Feel their combined currents and notice if you sense harmony among them. If not, ask the Stone Beings to harmonize in order to help you with this practice.
2. With the stones in your cupped hands a few inches in front of your mouth, softly breathe over them. On the out-breath, offer the Beings of these stones your good wishes and your willingness to work with them. On the in-breath, invite the Stone Beings to come into your heart and your energy field. Ask for their help in the process you are about to begin. Do this for several breaths, until you feel the connection has been made and it is time to continue.
3. Bring your hands and the stones to the center of your chest, at the level of your heart. Continue to breath consciously, offering yourself when you exhale, and inviting the Stone Beings into your heart as you inhale.
4. Using your imagination, picture yourself standing in the space in the center of your chest. You are standing next to a gate. It can look however you want it to look, or however your

unconscious displays it to you. It can be an arch with flowers, or a picket fence type gate, or a gate made of metal with bars and locks—whatever feels most true. It doesn't matter whether the gate appears to be locked, or shows that it was once locked and fortified. You are going to open it.

5. Now picture the image of yourself smiling and opening the gate, and then standing beside it again, with a hand held out in a gesture of invitation. When you have this image clearly, inwardly say, "This is the Gate of Forgiveness in my heart. Any being who wishes for forgiveness may come through this gate. I invite you." Repeat this until you see a being or beings coming forward.
6. As this begins to occur, watch carefully for who comes forward and observe them as they pass through the gate. Notice as many details as possible. See if you recognize them or not, and pay attention to whether any of them speak to you or look at you as they go through. Most of the time, this does not happen, but if it does occur, it will be significant.
7. Allow the process to flow, and continue to welcome all the beings who come to your gate. Notice your own emotions and attend to the effortlessness of how it feels to forgive without discriminating whether the ones coming to you "deserve" forgiveness or not. This is always important, and especially so if you happen to see *yourself* coming to the gate.
8. Eventually you will notice that the process is coming to completion. Gently and patiently allow the last beings to move through your gate. When it feels appropriate, inwardly say, "My Gate of Forgiveness is open, and it will remain open, even when I am not here watching. All beings are welcome to pass through and receive forgiveness." (This can be particularly helpful if you find that there seems to be an endless procession coming through, and that it is time for you to come out of the process.) It is also a good intention to set within oneself that the gate of one's heart is always open and ready to forgive.
9. If for any reason you do not feel comfortable leaving your gate open when you withdraw from this process, that is okay. It may mean you feel too vulnerable to do this, and that feeling could be valid. Or it might mean that there is work to be done around trusting that you are safe when you forgive. But you do not have to push yourself. Stay with what flows and feels good inside you. You can always come back and open your gate again. In this situation, simply send love and forgiveness out to any remaining beings and gently come back to normal consciousness.
10. As you come back from the process and open your eyes, once again thank the Stone Beings for their help and put the stones aside. Ground yourself, have a drink of water, or whatever you need to do. Then write in your journal about what you experienced and who came through your gate. Remember and write down as many details as possible. What did your gate look like? Did it change? How did you feel? Were you surprised by anyone who came through? Did any of them interact with you, and what was the interaction? Were there any beings whom you didn't recognize? Did you yourself come through the gate? How many came through—just one, a few, a few dozen, hundreds, thousands? Is this a practice you would like to do again? Can you imagine and feel comfortable with the idea of always leaving the gate of your heart open to all beings who wish for forgiveness? If you were to leave your gate open, how do you imagine it might change the way you feel in your daily life?

DISCUSSION

When I lead workshops, the Gate of Forgiveness is often one of the most moving and significant practices for those who attend. The stones we use, especially Celestite, Heartenite, Rosophia and Sauralite Azeztulite, readily draw people into a state of gentle receptivity and generosity of heart. The heart is activated, and the emotional body is calmed.

The envisioning of the Gate of Forgiveness is one that people seem to do quite readily. Even those who tend to have trouble visualizing quickly find their image of themselves standing beside their gate. Often they are surprised by the how the gate looks. This is a good thing, because such surprises mean that the Deep Self is paying attention and is participating in the practice. The same holds true when the process really begins and beings begin to come forward and pass through your gate.

It is amazing what a powerful and deeply needed thing forgiveness is. In my workshops, people have often reported seeing themselves come forward to go through the gate. Also frequently seen are family members, friends, spouses and others with deep emotional ties. Once an aborted fetus came through for a woman, asking her forgiveness for not becoming her child. Several times people have reported friends or family members who committed suicide coming to their gates to be forgiven. It is amazing to be present for some of the powerful healings that occur through this practice.

Another type of occurrence which has happened with some of the workshop participants is the phenomenon of people unknown to them coming through their gates to be forgiven. In some cases, only a few figures come through, but more frequently there are long lines of beings—hundreds or even thousands. In some people, the procession is deliberate and relatively slow-moving, but other people report a rush of figures literally pouring through their gates.

What is happening here? One possibility is that the many fragments of oneself which were cast into exile through countless incidents in one's life are all coming back into the heart. I believe this is sometimes the case, and in those instances, the participants display strong emotions of relief and joy. In the majority of cases, people who experience many beings whom they do not recognize pouring through their hearts do not report powerful emotions. They usually seem to be primarily *witnessing* an event which is of great importance to the beings pouring through their gates, but which is not personal to them.

The impression I have, and which many participants have expressed, is that these multitudes of beings are the souls of people who have died, and who need to experience forgiveness in order to move forward spiritually. Because this type of thing has happened every single time I have facilitated this process, my conclusion is that there is a huge need for forgiveness among the souls of a great many people who have died, and that an offering such as we make in the Gate of Forgiveness practice is of major importance to those souls. It is clear that all of us still living also need forgiveness in some area or another, and that we all need to forgive ourselves in order to become whole. Perhaps there is something similar going on in the soul realm. There is no doubt in my mind that the recurrent floods of souls coming through the hearts of participants who make the generous offer of unrestricted forgiveness indicates that such practices offer healing beyond what I had anticipated. Apparently, forgiveness is a great and transformative energy, and its effects are more profound than we may have imagined. I feel that more work should be done in this area, and I hope some readers of this book will get involved with it.

This train of thought takes me back again to spiritual alchemy and its precepts. As I keep emphasizing, it was believed by many alchemists that if the Great Work of the transformation and perfection of the *prima materia* (oneself, and the outer world, simultaneously) could be accomplished by even a single alchemist, *it could redeem the whole world and the entire cosmos.* When one realizes how much aid may be provided to beings in the afterlife by such simple practices as the Gate of Forgiveness, one begins to comprehend how enormous the potential may be, and one can glimpse that the vision of cosmic redemption held by the alchemists could actually be true. The third practice to be outlined in the next chapter will take us further in the direction of universal awakening and redemption.

14

Ascension of the Heart

Man is a transitional being; he is not final. The step beyond man is the next approaching achievement in the earth's evolution. It is inevitable because it is at once the intention of the inner Spirit and the logic of Nature's process.

–Sri Aurobindo

At times I feel as if I am spread out over the landscape and inside things, and am myself living in every tree, in the splashing of the waves, in the clouds and the animals that come and go, in the procession of the seasons. There is nothing with which I am not linked. Here everything has its history, and mine; here is space for the spaceless kingdom of the world's and the psyche's hinterland.

—Carl Jung

This perfection, this oneness of substance and consciousness and being, is like the world's golden memory, the blurred image that each one and each thing strives to conjure up and capture, the goad of the world's great Thirst, the driving force of its gigantic Need to be and embrace and grow. It is like a tenacious memory thrusting things and beings and even galaxies into a mortal embrace that would like to be an embrace of love, that would like to understand all, hold and encompass all within its circumference.

—Satprem

1. Phenacite, 2. Rosophia, 3. Moldavite, 4. Sauralite Azeztulite, 5. White Azeztulite, 6. White Danburite, 7. Vivianite, 8. Agni Gold Danburite, 9. Himalaya Gold Azeztulite, 10. Trulite Silica, 11. Golden Azeztulite.

In the next phase of alchemical transformation, the practice we will work with focuses our attention on the Third Conjunction. This is described as the event that can occur after the Second Conjunction, when the alchemist has fully united the conscious and the unconscious sides of his or her being, and the new Self of wholeness has come into existence.

The Third Conjunction refers to an even more profound stage, in which the whole and fully integrated Self of the alchemist unites with the Divine. One must work through imagination and intuition in attempting to envision this state of being. We will attempt to at least catch a glimpse of it through the processes initiated with this practice.

In most of the practices we work with in the Alchemy of Stones, we endeavor to combine the vibrational support of the Stone Beings with our three powers of Attention, Intention and Imagination. In doing this, we are emulating the ancient alchemists, who worked with these same powers, steering their efforts toward co-creative partnership with Sophia, the Being of Wisdom, the Soul of the World.

In our work, the stones and their currents are our link with Sophia and her Wisdom. After thirty-three years of this work, it is clear to me that stone energies are indeed emanations of healing, harmony and wisdom offered to us from the Soul of the World. What comes to us through the stones is always beneficial—always oriented toward the good of the whole. This is a fundamental quality of Sophia, as she has been described in sacred texts for over two thousand years.

Those of us who work spiritually with stones are like the alchemists in another way—we choose to act on our belief that we can *help* Sophia to evolve the universe to its highest expression. We do this by working to transform ourselves to our own greatest potential. Like the alchemists of earlier times, we understand the dictum from the Emerald Tablet stating, "that which is above is like that which is below." This means that all parts of the universe resonate with all others at all levels, and a change in oneself reverberates through all that is, influencing the evolution of everything. In this effort, we use the tools of our free will and our imagination, while allowing ourselves to be guided by the Wisdom of Sophia, which we glean from our inner experiences and the synchronicities that come to us. The Stone Beings act as direct sources of access to Sophia's wide spectrum of beneficial emanations, and we attune to them in order to do our work in harmony with her.

Most of us tend to locate our center of self-awareness in our heads. We think that our "I" lives in the brain, and that our consciousness is something that happens in the brain. That is what we have been taught in school. (Some thinkers, such as biologist Rupert Sheldrake, maintain that consciousness is *expressed* through our brain, nervous system and body, but that the *source* of our consciousness is in a domain beyond the physical world.) Furthermore, the idea that consciousness is a product of the brain was not always viewed as a truism, nor is that the case everywhere today.

We know something about our right and left brain hemispheres—that in most of us our rational, mechanistic thinking is associated with the left brain hemisphere, and our intuitive, musical and artistic qualities are usually expressed through the right brain hemisphere. But this is not our whole story.

In human beings, the Wisdom of Sophia expresses itself most clearly through the intelligence of the heart. As the ancient Gnostics, the alchemists, the poet Novalis, modern indigenous peoples, and countless others have long known, the heart is the Seat of the Soul. As biology tells us today, the heart contains more neuronal cells than muscle cells, so there is a physical foundation through which the heart's intelligence can be expressed. In my worldview, the heart is the proper center of our selfhood, and the place in us where our Deep Self resides together with Sophia—the source of the spark of our divinity.

As I see it, the great Third Conjunction—our ultimate destiny—will involve our thinking and our wisdom—through the brain and the heart—coming into union. In this union, the heart and its wisdom will ascend to its rightful seat of sovereignty—assuming its authority over the mental activities expressed through the brain. We will feel subjectively that the spiritual heart *actually rises up* through our chests in a surge of love and power, filling the interior of our skulls with Light, Love, Truth and Wisdom. Our way of being will change, and the most prominent sensation of our transformation will be that we experience our soul/spirit identity as an enlightened presence filling up the entire bodily corridor from the base of the heart to the top of the brain. It will ultimately fill our entire chakra column from root to crown, linking with the etheric chakras above our heads as well.

The dominion of the heart will not be felt by our old identity as if it has been overpowered by something. At the arising of the heart, our minds will rejoice in recognition that the Divine is truly in us, and has always been within us, and is our actual true Self. Our minds and brains will gladly surrender to the opportunity to be guided always by Wisdom, and to serve the heart's purposes, which are Sophia's purposes—Love, and the Enlightenment of the Universe. The Ascension of the Heart ends our loneliness, our fear and our confusion—all in a single event. Whatever we ask, we immediately understand. Wherever we look, we see another mirror of Divinity. This includes the "lower" parts of ourselves—our physical bodies, our wounds, our imperfections. It includes everything and everyone we encounter in the material world—not just in the spiritual realms. In this awakening, Darkness and Light, Matter and Spirit conjoin in sacred marriage. And the Earth—in resonance with the redemption of Sophia (for it is She who awakens in matter when our hearts arise)—will become the Philosophers' Stone, the living union of spirit and matter, the marriage of Heaven and Earth.

This is my vision of the ultimate potential of the Alchemy of Stones, and of our human destiny. It is a very high aspiration, but my heart affirms it. Something within me smiles, and is glad that I have even dared to express it.

There have been moments in my life in which these things happened, as I have described in this book. In my first mystical experience when I was eighteen years old, I was filled with Light that I knew to be a Divine presence, and for a brief time, I had the answer to every question I asked. In the Moldavite meditation and journey to the Great Central Sun, my heart chakra blossomed with Light, and that Light rose up to illuminate my brain and mind, as well as all of the chakras, above and below my heart. In the Moldavite experience, the new knowing I received was the activation of my capacity to feel and understand the spiritual energies of stones. I believe that these two experiences offered me a glimpse of what the Third Conjunction will be like, but, because the peak states of expanded consciousness and union with the Divine did not stay with me permanently, I would not say that I have fully reached the stage of the Third Conjunction.

So, how in the world do we create a practice that moves us in this direction? What stones should we ask to help us in this, and to what should we turn our imaginations? Fortunately, as has happened often in my life, I was given a clue through a synchronicity.

In the year 2006, my wife Kathy and I were traveling in Europe. I was accompanying her on a pilgrimage through France and Italy, visiting a number of the paintings and carvings of the Black Madonna—one of the forms of Sophia that was venerated in those countries during the Middle Ages and early Renaissance. On one particular day, we were visiting the Louvre, the great art museum in Paris, and we were hurrying along through several galleries, on our way to see the Mona Lisa. [A side note: The Mona Lisa is viewed in some esoteric circles as being an image of Sophia, rather than the portrait of an unknown woman, as is commonly believed. From this point of view, her enigmatic smile expresses the way Sophia looks towards humanity.]

Suddenly, a painting that I was about to walk past caught my attention. I stopped, turned to my right and gazed at it. The longer I stood there, the more the painting gripped me. Something deep within me was activated by this image. My heart started beating harder and there was an intense tingling in my third eye. Then the energy moved up from my heart and linked with my third eye, and the intensity increased. Soon there was what I would call 'a fountain of energy' flowing up through me and out the crown chakra at the top of my head. The painting was kindling something numinous and powerful. I had never experienced this kind of activation from viewing a piece of art. Only certain stones—such as Phenacite, Danburite, Azeztulite, Moldavite and Rosophia—had ever stimulated me in this way before, and perhaps not as strongly as this painting. I was transfixed, and I did not hurry off to see the Mona Lisa. I stayed with the painting for almost an hour, vibrating in a state close to ecstasy, feeling I never wanted to leave. We finally did go to view the Mona Lisa, and her eyes seemed to smile knowingly. I had just seen something that my soul (and Sophia) wanted me to see.

The title of the painting was *Mysteries of the Passion of Christ,* and the artist was Antonio Campi (c. 1522–1587). The painting depicted an array of scenes from the story of Jesus' crucifixion and resurrection, showing all of them on a single canvas. This juxtaposition of all these different moments from the Christ story felt strangely supernatural. It gave the visual impression that time had stopped, or become simultaneous. Soon, my attention was fixed on the top right portion of the painting, which showed the image of Christ's Ascension.

Why did this image affect me so strongly? In truth, I can't say why. What happened was deeper within me than my conscious thought can go. But I can at least say some things about the insights I experienced while gazing at it.

My wife and I were on a spiritual pilgrimage, and our intention was to become inwardly closer to Sophia by viewing numerous images of her in sacred art. In the months prior to our

trip, we had also been attending classes at Robert and Cheryl Sardello's School of Spiritual Psychology. In our studies about Sophia, I learned that the ancient Gnostics had believed that Sophia's divine partner is Christ, and that together they form a *syzygy*—a perfectly matched female/male pairing of the Divine emanations known as *aeons.* In some Gnostic texts, the mission of Christ is the rescue of Sophia's spirit from its imprisonment in matter. From this point of view, Sophia is one side of a holy union, rather than a completely separate being. Suddenly and surprisingly, on our Sophia pilgrimage, the other side of the syzygy made itself felt in this painting of Christ ascending. The Sophia side, in the guise of the Mona Lisa, seemed to have led us there. After all, had we not been on our way to see her, we might never have walked by Campi's painting!

[NOTE: The astronomical meaning of the word *syzygy* (pronounced *sizz*-uh-gee) is also worth considering in this context. In astronomy, a syzygy is: "a conjunction or opposition, especially of the moon with the sun." Here we are again, back in the imagery of alchemy! One could say that the alchemical Conjunction of the Sun and Moon (aka the King and Queen) which is so prominent in alchemical texts and emblems, echoes the pattern of this astronomical conjunction, as well as the Divine syzygy of Christ/Sophia, who are, in mythic terms, the King and Queen of the Universe.]

As I gazed at the painting, thoughts and images began to come to me. I remembered that the author Joseph Chilton Pearce had called Christ "the Great Being of the Heart." This memory came to me while my own heart was overflowing with intense energy, which was filling the center of my body and pouring out the top of my head. I understood that the portion of the painting that was most intensely attracting me was the part depicting Christ's Ascension. I sensed that what was happening within me was an Ascension in its own right. I felt sure that the pattern shown in this painting of the mythic story of Christ was meant to convey the *experience* of the Ascension of the Heart to viewers who were prepared to take that into themselves. I did not believe that what was happening in me was something I had earned, or that could be earned. It felt more like a gift of grace—an astonishing and surprising opening, triggered by a spiritual mystery, translated through the hands of an inspired artist 450 years earlier. This experience was so important to me that I have brought the image of Campi's painting into many of my subsequent workshops and books.

If we consider for a moment the fundamental "blueprint" or mythic "gesture" of the Jesus story, it fits several of the patterns we are considering in regard to our own spiritual evolution. Jesus, considered mythically, is a personification of the spiritual Sun (the Great Central Sun) or the Solar Logos. He is a Man of Light and perhaps most notably a personification of the Heart. Countless artistic renderings of Jesus depict his heart as visible *outside his chest,* emanating radiant Light, displaying visually the unbounded love and compassion from which he is said to have lived and taught.

One might say that crucifixion is more or less what has happened to the heart itself in human history. Love, which moves through the world in a gesture of generosity and trust, has been subjugated to the tyranny of the mental, calculating consciousness that responds to its fear of the unknown future by trying to master and control the world. This pattern is everywhere—throughout our political and economic structures, within our education systems, and deep down in the habits of our personalities. The magnificence of the Jesus story—as history or myth, however one may see it—is that it asserts the ultimate victory of the Heart, which neither avoids its enemies nor fights them, but which triumphs over death through its absolute love and trust. This pattern is offered to us as our way of transcendence.

To go a few more steps, let us remember that in the tale of Jesus, this Great Being of the Heart was crucified at a place called Golgotha, which means "the Hill of the Skull." The symbolism could not be clearer. The place where the the Heart—which holds our spark of the Divine, our Love—has been crucified, is the Skull—the seat of our mental, calculating consciousness.

Within our own bodies, the heart is our core. In fact, the word "core" is derived from the French word *coeur,* which means "heart". In fetal development, the heart is the first organ to form, and it starts to beat weeks before there is any discernable brain activity. Spiritually, the heart is the true Sovereign within us, the King or Queen of the realm of our being. Our fear is a consequence of our fragmented state, a condition in which the true Sovereign is not recognized, is denied and nailed to the Cross of matter. And this is strangely archetypal, as though the situation we are living in—the story we are living out—is so primal that it is portrayed in our anatomy. Our physical hearts are placed at the center point of our energy system, the "crossroads" of our bodies.

Yet the spiritual Heart, because it holds the Divine spark, cannot be contained, even by death. It can rise up, in our own psyches and bodies, and in so doing it illuminates the clouded mental consciousness. At that moment, if we *ask deeply* for it, (because love offers but does not compel), the "resurrected" Heart rises into its seat of Sovereignty at the center of our consciousness.

Metaphorically, energetically and perhaps even physically through neuronal channels, our Heart awareness rises into our skull, which illuminates our consciousness with golden radiance—the Light of the spiritual Sun—transforming our interior darkness into the dome of Heaven. Seeing fear dissolve into the joy of Love's victory, all the mental forces in us that sought to control the future, thereby putting the heart in bondage, recognize their true place as servants of the Heart's life-generating activity of blessing.

All of this can be seen in the image of Christ's Ascension as depicted in Campi's painting. It portrays Christ, the Being of the Heart, rising triumphant into the cranium-shaped vault of heaven. His entire body radiates Light, and in my view, his radiant body is the Light Body that we also seek to incarnate. The fact that this golden "cranium" is depicted among dark clouds, and is a portal into another realm, signifies the transformation of the "clouded" mental self through the Ascension of the Heart. If you look closely, you will see that the golden-domed vault in the painting is held up by a *host of beings.* This is symbolic of the willing service that is spontaneously offered by all aspects of ourselves—and by the Beings of the spiritual realms—when the Heart is recognized as the true Sovereign. The central cap in the top of the dome signifies the final doorway leading to the infinite Divine.

Below the Christ figure, there are lower, earthly figures being drawn up behind him, perhaps symbolizing that that the "lower" aspects of the self are carried up in the Heart's Ascension. Around the ascending Christ are four rejoicing angels. (In the Alchemy of Stones, the angels can be seen as representing the Stone Beings.) The great sphere in the center of the dome is the transfigured World—the World in its Body of Light. Its image contains a smaller sphere, the physical Earth, and the Sun and Moon above it, within the larger "World Sphere". The fact that the World Body has ascended along with the Christ figure reveals that our own transfiguration and ascension are intimately linked to that of the Earth. We don't ascend to leave the world. We ascend *together with the world.* The painting suggests this, inasmuch as it depicts the World Sphere lifted up into the heavenly dome by the ascending Christ. At the top of the dome is a golden capstone depicting the illumined crown chakra, the Gateway to the Great Central Sun, the Light of the Divine Source.

At the time of my experience, I was focused on ascension, and I can understand why, because I felt the inner ascension of my own heart. I was far more drawn to the ascension portion of the painting than I was to the darkness, suffering and death that was depicted on much of the rest of the canvas. Yet I now realize that this portion is important as well. In spiritual alchemy, we always work with both polarities.

In the mythic pattern embedded in the story of Christ, we are looking at suffering, death, resurrection and ascension. I have learned in my research that, in the early centuries of Christianity, the story also often included a journey to the underworld, undertaken by Christ during the three days that elapsed between his death and his resurrection. In these versions, it is in the underworld that the victory over death occurs. The transformation happens in the invisible depths. This is the only part of the story that Campi's painting does not show us. We see Christ emerging from the tomb, but we are not shown what happened in the underworld. In a sense, I believe it must be this way, because it is a mystery that goes beyond images.

I won't try to solve the mystery implied in the myth itself. However, I needed to bring in Christ's journey to the underworld, because if our own hearts are to ascend, we too must go into the depths before we rise.

All this is a lot to think about, but I wanted to set the stage here for the meditative practice I have named the Ascension of the Heart. I feel that this Ascension, which takes place simultaneously within our bodies, our consciousness, and the world, is a key to the Third Conjunction. The Ascension of the Heart is an alchemical transformation that unites our conjoined surface self and Deep Self with the Divine, creating the Philosophers' Stone. In its complete and perfect manifestation, it is the simultaneous redemption of the alchemist, the Earth, and the Universe.

At this point, we can go on to the practice itself. We will use both the image from Campi's painting and a group of stones that can support the kind of experience we are aiming for. Once again, I want to mention that I am not trying to espouse any religion. The pattern in the painting is archetypal, and viewing it that way allows us to avoid getting entangled in religious doctrines. It is brought into this practice in an attempt to *show an image*—something with which one's psyche can resonate—that speaks to the Deep Self, beyond the limitations of words.

PRACTICE: THE ASCENSION OF THE HEART

In this practice, we will work with the images in Campi's painting, as well as four stones chosen to accentuate the Ascension of the Heart. We will use *imagination* to envision the essence of what the painting signifies, and to implant its pattern within our bodies. We will use our concentrated *intention* to affirm that this pattern is a reality. And we will utilize our *attention* to observe and participate in everything that is evoked within us by this practice.

STONES TO USE:

Phenacite, White Azeztulite, Moldavite, Rosophia. I have selected these four stones to represent the four angels in the painting, supporting Christ's Ascension. On the energetic level, each of these stones resonates with the Ascension of the Heart. These are also the four stones shown on the cover of this book. Because of their power and the energy dynamic among them, I have designated them as the Four Cornerstones of the Alchemy of Stones. (See Chapters 29–32).

Rosophia and White Azeztulite represent the divine syzygy of Sophia and Christ. We have touched on this earlier. In a simplified sense, the White Azeztulite conveys the Light and Blessings of Heaven reaching "downward" into the world, and the Rosophia conveys the world's love, reaching "up" to meet the Light. This echoes the pattern of the Christ/Sophia syzygy.

Moldavite is known as the Stone of the Holy Grail—a legendary version of the Philosophers' Stone. Moldavite is literally a joining of Heaven and Earth, since it is a fusion of meteorite and earthly rock. Energetically, it is a catalyst of transformation, and it resonates powerfully with the heart.

Phenacite is a high-vibration stone of the realms of Light, and can activate the third eye, the crown chakra and the etheric chakras above the head. It also stimulates the heart chakra and brings Light to the emotional body. Thus, it supports the intention of this practice—bringing the heart's presence up through the chakra column and establishing its Wisdom as the sovereign center of our whole being.

ADDITIONAL STONES:

White Danburite, Sauralite Azeztulite, Agni Gold Danburite, Himalaya Gold Azeztulite, Golden Azeztulite, Trulite Silica, Vivianite. If you are drawn to do so, you can add any of these stones—or any other stones which "ask" to be included—to the four listed above. All of the ones I have mentioned are in harmony with the intention of this practice.

[NOTE: Because this practice is rather long and complex, I suggest that you consider recording the instructions and listening to them as you go through the practice. After doing it with the recording one or two times, you may be able to remember the steps well enough not to need it. Alternatively, you may want to ask a friend to guide you through the process, reading the instructions aloud to you.]

Instructions

1. Set up a quiet space where you can be undisturbed for an hour. Sit in a comfortable chair, with this book opened to the images of Campi's painting, placed so that you can see them without needing to touch the book. Gather the stones you will be using so they are within easy reach.
2. Pick up the stones you will be working with in this practice and hold two of them in each of your two cupped hands. Hold the Moldavite and Rosophia in one hand, and the White Azeztulite and Phenacite in the other. (Use your intuition to decide about the placement of any other stones.) With the stones in your hands a few inches in front of your mouth, softly breathe over them. On the out-breath, offer the Beings of these stones your good wishes and your willingness to work with them. On the in-breath, invite the Stone Beings to come into your heart and your energy field. Ask for their help in the process you are about to begin. Do this for several breaths, until you feel the connection has been made and it is time to continue.
3. Bring both of your hands and all of the stones to the center of your chest, at the level of your heart. (Keep them paired in each hand, as described above.) Continue to breathe consciously, offering yourself when you exhale, and inviting the Stone Beings into your heart as you inhale.
4. When you feel the presence of the stones' energies, keep your eyes closed and hold you're your attention in your heart, Allow yourself to imagine that you are in total darkness and silence. You are together with your heart, deep underground in the depths of the Earth. Continue to breathe, while holding the four stones over your heart.
5. When you have settled down into this place of darkness and utter silence, inwardly say to yourself, with sincerity, "I am alone in the realm of death." Then stay in the darkness and

silence. If you notice that any images come, bring back the darkness and silence and repeat, using your intention to make it real: "I am alone in the realm of death."

6. Stay in this place of nothingness and darkness. Let yourself feel it. Don't think. Simply be fully present in the darkness of the realm of death.
7. Now think seriously of the reality of your own death, while keeping the stones over your heart and your eyes closed. If you drift away from this or find that thoughts try to run away with you, bring yourself back to it.
8. When you have truly dwelt in this place, with real thoughts of your own death, bring your attention again into the center of your heart. Notice that you were never actually alone. You are within your heart, in the presence of your heart, even in the realm of death.
9. When you can feel this, inwardly ask the four stone Angels of Moldavite, Phenacite, Azeztulite and Rosophia to come to you within your heart space, and to bring all of their power. When you can feel them strongly, (hopefully, more strongly than you ever have before), welcome them into your heart, within this darkness of the Sacred Underworld. Feel their presence with you as the presence of four powerful Angels.
10. From the core of your heart, in the darkness where you are, with the Stone Beings supporting you, call out: "Being of my heart, Twin of my soul, come to me now and lift me up!" Stay in your heart, waiting. Look to see if someone appears. Call out again: "Being of my heart, Twin of my soul, come to me now and lift me up!" Repeat this and watch in the darkness for a spark of light, or a Being coming to you. Notice carefully who comes.
11. When you see the image and feel the presence of the Being of your heart, your soul's Twin, open yourself and *merge* with that One, who has always waited for you and has always loved you. Give yourself completely to that union, holding nothing back. When this truly occurs, you may feel a powerful surge of emotion, which can include both joy and sorrow, elation and grief. Over all of this will be the sense of reunion. Let yourself experience this fully, while keeping your eyes closed and remaining in the Sacred Underworld in the dark cave of your heart.
12. When you are ready, you will feel an inner prompting to open your eyes. Now, while staying linked with the stones and centered in your heart, look at the image of Campi's whole painting. Let the meaning of the painting, in all its complexity, enter into you. Imagine this powerful depiction of love, suffering, sacrifice and victory as your own soul's journey. Your own Deep Self, the Twin who is with you now, has loved, suffered and sacrificed, in this same way, for you. And now you are reunited.
13. Within the emotion and energetic potency of this moment, you may sense that something more is trying to happen. You may feel this as an inner suggestion or longing, now that you are joined with your Deep Self, to rise up as one. (Goethe said of this moment, "The desire for higher lovemaking sweeps you upward.")
14. Now bring your attention to the enlarged image of Christ's Ascension. Let yourself feel that something like this is beginning to happen inside you. The being that is the union of your everyday self and the Deep Self—the soul's Twin—is expanding, and golden light is radiating within your heart. Feel the energies of the four Stone Angels intensifying and supporting the growing inner radiance.
15. Agree inwardly to allow this radiance in your heart to rise up to your head. Keeping the Moldavite and Rosophia stones over your heart in one hand, bring the Phenacite and Azeztulite stones up to your crown chakra with the other hand. Pay attention to the currents of all four stones as they link the heart, throat, third eye and crown chakras. Feel your heart's energy and presence rising upward, filling your chakra column with golden Light.

16. Now, make an image of the ascension part of the Campi painting and overlay it on your own body. I suggest imagining that the golden skull/cloud shape be larger than your physical head, so that the base reaches to your heart. As you imagine that overlay, allow it to move into your body so that its image touches the sensations of the stone currents in your head and heart.
17. Hold this combination of the image and the feeling of the stone currents, keeping focus on the entire heart-to-crown area. Now remember the symbolism and feeling of the painting. Remember the joyfully upraised arms of the resurrected Christ. Remember the lower beings that are drawn up along with him. Remember the rejoicing angels around him, and the resurrected Light Body of the World that he lifts above him. Recall that he is the Being of the Heart, of your own heart as much as any other.
18. Bring attention to your heart center, allowing it to move upward toward your head. Remember all that is shown in the painting, while feeling the helpful currents of the four stones (your own four rejoicing angels), holding the heart's powerfully vibrating radiant field as it moves upward. Remember the gesture of the Heart as you allow it to rise—the generative gesture that loves and blesses all. As you are feeling all this, say to yourself, "All of this is happening in me." Go over the meaning and the feeling of the pattern you have created with the image and the stone currents, and repeat, "This is truly happening within me now."
19. Let go, and let everything you have imagined become real within you. It *is* happening now.

AFTERWARDS: There is no way to "complete" this practice, because, when it has become real, it never ends. You will, of course, open your eyes, put the stones down, close the book, etc. You will continue with your life. However, if this practice has spoken to you deeply, I encourage you to keep it going. If you want to take this as far as possible, carry the stones you used in this practice with you, and work with them again and again, repeating the practice as outlined above, or letting it evolve. Continue to place the image of the Ascension of the Heart into your body frequently, every day, whenever you can remember to do it. In its essence, I believe that this vision *is* happening now, and that by imagining, intending and attending to it, we are practicing the alchemy through which it can fully manifest.

There are other practices, other images and other rituals that one can create and utilize to facilitate the Ascension of the Heart. Because of the heavy cultural "baggage" around images such as those Campi portrayed, I repeat again that this is not an endorsement of a religion. It is an attempt to see *through* the religious iconography to the essential spiritual gesture behind it, and to make that gesture our own. If you find it preferable to use another image, by all means do so. It is our opening to the Heart's Ascension that we care about.

Another important opportunity: We need not see ourselves as alone in this process. If our hearts are ascending, so potentially are all others. (One of Jesus' famous purported sayings is, "If I am lifted up, I lift all people with me.") One way of recognizing and honoring this is to make a practice of seeing others as being within this process of the Ascension of the Heart. It is both impractical and potentially rude to start *telling* this to other people, but we can wordlessly imagine it when we look at them. I like to project the image of the Campi painting, overlaid on the other person, and say to myself, "This is also happening in her (or him)." This plants an invisible seed—in ourselves, perhaps in those we encounter and certainly within the soul body of the world.

Whether we or others are aware of it or not, the great spiritual process of the Heart's Ascension is unfolding, within us and around us. I have already mentioned this quote, ascribed to Jesus in the *Gospel of Thomas*. When he was asked when the Kingdom of Heaven would come, he is said to have replied: "The Kingdom of Heaven is spread out on the Earth, only men do not see it."

We are called to see this reality, and so to help give birth to it. In attempting this, we are embracing the Great Work, the *Magnum Opus* of the alchemists.

ALTERNATE PRACTICE: ASCENSION OF THE HEART BODY LAYOUT

For those who wish to work with a more complex (and possibly more powerful) array of stones to facilitate the Ascension of the Heart, I offer the list of stones below, and some slightly differing instructions. The process is basically the same as the one outlined above, except that one does it lying down, with the stones placed on the heart and third eye chakras, and adjacent to the root and crown chakras. Unless you can work out a way to see them while lying down, you'll have to visualize the image of Campi's painting from memory. It might be best to try this practice after having done the first version at least once. It may also be helpful to have someone place the stones on and around your body for you, and you can consider having them read the instructions to you as you go through the practice.

Once one is lying down with eyes closed and the stones are placed, one is instructed to feel the energies, and overlay the images on and within one's body, just as in the practice as outlined above. I suggest that you hold the same intentions and do the same affirmations. You may select music to go with this layout. For myself, I usually use recordings of Gregorian chants.

STONES TO USE:

ROOT CHAKRA: Anandalite, Tibetan Tektite
SEXUAL/CREATIVE CHAKRA: New Zealand Carnelian
SOLAR PLEXUS CHAKRA: Libyan Gold Tektite
HEART CHAKRA: Moldavite, Satyaloka Rose Azeztulite, Rosophia, Pink Azeztulite, Astaraline, Sauralite Azeztulite, Anandalite
"HIGH HEART" CHAKRA (between heart and throat): Morganite, Kunzite
THROAT CHAKRA: Azumar
THIRD EYE CHAKRA: Phenacite, Herderite. Brookite
CROWN CHAKRA: Danburite, Satyaloka Yellow Azeztulite, Satyaloka Clear Azeztulite, Circle Stone, Natrolite, Anandalite

Workshop participants often report dramatic experiences with this layout. Some people find that they need to do some work on grounding themselves afterwards. I suggest water, food, standing outdoors in bare feet, and using stones such as Hematite and Black Tourmaline when grounding is needed.

DISCUSSION

The Ascension of the Heart practice is designed to alchemically combine the three powers of imagination, attention and intention, along with Campi's profound symbols, and the energies of the Four Cornerstones of the Alchemy of Stones. The purpose of this is to try to create the conditions in which one may enter into the Second and Third Conjunctions of spiritual alchemy. (I have chosen to invoke both the Second and Third Conjunctions in this practice, because most of us need to establish or refresh our union with our Deep Self in order to be prepared for the Third Conjunction.) Such experiences are associated with the third phase of alchemy, the *rubedo* (the redness) that is linked with the manifestation of the Philosophers' Stone. In this context, as we have discussed elsewhere, the Philosophers' Stone is the fully individuated Self, joined with the Divine.

I used Antonio Campi's painting, *Mysteries of the Passion of Christ* as a symbolic template for this transformation, primarily because of the spiritual experience it triggered in me. Also, I know of no better example for displaying the radical metamorphosis of the third Conjunction. In the instructions, I tried to invoke an imaginal journey that would echo this pattern, anchoring it into one's conscious mind, one's Deep Self, and one's body. The energies of the stones help to create a resonant connection into the subtle body and the physical body. It is important to do this in order to "make it real." Although it is quite a high aspiration to attempt to connect with the Third Conjunction, I feel that even achieving the "echo" of such an experience is worthwhile.

It is possible to get too attached to the *content* of an image such as the Campi painting, forgetting that we are trying to *see through* the image to the pattern of spiritual reality that lies beneath it. It is this underlying pattern that we are aiming toward. There are alchemical emblems that also portray the Third Conjunction. The adjoining picture shows one such alchemical portrayal.

Look at the alchemical emblem and notice the similarities to the Campi painting used in the Ascension of the Heart practice. We see again the gray clouds that surround the miraculous opening in the sky. Within the opening, there is a globe of golden light. There is an obvious line of transition between the mundane world and the Divine reality above. In the Divine realm, the radiant golden hemisphere is filled with angelic beings, just as the golden dome was in the Campi painting. Near the top of the golden hemisphere, in both pictures, we see a gold 'capstone' with an inscription of sacred letters, indicating the gateway to the Divine Source.

This alchemical emblem depicts the fulfillment of the Great Work. We can see in many places the various pairs of opposites in symmetry with one another. There are the Sun and Moon, the male and female, day and night, and other such pairs. In the center of the image, we see the alchemist, wearing a garment that is half black and half white, indicating that he has accomplished the conjoining of the opposites within himself. The opposing pairs arrayed around him show that he has balanced the forces within and without. The opening above him to the miraculous higher realm of the Divine has come about in synchronous resonance with his individual achievement of Conjunction. And we see the mystic union of Heaven and Earth in the central golden radiance that unifies the Above and the Below. (Could this signify the Great Central Sun?) I believe that this emblem and Campi's painting are both symbolic portrayals of the pattern of alchemy's Third Conjunction, which is, in human terms, the Ascension of the Heart.

Let's review for a moment the three basic stages of spiritual alchemy. The *nigredo* (the blackness) is the first stage, and is associated with the beginning of the work. At the beginning, one is filled with all sorts of impurities and negative attachments, as well as an unrefined sense of self. One's ego is predominant. Going through the effort of becoming conscious and dissolving all the pollution is difficult and unpleasant. There is suffering, and if one goes all the way down into it, one may experience the Dark Night of the Soul. The First Conjunction of the surface self with the Deep Self can be viewed as the culminating release from the nigredo.

The second stage is associated with the Light of expanded consciousness that is brought about through the First Conjunction. Because of this Light, the stage is known as the *albedo* (the whiteness). One is, as this point, a whole and individuated human being. As the fulfilling step in this stage, one's surface self and Deep Self can permanently unite in the Second Conjunction.

Where does one go from there? The pattern of spiritual alchemy tells us that there is a third stage to be manifested, the *rubedo* (the redness). The red color is reminiscent of the blood, of the vitality of physical life. As my friend Danny Deardorff liked to say, "The rubedo is the revalorization of the flesh." [The dictionary tells us that "revalorization" is: "the process of setting a new value."] This "setting a new value" means that, after the suffering, purification, awakening and expansion of the first two stages, the third stage is to bring all the grief and glory of the alchemical journey back into one's body, to "make it real." When this is done sufficiently, one is potentially ready for the Third Conjunction, in which one's whole Self rises and unites with the Divine.

Here again, we can note the appropriateness of Campi's painting and the pattern of the Christ mythos. In the Christ story, religious doctrine emphasizes that Christ's Ascension was *bodily,* not only spiritual. This tells us that, alchemically speaking, he had reached the stage of the rubedo and it was then possible for him to ascend in his "revalorized" flesh and unite with the ultimate Divine.

However impossible or unlikely it may seem that something like this could occur for us, it is the pattern toward which alchemy aspires. And it is what I think humanity and the Earth can do together. This is what it means when I write, for example, that if and when all the Quartz in the Earth's crust embodies the energies carried by the Azeztulites, the Earth will become a Planet of Light. And we will necessarily transform at the same time.

The idea in alchemy that the Philosophers' Stone could change lead into gold is a way of stating metaphorically that transformation is contagious. (Thinking back to our discussion of fractal geometry, we can recall that this mathematics validates the idea that contagious transformation, in which a tiny pattern becomes the basis for a new system, is the way nature operates.) The alchemists believed that by enacting, in their small-scale experiments, patterns of metamorphosis and evolution that echoed those sought by Sophia, they could accelerate and enable those changes on a global and even a universal scale. We have been attempting the same kind of thing by going through practices such as the Ascension of the Heart with the Stone Beings.

I know that this chapter has been a challenging one. It was, in many ways, the most difficult one for me to write. I think that is because we are trying to approach the mystery at the heart of alchemy, which is the mystery at the heart of the world.

I sometimes get little clues. They often come as things I stumble upon without looking for them. (I'm sure all my readers know what that is like!) Last night, I was restless at bedtime and picked up a book—*The Martian Chronicles,* an old science fiction novel by Ray Bradbury. As I read, I came upon this line: "Science is no more than an investigation of a miracle we can never explain, and art is an interpretation of that miracle."

Alchemy offers a third approach: *We attempt to join forces with that miracle.*

The three stages of alchemy, the Three Conjunctions, and the 'third thing' that arises when a set of polarities is transcended, also exemplify the idea of "triality," the "threeness of things." This principle resonates through the very heart of alchemy, and we will explore it in the next chapter.

15

Triality, Transcendence & Transformation

Between the conscious and the unconscious, a third thing has put up a swing:
all earth creatures, even the supernovas, sway between these two trees,
and it never winds down.
Angels, animals, humans, insects by the million, also the wheeling sun and moon;
ages go by, and it goes on.
Everything is swinging: heaven, earth, water, fire,
and the Secret One, slowly growing a body.
Kabir saw that for fifteen seconds, and it made him a servant for life.

—Kabir, *The Swing*

The Jungian psyche is no longer based on matter or the brain or mind... but on soul... as a third reality between... the mind... and matter.

—Roberts Avens, *Imagination Is Reality*

In our exploration of the Alchemy of Stones, and the transformations we seek, I have been giving a lot of emphasis to the dynamics of polarities. I recounted my experience from college, when the polarity between my views of what was real and what was "only a dream" came into a high degree of tension. This was due to the huge synchronicity of my seeing the horse-cloud from my recurrent childhood dream floating in the sky of the "real" world, moments after I had described that dream to my roommate. The sudden intensification of that tension shattered my materialistic view of reality, and from my fear, I called out to a "third thing"—to God—for help. In the next moment, spiritual Light washed through my body, turning terror into ecstasy. The "third thing" had arrived. In Jung's terminology, I had experienced the Transcendent Function—the movement beyond dualistic polarities to a greater awareness that encompassed them.

There is thus a kind of numinous resonance about the "threeness" of things, and examples can be found in a multitude of places, both inner and outer—from the physical body to the highest spiritual realms. Author Daniel Deardorff calls this ubiquitous phenomenon *triality.* In his (highly recommended!) book, *The Other Within: The Genius of Deformity in Myth, Culture and Psyche,* he gives numerous examples of fundamental threesomes: heaven, earth and underworld; instinct, intellect and inspiration; past, present and future; and the triune (three-part) brain, with its reptilian, mammal, and human layers. Mr. Deardorff's drawing of the Triple Oroborous (opposite) gives us an alchemical image of this omnipresent pattern.

I think it is important at this point to give attention to the fact that the opposites depicted in alchemical drawings—as well as those we choose to work with inwardly for self development—are engaged in order to evoke the emergence in our consciousness of a "third thing." We can call it the Seat of the Soul, the spiritual Heart, the Deep Self, the Divine, or any of a plethora of other names. The movement toward the third thing is the movement of transcendence, and all of our work involving the holding of the opposites is aimed at that.

The experience of transcendence—the shifting of one's center of awareness to a new perspective that goes beyond and encompasses all polarities—leads to a radical and greatly beneficial transformation.

We could say that the movement from duality into triality is the movement from ignorance into *gnosis,* from bondage into freedom, from fragmentation into wholeness, from anxiety into ecstasy. It can be felt in any and all of these ways. When this transcendence lasts for more than a passing moment and becomes one's way of being, a great alchemical transformation has occurred: the "lead" of one's fragmented self has become the "gold" of wholeness.

As I thought about this, I began to notice even more trialities that relate to our work and enrich the alchemical worldview that I am trying to illustrate. There are, for example, the Three Conjunctions mentioned in the previous chapters, with the Third Conjunction bringing about the transcendent goal of a mystical union of the human individual and the Divine. In Chinese alchemy and in Taoism, there is the Yin/Yang symbol, half black and half white, with the "third thing" present as the *circle which encompasses both.* There are also the Three Human Powers of Attention, Intention and Imagination that we use in all of our stone practices (and which we aspire to use consciously at all times). We use these three powers to enhance our inner and outer lives through practicing co-creation with Sophia.

I have already mentioned the Seat of the Soul described by Novalis, which exists as a third realm, where the inner and outer worlds overlap. We can relate that to the Marie Louise von Franz's statement, which I quoted earlier: "The individuated person lives in the world of active imagination, and the ego does not identify with the outer world, nor with the inner world, *but with the imaginative world, which includes both of the others.*" The "imaginative world" of von Franz is the same as Novalis' "Seat of the Soul." Both writers emphasize the significance and transcendent quality of this third realm, which incorporates the polarities within itself.

THREE STAGES IN THE ALCHEMY OF STONES

Significantly for our work, there is a famous alchemical triality which involves the colors black, white and red.

Black, white and red have myriad associations across many cultures. In fact, the study of human languages has revealed that all languages have words for the colors black and white, with the third most commonly named color being red. Other colors are less frequently given their own names. One could say that red, white and black are the archetypal colors.

It is interesting to note that many old fairy tales make use of these three colors as symbolic motifs. The most famous of these is the Grimm Brothers' tale "Snow White," which begins with Snow White's mother asking for a child who is "white as snow, as red as blood, and as black as ebony wood." In this story, Snow White is eventually able to transcend death, through the transcendent shift we call love, in which the male and female polarities merge. (The transcendence of death was, of course, one of the great aspirations of the alchemists.)

Of the many of symbols associated with these colors in myth, some of the most vivid are these: black for feces, white for milk or semen, and red for blood. These are the three fundamental substances or "liquids" produced by the human body.

The three colors black, white and red signify the three major stages of inner alchemy, and are known in alchemical language as *nigredo* (black), *albedo* (white) and *rubedo* (red). Each of these stages is necessary for the alchemical transformation of the self, and for the corresponding transformation of the world.

The three practices we have gone through in the previous chapter have touched on these three stages, and I want to once again discuss the three stages and how they relate to those practices, and to our work in the Alchemy of Stones.

The first alchemical stage was called *the nigredo,* meaning "the blackness" or "the darkness." It was associated with the beginning of the work, and with the initial chaotic state of the *prima materia*—the "first matter" with which alchemy begins. The prima materia is frequently represented by a lowly physical substance to be transformed, or the darkness of the alchemist's consciousness in the beginning. The prima materia and the nigredo are both metaphorically associated with feces—the chaotic, dark, unpleasant but fertile substance produced by the human body. Without the fertile darkness, the work cannot begin. Thus, our dark, disagreeable qualities—the things we think the least of—are the places where the seed of the Self is hidden. The importance of working first with dark interior "soil" is emphasized within the word "alchemy" itself. *Al-khem* is Egyptian for "the black earth."

The nigredo often refers to difficult inner experiences of confrontation with one's shadow side. Experiences of fear, shame, grief or illness can be manifestations of the nigredo stage. The "Dark Night of the Soul" which is discussed in many spiritual traditions is an immersion in the nigredo.

The alchemists knew that the treasure they sought to create could not be made without experiencing the nigredo. We all know that, in our everyday lives, there is nothing to be gained by turning our backs on the darkness. It must be faced, in order for us to consciously receive its wounds and its blessings. It is appropriate that this stage comes first, because we cannot grow or become whole while ignoring or supressing the shadow.

In the Chapter 12, I described the practice: "Calling the Lost Parts Back from Exile." In it, we focused attention on what I termed our "worst" traits, and, with the support of specially selected stones, we inwardly expressed *gratitude* for the parts of ourselves which we had previously judged negatively and "exiled." To put one's attention on one's "worst" qualities is to consciously feel the discomfort of facing them and including them as aspects of our identity—something we seldom do. In essence, the "Lost Parts" practice is a conscious entry into the nigredo. We are facing our darkness, without rejecting it. In fact, by expressing gratitude, we are inviting our darkness into our hearts.

In spiritual alchemy, we work with our hearts all the time. The heart is the inner vessel that is capable of transforming whatever substance we bring into it. It is like the fiery stove or furnace that the ancient alchemists used to melt and transmute physical substances. The heart is the home of our innate Wisdom. It is the place of truth where Sophia dwells in us. Thus, when we invite our darkness there, we must feel it fully and truthfully.

The alchemists, knowing the necessity of all three stages of the Great Work, entered the nigredo stage voluntarily, without knowing when, *or whether,* they would emerge from it. We must also do this, if we seek transformation. One of the great benefits of working with the stones is that their clear, steady vibrations can both accelerate and stabilize our inner processes.

Stones that resonate with the nigredo stage, and which aid one when that stage is present, include: Black Tourmaline, Master Shamanite, Nuummite, Black Azeztulite, Black Tourmailne Azeztulite, Mystic Merlinite, Black Merlinite, Smoky Quartz, Tibetan Black Quartz, Black Obsidian and Black Jade.

A practice such as "Calling the Lost Parts Back from Exile," can evoke an experience of the nigredo stage. It is, in my experience, a temporary and safe entry into this territory, and I believe the stones act in the same manner as a shaman's spirit helpers, facilitating and guarding one through the inner processes we must undergo. I can say that, in my personal history, experiences of the nigredo have been incredibly fertile and fruitful for my awakening and growth, even though they are difficult. (Or, more likely, *because* they are difficult!) If you engage the Lost Parts practice with sincerity and openness, I believe you'll understand what I mean.

In my workshops, participants who go through the Lost Parts practice sometimes report that they experienced a descent into grief, regret or despair, which at some point transforms into an uplifting feeling of moving into Light. This shift is the transition from the nigredo into the next phase, the *albedo.* In Jung's words, "the nigredo gives way to the albedo . . . the ever deepening descent into the unconscious suddenly becomes illumination from above." Again, I will point to the mystical experience I had in college. It began with a disturbing descent into my inner darkness, and, at the pivotal moment, I was suddenly filled with numinous Light.

After the dark night of the nigredo stage in spiritual alchemy, there comes a second phase, known as the *albedo,* or "the whitening." This corresponds to our inner experiences of Light, and to purification. It can be associated with a feeling or memory of connection to the Divine, with a desire to be of service to others, and with a shift towards a greater level of integrity. We might say that, by reclaiming the parts of ourselves which were exiled in the subconscious, we are freed from being chained to our darkness through our denial of it.

In terms of bodily metaphors, the albedo is associated with milk or semen, the two "white" liquids produced by the human body. Although they are excretions of the body, both are of a much more refined and purified nature than feces, and both are associated with the birth of a child. We can use these images to help us feel qualitatively the differences between the nigredo and albedo.

The albedo stage can be associated with the activation of the upper chakras, and with visionary experiences. In this phase, we may want to meditate a lot, and we may naturally express love and empathy in our relations with others. People doing charitable volunteer work, *reiki,* or other types of healing, may be expressing the albedo. In the albedo stage, when we are not feeling an immediate connection to the Light, we are seeking one.

In the Alchemy of Stones, the albedo stage can be evoked and supported by stones such as the following: White Azeztulite, Sauralite Azeztulite, Satyaloka Clear Azeztulite, Celestite, Natrolite, Brookite, Phenacite, Danburite, Lemurian Light Crystals, Nirvana Quartz and other upper chakra stones.

In Chapter 13: Forgiveness, I described a practice called "The Gate of Forgiveness," and I suggested using some of the stones listed above. As in all of our transformational activities with stones, we worked through the heart. We set up an imaginal "gate" in the heart and invited all beings who wished to experience forgiveness to come through it. If you have tried this exercise, you probably know now how readily the beings come forward to accept this offer.

The Gate of Forgiveness is a practice meant to evoke an experience of the albedo. It is an exercise in sincere and selfless giving, done imaginally, with the help of the Stone Beings. Inviting *all* beings who wish to experience forgiveness to come through the gate of our hearts is a ritual that purifies us. By being non-discriminating in our invitation, and then witnessing what happens, our habit of judging and deciding who *deserves* forgiveness (which stops us from ever *feeling* a genuine forgiving gesture) is bypassed. We discover how simple forgiveness can be, and how good it feels. Experiencing this is a purification. It can lead to an important new recognition: Forgiveness is what heals. If we wish to heal ourselves and others, and if we wish the world to be healed, everything must be forgiven.

[**NOTE**: I have witnessed hundreds of people engaging in the Gate of Forgiveness practice. I want to mention some revelations this has brought to me. First, the immediate and virtually universal experience of participants was that beings indeed came to their gates. Many were surprised to see large numbers of souls pouring through their hearts, most of whom they did not recognize. This surprised me, too, and it convinced a stubbornly skeptical part of me that the beings we meet in the imaginal realm are *really there.* We are not making them up. And it revealed that the healing gesture of forgiveness is needed there as much as it is in the material world. It also showed me that the imaginal realm is a place where souls exist after death, or perhaps more accurately, it is a "middle ground" where they can meet us.]

The Light that enters in the albedo stage can be deeply comforting. In my mystical experience in college, and in the Moldavite journey to the Great Central Sun, it was ecstatically comforting to be filled with the Light. Purification through this kind of grace feels wonderful, especially in comparison to the disconcerting confrontation with darkness and chaos experienced in the nigredo. The inner clarity and restructuring that goes with the "higher consciousness" of the albedo phase can make one feel as if the ultimate goal has been attained.

But we have not yet reached the completion of our alchemy. In the albedo, we are often high in the realm of Spirit, but far from the Earth. By this, I mean that we may experience the albedo as transitory phenomenon. This points to the necessity *of grounding the Light into physical life.* In order to truly complete the Great Work of alchemical transformation, we must *incarnate* our awakened awareness and *live it in the world,* with commitment and passion. After the albedo stage of purification, we still need to become as physical and "solid" as a stone—the Philosophers' Stone. The phase in which this transformation occurs is known as the *rubedo.*

> *[In the] state of "whiteness" [albedo] one does not* live *in the true sense of the word. It is a sort of abstract, ideal state. In order to make it come alive it must have "blood", it must have what the alchemists called the* rubedo, *the redness of life. Only the total experience of being can transform this ideal state into a truly human mode of existence. Blood alone can reanimate a glorious state of consciousness in which the last trace of blackness is dissolved, in which the devil no longer has an autonomous existence but rejoins the profound unity of the psyche. Then the* opus magnum *is finished; the human soul is completely integrated.*
>
> —Carl Jung

The albedo state is one of lofty experiences, high ideals and spiritual aspirations, while the nigredo is one of chaos, loss, grief and despair. In most, if not all cases (and certainly in my own life), the path from black to white to red is not a straight line of ever-improving experiences. As Jung taught, the transcendent function, which brings a great expansion to another level of being, is preceded by a "shuttling back and forth" between the opposites. As we saw in our discussion of the caduceus symbol, the pattern leading to transcendence involves a continual *intensification* of the tension between the opposites. This is necessary in order to build up sufficient energy to trigger the transcendent function.

In practice, this often means that an experience of the albedo is followed by a descent back down into the nigredo. (Recall also that the initial movement to the Light of the albedo is most often preceded by the "dark night" of the nigredo). When we are immersed in the nigredo once again, we are in darkness, but the memory of union with the Light draws us back. Most often in these times, there is more of our shadow to embrace and integrate, at which point insight and/or grace elevates us into "the whiteness" once again.

Why do we fall back down to the nigredo? There are many reasons, but one of them, in my own experience, is a sense of grief that comes when we "lose" the Light. In my most powerful spiritual experiences, there was a feeling of, "Aha! I am here, I understand everything. I am ecstatic, and I am always going to feel like this." And then the experience passed away. Somehow the sense of union with the Divine sooner or later faded out and I was merely (mostly) my old self again.

This, of course, plummeted me downwards. How was it possible that I could "lose" the intense, immediate awareness of the truth that I was loved and held in the Light of the Divine? If the feeling was true, how could it ever go away? Did its passing mean that it was an illusion? Was the Light just a safety mechanism—a circuit breaker in my brain that was tripped by fear and despair? Could that be all there is to it? When these questions are asked, one is already down in the pits of the nigredo. And one usually has to dwell there for a while before managing to rise again.

The above is a little sketch of the "shuttling back and forth" between the opposites that occurs in the first two phases. We identify ourselves with first one side of the darkness/light polarity and then the other. Our habit of one-sidededness—stemming from the viewpoint of duality (light *versus* darkness)—continues. And if things go "well" (from the alchemical perspective) one's internal tension *increases.* If we do not go all the way through this process, we will most likely get stuck—either in a hopeless surrender to darkness, or in a naïve clinging to light. (I would guess that at least some atheist/materialists are stuck in a pessimistic darkness, while at least some of us who embrace New Age spirituality are mistakenly adhering to an ungrounded optimism and attachment to light.)

Fortunately for us, trialty—not duality—is the pattern of reality. Spiritual alchemy tells us that there is an overriding potentiality which transcends our vacillation between the darkness and the light. It expands our perspective beyond polarities, into a new consciousness that includes both sides within a greater whole. When we do more than think about this new consciousness—when we *live* it bodily, emotionally and imaginally—we have entered the rubedo phase.

The rubedo, when it is truly lived, is the culmination of spiritual alchemy. It coincides with the creation of the Philosophers' Stone. The Stone can be viewed as the Divinity, fully incarnated in the human being. To be 'fully incarnated' means to be utterly, irrevocably committed and conjoined. This is closely akin to what author/alchemist Jeff Raff called the Third Conjunction. The Self is born as a permanent unity of human and Divine, including light and darkness, and all other polarities, within and without. It can no more dissolve and fade away than a stone can become water. One's deepest identity has transformed–body, soul and spirit. In this state, every cell sings the song of its true ecstasy. Joy and sorrow, darkness and light, are notes in its melody, and one would no more cling to them than would a musician choose to play only one note.

The practice called The Ascension of the Heart, which I described in the previous chapter, is a practice that aims to bring one into the rubedo, or at least to help one see it from afar.

To begin with, we center ourselves in the heart, and we use four stones which resonate with the heart chakra: Moldavite, Phenacite, White Azeztulite and Rosophia. This heart-centering is important for many reasons, including that the heart is the epicenter of the circulatory system, carrying our blood (which embodies the "redness" of the rubedo) throughout the body. If we are to actually *incarnate* our awakened awareness, it must flow into every cell. In Jung's words, "Blood alone can reanimate a glorious state of consciousness . . ."

Moldavite is a particularly appropriate stone for stimulating the transformational rubedo stage. Its formation as a fusion of a meteor with earthly rock is resonant with the radical transformation of the rubedo. So is the fact that this fusion occurred as the result of an intense, explosive collision which literally brought "heaven" and "earth" together. Moldavite's resemblance to the fabled Stone of the Holy Grail—the Emerald that fell from the sky—is closely akin to the Philosophers' Stone of alchemy.

Other stones that resonate with the rubedo stage are Libyan Gold Tektite, Tibetan Tektite, Agni Manitite, Bloodstone, Prophecy Stone, Healerite, Heartenite and Seraphinite.

Another aspect of the "redness" is passion, and the heart is the center of all our genuine passions. Courage, too, is a quality of the rubedo, because to live our Divine identity involves letting go of all "safety nets," and this requires the heart's courage. (The word "courage," like the word "core" that I mentioned earlier, comes from the French word *coeur,* meaning "heart.")

Going further, the utilization of Campi's painting, *Mysteries of the Passion of Christ,* brings to this practice a mythic image that evokes the fullness of the rubedo stage in its most powerful archetypal form. [I wish to again remind readers that I am discussing the mythic pattern and symbolic meaning of the story of Christ. I do not go to church or call myself Christian, but at the same time, I love and revere the Christ story, and I can feel its numinosity.]

I brought Campi's painting into this book because I wanted readers to use the image of Christ's Ascension as an imaginal talisman to evoke transcendence within themselves. And when one looks at the entire painting, one can see in a single image the pattern of the life and death of Jesus, his victory over death, and his ultimate bodily ascension, as Jesus Christ, into the golden dome of Heaven—bringing the Earth and humanity with him.

This image is the most powerful symbolic rendering of the rubedo state that I have encountered. The figure of Christ is of a human being who is simultaneously an incarnation of God.

The pink-gold light around his ascending body is the color of the illumined heart. His ascension brings the heart's love into the skull-shaped opening in the clouds—overcoming mental duality with the heart's mystical transcendence. In us, when the heart "ascends" to its sovereignty over the whole of our being, its energy and light fill the entire bodily column from our chest to the top of our heads and beyond, and down through our feet to the Earth. In this transformational fulfillment, the well-known inner struggle between our right and left brain hemispheres (which physically mirrors the longstanding conflict between the "rational" and "intuitive" sides of our nature), is enfolded in an ocean of compassion. This is "the peace that surpasses all understanding." All dualities are resolved, and the goal of alchemy has been achieved. (This is mirrored by the colors in the painting: The surrounding sky of lead-colored grayness has given way to an atmosphere of golden light.)

In simpler terms, the Ascension of the Heart practice aims us toward the rubedo through the use of stones energies and symbolic imagery, combined with one's own powers of attention, intention and imagination. Remembering the basic alchemical dictum, "as above, so below," we use the "highest" possible example—Christ's Ascension—to try to kindle its resonant likeness in ourselves.

People have asked me, "Isn't this idea of the Ascension of the Heart a departure from the body? Isn't the idea of Ascension another attempt to escape from darkness (nigredo) by going into the light (albedo)?"

My most candid answer is, "Yes, but no." The word "ascension" seems to point to an attempt to fly over the troubles of life, and the Campi painting seems to depict Christ's ascension into the sky. But in the practice we are discussing, *everything happens within the body.* We are not trying to send our souls flying up to the Light. We are envisioning the ascending Christ image within our own bodies. We are imagining, and intending, that the Divine shall incarnate within us.

The alchemists envisioned that the world was moving towards an evolutionary goal. They believed that their active cooperation could aid the Soul of the World in realizing that goal. They trusted that by participating and co-creating, they would share in the cornucopia of blessings accompanying the goal's realization. They named the manifestation of the goal the Philosophers' Stone, and it was imagined as a Divine substance, with many beneficial powers. In some alchemical engravings, Christ was depicted as *the filius philosophorum* (child of the philosophers), another name for the Philosophers' Stone. Whether the Divine "substance" was an "outer" thing such as a physical stone, or whether it was the imaginal presence of Christ, or the Divine spark in the alchemist himself (or herself)—or if it was somehow all three at the same time—was a mystery that mattered less than the all-important achievement of the goal.

The idea of the incarnation of the Divine within a human being can seem to be a rather high-flown mystic notion. How real is it? Jung was careful with his words because he did not want his psychology to be viewed as unscientific mysticism. His word "individuation" was used to signify the state of human wholeness. Yet if, as Jung also said, there is a divine spark at the core (heart) of our being, then "wholeness" *exactly* means the incarnation of the Divine. And this is the rubedo state in alchemy. The divine spark has enflamed a passion in our hearts and in our very blood, and we live out our lives in the liberated expression of that passion.

The Ascension of the Heart practice is meant, for those ready to commit to it, to be extended and amplified in the hours, days and years after we first enact it in meditation. It is suggested that we continue to carry with us the stones we used when we first did the practice. One is also encouraged to continue to envision *within one's body* the image from the Campi painting, while affirming, "This is happening in me." Going even further, we can imaginally place the same image as a blessing/offering into the bodies of everyone we encounter, while inwardly affirming, "This is happening in her (or him)." As in most or all alchemical practices, we engage in a process of transformation through feedback, as symbolized in the image of oroborous.

Each repetition of the practice—each visualization and each affirmation of our intention—enfolds all our previous iterations of it. In alchemy (as in the fractal geometry of Chaos Theory), these repetitions are never mere duplications—they are refinements and purifications that lead ultimately to a radical transformation. And then, perhaps, it may all begin again, but from a new starting point.

The triple oroborous at the chapter's beginning has been designed to encompass, in a single image, the essence of the three alchemical stages—nigredo, albedo, rubedo—and their eternal evolutionary flow. In this chapter, we have looked at the idea of triality as a fundamental quality of reality. I want to end here by affirming that we ourselves consist of the triality of spirit, body and soul. Spirit is our divine spark, body is our physical expression, and soul is the "third thing" that joins the other two. We live in three worlds—heaven, earth, and the imaginal realm that links them.

Stones, too, have their own triality. This is what makes them, for me, the best allies in our alchemical journey. As angelic entities, they exist in the realm of spirit. As physical objects, they are the most *tangible* spiritual talismans one can ever work with. And the stone currents, in my view, exist in the overlapping realm of subtle matter/energy—the realm of soul. When we attend to that realm, we can feel, see and converse with the Stone Beings. This teaches us how to live in the Seat of the Soul, and it is from this place that we can engage and co-create with Sophia.

In the next chapters, we are going to explore the "third realm" that links the worlds of matter and spirit. This is the Imaginal Realm, the domain where we encounter the Stone Beings and discover our own psychoid/imaginal form—the Subtle Body.

16

Stone Beings & the Imaginal Realm

> *The alchemists wove [intuitive imagining] . . . and scientific "fact" into a single world. They could not, or perhaps did not care to interfere with their own imaginative activity. For example, by considering silver as "seed" of the moon or copper as "seed" of Venus or lead as "seed" of Saturn, they disregarded the distinction between the organic and inorganic kingdoms. To the alchemists,* "seeds are **living forces with encoded intentionality** . . ." *These ore-bodies were not dead matter to be pushed around, but vital seeds, embodiments of soul; not objective facts, but subjective factors." In this way the alchemical view "incorporated into its theoretical premises what modern science is now stating as new: the observer and the observed are not independent of each other."*
>
> —Roberts Avens, *The Imaginal Body*
> [Quoted phrases are from James Hilman. Emphasis is mine–RS]

> *The transformation of lead into gold is the release of soul into its imaginal realm—its liberation from entrapment in the leaden literalism of scientific fact, or the suffocating dogma of a philosophical ideal.*
>
> —Roger Brooks, *Pathways Into the Jungian World: Phenomenology and Analytical Psychology*

At this point, we have come quite a good distance along the path of the Alchemy of Stones. Now that we are getting closer to the "top of the trunk" of our alchemical tree, where things begin branching out into a variety of different activities, I think it's a good time to take a look around. I want to unpack some thoughts about the realm we have entered in preparation for exploring it further.

I have asked you to imagine—and to proceed from the viewpoint—that all of reality has consciousness at its foundation. By "consciousness," I refer to awareness—both "conscious" and "unconscious." We can say that matter emerged as an expression of this consciousness. Or we may agree with the Buddhist perspective of "interdependent co-arising"—the idea that matter and consciousness arise simultaneously, and cannot exist independently.

From the alchemical viewpoint, as described in the Roberts Avens quote above, a world arising from consciousness is one in which imagination is naturally at home, and in which imagination would naturally have an influence on "physical matter"—the stuff from which scientific "facts" are derived. In truth, imagination is fundamental to all of our experience of reality. As Jung said,

Aquamarine crystal reveals its inner "face" in its reflection

"the world exists only so far as we are able to make an image of it." This is exactly what the alchemists believed. Thus, the worldview of panpsychism ("soul everywhere") is very much the alchemical worldview. This can be hard for us to understand, because we are so enmeshed in our habitual concept of reality that we forget that it is all an image. (But this does *not* mean that it is unreal.)

Stones, and all things in the world—from atoms to elephants to galaxies—express and embody the fundamental consciousness at the root of everything, and all of them have their own identities. Whether they have individualistic egos like we do is another question, but we can say that every center of consciousness, expressed as any self-organized object or creature, is a "self." From this understanding, we recognize that both we and the stones we work with have selfhood—both human beings and stones are centers of consciousness. This is why I call them Stone Beings.

The underlying selfhood of all things, including us, can be designated by the word "soul." Although soul pervades our whole being, the Seat of the Soul, as Novalis said, is the space of awareness "where the inner world and the outer world meet." This is the subtle or imaginal realm, which partakes of the qualities of both matter and spirit. In the human body, this corresponds most directly to the heart. The intelligence expressed through our hearts is the intelligence of the soul. Although we also have a mind and a body, and are connected to the Divine in our spirit, the soul is where the spark of Wisdom exists in us. This is where our sincere and "heartfelt" intelligence comes from.

I hold with the insights of the alchemists, the Gnostics, the Sufis and a variety of other spiritual traditions—that there is a Soul of the World. In the Alchemy of Stones, we follow the tradition of using the name Sophia to designate the World Soul. We remember that Sophia is the ancient Greek word for Wisdom, and we understand that Sophia is the living Wisdom who is expressed in what we perceive as the intelligence, beauty and harmony of the world. Sophia is a vast, yet intimate, intelligence who is embedded within every object and every process in the world. And when we say "world" we might be better off saying "universe," because the harmony of Sophia's Wisdom reaches far beyond the Earth. (If we wish to address only the soul of the Earth, we might use the name Gaia, while knowing that Gaia is one of Sophia's faces, just as all souls can be seen as aspects or expressions of Sophia.) Our own souls can also be viewed as emanations of Sophia, even though we are, at the same time, individual selves. We contain a holographic spark of Sophia's divine wisdom, while still existing as our "separate" human identities. (To me, this is one of life's greatest and most wonderful mysteries!)

When we work with the Stone Beings, we could say that we are working with Sophia's "angels." Angels have been traditionally conceived as being divine messengers, and the stones carry the sincere and benevolent "messages" of Sophia to us when we turn our attention to them and invite them into us. These messages are experienced as what we call the energies or metaphysical qualities of the stones. When they reach us, we may sense them as currents of vibration, of heat, of emotion and feeling, as images, sounds, scents, tastes, words and even as imaginal figures in human forms. Each of these modalities is real, symbolically expressing the "message" of that stone, and can be enhanced through meditative practice.

Because we are operating in the realm of soul, we center ourselves in our hearts when we work with the Stone Beings. The practice of engaging a Stone Being through the heart can easily be synchronized with our breathing. On the exhale, we offer ourselves for relationship with the Stone Being, with a benevolent inner gesture of appreciation and well-wishing. With the inhale, we open our hearts in invitation, holding the intention that we trust the Stone Being, and that we appreciate the opportunity to receive whatever it offers. (This pattern is essentially the same as the one I described earlier as the Activity of Blessing, and it automatically centers us in the soulful sincerity of the heart.) Setting the stage in this way lays the groundwork for genuine and helpful relationship between ourselves and Sophia, through her angels, the Stone Beings.

Another important way to think about how we should view the Stone Beings is implied in the above paragraph quoted from Roberts Avens and James Hillman. Just as metals were envisioned alchemically as "seeds" of planetary energies, the stones we work with can be viewed as "seeds" of their own particular energy patterns. When we invite the stone's currents into our hearts, we are "planting" those seeds within our souls—within what is called the subtle body, or the imaginal body. This is where the potential qualities carried in the stone "seeds" can grow and flower. When we endeavor sincerely to do this, we are co-creating with the Stone Beings through True Imagination.

To quote again the core phrase from Avens: "To the alchemists, 'seeds' *are living forces with encoded intentionality . . .*" This is an excellent metaphor. The DNA in the seed of a plant facilitates the formation of the organic building blocks it needs to grow to maturity. (The actual "blueprint" of the fully developed organism most probably exists in the subtle-imaginal realm in what biologist Rupert Sheldrake calls the "morphic field" of each species. The physical DNA may simply attune to this blueprint and transmute it into physical expression.) The life force or vital energy of the seed is the plant's *encoded intention* to live and develop.

So, when the alchemists called copper the "seed of Venus" they were saying that the pattern of intentionality (the energy) of copper was akin to the energy pattern associated with Venus in astrology. Working alchemically with copper could enable the alchemist to *manifest* the energies of Venus. Following the alchemists' thought, we can say that the stones are also "seeds," on the soul/imaginal/subtle level of reality.

What I and other authors have been calling the "metaphysical qualities" or the "energies" of stones *are,* to borrow Avens' phrase, the "living forces of encoded intentionality'" of the Stone Beings. Every kind of stone has a different set of metaphysical qualities, which means that every species of Stone Being has a different pattern of intention—its own purpose and destiny.

There is a word for this encoded intentionality. It is the word *entelechy* (pronounced en-TELL-a-key), which the dictionary defines as, "the realization of potential; the development and functioning of an organism or other system or organization." In philosophy, entelechy means, "the soul."

It is interesting to consider that entelechy can mean both "the soul" and "development and functioning of an organism . . ." It seems to suggest that "soul" is always impregnated with "encoded intentionality"—with purpose.

From this I want to underscore the point that *we meet the Stone Beings within the realm of soul, which is also the imaginal realm,* AND *the realm of subtle matter/energy and subtle bodies.* This is the same territory that I referred to earlier in the book as the psychoid realm, where the physical and spiritual worlds overlap. All of these terms refer to the same domain of experience—the same reality.

We may feel physical bodily sensations from holding a stone, but *stone energies are not quite physical.* They are patterns originating in the realm of pure Spirit, which we experience in the world of soul—the imaginal/psychoid realm of subtle matter-energy. We must use our own attention, intention and imagination to enter into rapport with the Stone Beings in this realm. Sometimes our connection can happen as quickly as picking up a stone and holding it. But this establishing of rapport—this attunement—is nonetheless what is going on. We are linking with the Stone Being through our subtle body, within the soul/imaginal/psychoid realm. And if we are well-enough attuned—with ourselves and with the stones—throughout our various levels of selfhood, we notice the "vibes" or other manifestations of our connection with the stone.

This is why I am sure no mechanical or electronic instrument will ever be able to measure what we experience as stone energies. (Of course, materialists will say that if it can't be measured with instruments, it isn't real.) The New Age authors who say that stone currents are, for instance, "electromagnetic energies" tend to confuse the issue. The realm of soul is much greater than the purely "physical" world in which electromagnetic energies occur. And physical instruments cannot measure something that exists in a higher level of reality.

Electromagnetic energies, and all phenomena we designate as "physical" exist *within* the much vaster world of the soul—the imaginal domain. They are *secondary* phenomena within the *primary* realm of True Imagination. Our perception of stone energies is a *direct* experience in the subtle/psychoid/imaginal/soul realm. That is what makes this work so unique and exciting. Soul-to-soul contact nourishes and enlivens soul.

[NOTE: Having repeatedly used the four closely related terms—soul, imaginal, psychoid, subtle—for the domain we are exploring, I will try to write in less cumbersome language from here onwards, using only the words that I feel best apply in each instance. However, it is still important to hold in mind that all four of these overlapping ideas are implied.]

Why do we find our contact with stone energies so compelling? Why do we bother to meditate with them and try to understand their spiritual qualities? Because *we aspire to fulfill our own entelechy*—our own encoded intentionality—through receiving what the stones' energies offer us. And there is more to this. By engaging with the Stone Beings, we can help them fulfill *their* purpose—their encoded intentionality. This mutual nourishment is what the Activity of Blessing looks like in regard to our relationships with stones. It is yet another example of the co-creative feedback loop symbolized by the oroborous.

As we approach the idea of co-creation from this direction, we find ourselves yet again facing one of the mysteries of the universe: The more attention we give to beings in the imaginal realm, the more real they become! And this is not simply our "fantasy" becoming more vivid. It actually happens, and manifests in a multitude of ways.

Psychologist, alchemist and author Jeffrey Raff has described this phenomenon in his book *Ally Work*. Raff does a lot of work in the imaginal/psychoid realm, and in *Ally Work* he focuses on practices by which we can meet and develop a relationship with the being he calls the Ally. He describes the Ally as, "my divine partner, twin of my soul." (I believe the Ally has much in common with what I call the Deep Self, though the two terms may not be exactly synonymous.) Raff uses Jung's practice of *active imagination* to enter the subtle/imaginal realm and relate with beings such as the Ally, Sophia, etc. Our own meditative encounters with the Stone Beings occur through very similar processes.

Raff notes that the attention one gives to the Ally helps that being to manifest more and more vividly in the imaginal realm. As this occurs, one's own capacity of imaginal perception is enhanced, and one's ability to access the Ally is also strengthened. Raff writes: "Perception is related to attention and it is through the act of seeing an imaginal entity that the entity becomes more real. The more I see the Ally, the more real the Ally becomes. The Ally then presents itself to me in the way it wishes to be seen and, by my seeing it, becomes more clearly what it first presented."

This circular-sounding feedback loop of mutual nourishment through mutual imagining is an instance of the oroboric nature of co-creative activity. The more we perceive, the more there *is* to perceive. Attention, intention and imagination combine as the creative power of the human being. And because we are meeting real spiritual beings in the overlapping subtle/imaginal realm, which encompasses both spirit and matter, our creative power combines with theirs to bring forth vivid reality out of mere potential.

Another quote from Raff: "At the same time that my perceptual skills increase, the Ally too transforms, becoming more real and less ethereal. As we develop objective reality and the felt sense, the Ally becomes more present and substantial, as if, through our increased perceptual ability, the Ally takes on more substance. It is not clear if the Ally's incarnating improves our imaginal skill or vice versa, but that is not important. What is important is that the relationship grows as perception does, and as the relationship grows, so does perceptual skill."

In this longer quote from Raff, the activity of co-creating in the imaginal realm is described in greater detail:

> *How can the Ally become more real if it is already real?*
>
> *To understand what I mean, it is necessary to recall our map of reality. The upper world of pure spirit remains unknown to us. Spiritual beings such as the Ally enter the imaginal world in order to be perceived. By the same token, we enter the imaginal world in order to perceive them. However, the Ally does not enter the imaginal world all at once. It is as if the image it creates for itself can only hold a certain amount of the Ally's energy, so it remains relatively weak and indistinct. When a person enters the imaginal realm, he or she brings along a certain amount of skill or knowledge that facilitates perception of an imaginal figure. A person with more skill may perceive more clearly than someone who has less skill. As our skills increase we can discern more of the imaginal space. In the same way, the Ally has a limited ability to incarnate in the imaginal realm and only if that capacity increases does it become more apparent in every way. As Ally work progresses therefore, the Ally image becomes stronger and holds more of the energy of the Ally, so that the Ally* incarnates *in the image. As a result the image gains in power and distinctiveness. It seems to the partner that his or her Ally has become more real. Just as it is our goal to increase our perceptual abilities, it is the Ally's goal to bring more of its personality into the image it has forged. Ultimately the image and the Ally are one.*
>
> —Jeffrey Raff, *Ally Work*, pgs 43-44) [roman mine–RS]

Raff's explanation makes vividly clear that the Ally is a real being who wishes to work with the human partner. The initial image into which the Ally's energy gradually enters is like an artist's preliminary sketch of what will ultimately become a complete painting. But in this case, the effort is co-creative. The Ally's initial "sketch" gives the human being something to work with, and as the human partner contributes attention, intention and imagination to the relationship with the Ally, the sketch becomes more vivid. With a more vivid image, more of the Ally's fullness can manifest, and so on. This reciprocal feedback is akin to the image of the double oroborous. And the "third thing" which is greater than the parts is the *relationship* that is being nourished through the co-creative activity. This can eventually become a full-fledged *conjunction*—a mystic union of the human self with the divine twin.

In our work with stones, the same sorts of processes unfold. I'll share an example. I have told this story elsewhere, so I'll make it brief.

THE EVOLUTION OF AZEZTULITE

Of all our stones, the one that came to us in the most unusual fashion was Azeztulite. We were told by our friend Naisha Ahsian that during her meditations she had encountered a group-soul angelic entity—the Azez. The being(s) communicated that "Azez" referred to the Nameless Light of the Great Central Sun, which they served. The Azez urged Naisha to alert me and Kathy to their prediction that we would soon encounter a stone which they had "activated" to carry the Nameless Light energies. The beings advised that the stone, when found, should be called Azeztulite. Through Naisha, we were told that Azeztulite had the potential to become a source via which much spiritual Light could come into people who worked with it, and to the Earth. The Azez also foretold that, as their agenda unfolded, more and more varieties of Azeztulite would be discovered in various locations around the globe.

In a matter of months from Naisha's initial encounter with the Azez, the first Azeztulite stones came into our hands, in (of course!) a highly synchronistic way. And during the ensuing years, thousands of people acquired Azeztulite through our company, Heaven and Earth. Their reports verified Azeztulite's original description as a stone of spiritual Light. And Azeztulite was subsequently discovered in over a dozen different locations around the world (so far).

In the real-life story above, we might notice several elements that correspond to the discussion in this chapter:

1. Naisha's meditative encounter with the Azez occurred in what I would now call the imaginal realm. She was also able to go back into that space and engage with them several more times. Since then, other people, including myself, have encountered these beings in meditation and dreams. (Readers may recall that, in one dream, the Azez appeared to me as a threesome, cheerfully advising me to, "Dance or die!")
2. The stones which came to us, and which we named Azeztulite, per the instructions from the Azez, were most definitely what the alchemists would have termed "seeds." They were *"living forces with encoded intentionality"*—namely, to bring spiritual Light to humanity and to the Earth. People who feel the currents of Azeztulite would almost unanimously agree with this description, and we have many letters which testify to that. It is interesting that in Naisha's initial report of her encounter, the being(s) described themselves as angelic and used the word Azez to refer both to themselves and to the energy they served. This energy is their "message". The being(s), the stone, and the "message" (i.e. the coded intentionality and/or purpose) are all one.
3. The Azez (and all the Stone Beings) are "angelic"' because they are beings of pure spirit who enter the imaginal realm, the realm in which meditation occurs, in order to work co-creatively with humans to *manifest their message* on all levels of reality.

MANIFESTING THE MESSAGE

Perhaps the most interesting aspect of this story is something we observed with the Azeztulite stones and the way people responded to them. In the beginning, Azeztulite appealed almost exclusively to people who were pretty far along the crystal path, and who had highly developed sensitivities to stone energies. Other people usually couldn't feel Azeztulite's vibes, and were not as strongly attracted to it. However, the highly sensitive people responded very powerfully to the stones, frequently with tears and strong emotions. Even those who had not heard any of the Azeztulite story reported inner experiences of a beautiful and holy Light.

Over time, as more and more people encountered and acquired Azeztulite, *it became easier and easier for people to feel its energies.* This led to an explosion of interest in Azeztulite, which quickly became our most popular stone. At the mineral shows we attended, I experimented with handing pieces of Azeztulite to a wide variety of individuals, including those who disbelieved in the whole idea of stone energies. During this period, I observed many instances in which people who expected nothing to happen were surprised (even shocked) and deeply moved by the experience of feeling stone energies for the first time. This phenomenon continues to this day, and, if anything, it is getting stronger.

This observation—that, over time, it has become easier for more people to perceive the energies of certain stones such as Azeztulite—is demonstrative of biologist Rupert Sheldrake's theory of morphic resonance and the building of morphic fields of consciousness. It has been reported that after researchers taught rats to run a maze at Harvard, rats in Britain seemed to draw upon that knowledge and learned the maze more quickly. Sheldrake also found evidence that people who wait to work Tuesday's newspaper crossword puzzle on Wednesday can solve it more easily, theoretically because thousands of others had already solved the same puzzle, and there was a "memory" of solving the puzzle in the human morphic field.

Such observations have profound implications in regard to our picture of reality and in regard to the insights of the ancient alchemists. Remember their assertion that when one alchemist succeeded in creating the Philosophers' Stone, this event had the potential to redeem the entire cosmos. (This kind of universal redemption is essentially the entelechy—the encoded intentionality—of Azeztulite.) From the point of view of morphic resonance, the idea of a single alchemist influencing the morphic field of the cosmos is plausible.

From the point of view of the Alchemy of Stones, the more people who consciously work with Azeztulite (or any other stone), the more powerful the influence of the human/stone co-creative intention will become. It will not only become easier for more people to feel the stone, but also the entelechy or encoded intentionality of the stone will manifest more fully.

One interesting thing that we have witnessed and experienced repeatedly points to the idea that the Azez are indeed present in the imaginal/psychoid realm of subtle matter-energy. Over the past twenty-five years, Kathy and I have exhibited and sold Azeztulite and many other stones at trade shows and at my workshops. At these events, I have introduced Azeztulite to literally thousands of people and have told the Azeztulite story countless times.

During these conversations, there often comes a point at which I suddenly get an "energy rush" that gives me head-to-toe goose bumps. When I mention it to the customer(s), it usually turns out that he, she, or they felt the energy and got the goose bumps at the same moment that I did. Sometimes they have mentioned it before I did. This has happened hundreds of times. I have come to view this experience as the presence of the Azez, making themselves known to us as we discussed them and their mission. The fact that we quite literally *felt them* (even without having intended to), and that we all had bodily symptoms in unison, convinces me that the Azez were truly with us, in the in-between psychoid region of subtle matter-energy. I am sure that we felt their presence through our own subtle bodies, and that the physical symptoms occurred in resonance with that. (This kind of thing can also happen with other stones, but I have experienced it the most with Azeztulite.)

Another aspect of the manifestation of the message (the encoded intentionality) of the Azez and Azeztulite is the fact that, true to the prediction given to us through Naisha over twenty-five years ago, more stones carrying the Azeztulite energies have been discovered around the world. I have found several of them myself, and in each case, I have felt that I was guided to them by inner urges and intuitive promptings, as well as by synchronicities in the "outer" world. Perhaps the Azez are also involved in giving me these psychic "nudges." Whether they are directly responsible or not, their original prediction has continued to manifest.

All of the details I have mentioned here are related to Raff's idea that perception feeds manifestation, and manifestation feeds the enhancement of perception, which then nourishes even more vivid manifestation, and so on, *ad infinitum.* It also underscores that when we encounter the Stone Beings in the imaginal realm, we are meeting actual beings, who have gifts to give us, and who desire the gifts we can offer them. In both cases, these gifts are related to the realization of the entelechy—the *soul purpose* of both the Stone Beings and ourselves.

In my view, the Alchemy of Stones is a particularly wonderful path of spiritual alchemy, because the Stone Beings, unlike many other entities one can meet in the imaginal realm, are grounded in physical reality. The stones have utterly solid (and beautiful!) physical bodies that are nonetheless endowed with powerful subtle energies. And like ourselves, and Raff's Ally, the Stone Beings can manifest in the imaginal realm, both as energies and in the forms of their subtle bodies.

As we practice our co-creative alchemy with the Stone Beings, their subtle bodies are enhanced—they become more vivid, more fully developed and more powerful. And because we are involved with them in a mutually beneficial feedback loop, we discover that our own subtle bodies are becoming stronger and more active at the same time. This development of the subtle body is one of the key aspirations of spiritual alchemy, and it is something that brings us through a profound process of transformation.

17

The Subtle-Imaginal Body

It is clear enough . . . what the ultimate aim of alchemy really was: it was trying to produce a corpus subtile [subtle body], a transfigured and resurrected body, i.e., a body that was at the same time spirit.

—Carl Jung, *Collected Works* 12, para 511

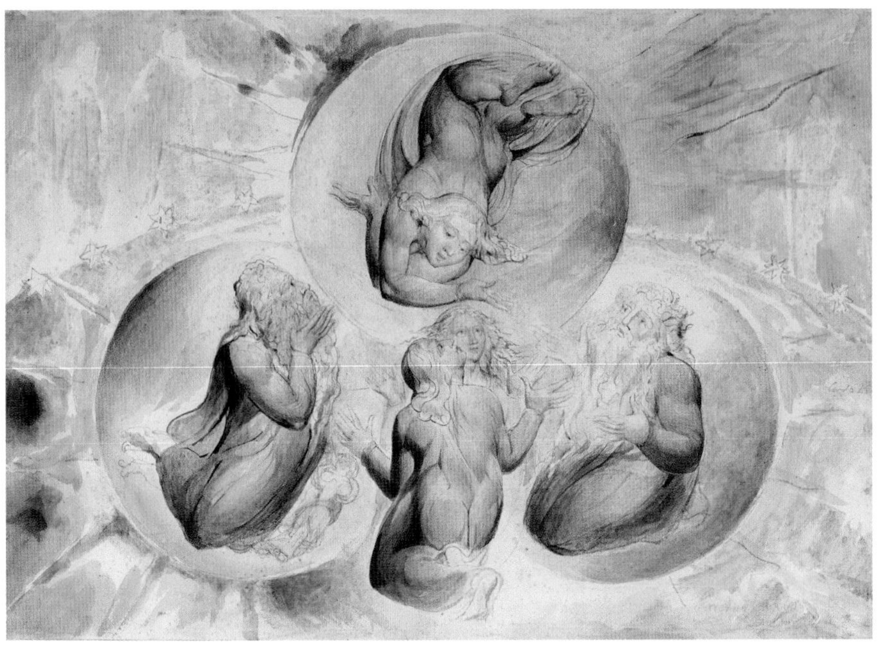

There is another possibility, that of the subtle body, a fine material veil of the soul, which cannot exist so to speak without a body. This is the "corpus glorificationis" (glorified body), the transfigured body, which is our future portion.

—Carl Jung, ETH, Lecture XIV, page 115.

In the quotes above, Jung indicates that the building of the subtle body was, in a sense, synonymous with the creation of the Philosophers' Stone, the ultimate goal of alchemy. He also hints that the manifestation of the subtle body is our destiny—our "future portion." Thus, it would be hard to overestimate the significance of the fact that working with stone energies can enhance and strengthen the subtle body. It is also interesting to note that Jung viewed the subtle body as something that must be *produced.* It is not simply a given, but is something that we only have in *potential.* It is rather like an embryo, which can, but may not, fully develop. In the case of one's subtle body—unlike a physical embryo—the process of development must be done consciously and intentionally. Fortunately, because of the Stone Beings and Sophia, we do not have to do our work alone.

Before committing oneself to a lengthy and somewhat tenuous inner process, it is fair to ask ourselves, "Is all this for real?" I have certainly asked myself that question at many points on my path, and when I have truly looked, the answers I have discovered have always encouraged me to continue. So let's look at this question together.

ABOVE: Painting by William Blake: Saint Peter, Saint James and Saint John with Dante and Beatrice

EVIDENCE FOR THE REALITY OF THE SUBTLE-IMAGINAL BODY

We have already given consideration to the idea that what we experience when we feel the currents of stones is subtle energy or subtle matter-energy. The distinctive patterns of the Stone Beings and ourselves in the subtle/imaginal/psychoid realm are our subtle bodies—our soul bodies. One of the things that makes alchemy an ideal paradigm for our work with stones is that the alchemists were highly aware of the imaginal realm, and they utilized the three powers of attention, intention and imagination in all of their endeavors. They worked inwardly to manifest transformation in both the inner and outer aspects of themselves and the substances used in their endeavors.

At this point, I want to offer evidence to drive home the point that the subtle-imaginal body is real, and that in recognizing this we gain a golden opportunity to live with much greater freedom, personal power and understanding. I am sure most readers of this book already have a certain sense of agreement with this idea, and some may already be working extensively with the subtle body. In my own case, even though I would always have agreed with the idea of having a subtle-imaginal body, I didn't necessarily "feel it" as my living reality. My unconscious attachments to the materialist worldview got in the way, even though I did not consciously believe in materialism. It took much study, practice and contemplation to get to the place at which I suddenly thought, in regard to the subtle body: "Aha! Of course! Now it all makes sense!" The evidence below is meant to help bring you to the same place.

Our subtle bodies are in close relationship with our physical bodies, and they affect one another all the time. In a certain sense, one could say that both the physical body and the subtle body are complex living patterns that are intertwined with one another. The subtle body is finer and more mutable. Because it exists in the imaginal realm, we can learn to influence the subtle body's patterns through working with focused imagination. (Once again, the three human powers of attention, intention and imagination come into play.)

METAPHYSICAL HEALING

One of the ideas common to many metaphysically oriented healing modalities is that if we are able to correct a problematic pattern in the subtle-imaginal body, the correction can resonate into the physical body.

In shamanic healing, this is exactly what happens. The shamanic practitioner is usually someone with a gift of inner vision that facilitates her perception in the imaginal realm. With appropriate training, she can enter and familiarize herself with the various shamanic worlds and can become acquainted with Spirit Helpers—beings who manifest in the imaginal realm—who are willing to aid the shamanic practitioner in her intention to help people heal.

In a typical healing session, the shaman will view her client's subtle-imaginal body and will recognize where the client's pattern needs to be corrected. There are a variety of images that the shaman may see, indicating different sorts of problems. Physical illnesses such as cancer may show themselves as dark splotches or gray areas in the client's imaginal body, or in other ways. Different types of images may indicate negative attachments, "implants," soul loss, or other issues.

The shaman's "view" of the client's imaginal body may not be strictly visual, and may be "felt" more than "seen." But we are still talking about "image." (An inner image can manifest in a variety of ways.) The shamanic healer may work independently, utilizing her own imaginal body. Or she may work with Spirit Helpers who can assist, or even do the work themselves. I have experienced a number of shamanic healing sessions with my wife Kathy, and I have frequently seen them produce dramatic improvements, both in myself and in her other clients.

My point here is not to attempt to fully summarize shamanic healing, but to show how this form of healing, which is humanity's oldest healing modality, works in the imaginal realm of subtle matter/energy to bring about healing on all levels.

Additional metaphysical healing modalities that work on the subtle-imaginal body include Reiki, EFT, Polarity Therapy and numerous others. Many body workers, osteopaths and chiropractors work with "energy balancing," which is something that occurs on the subtle body level. Acupuncture works through subtle body channels called the meridians. (The acupuncture points do not directly correspond to neural structures or blood vessels, but to dynamic patterns existing in the subtle body.)

THE PLACEBO EFFECT

In mainstream medicine, the "placebo effect" is one of the best-known and least-understood phenomena. In medical studies in which some patients are treated with inert substances (placebos) such as sugar pills or saline injections, patients improve, even though no physically active "medicine" was given to them. This has been something of an embarrassment to orthodox doctors, who often dismiss the positive results, even though the average effectiveness of placebos has been shown to be about 30% to 50%, and in some cases even higher.

The placebo effect has been studied extensively, because new medications are typically tested against placebos. If the actual drug is not significantly more effective than the placebo, it is thought to be an ineffective treatment. However, if the medication is, for example, 60% effective and the placebo is 50% effective, the medication is usually credited with having caused the entire positive effect, even though a placebo effect may have caused most of it.

A few facts to dramatize this:

1 The U.S. Department of Health reports that 50% of severely depressed people get better if they take an antidepressant like Prozac, while 32% of depressed people get better if they take a sugar pill they *think* is an antidepressant. An analysis of thirty-nine studies done between 1974 and 1995 showed that, among depressed patients treated with drugs, psychotherapy, or a combination of both, 50% of the drug effect was due to the placebo response.

2 A placebo presented as a stimulant will have a stimulant-type effect on heart rhythm and blood pressure, but when the same placebo is administered as a depressant, the opposite effect occurs. Studies have found that the color and size of the placebo pill make a difference, with "hot-colored" pills working better as stimulants while "cool-colored" pills work better as depressants. Placebo capsules rather than tablets seem to be more effective, and size can make a difference. One researcher has found that big pills increase the effect. A silver-coated capsule got some of the best recorded results. Placebo injections appear to be more effective than pills, and placebo surgery gets even better results.

3 Placebos have shown benefits in treating chronic pain, Parkinson's Disease, cancer, chronic fatigue syndrome, migraine headaches and a vast number of other conditions.

4 There is a complementary negative phenomenon called the *nocebo* effect. When patients anticipate a side effect of a medication, they can suffer that effect even if the "medication" is actually an inert substance. One article that reviewed thirty-one studies on nocebo effects reported a wide range of symptoms including nausea, stomach pains, itching, bloating, depression, sleep problems, loss of appetite, sexual dysfunction and severe hypotension.

5 Both the placebo and nocebo effects can induce measurable changes in the body and the brain.

6 Placebos have been shown to produce beneficial effects *even when the patient is aware that the treatment is a placebo.* This suggests that the subconscious mind and the subtle body are responding to the placebo, even though the conscious mind is aware that the substance is not a "real" medication.

So what does all this have to do with our discussion of the subtle-imaginal body? In my view, the reason for the placebo effect is that *the imagination of the patient is shifting the patterns in the subtle-imaginal body,* and this change results in a corresponding beneficial physical outcome. The same sort of thing occurs in reverse when the nocebo effect generates a detrimental physical outcome.

It is likely that the greatest part of this is occurring subconsciously. People have become accustomed to taking pills or injections when they are ill, and one's subconscious associates receiving such treatments with being healed. The subconscious mind *imagines and therefore "intends"* the beneficial change, and *the subtle-imaginal body responds* in accord with the imagined/intended pattern. The physical body senses the change in its subtle body counterpart and is influenced in the direction of the imaginal pattern. (This description may make the subtle and physical bodies seem more separate than they really are. I suspect they are not separate at all, but this is something to be discovered through experience.)

So, why don't placebos always work? And for that matter, why do shamanic healings, reiki, or prescription drugs sometimes fail to produce cures? I think it is likely that the subtle-imaginal body *influences* the physical body, but does not control it. Or our vacillations may undermine the potential cure: in the course of an hour or a day, one may consciously or unconsciously imagine a variety of different things in regard to one's ailments, ranging from strong confidence to intense anxiety. Such variations might act to confuse or undermine the potential benefits of any treatment. (The Chinese alchemists believed that most people's subtle bodies are relatively weak and undeveloped, and that meditative practice can produce much better results.)

However, the important insight for our purpose now is that *the placebo effect strongly indicates the reality of the subtle-imaginal body,* and it suggests that this body responds when attention, intention and imagination are focused on it. When we realize this, a whole range of possibilities opens up, and we can begin to picture new ways to facilitate healing in ourselves and others.

HOMEOPATHIC MEDICINES

Homeopathy is a system of alternative medicine developed in 1796 by Samuel Hahnemann, based on the alchemical doctrine of *like cures like.* This idea suggests that a substance which causes the symptoms of a disease in healthy people would *cure* similar symptoms in sick people. Homeopathic medicines involve diluting the original substance repeatedly, often until there is no discernible trace of the physical substance remaining in the remedy.

From a materialistic standpoint, homeopathic medicines could not possibly work, since there is no measurable "medicine" in most of them. Orthodox doctors typically ascribe any positive effects of homeopathic remedies to the placebo effect.

I have personally found that homeopathic remedies can work very well. I take Arnica Montana for muscle pain, Ledum Palustre for insect bites, Pulsatilla for nasal congestion, etc. The three remedies I have named here have worked for me many times, and for others who tried them at my suggestion. (Ledum Palustre in particular relieves the discomfort of insect bites in minutes.)

How is this possible? Are homeopathic remedies simply placebos?

Even if homeopathic remedies were nothing more than placebos, their effectiveness would still support the contention that the subtle-imaginal body is real, just as the effects of placebos do. However, I think there is more to this.

Earlier I made the assertion that every self-organized object or creature is a "self," existing in the realm of soul. The domain of soul is the same as that of the subtle-imaginal body. Our soul can be called a pattern of selfhood, and from the perspective I am taking, all of the substances from which homeopathic remedies are derived have their own particular pattern of soul qualities. You could call these their identities, their entelechies, or their encoded intentionalities. (With stones, we call such patterns their metaphysical qualities.)

A homeopathic remedy may be diluted until it contains no measurable trace of the original physical substance, but in the imaginal realm *it could still resonate with and invoke the subtle body of the substance.* When we take the remedy, we engender a conjunction of our own subtle body with that of the substance associated with the remedy. Then our own subtle body's pattern will shift in response to the presence of the imaginal pattern of the remedy substance. Since homeopathic remedies frequently utilize substances that cause the symptoms we want to get rid of, it seems that the interaction between the subtle-imaginal bodies of the substance and oneself triggers something like an *immune response* in one's subtle body. This can then produce a resonant effect in the physical body, relieving one's symptoms.

Once again, I have gone into discussing homeopathy primarily to offer more evidence for the reality of our subtle-imaginal bodies. However, there are also implications for how we may engage with the Stone Beings and their energies for healing. I think a pattern similar to the one described for homeopathy may be a useful way of picturing what happens when we do stone layouts or carry a stone for the purpose of healing.

OTHER EVIDENCE FOR THE SUBTLE-IMAGINAL BODY

1. **PHANTOM LIMB PHENOMENON:** A phantom limb is the sensation that an amputated or missing limb is still attached. Approximately 60% to 80% of individuals with an amputation experience phantom sensations in their amputated limb, and the majority of the sensations are painful. Phantom sensations may also occur after the removal of body parts other than the limbs, e.g. after amputation of the breast, extraction of a tooth (phantom tooth pain) or removal of an eye (phantom eye syndrome). Animals also appear to experience this. A Wikipedia article on phantom limb includes a video of a cat attempting to scoop litter with a missing leg that had been amputated months before. I believe that the phantom limb phenomenon offers some of the strongest evidence of the reality of the subtle-imaginal body.
2. **VISUALIZATION FOR HEALING:** Guided imagination has been shown to be beneficial in treating headaches, coronary artery disease and chronic pain; also in ameliorating the symptoms of chemotherapy-induced nausea, vomiting, and localized physical pain in patients with cancer. If my premise is correct, the visualizations would change the patterns in the subtle-imaginal body, thereby beneficially influencing the physical body.
3. **VISUALIZATION FOR SPORTS PERFORMANCE:** In 1984 the Russians realized that Olympic athletes who mentally rehearsed their sport experienced a positive impact on their performance. Since then, this effect has been documented by thousands of athletes in virtually every sport. In my view, visualization rehearsals such as these implant a desired pattern in the subtle-imaginal body, which then aligns with the physical body, and the result of their harmonious accord is improved performance.
4. **NEAR-DEATH EXPERIENCES:** Most readers know of the phenomenon of near-death experiences, a person who has clinically "died" or is close to death finds himself or herself outside the body, awake and aware of the surroundings. Sometimes the experiencer reports having a body-image, and at other times the person seems to be simply a point of awareness, often hovering over the physical body. However, even when a body-image is not perceived, the experiencer typically has the senses of vision and hearing, and the ability to move about. Being able to see and hear events in the physical world (and often in realms not discernable to everyday consciousness) are attributes that clearly suggest the existence of the subtle body.
5. **ASTRAL TRAVEL:** Astral travel is a term used to describe a person's self-willed travel without the physical body to other places in the physical world (and sometimes elsewhere). It typically involves visualization and/or perception of an "astral body" which closely resembles what I have been calling the subtle-imaginal body. Untold thousands of people have

engaged in this practice, including the well-known author Robert Monroe who published several books on the subject. Astral travel has been known and practiced for thousands of years, and in a variety of cultures, including the ancient Egyptians, Greeks, Chinese, Hindu, Native American, Inuit and Japanese cultures, among many others.

6 **APPARITIONS:** Apparitions are perceptual experiences of non-physical beings. Most often these are the souls of deceased people. Mediums who work as spirit communicators for clients who hope to contact friends or relatives who have died frequently "see" the deceased in an imaginal body form. When the medium describes the image to the client, the deceased person is frequently recognized. In other cases, friends or relatives have their own visions of the person who has died. Often, the imaginal body image shows the deceased individual looking much younger and healthier, frequently to the surprise of the experiencer. All of these apparitional experiences indicate the reality of the subtle-imaginal body.

Various esoteric systems assert that we have not one but several non-physical bodies—astral, etheric, subtle, causal, etc. I do not dispute these ideas, but neither am I expert enough to validate or write about them. I also feel that to do so would complicate things and take us too far afield from our focus on the Alchemy of Stones. For my purposes in this book, it is sufficient to simply work with the idea of a subtle-imaginal body. I tend to think that if we can begin with this as our strong assumption, our actual experiences will reveal the reality of the situation. This, I believe, is preferable to making an overly complex set of mental "maps."

THE SUBTLE-IMAGINAL BODY IN ALCHEMY

As we have seen, alchemists were very much engaged with imagination as a creating force in their work. Jung and the alchemists believed that the aim of alchemy was to take "material" which begins in a chaotic state and, through inner and outer processes of purification and transmutation, bring forth the same material, but in its perfected state. The perfected material was called the Philosophers' Stone, as we have discussed. Jung further stated that the Philosophers' Stone was identical with the whole and integrated Self. The Self or Philosophers' Stone was formed in the alchemical Third Conjunction, in which the individual human being, having come to a state of wholeness in the human personality, joins with its own divine spark, giving birth to a new and greater being. The alchemists and Jung both insisted that the Philosophers' Stone or Self was always present in latent form, even within the chaotic state in which the material began. Alchemy as a whole, especially spiritual alchemy, was always directed toward facilitating this great transformation.

There is more to this than a purely "inner" experience. In the quote that begins this section, Jung asserts that the ultimate aim of alchemy was, "to produce a *corpus subtile* [subtle body], a transfigured and resurrected body, i.e., a body that was at the same time spirit." Here we see that the culmination of the alchemical endeavor was envisioned as bringing forth a new body—in Jung's words, "the *corpus glorificationis* (glorified body), the transfigured body, which is our future portion." This perfected and enlivened body would be a human-divine incarnation centered in the subtle-imaginal realm. Jung tells us that this is our "future portion"—our ultimate destiny.

The renowned 16th century alchemist Paracelsus delineated the distinctions between the physical body and the subtle-imaginal body, as well as their unity:

> *Man has also an animal body and a sidereal [subtle-imaginal] body; and both are one and are not separated. The relation between the two is as follows. The animal body, the body of flesh and blood, is in itself always dead. Only through the action of the sidereal body does the motion of life come into the other body.*

We might initially be shocked by Paracelsus' assertion that "the animal body . . . is in itself always dead." However, what he is saying is that our physical body is animated by the soul. In fact, the word "animation" is derived from the word *anima,* meaning soul. Without the soul's presence, the physical body cannot live. I tend to agree with Paracelsus. (A world of living bodies without souls sounds like a world of zombies, which can, in a sense, come about when we forget our vital connection with soul.)

Paracelsus uses the term "sidereal body" for what I am calling the subtle-imaginal body. The meaning of "sidereal" is: "of, or relating to, the stars." Earlier in this book, I quoted another saying of Paracelsus: "Imagination is the star in man." When we consider these two quotes together, we notice that Paracelsus is basically describing the subtle-imaginal body as a "star body." Further, since "imagination is the star in man," we can conclude that Paracelsus is telling his readers that the sidereal body is the "star body," aka the body of imagination—the subtle-imaginal body.

One of the complications in working through the writings on the subtle-imaginal body is, as I have mentioned, the plethora of different names for it. One of the names is "astral body," which is linked in meaning to the concept of the sidereal [star] body that Paracelsus expressed. A Wikipedia article about the astral body states: "According to [Rosicrucian author] Max Heindel, the term 'astral body' was employed by the medieval Alchemists because of the ability it conferred to traverse the 'starry' regions. The 'Astral body' is regarded as the 'Philosophers' Stone' or 'Living Stone' of the alchemist, the 'Wedding Garment' of the Gospel of Matthew, and the 'Soul body' that Paul mentions in the First Epistle to the Corinthians."

I was interested to see the Biblical references, but what really excited me in finding these quotes was the image of a "'star body" that could "traverse the starry regions." I was suddenly reminded of two powerful visionary experiences from my past.

THE SUBTLE BODY AS A SPHERE OF LIGHT

Many years ago, when I was in my twenties, I practiced Trasnscendental Meditation. This is a type of meditation in which one quiets one's self-talk and other distracting mental activity by inwardly repeating a sacred word—a mantra. (The Beatles band members famously involved themselves with T. M., and its founder, Maharishi Mahesh Yogi.) Though I eventually discontinued the practice, I had one experience that stands out in my memory.

Around dusk on warm a summer day, I lay down on my bed to do my twenty minutes of meditation. I closed my eyes and began to inwardly repeat the mantra. After some length of time, I forgot about the mantra and dropped into an utter silence,

Suddenly I was in another place, another realm. I was in an unbounded space of diffuse silvery light, and I was not alone. Beside me were two beings who appeared as spheres of white light, with overtones of gold. I became aware that my own "body" was also a sphere of gold-white light.

The other spheres were communicating with me telepathically. We were discussing the fact that I was about to descend into a physical body to be born on Earth. One of the beings wordlessly "said" to me something that more or less corresponded to these words: "Of course, you realize that when you do this, you will forget what you are."

I agreed that, yes, I knew this.

In the next instant, my "sphere" of self-awareness shot down—seemingly from a vast distance—the length of a long, thin silver thread that took me to the Earth, and into the body, in infant form, that became "me."

In the room where I lay on the bed, my eyes opened. I was both shaken and thrilled by the experience I had just had. I felt that I had recalled a vivid pre-birth memory. To this day, it remains one of my clearest recollections.

Readers of this book may recall from Chapter 1 the story of the first meditation in which I felt the energies of Moldavite. In that experience, I went on a visionary journey to a golden star (that I later identified as the Great Central Sun), and in that vision I suddenly saw my own spherical Body of Light:

> *At one point, I saw a golden star far away, and I knew that I wanted to go to it, so I willed myself there. In a short time, the golden star had become an immense golden sun, and it emanated a light that felt holy. Then I noticed that there were thousands, or perhaps millions, of golden orbs circling the golden sun, each with a thin gold thread linking the orb to the Sun. The orbs seemed to be alive, like a procession of souls, circling in adoration around the golden Sun. I was deeply moved by this vision, and I wondered if the golden orbs were really souls. At that point, I also wondered what my own body might look like in this place. I turned my attention downward, toward where my chest would have been, and was surprised to see another golden orb about twelve inches in diameter, encompassing the space around my heart. And there was a golden thread that linked my own orb to the great golden Sun.*
>
> *I was filled with awe and wonder, and my thoughts became silent. Then I suddenly heard a deep, resonant voice—perhaps like the voice of an angel—saying clearly, "The Light you seek without is identical to the Light within."*
>
> *In the next moment, several things happened. I suddenly realized that the golden orbs were souls, and that I was one of them . . .*

Painting by William Blake *Stepping Out of the Sun*

I recount these events here because the experience of being embodied as a sphere of light is not just my own. It is one of the classic descriptions of the subtle body, and it may be utilized in our meditations in the Alchemy of Stones.

In the book *The Subtle Body in the Western Tradition,* author G.R. Mead quotes a variety of sources from the ancient Greeks and Romans. One of these is the Platonist Philoponus, who wrote:

> *There is, moreover . . . another kind of body, that is forever attached to the soul, of a celestial nature, and for this reason everlasting, which they call radiant (*augocides*) or starlike (*astroeides*) . . . the matter of celestial bodies is not of the four elements, but there is another kind of body—the fifth element, or quintessence, and its form (*eidos*) is spherical.*

Mead also quotes the Roman Marcus Aurelius, who wrote:

*The sphere of the soul is radiant (*augocides*) when it is neither extended to any object, nor is contracted inwards, nor is convoluted, nor collapses, but when it is made to shine with that light whereby it sees the truth—the truth of all things, and the truth in itself.*

Mead goes on to say:

In classical Greek, augoeides *is an adjective meaning "possessed of a form of* auge"*—that is, of a form of splendor, radiance; hence brilliant, shining, radiant, ray-like, luciform, glorious, etc.*

I'll use one last excerpt from Mead, in which he quotes the ancient Greek Platonic teacher Damascius, who wrote:

*In Heaven indeed, our radiant (*augocides*) portion is full-filled with heavenly radiance (*ague*)—a glory that streams throughout its depths, and lends it a divine strength.*

In discovering Mead's book on the subtle body, I was struck by the close similarity between these ancient descriptions of the subtle body (soul body) and my own experiences, which occurred spontaneously and without my having read any such descriptions before.

All of this suggests to me that Paracelsus and the other medieval alchemists were correct in calling the subtle-imaginal body a "star-body," and asserting that it conferred the ability to travel the starry regions. And although we can see that the Sphere of Light is one of the subtle-imaginal body's possible forms, it is good to remember that this body can express itself through various patterns and images, and is not limited to any one of them.

Mead's book confirmed to me that the image of my "body" in my Moldavite journey was quite real. I already believed that the experience had really happened, because it was the event that "switched on" my sensitivity to the energies of stones. Nonetheless, discovering that many others throughout history had described the subtle body as a Sphere of Light provided additional validation. And, of course, the Moldavite, as it "buzzed" in my hand, was the trigger for the sudden infusion of spiritual Light that opened all my chakras and filled me with bliss. Thus, we are once again brought around to the realization that the Stone Beings we work with in the Alchemy of Stones do indeed convey subtle energies which affect our subtle-imaginal bodies in highly noticeable and beneficial ways.

I want to ask you to pause a minute and feel this. You have a subtle-imaginal body, and it is even now being affected by the images conjured within you by the words you are reading. If it's convenient to do so, go and pick up one of the stones in your collection, close your eyes, bring it to your heart and invite its energy into you. When you feel this energy, you are sensing with your subtle-imaginal body, and you are experiencing the exchange between yourself and the Stone Being. As angelic emissaries of Sophia, their gestures to us are motivated by love and generosity, and the currents we feel from them are good for us.

We may be drawn to one or another stone at various times, and I believe that this is due to our Deep Self guiding us to what we most need in a particular moment. Our "need" is continually steering us toward healing and wholeness—the realization of our entelechy. It is always important to be mindful of our inner promptings when we choose stones to work with. Our intuition tends to be more accurate than our preconceived notions.

PRACTICE: TAKING A JOURNEY WITH A STONE BEING IN THE SPHERICAL BODY OF LIGHT

In this practice, we visualize our Subtle Body as a Sphere of Light, and we allow ourselves to travel in it to the "starry regions." We are not necessarily trying to choose a particular place or goal for this journey. Rather, we will allow ourselves to be guided by the Stone Being that we work with.

As I have mentioned elsewhere, each stone can be said to have its own "world." This is a "place" in the subtle/imaginal realm where one can visit with a Stone Being in its own territory. This potentially allows the Stone Being the freedom to fully express its nature and deliver its messages to us. It can offer us particularly vivid experiences that are rich in symbolic meaning. Journeying to the world of a Stone Being can bring about a full immersion in the energies of that stone, leading to insights, healings, and/or a mutually enriching rapport that nourishes both sides.

For this practice, you will need a notebook and a pen to take notes of what occurs. You may even want to have some colored pencils or other drawing supplies at hand, in case you want to sketch any images from the world of the Stone Being.

In this meditative practice, you should find a place where you won't be disturbed for a least half an hour. You may wish to use music, but this is optional. If you play music, use something that feels like it supports your intention, and don't use anything with lyrics that will distract you.

1. Begin by placing the intention in your heart that you desire to journey with a Stone Being to it's world. When I do this, I like to affirm that I want to take whatever journey is for the highest good. Then I release that intention and trust the process as it unfolds.
2. Next, go to your collection and choose the stone with whom you wish to journey. Or, if you are open to it, let the Stone Being choose you. To do this, just look through your stones with a soft focus, and pay attention to your intuition. When you find yourself drawn to a particular stone, that's the one! (If it's more than one, this may be a signal that you should go on more than one journey.)
3. Find a comfortable chair or a quiet place to lie down. Do the Breath of Blessing over the stone and then bring it to your heart. As you breathe with the stone nestled at your chest, invite the Stone Being into your heart as you inhale. Then, as you exhale, offer your friendship and trust to the Stone Being.
4. When you feel the vibrations of the stone, center your attention in your heart, and address the Stone Being with this intention: "Please take me to your world, and show me what is most beneficial for me to see or understand." (If you wish to make a different request, you can do so. However, I do recommend that you ask the Stone Being to take you to its world. You can ask the Stone Being to take you to its world for healing, insight into a problem, purification of your Light Body, etc.)
5. Visualize a sphere of Light surrounding your heart. This is one form of your subtle body, your Body of Light. Now visualize a sphere of Light surrounding the stone you are holding. There is a filament of Light connecting the two spheres.
6. Now imagine that the two connected spheres are floating up together, leaving their physical forms behind. See your two Spheres of Light going up higher and higher. As you lift up, place your viewpoint inside your Sphere of Light. At this point, you will see the Sphere of the Stone Being, but you may not see your own.
7. Allow the experience to unfold as it will. Envision that you are out among the stars in your Sphere of Light, linked with the Sphere of Light of the Stone Being. Pay attention to everything you see and to all that occurs.
8. Eventually, you may see that you are getting closer to a specific star and/or planet. Allow this to happen. At some point, you and the Stone Being will "land" in the Stone Being's "world."
9. From this point onwards, everything you experience in this world is an aspect of the Stone Being itself. Allow the experience to continue. If you feel that nothing is happening or that you are stuck, you can try asking the Stone Being again to help you with your request.

10. At this point, let yourself explore the possibilities. Observe what happens. The Stone Being may appear to you in a different form. It may communicate something to you in words, images, or an exchange of energy. Your own form may continue to be a Sphere of Light, or it may change. (You might discover that your Sphere of Light is for traveling, but that you assume a human form, or another form, when you are in the Stone Being's world. Anything is possible here, and *everything* that happens has a meaning.)
11. You can dialog with the Stone Being if you wish. Try it and see how it works. Remember, according to Paracelsus, dialog with an "invisible" ally was the essence of alchemical meditation.
12. When the experience—however it manifests—feels complete, thank the Stone Being and ask it if it wishes to journey back to this world with you. In most cases, it will do so, but if it declines, don't be concerned. You can find your way back in your Sphere of Light, and the Stone Being may be letting you "fly solo" for just that reason.
13. When you return to your body, allow yourself to get comfortably grounded. You may want to wiggle your toes, etc. Then take notes right away of what you saw, heard and felt. Also, you can make sketches of the Stone Being's world, or things you were shown.

With practice, most people find it quite easy—and often fascinating—to takes these journeys with their Stone Being friends. Envisioning the Sphere of Light and traveling in it can strengthen it and can lead to more and more vivid experiences. The Stone Beings shower us with helpful energies, and this facilitates our manifestation of a stable and coherent subtle body.

We all have a subtle-imaginal body, but what is its condition? Is it already finished and perfect, or is it in something more like the initial chaotic state of the alchemical *prima materia?* Since we are envisioning the subtle-imaginal body as the body of the soul, we must consider that its pattern would reflect all of our psychic imperfections, emotional wounds, addictions, phobias, and so forth—as well as our strengths. This is indeed what the shaman or a gifted healing practitioner perceives when she focuses attention on a client's subtle body. Spiritual alchemy works on healing, purifying and transmuting the psyche, of which the subtle-imaginal body is the expression. So we can agree here with Jung that our goal is to bring forth our subtle body, in a transfigured and glorified incarnation.

It may worry us a bit to think that our subtle body has not yet manifested in its full potential, and that we may have to go through a long process of focused intention and effort to heal and transform it. Nonetheless, this is what the alchemists believed, particularly the ancient Chinese alchemists. We'll take a brief look at some of their ideas and practices, and we may decide that we are not faced with a difficult chore, but with an amazing adventure.

[**NOTE**: In the Dedication of this book to my friend Daniel Deardorff, whose work I have mentioned or quoted in several places, I wrote that Danny died a few months before the book went to press. Consequently, he never got to complete the Introduction I had asked him to write. However, after his passing, we were able to reconnect with one another, and he did provide the inspiration and imagery for the Introduction I wrote.

Some days later, I connected with Danny again. This time, we were able to inwardly "speak" to each other, and we had what was, to me, an astonishing conversation. Part of it involved the subtle body and the way stone energies can affect it, as he viewed these things from his perspective in the soul realm. I have transcribed the conversation, which readers can view in the back of this book. It is labeled Appendix A.]

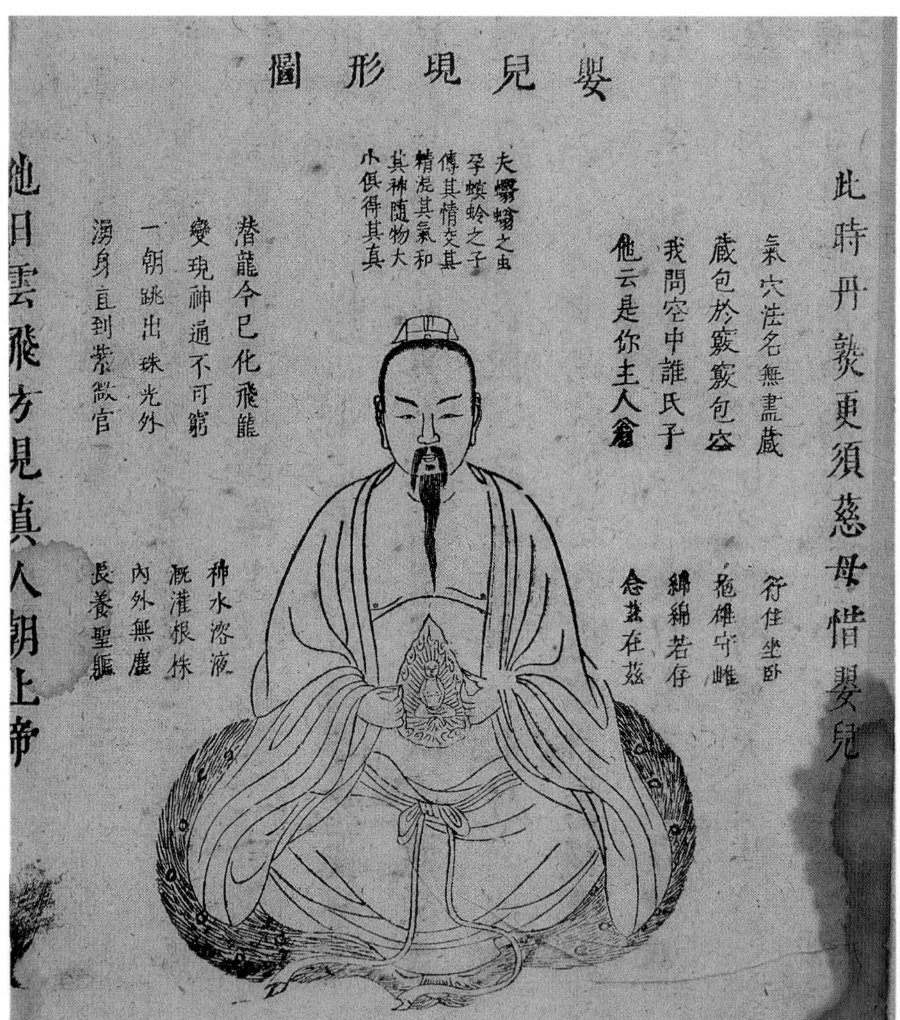

The seed that is present from the beginning, but in latent form, [is called, in Jungian psychological language] the Self. Jung has often compared it, being there from the beginning, with the lattice of a crystal, which though invisible, is present in the solution from the beginning. If for a moment we consider the making of the subtle body as if it were a crystal, the Chinese idea would roughly be that the crystal itself could never form in the solution unless we spend the most profound meditation and concentration upon it, which would enable it to become visible, hard and strong, in the shape predestined from the beginning for that particular crystal.

This necessary concentration on the growth process is expressed in China through many images. Only to mention one: a sage is depicted in deepest meditation, in whose heart a small child is forming. (This is of course the Divine Embryo which is mentioned in The Secret of the Golden Flower, *but is also symbolized in other ways, like the Golden Lotus.) This little child is nourished and cared for there, until at last it is ready to float through the cranial cavity, into the heights of the new Divine birth. This, Wilhelm says, is an image that represents emerging into another order of time, where we can see the whole of life, as from another dimension, and yet at the same time remain energetically* connected *with our present life in our present order of space and time.*

—Barbara Hannah lecturing regarding the Chinese text *The Secret of the Golden Flower,* translated by Richard Wilhelm

The Subtle-Imaginal Body, Chinese Alchemy & Immortality

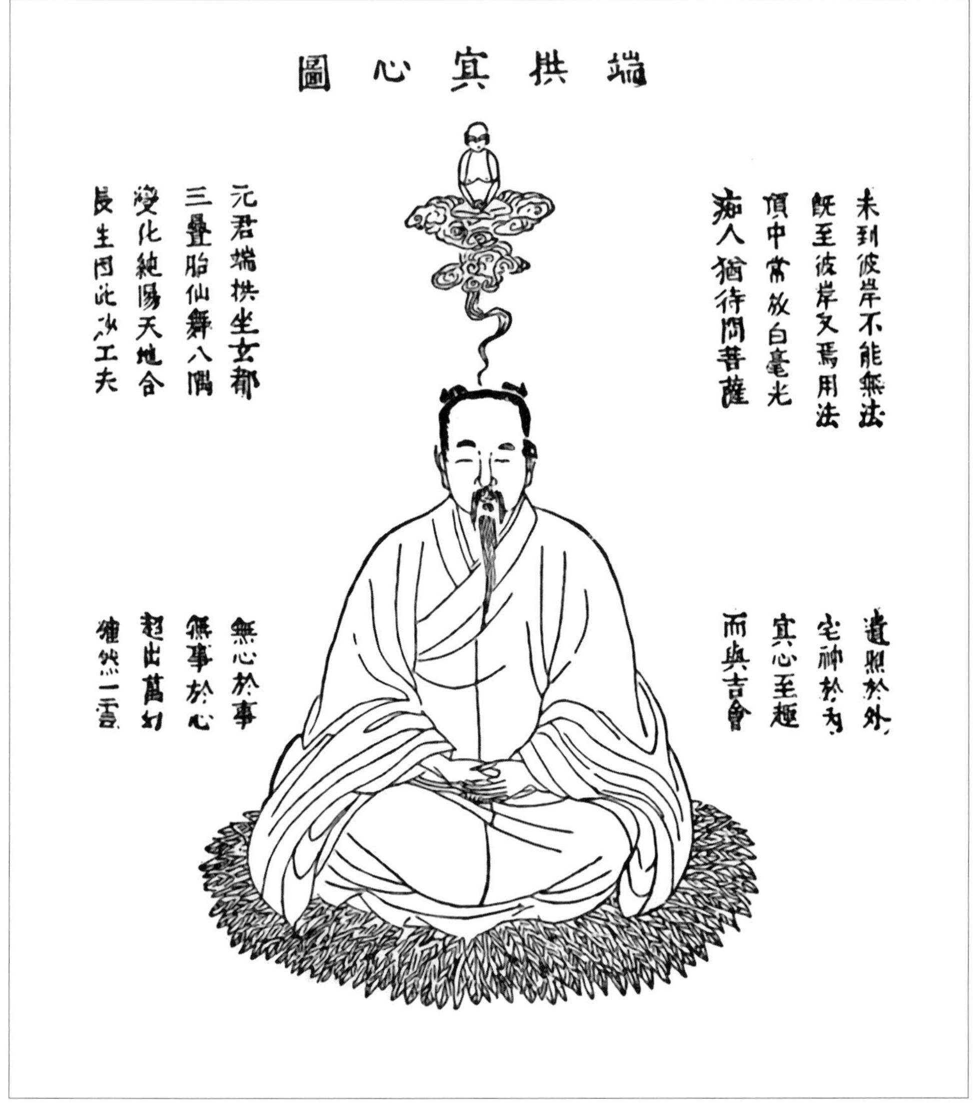

According to the Sinologue [expert on Chinese culture] Richard Wilhelm with whom Jung collaborated by writing an important commentary on the ancient alchemical text, "The Secret of the Golden Flower," Confucius held that spirit, far from being something that grows naturally in man, must be acquired in the course of life by strenuous effort. In Wilhelm's words, the spirit:

> *"... leads a somewhat precarious existence unless it has been so concentrated in the course of life: that it has already 'built itself a kind of subtle body of a spiritual nature,' made as it were of thoughts and works, a body that gives consciousness a support when it has to leave its former assistant, the body. This psychic [subtle-imaginal] body is at first very delicate, so that only the very wisest men can preserve it and find their refuge in it after death."*

> *What we gather from this passage is that "immortality" is the result of a creative effort: a process of* crystallization *and transformation of the psychic seed which is reborn in the form of a new body, called the "diamond body" in Chinese alchemy (the "diamond thunderbolt" or the* dorje *of Tibetan Buddhism). According to Jung, the new body symbolizes the perfect state where masculine and feminine are united; it corresponds to the* corpus incorruptible *[incorruptible body] of the medieval alchemy, which in turn is identical with the* corpus resurrectionis *[resurrection body] of the Christian tradition.*
>
> —Roberts Avens in *The Imaginal Body*, pgs 187-188 [emphasis mine–RS]

> *The* coniunctio *[conjunction] in alchemy is a union . . . of the spiritual and material principles, from which a perfect body arises, the glorified body after the Last Judgement, the resurrection body . . . This means an eternal body, or the* subtle body, *which is designated in alchemy as the Philosophers' Stone, the lapis* aethereus *[etheric stone] or* invisibilis *[invisible stone].*
>
> —Carl Jung, ETH Lectures, page 159

> *It seems to me that we are at the end of an era. The splitting of the atom and the nuclear bomb bring us a new view of matter. As physical man cannot develop any further, it would seem that this particular evolution ends with man. Like the caterpillar dissolves and turns into a butterfly, it is conceivable that the physical body of man could change into a more subtle body. It might not be necessary for him to die to be clothed afresh and be transformed.*
>
> —Carl Jung, *Conversations with C.G. Jung*, page 63

> *Your subtle body is the whole of the integrity of your consciousness as you have built it in your life, through the efforts of engagement with Spirit—through winding the golden threads that you notice as you follow your path.*
>
> —Daniel Deardorff, personal conversation with Robert Simmons

Although immortality was one of the goals of alchemists from various traditions, it was the main focus of Chinese alchemy. As we see in the above quotes from Avens and Hannah, the immortality envisioned in Chinese alchemy was not centered on infinite preservation of the physical body as we know it. Although the Chinese alchemists did focus on cultivating longevity, the vehicle of immortality they sought to bring into the realization of its full potential was what I have been calling the subtle-imaginal body, the body of the soul.

In Chinese philosophy, there are a number of varying concepts for the soul, as well as different systems asserting that individuals have from two to ten souls. I will not try to sort out or explain these. However, one of the simpler systems suggests two souls—one attached to the physical body and one linked to the heavenly realms. The physical body was viewed as being sustained by food and medicines, while the heavenly body was nourished by the cultivation of *chi* (spiritual life-force). Healthy living, which included wholesome food, a good environment and a virtuous life encouraged physical longevity. Cultivation of *chi* enlivened and strengthened the heavenly body. In the culmination of the Chinese alchemical endeavor, these two bodies became a unified whole, with an enlightened consciousness as well as powers that resulted from its transcendence of all limitation. The new body was centered in the subtle/imaginal/psychoid realm, but could manifest in the physical world or travel to the realm of the gods.

> *Running through popular Chinese alchemy was the belief that it was possible to attain a bodily immortality; that the body could be so rarified that it took on the attributes and possibilities of a spirit. It was not merely a matter of arresting the normal processes*

> *of aging and decay but, through a lifetime of practices, creating a new subtle body, capable of "flying on the wind," of being in more than one place at once, immune from harm from fire, water or weapons and able to assume invisibility; in fact having all the supernatural powers.*
>
> —Jean Cooper, *Chinese Alchemy: Taoism, the Power of Gold, and the Quest for Immortality*

These ideas make sense within the framework of the subtle-imaginal body as I have been describing it. The subtle-imaginal realm is a reality that bridges the domains of physical matter and pure spirit, and it is a domain in which physical "laws" do not hinder a being's movements. How does this aspiration of the Chinese alchemists connect with our work in the Alchemy of Stones? I believe that the idea of the union of the two souls (the physical and the heavenly) described above, leading to the birth of a new being, is much the same as the alchemical Third Conjunction we have described in an earlier chapter. Both lead to the manifestation of a Self that embodies the union of spirit and matter, and has transcended all limitations.

Further, when we perceive the energies of stones, we are receiving a flow of subtle matter/ energy that nourishes our subtle body. This simultaneously stimulates our awareness of the Stone Beings with whom we can interact and co-create in that realm.

Of course, I also find provocative the fact that both Avens and Hannah utilized the idea of the formation of a *crystal* to illustrate the coming-into-being of the perfected subtle body (aka the Philosophers' Stone). In my earlier book, *Stones of the New Consciousness,* I wrote about scientific discoveries regarding the liquid crystal nature of our physical bodies; I discussed the theory that bringing the Liquid Crystal Body Matrix into higher degrees of coherence (i.e. greater crystallinity) has the effect of enhancing all of the higher (and deeper) capacities of human consciousness.

When we invite stone energies and give attention to their effects, we can feel the inner harmony they bring into us. This is the subjective experience of increased coherence in our own liquid crystal nature. In other words, meditating with stones enables one t*o become more like a crystal.* Such practices cultivate and vivify the subtle body, stimulating the emergence of latent capacities and potentially enabling one to exercise "all the supernatural powers." To me, this strongly parallels alchemical ideas from both Europe and China.

The ancient Greek philosopher Philiponus tells us that, according to Aristotle: "'The everlasting sublime body partakes of transparency; and he calls it the out-flow of the spheres [heavenly regions], for all of them are transparent.' It pertains to the crystalline."

So, once again we have an association of the "sublime" body of the soul with the qualities of a crystal.

Now, back to Chinese alchemy. I want to return to Barbara Hannah's quote at the beginning of this section and consider the part of it that describes an alchemical drawing: ". . . a sage is depicted in deepest meditation, in whose heart a small child is forming . . . This little child is nourished and cared for there, until at last it is ready to float through the cranial cavity, into the heights of the new Divine birth."

The 'Divine birth' is the culmination of the alchemical process, which Jung's quote above describes as, ". . . a union . . . of the spiritual and material principles, from which a perfect body arises, the glorified body after the Last Judgment, the resurrection body . . . This means an eternal body, or the *subtle body,* which is designated in alchemy as the Philosophers' Stone . . ."

Now I want us to consider several images, so we can try to understand more vividly within ourselves what is being described, and what is possible.

The larger image on page 158 at the beginning of this chapter depicts the Chinese sage mentioned in Hannah's quote, with the small child forming in the heart. The meditator directs his attention, intention and imagination to his heart, encouraging the formation and continuous enhancement of the child-image. This is akin to our focusing on the Deep Self in our own hearts. Like the embryo upon whom the sage is meditating, our Deep Self must be nourished by our attention and love. Doing this as a practice is like planting, watering and shining light upon a seed—what is at first a mere potential begins to grow. In this case, the seed is the divine spark of our Deep Self.

The smaller image on page 159 shows the fulfillment of the Chinese alchemical process. In this image, the sage's center of awareness has moved into the image of the newborn Divine child which hovers "above" the earthly body. Again, from Hannah: "This . . . is an image that represents emerging into another order of time, where we can see the whole of life, as from another dimension, and yet at the same time remain energetically *connected* with our present life in our present order of space and time."

In a drawing, it is difficult to depict the fact that this new center of self-awareness is not merely hovering in the air over the physical body. However the image of the child seated on a magical-looking "cloud" indicates that the sage himself is now "above and beyond" the corporeal body in a more profound sense. His center is now in the vastly greater and different world which I have described as the subtle-imaginal realm. Yet, as Hannah says, there is still a connection to our corporeal life, and to "our present order of space and time." This is symbolized by the tail of the cloud remaining connected to the meditator's head.

The divine birth of the meditator into the subtle-imaginal body marks the inception of a new life. The human personality has come into the Third Conjunction with the Deep Self, and, as in our physical birth, the Child—the true Self—has emerged into a new world. The world one has known does not disappear, but the Self is centered in "... another order of time, where we can see the whole of life, as from another dimension..."

We might say that from the perspective of the spiritual alchemist who has achieved this union, the world of space and time that one has known is now *encompassed* within a larger reality—"another order of time." A possible name for that newly-entered order of time might be *eternity*. And we can imagine that an existence centered in eternity would be what the alchemists have referred to as immortality.

From the perspective of both Western and Eastern alchemy, this is not the same as "life after death." It is an achievement of rebirth into a higher order of existence, within one's physical lifetime. Jung puts it this way in the quote above: "Like the caterpillar dissolves and turns into a butterfly, it is conceivable that the physical body of man could change into a more subtle body. It might not be necessary for him to die to be clothed afresh and be transformed."

This may appear to be something that is far away from the lives we are living day-to-day. When we look at our usual habits and routines, and when we consider the things upon which the majority of people seem to place their focus, the chasm separating us from the wisest and most successful of the alchemists and sages seems huge indeed. Yet there is nothing closer to us than the soul, and nothing more intimately a part of us than the subtle-imaginal body. Every time we tune in to a crystal we can feel the mysterious currents of energies that no machine can measure. We can sense the thrill of recognizing the presence of spiritual beings who want to co-create with us. And when we look within, we can feel our longing for union with the divine spark in our depths. And this longing may actually be coming *from* the Divine in our depths, *longing for us.*

Before we leave this image of the Chinese sage and the divine embryo that he nurtures in his heart until it is ready to ascend, I want to bring in another image for comparison. This is one we have looked at earlier in the book. It is the image of the Ascension of Christ in the Renaissance painting by Antonio Campi, *Mysteries of the Passion of Christ.* I presented this image in Chapter 14.

It may be worthwhile to look back at the passage in which I described the painting and its meaning in some detail. [see pgs 121–123] What I want to call attention to here is that the essen-

tial pattern or "gesture" depicted in Campi's painting echoes the gesture we see in the pair of Chinese alchemical pictures. In each of these representations, we are viewing an Ascension of an enlightened consciousness into a higher order of existence. In both cases, a "being of the heart" rises from the heart into the cranium.

In the second of the Chinese drawings, the Divine Embryo is shown *having already ascended* through the top of the cranium into a heavenly realm. In the Campi painting, we see Christ, the Great Being of the Heart, in the *process of ascending.* He radiates divine Light, which fills the supernatural skull-shaped opening that has appeared among the mundane gray clouds. From the story of Christ's ascension, we know that, like the Chinese Divine Embryo, the Christ figure will continue upward through the "doorway" in the top of the golden skull-dome, to ultimately dwell in a higher order of reality—to experience a "new Divine birth" into eternity.

When I presented Campi's painting as a focus for our meditation practice, Ascension of the Heart, I suggested that you imaginally place the gestural essence of the painting within your own body, while affirming, "All of this is happening in me." We could do the very same thing with the two Chinese alchemical drawings, using the same affirmation. In both representations, I view the images as depicting what is essentially *the same inner event,* and I believe that the purpose of both of these is to *bring forth that inner event in those who view and contemplate them.* The fact that these two artistic renderings—independently created, far from one another is space and time—are so alike in their essence, hints that the underlying phenomenon they display to us is real. Though we do not literally see these events in the mundane world, they are inner realities of the soul.

A PRACTICE FROM CHINESE ALCHEMY

In Chapter 8, I touched on the Taoist practice known as the Microcosmic Orbit or the Circulation of the Light. In this practice, *chi* energy is imagined and willed to follow an oroborous-type path in one's body. As one inhales, one draws the vital *chi* energy from the area of the tailbone up the back along the spine and over the top of the head. As one exhales, one envisions and attempts to feel the *chi* flowing downwards along the front of the body and back to the tailbone area. This is the basic pattern, although there are many aspects of this practice which I am not describing here. (For a good layman's explanation of the Circulation of the Light, see Alchemy Lab's online article: https://www.alchemylab.com/circulation_of_the_light.htm)

The Circulation of the Light practice was aimed at magnifying and multiplying the subtle matter/energy (*chi*) in the practitioner's subtle body so greatly that it became strong enough to function as a body of immortality. Once again, we see that the means of self-transformation involve attention, intention and imagination.

In my own personal view of reality, I do not believe, as some interpreters of Chinese alchemy suggest, that if one does not engage in chi-building practices such as the Circulation of the Light, the individual soul will decompose after death and dissolve out of existence. My hypothesis is that we will continue to exist after death and to reincarnate. Each life provides the opportunity to do the inner and outer work that

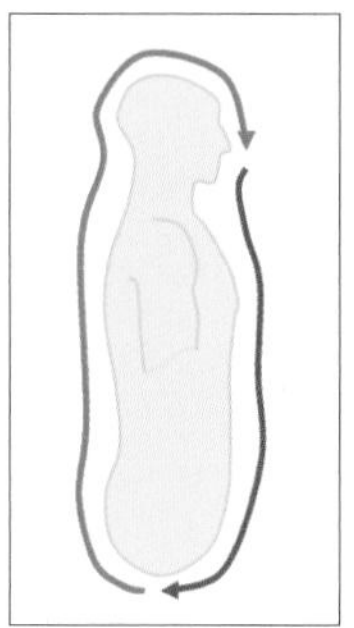

The Microcosmic Orbit

can lead to wholeness, and I think we get more than one opportunity to do this. (And, like many people, I *remember* parts of some past lives!)

However, I agree with the Western alchemists that it is worthwhile to engage in the effort to assist in Sophia's work. I think we are called to work co-creatively for the beneficial transformation of ourselves and our world. I also envision that the unification of the self through the Transcendent Function and the Three Conjunctions may bring forth a new Self that is a bridge between Heaven and Earth, free to move in all realms. Such a being would not need to reincarnate, because the goals of incarnation will have been achieved. And from the standpoint of the life we have known, that Self would be "immortal"—a dweller in eternity.

THE RAINBOW BODY

Among the lore of the spiritual traditions of the East there is something known as the Rainbow Body. The Rainbow Body is primarily associated with Dzogchen Buddhism, although the phenomenon has been reported in other spiritual traditions, such as Vajrayana Buddhism.

In Dzogchen Buddhism, some practitioners embark on a practice known as Thodgal, which translates as: "direct crossing", "the direct approach" or "leapover." The effect of this practice is said, "to enable a person to actualize all the different aspects of enlightenment within themselves in one lifetime." In Thodgal, the practitioner, "works directly with the clear light that dwells inherently, 'spontaneously present,' within all phenomena."

A Wikipedia article on the Rainbow Body tells us:

> *The ultimate fruition of the Thodgal practices is a body of pure light, called a rainbow body. If the four visions of Thodgal are not completed before death, then during death, from the point of view of an external observer, the dying person starts to shrink until he or she disappears. Usually fingernails, toenails and hair are left behind. The attainment of the rainbow body is typically accompanied by the appearance of lights and rainbows. Exceptional practitioners are held to realize a higher type of rainbow body without dying. Having completed the four visions before death, the individual focuses on the lights that surround the fingers. His or her physical body self-liberates into a nonmaterial body of light (a Sambhogakāya) with the ability to exist and abide wherever and whenever as pointed by one's compassion.*

The Rainbow Body of Padmasambhava

Considering this description, I am struck by the similarity of some of its features to the process engaged in by the Chinese sage in the drawings we have discussed a few paragraphs ago. The critical feature, from my perspective, is the attainment of a "body of light" that can "exist and abide wherever and whenever as pointed by one's compassion." The consciousness of the enlightened practitioner, and his light body, is centered, in my view, in the subtle-imaginal realm. The fact that observers report seeing lights and rainbows in connection with this event suggests that it is what Jung and some of his disciples would term a *psychoid* phenomenon—something that happens in a realm that overlaps or conjoins the world of matter and the world of pure spirit.

The 8th century Buddhist master Padmasambhava was said to have achieved the Rainbow body, along with his consort Mandarava. Here is a brief account from Wikipedia

(Note also the image (opposite page) from a Tibetan Thangka, depicting Padmasambhava in his Rainbow Body form):

> *In Rewalsar, known as Tso Pema in Tibetan, [Padmasambhava] secretly taught tantric teachings to princess Mandarava, the local king's daughter. The king found out and tried to burn him, but it is believed that when the smoke cleared he just sat there, still alive and in meditation. Greatly astonished by this miracle, the king offered Padmasambhava both his kingdom and Mandarava.*
>
> *Padmasambhava left with Mandarava, and took to Maratika Cave in Nepal to practice secret tantric consort rituals. They had a vision of buddha Amitāyus and achieved what is called the "phowa rainbow body," a very rare type of spiritual realization. Both Padmasambhava and one of his consorts, Mandarava, are still believed to be alive and active in this rainbow body form by their followers.*

Over many centuries, there have been eyewitnesses to the Rainbow Body phenomenon. The meditation manual *Heart Drops of Dharmakaya*, by the Tibetan teacher Shardza Tashi Gyaltsen, "contains an eyewitness account of his main students' bodies shrinking and rainbows appearing in the sky at death." In other related literature, one can find similar accounts of people witnessing a Rainbow Body.

I am not any kind of expert on Buddhism. In writing about this, I view myself more as a sort of spiritual detective, looking for clues that can shed light on the mysteries that interest me (and, hopefully, my readers). Considering the above account of the Rainbow Body, as well as the earlier discussion of the disciplines leading to various manifestations of a "body of light" centered in the subtle-imaginal realm, we see a common thread in terms of how the phenomenon is described, as well as the profound shift of consciousness that goes with it. These accounts also suggest that such an attainment requires great discipline and devotion.

THE ROLE OF THE STONES & THE EARTH

At this point, let us presume that the above assertions about the requirements for forming the Body of Light are all true. I accept that they are accurate, especially in historical terms. But I want to add another element to the mix. To the best of my knowledge, none of the traditional accounts of these great human transformations take the Earth into account as a Being who is also seeking enlightenment and transformation. But we who are involved with the stones in our spiritual lives are aware that the transformation we are already experiencing is not something we are doing alone. Certain stones—Phenacite, White Azeztulite, Satyaloka Clear Azeztulite, Natrolite, Anandalite, Lemurian Light Crystals, and others—facilitate the infusion of the Clear Light into our subtle bodies. Numerous stones—Cinnazez, Green Jade, Cuprite, Red Fire Azeztulite, Ruby. Zircon, Red Jasper,and others—can increase our *chi* or life force, enhancing practices such as the Circulation of the Light, or other similar techniques. Still other stones—Rosophia, Sauralite Azeztulite, Morganite, Kunzite, and others—nourish the heart center, and may facilitate the development of what the Chinese alchemists called the Divine Embryo.

Through relating with the Stone Beings, we can accelerate our inner evolutionary processes, perhaps bringing about results akin to those sought by the meditators in the spiritual traditions of the East. To me, it feels like the stones boost the energies in our subtle bodies in ways that may allow us to transform, perhaps without needing to exert the prodigious forces of will described in the Chinese and Tibetan traditions. I do not know this for a fact, but my intuition leads me to this hypothesis. I believe that the imagination, attention and intention of the Earth—the Soul of the World—are attuned to this same potential.

The Western alchemists, whose paths were most akin to the ones we take in the Alchemy of Stones, repeatedly asserted that they worked always in co-creative collaboration with Sophia, the Soul of the World. They accepted the Gnostic idea that one aspect of Sophia was, in a certain way, bound unconsciously in matter. At the same time, they attempted to follow Sophia's wisdom in conducting their work, stating that without her Wisdom, they could never succeed. In regard to this, Jung wrote, "for the alchemist, the one primarily in need of redemption is not man, but the deity who is lost and sleeping in matter."

I agree here with Jung and the alchemists. Readers may remember from an earlier chapter that what brought me into the alchemical worldview were my two dreams of Sophia. In both of those dreams, it was clear that Sophia is a divine being, and that she needs human help in order to fully manifest who and what she is. I differ from the Chinese alchemists, in that I do not view the attainment of personal immortality or power as the most important goal. My primary reason for describing their practices was to dramatize the reality of the subtle-imaginal body, and to offer a glimmer of how profound one's own alchemical transmutation can be. But as Jung pointed out, the most important aspiration of alchemy is the redemption of She who is "lost and sleeping in matter."

The redemptive power in the universe is love. When we invite a Stone Being into our heart and feel its currents filling us, we are receiving the outpouring of the life-giving love of the Soul of the World. When we love the Earth through loving the stones (or even without the stones), we are loving Sophia, and we are infusing her with life force, just as surely as when a stone's currents enter and vitalize us. This is co-creation, and mutual redemption. It is a feedback loop, an oroborous of mutual blessing that creates synchronicities and miracles.

The world is changing, as are we. The Stone Beings are more awake than they have ever been in history, and more of us are awake to them than has ever been the case before. All of this is accelerating. I believe we are approaching a cusp of transformation—a point at which both we and the Earth may make a great leap into a whole new way of being, in which our very identities will undergo a profound metamorphosis. Will the new reality be centered in the subtle-imaginal realm? Will matter become spiritualized while spirit materializes? I think we are moving in that direction, but none of us can foresee what that will be like. Our task, our joy, and our own redemption is to keep on loving, and to trust.

Tibetan Buddhist Symbol
for the Rainbow Body

**PADMASAMBHAVA
GAINS A RAINBOW BODY**

his disciples stand around
looking into the sky,
the good students ecstatic
over his success
and their own potential,
the average students scratching
their heads for now they have
no teacher . . .
the poor students sad
that they have learned
nothing until today

—David Schafer

19

Manifestations

> *Concerning matter, we have been all wrong. What we have called matter is energy, whose vibration has been so lowered as to be perceptible to the senses. There is no matter.*
>
> —Albert Einstein

Earlier today, I was working on revisions and corrections to the manuscript of this book. It took me an hour or so to complete my review of the preceding chapter on the subtle body and the Rainbow Body, and to begin proofreading this one. Then I put down my work and left the house with my wife, Kathy, because we had some errands to do in a town about thirty miles from where we live.

It was a lovely drive through the green New Zealand countryside and the sun was shining, even as a light spring rain fell from scattered clouds.

Suddenly, as we rounded the curve past a high hill, we were stunned at the sight of an ultra-bright double rainbow right in front of us! It may have been the most vivid rainbow I have ever seen. And the angle of the sun above and behind us made it seem as if the rainbow's ends touched the ground less than a hundred yards from either side of the road.

We kept driving toward the rainbow, and as we drove, it seemed to grow even brighter and more vivid, and the second bow became more clearly visible. Both of us were delighted by the unexpected beauty we had encountered on our little journey.

Then I suddenly laughed out loud. Of course! My head had already been full of rainbows–the Rainbow Body from the chapter I had just finished, and the Rainbow Orbs that are described later in *this* chapter! How funny—and how mysterious—this playful synchronicity felt to me! How easy it was for me to view this event as one of Sophia's gestures! My life is punctuated by many of these moments, and I interpret them as Sophia's way of reminding me that she is totally with me, aware of me, and always dancing.

Another funny thing—before leaving the house, I had been wondering how to introduce this chapter. On the drive, I got my answer!

It goes without saying that a materialist would mock my interpretation. But the alchemists, and many indigenous peoples, would not.

In my view, this anecdote offers an example of perceiving the world through the alchemical lens of True Imagination. This is a viewpoint one utilizes by one's own conscious choice, for the purpose of co-creating with Sophia. At first, I simply enjoyed the rainbow as a beautiful event in the everyday world. Then I recalled that, only a few minutes earlier, I had been preoccupied—with my "head full of rainbows." I suddenly saw the synchronicity, and my "lens" immediately shifted. I recognized that the rainbow had meaning as well as beauty. And the meaning was personal to me—reminding me of the intimacy and playfulness that imbues the way in which we are known and cherished by the Soul of the World.

It seems to me that this is a good place in the book to emphasize once again that True Imagination is essential, if our alchemical efforts are to succeed and if our experience of life is to be meaningful to us. Without this element, *we cannot contribute our share of what is necessary to make the meaning real.* We cannot dance with Sophia. Here again is the quotation that addresses this, from the German Romantic philosopher Novalis:

> *The world must be romanticized. In this way the originary meaning may be found again. To romanticize the world is to make us aware of the magic, mystery and wonder of the world; it is to educate the senses to see the ordinary as extraordinary, the familiar as strange, the mundane as sacred, the finite as infinite.*

I love that Novalis tells us that we must *educate* our senses! They have already been educated by our culture into seeing the world as ordinary, familiar and mundane—in other words, meaningless. That meaninglessness is the *interpretation*—the "explanation" of reality we have been told is true—but it is *only* an interpretation. Ironically, meaninglessness is the "meaning" that materialism conveys upon reality.

And by the way, Einstein's quote above puts the materialists on shaky ground indeed, since this genius of physics tells us, "There is no matter."

But there *is* meaning, and the making of it comes out of our dance with Sophia. Here again is what the great Jungian analyst Marie Louise von Franz tells us about the way reality displays itself to someone who has reached the state of wholeness that the Jungians call Individuation:

> *Normal ego consciousness would be replaced by an* imaginative consciousness *that beheld the world through the eyes of imagination. It would see underneath the apparent solidity of ordinary reality to the* meaning hidden there. *It would* behold the spiritual powers at play *in ordinary life, and it would posses* the freedom that perceiving symbolically bestows.

To me, the rainbow this morning was an example of "the spiritual powers at play in ordinary life." There are uncountable numbers of such examples, as we see when we "behold the world through the eyes of imagination." Our whole endeavor with the Stone Beings has True Imagination at its core. This is essential, if we are to adequately receive and interpret the gifts that come to us through the stones, and through the gestures Sophia makes to us.

THE LABYRINTH & THE RAINBOW ORBS

Now I want to look back a few years to something that surprised and amazed me . . . twice. In 2008, I was working extensively with several types of Azeztulite, as well as with Rosophia. Kathy and I were excited by the powerful experiences that people all over the world were having with these stones, and I had done my best to acquire as many of them as possible. As with most types of stones, only the best ten percent or so were suited to making polished pieces—spheres, wands, beads, jewelry, etc. That meant that we had quite a lot of material that was energetically powerful, though not aesthetically spectacular. I wondered what we should do with it all. As usual, I tried to imagine how to amplify and enhance the stones' energies and effects.

One afternoon, while I sat idly on our deck, an inspiration hit me. I suddenly envisioned a labyrinth made completely out of Azeztulite and Rosophia stones, and I knew I wanted to build it—right now! I felt sure that a concentric, winding labyrinth path made from these intensely powerful stones would bring about vivid and beneficial experiences for people who walked it. I was so obsessed with the idea that I immediately had all of the "surplus" Azeztulite and Rosophia stones brought to our house. I worked for hours each day, often into the evening, intuitively placing the stones in the thirty-seven foot diameter pattern.

In a couple of weeks, the labyrinth was complete, and it did indeed have powerful effects on us, and on many other people. A bit surprisingly, it was not overwhelmingly intense for most of us. Instead it was deeply and profoundly peaceful, often bringing the mind into a state of inner silence. It was also pleasurable—it made us feel good after we had walked it.

There is more I could say about the labyrinth, but I want to skip ahead to the first big surprise. On the second floor of our house, we had a deck that overlooked the lawn where the labyrinth was, next to a stream and its waterfall. On one lovely autumn morning, I decided to take a picture of it all from my elevated vantage point. Then I put the camera in a drawer and thought no more about it.

Some weeks later, Kathy and I were looking through our pictures, and we saw the labyrinth photo. Both of us were stunned by what it revealed: seemingly hovering above the labyrinth was a huge rainbow-colored orb! Looking closely, we saw a similar-sized but fainter orb that appeared to be either emerging from or entering the ground at the center of the labyrinth.

We had seen a number of quite different orb photos elsewhere, and we knew that many people thought of these as "spirit photography." But never before had we encountered *rainbow orbs,* or any orbs of such a large apparent size.

Looking at the photo triggered my memory of having read about the Rainbow Body phenomenon, and I wondered if this could be related to it. I had snapped a second photo of the labyrinth right after I took the first one, and the brighter of the rainbow orbs appeared in that one too, in a slightly different location.

I was intrigued by the proximity of the rainbow orbs to the Azeztulite and Rosophia labyrinth. Could placing these stones in this concentric pattern have created an "energy portal" which could be used by some sort of spiritual beings to enter and leave the material world? Or were these the Rainbow Bodies of enlightened human beings? Or was this something else entirely? We did not rule out the possibility of the image being an optic glitch of some sort, though we looked online for other images like ours and could not find them.

Two years later, we organized a four-day workshop for me to present. It was entitled *Stones of the New Consciousness,* and the program was based on the ideas presented in what was then my newly-published book of the same title. The event was held at a hotel and conference center in Vermont, and one of the hotel's features was a large green lawn. We requested and received permission to build a special Azeztulite and Rosophia labyrinth there, just for the four days of our event. It was to be a temporary "twin" of the one at our home, and all the participants would have the opportunity to walk it. During the workshop, I told the story of the first labyrinth and showed the picture with the rainbow orbs.

The event went well, and the experience of walking the labyrinth was a favorite of many participants. A few days afterwards, one woman who had been at the workshop sent me some photos of the labyrinth. She had taken them in the early morning after the event, before we disassembled it. She was excited and amazed—as we were—to discover that *there were rainbow orbs above this labyrinth too!* The rainbow orb photo shown at the bottom of the page facing the beginning of this chapter is one of the ones she sent to us. Once again, the orb appears right over the labyrinth.

The rainbow orb photo shown here is one of the photos she sent to us.

I find it intriguing that these photos show the rainbow orb images in conjunction with the only two Azeztulite-Rosophia labyrinths ever created.

Now, go back for a moment and look at the image of the Rainbow Body of Padmasambhava on page 164. Notice the similarity of the stylized wavy "rays" in his Rainbow Body to the wavy rainbow patterns in the orb photos from the Azeztulite labyrinths.

Again, I have looked for other photos with orbs like these and have not found them. Although I suppose it is possible that these are optical anomalies, I am tempted to think of them as representing something more profound.

And what is that? Is this an Ascended being like Padmasambhava, or something else? I still can't say that I know, but I want to mention an idea proposed by Robert Sardello. At the 2008 Sophia Conference, Robert presented a talk that included slides of several types of so-called "paranormal" phenomena. Among them were crop circles, UFOs, and orb photos. Robert suggested that all of these phenomena are "Sophianic interventions." By this he meant that Sophia creates these unexplained events to jolt us out of the artificial and superficial "reality" of things that are "known." Our everyday worldview, with its commonplace explanations for everything, is keeping us in a trance that prevents us from being present to the deep mystery of the world—of which Sophia is the deepest.

I want to invite you to contemplate this for a few minutes. Most of us already have "explanations" in our minds for these phenomena, even if we don't think about them very often. For example, we may tell ourselves that UFOs are hallucinations, government aircraft, or perhaps that they are travelers from other worlds or other dimensions. We might presume that crop circles are hoaxes perpetrated by people, or that they are communications from extraterrestrials. We might believe that orb photos are images of discarnate spirits, or optical illusions caused by dust or moisture in the air or on a camera lens.

It doesn't matter what our "explanation" is, or whether it is right or wrong. What does matter is that we create such explanations in order to *avoid confronting the mystery at the heart of the world.* What we call our normal "worldview" is basically a mental box full of explanations that give us the illusion that we comprehend reality. In a certain way, maybe this is okay. Perhaps we need such explanations in order to navigate our everyday lives. But perhaps, if we did not invest ourselves so deeply in our *concepts* of the world, the *numinous living presence* of the world—the Soul of the World—could enter into us. If we want to truly be present spiritually—if we want to be sharply and vibrantly awake rather than comfortably half-asleep—we have to remember that our commonplace worldview, or even our unconventional set of New Age ideas, is too small to encompass the world.

When we experience a "Sophianic intervention," the most important thing to do, as Robert Sardello insisted, is *not to throw an explanation around it.* Stand there with your eyes bugged out and your mouth hanging open, and *stare into the mystery!* Feel it. Let it disassemble your worldview, right before your eyes.

Let's go back and visualize the Campi painting for a moment. Imagine that you are standing outside looking at the sky, and suddenly a huge hole opens in the clouds, appearing as a dome filled with golden light and moving figures. (Let's not even put Christ in the image, because "recognizing" him might throw an "explanation" over it all.) Now, there you stand with the "impossible" right in front of you. You blink, but it doesn't go away. How do you feel?

In his talk, Robert Sardello was trying to show us the difference between wearing our usual protective overcoat of explanations and standing naked before the truth of our experience. It is hard to do this, because we are unconsciously quite fearful of the world, if we don't give ourselves a reassuring explanation for it. In several of his books, Joseph Chilton Pearce quotes American philosopher Susanne Langer: ". . . our greatest fear is of 'collapse into chaos should our ideation [worldview] fail us.'"

Think back to the story I told at the beginning of this book. At eighteen years old, late at night, in an atmosphere of introspection and self-doubt, I described my most recurrent childhood dream to my college roommate. Moments later, I randomly looked out a window, and was stunned to see the central image of that dream, manifested as a huge, white horse-shaped cloud.

That event was my own personal "Sophianic intervention." I stood confronting what was, to me, the impossible. I blinked, but it didn't go away. I was terrified. And then my "ideation"—my worldview and "myself"—collapsed in a thousand pieces.

But this was not the end. I did not die or go insane. From my terror, I cried out to the Divine, and in the next moment I was suddenly filled with Light. And with the Light came the ecstatic certainty of being held in the love of something vast and wonderful beyond conception. It was still an unfathomable mystery, but it was nothing to fear. And during the ecstasy of that event, my fear was banished utterly. I would now say that the one whose Light and love enveloped me was Sophia. At the time, I thought it was "God," but I am not sure now how much the distinction matters.

The thought may by now have occurred to you that this book constitutes yet another "explanation" for the mystery at the heart of the world. In one way, it is precisely that, and this is the place in the book where I want to call your attention to it. If we take the imagery and ideas of alchemy literally, or if we view alchemy as simply a symbolic explanatory "overcoat" to cover our naked ignorance of what reality actually is, then we have missed the boat again. If we work with the energies of stones and imagine the Stone Beings as if they were "things" we can define and "know," we have replaced their mystery with a narrative. This is a slippery area, because we tend to do these things unconsciously and automatically. And there is always the problem of using language to reach toward any real knowing—language itself tends to substitute words and ideas for immediate experience. We do it every day.

What is our alternative? Why is the alchemical worldview any better than materialism?

Our alternative is to remember that the images we perceive of the Stone Beings, or other beings in the subtle-imaginal realm—whether they are visual, tactile, auditory, etc.—are symbolic, like masks worn by people in a play. The "mask" does not need to be physical—it can simply be the "identity" of the fictional character. The masks in a good play are indicative of the qualities of the characters, so they are useful for understanding what is occurring. But it is a mistake to forget that we are looking at masks, and that the masks *both reveal and conceal* the Actors behind them. What I am describing is like what we see in myths: the *images* of the gods are masks through which Divine energies are expressed in ways we can relate with. (This may be why the mythologist Joseph Campbell's titled one of his books *The Masks of God.*)

The alchemical worldview does not have to obscure our experience of spiritual reality. (It differs here from the mindset of materialism which denies that there *is* any spiritual reality.) If we look at spiritual alchemy *as a recipe book* for "cooking up" experiences that will bring us face-to-face with the Divine Mystery, then our task is simply to follow the recipes and "taste" the results. No one would read a recipe and believe that they were tasting the food, and no one should imagine that any set of concepts—any worldview—encompasses reality.

Small children do not have the firmly entrenched worldviews that adults do, and we can see the complete wonder and delight with which they at times experience the world. This may point us toward the truth within the Christian saying attributed to Jesus, "Unless you change and become like little children, you will never enter the kingdom of heaven." (Matthew 18:3)

I like the alchemical approach because it acknowledges the Divine Mystery and attempts to engage with it. The alchemists understood intuitively that the means for fundamentally transforming themselves and the world (metaphorically, from "lead" to "gold") would have to involve this Mystery. Somehow—perhaps through their own encounters—they knew that the Mystery was benign, loving and wise. They followed the Gnostics and other ancient wisdom traditions by referring to the Mystery with which they aspired to engage by the name Sophia. This name is a mask, but She is real. And She loves us.

We are all blessed with Sophianic interventions. Every synchronicity we experience is just such a gesture from Sophia, and the mystification, pleasure or thrill we feel when these things occur is coming from the fact that we have momentarily glimpsed the numinous reality behind our curtain of presumed normalcy. Every time we feel the "currents" or "energies" of a stone, we are feeling the touch of Sophia. If we can shed our habit of immediately grabbing hold of the nearest convenient explanations—even the New Age ones—we come nearer to Her. This approach to the Divine Mystery is a key element that can lead us to the union of opposites in the psyche that the alchemists called Conjunction.

In my case, back when I was eighteen, the opposites that were in conflict in my psyche were my concepts of "dream" versus "reality" and "inner" versus "outer." Only when my old worldview—in which these opposites could not co-exist—collapsed in the presence of the "impossible," did I call out to something greater. Then, in the mystic ecstasy of the Light that filled me, I understood that what had happened was destined (though not "fated") to happen, and that the inner and outer worlds are one. But please don't read this paragraph and think that I have "explained" anything. All I am trying to do is nudge you (and myself) closer to the Mystery.

The stone energies, as familiar as they may seem, are just as deeply mysterious as the other phenomena I have described. The fact that we take pleasure in them and that they are readily accessible to us does not make them any less astonishing. But the stones do show us that Sophia is intimate and loving as well as vast and unfathomable. And they hint to us that Heaven and Earth are one.

Even Carl Jung, the great psychologist who resurrected alchemy from obscurity, was aware that the Mystery he studied might be unsolvable:

> *As some alchemists had to admit, that they never succeeded in producing the gold or the stone, I cannot confess to have solved the riddle of the* **conjunctio** *[conjunction] mystery. On the contrary, I am darkly aware of things lurking in the background of the problem—things too big for horizons.*
>
> —Carl Jung, letter (1957)

We are within a mystery, whether we know it and work with it or not. And we don't know whether we will achieve the goals of alchemy fully or not. But like the alchemists, we may still be of benefit to the world, and to Sophia, and we may enhance our relationship with wisdom. Jung achieved all of these, as did Paracelsus and other alchemists, and as poets, mystics, teachers, storytellers and lovers all may do.

Having come to the top of the trunk of our alchemical tree, and having glimpsed the overhanging mystery of the starry regions and of eternity behind them, we can begin our exploration of the branches of the tree. Here we will find many things that we can do. Yet, as we continue, it is crucial to remember that we are always working with the unknown.

We tend to fear the unknown, and even when we don't, we are always trying to get rid of it and "know about" whatever the subject may be. In the everyday world, as I have said, this kind of knowing seems necessary. However, what the alchemists were seeking, and what we seek, is *gnosis.* The word gnosis means "knowing," as distinct from "knowing about." Someone else may "know about" your spouse or your child, but you *know* them. Gnosis is intimate knowledge, soul knowledge that comes through *uniting* with the other. Even in close human relationships, this kind of knowing is limited. However, when we experience union with the Deep Self, or with spiritual beings such as the Stone Beings, we can and do enter into gnosis.

Gnosis—knowing through union—transcends "facts" and "information." If I were to tell you about the energies of one stone or another (as I do, and will continue to do), you would "know something about" that type of stone. But when you hold it, offering yourself for relationship, if something happens in which you meet the Being that expresses itself through that stone, that is a moment of gnosis. And if you know the Stone Being in this way, you will *be known* as well, and feeling yourself *being known* is another entry into gnosis.

For example, when we hold a stone and feel its currents, we tend to believe that "we" are experiencing "it." But as I have mentioned, I think such experiences are occurring through the conjoining of our subtle bodies with the subtle bodies of the Stone Beings. So the phenomenon of our connecting with them is both "knowing" them and "being known"' by them, through spiritual communion. When you "feel something" with a stone, you are feeling *all of that!*

If you will use imagination to *enter into* what I have been describing here, you may get a hint of what I am trying to point to. In the Alchemy of Stones, this is Conjunction—the mystery that Jung himself confessed he had not been able to completely unravel. It seems likely that we will never fully understand it either, but that does not mean that we cannot experience it. And we need to do so—multiple times and at ever-greater depths—for our own sake, and for the sake of Sophia and the Earth.

The path of the Alchemy of Stones leads to wholeness, and there is much to discover and experience along the way. The next chapters will take us down avenues that branch out from where we are now, yet like the oroborous, they will bring us around and back to the center. That is the place of Conjunction, where inner and outer, Heaven and Earth, and all of the opposites unite. It is where we are truly whole, united with our Divine spark, and with the Soul of the World. If and when this wholeness and union become "as solid as a rock" we will have co-created the Philosophers' Stone.

An interesting . . . Wait! What?! That's unbelievable!

Okay, Dear Reader, I have to let you in on this... It is still the same day that I saw the ultra-bright rainbow on my drive with Kathy, and I had just finished my review and corrections for this chapter. I was writing the concluding paragraph when I happened to glance up from the computer, and . . . yes, you guessed it! *There was the rainbow* ***again,*** right in front of me as I looked out the window behind the video screen. This time, it appeared in a clear blue sky, and it arched over the almost-full moon. I had my camera beside me, so I took a picture of it. A few minutes later, it was gone. Have a look:

Remember what I said about the intimate and playful nature of Sophia's synchronistic dance with us?

BULLETIN

There is a Mystery at the heart of the world.

This has been a Bulletin from SNN—the Synchronicity News Network.
We now return you to Robert's book:

An interesting likeness to the spherical Body of Light and the Rainbow Orbs can be found in another numinous form—the mandala. In the next chapter, we will explore the mandala, which Jung described as the archetypal image that "signifies the wholeness of the Self." In doing so, we will encounter mandalas from various cultures, from inner visions, and from nature. We will learn to create mandalas that express our sense of the qualities of specific Stone Beings. And we will experiment with constructing mandalas of multiple stones—from palm-size templates to labyrinths—utilizing their synergy of energies for healing, awakening and transformation.

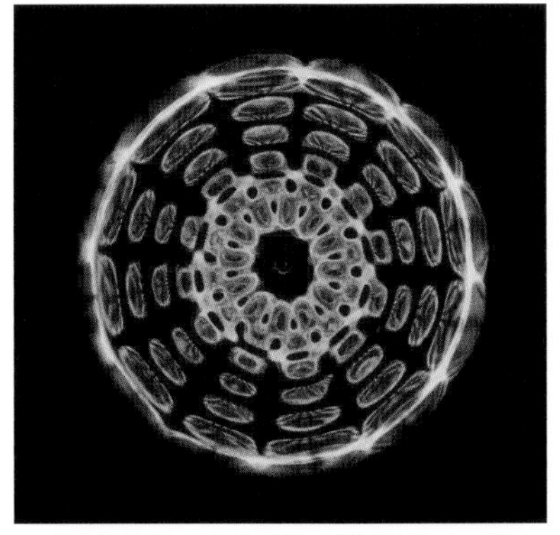

Stone Mandalas: Synergies of Energy & Meaning

The adventure of the Alchemy of Stones is a journey into wholeness and unity with the Divine, for ourselves and for the world. As we begin to branch out into areas of activity that will carry us along our path, with the aid of the Stone Beings, our movement into the consideration of stone mandalas is a natural one. Mandalas symbolize wholeness and the human connection with the Deep Self. The goal of spiritual alchemy is to fully actualize that connection.

As our allies in this work, the Stone Beings can be combined in mandalas (grids or templates) of synergetic energy patterns that amplify their beneficial influence. And in our alchemical meditations, the Stone Beings will sometimes reveal themselves to us in imaginal mandala forms. We will explore both of these potentials in this chapter and the next one.

Before we dive into this exploration, I want to offer some relevant quotes that explain what a mandala is, and what its spiritual significance can be.

> *Mandala: a circular design containing concentric geometric forms, images of deities, etc. and symbolizing the universe, totality, or wholeness.*
>
> —YourDictionary.com

> *Mandalas are a type of religious and spiritual art with a deep significance for many people. As a symbol of the cosmos or universe, a traditional mandala is a square containing a circle, and the entire design is symmetrical and balanced. Some spiritual traditions use mandalas for meditation or for marking a spiritual space. The word mandala itself simply means "circle" in Sanskrit.*
>
> —Vocabulary.com

> *Despite its cosmic meanings a yantra [mandala] is a reality lived. Because of the rela-tionship that exists in the Tantras between the outer world (the macrocosm) and man's inner world (the microcosm), every symbol in a yantra [mandala] is ambivalently resonant in inner/outer synthesis, and is associated with the subtle body and aspects of human consciousness.*
>
> —Wikipedia article on the Mandala in Hinduism

TOP LEFT: Sound pattern of the word "Agni"; RIGHT: Pyrite dollar; BOTTOM: Chartes Labyrinth

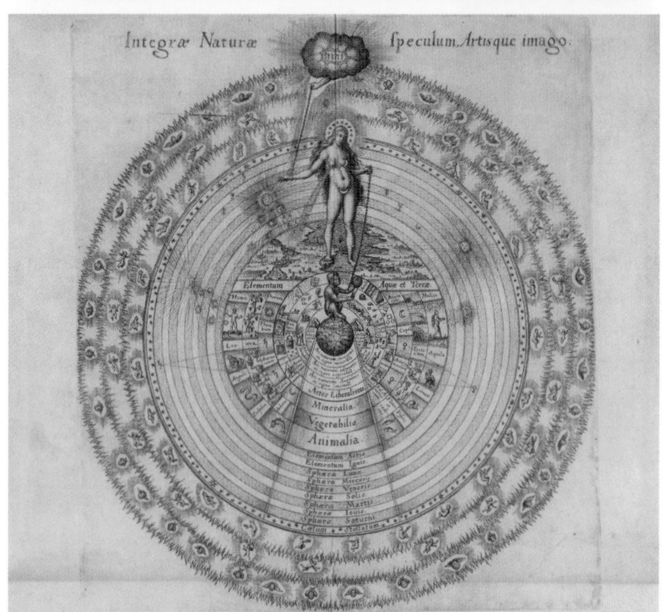
Integræ Naturæ
speculum Artisque imago.
Elementum
Aque et Terræ
Mineralia
Vegetabilia
Animalia

The word "mandala" is from the classical Indian language of Sanskrit. Loosely translated to mean "circle," a mandala is far more than a simple shape. It represents wholeness, and can be seen as a model for the organizational structure of life itself—a cosmic diagram that reminds us of our relation to the infinite, the world that extends both beyond and within our bodies and minds. Describing both material and non-material realities, the mandala appears in all aspects of life: the celestial circles we call earth, sun, and moon, as well as conceptual circles of friends, family, and community.

—themandalaproject.org

Carl Jung, the father of analytical psychology, and one of our chief guides in our exploration of spiritual alchemy, also worked with mandalas, which he envisioned as diagrams that could both express and invoke the wholeness of the Self:

In the products of the unconscious we discover mandala symbols, that is, circular and quaternity figures which express wholeness, and whenever we wish to express wholeness, we employ just such figures.

—Carl Jung, *Memories, Dreams, Reflections*

I sketched every morning in a notebook a small circular drawing, . . . which seemed to correspond to my inner situation at the time. . . . Only gradually did I discover what the mandala really is: . . . the Self, the wholeness of the personality, which, if all goes well, is harmonious.

—Carl Jung, *Memories, Dreams, Reflections*

My mandalas were cryptograms concerning the state of the self which were presented to me anew each day. In them I saw the self–that is, my whole being . . .

—Carl Jung, *Memories, Dreams, Reflections*

The mandala is an archetypal image whose occurrence is attested throughout the ages. It signifies the wholeness of the Self. This circular image represents the wholeness of the psychic ground or, to put it in mythic terms, the divinity incarnate in man.

—Carl Jung, *Memories, Dreams, Reflections*

In a previous chapter, we looked at one of the possible forms of our subtle/imaginal body—a sphere of light. In the context of the worldwide use of the circular form in mandalas as a symbol of the wholeness of the self, the idea that our soul might naturally appear in the subtle/imaginal realm as a sphere is fascinating. In a wide array of cultures, the circular patterns known as mandalas have been utilized as spiritual talismans and meditative aids, leading one to the truth of one's soul essence.

Jung said that the mandala is a symbol of wholeness, with the Self as center. In previous chapters, I described the spontaneously occurring photographic images of rainbow orbs in an Azeztulite and Rosophia stone labyrinth. I also recalled my two inner experiences of the spherical subtle body. These subtle body orbs are reminiscent of mandala shapes, and the labyrinth itself is a kind of mandala. Perhaps "mandalas" as symbols of wholeness actually do mirror the natural phenomenon of the subtle body. Perhaps the subtle body is an inner mandala that displays the state of one's being, as were the mandala drawings Jung created every day. And it may be that our subtle bodies can only manifest in a stable and powerful way when our wholeness has been brought forth.

OPPOSITE TOP: Tibetan sand mandala; MIDDLE: Alchemist Robert Flood, Integrae Naturae; BOTTOM: South window of Chartes Cathedral. THIS PAGE TOP: Golden Flower mandala; BOTTOM: Moon jellyfish

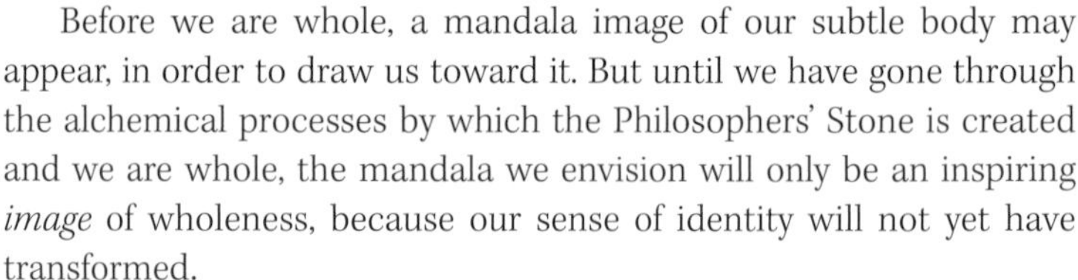

Before we are whole, a mandala image of our subtle body may appear, in order to draw us toward it. But until we have gone through the alchemical processes by which the Philosophers' Stone is created and we are whole, the mandala we envision will only be an inspiring *image* of wholeness, because our sense of identity will not yet have transformed.

According to author Barbara Hannah, who described this type of process in Chinese alchemy, when the metamorphosis occurs, one moves into *identification* with the subtle body. One's sense of selfhood will be centered there, and one will be living in a "new order of time." (see Chapter 18) In this situation, we might find that the most natural form of the subtle/imaginal body is spherical, as I saw it in my two meditative experiences.

However, the subtle body may be capable of taking on many forms, with the spherical form being simply its "resting" state. What we understand about the subtle/imaginal realm indicates that images can transform readily in that world, and an unlimited range of expressions might be available to one who is centered there. This may be related to the spiritual folklore of the East, which tells us that a Master can appear in human form, or any other form, and can even appear in more than one place at a time. Having full command of oneself in the subtle/imaginal realm—the realm of image—would allow for such occurrences.

The round or sphere-shaped mandala of the Self is also resonant with the "divine embryo" which the Chinese alchemists worked to manifest. And thinking of the orb/mandala shape, it is very much like the circular form of a biological human embryo at the moment of fertilization.

Author Barclay Powers has maintained that the first few cells of the human embryo are in some sense the image of the divine embryo (our "original face"). The first four cells of the human embryo form a quaternary, which was the pattern at the center of many of Jung's mandalas in the *Red Book,* which recorded his deepest spiritual experiences. The pattern created by the first eight cells is flowerlike, and is reminiscent of the well-known "Flower of Life" mandala pattern. If we view the image of the mandala-shaped early embryo as our "original face," then we can also envision that the sphere of golden light, as I experienced it in my Moldavite vision, is the "Golden Embryo"—the eternal subtle body of wholeness—the image of the Deep Self.

TOP ROW, LEFT TO RIGHT: Yarn Mandala, Mexico; Mayan Compass; Human Embryo; Navajo Sand Painting; LEFT COLUMN, TOP TO BOTTOM: Golden Temple, Nepal; Street Mandala, India; Snowflake; Trapiche Emerald; Alchemical Mandala

The journey to the Great Central Sun, which I spontaneously experienced during a meditation with Moldavite (see Chapter One), and which awakened my capacity to perceive stone energies, was an inner mandala experience. The Great Central Sun as I saw it is an imaginal-realm representation of the wholeness of the Deep Self—the Divine which is incarnated in us. Thus its size was huge, and yet it's holographic replica was inside me.

A WORLD OF MANDALAS

Our world is full of mandala forms, and these patterns speak to us. When we gaze upon the radial symmetry of a snowflake, a flower, a jellyfish or a sea star, we find them beautiful. The natural round and radiating form of a Pyrite "sun dollar" gives us pleasure in a way not unlike that which we experience viewing human creations such as a labyrinth in a garden, or a Rose Window in a cathedral. Why do we feel this way?

The mandala is, as Jung wrote, a primary symbol of wholeness. One way for us to confirm this in ourselves is to view some mandala images and notice how they make us feel as we look at them. I hope you will take a moment now to tune in to the mandala images shown on these pages.

If you are like me, you will notice a growing interest and pleasure arising in yourself as you view these mandalas and mandala-like natural forms. Although mandala patterns are by no means the only patterns we may find beautiful, I believe that they express a universal form that speaks to our depths, and which calls the Deep Self into our conscious awareness.

It is interesting to ponder the fact that our own DNA, the coded molecule carrying our physical "blueprint" in every cell, is also a mandala-type pattern. Perhaps this is physical evidence that mandalas resonate with our wholeness, right down to the molecular level!

MANDALAS IN SPIRITUAL PRACTICE

Most of us will most likely have first heard of mandalas in the context of their utilization in the meditative practices of Buddhism and Hinduism. We will not spend much time here, as I do not want us to lose our way in the multitude of images and information in this domain. But in hopes of enhancing our understanding of mandalas in our work with stones, we will touch briefly on this area.

A Wikipedia article on mandalas asserts that, in Hindu practice, the yantra [mandala] represents "the abode of the deity" and "calls the deity into the presence of the practitioner . . . " This is an excellent description of the mandala as a portal to spiritual encounters in the imaginal

TOP RIGHT: DNA Cross Section; LEFT TO RIGHT: Sri Yantra, India; Kalachakra Sand Mandala, Tibet; Stained Glass Window, France

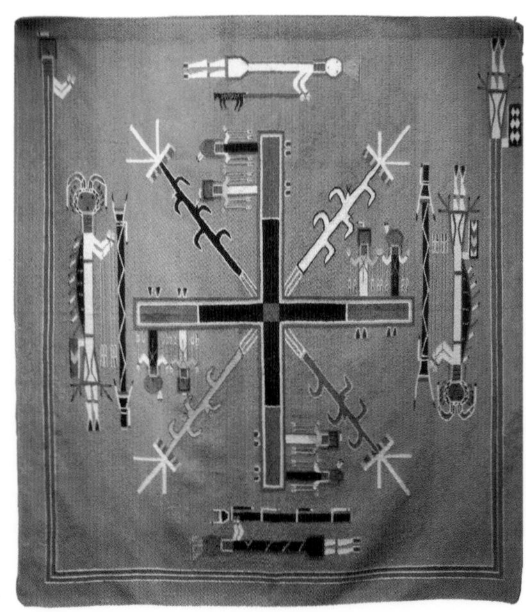

Navajo Rug, USA

realm. The physical rendering of the mandala acts as a visual doorway through which one can connect with a spiritual entity, by means of the contemplation of its subtle/imaginal body pattern. The statement that a yantra mandala is viewed as *the abode of the deity* is especially interesting. The mandala pattern is where the *deity resides*—the form within which its essence is contained—in the imaginal/subtle/psychoid realm. Viewing the pattern also *calls the deity into the meditator's presence.* Thus the mandala image is a true doorway, operating in both directions between the physical and spiritual realms. And, as we have said, the imaginal domain *implicitly "contains" both the physical and spiritual worlds.*

It is important, as we prepare to work with the Stone Beings via mandalas, to remember that the physical mandala, whether it be a drawing or a stone grid, is *a doorway into experience* within the subtle/imaginal/psychoid domain. The physical mandala can be understood as its "surface," in the same way that we recognize the surface of the ocean. With both the mandala and the ocean, one must "dive in" to actually experience what awaits us. With a stone mandala, our aim is to *meet the consciousness* beneath it, and for this we must use our power of True Imagination.

This is equally true in the way mandalas are used in Buddhism. A Wikipedia article states, "The mandala is 'a support for the meditating person', something to be repeatedly contemplated to the point of saturation, such that the image of the mandala becomes fully internalized in even the minutest detail, and can then be summoned and contemplated at will as a clear and vivid visualized image." In Tibetan Buddhism, certain mandalas serve as two-dimensional "blueprints" of three-dimensional or multi-dimensional "palaces" which have been created in the imaginal realm, and which the meditator can enter through the kind of "saturation" described above. Practitioners are often admonished to remember that the physical mandala is relatively unimportant, except as it serves to bring the meditator's consciousness into the true mandala, as it exists in the inner world, among the divine energies.

MANDALAS OF SOUND: CYMATICS

As we approach the making of stone mandalas to bring forth synergies of energy and meaning, we may deepen our appreciation for the vibrational/energetic nature of mandalas by noting the new science of Cymatics.

The word Cymatics comes from an ancient Greek word meaning "wave." The term was coined by Hans Jenny, a follower of Rudolph Steiner's anthroposophy.

Wikipedia tells us: "[Jenny] claimed the existence of a subtle power based on the normal, symmetrical images made by sound waves . . . According to Jenny, these structures, reminiscent of the mandala and other forms recurring in nature, would be a manifestation of an invisible force field of the vibrational energy that generated it. He was particularly impressed by an observation that by intoning a vocalization in ancient Sanskrit of the word Om (regarded by Hindus and Buddhists as the sound of creation) lycopodium powder [spread out on a metal plate] formed a circle with a centre point, one of the ways in which Om had been represented." This observation takes what we have already noted about visual mandalas into the realm of sound, and it suggests that mandalas are representative of fundamental patterns in the realm that unites spiritual and physical reality.

It is also remarkable that in Jenny's experiments, the sound of Om, which has been held for thousands of years as a symbol of the fundamental wholeness of All-That-Is, brings forth a physical mandala form that is a natural symbol of that very wholeness. In this ancient symbol, the outer circle represents the All, while the central point represents each individual center of consciousness.

Since Jenny's day, the technical precision of Cymatics has increased dramatically. There is now a device called the CymaScope which projects sound vibrations onto water in a circular dish, and which records the patterns that are produced. The patterns can be enhanced with light, and the results are visually stunning mandala images that "can be considered as analogs of the sound or music." In short, the CymaScope makes music (and other sounds) visible. (For more about Cymatics and the Cymascope, visit www.cymascope.com)

There is much to learn in the field of Cymatics, but for our purposes, I simply want to show that the type of pattern we call a mandala is something that exists in multiple manifestations, throughout the physical, spiritual and imaginal realms. We not only see mandala forms in nature and through the inner eyes of our imaginations—we are also immersed in a world of sound, which could be described as an ever-flowing river of patterned mandala-shaped vibrations.

One other point I want to mention is that the cymatic researcher John Stuart Reid has suggested that sound patterns are *spherical,* rather than wave-shaped (as traditional science tells us). If this is so, then they may echo the pattern of the "spherical subtle body" discussed earlier. In spiritual terms, sound itself may be a living thing!

It is my view that we can take these ideas a very long way, all the way into the realm of the Stone Beings. The currents and

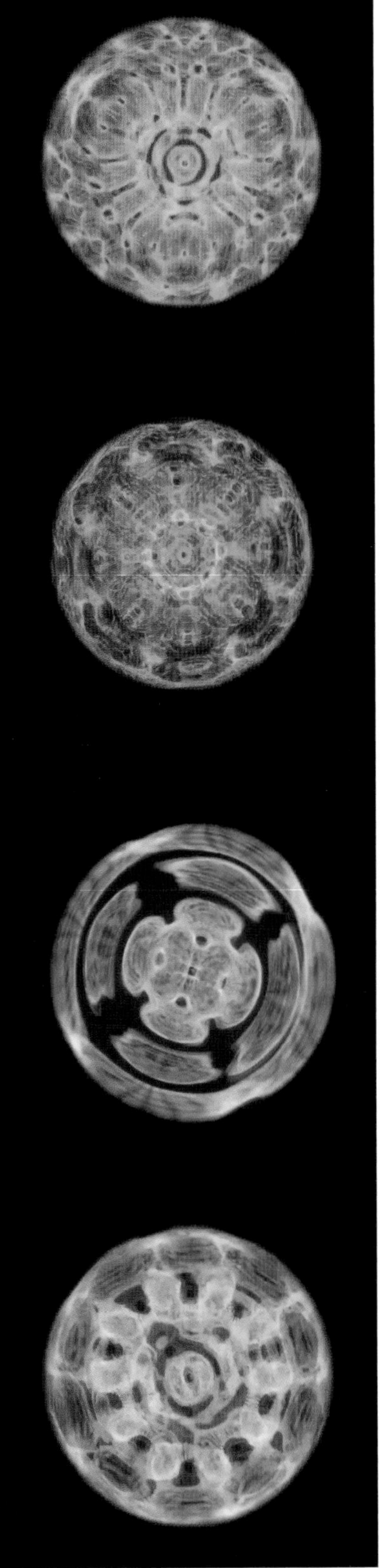

TOP TO BOTTOM: The author's voice singing; Om; Love; Azez

Azozeo

energies of stones are vibrational, and may readily be visualized as mandalas. I think our exploration of mandalas thus far has given us enough evidence to hypothesize that it is natural for physical, imaginal and spiritual energies to manifest in mandala patterns. (The closest analog to stone energies may be the sound mandalas revealed by Cymatics.)

Like the Hindus who utilize mandalas to "call the deity," we can ask the Stone Beings to reveal themselves to us in mandala form. This is remarkably easy to accomplish, perhaps because mandalas are truly archetypal forms that underlie the nature of reality. And as we do this, we may then learn to enter the realms on the Stone Beings and commune with them through contemplation of their mandalas. That is where we are going next!

PRACTICE: MAKING MANDALAS OF THE STONE BEINGS

In this Practice, we will use the form of inner dialog described by Paracelsus as Alchemical Meditation. The goal is to inwardly see and/or feel, and then draw, a mandala that represents the image and essence of the Stone Being we are working with. This practice can deepen our relationship with the Stone Being, and can increase our capacity for experiencing its energies and consciousness. Just as, for the Hindus, a mandala serves as the "abode of the deity" and "calls the deity into the presence of the practitioner," the mandala we co-create with the Stone Being will become for us a means of access to that Being in the imaginal realm.

Before beginning this practice, it will be necessary to gather some materials. You will need paper, as well as some colored pencils, markers or crayons. I suggest having several sheets of paper with a large circle pre-drawn on each of them. (You may want to use a compass, or trace around a plate or bowl.) This will give you a starting point when you are ready to begin your drawing of this Stone Being Mandala.

[**PLEASE NOTE**: It *does not matter* whether you are good at drawing or not. We are not making art—we are making spiritual talismans for relating with a Stone Being. It does not make a difference how "good" the image is. What matters is the ability of the image to function as a doorway, bringing you *through* it, into an experience of the presence of the Stone Being. For that, you only need to free yourself from "judging" the mandala, and simply allow the Stone Being and your Deep Self to guide your hand. Just as a simple pair of perpendicular lines can evoke the Christian cross and all the feelings that go with it, a simple mandala—made with no particular artistic skill—can connect you immediately with the Stone Being that it represents. So, once again, DO NOT start with a pre-conceived image or concept! Let the process take you through unknown territory and allow the mandala to "draw itself."]

1. Before beginning, choose a stone from your collection. It is ideal to *let the stone choose you* by viewing a number of different crystals and stones on a table or shelf, and waiting to see which one "calls" you for this exercise. (It's best if you hold or visualize the idea of what you will be doing when you approach the stones.)

2. Start the process in the same way we have been beginning most of practices so far–by looking at the stone and sensing it with all your senses. Breathe over the stone, offering your love and appreciation with the out-breath and gratefully receiving whatever the Stone Being may offer you with the in-breath. This is meant to initiate a resonance between yourself and the Stone Being.

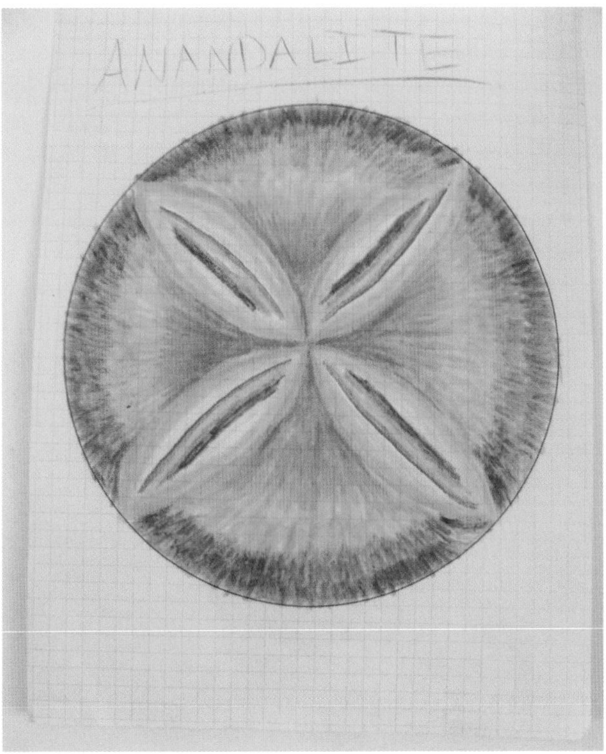

Anandalite

3. Continuing the breathing as a rhythm of offering and invitation, Close your eyes and pay attention to the interior of your body. Notice when and where the energies of the Stone Being begin coming into you, and pay close attention to how they feel and what they do.
4. Hold the stone at the center of your chest, at the level of your heart. On the in-breath, imagine that the image and essence of the stone is moving into your heart, uniting with your love and appreciation. Gratefully receive the qualities and energies of the stone.
5. When you feel ready, and can sense the stone energies resonating with yours, place your attention and intention in your heart and ask the Stone Being: "*Please show your nature and your spiritual qualities to me as a mandala image, or as feelings I can translate into a mandala image.*"
6. Pay attention to any colors, patterns, images or symbols you see, and to feelings or emotions, etc. Envision a Circle of Light, and *invite the Stone Being to show itself to you within that circle.* Continue to visualize the Circle of Light and wait to see if a pattern coalesces within it. If this occurs, give your full attention to the image, utilizing all modes of inner perception, including physical sensations and emotions. Then, when you are ready, you can go to the next step. [**NOTE**: You may find it is necessary to ask more than once, or you may find that the Stone Being wants to dialog with you rather than showing you a visual pattern. It is important to hold your intention, but with a sufficiently light touch so that you can pay attention to the Stone Being and engage with it in whatever way the experience evolves.]
7. Stay with the inner experience until it feels complete. Depending on whether you are able to keep the connection while drawing, you can begin doing so, or wait until you have thanked the Stone Being and withdrawn.
8. Draw the stone's *qualities* on the mandala paper. (If the Stone Being revealed its image within the Circle of Light that you envisioned, you can simply try to draw what you saw,

but try to do so while staying in the realm of feeling.) Draw intuitively, not allowing any preconceived ideas to take you away from the experience. Draw the energies, express visually the experience of everything you perceived. Remember you are making a spiritual portrait or diagram of the essence of the Stone Being. Choose colors that resonate with the feelings you noticed. Allow your Deep Self—your so-called unconscious self—to guide you in drawing. Don't try to control what happens. Let IT control you.

If you wish, you can make a second or third version of your drawing. You may want to do this if you have sketched the initial image quickly in order to get the gist of it on paper before losing the feeling of the experience. (Jung did this with his own mandala drawings.)

9. When your mandala drawing session feels complete, hold the stone to your heart once again and inwardly thank the Stone Being, offering your love and appreciation. Write the name of the stone somewhere on the page, and perhaps the date when you made the drawing. (You may want to try this exercise again at a later time and be able to compare the mandalas to one another.)

[**NOTE**: Adjoining this part of the text you can see reproductions of several mandalas of Stone Beings which were produced by participants at my Intensive Workshops. In the workshop setting, things are done rather quickly, in order to provide as many different experiences as possible during the event. However, when you do this in your own environment, you can take as much time as you need. Each of these mandala drawings was made by a different person, and you can see the great diversity of expressive styles they used. Also, I have shown some examples of mandalas that represent the same species of stone, but which were drawn by different individuals. Look at them with your full and relaxed attention. Can you see that the same Stone Being is being evoked, even though the mandalas all look different from one another?]

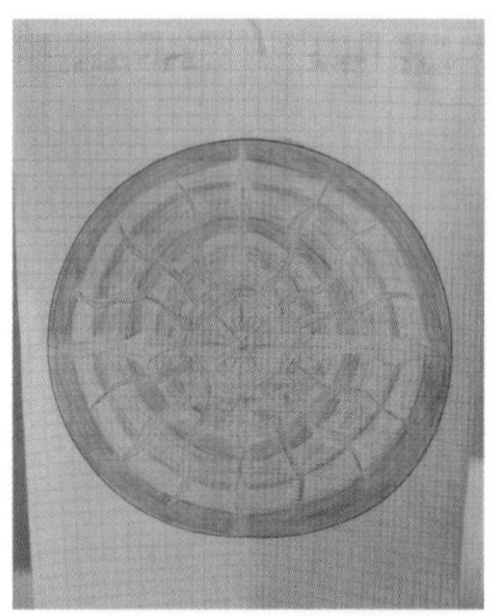

Danburite

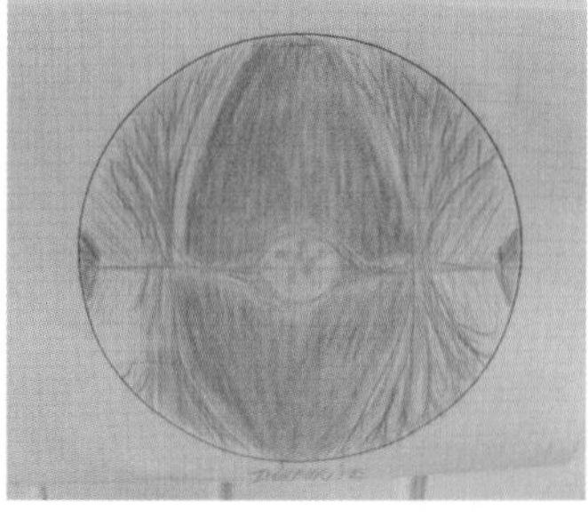

Danburite

Lemurian Light Crystal

Lemurian Light Crystal

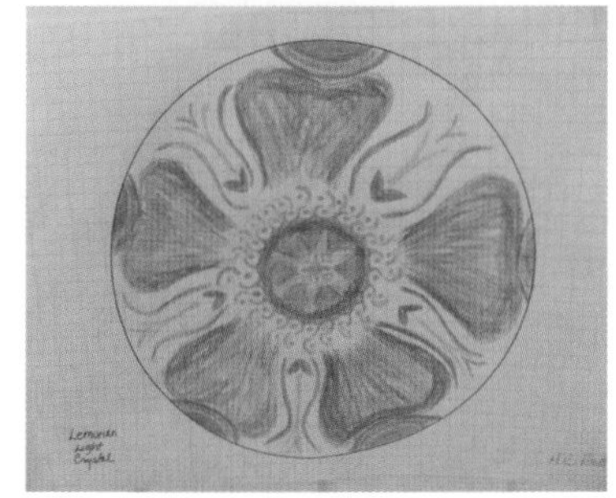

Lemurian Light Crystal

Master Shamanite

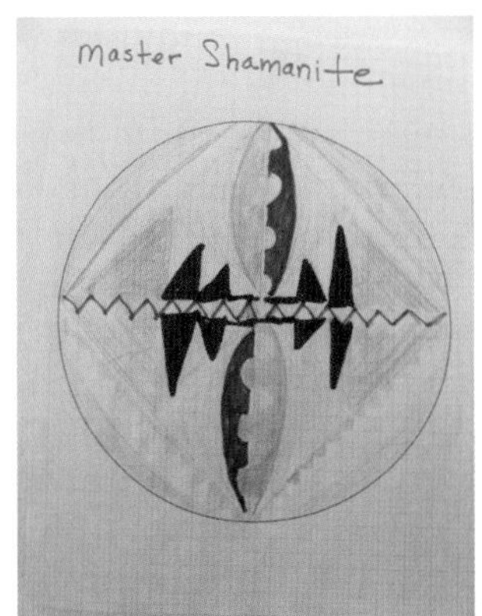

Master Shamanite

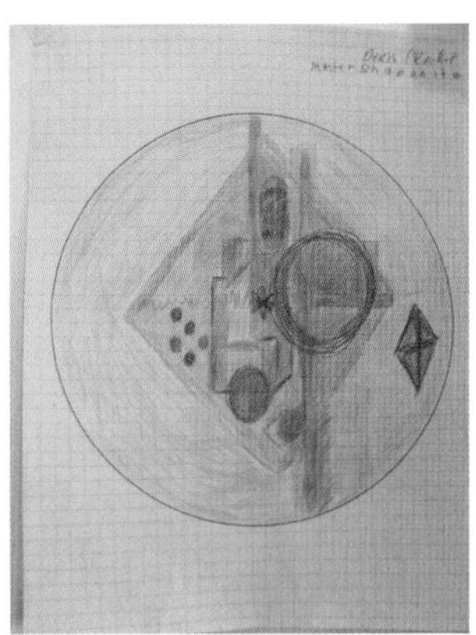

Master Shamanite

Moldavite

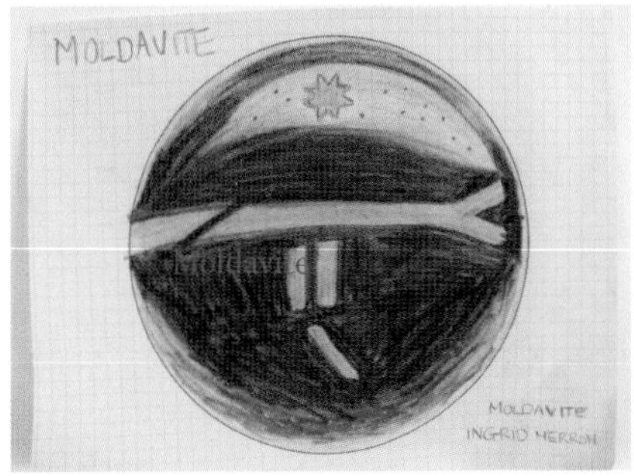

Moldavite

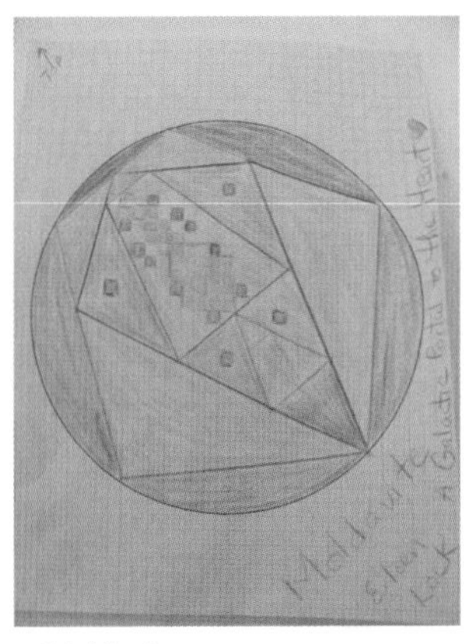

Moldavite

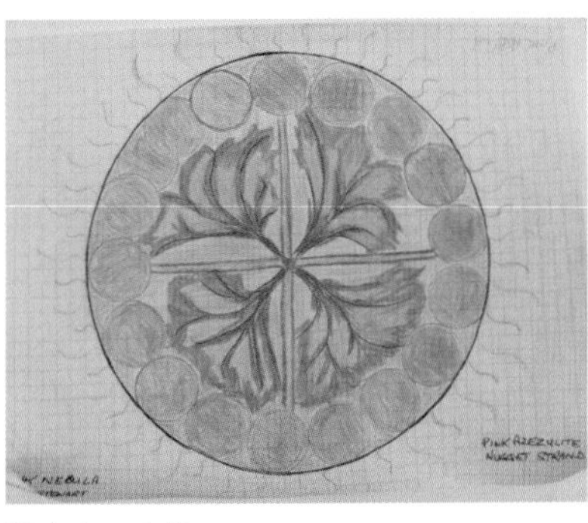

Pink Azeztulite

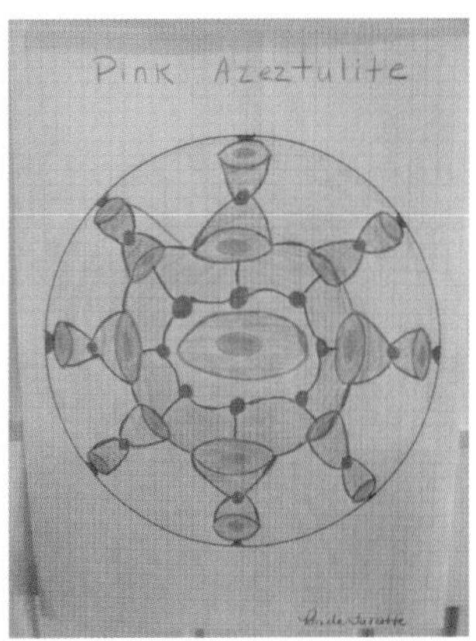

Pink Azeztulite

Rosophia

Rosophia

Satyaloka Clear Azeztulite

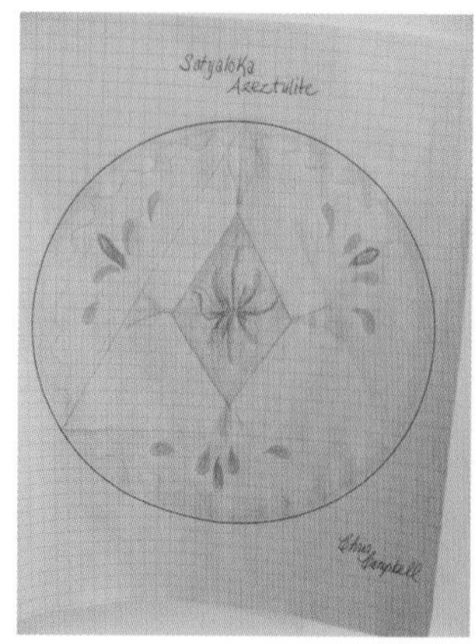

Satyaloka Clear Azeztulite

Satyaloka Clear Azeztulite

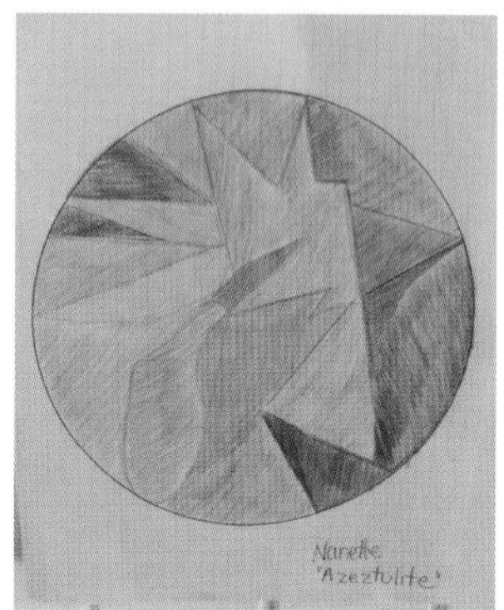

White Azeztulite

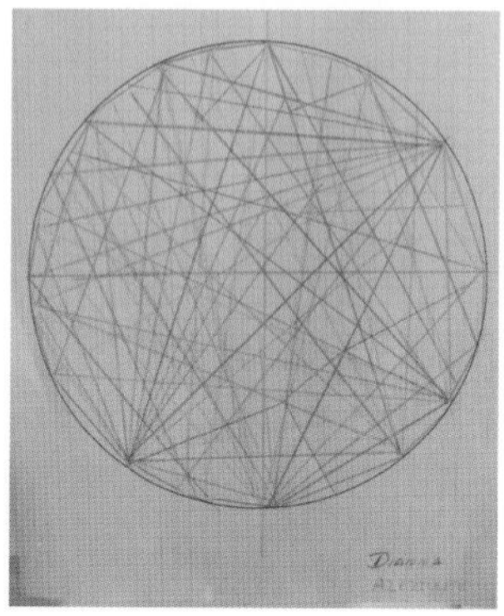

White Azeztulite

21

Working with Mandalas & the Stone Beings

> *The question arose repeatedly: What is this process leading to? Where is its goal? From my own experience, I knew by now that I could not presume to choose a goal which would seem trustworthy to me. It had been proved to me that I had to abandon the idea of the superordinate position of the ego. After all, I had been brought up short when I had attempted to maintain it . . . I was being compelled to go through this process of the unconscious. I had to let myself be carried along by the current, without a notion of where it would lead me. When I began drawing the mandalas, however, I saw that everything, all the paths I had been following, all the steps I had taken, were leading back to a single point—namely, to the mid-point. It became increasingly plain to me that the mandala is the center. It is the exponent of all paths. It is the path to the center, to individuation [wholeness].*
>
> —Carl Jung, *Memories, Dreams, Reflections*

After you have co-created a mandala of a Stone Being, the next stage is to begin working with it meditatively. As with the Hindu mandalas which represent various deities, a primary purpose of making a stone mandala is to co-create an image that enhances communication and the exchange of blessing energies between yourself and the Stone Being. It is a little like installing a window between two rooms—now that it is there, it is important to look through it! And in this case, it is important to love through it, bless through it, dialog through it, and build relationship through it. To help you get started with this, I will describe two suggested exercises.

EXERCISE ONE: SET UP AN ALTAR: After you have completed a mandala of a Stone Being, find a table or shelf that you can designate as sacred space. Clear the space and do not let things clutter it up. Maintain the sacred space.

Place the mandala onto the table or shelf. I suggest that you also put a piece of the actual stone in the center of the mandala. Create a ritual in which you affirm your appreciation to the Stone Being, and reiterate your wish to deepen your relationship with that Being.

From this point, there are many ways to go. I suggest that you come to the altar several times a week and bring a little offering. The best offerings are often things you go out and find in the natural world—twigs, feathers, little rocks, whatever calls to you. Each time you make an offering, spend a couple of minutes gazing down into the mandala with the stone at the center.

Imagine that you are looking at a fuzzy image of the Stone Being's essence, soul, and/or its subtle body—as if you were seeing it through a mist, or through wavy glass. Look *through* the mandala and try to see and feel the Being.

If you are able to feel a link with the Stone Being, the next step is to try engaging in a dialog with it. Ask the Being questions about its qualities and about the kind of work you might do together. Let the Stone Being know what you would like to ask of it, or to co-create with it. You might want to work with it in self healing or healing someone else. Or perhaps you may wish to enhance your psychic abilities and intuitive perception. Let the Stone Being know this, sending your wish or intention through the mandala and listening inwardly for what comes back. Feel free to ask the Stone Being if it is willing and able to help you. Also, ask the Stone Being what it wants or needs from you. Often it will request assistance in expressing itself more fully in the imaginal realm. This is something you can give it quite easily through meditation with the stone and/or its mandala.

When you feel you have completed this stage and that you have a solid connection with the Stone Being, you may disassemble the altar and take the offerings back to where you found them (more or less). If they are bits and pieces from the outdoors, take them out into nature and let them go.

One variation that you may wish to try in the altar exercise is to bring in a photo of yourself and place it in the center of the mandala. This is basically a way of offering yourself for relationship with the Stone Being, and it should be accompanied by your focused intention, poured through the mandala to the Stone Being. I suggest trying this if you have gone through the steps listed above and are not feeling that the connection has really been made. You can take this further by adding other offerings, such as a lock of your own hair, or a small Quartz crystal that you have programmed with your intention for relationship with this Stone Being. And be sure to open the door to your own intuition, which often will show you the precisely appropriate things to do.

Mandala Altar for Moldavite

EXERCISE TWO: JOURNEY INTO THE MANDALA. The primary purpose of the first exercise was to establish and strengthen your relationship with the Stone Being, who is represented by the mandala you co-created with it. To take this further, I suggest using the mandala drawing as a window into the world of this Stone Being. Every species of Stone Being has its own world in the imaginal realm, and you can learn to travel there through the mandala.

For a process such as this, I suggest sitting down in a comfortable chair with the mandala in your hands. You may also hold or wear a piece of the stone itself, but this is not the main focus. We want to work through the mandala.

Gaze into the mandala with your eyes soft-focused. Hold your intention to visit the Stone Being in its world. Relax and allow your attention to flow into the center of the mandala, as if you were descending down into a mine shaft or a well. (If meditation music—or even shamanic drumming—aids in this process, feel free to utilize it.) When you reach the bottom of the well or shaft, look for a light somewhere around you. Follow an inner passageway towards the light until you emerge. When you come through, look around and see what this world is like. Perhaps the Stone Being will be waiting there for you, or you may have to go on a search. When you see a being you feel you recognize, ask if it is the Being of the stone. If so, you may then do any number of things together. I will not speculate on the content of your journeys, because I don't want to limit them. However, I hope you will write down an account of them afterwards.

When your journey into the world of the Stone Being feels complete, offer your thanks, say your farewells and retrace your path, emerging back up through the mandala and into this world.

You may go into such journeys with any intent you wish—healing, learning, etc.—or with no agenda other than to explore and deepen your relationship with this Stone Being. You may even ask a Stone Being with whom you have a deep rapport to introduce you to Sophia. All of these things are possible. How deep you go can depend on practice, focus, imaginative ability, and sometimes on pure Divine grace.

In some cases, you may feel drawn to try this same type of journey with the mandalas of various different Stone Beings. I think this is a very good idea. There are many stones to meet and many worlds to travel.

GREATER POSSIBILITIES: The potential ways you can work with mandalas of the Stone Beings are limitless. I encourage readers to let the stones themselves make suggestions, and to listen also to your own Deep Self for inspirations. Making these mandalas is an excellent way to enter into instant co-creative activity with a Stone Being. It also illuminates the nature of these beings in one's consciousness.

Over time, you may discover that the energies you would typically feel from holding a particular stone are also evoked by contemplating its mandala. That is how mandalas of all types function when one puts sufficient time and attention into practicing with them. One important thing to remember is that the energies of the Stone Beings are not limited by space and time, and may be called upon, if one has a rapport with them, even when a physical stone is not present. The mandala provides a stepping stone into developing this type of rapport.

For those who try making mandalas of the Stone Beings at least a few times, and who find that they enjoy the results, I would encourage co-creating mandalas of all of the stones in one's collection, or at least those that are one's favorites. By doing this, one co-creates an array of the worlds of various Stone Beings, resulting in a Cosmos of Stones in which one can journey and participate whenever one wishes. It is possible to eventually live "with one foot in each reality" so that one is in touch with the world of one's daily life and the worlds of the Stone Beings, all at the same time. This is a powerful path for expanding one's consciousness, potentially leading to the ultimate union which the alchemists sought.

STONE ENERGY MANDALAS: TEMPLATES, GRIDS, LAYOUTS & LABYRINTHS

> *Material things are laden with* mana *[spiritual power] . . . they are divine things. What is divine? Materials are divine; therefore, if we use any kind of matter, we use a god, or a Godhead full of* mana, *and by mixing materials, divine powers are mixed and a divine power is exerted, or we bring forth changes within the realm of divine powers. All Egyptian techniques were used in that magical and religious spirit.*
>
> —Marie Louise von Franz, *Alchemical Active Imagination*

Having looked at making mandala drawings to link us with the energies and consciousness of individual species of the Stone Beings, we can move on to discussing the creation of mandalas utilizing multiple types of stones. These mandalas work in a different way from our mandala pictures. Rather than aiming toward understanding and relating with a single Stone Being, we are working with combinations of a variety of stones, and our efforts are aimed at bringing about certain effects. This echos the ancient Egyptian alchemical work referred to in the quote above. When we combine different stones in mandalas, we are bringing synergistic patterns of divine energies into our environment, and we are simultaneously co-creating those patterns in the subtle/imaginal/ psychoid realm.

One can view the creation of these harmonies of stones as being somewhat akin to the composition of music. The musical composer draws upon knowledge of a multitude of vibrational frequencies (musical notes) as well as an array of different instruments which can express these notes in different ways. A musical composer also works with an idea of the experience (or set of experiences) she or he intends to evoke in the listeners.

As we start to compose a stone template or grid, we do many of the same things, and we draw our vibrational "notes" from the variety of minerals and crystals available to us. Also, we notice that there are often a number of stones that emanate the same or similar frequencies, though each has its own "voice." Thus, we can bring together stones that emphasize a specific energetic "tone," or we can build a more complex pattern that involves a "chord" of different stone vibrations.

The difference between a stone template and a stone grid, as I loosely define them, is primarily one of size. A template is usually something that can be easily held in one's hand or placed on one of the chakras in a body layout. A grid is often larger, ranging from six inches to an almost unlimited size. (Some people construct stone grids around their entire properties, and I have participated in projects for gridding whole cities (Washington, D.C. in particular). Another distinction is that a stone template always has a base, whereas stone grids can be created either with bases or without them.

In making templates, I use glue or putty to attach small stones and gems onto a larger (often palm-size) stone base. When I am making a template that I want to keep for a long time I frequently glue the stones in place, if the size of the project makes that practical. (On occasion I also make temporary grids that are designed to be used for a specific time period, like the Tibetan sand mandalas.)

The stone combinations one can use to build templates are unlimited. I have worked creating gemstone templates for a number of years, and I find it to be a fascinating activity. Usually I begin with a purpose in mind, in terms of the effects I am hoping to facilitate, and then I meditate on the idea, while staying close to my collection of stones. Frequently I find that the Stone Beings will "talk" to me, usually by generating images in my mind's eye, letting me know which stones are volunteering to come together in the piece I want to make. Sometimes I am surprised by the images that come to me, but I almost always follow the suggestions I receive, and the effects have been good. I recommend this method when you want to compose your own templates. It helps you to be more open to co-creative influence from the Stone Beings and your own Deep Self than planning the template "logically" before you sit down to do it.

What should one use for the base of a stone template? Most of the time, I use some type of stone for the base. Most often, I work with Selenite bases because Selenite tends to amplify the energies of the entire combination, and to harmonize them. In other instances, I may choose a base stone that I want to act as a particularly strong influence in the piece. It is also good to work with a clear Quartz base for overall amplification, although these have become scarcer and more expensive than the Selenite.

In the following pages, a number of gemstone templates are shown, and their stone combinations are listed next to them. As you view them, relax and let your eyes go into a soft focus. Take enough time to connect with some of the templates energetically through their photographs. This technique actually works, and you can connect with the Stone Beings in a particular piece by pouring your attention into the image of the template. This is very much like the way that meditators go into a mandala to enter "the abode of the deity." In this case, one is entering the vibrational abode of the Stone Beings combined in the template. When you make or buy templates of your own, you can also use them as windows into the realm of the Stone Beings. For most people, it is easier to work through the physical template than the photo of one, but either way can work.

One last thought before you go on to view the template images: Remember the idea that some of the traditional Tibetan mandalas were conceived as "blueprints" of inner temples or palaces in the imaginal realm? When we create a template, we are building a "vibrational temple" of stone energies. When we hold the template or place it on our body, we are inviting the vibrational pattern of that temple into ourselves, and we are simultaneously *entering* that temple. Within the temple are all of the Stone Beings who are represented in the piece. If one has worked with them in a co-creative way, one may be able to inwardly see or feel their combined presence, and perhaps even to discern them individually. One may even be able to go inside the temple and experience its healing or imaginative qualities. After all, the word "template" has the word "temple" within it!

So, as you view the images, and when you work with physical stone templates, I invite you to use your power of True Imagination to enter them imaginally and experience them as deeply as you can.

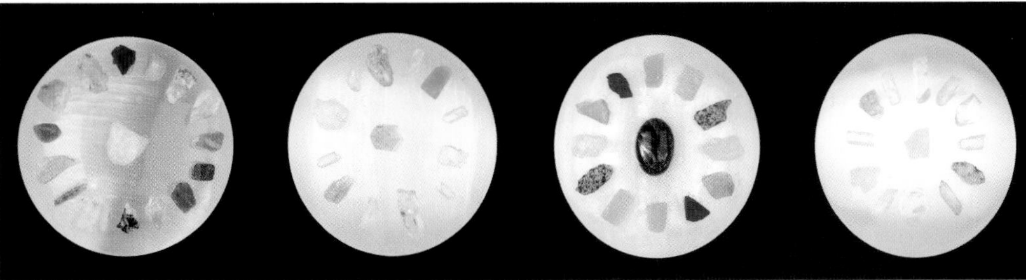

AZEZTULITE 16: Selenite base with sixteen different varieties of Azeztulite

ANGELIC REALM: Selenite base with White Azeztulite, Angelite, Lithium Light, Angel Aura Quartz, Petalite, Azumar, Danburite, Magnifier Quartz

HEALING POWER: Selenite base with White Azeztulite, Healerite, Guardianite, Crimson Cuprite, Seraphinite, Azumar, Auralite-23

ASCENSION 7: Selenite base with White Azeztulite, Phenacite, Herderite, Danburite, Natrolite, Petalite, Satyaloka Clear Azeztulite, Magnifier Quartz

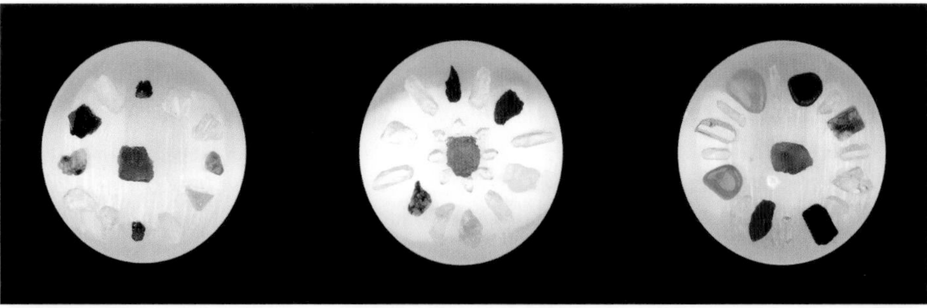

SYNERGY 12: Selenite base with Moldavite, Phenacite, Tanzanite, Danburite, White Azeztulite, Natrolite, Scolecite, Brookite, Satyaloka Clear Azeztulite, Petalite, Tibetan Tektite

ALCHEMICAL TRANSFORMATION: Selenite base with Black, Red Fire, White, Himalaya Gold, Black Tourmaline and Satyaloka Clear Azeztulites, plus Moldavite, Herkimer Crystals, Magnifier Quartz

SUPER CHAKRA HARMONY: Selenite base with Black Tourmaline, Red Fire Azeztulite, Carnelian, Golden Apatite, Moldavite, Azumar, Lapis, Auralite-23, Danburite, Magnifier Quartz

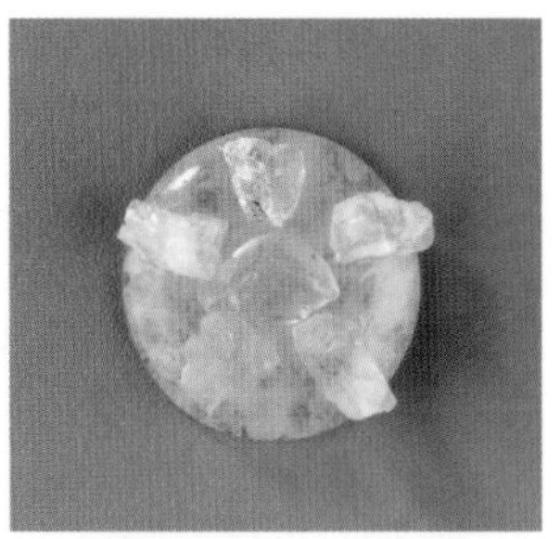

ASCENSION 7: White Azeztulite base with Petalite, Satyaloka Azeztulite, Danburite, Nirvana Quartz, Golden Azeztulite, Satya Mani Quartz

EARTH MAGIC: Mystic Merlinite base with Fulgurite, Black Tourmaline, Nuummite and Master Shamanite

PHILOSOPHERS' STONE: Rosophia base with Moldavite, White Azeztulite, Himalaya Gold Azeztulite, Master Shamanite

HEALING: Sanda Rosa Azeztulite base with Morganite, Seraphinite, Healer's Gold

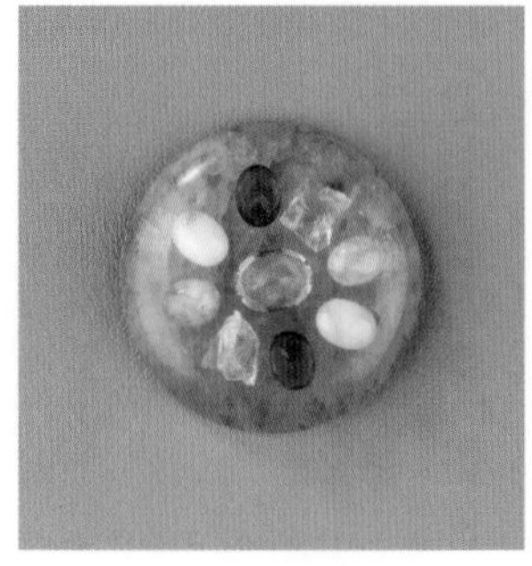

GREAT CENTRAL SUN: Himalaya Gold Azeztulite base with Libyan Gold Tektite, White Azeztulite, Moldavite, Agni Gold Danburite, North Carolina Clear Azeztulite

POWER OF THE AZEZ: White Azeztulite base with North Carolina Clear Azeztulite, Pink Azeztulite, Himalaya Gold Azeztulite, Satyaloka Azeztulite, Sanda Rosa Azeztulite, Golden Azeztulite

Sometimes a small grid (or super-template) can be built on a gemstone base, like the Moldavite, Quartz and Amethyst one pictured at the beginning of this chapter. More often, we have to use a different material as the base for stone mandalas that are larger than palm size.

One material that makes an excellent base for stone grids is tempered glass. I like to use the standard size ten inch squares that are available from store display companies and some glass suppliers. Tempered glass is durable and scratch resistant, and is composed of approximately 70% quartz. This makes it a good conductor for stone energies, although I do not feel that it amplifies them, as natural Quartz and Selenite do.

Another benefit of using the tempered glass squares as bases for stone mandala grids comes from their shape. One of the quotes at the beginning of Chapter 20 tells us that "a traditional mandala is a square containing a circle, and the entire design is symmetrical and balanced . . ." And Jung stated: "In the products of the unconscious we discover mandala symbols, that is, circular and quaternity figures which express wholeness, and whenever we wish to express wholeness, we employ just such figures." In alchemy, one of the metaphors for producing the Philosophers' Stone was known as "squaring the circle." So, if we begin a stone grid with a glass square as a base, and then create a circular array of stones on the base, we are evoking this archetypal pattern of wholeness through the mandala that we create. Below are two photographs of these glass-base stone mandalas.

HEALING GRID ON TEMPERED GLASS: with Sauralite Azeztulite (center), Healerite, Azumar, Amazez, White Azeztulite, Vitalite, Seraphinite, Shungite

SYNERGY 12 GRID ON TEMPERED GLASS: with Moldavite, Phenacite, Tanzanite, Danburite, White Azeztulite, Brookite, Scolecite, Petalite, Tibetan Tektite, Natrolite, Herderite, Satyaloka Clear Azeztulite

Another type of stone mandala has been made possible through the availability of laser-etched wooden mandalas. The ones I work with are made from thin birch plywood, and are available in a variety of different designs. The laser etching allows these pieces to be quite detailed and intricate, without making the cost prohibitively high.

I like the use of these wooden bases, because my sense is that natural materials like wood do not diminish or interfere with stone energies. The visionary inventor Willhelm Reich utilized wood and other organic materials in his orgone accumulators, which were subtle energy devices. This also speaks to the idea that wood can work harmoniously with stones in creating our mandalas. (We will explore orgone devices in a Chapter 26.)

Another virtue of the laser etched wood mandala bases is the fact that they already contain intricate and symbolically meaningful mandala designs. Thus they already carry a degree of

imaginal power which can work on one's consciousness, facilitating the spiritual experiences to which one aspires.

On the left, there are photos of several of the wood-based Mandala Crystal Grids that I have made. As with all such pieces, I recommend working meditatively and co-creatively with the Stone Beings in designing your own pieces.

LARGER STONE MANDALA GRIDS

One can co-create larger Stone Mandala Grids on a table top, floor or other flat area. The same basic techniques for stone selection and patterning can be used in these larger grids. When I make grids such as these, they are usually temporary and are meant to enhance the energies of a meditation altar, healing room or other area designated as sacred space.

The primary benefits of these larger grids have to do with building a more powerful energy field by bringing in larger stones, a greater number of stones, and (if one chooses) a wider variety of stones than are typically included in smaller grids and templates.

When building a larger grid, it is ideal if one meditates before beginning, asking for the participation of Sophia and the Stone Beings. Then, as much as possible, one should do the stone placement in silence and without outer distractions, keeping one's intention and attention linked to the guiding impulses that one receives. When this is done, the effect can often be astonishing, as one recognizes that one is truly participating in *co-creation* with these beings.

Opposite are photos of a tabletop Stone Mandala Grid that I have made. I invite you to take a few moments to contemplate each one, and allow their energies to meet you in the imaginal realm.

FROM TOP TO BOTTOM

CHAKRA POWER, with Amethyst, Lapis, Aquamarine, Aventurine, Citrine, Carnelian, Garnet, Satyaloka Clear Azeztulite, Amazez, Tanzanite, Azumar, Moldavite, Himalaya Gold Azeztulite, Pink Fire Azeztulite, Red Fire Azeztulite, Rose Quartz, Satyaloka Clear Azeztulite

POLARITY HARMONY, with Black Tourmaline Azeztulite, Guardianite, Black Azeztulite, White Azeztulite, Satyaloka Clear Azeztulite, Black Tourmaline, Lemurian Light Crystals

HEART OF LOVE AND LIGHT, with Heartenite, Satyaloka Rose Azeztulite, Rosophia, Super Pink Kunzite, Pink Petalite, Pink Azezetulite, Rhodocrosite, Rose Quartz, Lilac Lepidolite

HEALING POWER, with Healerite, White Azeztulite, Healers Gold, Seraphinite, Sugilite, Infinite, Guardianite, Hiddenite, Chrysoprase, Vitalite, Auralite-23, Crimson Cuprite, Kaurilite, Lemurian Light Crystals

ASCENSION, with Herderite, Phenacite, Danburite, Moldavite, White Azeztulite, Natrolite, Satyaloka Clear Azeztulite

OPPOSITE

DESK-TOP STONE MANDALA GRID. The intention of this one is for worldwide awakening, healing and wellbeing. Stones: Azozeo Phenacite, Rutilated Quartz, Moldavite, Amethyst, Ajoite, Clear Quartz, White Azeztulite, Azumar, Healerite, Rhodocrosite, Sauralite Azeztulite, Labradorite, Orange Calcite, Amazez, Celestite, Lepidolite, Golden Azeztulite, Tibetan Black Quartz, Kaurilite, Pink Calcite, Rose Quartz, Citrine, Andean Green Quartz, Rosophia

Another sort of stone grid that I work with is for the ballrooms or auditoriums where I offer my Intensive Workshops. Before the participants arrive for these events, I go in with one or two helpers and set up a stone energy grid around the perimeter of the entire space. In doing this, I always ask for the co-creative participation of the Stone Beings that will be in the grid, and all the Stone Beings whom we will work with during the event. As I am placing the stones around the room, I hold the intention of energizing the space with the purest spiritual Light, and keeping the area clear of any disharmonious energies. I usually take an additional step at the beginning of my workshops: When everyone is assembled on the first day, we chant Om together and all of us join in emphasizing our intentions—to work co-creatively with the Stone Beings to charge our sacred space and to keep it clear. In these group activations of the grid, we also always invite the Stone Beings to join us. We then do all of our work for the next few days within the sacred space of this powerful mandala.

We can take this process of co-creating large stone mandala grids as far as we want to. My company, Heaven and Earth, has supplied Azeztulite and other high vibration stones to a number of people who were planning to build outdoor stone energy grids around their properties. The reports we received from them were all highly positive; and the people could certainly sense a beneficial difference in the vibrational feeling of their environment.

One example is that of one of my workshop students, Steffny Wallace, who created an Azeztulite grid on her lavender farm to enhance both the growth and the healing qualities of her lavender. She later wrote to tell us that the results were even more wonderful than she had imagined. One big surprise was that, having been in the presence of Azeztulites from our labyrinth, her lavender plants matured fully in the first year, when she had been told to expect it to take two to three years before she could start to harvest them. She told us that the Azeztulites helped her to grow top quality lavender of a remarkably high spiritual vibration. Steffny also experienced a number of direct communications with the Azez, who offered blessings and guidance for her and her community. (To read a more detailed account of her experiences, see the testimonials page on our website: www.heavenandearthjewelry.com/testimonials.aspx)

I mentioned earlier that I have been involved in gridding Washington, D.C. with stones. This is another project in which Azeztulite was used. A group of people who envisioned placing stones of spiritual Light around that city came to me as a source for stones of very high vibration. After some discussion, we supplied a quantity of Azeztulite pieces for their project. I hope (and hold the intention) that this installation is working beneficially for the good of the world. As I write this, my feeling is that more stones and more people are needed. Perhaps this mandala needs to be strengthened, both with stones and with the energy of human participants. The vision I see is that, if people choose to do this, they will be intuitively guided in regard to where the stones should be placed. Although the classic mandala forms are symmetrical, I believe that in a living mandala such as this, the intention of those who are co-creating it will be more important than the geometrical symmetry.

[NOTE: For those who live in the D.C. area, or who will be traveling there, and who would like to get involved: send an email to heavenandearth@earthlink.net, and someone will get back to you. We also invite communication from those wishing to create mandalas of this scope in other parts of the world.]

STONE LABYRINTHS AS MANDALA GRIDS

Some of the largest and most powerfully charged stone mandalas I have personally experienced are labyrinths. For readers who are unacquainted with labyrinths as sacred spaces of meditation and spiritual experience, I will offer this quote from labyrinthsociety.org:

LEFT: Azeztulite/Rosophia Labyrinth, Vermont, USA
BELOW: Rose Quartz indoor Labyrinth, Italy

A labyrinth is a meandering path, often unicursal [single-path], with a singular path leading to a center. Labyrinths are an ancient archetype dating back 4,000 years or more, used symbolically, as a walking meditation, choreographed dance, or site of rituals and ceremony, among other things. Labyrinths are tools for personal, psychological and spiritual transformation, also thought to enhance right-brain activity. Labyrinths evoke metaphor, sacred geometry, spiritual pilgrimage, religious practice, mindfulness, environmental art, and community building.

I have already mentioned, in connection with the rainbow orb phenomenon, the Azeztulite and Rosophia labyrinths I was involved in creating. When the idea for the first of these labyrinths came into my mind, it was a completely unexpected inspiration. However, once the image came to me, I felt compelled to build it.

That mandala/labyrinth was the site of many extraordinary spiritual experiences. I walked it many times, and could always feel a calm and powerful resonance within it. My wife Kathy commented that walking into the labyrinth felt as if she was entering a sphere of Light, which extended into the air above her and the earth beneath her feet.

When the second Azeztulite and Rosophia labyrinth was built for my Stones of the New Consciousness Intensive in 2010, the power of that installation was much like that of the one at our home. Numerous participants at the workshop spoke of their experiences in the labyrinth as the peak moments of their time at that event.

In The Alchemy of Stones, we recognize that the imaginal world—the great realm that encompasses both physical and spiritual reality—is the domain in which symbols and images

TOP: Stone Labyrinth at Te Moata Retreat Center, New Zealand; BOTTOM: Chartres-style Labyrinth with river stones and White Azeztulite, Benson, North Carolina

carry the power that weaves spirit and matter together. The labyrinth itself is a symbol of spiritual meaning that resonates many centuries into the past, and forward into eternity. The website crystalinks.com tells us:

> *A labyrinth is an ancient symbol that relates to wholeness. It combines the imagery of the circle and the spiral into a meandering but purposeful path. It represents a journey to our own center and back again out into the world.*

Thus, the spiritual purpose of the labyrinth is closely akin to that of our work in the Alchemy of Stones. Our alchemical journey is aimed at realizing and embodying our wholeness, and it involves "a journey to our own center and back again out into the world." That is what we have referred to in alchemical terms as Conjunction, and one might imagine the Three Conjunctions (which lead ultimately to fulfilling our wholeness in union with the Divine) as three journeys through the labyrinth of the world, each at a deeper level. After each of these voyages, we emerge into the world at a different stage of transformation.

Our meditative processes with stones involve rituals which are resonant with the pattern of the labyrinth. In ritual, we symbolically enact the inner process that we hope to activate. For example, the blowing of our breath over a stone as we begin a meditation is a ritual offering of our spiritual essence to the Stone Being. The physical breath symbolizes the offering of essence. By performing the "surface" ritual physically while holding the imaginal intention for the deeper event to occur, we call that event into our reality. Thus, each of these rituals is a journey to the center and back. The labyrinths built into the floors of sacred sites such as Chartres Cathedral were created in order to facilitate the experience of going inward to the Divine center, and returning to the world as a transformed human being. Our meditative work with stones carries essentially the same intention.

With all of this in mind, one can see how powerful it could be to use the mandala pattern of the labyrinth in combination with our work with stones. This idea is what captured my imagination and motivated me to build the Azeztulite and Rosophia labyrinths. The ritual pattern of the journey was present in the labyrinth path. And the currents of the stones provided a sphere of resonant energy that made one vividly aware that the "walk" was simultaneously taking place on multiple levels of reality. This environment provided an ideal atmosphere for spontaneous experiences of spiritual awakening and transformation.

But what if you do not have access to a labyrinth made out of high-vibration stones? Don't be concerned! One can devise and partake of profound rituals and powerful experiences by simply carrying a chosen stone as one walks any sort of labyrinth. I recommend holding the stone over one's heart during the walk, and working with the feedback loop of offering and receiving love and appreciation—to and from the stone—through one's breath. If you are focusing and utilizing your three powers of attention, intention and imagination while you do this, you are likely to have experiences of great power and significance for you.

THE AZEZTULITE & ROSOPHIA WORLD LABYRINTH

The alchemists aimed their intentions toward the spiritual fulfillment and redemption of themselves and the world. How can we do this now? There are countless ways for us to express this intention, and to make rituals that plant the seeds of this intention. Of all such rituals in which I have participated, perhaps the longest and most ambitious was the one that we named the Azeztulite and Rosophia World Labyrinth.

This project began in 2011, when my wife and I were preparing to move from Vermont, USA, to New Zealand. We loved our Azeztulite and Rosophia labyrinth, and we did not want to leave it behind. But we had no open land in New Zealand where we could set it up. What to do?

Once again, an inspiration arrived, and this time it was a simple one. I suddenly saw—and felt with complete certainty—that the thing to do was to distribute the stones from our labyrinth to people all over the world. We would suggest that each person who acquired one of the stones should "plant" it in an appropriate place, holding the intention that it would resonate with all of the other stones from the labyrinth, and would bring harmony and awakening to the whole Earth and all its beings. Together, we would spread the labyrinth over the whole planet–the Azeztulite and Rosophia World Labyrinth.

I felt sure that every stone from this labyrinth was highly charged, both because of the types of stones that they were, and because of the many experiences in which they had been involved. They were also perfectly harmonized with one another. In line with the alchemical maxim, "As above, so below," perhaps this ongoing ritual with many participants would help to influence and accelerate the worldwide spiritual transformation which is our common vision.

At first we were only sending out the whole stones as they had been when we took the labyrinth apart. Later, in response to many requests, we broke some of the stones into smaller pieces. Some we cut and polished and made into pendants. Others we made into pocket-sized tumbled stones. All of this was done to make the stones accessible to people, to use in the ways that most strongly drew them.

In the years since the project began, people from dozens of countries have claimed their stones and joined their intention with ours. Most of the spots where the stones have been placed are outwardly unremarkable, but they are often places that are much loved by those who brought them there. In some instances, people have taken their stones to areas that are terribly stressed by pollution or disasters, such as Hiroshima and Fukishima in Japan. Others have been set in power spots and on ley lines, to contribute to the wellbeing of the Earth. Now we can truly say that our first labyrinth has become a world labyrinth, and wherever we walk in our life's journey, we are all within it.

[**NOTE**: As of this writing, we still have some of the World Labyrinth stones. Those interested are invited to see them online at heavenandearthjewelry.com, or send an email inquiry to: heavenandearth@earthlink.net]

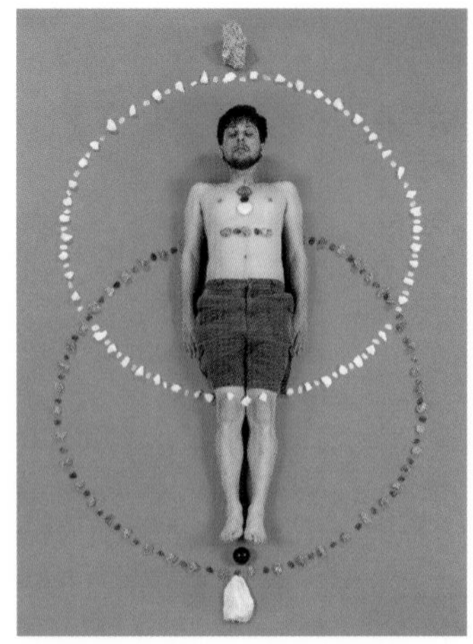

STONE MANDALA BODY LAYOUTS

Body layouts are one of the best known practices through which one can experience the energies and influence of multiple stones simultaneously. We will describe and explore a number of these in the next chapter. However, the idea of the mandala can also be applied to stone body layouts, as the pictures on the left display.

The benefit of doing this type of body layout/grid is that the stones are not confined to being in contact with the body, and the person receiving the layout is within an energy field, created by both the stones themselves and the symbolic resonance of their patterns in the subtle/imaginal realm. The stones carry their individual and combined meanings and energies, as do the mandala patterns.

In the next chapter, we will delve more deeply into stone "body layouts" for healing and spiritual activation. We will work with the traditional approach of placing appropriate stones on the chakras and meridian points, as well as in the body's surrounding subtle energy field.

In Chapters 23 and 24, we will discover that we can also influence an individual through working with stones placed on a *photographic image* of the body. These sorts of stone layouts represent a significant departure from what has been done in the past, and they open up a myriad of exciting possibilities. I call them Photonic Stone Layouts.

FROM TOP TO BOTTOM
MANDALA GRID HEAVEN AND EARTH (VESSICA PISCES), STONES: Rosophia, White Azeztulite, Master Shamanite, Phenacite

MANDALA GRID MERKABA, STONES: Merkabite Calcite, Selenite Wands, Mystic Merlinite, White Azeztulite, Cryolite, Petalite, Phenacite, Spanish Aragonite, Datolite, Tibetan Tektite, Darwinite, Moldavite, Libyan Gold Tektite, Sanda Rosa Azeztulite, Natrolite, Circle Stone;

MANDALA GRID FULL ASCENSION, STONES: White Azeztulite, Golden Azeztulite Crystals, Pink Azeztulite, Himalaya Gold Azeztulite, Sanda Rosa Azeztulite, Satyaloka Azeztulite, Selenite Wands, Nirvana Quartz, Petalite, Creedite, Cinnabar Quartz, Crimson Cuprite, White Danburite, Agni Gold Danburite, Mystic Merlinite, Tibetan Black Quartz, Circle Stone, Phenacite, Moldavite, Moldau Quartz, Prophecy Stone, Fulgurite, Spanish Aragonite, Satya Mani Quartz

22

Stone Body Layouts for Healing & Visionary Experience

Many other cultures have developed traditions of crystal healing over time, including the Hopi Native Americans of Arizona and Hawaiian islanders, some of whom continued to use it as of 1997. The Chinese have traditionally attributed healing powers to microcrystalline jade.

—Wikipedia https://en.wikipedia.org/wiki/Crystal_healing

TOP: Participants in the 2016 Alchemy of Stones intensive in Vermont during Stone Body Layouts Practice; BOTTOM: Participants in Robert Simmons' 2019 Workshop in Japan work on Stone Body Layouts.

We have already touched on much that is related to working with stones for purposes of healing, and for the evolution of one's consciousness. That is what the Alchemy of Stones is all about. In this chapter we will go into one of the "cornerstones" of modern spiritual work with crystals and minerals—Stone Body Layouts.

The most basic idea involved in this type of work is that, because both stones and people have subtle energy vibrational fields, one can affect the state of a person's field—and ultimately their health and consciousness—through bringing together the individual's field with the fields of appropriate beneficial stones. Since the human energy field is closely linked with the physical body, it seems to make sense to try to bring about the desired changes and benefits through placing stones on or near the body. Most of us find it easier to feel stone energies when we are holding or touching the stone. Placing stones at various points on the body is a way to orchestrate a coordinated overall 'chord' of vibrational energy that can benefit the recipient. (In the next chapter, we'll discover a way to do stone layouts remotely, but for now we will stay with the conventional method of placing stones on and around the physical body.)

Stone Body Layouts are easy to do. Hundreds of thousands (or millions) of people have experienced them. When I offer my Intensive Workshops, we always include Body Layout sessions where participants pair off with partners to do the work. These sessions often prove to be among the high points of the entire four days for many attendees. Because I believe my readers will almost all have heard of Stone Body Layouts before, or have read about them in other books, I will touch only lightly on explanations, and concentrate on several recommended layouts that we can do.

USING THE THREE HUMAN POWERS IN STONE BODY LAYOUTS

In the Alchemy of Stones, we work co-creatively with the Stone Beings and Sophia in all of our practices. To do this, we focus on utilizing our capacities of attention, intention and imagination. When one is getting ready to either give or receive a stone body layout, it is important to bring one's awareness into harmonious accord through consciously focusing one's full attention on what one intends to do. This will automatically bring in the faculty of imagination which spontaneously "pictures" what one intends. This may seem obvious, but I am mentioning it because it is important to give oneself fully to the process and outcome one wishes to co-create. By using one's focused will to pour oneself into the practice, one's energies are more highly activated, and are more available for connection with the Stone Beings.

One helpful way to think about this is to envision these practices as *rituals* of healing and/or consciousness expansion. In a spiritual ritual, one would not allow oneself to become distracted by outside events of random thoughts. (One would not, for example, have the television turned on, or be making dinner plans!) The more focused one can be when giving or receiving a stone layout, the more effective it can be.

It is also important to do these practices utilizing what Robert Sardello has called the "soft will." Even though I have emphasized the need for undistracted focus and for imagining what one wishes to accomplish, one must not allow one's intention to become rigid or "hard." Doing this will eliminate the possibility of co-creating with the Stone Beings, because their input will be screened out by the way the "hard will" tries to control the process. Even when we think we want to co-create with the stones, a too-intense focus of intention will undermine our efforts. What I tell myself to do is: "Pour yourself into this with every inhalation, and surrender it all when you exhale." One does not need to follow this pattern with absolute precision, because trying to do that is another gesture of the "hard will." But it is helpful to remember to imagine what is happening and then let go into the experience of what actually occurs.

I'll give a quick example here. I recently decided to do a simple layout on myself for the purpose of purifying the energies in and around my first and second chakras. I had been aware of stagnant energies in those areas for almost a year, and of some physical discomfort that went along with that situation. None of the traditional healing modalities I tried had helped me much. Suddenly, in a random moment, I received a strong impulse to do a body layout with two pieces of Sauralite Azeztulite–one at the root chakra and one at the heart chakra.

As I lay on the floor with the two Sauralites in their respective placements, I first concentrated on my breathing, inviting the Stone Being of Sauralite into my subtle body field as I inhaled, and offering myself for relationship with Sauralite as I exhaled. This brought me into attunement with Sauralite's energies, which I experienced as a relaxing "Ahhhhhh . . ." sensation, which flowed through my whole body.

Next I saw a spontaneous inner image that suggested to me that I should visualize and invite the Sauralite energy to circulate as a figure-eight current, pouring out of both stones, moving through and around my body, in rhythm with my breathing. (I always follow these inner impulses, whether they come from my Deep Self or from the Stone Beings.) As I did this, I felt a lovely and pleasurable intensification of the Sauralite energies. After just a couple of minutes, I noticed that my discomfort had lessened considerably, and after perhaps ten minutes, it was completely gone! Nothing I had tried—from homeopathics to herbs to prescription medication—had given me that kind of relief. Further, the energy in my first and second chakras was flowing—no longer stagnant.

This incident marked my first clear recognition of Sauralite Azeztulite as an important spiritual healing stone. Up to that time, I had imagined it was primarily for inner Light, consciousness expansion and opening the heart to love. (Of course, there is a very healing quality to the energies of spiritual Light and love!) This event reminded me that it's best not to become too attached to one's previous conception of what the energies of a stone such as Sauralite can do.

The point I want to make with this story is that in doing stone body layouts, working with the "soft will" is very helpful. One needs to use a degree of will simply to conceive of one's intention and follow it. Yet one must also be ready to surrender to the energy, and to follow intuitive impulses. And one must be ready to accept and go along with input from the Stone Beings and from one's Deep Self. By doing so, the effects of the stone body layout are a co-creation, and this is where healing or expanding awareness with the help of stones can really happen.

PRACTICES: THREE STONE BODY LAYOUTS FOR ALCHEMICAL TRANSFORMATION

The next three stone layouts are meant to be done in sequence, as enactments of the process of alchemical transformation. The idea here is to first clear, cleanse, heal and purify the subtle body and the physical body, bringing them into harmony and wellbeing. When this process has been initiated, the next phase is to call forth the alchemical unification of the surface self and the Deep Self. One of the terms I use to describe the third stage, in which the unified Self joins with the Divine, is Vibrational Ascension. The ancient alchemists called it the creation of the Philosophers Stone. I have named the first layout Purification and Healing. The second one is called Conjunction with the Deep Self, and the third layout is called Vibrational Ascension: Creating the Philosophers' Stone.

It is easiest if you can arrange to do these layouts with a partner, and it is ideal if each of you can experience both giving and receiving the layouts. In my workshops, we have found that both givers and receivers have had profound experiences. The instructions below will assume that the layouts are being done with partners.

For each of these layouts, I have chosen the stones I feel are best suited to create the vibrational "chord" that corresponds to or resonates with the mind/body patterns that their names describe. The imaginal aspects of these processes are also meant to bring one into these states of consciousness.

I want to mention here that body layouts such as these do not "do the job" *for* you. Nothing I know of can automatically heal you, awaken your union with the Deep Self, or cause Vibrational Ascension. However, the vibrational "chords" of each of these layouts expose your body, mind and soul to energy patterns that can suggest and kindle major shifts in your way of being. They can work somewhat like a homeopathic remedy or acupuncture treatment that uses subtle energy patterns to trigger a physical healing response. These stone body layouts infuse the deeper levels of one's being with synergistic energy configurations that facilitate the realization of one's intention. I want to stress that all such work is done through co-creation. The stone combinations in the three layouts offer us vibrational fields that support each of these stages of transformation. Our part as spiritual alchemists is to utilize our powers of attention, intention and imagination to resonate as deeply as possible to the patterns the stones present to us, and to release our old and outmoded ways of being. Our conscious participation allows new and better patterns to form, in resonance with the vibrational "chord" that each layout "sings" into one's being.

I like to say that the stone layouts "sing" their combined qualities into us, because this sort of image reminds us that the Stone Beings have "voices" that we perceive as their energies. And, as with music, we can "hear" it without really listening. Or, more powerfully, we can *invite* the "music" to flow through us and transform us. Often, it takes practice and repetition to fully take in what is offered to us, and to make it our own. But the gifts of the Stone Beings are continually available, whenever we invite them.

To sum this up, I am saying that these three stone layouts (and all stone body layouts) *suggest* beneficial bodily and spiritual changes, but they don't compel them. We can feel their energetic "suggestions," but we must affirm and allow them to enter us and shift our patterns. And because we are such multi-layered beings, it may take some time and repetition for our many levels of self to understand and accept the changes we desire.

So, with the next three layouts, I urge you to do them in sequence, at least for the first time through. This is the order in which the transformational steps most frequently take place, and the sequence will give that pattern as a suggestion to your Deep Self. Since most or all of us must approach such profound transformations more than once in order to fully enact and integrate them, you may wish to do these layouts a number of times. Trust your intuition in regard to how often and how many times to do them. And remember that the Great Work of spiritual alchemy is always ongoing, and is a way of being to be cultivated full-time. When we aim for transformation as a constant activity, we get further than we do if we just 'do an exercise' and then go back to our old habits.

SUBSTITUTING STONES

Regarding the stones listed for the layouts, I have chosen what I view as the optimal stones for each process. However, you are free to make substitutions if you do not have all of the stones on my lists. I suggest working with the Dictionary of Stones and the Index of Stone Properties at the back of this book to help you make choices for substitutions, as well as for designing your own layouts.

At a bare minimum, you can use a piece of common Quartz to substitute for any missing stone, and simply program it to carry the energy stream of the stone it is replacing. Do this meditatively, as an invitation to the Being of Quartz, and to the Being of the stone for which a substitution is being made. Imagine the two Stone Beings making an agreement to do this, and offer that image as your intention to the two Stone Beings and to Sophia. Visualize it as clearly as possible, offer it through your "soft will" as your desired outcome, and then surrender to whatever unfolds.

ALCHEMICAL BODY LAYOUT 1: PURIFICATION AND HEALING

PLACEMENT OF STONES (shown on diagram below)

SOUL STAR (8th) about 6 inches above the crown: Petalite, Violet Flame Opal, Amazez, Tibetan Tektite
CROWN (7th) CHAKRA: Black Merlinite, Black Tourmaline Azeztulite
THIRD EYE (6th) CHAKRA: Nuummite
THROAT (5th) CHAKRA: Azumar
HIGH HEART TRANSITION POINT (4th TO 5th): Auralite 23
HEART (4th) CHAKRA: Deva Quartz Green Phantom, Vitalite, Green Taralite
SECOND TRANSITION POINT (3rd TO 4th): Healerite, Shungite
SOLAR PLEXUS/WILL (3rd) CHAKRA: Golden Healer Quartz
FIRST TRANSITION POINT (2nd TO 3rd): Black Obsidian, Shungite (first half of session); Healer's Gold, Shungite (second half of session)
SEXUAL/CREATIVE (at navel) **(2nd) CHAKRA:** Healers Gold, New Zealand Carnelian
BASE (1st) CHAKRA: Cinnazez, Guardianite
EARTH STAr (at feet): Master Shamanite, Black Azeztulite, Tibetan Tektite
HANDS: White Azeztulite, Quartz Point (one piece of each in each hand)

Body Layout 1: Purification and Healing

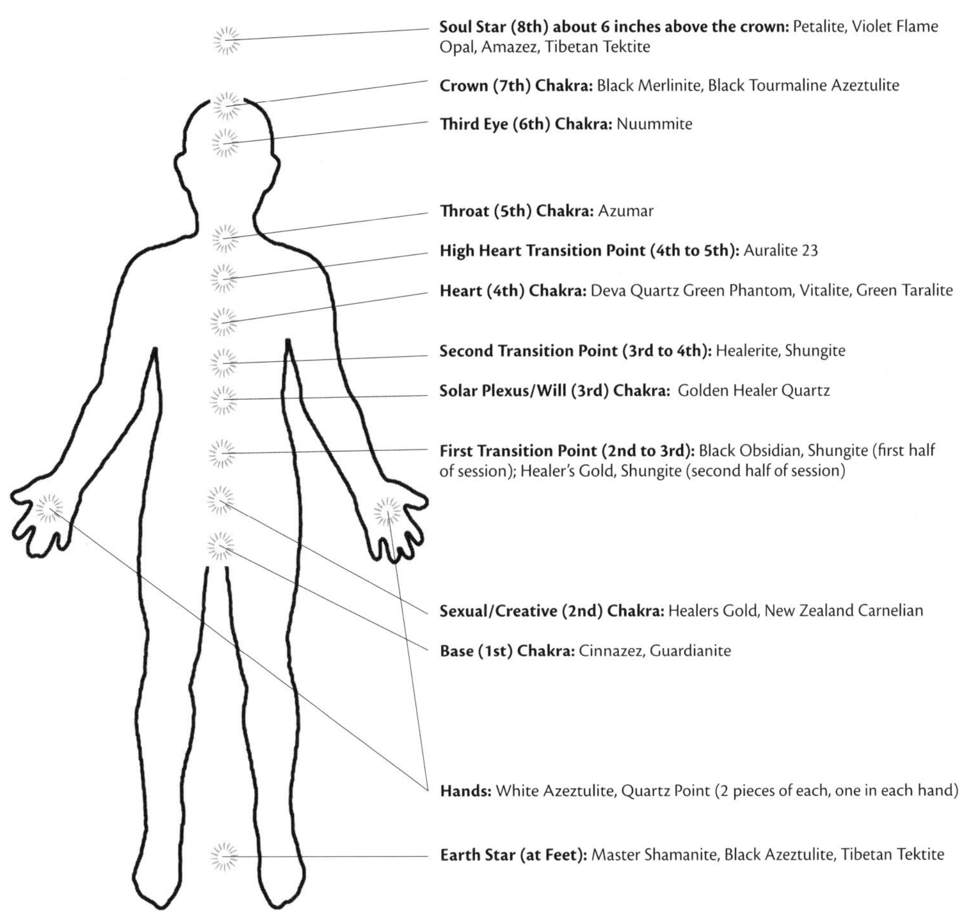

The Alchemy of Stones™ Stone Body Layout

BEFORE BEGINNING, get out the stones listed above and shown on the diagram. Arrange them in a row alongside the receiver's body. When this is finished, both people should go into meditative silence. (Notice that this layout requires working with different stones at the First Transition Point during the two halves of the process. During the first segment, you'll place Black Obsidian and Shungite on the First Transition Point, and replace the Black Obsidian with Healer's Gold for the second segment.)

If you are GIVING the Layout:

1. Close your eyes, and begin by centering yourself in the heart.
2. Next, keep your eyes closed and do the Heart Appreciation practice. (We have also called this the Activity of Blessing.) As you inhale, invite the person who will receive the Stone Layout, and all of the Stone Beings you will be working with, into your heart. On the exhale, offer your love and appreciation out to all of them. Follow this breathing for about a minute, or until you intuitively know you have attuned to the other person, and to the stones.
3. When you have entered into the state of Appreciation, open your eyes and look at your partner. Stay in the place of love and appreciation, and take several deep, relaxed breaths, imagining currents of blessing circulating between you and your partner. See the flow emanating and circulating from your hearts.
4. Staying in this state, (and going back into conscious circulation of heartfelt blessing if you forget or lose focus), begin placing the stones on your partner's body, as shown in the diagram. You can start from the top or bottom, or at any point.
5. As you place the stones in their appropriate places, hold the intention of being of benefit to your partner's process of dissolving old and outmoded patterns, as well as inviting new and healing patterns of energy into all levels of her or his being.
6. VISUALIZE this happening while you are doing this. NOTICE if the things you begin to see are different in any way from what you expected.
7. ALLOW whatever happens. Your job is to hold the intention of being of service to your partner and his or her Helping Spirits.
8. When you have placed all of the stones on your partner, sit quietly near him or her, and stay in the circulation of blessing. Take inner note of anything you see or hear inwardly.
9. This process has two segments. (You may choose to utilize background music to accentuate the intentions. If so, I suggest a stronger, more dramatic music for the first segment and a softer, more soothing music for the second segment. Try out the music and get your partner's agreement before doing the layout.) During the first segment of this layout, VISUALIZE your partner having any unhelpful blockages, dysfunctions or habit patterns broken up into smaller and smaller pieces, which disappear into a soft, golden white light that is near or around your partner.
10. When you have finished the time allotted for the first segment (or when the music changes), gently EXCHANGE the Black Obsidian at the first Transition Point for a piece of Healer's Gold. When this has been done, sit beside your partner and VISUALIZE beautiful healing energy and Light entering your partner and filling him or her with new and loving healing energies. See the seeds of beneficial energy patterns forming and filling your partner. Take note of any visions, words or information that come to you.
11. While observing all of this, hold the intention for your partner to experience transformational healing for his or her highest good.

12. When the session feels completed, gently remove the stones and allow your partner to come back. Don't speak at first. When your partner's eyes open, greet him or her silently. You will both know when you are ready to exchange words.
13. I recommend that both Giver and Receiver take a few minutes to write down what was felt, seen and experienced during the process. After that, you may compare and discuss the process if you wish to.

If you are RECEIVING the Layout:

1. Lie down on your back and get yourself comfortably situated.
2. Close your eyes, and begin by centering yourself in the heart.
3. Next, keep your eyes closed and do the Heart Appreciation practice. (We have also called this the Activity of Blessing.) As you inhale, invite the person who will be giving the Stone Layout, and all of the Stone Beings you will be working with, into your heart. On the exhale, offer your love and appreciation out to all of them. Follow this breathing for about a minute, or until you intuitively know you have attuned to the other person, and to the stones.
4. When you have entered into the state of Appreciation, open your eyes and look at your partner. Stay in the place of love and appreciation, and take several deep, relaxed breaths, imagining currents of blessing circulating between you and your partner. See the flow emanating and circulating from your hearts.
5. Then close your eyes, remembering the circulation of blessing. Visualize blessing and light coming into your heart and into your body through your partner, and through the stones being placed.
6. Remain attuned to your whole body, and welcome the currents of the stones. As you breathe in, allow more and more Light to come into every part of your body, and into each cell.
7. The first segment of layout session is for breaking up, dissolving and discharging the outmoded patterns to be released. (You may want to use some percussive or somewhat dramatic background music.) During the first segment of this layout, VISUALIZE yourself having any unhelpful blockages, dysfunctions or habit patterns broken up into smaller and smaller pieces, which disappear into a soft, golden white light that is near or around you. Surrender to this process, and allow the dissolution to take place. Notice the dissolving, and allow any information you need about it to be revealed to you.
8. The second segment of the layout session is for healing, replenishment and the formation of new, beneficial energy patterns. When the time allotted for the first segment is over (or when the music changes), notice the shift in the energies when your partner exchanges the Black Obsidian at the first Transition Point for a piece of Healer's Gold. VISUALIZE beautiful healing energy and golden Light entering you and filling you with new and loving healing energies. See the seeds of beneficial energy patterns forming and filling your body and your energy field. Take note of any visions, words or information that come to you. Allow the golden Light to permeate you with healing and uplifting energies. Notice what happens, and remain centered in your heart. If the process begins to take on a life of its own, go with it. This is what we hope for.
9. Stay with the energies that you experience, allowing this particular healing session to reach its natural completion.
10. When you feel the process is complete, gently focus your attention on you physical body. Thank the Stone Beings and spirit helpers for working with you. Wiggle your toes to bring yourself fully back into your physical body.

11. Stay in silence until your healing session feels completed. When you are ready, open your eyes. Don't speak right away. Greet your partner silently. You will both know when you are ready to exchange words.
12. I recommend that both Receiver and Giver take a few minutes to write down what was felt, seen and experienced during the process. After that, you may compare and discuss the process if you wish to.

ALCHEMICAL BODY LAYOUT 2: CONJUNCTION WITH THE DEEP SELF

PLACEMENT OF STONES (shown on diagram on page 209)

SOUL STAR (8th) about 6 inches above the crown: Fulgurite, Guardianite, Auralite 23
CROWN (7th) **CHAKRA:** Tibetan Tektite, Anandalite
THIRD EYE (6th) **CHAKRA:** Phenacite
THROAT (5th) **CHAKRA:** Black Merlinite
HIGH HEART TRANSITION POINT (4th to 5th): Rubellite Tourmaline; Lepidolite
HEART (4th) **CHAKRA:** Moldavite, Honey and Cream Azeztulite,
SECOND TRANSITION POINT (3rd to 4th): Celestite
SOLAR PLEXUS/WILL (3rd) **CHAKRA:** Vortexite
FIRST TRANSITION POINT (2nd to 3rd): Petalite
SEXUAL/CREATIVE (2nd) **CHAKRA:** New Zealand Carnelian, Shungite
BASE (1st) **CHAKRA:** Mystic Merlinite, Vitalite
EARTH STAR (at Feet) : Tibetan Tektite, Anandalite
HANDS: Rosophia, White Azeztulite (one piece of each stone in each hand)

BEFORE BEGINNING, get out the stones listed above and shown on the diagram. Arrange them in a row alongside the receiver's body. When this is finished, both people should go into meditative silence.

If you are GIVING the Layout:

1. Close your eyes, and begin by centering yourself in the heart.
2. Next, keep your eyes closed and do the Heart Appreciation practice. (We have also called this the Activity of Blessing.) As you inhale, invite the person who will receive the Stone Layout, and all of the Stone Beings you will be working with, into your heart. On the exhale, offer your love and appreciation out to all of them. Follow this breathing for about a minute, or until you intuitively know you have attuned to the other person, and to the stones.
3. When you have entered into the state of Appreciation, open your eyes and look at your partner. Stay in the place of love and appreciation, and take several deep, relaxed breaths, imagining currents of blessing circulating between you and your partner. See the flow emanating and circulating from your hearts. If you will be using background music in this session, it can begin at this point.
4. Staying in this state, (and going back into conscious circulation of heartfelt blessing if you forget or lose focus), begin placing the stones on your partner's body, as shown in the diagram. You can start from the top or bottom, or at any point.
5. As you place the stones in their appropriate places, hold the intention of being of benefit to your partner's process of coming into Conjunction and Union with his or her Deep Self. Call upon your own Deep Self, and the Deep Self of your partner. Allow the call to come from your heart, and share in the longing for union from BOTH sides of the relationship with the Deep Self, both for you and for your partner.

Body Layout 2: Conjunction with the Deep Self

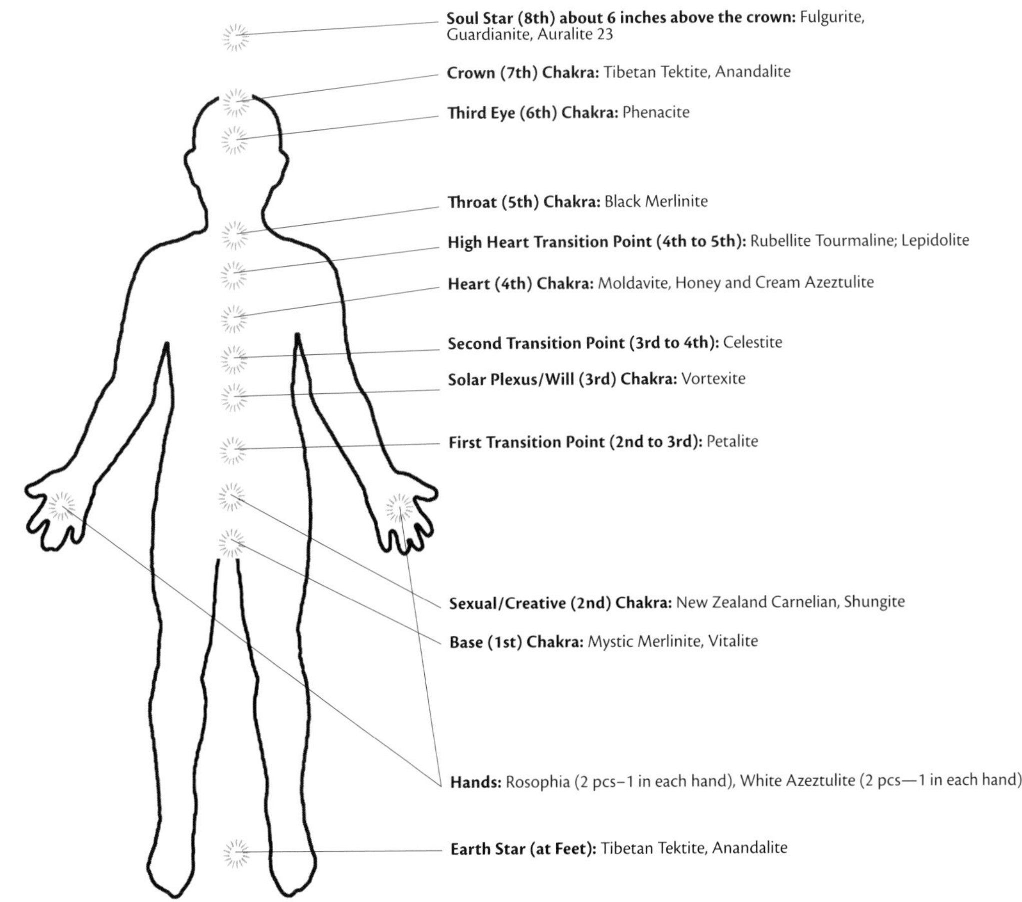

The Alchemy of Stones™ Stone Body Layout

6. Begin placing the stones on and around your partner, continuing to circulate blessing energies with your breath. As you do so, visualize images of reunion, of joyful reunification, of the conscious self with the deep identity within the unconscious. This can be for yourself and your partner, and everyone in the room, all simultaneously.
7. Allow whatever happens. Your job is to hold the intention of being of service to your partner and his or her Deep Self, to encourage and welcome their reunion.
8. When you have placed all of the stones on your partner, sit quietly near him or her, and stay in the circulation of blessing. Take inner note of anything you see or hear inwardly. Also be prepared to welcome your partner's reunion with the Deep Self. It can happen at any time.
9. Allow the music to flow through you both, and to act as a call to the Deep Self. Remain alert, yet also surrender to the unfolding of the process. If you experience the presence of the Deep Self, within yourself or your partner, you do not need to try to stay separate from what is happening in order to write things down. You won't forget, and it is important to be present for this.
10. If your partner goes into an emotional place, stay present with him or her, and hold sacred space, providing a safe and protected environment.
11. When the session feels complete (after the music ends, if you are using music), gently remove the stones and allow your partner to come back. Don't speak. When your partner's eyes open, greet him or her silently You will both know when you are ready to exchange words.

12. I recommend that both Giver and Receiver take a few minutes to write down what was felt, seen and experienced during the process. After that you may compare and discuss the process if you wish to.

If you are RECEIVING the Layout:

1. Lie down on your back and get yourself comfortably situated.
2. Close your eyes, and begin by centering yourself in the heart.
3. Next, keep your eyes closed and do the Heart Appreciation practice. (We have also called this the Activity of Blessing.) As you inhale, invite the person who will be giving the Stone Layout, and all of the Stone Beings you will be working with, into your heart. On the exhale, offer your love and appreciation out to all of them. Follow this breathing for about a minute, or until you intuitively know you have attuned to the other person, and to the stones.
4. When you have entered into the state of Appreciation, open your eyes and look at your partner. Stay in the place of love and appreciation, and take several deep, relaxed breaths, imagining currents of blessing circulating between you and your partner. See the flow emanating and circulating from your hearts.
5. Then close your eyes, remembering the circulation of blessing. Visualize blessing and Light coming into your heart and into your body through your partner, and through the stones being placed.
6. Remain attuned to your whole body, and welcome the currents of the stones. Feel the benevolent, loving Wisdom of Sophia and the Stone Beings pouring into you through the stones. As you breathe in, allow more and more Light to come into every part of your body, and into each cell. INVITE this flow to increase and from your Heart, call out to your Deep Self. Ask it to come and join you.
7. Now be aware that there is also darkness present. It is not negative or threatening. It is a nourishing darkness where your Deep Self dwells. Allow yourself to visualize both Darkness and Light within you, within every cell, and allow the Darkness and Light to circulate with one another in mutual blessing.
8. Notice that within the mingling Darkness there is a powerful presence that sees you, knows you and loves you. It is your Soul, your very own Deep Self. It has been waiting for many years for this moment, the moment of your reunion, and of your joining together.
9. Notice that there is also a beautiful, loving presence within the Light that is circulating inside you. That is the presence of pure Spirit. Allow the Light presence and the Deep Self which has dwelt in the darkness to celebrate and dance together, within your heart, your body and your energy field, within every fiber of your being.
10. Stay with these intentions and visualizations until the process takes on a life of its own. If the process does begin at any time to take on a life of its own, go with it. (If it goes off into fantasy or a dreamlike state, notice that and bring yourself back to the intention of reunion with the deep Self.) And if the Guest, your Deep Self, makes itself known, WELCOME IT.
11. If you have chosen music to assist in providing a helpful acoustic environment for the reunion with the Deep Self, let it become the soundtrack to a joyful encounter.
12. If you become emotional, don't hold it back. Let yourself feel everything. It is part of the reunion.
13. If you experience the feeling that there are two people inside you, stay calm and allow it. If this occurs, you should also feel the presence of love. That is your way of identifying that the second presence is that of your own Deep Self.

14. If you have the opportunity, see if it is possible for you to have a dialog, and enter into conversation with your Deep Self. (The Sufis valued this ecstatic conversation above all else.)
15. Sometimes your Deep Self will show you images, or even past life memories. Stay calm and allow them, as long as they do not take you away from your Deep Self. If they do, it is better to gently withdraw from them and go back into rapport with your Deep Self. This is the experience of Conjunction, and it has the capacity to bring you into a new way of being through the Transcendent Function.
16. When you feel the process is complete, gently return to your physical body. Thank your Deep Self, the Stone Beings and Sophia for working with you. Wiggle your toes to bring yourself fully back into your body.
17. Stay in silence until this session feels completed. When you are ready, open your eyes. Don't speak right away. Greet your partner silently. You will both know when you are ready to exchange words.
18. I recommend that both Receiver and Giver take a few minutes to write down what was felt, seen and experienced during the process. After that you may compare and discuss the process if you wish to.

NOTE: If your experience was not one of conscious reunion with your Deep Self, it simply means that more has to happen to bring about that reunion. You may need to do the practice more, and to pay attention to your Deep Self as a daily intention. Sometimes we need special circumstances for the reunion to happen fully, but hold to your intention, with as much feeling as possible.

ALCHEMICAL BODY LAYOUT 3:
VIBRATIONAL ASCENSION—CREATING THE PHILOSOPHERS' STONE

PLACEMENT OF STONES (shown on diagram on page 212)
SOUL STAR (8th) about 6 inches above the crown: Danburite, Natrolite, Anandalite,
CROWN (7th) **CHAKRA:** Azozeo Phenacite, New Zealand White Azeztulite, Amazez, Satyaloka Clear Azeztulite
THIRD EYE (6th) **CHAKRA:** Circle Stone, Phenacite
THROAT (5th) **CHAKRA:** Azumar
HIGH HEART TRANSITION POINT (4th to 5th): Pink Azeztulite, Deva Quartz
HEART (4th) **CHAKRA:** Sauralite Azeztulite, Satyaloka Rose Azeztulite
SECOND TRANSITION POINT (3rd to 4th): Revelation Stone, Datolite,
SOLAR PLEXUS/WILL (3rd) **CHAKRA:** Himalaya Gold Azeztulite,
FIRST TRANSITION POINT (2nd to 3rd): Lithium Light, Sanda Rosa Azeztulite,
SEXUAL/CREATIVE (2nd) **CHAKRA:** Pink Fire Azeztulite, Cinnazez
BASE (1st) **CHAKRA:** Red Fire Azeztulite, Black Tourmaline Azeztulite
EARTH STAR (at feet): Anandalite
HANDS: White Azeztulite (2pcs) Vortexite, Shungite

If you are GIVING the Layout:

1. Close your eyes, and begin by centering yourself in the heart.
2. Next, keep your eyes closed and do the Heart Appreciation practice. (We have also called this the Activity of Blessing.) As you inhale, invite the person who will receive the Stone Layout, and all of the Stone Beings you will be working with, into your heart. On the exhale, offer your love and appreciation out to all of them. Follow this breathing for about a minute, or until you intuitively know you have attuned to the other person, and to the stones.

Body Layout 3: Vibrational Ascension–The Philosophers' Stone

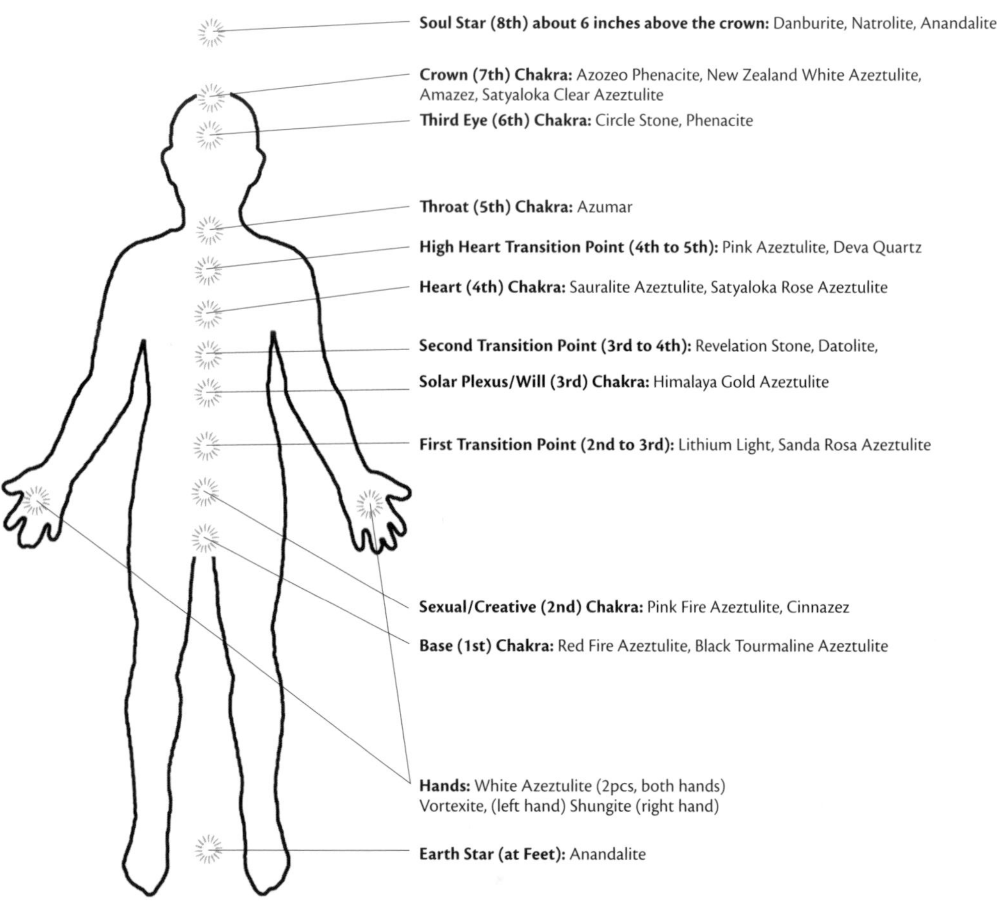

The Alchemy of Stones™ Stone Body Layout

3. When you have entered into the state of Appreciation, open your eyes and look at your partner. Stay in the place of love and appreciation, and take several deep, relaxed breaths, imagining currents of blessing circulating between you and your partner. See the flow emanating and circulating from your hearts. If you will be using background music in this session, it can begin at this point.
4. Staying in this state, (and going back into conscious circulation of heartfelt blessing if you forget or lose focus), begin placing the stones on your partner's body, as shown in the diagram. You can start from the top or bottom, or at any point.
5. As you place the stones in their appropriate places, hold the intention of being of benefit to your partner's process of raising his or her vibrational level to the highest possible frequencies, in complete alignment with Sophia.
6. After you have placed the stones, sit down near your partner, and give him or her your full attention, with eyes open or closed as feels best to you. VISUALIZE your partner's body filling up with more and more Light. SEE the seed of his or her Divine Radiance begin as a point in the center of his or her heart, and IMAGINE that Light becoming like a small Sun, growing in its radiance, spreading through the Liquid Crystal Body Matrix, turning every strand of DNA into a spiral of Light. The Light may be one color or many colors, or even a rainbow of Light.
7. As you visualize your partner's body filling with Light and radiating Light, call upon the Stone Beings, the Azez, Sophia and your partner's Deep Self to join in the birth of the Divine Child within your partner, as a new identity—the True Self.

8. IMAGINE your partner's whole being vibrating at a higher and higher level, completely aligned with the single pure intention of union with the Soul of the World.
9. Allow yourself to go with the process, holding your intention while also observing whatever occurs inwardly and outwardly. You may see or feel things beyond the parameters of these visualizations.
10. Continue to hold sacred space for your partner throughout the process. When the music ends, if you use music,continue to hold space for your partner.
11. When the session feels completed, gently remove the stones and allow your partner to come back. Don't speak at first. When your partner's eyes open, greet him or her silently. You will both know when you are ready to exchange words.
12 I recommend that both Giver and Receiver take a few minutes to write down what was felt, seen and experienced during the process. After that you may compare and discuss the process if you wish to.

If you are RECEIVING the Layout:

1. Lie down on your back and get yourself comfortably situated.
2. Close your eyes, and begin by centering yourself in the heart.
3. Next, keep your eyes closed and do the Heart Appreciation practice. (We have also called this the Activity of Blessing.) As you inhale, invite the person who will be giving the Stone Layout, and all of the Stone Beings you will be working with, into your heart. On the exhale, offer your love and appreciation out to all of them. Follow this breathing for about a minute, or until you intuitively know you have attuned to the other person, and to the stones.
4. When you have entered into the state of Appreciation, open your eyes and look at your partner. Stay in the place of love and appreciation, and take several deep, relaxed breaths, imagining currents of blessing circulating between you and your partner. See the flow emanating and circulating from your hearts.
5. Then close your eyes, remembering the circulation of blessing. Visualize blessing and Light coming into your heart and into your body through your partner, and through the stones being placed.
6. VISUALIZE your body filling up with more and more Light. SEE the seed of your Divine Radiance begin as a point in the center of your heart, and IMAGINE that Light becoming like a small Sun, growing in its radiance, spreading through the Liquid Crystal Body Matrix, turning every strand of your DNA into a spiral of Light. The Light may be one color or many colors, or even a rainbow of Light.
7. As you visualize your body filling with Light and radiating Light, CALL UPON the Stone Beings, the Azez, Sophia and your Deep Self to join in the birth of the Divine Child within yourself, as a new identity—the True Self.
8. IMAGINE your whole being vibrating at a higher and higher level, completely aligned with the single pure intention of union with the Soul of the World. FEEL the PRESENCE of Sophia within every atom of your being. Allow yourself to surrender into union with Her.
9. Allow yourself to go with the process, holding your intention while also observing whatever occurs on all levels. You may see or feel things beyond the parameters of these visualizations.
10. Continue to attune yourself to the stone energies and to the Light throughout the process. When the music ends, (if you are using music) you may wish to stay with the process for another minute or two.

11. As you begin to come back, thank Sophia and the Stone Beings for the gift of this experience. It is suggested that you practice holding the intention for this Union to become your new way of being.
12. When you feel the process is complete, gently focus your attention on your physical body. Thank the Stone Beings and spirit helpers for working with you. Wiggle your toes to bring yourself fully back into your physical body.
13. Stay in silence until your session feels completed. When you are ready, open your eyes. Don't speak right away. Greet your partner silently. You will both know when you are ready to exchange words.
14. I recommend that both Receiver and Giver take a few minutes to write down what was felt, seen and experienced during the process. After that you may compare and discuss the process if you wish to.

Additional Notes for those giving Stone Body Layouts

If you feel a strong intuition about making a different stone placement than the positions shone on the diagrams, or if you intuit a need for any other stones to be added to the layout, you are free to make such changes. But please be sure that this is coming from somewhere beyond your personal self. If in doubt, just follow the pattern as has been set up in the diagrams. This is for your partner's benefit. Before beginning, you should ask your partner's preference—whether to allow intuition to be followed or if he or she is more comfortable following the practice as it is outlined. (if you are receiving the layout, check inwardly with your heart intuition to see what will be best for you.)

Also, if those of you giving the layouts have any visions or information to share with your partner after the Practice, make notes to yourself about them, and ask your partner before sharing them. It is sometimes more appropriate for your partner to process the experience for some time before getting input, and at other times such information can be quite helpful.

There are a great many different processes than can be initiated through Stone Body Layouts. Using the human powers of attention, intention and imagination, in co-creative unity with your Deep Self, the Stone Beings and Sophia, there is literally no limit to what you can do, and where you can go. I have described in detail three layouts that were designed to support three major stages of alchemical self-transformation. This transformation is, in my view, the fundamental purpose of spiritual alchemy.

But the world is wide, and the energy patterns we can experience with the Stone Beings are unlimited. So now I will offer suggestions for some additional Stone Body Layouts. If you have read through the instructions for the three processes above, I'm sure you understand the ways I recommend for entering into these processes and for carrying them through to completion. So, in the following pages of this chapter, I am simply going to provide the names, stones and diagrams of these layouts, and I'll leave the rest of the details up to you. I hope you will feel free to design your own Stone Body Layouts. After all, the Great Work of the Alchemy of Stones can only be achieved by a combination of both study AND practice! (If you would like to get a blank copy of our Body Layout diagram, go to www.heavenandearthjewelry.com and enter *Body Layout diagram* into the search function.)

NOTE: When designing your own Stone Body Layouts, I encourage you to make use of the Dictionary of Stones and the Index of Stone Properties in the back section of this book. And I suggest allowing your intuition to guide you. Sometimes the best stone for a particular need or placement in a layout will seem to leap off the page at you. Let unexpected clues and synchronous incidents guide you. Allow the Stone Beings to jump off the page and grab your attention. Then work with them co-creatively for the highest good. This is part of the fun of our transformative evolution. In the Alchemy of Stones, we do serious work . . . lightly.

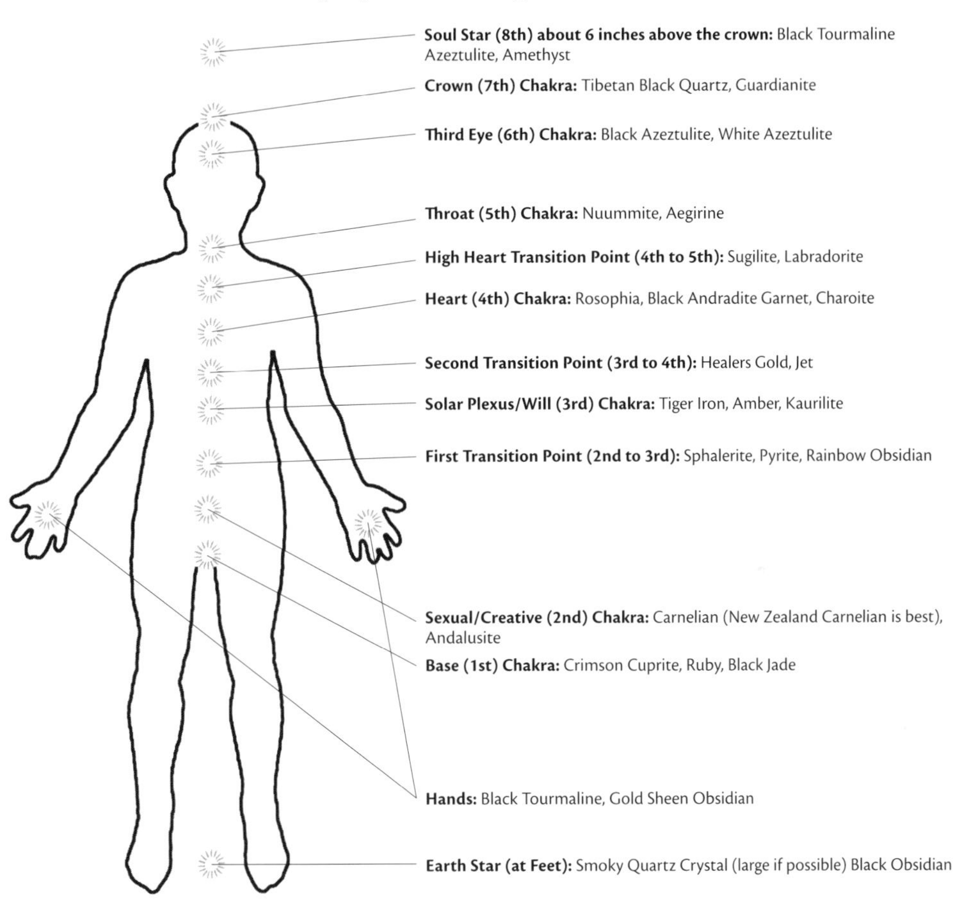

The Alchemy of Stones™ Stone Body Layout

Body Layout: Spiritual Healing for the Physical Body

Soul Star (8th) about 6 inches above the crown: White Azeztulite, Selenite

Crown (7th) Chakra: Lemurian Seed Crystal,

Third Eye (6th) Chakra: Charoite, Sugilite

Throat (5th) Chakra: Iolite, Aquamarine

High Heart Transition Point (4th to 5th): Blue-Green Azeztulite, Green Fire Azeztulite

Heart (4th) Chakra: Seraphinite, Emerald, Bloodstone

Second Transition Point (3rd to 4th): Healerite, Healers Gold, Prehnite

Solar Plexus/Will (3rd) Chakra: Kaurilite, Amber, Jet

First Transition Point (2nd to 3rd): Unakite Jasper, Seriphos Green Quartz

Sexual/Creative (2nd) Chakra: Mook Jasper, Carnelian

Base (1st) Chakra: Cuprite, Goethite, Ruby Zoisite

Hands: Healerite, Healers Gold, Sanda Rosa Azeztlite

Earth Star (at Feet): Black Tourmaline, Hematite

The Alchemy of Stones™ Stone Body Layout

Body Layout: Emotional Healing and Forgiveness

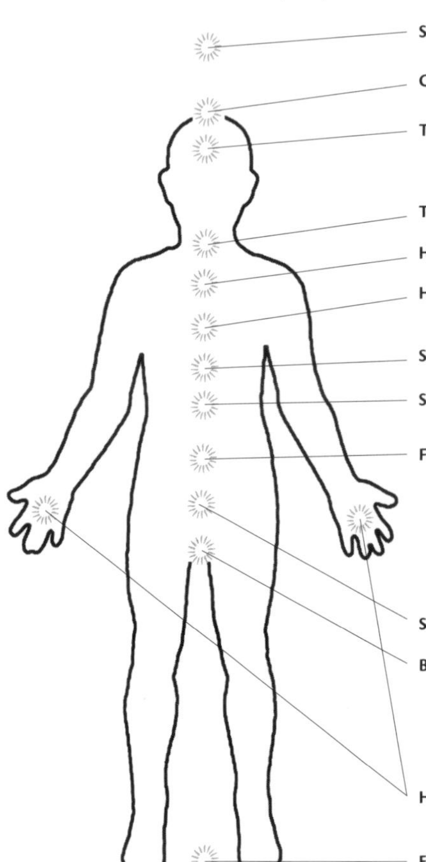

Soul Star (8th) about 6 inches above the crown: Anandalite

Crown (7th) Chakra: Ajoite, Azumar

Third Eye (6th) Chakra: Sauralite Azeztulite

Throat (5th) Chakra: Larimar, Azumar

High Heart Transition Point (4th to 5th): Lepidolite, Pink Opal, Pink Amethyst

Heart (4th) Chakra: Rosophia, Kunzite, Dioptase, Gaia Stone

Second Transition Point (3rd to 4th): Healerite, Gaspeite

Solar Plexus/Will (3rd) Chakra: Pink Fire Azeztulite, Pink Calcite

First Transition Point (2nd to 3rd): Pink Azeztulite, Stichtite

Sexual/Creative (2nd) Chakra: Rhodocrosite

Base (1st) Chakra: Crimson Cuprite, Eudialyte

Hands: Rose Quartz, Amazonite, Angelite

Earth Star (at Feet): Dravite (Brown Tourmaline), Healers Gold

The Alchemy of Stones™ Stone Body Layout

Body Layout: Embodying Love

Soul Star (8th) about 6 inches above the crown: Rose Quartz (large raw chunk)

Crown (7th) Chakra: Stilbite, Danburite

Third Eye (6th) Chakra: Lilac Lepidolite, Bixbite

Throat (5th) Chakra: Azumar, Angelite

High Heart Transition Point (4th to 5th): Kunzite, Tugtupite, Morganite

Heart (4th) Chakra: Emerald, Rosophia, Sauralite Azeztulite

Second Transition Point (3rd to 4th): Pyromorphite, Healerite, Pink Amethyst

Solar Plexus/Will (3rd) Chakra: Seraphinite, Hiddenite

First Transition Point (2nd to 3rd): Pink Sapphire, Rhodonite,

Sexual/Creative (2nd) Chakra: Rhodochrosite, Pink Tourmaline

Base (1st) Chakra: Lepidocrocite, Muscovite

Hands: Pink Azeztulite, Rosophia, Rose Quartz, Morganite

Earth Star (at Feet): Rose Quartz (large raw chunk)

The Alchemy of Stones™ Stone Body Layout

Body Layout: Interdimensional Travel

Soul Star (8th) about 6 inches above the crown:
Clear Quartz Crystal (programmed)

Crown (7th) Chakra: Scolecite, Circle Stone

Third Eye (6th) Chakra: Phenacite, Herderite, Brookite

Throat (5th) Chakra: Cavansite, Siberian Blue Quartz

High Heart Transition Point (4th to 5th): Aqua Aura Quartz, Heulandite

Heart (4th) Chakra: Clear Apophyllite, Green Apophyllite,

Second Transition Point (3rd to 4th): Sphene, Rutilated Quartz

Solar Plexus/Will (3rd) Chakra: Himalaya Gold Azeztulite, Natrolite

First Transition Point (2nd to 3rd): Pietersite, Merkabite Calcite

Sexual/Creative (2nd) Chakra: Barite, Rhodizite

Base (1st) Chakra: Cerrusite, Fairy Wand Quartz

Hands: Danburite, Clear Apophyllite, Phenacite

Earth Star (at Feet): Cassiterite, Stellar Beam Calcite

The Alchemy of Stones™ Stone Body Layout

Body Layout: Connecting with the Angelic Realm

Soul Star (8th) about 6 inches above the crown: Amethyst, Angel Aura Quartz Cluster

Crown (7th) Chakra: White Azeztulite, Danburite

Third Eye (6th) Chakra: Phenacite, Lemurian Light Crystal

Throat (5th) Chakra: Angelite, Ellensburg Blue Agate

High Heart Transition Point (4th to 5th): Ajoite, Celestite

Heart (4th) Chakra: Seraphinite, Morganite

Second Transition Point (3rd to 4th): Seriphos Green Quartz, Selenite

Solar Plexus/Will (3rd) Chakra: Agni Gold Danburite,

First Transition Point (2nd to 3rd): Prehnite, Hemimorphite, Selenite

Sexual/Creative (2nd) Chakra: Creedite, Smithsonite

Base (1st) Chakra: Covellite, Angel Wing Blue Anhydrite

Hands: Danburite, Angelite, Selenite

Earth Star (at Feet): Smoky Elestial Quartz, Selenite

The Alchemy of Stones™ Stone Body Layout

Body Layout: Spiritual Enlightenment

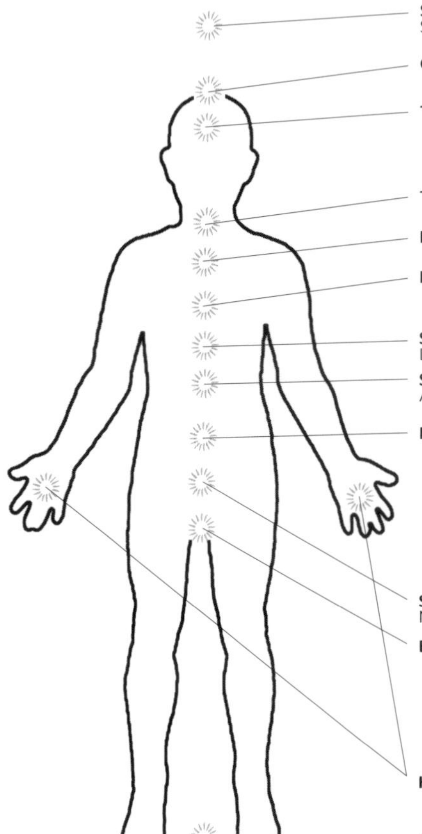

Soul Star (8th) about 6 inches above the crown: Lemurian Light Crystal, Satyaloka Clear Azeztulite, Tibetan Tektite

Crown (7th) Chakra: Circle Stone, Danburite, Natrolite

Third Eye (6th) Chakra: Phenacite, Brookite, Herderite

Throat (5th) Chakra: Nuummite, Labradorite

High Heart Transition Point (4th to 5th): Morganite, Kunzite, Pink Amethyst

Heart (4th) Chakra: Rosophia, Sauralite Azeztulite, Moldavite

Second Transition Point (3rd to 4th): Nirvana Quartz, Libyan Gold Tektite, Selenite

Solar Plexus/Will (3rd) Chakra: Agni Gold Danburite, Himalaya Gold Azeztulite

First Transition Point (2nd to 3rd): Pietersite, Revelation Stone, Selenite

Sexual/Creative (2nd) Chakra: Angel Aura Quartz, New Zealand Carnelian, Infinite

Base (1st) Chakra: Master Shamanite, Tibetan Tektite, Empowerite

Hands: Phenacite, Satyaloka Clear Azeztulite Lemurian Light Crystal

Earth Star (at Feet): Black Azeztulite, Black Tourmaline Azeztulite

The Alchemy of Stones™ Stone Body Layout

Body Layout: The Nameless Light

Soul Star (8th) about 6 inches above the crown: Amazez Azeztulite

Crown (7th) Chakra: Satyaloka Clear Azeztulite

Third Eye (6th) Chakra: White Azeztulite

Throat (5th) Chakra: Honey and Cream Azeztulite, Azumar

High Heart Transition Point (4th to 5th): Blue-Green Azeztulite

Heart (4th) Chakra: Green Fire Azeztulite, Sauralite Azeztlite

Second Transition Point (3rd to 4th): Golden Azeztulite, Satyaloka Rose Azeztulite

Solar Plexus/Will (3rd) Chakra: Himalaya Gold Azeztulite, Satyaloka Yellow Azeztulite

First Transition Point (2nd to 3rd): Cinnazez, Himalaya Red-Gold Azeztulite

Sexual/Creative (2nd) Chakra: Pink Azeztulite, Pink Fire Azeztulite

Base (1st) Chakra: Red Fire Azeztulite, Black Azeztulite, Himalaya Red Azeztulite

Hands: White Azeztulite, Satyaloka Clear Azeztulite, Blue-Green Azeztulite

Earth Star (at Feet): Sanda Rosa Azeztulite, Black Tourmaline Azeztulite

The Alchemy of Stones™ Stone Body Layout

23

Photonic Stone Layouts

In spite of the criticisms, skepticism, and disbelief, the [radionic] methods originated by [Dr. Albert] Abrams have been refined by a number of investigators and appear to yield reproducible results. The equipment utilizes subtle energies that are not yet fully understood, and the energies involved are very small, as in homeopathy. This does not mean that the concepts should be rejected, for the history of medicine teaches us that what is heresy for one generation can become a dominant paradigm in the next.

—James L. Oschman PhD, *Energy Medicine*

I realized while at the workshop that this is really what I'm meant to do and how I am supposed to help people! Since being home, I have developed a website where I can offer Photonic Crystal Treatments and other energy work. I have done four Photonics sessions since returning home and have had amazing feedback.

—M.E., participant in Alchemy of Stones Intensive, 2016

The Photonic Layouts are a brilliant idea, and I am definitely going to incorporate them into my practice with horses and humans!

—Jeanie Shepherd, participant in Alchemy of Stones Intensive, 2016

In June of 2016, as I was gathering materials and doing experimentation in preparation for writing this book, I facilitated an Alchemy of Stones four-day intensive workshop in Vermont, USA. Perhaps the most amazing (maybe even revolutionary) activity we engaged in at that event was something I called "Photonic Stone Layouts." I used the term "photonic" to denote several things this practice brings together. What we did could be seen as a form of "radionics" which I'll describe below. Also, we worked with photographs—hence the "photo" in "photonic." So photonics could be described as the practice of using photographs in doing radionics.

But there is also a more subtle meaning here. In my view, we were working all along with the energy of *consciousness*, and one phenomenon that can be used to describe consciousness is *light*. When we "shed light" on something, we are bringing information that was not previously known into the realm of consciousness. And, of course, the fundamental unit of physical light is called a "photon," or light-particle. One could also call a particle of spiritual Light (or energy) a Photon. So, a Photonic Stone Layout is a way of working with the consciousness of stones, combined with our own consciousness, using a photograph in place of the physical body, and engaging with the energies of spiritual Light that we call "stone energies."

What did we actually do? Before the Intensive, I sent letters out to all the participants, asking them to bring an 8 x 10 inch photo of themselves to the event. I didn't tell them why. In the meantime, the Heaven and Earth staff prepared a special bag of small stones for each participant. My plan was simple: I would give out the bags of small stones, and at a certain point in the workshop, we would choose partners and do "body layouts" of these small stones for one another. However, instead of placing the stones physically on our partners, we would ask the partner to lie down with eyes closed while we placed the tiny stones, in layout configurations, *on the photograph* of our partner. Afterwards, we would have a discussion of the effects of the process . . . if any.

Photonic Body Layout

I had good reasons to believe there would be some very noticeable effects because, of course, I knew from experience that people receiving stone body layouts feel a great deal of energy, and also experience numerous other things. And I was pretty certain from my research that doing a layout on the photographs would have effects similar to giving the same layout directly on the body.

Did it work? In a word, yes! Quite amazingly well. But before I go on to that, let's have a look into the history and principles of radionics, the practice that inspired the Photonic Stone Layouts.

I quote below from *The Secret Life of Plants,* where I began my research into radionics:

> *At the end of the 19th century Dr. Albert Abrams, the son of a successful San Francisco merchant from whom he had inherited a vast fortune, traveled to Heidelberg to study medicine. In Naples young Abrams watched the famous Italian tenor Enrico Caruso flick a wine glass with his finger to produce a pure tone, then step back and by singing the same note, shatter the glass. This impressive feat awoke in Abrams the idea that he might have stumbled on a fundamental principle that could be tied to medical diagnosis and healing.*

Abrams went on to develop a technique of medical diagnosis using samples of tissue from patients, and another person as a stand-in, or "resonator" for the patient. Abrams had great success with this technique, though he was attacked by the medical establishment of his day. (Abrams called the technique "radionics" because in his time the information that led to his diagnoses was imagined to be carried by radio waves. This was not the case, and I believe now that all radionics work directly at the level of *the consciousness which underlies physical reality.*)

Some years later, William Knuth investigated Abrams' work, and this led to his experiments with "radionic" pest control. He too experienced amazing success. In his work, he exposed photographs of farmers' fields to tiny amounts of pesticides, while "charging" the photograph with a radionics machine. In many cases his treatments succeeded far better than the direct application of pesticides, at a far lower cost, and without damaging bees and other beneficial insects. Somehow, his treatments apparently caused the unwanted insects to die or disappear.

In one amazing experiment, Knuth took a photograph of an insect-infested corn field, cutting off one corner of the image before treating the rest of the photograph radionically. In *The Secret Life of Plants,* it was reported that 80 to 90% of the pests died or disappeared from the part of the field represented by the treated portion of the photograph. However, the area which had been cut off of the photograph remained fully infested! Soon, pesticide companies enlisted government authorities to put Knuth and others in this field out of business, claiming their results could not be replicated by "disinterested agencies."

As an important side note, even if it was true that "disinterested agencies" failed to get positive results, it actually *magnifies the importance of consciousness* within the process. As was seen later, it was the *intention* of the experimenters, rather than the effectiveness of their electronic devices, that was primarily responsible for their very real successes. This is highly important in our work with stones because we are engaging with the Stone Beings *co-creatively,* and we are most definitely working through intention within the underlying level of our shared consciousness.

Even though many radionics experiments worked, no one fully understood why. The British engineer George DeLaWarr performed many successful experiments involving the radionic treatment of photographs of garden plots. In most cases, he treated the photographs with fertilizers rather than pesticides, and the garden plots in his "treated" photographs typically produced huge crop yields compared with those of adjoining untreated plots.

DeLaWarr wondered whether treating an inert mineral substance, such as vermiculite, and then mixing it into soil, would produce similar positive results. In these experiments, garden plots with "treated" vermiculite produced much bigger yields than identical plots mixed with "untreated" vermiculite. However, when outside plant breeding companies tried to reproduce his results, it didn't work. Some people assumed this meant that DeLaWarr had been faking his results, but this was not true.

Undaunted, DeLaWarr leapt to the insight that it was the *expectation* (aka *intention*) that the treated plants (or plants grown with treated vermiculite) would do well that was primarily responsible for his successes. "Disinterested" parties did not have such intentions, so no remarkable results came about when they did the very same processes but in a "disinterested" way. Ultimately, DeLaWarr performed another vermiculite experiment in which workers were simply told that one batch of vermiculite was treated while another wasn't (but neither batch was exposed to a radionics machine). As we might imagine, the garden plot in which the workers expected (intended) for the plants to flourish produced dramatically better results without any use of a radionics machine whatsoever.

From *The Secret Life of Plants:*

> *When DeLaWarr realized that the real key to getting plants to flourish was simply* asking *them to do so, he published an article entitled "Blessing Plants to Increase their Growth." Readers of the article were asked to work with bean seeds, to hold them in their hands and "invoke a blessing," visualizing them growing and thriving. Hundreds of readers reported successful results.*

I was greatly excited when I read the research summarized above. It was clear to me that the people working with "radionics" had stumbled onto something far more significant than even they had imagined. Rather than finding a way to manipulate matter through electronic machines and "radio" waves, they had produced dramatic results in experiments where the true cause of their success was their own *intention,* acting through the medium of consciousness! In order for their results to make sense, it also meant that the consciousness of the various experimenters and workers was somehow linked with the living plants and insects they were trying to affect. It meant that *consciousness is fundamental*—the underlying substrate of reality—and that matter (the whole outer universe) is the manifested aspect or expression of the primary consciousness. (This is completely aligned with the assertion of ancient alchemists that in order to change outer reality, one must go to the source, the *prima materia,* or "first matter." I would suggest that the "first matter" referred to in this context is *the subtle matter/energy of consciousness* that is present in the imaginal realm.)

I want to call the readers' attention to the fact that DeLaWarr's experiments utilized what I am calling the three alchemical human powers of attention, intention and imagination. In doing their experiments, the *attention* of DeLaWarr's helpers was fully engaged. Their *intention* and *imagination* were focused through the expectation that the radionically treated garden plots would perform better. The results recorded from these experiments strongly support my contention that these three powers can profoundly affect events in the physical world.

I was also highly excited to see that the "Activity of Blessing," as I have called it, was the important factor in the seed-germinating experiments. It is the positive intention of mutual blessing between ourselves and the Beings of the Stones that is at the core of all my ideas of working co-creatively with them. If our efforts toward healing and the expansion of our awareness are to bear fruit, we must approach all beings, from humans and animals to plants and stones, with respect and benevolence, along with our focused intention. Like the alchemists, we must clearly *intend* the results we wish to achieve, inviting our co-creating partners to join us. And we must simultaneously release any effort to "control" the response of whatever beings we are working with. All of this is implicit in the Activity of Blessing.

Widely known programs utilizing creative visualization (such as those recommended by Shakti Gawain, or in the book, *The Secret*) are, in my view, working to modify outer reality through the use of focused intention. The successful results which are sometimes achieved are due, I believe, to shifts in the underlying subtle/psychoid/imaginal realm of consciousness, which then manifest in the outer world.

However, many such programs have results that fall far short of the expectations people have for them. Why? Perhaps the most common reasons would be the distraction of attention, the diminishment of intention, and/or the inconsistency of imagination. However, the ancient alchemists had another answer to this. The alchemists believed that their efforts at the transmutation of themselves and the world would always fail, *unless they worked cooperatively (co-creatively) with Sophia,* the Soul of the World.

As we have seen, the ultimate goal of spiritual alchemy was the creation of the Philosophers' Stone. (In ancient Greek, *philo* = love and *sophia* = Wisdom, the Soul of the World.) An alchemical *philosopher* is one who relates to the Soul of the World through love. And love is the combination of benevolent intention and surrender. This is the essence of co-creation. To create the Philosophers' Stone was to forge an unbreakable co-creative relationship with Sophia. The *relationship,* when it is constantly present in one's conscious awareness and when it has become so strong it can never be broken, *is* the Stone. The Philosophers' Stone was said to convey many extraordinary powers, from the transmutation of metals to healing, rejuvenation, and even immortality.

We can see from the history of radionics that there is indeed an underlying consciousness around us, with which we can relate, and through which we can bring changes into outer reality. How much more effective could our efforts be if, like the alchemists, we focused intently on developing a strong relationship with that underlying consciousness of Wisdom, in all of Her myriad expressions?

Among those myriad expressions in the intimate vastness of Sophia's consciousness are the Stone Beings. What is a "being?" From one point of view, a being is a persistent pattern of consciousness, which may be embodied in a physical form. Stones are "beings" whose physical form persists far longer than ours . . . although, as patterns of consciousness, we and the Stone Beings might both be eternal. (Regarding this, some alchemists, particularly the Chinese, believed that we humans have to *work* for spiritual immortality, as we discussed in Chapter 18.)

In any event, stone energies are very coherent, persistent and dependable. They are stable expressions of consciousness, whereas we humans, with our fluid nature, tend to be more unstable. The alchemists worked to join with Sophia so they could *become* the Stone—a pattern of consciousness that was both "immortal" (permanently stable) and capable of transforming matter in the physical domain through co-creation with Sophia.

The stones, in my view, are like helpful angels of Sophia who are able and willing to provide guidance on the path of our evolution and transformation by offering us "vibrational information"—patterns with which we can resonate to help ourselves become more stable, coherent, creative, healthy and powerful. Thus, they offer great assistance to us. This is also of great service to the Soul of the World, because she desires and needs us to co-create the New Earth with Her.

Now, back to the Alchemy of Stones Intensive and the Photonic Stone Layouts!

When our group at the AOS Intensive did the Photonics Body Layouts, we worked with focused intention for the benefit of our partners receiving the layouts, as well as opening ourselves to the intuitions that came to us in regard to the appropriate placement of the stones. We also carried an overall focused intention to invoke the participation of the Stone Beings and Sophia, along with a surrender of any expectations of how that might manifest. This is the basic pattern for co-creation.

Those who were to receive Photonic Stone Layouts lay down with eyes closed, while those administering the layouts worked intuitively with pendulums to choose the appropriate stones from their Photonic Layout Kits. Everyone attempted to sense the most beneficial placements of the stones on the photos of their partners. We all spent whatever time was necessary to complete this.

Although I was facilitating the event, I ended up placing stones for a participant who had no partner. When I placed a tiny Rosophia stone on the heart chakra of her photograph, she spontaneously said, "Ohhh! My heart just opened!" That was my personal validation that the process works, and works very powerfully.

After both partners had received and given a Photonic Layout, we opened up the whole group for discussion of what had happened. Virtually everyone in the group of 182 people had felt the energies of the stones within their own bodies, even though the layouts were done on their photographs. By this time, it was late evening, so I sent everyone off to sleep, suggesting that they take their photographs to their rooms and keep their layouts in place for the entire weekend. I felt this would allow the Stone Beings to work on them (and with them) through the connections established by the layouts, and to continue working through the whole weekend. Checking in with everyone the next morning, and later in the weekend, I learned that most of the participants continued to feel and to perceive a benefit from their Photonic layouts for the entire duration of the event.

In 2019, Kathy and I went to Japan to offer workshops in Tokyo and Osaka. I was eager to try the Photonic Layouts again, so they were included on the agenda in both cities. Once again, virtually all the participants reported being able to feel powerful energetic effects from these layouts, whether they were receiving or giving them. Also, at these events, the Photonic layouts were left in the workshop room overnight, instead of being taken to the participants' homes or hotel rooms. Nonetheless, over 90% of the participants reported feeling the energies of their layouts working on them through the night. In fact, a number of people said the effects were so powerful that they were kept awake by them!

After these confirmations, I realized that there are a number of promising avenues for working with stones in this way:

1. We can work on ourselves, using our own photographs and placing stones where our intuition guides us. Using intention and intuition, we can set up patterns of stones whose energies can benefit us all the time, not just during an hour while we lie down. This can continue indefinitely, and a layout can also be modified over time. Photonic Layouts are not limited in time span, or by the location of the person.

2. We can do Photonic Stone Layouts for other people, whether we are with them or not. All one needs is the person's photograph (preferably an 8 x 10 inch image, with the person lying down) and his or her permission to do the layout. [**NOTE**: Permission is very necessary, for both ethical and practical reasons. First, it is unethical to perform any sort of energy work on someone without his or her knowledge and permission. Second, without the person's permission, there is no co-creating with that person. It is more like an imposition of one's own will. That can be dangerous, and may be why such practices—when negatively directed (as in sorcery), or simply when done without permission—can trigger a "boomerang" effect on those who try it. Not recommended!]

3. We can use Photonic Stone Layouts on photographs of pets, gardens, properties, areas of land, bodies of water, countries, or even the whole Earth. If we are using our benevolent focused intention of blessing, and are asking the Stone Beings and Sophia to co-create with us, amazing and wonderful results can be achieved. [Note in regard to the caution about permission: With animals, plants, land, bodies of water, etc., one is recommended to ask inwardly and listen for the felt sense of an answer. Then, the layout should be done as an offering, not an imposition, and one can affirm one's agreement that the offering is simply an offering, not an effort to impose one's will. I recommend this when it is not possible to

directly ask verbally for permission, and I want to emphasize that it is important to be receptive and honest when listening for the inner response.]

4. We can use Photonic Stone Layouts for any beneficial spiritual purpose. The Stone Beings are very powerful, as are we. They (and we) can even bring about effects for the entire Earth. I personally believe that we are being called by Sophia to join in co-creating the Vibrational Ascension of Earth and all beings here. One way of performing this magic of spiritual alchemy is to work with a Photonic Stone Layout, using a photograph of the Earth. This can move us toward the achievement of what the alchemists called the Great Work (the *Magnum Opus*) and the creation of the Philosophers' Stone. From one point of view, the Philosophers' Stone is the Ascended Earth, and from another viewpoint the Philosophers' Stone is the union of the alchemist with Sophia. Actually, I believe that these viewpoints both refer to different aspects to the very same outcome!

PHOTONIC LAYOUT KITS

After the Alchemy of Stones Intensive, I wanted to bring what I view as an exciting new discovery into the community of stone lovers, especially those whose work with stones includes healing and the expansion of awareness. I feel Photonic layouts can help us engage with the Stone Beings to bring about a wealth of beneficial outcomes, and through this practice we have a golden opportunity for learning to work co-creatively with the Stone Beings and Sophia.

The principles are available to everyone, and you can use any stones that feel appropriate to you. The full Photonic Stone Kit that we used in the 2016 Intensive contained forty high-vibration stones, including: Guardianite, Black Tourmaline, Amazez, Amethyst, White Azeztulite, Satyaloka Clear Azeztulite, Auralite-23, Petalite, Black Tourmaline Azeztulite , Violet Flame Opal, Magnifier Quartz, Azumar, Rose Quartz, Rosophia, Danburite, Lithium Light, Honey and Cream Azeztulite, Pink Azeztulite, Himalaya Gold Azeztulite, Satyaloka Rose Azeztulite, Celestite, Healerite, Healers Gold, Hematite, Empowerite, Vitalite, Moldavite, Cinnazez, Red Fire Azeztulite, Master Shamanite, Pink Fire Azeztulite, Black Azeztulite, Mystic Merlinite, Tibetan Tektite, Phenacite, Circle Stone, Natrolite, Scolecite, Fulgurite and Revelation Stone. The pieces are small but that's ideal for this sort of work.

[**NOTE** The Photonic Stone Kit mentioned above can be viewed and/or purchased at my company's website: www.heavenandearthjewelry.com]

PRACTICE: PHOTONIC LAYOUT FOR HEALING

(or other purpose of your choosing)

Instructions:

(**NOTE** These relate to working with a partner in a group setting, as we did at the Alchemy of Stones Intensive. You can adapt these instructions as you wish for other situations. You can, for example, do a similar layout for yourself, or for a person who is not present, if you have their photo and permission. Ideally, the photo should show the subject lying down, and should look directly down from above.)

1. **BEFORE BEGINNING THE LAYOUT:** Gather together an array of small stones from your collection, or from a Photonic Layout Kit, or a combination of the two. Draw a diagram of a human body form on a piece of paper so that the position of the stones in the layout can be recorded. (You can work with something like the outline used in the Body Layouts in Chapter 22.) You will need some poster putty so the stones can be temporarily affixed to the photograph. You may want to have a pendulum available for the use of the person

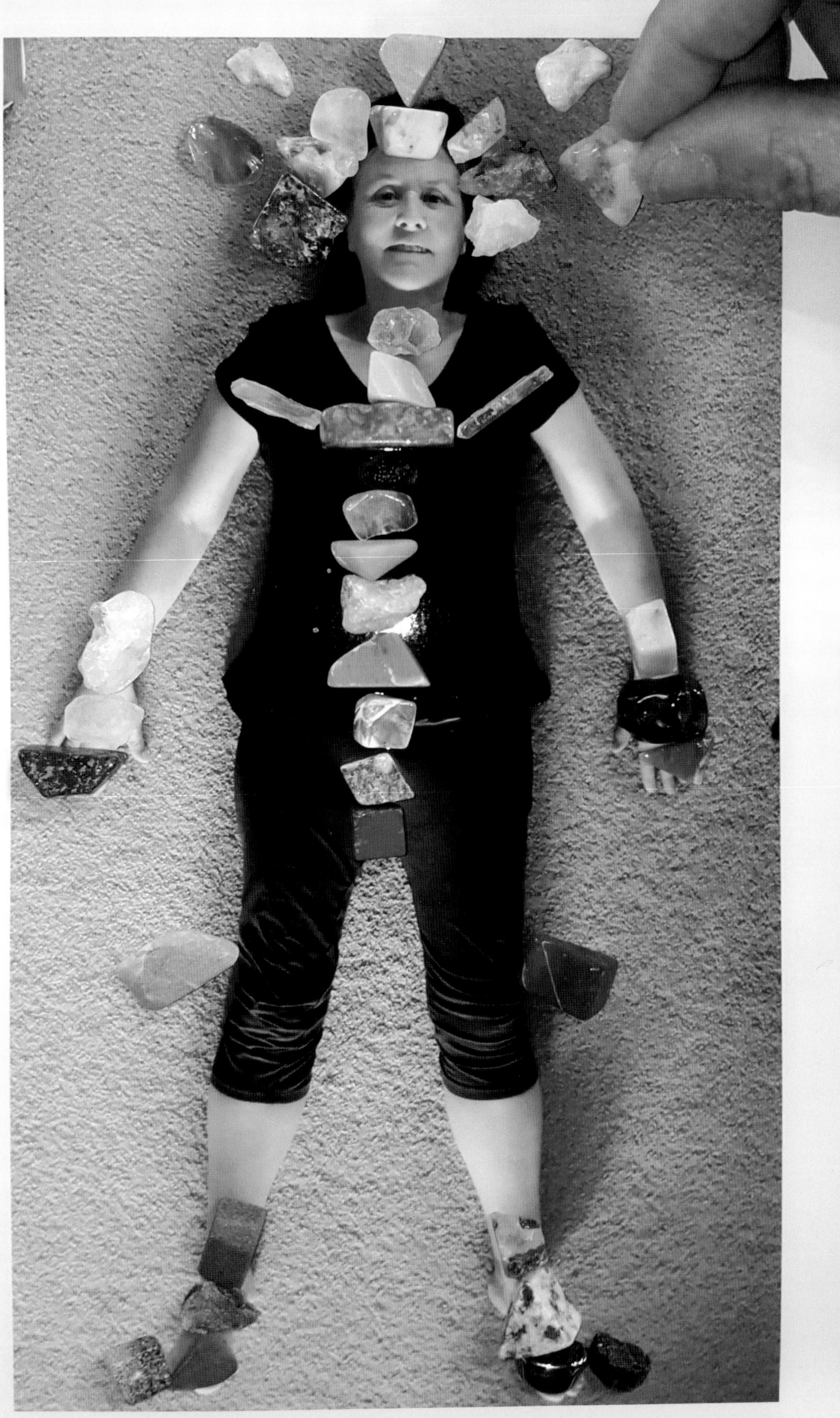

giving the layout. This can help some people to intuitively select the best possible stones and placements.

2. Choose a partner, discuss with the partner your intention for the layout.
3. Decide, tell your partner, and write down the intention for your layout. (i.e., physical healing, emotional healing, purification of the subtle body, or any other type of healing intention you choose.)
4. Decide who will receive their layout first.
5. Both partners should center themselves in the heart.
6. If you are receiving the layout, tape your photo to a tray or a stiff piece of cardboard. Have your full array of small stones ready and at hand so that your partner can intuitively choose the appropriate ones for placement on your photo. Get into resonance with the photo of yourself through breathing and blessing, offering and requesting, giving and receiving. It is helpful to move into harmony and love for oneself when one is about to receive a photonics layout. After this, lie down with closed eyes and remain in a receptive frame of mind. Pay attention to all sensations in your body and your energy field, as well as any imagery or guidance that comes to you. Do not open your eyes or talk until the partner giving you the Photonic layout calls you out of meditation.
7. If you are the one who will be giving the layout for your receiving partner, get into resonance with the array of stones, and also with your partner. Touch your partner, engage him or her with open eyes and breathe together with both the stones and the partner, offering and receiving, with the intention of blessing.
8. If you are giving the Photonic layout, hold in mind the intention of your partner for the layout, and align your own intention with it. Then begin from either the top or bottom of the image, and place stones at each chakra, as you are guided to do for that person. You can touch the photo to connect with that area and you can touch whatever stones you are drawn to in order to feel the appropriate choice. Or, you can use a pendulum to choose the appropriate stones, and to see how it feels afterwards.
9. As you select and position the stones, use the poster putty to stick them onto the photo in their appropriate placements. Note: You may find that you are guided to put one or more stones in places on the photo that are outside the outline of the body image. Such placements may correspond to areas of the person's energy field. I suggest that you follow your intuition in regard to all of the stone placements, no matter where they "want" to go.
10. Make a written note, on the receiving partner's body diagram paper, of which stones go at each location. You can do this after you have placed them all, or as you go along. This provides a useful record of the layout.
11. When finished placing the stones, spend a moment to bless the whole layout. Then sit quietly for a few minutes, allowing your partner to "absorb" the Photonic layout. During this time, pay attention and remember any sensations, imagery or guidance that come to you.
12. When the time feels appropriate, the giver of the layout should softly call the name of the receiver, to bring him or her gently out of the meditative state.
13. At this point, both giver and receiver should write down some notes about the experience. Afterwards, you may describe to one another how you experienced the process. This can be quite beneficial, because helpful images and insights may come to either or both of you.
14. When this is finished, those who received the Photonic layout may wish to remove and put away the stones. On the other hand—and this is my usual suggestion—one may have the sense that it will be beneficial to leave the layout in place on the photo for some period of time. This is one of the special advantages of Photonic layouts over regular stone body

Photonic Body Layout for ______________________ Date ______________

Goal(s)

Stone Placement

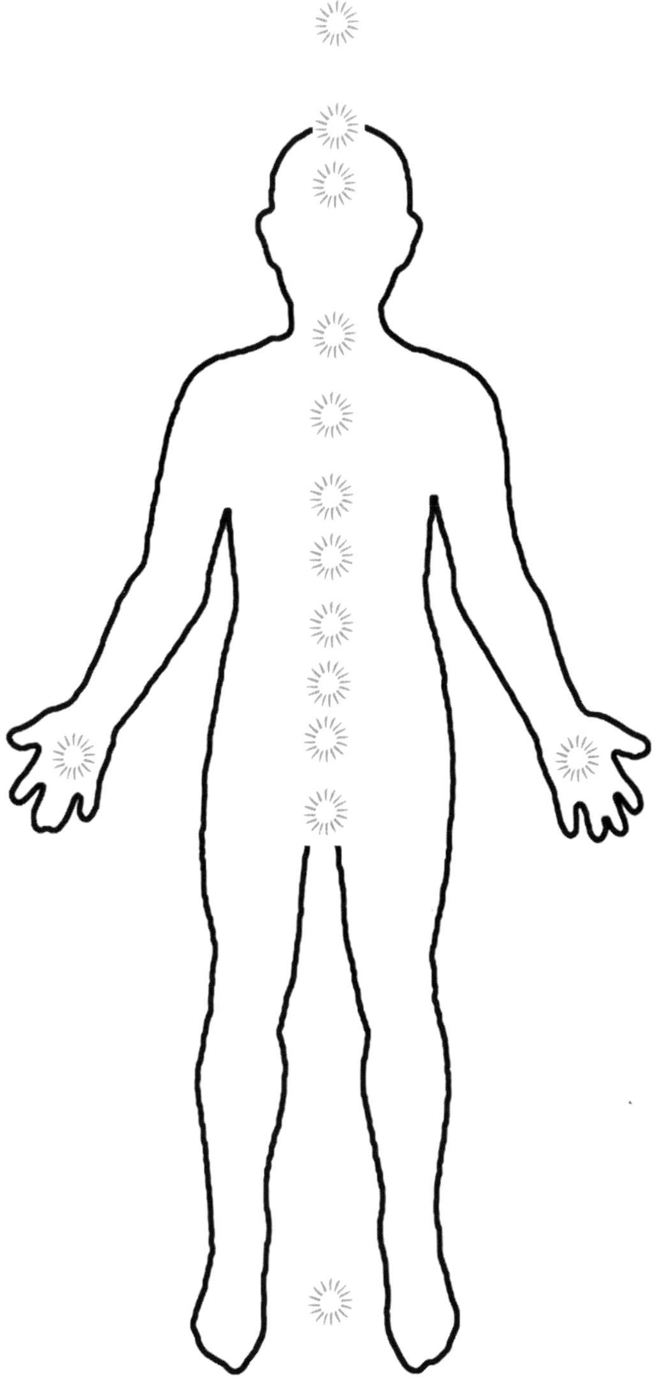

If a photo of the person is not available, or if the image is not of the person's whole body, you can use a "generic" layout diagram like this. Write the person's name on the page and/or attach whatever photograph is available. Then place the stones in appropriate positions on the diagram. You can copy this diagram or get it digitally from the Heaven and Earth website. Search for "Generic Photonic Body Layout."]

layouts—they can be continued for an indefinite amount of time, allowing the stones to do their work with us much longer. If you do continue your layout for days or weeks, I suggest that you pick up the photo, still attached to its backing, and sit with it in contemplation, inwardly focusing on your intention, intensifying it through imagining the purpose of the layout in a stage of complete fulfillment. Do this until you feel the process is complete.

15. After the initial process of placing the stones in the layout and allowing the process to begin, the partners may wish to reverse the roles of giver and receiver and go through the process again. In this way, both people have the opportunity to receive a photonics layout, and to give one.

ADDENDUM: Please note that in photonic layouts where both partners are present, it is possible to do things to enhance one's resonance with one's partner that we cannot do in the same way when we work with a distant person, or a place, etc. When doing a photonic layout for someone or something which is not present, remember to use intention and imagination to create the strongest possible resonance. As Alchemical Stone Healers, our purpose is to bring about a successful outcome, rather than to be "disinterested observers." So pure intention is necessary.

Once intention has been set, and the stones are in place to carry the intention, we can release it. We do not need to keep thinking about it, and it is better not to, because we might create doubt, which is counterproductive. Trust that the stones will hold the intention we have set in motion. That is a big part of their role.

Now that we have explored the ideas behind Photonic Stone Layouts and have worked with a healing layout for a person, we can move on to experiment with more Photonic Stone Layouts. The intentions for the layouts in the next chapter involve the healing and awakening of the Earth, the activation of our DNA, and the co-creation of the alchemical *Magnum Opus*.

24

Photonic Layouts for Earth Ascension & DNA Activation

As an aspiring spiritual alchemist, I am always carrying the intention for enlightenment and union with the Divine to occur for myself, for humanity, and for the Earth. This is in accord with the words of Paul Levy, which I have quoted earlier (and which I have posted on the wall in several rooms of my home):

> *Alchemy is a timeless, sacred art, as the alchemists' art is to become an instrument for the incarnating deity to make itself real in time and space.*

Thinking about Levy's aphorism, it occurs to me that the Divine is already real in the realm of pure spirit, and in the subtle/imaginal realm. If there is a place where the presence of the Divine is yet to fully manifest, it is in our physical reality—the realm of time and space. As I have written, all of my inner encounters with Sophia have shown me that, even though she is vast and wise beyond our understanding, *she needs our help* if she is to achieve her fulfillment.

ABOVE: Workshop participant in Japan assembles a DNA Activation and Earth Ascension Photonic Layout.

How can we help Sophia to achieve the transformation she seeks—making herself real in time and space? Everything I try to do in spiritual alchemy has this intention at its core. I can also see that Sophia's manifestation in time and space is *the same event* that one might describe as the enlightenment of oneself, humanity and the Earth. You could say that we are all riding the same oroborous!

The Photonic Stone Layouts described below are intended to nudge these great aspirations closer to their realization. As we engage with them, their immediate effects may seem quite powerful to us as individuals, yet insufficient to transform our whole world.

When such thoughts come to me, I admonish myself to follow the lead of the alchemists and cultivate the virtues of patience and purity of intent. I am reminded of the weeks and months these ancient practitioners would tend to the flasks on their stoves, patiently observing the slow transformation of the substances inside.

So, our task is to continue our work and appreciate the blessings that come to us, and to offer ours back to the world. Our love is the alchemical fire in the furnace of our hearts. We never know just when or how the Great Transformation may occur.

While we're watching for that moment, let's do some Photonic Stone Layouts that help us magnify the power of our intentions!

PHOTONIC EARTH ASCENSION LAYOUT

I've designed another Photonic Stone Layout Kit, one with a very special purpose. I call this one the Photonic Earth Ascension Kit. It's purpose is to facilitate the Vibrational Ascension of the Earth and all beings who live on this planet. The kit contains small pieces of twelve different

Photonic Earth Ascension Layout

types of Azeztulite, plus ten pieces of Magnifier Quartz, which are meant to amplify the effects. The kit also includes an image of the Earth, upon which the layout can be placed. I suggest that you work intuitively or with a pendulum to choose the spots for placing the stones on and/or around the Earth's image, holding the intention for the highest good of the Earth and all beings here. Personally, I feel that this may be the most important activity one can engage in at this time, at least in regard to working with stones.

Those who know the story of Azeztulite will recall that the Azez is the name for the angelic group soul that serves and proliferates the Nameless Light energies that are emanated by the Great Central Sun. This energy comes through all Azeztulites, and I identify Azeztulite stones based on whether it is present. "Azez" is also the term for the Nameless Light itself. The agenda of the Azez is to work co-creatively with human beings for the purpose of imbuing all the Quartz in the Earth's crust (over 25% of the crust of the entire planet) with the Nameless Light energies. In other words, their mission is to turn all of the Quartz in the Earth into Azeztulite, thereby transforming the Earth into a Planet of Light. To me, this is a profound portrayal of Vibrational Ascension. And when it occurs, we will ascend simultaneously with the Earth. It does not mean we will leave the Earth—it means that we will join with the Earth in becoming filled with spiritual Light. This is planetary enlightenment.

As we have seen, one of the major insights of spiritual alchemy is that the universe works through feedback. That is why a major symbol of alchemy is the Oroborous—the snake that devours its own tail. That image portrays feedback in a powerful way, and all of Nature's processes partake of it. Thus, when we place Azeztulite—a stone of spiritual Light which comes from the Earth but which has been activated by heavenly beings—upon an image of the Earth, we are initiating a feedback loop. It is fueled by our love and our benevolent intention, along with the Light of the Azez and the love of Sophia, Soul of the World. It may well be that this simple act of intention, *amplified* by the Azez and Azeztulite, and *multiplied* by as many people as are willing to implement it, will be enough to actualize the potential of the Earth to become a Planet of Light.

This is a rather mind-boggling idea to contemplate, but I urge everyone reading this to consider it deeply. We saw at the Alchemy of Stones workshop in 2016 (and in the 2019 workshops in Japan) that the Photonic Stone Layout process works. Since we know that it works, we must use our imaginations to try to picture the absolute highest and best use of this understanding, and the co-creative potential we have. I can think of nothing more wonderful (or necessary!) than participating in the possibility of co-creating Earth's Vibrational Ascension and enlightenment. All I have learned about alchemy tells me that human participation is absolutely essential. Without it, the Divine cannot "impose" enlightenment upon the world, any more than we can "impose" healing on someone who does not wish to be healed. I invite all those who feel called to this possibility to join in this great experiment, the Great Work, the *Magnum Opus.* I think it's going to be profound, astounding, fantastic fun!

PRACTICE: CREATING A PHOTONIC EARTH ASCENSION LAYOUT

1. Choose the stones you will be working with. In the Photonic Earth Ascension kits I have designed, these are the stones included: Satyaloka Clear Azeztulite, Pink Azeztulite, Sanda Rosa Azeztulite, Cinnazez, Amazez, Satyaloka Rose Azeztulite, Satyaloka Yellow Azeztulite, Himalaya Gold Azeztulite, Red Fire Azeztulite, Pink Fire Azeztulite, Black Azeztulite, White Azeztulite (2 pieces), Magnifier Quartz Crystals (12 pieces).
2. Lay the stones out beside the spot where you have placed the photo of the Radiant Earth. I recommend doing this on your altar, or in your sacred space. If you do not have such a place set aside, you can "sanctify" a space by doing a little ritual of purifying the place where the

layout will be, using sage or Palo Santo and a prayer in which you ask for the space to be clear and blessed. Ask your guides, the Soul of the Earth, and the Stone Beings to assist you in the ritual of sanctification, as well as with the layout you will do.

3. Enter the inner state of True Imagination by visualizing your intention for the awakening, transformation and Vibrational Ascension of the Earth and of all beings who are part of the Earth. Ask for Sophia, the Earth and the Stone Beings to co-create this reality with you.
4. Now, staying in silence and remaining mindful of your intention and of the presence of all the other beings who are working with you, begin placing the stones on the photo of the Earth. Let your intuition and inner guidance tell you where to place each stone. See the light around the Earth's image, and imagine that the real Earth where you are standing is beginning to awaken and to emanate a radiance of spiritual Light. Envision that what you are doing symbolically with the photograph is simultaneously happening all around you. Envision the Earth becoming a Planet of Light.
5. When you have finished laying out the stones, stop and contemplate the pattern and the meaning you have asked it to help manifest. Feel in your heart how you might experience the reality of this manifestation. Imagine what the synchronous awakening and transformation of yourself and the Earth might feel like.
6. Inwardly or outwardly (or both), say a phrase such as, "May it be so!" And after a few moments, when the energy feels right, say, "It is done!"
7. At this point, release the focus of your intention and let everything go. This is the moment of surrender that allows your spiritual partners to do their part, in harmony with the intention you have set. It is important to release any expectations, because the results of such ritual practices of co-creation are rarely identical to what we originally imagined. Often, they are far better! In any case, it is important to hold the essence of your intention, but to let go of expectations as to the form in which it may manifest.
8. When you are ready, you may depart from the sacred space and go on with your day. Before you do so, you may want to sit in the room with this layout and write down what you felt or saw inwardly as you created it. These practices affect the spiritual alchemist (you!) just as much as they affect the subject upon which you have focused your intention. Remember, Vibrational Ascension is meant to happen for *you and the Earth,* simultaneously!
9. I suggest keeping this layout in place for some time, and coming back to it frequently. If you simply set it up and leave it, you may forget about it. This lessens your co-creative power, because you will have let your attention and intention dissipate. It is good to go back to the layout each day, or at least every few days. When you return to it, recharge it by re-envisioning it, and reaffirming your intent for this to become real in the world, in the best possible way. Before leaving, once again say, "May it be so!" and, "It is done!" or other words of your choosing.
10. Eventually, you may feel it is time to take the layout down. Do not resist this feeling. Your intuition may be telling you that this iteration of the process is complete. Or you may sense that it is time to repeat the layout once again, perhaps with the stones in a different pattern, or with some new stones included. Don't hesitate to follow these intuitive promptings. Part of the benefit of all these processes is to teach us how to know the voice of the Deep Self, as it speaks to us with intuitive impulses. This very thing is an aspect of the Vibrational Ascension we are seeking.

DNA VIBRATIONAL ASCENSION LAYOUT

In the Alchemy of Stones, as in the spiritual alchemy of past centuries, we recognize the interdependence of spirit and matter. We hold the alchemical worldview that matter is holy and spiritually alive, that the Earth has a Soul, and that our physical bodies are a microcosm of the world that can resonate with the whole. As the alchemists said, "As above, so below. As below, so above." The Photonic Stone Layouts, and all of our work with stones, are based on these principles. The vision of co-creating the simultaneous Vibrational Ascension of ourselves and the Earth is also grounded in these ideas. In our efforts to facilitate this great transformation, we work both physically and symbolically, utilizing the three human powers of attention, intention and imagination. We do this in conjunction with the Stone Beings, in both their physical and spiritual aspects.

About a year after envisioning the Photonic Earth Ascension layout described above, another inspiration came to me. I suddenly saw the radiant Earth with the image of a cross section of human DNA superimposed over it. I strongly sensed that this was an excellent picture to

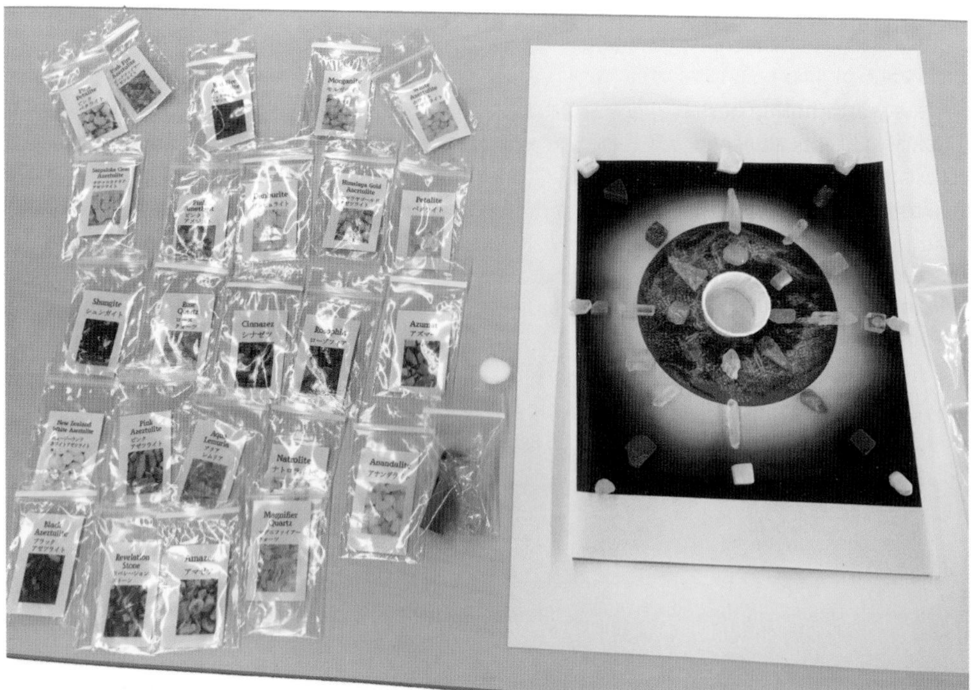

symbolically display the intention of the simultaneous Vibrational Ascension of ourselves and the Earth. I felt guided to make such an image and to enhance it with stones in a new Photonic Layout. As with all my practices involving layouts, it was to be done in ritual space, holding the vision and intention of what was desired.

A little later, an additional insight came to me. I realized that, for any person who chose to do this Photonic Layout, the way to "personalize" it and maximize its co-creative power would be to *include a sample of one's own DNA* in the layout! I felt certain that this addition would intensify the effects of the layout on both oneself and the Earth. I knew that our DNA is liquid crystal, and has an energetic resonance with the currents of the stones.

I also remembered Cleve Backster's research into Primary Awareness. Although his most famous experiments involved hooking a polygraph to plants, he also tested many other living substances, including human saliva, which contains our DNA. Backster found that saliva, taken from the cheek and hooked up to a polygraph machine, would react to experiences undergone by the person it came from. Backster showed that a person's saliva would display signs of distress on the polygraph when that person was in a stressful situation, even hundreds of miles away. This told me that, by placing a sample of one's DNA on the photonic layout I had envisioned, one could achieve a much more intimate personal connection with the stone energies of the layout, as well as its symbolic power.

The purpose of the DNA Vibrational Ascension Layout is similar to that of the Photonic Earth Ascension Layout. The principle difference is that it more strongly links the stone energies and the energies of the image with one's individual self. Also, this layout directs these energies into the DNA of the person and of the human species at large, as well as into the Earth and all living beings here.

Ascension is an event that encompasses the entire physical body, as well as one's subtle/imaginal body. It is not something that merely occurs "in one's head," or only in the spiritual realms. From the alchemical perspective, Vibrational Ascension is the Great Conjunction, the Marriage of Heaven and Earth. When we experience this as individuals, we witness and partake of this great cosmic union. When we build a Photonic Stone Layout of this type, incorporating our DNA into the pattern, we are inviting the energy of Vibrational Ascension into every cell of our bodies.

It is worth noting here that every DNA molecule in one's body naturally emits light—real physical light—as an aspect of the life process. This has been scientifically measured and verified. It can be useful to remain mindful of this as one does the practice below, because it can help to overcome unintended mental resistance to fully committing oneself to this co-creation. If our minds know that our DNA is already radiating light, then it seems that much more believable that we can turn up its intensity!

PRACTICE:
CREATING A DNA VIBRATIONAL ASCENSION PHOTONIC LAYOUT

1. Choose the stones you will be working with. In the DNA Vibrational Ascension Photonic Layout kits I have designed, these are the stones included: White Azeztulite, Petalite, Danburite, Phenacite, Satyaloka Clear Azeztulite, Blue-Green Azeztulite, Nirvana Quartz, Lemurian Light Crystal, Satya Mani Quartz, Selenite, Celestite, Scolecite, Healerite, Healers Gold, Kaurilite, Jet, Shungite, Magnifier Quartz (16 pieces)
2. Lay the stones out beside the spot where you have placed the photo of the DNA/Radiant Earth. I recommend doing this on your altar, or in your sacred space. If you do not have such a place set aside, you can "sanctify" a space by doing a little ritual of purifying the place where the layout will be, using sage or Palo Santo and a prayer in which you ask for the space to be clear and blessed. Ask your guides, the Soul of the Earth, and the Stone Beings to assist you in the ritual of sanctification, as well as with the layout you will do. Ask the DNA in every cell in your body, and in all life on Earth, to participate in this co-creation with you.
3. Enter the inner state of True Imagination by visualizing your intention for the awakening, transformation and Vibrational Ascension of the Earth and of all beings who are part of the Earth. Envision your DNA emitting more and more Light, increasing in intensity through the entire process. Ask for Sophia, the Earth and the Stone Beings to co-create this reality with you.
4. Now, staying in silence and remaining mindful of your intention and of the presence of all the other beings who are working with you, begin placing the stones on the photo of the Earth. (I suggest that you place the Selenite at the center of the layout, and that you use a cotton swab to collect a little saliva from the inside of your cheek, which you then wipe on the Selenite. The Selenite has the quality of connecting and amplifying all the stones in your layout, so it is a good place to put your DNA sample. Whenever you take the layout apart, you can wash the Selenite and re-use it.) As you position the rest of the stones, let your intuition and inner guidance tell you where to place each one. See the light around the Earth's image, and imagine that the real Earth where you are standing is beginning to awaken and to emanate a radiance of spiritual Light. Place attention inside your body, and imagine that from the DNA in every cell, greater and greater Light is streaming out. Envision that what you are doing symbolically with the photograph is simultaneously happening within you and around you, throughout the Earth and all living creatures. Envision the Earth becoming a Planet of Light, and yourself and all others becoming radiant beings.
5. When you have finished laying out the stones, stop and contemplate the pattern and the reality you have asked it to help manifest. Feel in your heart how you might experience the actualization of this intention. Imagine what the synchronous awakening and transformation of yourself and the Earth might feel like. Imagine this with all your cells, and listen to the singing of the Light that pours out of them.

6. Inwardly or outwardly (or both), say a phrase such as, "May it be so!" And after a few moments, when the energy feels right, say, "It is done!"
7. At this point, release the focus of your intention and let everything go. This is the moment of surrender that allows your spiritual partners to do their part, in harmony with the intention you have set. It is important to release any expectations, because the results of such ritual practices of co-creation are rarely identical to what we originally imagined. Often, they are far better! In any case, it is important to hold the essence of your intention, but to let go of expectations as to the form in which it may manifest.
8. When you are ready, you may depart from the sacred space and go on with your day. Before you do so, you may want to sit in the room with this layout and write down what you felt or saw inwardly as you created it. After leaving the sacred space remember to re-create this vision in your imagination as frequently as possible. Do this as vividly as you can, but without attachment to specific results. Eventually (or perhaps right away) you will begin to feel what this is actually like. This is why releasing expectations is crucial. If we hang on to them, we may miss the real thing when it occurs. Often, such things begin very gently and subtly, but if we give attention to them without trying to control them, they grow.
9. I suggest keeping this layout in place for some time, and coming back to it frequently. If you simply set it up and leave it, you may forget about it. This lessens your co-creative power, because you will have let your attention and intention dissipate. It is good to go back to the layout each day, or at least every few days. When you return to it, recharge it by re-envisioning it, and reaffirming your intent for this to become real in the world in the best possible way. Before leaving, once again say, "May it be so!" and, "It is done!" or other words of your choosing.
10. Eventually, you may feel it is time to disassemble the layout. Do not resist this feeling. Your intuition may be telling you that this iteration of the process is complete. Or you may sense that it is time to repeat the layout once again, perhaps with the stones in a different pattern, or with some new stones included. Don't hesitate to follow these intuitive promptings. Part of the benefit of all these processes is to teach us how to know the voice of the Deep Self, as it speaks to us with intuitive impulses. This very thing is an aspect of the Vibrational Ascension we are seeking.

[**NOTE**: Photonic Stone Kits for the layouts mentioned above can be viewed and/or purchased at www.heavenandearthjewelry.com. The Photonic images of the Radiant Earth, and of the DNA/Radiant Earth can be downloaded free at the same website. I encourage you to try them out! Remember, you do not have to use the kits. You can also select your own array of stones to do these practices.]

PHOTONIC STONE LAYOUTS FOR EVERYTHING ELSE

Part of what makes photonic Stone Layouts such a fantastic addition to one's alchemical tool kit is that they can be utilized for virtually any purpose. Like any ritual practice, a Photonic Stone Layout can focus and enhance your capacity for manifesting your intention. However, in this case, we are enlisting the co-creative energies of the Stone Beings and Sophia, which make a huge difference.

The layouts I have described above are oriented toward what I think of as the highest aspirations to which we address ourselves as spiritual alchemists. I have described them in detail because, to me, it is important to work toward these transformational potentials.

However, even the ancient alchemists embraced a diversity of goals. Paracelsus spent a great deal of his time and energy on healing his patients. The pioneers of radionics were modern-day alchemists seeking to benefit food production and other objectives which were considerably more mundane than planetary spiritual transformation.

I believe that all these goals are worthwhile in their own right, and that pursuing them also facilitates our transformation. Practice helps us become familiar with the sort of work we are doing. Our capacities for subtle perception and for co-creative manifestation improve as we use them more frequently.

With all this in mind, I encourage those who have an interest in Photonic Stone Layouts to try them for a variety of purposes. Below I will list some suggestions for the kinds of thing one can do. But the possibilities are truly endless.

If you have read and considered the processes I described in this chapter (and especially if you have tried them out), I think you are ready to design and carry out your own Photonic Stone Layouts. I suggest you start out by using some notes, or writing out the details of the processes you decide to do. Then get what you think is a good photograph of whomever or whatever you want to be the focus of your layout, and print it out in a size large enough to accommodate the stones you'll be using. Gather a good variety of stones you feel are appropriate for the intention you want to manifest. The Index and Stone Dictionary in the back of this book can help you choose the most appropriate stones. You can refer to the layout practices described above to aid in planning your process. Here is a selection of possible applications:

1. **WORKING WITH PEOPLE AT A DISTANCE:** You can do a photonic layout for a friend or client anywhere in the world. Simply get his or her photograph, as well as the agreement of the person. Ideally you should know what the person's goal is for the layout you will do. It can be helpful to agree on a time for the session, so that the recipient can perhaps be alone and in a relaxed and receptive frame of mind. This may increase the effectiveness of the layout, and can facilitate the recipient's being able to sense the energies and inner shifts that the layout produces. You should also agree with your friend or client on the length of time the layout will be used. It can be for as little as an hour, or it can be for a week, a month, or as long as you like. (Remember to "recharge" layouts regularly when they are to be kept going for days or weeks.) it is a good idea for both you and the recipient to keep notes or a journal of what occurs during the course of the layout.

2. **HEALING AND HELPING PETS:** Begin with a good photo of the animal, and before creating a Photonic Stone Layout, do a meditation in which you ask the animal's permission. Be sure you have heard a clear inner "Yes" before doing anything else. If you get a "No," you can ask why, but do not force the issue. You can always try again later. Once you have received permission, you can follow the same general procedures you would use in doing a layout for another person. If this is your own animal, keep notes about any effects you can observe. You may also go back to meditation and ask for feedback directly from the animal. This sort of practice can have the added benefit of teaching you how to connect psychically with your pet, and with other animals. If the animal lives with you, you may wish to get a saliva sample to add to the layout. This can intensify the layout's connection to the animal, in addition to the photo.

3. **IMPROVING WELLBEING OF THE GARDEN:** Print out a photo of the plant, garden plot or area of land you intend to treat. As before, go into meditation and ask permission. If you get a "Yes," you may proceed as with the other layouts. Remember that the early radionics researchers used their practices to dispel pests from fields as well as to "fertilize" garden plots. Use your imagination and intuition to see what is most appropriate and helpful.

4. **WORKING TO ALLEVIATE POLLUTION AND CONTAMINATION:** This is something that both I and my friends have tried. In this instance, you can use a photo of a polluted area. If it is not possible or convenient to take a photograph yourself, a satellite photo that you find online

can be suitable. As always, ask for inner permission from the spirit of the land before you begin. As you do this type of layout, I suggest that you envision the land or area in a state of wholeness and wellbeing, and hold that intention, rather than focusing on the toxins in that environment. Sometimes paying too much attention to toxic conditions can inadvertently give them more energy. (The same holds true in healing layouts for people, pets, animals and plants. Hold the image of health rather than focusing on the illness or imbalance you hope to alleviate.)

5. **SEEDING CITIES AND COUNTRIES WITH CURRENTS OF HARMONY:** Crime, war, poverty and other social ills are spread out around the Earth. If you feel an inner call to facilitate the healing of such situations, you may design Photonic Stone Layouts to treat them. The process is, once again, similar to those already discussed. Ask for permission to treat the area where the disharmony exists, and work intuitively to make a beneficial layout on a photograph of that place. Once again, satellite photos are readily available and can be quite useful. Visualize these places with currents of harmony permeating everything, and ask for co-creative participation from the Stone Beings, Sophia, and from the souls of all those in these places who wish for harmony. This is a delicate matter, and one should approach it carefully. However, if one is impeccable in one's intent, it is possible to act as an invisible influence towards the good. (**NOTE**: Such practices are not meant to substitute for political or charitable work in these places. However, a Photonic Stone Layout can be viewed as a kind of prayer in which one seeks to recruit spiritual help for the good of the situation. Prayer alone may not eliminate these ills, but its influence has been shown to be beneficial in many arenas. I believe the Photonic Stone Layouts, when carried out with sincerity and love, can be at least as powerful as prayer.)

It is said in many spiritual traditions, as well as by those who have experienced moments of enlightenment, that everything is connected. Jung and the alchemists believed that *symbols* connect the inner and outer realms of existence in a web of meaning. In our Photonic Stone Layouts, we utilize the *image* of whatever or whomever we wish to help as a meaningful symbol. We then *treat the image,* with the aid of the Stone Beings and Sophia, in order *to help who or what the image represents.* The efficacy of such treatments both depends on and validates the universal connectedness of All That Is.

Perhaps the one substance that universally weaves the Earth and all of life together is water. All life partakes of water, and water can be viewed as the very blood of the Earth herself. Water circulates through oceans, air, rivers, lakes and streams, as well as in our cells and in our tears. Our own blood and tears are salty, like sea water. And water has been used as a symbol pointing to our emotions, our unconscious, and our souls. With all this to inspire them, is it any wonder that ancient alchemists such as Paracelsus sought to create elixirs, letting water carry healing herbs and substances into the bodies of their patients? In the Alchemy of Stones, we also create elixirs, charged with the potencies of the Stone Beings. We will dive into these waters in the next chapter.

25

Stone Elixirs & Crystal Waters

Water is a primordial element which underlies creation myths and stories around the world. The Egyptian Heliopolitan creation story recounts that the sun-god Atum (Re) reposed in the primordial ocean (Nun). In Assyro-Babylonian mythology, first the gods and subsequently all beings arose from the fusion of salt water (Tiamat) and sweet water (Apsu). The holy books of the Hindus explain that all the inhabitants of the Earth emerged from the primordial sea. At the beginning of the Judeo-Christian story of creation, the spirit of God is described as stirring above the waters, and a few lines later, God creates a firmament in the midst of the waters to divide the waters (Genesis 1:1–6). In the Koran are the words "We have created every living thing from water."

—Professor Christopher I.C.E Witcombe, "Water and the Sacred"

Elixir: In Alchemy, a substance thought to be capable of changing base metals into gold. The same term, more fully elixir vitae, *"elixir of life," was given to the substance that would indefinitely prolong life—a liquid that was believed to be allied with the Philosophers' Stone.*

—Encyclopedia Britannica online:
https://www.britannica.com/topic/elixir-alchemy

Besides the legendary "Philosophers' Stone," [alchemical life elixirs] have been the goal of all alchemical research—the 'High Arcana' of alchemy. These life elixirs as well as the legendary Aurum Potabile, *made from gold, represented universal remedies and preparations meant for unfolding our awareness . . . The most astonishing fact is that the alchemical life elixirs are by no means remedies in the modern medical sense, but purely energetic essences. They act on the energy field of man and animal—on the etheric substance, the soul and the spirit—and not directly on the body. The second great discovery in the ancient alchemical scriptures is how these different essences made of metals and gems influence the aura and chakras. It is the discovery of the old chakra system of alchemy.*

—Ulrich Arndt, in "Alchemy and Paracelsus Medicine," Horus Media online: http://www.horusmedia.de/2004-paracelsus/paracelsus-en.php

The Alchemy of Stones is, in my view, more than an idea, a book, or a set of practices. For those who truly internalize the implications of the phenomena of stone energies and our capacity to relate with the Stone Beings and Sophia, these things create a profound shift in our way of being. We deepen, we open, and we begin to recognize and affirm the multitude of threads that comprise the vast web of living connections in which we are embedded.

During our alchemical journey thus far, we have seen that reality is far deeper than the surface world of the merely physical. We have learned that we can meet the Stone Beings and the Soul of the World in the subtle/imaginal realm, and that this realm encompasses both the physical and the spiritual worlds. We have seen that our experience of the currents of the stones takes place initially in that subtle/imaginal realm, and that the effects of connecting with stones in that domain can resonate into all aspects of our being. We now understand that our three human powers of attention, intention and imagination can be utilized co-creatively with Sophia and the Stone Beings to instigate spiritual awakening and transformation in ourselves and our world. We have discovered Sophia's creative method of Transformation Through Feedback, which is manifested in the evolutionary patterns of nature.

In the last few chapters, we have begun considering a widening range of practices in which we can engage, in order to link with the stones and enhance their effects. We have explored Mandalas, Stone Body Layouts and Photonic Stone Layouts. All of these modalities partake of our three human powers, and all of them are fundamentally rooted in the subtle/imaginal realm.

The ancient alchemists, like the spiritual alchemists of today—including those of us who have embraced the Alchemy of Stones—were working simultaneously with both spirit and matter. They recognized, as we do, that it is false to try to separate them, and that such separation isolates us from our own souls and the World Soul. When we conjoin spirit and matter in the way we conceive of ourselves and our world, the sacred returns from exile, and we take a great step on the path to wholeness.

As we approach the next set of alchemical activities—those involved in making and using stone elixirs and crystal waters—it is important to contemplate how everything we have explored so far weaves together and informs what we are about to do. It is so simple to make stone-charged waters that we might easily miss their significance. Through producing and using these water-based stone potions, we are uniting the resonant patterns of the Stone Beings with our own. We are inviting these patterns to manifest in every cell of our bodies. We are volunteering for transformation.

The alchemists intuitively grasped that there is a "divine blueprint" of human wholeness which would, if fully realized, manifest as an individual who is healthy, free from disease, filled with vitality, spiritually awakened and overflowing with love. Some of the most gifted practitioners, such as Paracelsus, imagined that it would be possible to create elixirs that could carry the divine blueprint into a person and affect its full manifestation. Many even believed that such a preparation might confer physical immortality. This was at the root of the alchemist's quest for the *elixir vitae,* "elixir of life." These early pioneers of medicine made numerous discoveries that

17th Century Alchemists and Elixir of Life

are still in use today. They also made many mistakes, some of which proved toxic or even fatal. We will not try to re-create their work or follow their old recipes, but we will take inspiration from their insights and endeavor to make discoveries of our own.

As background, here are a few excerpts from my book, *Stones of the New Consciousness:*

Human beings are about seventy percent water, and water is something we must constantly take into our bodies in order to live. Though one can live a month or more without food, one will die in as little as a few days without water. Water moves through us, builds our tissues, cleanses our organs and makes up much of our blood, which carries nourishment to all the cells. Without the proper amounts of water, our digestion, nerve impulses, thinking, sensing and even breathing cannot function. Water is everywhere in us, and, in fact, is *us more than any other substance.*

Homeopathic medicine works on the principle that water, which is used in preparing the remedies, has a "memory" of the presence of the substance introduced into it. Dilution does not degrade the memory. (In fact, it increases its potency, according to homeopathic principles.) It has been established that water molecules fall into discrete and specific patterns of alignment in the presence of a foreign substance. When the substance is removed, the water retains those patterns, and it transfers them to water which is later added to the original batch.

Water is an ideal medium for the introduction of the vibrational patterns emanated by stones. It crystallizes in a hexagonal pattern similar to that seen in Quartz and numerous other minerals. It is tremendously sensitive, as has been shown through a gamut of research, ranging from the rigorous experiments of molecular biologists to the more spiritually based research of Japan's famous Dr. Emoto.

It is clear that we will most likely benefit from taking in water that has been intentionally imbued with positive qualities. Even something as simple as Dr. Emoto's practice of writing words on bottles of drinking water is promising—write the words "good health," "happiness" and/or "prosperity" on your jug of drinking water and watch the results. But is there an even better way?

Of course, my answer to the rhetorical question above is, "Yes!" For all of the reasons we have discussed thus far, I now believe that the alchemical approach of co-creatively engaging the Stone Beings and Sophia will enhance both the power and the appropriateness of the elixirs and drinking waters we make. So let's set up our alchemical "laboratory" and get started!

A WORD OF CAUTION

Before I offer any directions or recipes, I want to make it clear that you must take responsibility for being sure that the waters and elixirs you make contain no toxins. Some minerals are toxic to take internally, perhaps even in the amounts that might leach into water when the stones are soaked. Stones that contain mercury, lead and copper are to be handled especially carefully. If you wish to make potions using the energies of these stones, I recommend utilizing the two-bottle method, which I describe below. Radioactive minerals such as uranium should be completely avoided. There are websites and online articles that list a number of toxic minerals. If you are unsure whether a stone might be toxic, use the two-bottle method. You can also set up a stone grid around your water container. This is an easy way to avoid letting any possible toxins into the water you are treating. The stone energies from the grid will manifest as a field that surrounds and penetrates the container, so that you need not have any of the stones physically touch the water.

The basic means by which we introduce the energetic currents and patterns of one or more stones into a container of water is to simply place the stones in the container with the water. Stones such as Quartz, Rose Quartz, Amethyst, Azeztulite and many others are safe to work with in this way, providing that the stones have been washed well. (The exception among the Azeztulites is Cinnazez, which contains mercury.)

THE TWO-BOTTLE METHOD: In situations where you want to use a mineral that may potentially be toxic, simply place the stone inside a small glass container with a screw-on lid, fill it with water, and screw the cap on tightly. Then rinse off that bottle and immerse it a larger glass container with the water you will actually use for your elixir. Add any other non-toxic stones you want to include to the larger container of water, and then go through whichever charging process you have chosen. When you are finished charging the water in the larger vessel, remove the sealed bottle and any other stones. Pour the water from the sealed bottle down the drain, remove the stone and wash the bottle. Rinse off all stones that you have used and put them away.

There are two reasons for using water inside the small sealed bottle. One is that when it is full of water it will sink rather than float in your elixir water. The other is that I feel that the water inside the sealed bottle, which is in contact with the stone, will be fully charged, and will help to transmit the charge through the glass and into the water you will use for your elixir.

CRYSTAL WATERS VERSUS STONE ELIXIRS: I believe that more or less the same processes can be used to create crystal waters and stone elixirs. The potential differences between the two are concerned with preservation and potentization. Crystal waters are meant to be used more or less immediately. One can drink them or use them externally as soon as you feel the charging process is complete. Elixirs are usually bottled and kept for use over a longer period of time. Therefore, I typically use some type of preservative (usually alcohol) when making and bottling a stone elixir.

When I make stone elixirs, I also frequently "potentize" them in the same manner used for homeopathic medicines. I first remove the stones from the container of charged water. Then this water is shaken up or agitated in some way, to fully circulate the subtle energy patterns of the stone(s) and to stimulate the water itself. Then this water is diluted with untreated water, in a ratio of 1 to 9. So for each ounce of the original water, another nine ounces of untreated water is added. Then the mixed water should be agitated again. If one wishes to further potentize the water, this process may be repeated, starting with some of the potentized water and again diluting it in the 1 to 9 ratio. This can be done as many times as one wishes. In homeopathy, it is believed that each potentizing dilution *increases* the power of the remedy. I have not done thorough tracking of this with stone elixirs, but I do feel that at least one round of potentizing is beneficial.

After the potentizing process, I add alcohol (usually a good, clean vodka or brandy) until the mixture is about 10% alcohol. This has, in my experience, worked quite well to preserve the elixirs. I can't say whether this preservation will last indefinitely, so I suggest that you check your elixirs each time you use them, and make sure they have not deteriorated.

I have experimented with various ways of applying stone elixirs. One can put a few drops under the tongue, as one might do with an herbal tincture or a liquid homeopathic remedy. Elixirs can also be applied externally, placing a few drops on the skin at the appropriate chakras or meridian points. A third method is to use the elixir as an "aura spray." To do this, one simply decants the elixir into a spray bottle and uses it as a "mist" in one's auric field. Somewhat surprisingly, many people in my workshops have reported that the aura sprays have produced the most immediate and powerful effects.

At this point, I am going to describe some suggested processes for infusing water with the currents of stones. Once the water has been exposed to the stone energies, use your own feeling sense to decide when the process feels complete. Generally, I like to allow the water and stones to sit overnight. After that you may use the water as a crystal water or take the next steps of potentizing and preservation to create an elixir. (In all cases, make certain that there is no chance of toxicity.) To avoid having to use cumbersome language, I am henceforth going to refer these waters as "elixirs."

A BASIC PRACTICE FOR MAKING STONE ELIXIRS

1. Consider the aspiration or goal you have for the elixir you want to make. You may wish to have an elixir of an individual stone, in order to have the purest possible presentation of it qualities. Or you might decide to concoct your own "recipes" for elixirs that use combinations of stones. Whatever your choice, select the stone or stones (or better yet, ask for volunteers!) Get a glass jar or bowl that holds at least a quart of water. (If you are using the double-bottle method, have the small bottle with you as well.)
2. It is good to do this practice in ritual consciousness, and in a place you have set aside as sacred space. Have a comfortable chair at hand where you can meditate with your stone(s) and the container of water.
3. Sit in the chair and hold the container of water in your lap, with the stone(s) beside you. If you prefer, you can sit with a small table in front of you. Place your hands on the side of the container, center yourself in your heart, and begin with some deep breaths. When you feel centered, begin the Activity of Blessing, in rhythm with your breathing. As you inhale, invite the soul essence of the water into your heart. As you exhale, offer your love and blessing to the water.
4. Keeping the water bowl on the table or in a stable position on you lap, pick up the stone(s) you will use in making the elixir. Do the Activity of Blessing with the Being(s) of the stone(s), just as you did with the water. Invite the Stone Being(s) to infuse the water with their essential qualities, in co-creative union with your own intention.
5. When you feel the inner prompting to continue, gently place the stone(s) into the bowl of water. Continue to breathe in the circulation of invitation and blessing. Now, focus your attention on the bowl with the stone(s) in it. Imagine and visualize the subtle energies of the stone(s) permeating the water, changing the water's subtle energy patterns and its molecular alignment. Imagine that the water is transforming in harmony with the nature of the Stone Being(s) and in accord with your intention.
6. When you feel the activation of the water is complete, thank the water and the Stone Being(s) and go back into a gentle meditative space until you are ready to come back to normal consciousness. The next steps can be done on the following day, or whenever you sense that the process of charging the water is complete.
7. Begin the next phase of this process by carefully removing the stones from the glass container. You can use a slotted spoon or tongs to do this. To potentize the charged water, agitate it by shaking it (if the glass container has a lid) or by stirring it in a clockwise direction. Either way, the agitation should be fairly vigorous.
8. Now measure out a portion of the charged water into a small container and pour it into a glass container that is large enough to contain ten times that amount. Then fill the small container nine more times, pouring the water into the larger container. Afterwards, agitate all the water in the larger container. You now have a potentized stone elixir. (**NOTE**: You can repeat this process as many times as you wish, and thereby potentize the elixir to a higher degree. According to homeopathic principles, this can increase the strength of the elixir. It could also cause you to end up with a LOT of charged water. You can use this however you wish, though you may not want to bottle all of it! Alternatively, you can just use a small amount of water from each potentization, and discard the unused portions. Or use the excess water on your garden or house plants, and see how they like it!
9. If you want to preserve the elixir for some time, add enough vodka or brandy to bring the mixture up to 10% alcohol. Then you may wish to decant it into glass dropper bottles or

spray bottles. (If you don't want to use the alcohol, you can keep the elixir for quite some time by storing it in a glass container in the refrigerator.)

ENHANCEMENTS FOR STONE ELIXIRS

The process outlined above is my basic recommended way of making Stone Elixirs. However, there are a number of additional things you can do to enhance their efficacy. As you read through the list below, you will see that these enhancements build upon other ideas and techniques we have considered in earlier chapters.

There is truly no limit to the enhancements that can be devised to make more powerful Stone Elixirs, or to refine and focus their purpose. For example, elixirs can be made which are for one particular person, or a group of people, a pet, a specific piece of land, etc. And the list below is merely a sample. I encourage readers to work intuitively to devise the elixirs best suited to your aspirations.

Here is a short list of my ideas for Stone Elixir enhancements:

1. **CREATE A MANDALA THAT EXPRESSES THE NATURE OF THE ELIXIR YOU WANT TO MAKE:** Look back at the practice for creating Stone Mandalas, sit down and do a similar process for the elixir you plan to make. Choose the stone or the group of stones that you will use to charge the water. Then envision the purpose of the elixir (healing, angelic communication, protection, etc.). Call upon whatever Stone Being(s) you will be working with, while holding the stones to your heart. Ask the stone(s) to reveal to you the highest possible manifestation of the elixir, and ask to be guided in creating a mandala that expresses this. Then draw the mandala, keeping your focus soft and working with your "soft will," When the mandala is complete, place it on the altar or table where you will be charging the water. When you have charged the water initially, set the glass container on top of the mandala and allow the stones and the mandala together to charge the water to its highest potential. Before removing the stones and water, I usually let the container stay in place overnight.

2. **INCREASE THE POWER OF YOUR ELIXIR WITH A STONE GRID:** On your altar space or table, lay out a mandala-shaped grid of stones to increase the concentration of stone energies in the water. When I do this, I lay out the grid around the circumference of the vessel in which the water will be charged. I usually use the same varieties of stones in the grid that will be inside vessel charging the water. Sometimes I will include additional stones such as Selenite or Magnifier Quartz in the grid, because of their ability to intensify and unify the currents of the stones inside the vessel. One can even place a stone mandala under the vessel, and a stone grid around it, combining the influences of both.

3. **USE A PHOTOGRAPH ATTACHED TO THE GLASS VESSEL TO FOCUS THE ELIXIR:** This idea makes use of the radionic/photonic principles we have seen in the previous chapter on Photonic Stone Layouts. If you wish to create an elixir to specifically benefit yourself or another individual, this can be done by attaching a photograph of the person to the vessel in which the elixir water will be charged. As with the Photonic Layouts we discussed earlier, it is important to focus your attention, intention and imagination on the photograph, the stones and the water, holding the pattern of the highest good for whoever will receive the elixir. (Remember, this is always a co-creation. The stones don't "do it for us." Our participation using our three human powers is essential.) In instances such as these, I like incorporating Photonics into the elixir making process, as I feel it greatly facilitates directing the elixir's energies to where they are meant to go, and increases the beneficial effects to that individual. Another thing to keep in mind is that you can use a photo with two or more people, and the elixir will be directed toward them. Similarly, you can use Photonics to direct an elixir for the wellbeing of a pet, a plant or garden, a body of water, a forest, an area of land or for the whole Earth. You can then give 'doses' of the elixir in drinking water, or by applying the

charged water upon whatever the subject of the elixir may be. This sort of work has limitless applications. As a final note, it is possible to combine all three of the ideas discussed here—you can make an elixir on top of a mandala, with a stone grid surrounding it and a photograph taped to the vessel. There is great potential synergy in combining these techniques!

4. **PLACE YOUR ELIXIR-MAKING VESSEL INSIDE A PYRAMID POTENTIZER:** For those who wish to make the most potent elixirs possible, I recommend charging the water in the elixir vessel in the center of a copper pyramid. The pyramid's energy field has long been recognized in the metaphysical community as being a powerful means of charging, healing and preserving food, water, people and even physical objects such as razor blades. I have been designing and building copper pyramids filled with high-energy stones for over twenty years, and I have found their energies to be remarkable. In the 2016 Alchemy of Stones Intensive, we tried out a process of making Stone Elixirs inside large copper pyramids, and the resulting potions were used with much success in processes that occurred later in the workshop (more on that below). Once again, I suggest that those who wish to maximize the power in their elixirs may wish to combine all four of these ideas in making focused elixirs of the highest potency possible.

MAKING STONE ELIXIRS IN A GROUP SETTING

In the first Alchemy of Stones Intensive, we engaged in a group process through which we created four different Stone Elixirs, with 182 people contributing their focused intentions—blending both their intentions and their elixir waters together. This was the most powerful and uplifting process of its kind that I have ever experienced, and I want to describe it briefly. I think that in reading this, you will get a glimpse of how far one can take the alchemical activity of creating Stone Elixirs, and how powerful it can be—both as a group process and in the products that the process creates.

Before the event began, the Heaven and Earth team and I set up four large copper pyramids in the four corners of the ballroom where we held our sessions. We had filled each pyramid with a different set of stones, and we also laid out more of these stones on the floor at the corners of each pyramid. One pyramid was filled and surrounded with stones for protection and purification. Another contained an array of stones that focused on healing. The third pyramid had stones for the enhancement of love. The fourth pyramid featured stones chosen to facilitate vibrational ascension.

On the first evening of the Intensive, all the participants were given small bottles of spring water and told not to open them. As the last process of the day, I asked everyone to take out their bottles, close their eyes, and hold the bottles at the center of their chests. Then we all closed our eyes, took a few deep breaths and entered into the Activity of Blessing, with our intention focused on the water. We invited the water into our hearts and offered our love and blessing to the water.

After blessing the water together, I asked everyone to maintain silence while we continued the process. I pointed out the four pyramids, in which our staff had placed four very large glass jars with open tops. Everyone was to visit each of the four pyramids, and while holding the water, themselves and all those in the room in a state of reverent appreciation, slowly circulate around the room, visiting each pyramid. Everyone was instructed to pour a little of the water from their bottle into each of the four jars within the four pyramids. There were signs that designated them as Protection and Purification, Healing, Love, and Vibrational Ascension. (Each jar also contained the pieces of all the types of stones that filled the pyramids.) It took almost two hours for the 182 people to complete this part of the process, but it was done very well—silently and beautifully.

When this was finished, everyone went off to bed and we covered the tops of the big jars, leaving them inside the pyramids to charge the water overnight. The next morning, our staff decanted each of the big jars, potentized the waters, mixed in vodka to bring the alcohol content up to 10%, and filled up a dropper bottle of each of the four elixirs for each participant. (A rather monumental effort!) We later gave out the four elixirs to each participant, telling them to bring the elixirs back on the final day of the Intensive.

On the last day, our group did Stone Body Layouts, similar to those described in this book. The layouts were for the same four purposes as the pyramids and the elixirs—Protection and Purification, Healing, Love, and Vibrational Ascension. We did the layouts in pairs, with partners. Each person receiving a stone body layout was directed to take a few drops of the corresponding elixir before the layout began.

After we finished, we discussed the effects of the elixirs and the layouts on the participants. It was immediately clear that virtually everyone felt strong effects from the elixirs as well as the stones. Even those giving the layouts expressed this sentiment. I encouraged everyone to prolong and enhance the effects of the elixirs, the stone body layouts and the entire event by continuing to use the elixirs over the following weeks and months.

There are a multitude of synergies created in a process like the one I have described here. An important one involves the blessing of the waters, and the subsequent blending of all of our bottles of spring water together. I believe this enhanced our shared purposes, and also served to bond us together as a group. When people received the four bottles of elixirs, in addition to the energies of the stones, the elixirs were also charged with the co-creative power of all 182 people! It was also of great benefit to be able to prolong the effects of the pyramids, the body layouts and the entire event by continuing to take the elixirs afterwards.

"RECIPES" FOR MAKING YOUR OWN STONE ELIXIRS

THE ALCHEMY OF STONES ELIXIRS: These four lists of stones are the ones which were used to make the four elixirs at the 2016 Alchemy of Stones Intensive discussed above. [**NOTE**: When a recipe includes Cinnazez, please use the double-bottle method for that stone. I also suggest you consult online references for any stone that you are not certain is non-toxic.]

Alchemy of Stones Elixir–Purification and Protection: Guardianite, Black Tourmaline, Shungite, Black Tourmaline Azeztulite, Obsidian, Smokey Quartz, Amazez, Black Azeztulite

Alchemy of Stones Elixir–Healing: Healerite, Healer's Gold, Azumar, Seraphinite, Golden Healer Quartz, Auralite-23 [double-bottle method is suggested for Seraphinite]

Alchemy of Stones Elixir–Love: Rose Quartz, Rosophia, Pink Azeztulite, Morganite, Kunzite, Rhodonite, Pink Amethyst, Rhodocrosite

Alchemy of Stones Elixir–Vibrational Ascension: Sanda Rosa Azeztulite, Amazez, Cinnazez, Pink Azeztulite, Himalaya Gold Azeztulite, Honey and Cream Azeztulite, Golden Azeztulite, Black Azeztulite, Satyaloka Clear Azeztulite, Satyaloka Rose Azeztulite, Satyaloka Yellow Azeztulite, Sauralite Azeztulite, Red Fire Azeztulite, Pink Fire Azeztulite, Sedona Azeztulite [double-bottle method is suggested for Cinnazez]

MORE STONE COMBINATIONS FOR MAKING YOUR OWN ELIXIRS: The following lists of stones offer a substantial array of the combinations that I have put together for a wide variety of purposes. The names given to each combination are indicative of their intended effects.

Ascension Seven: Phenacite, Herderite, Scolecite, Brookite, Natrolite, Petalite, Azozeo White Azeztulite

Synergy Twelve: Moldavite, Phenacite, Tanzanite, Danburite, Petalite, Natrolite, Herderite, Scolecite, Brookite, Tibetan Tektite, Azozeo White Azeztulite, Azozeo Satyaloka Clear Azeztulte

Alchemical Radiance: White Azeztulite, Rosophia, Moldavite, Cinnabar Quartz, Sanda Rosa Azeztulite, Agni Gold Danburite [double-bottle method is suggested for Cinnabar Quartz]

Angelic Connection: Angel Aura Quartz, Rose Quartz, Sanda Rosa Azeztulite, Angelite, Agni Gold Danburite, Vermont White Azeztulite, Petalite, Sugilite, Moldavite, Satya Mani Quartz, Amethyst, Seraphinite [double-bottle method is suggested for Seraphinite]

Body of Light: Herderite, Vermont Azeztulite, Agni Gold Danburite, Golden Azeztulite, Sanda Rosa Azeztulite, Phenacite, Pink Azeztulite, Petalite, Satyaloka Azeztulite, Clear Danburite, Satya Mani Quartz, Himalaya Gold Azeztulite, Rosophia

Compassionate Heart: Morganite, Rhodocrosite, Rosophia, Danburite, Celestite, Petalite, White Azeztulite

Creative Manifestation: Radiance Jasper, Phenacite, Moldau Quartz, Golden Labradorite, Amber, Moldavite, Agni Gold Danburite, Zincite, Red Garnet, Spessartine Garnet, Citrine, African Green Garnet, Carnelian

Devas and Nature Spirits: DevaQuartz Green Phantom Crystal, Healerite, Dragon Blood Jasper, Aventurine, Stonehenge Bluestone, Seraphinite, Bloodstone [double-bottle method is suggested for Seraphinite]

Dispelling Negative Energies: Guardianite, Black Tourmaline, Black Azeztulite, White Azeztulite, Black Tourmaline Azeztulite, Master Shamanite

Divine Love: Morganite, Alexandrite, White Azeztulite, Emerald, Pink Tourmline, Green Tourmaline, Bi-color Tourmaline, Redberry Quartz, Red Aventurine, Moldavite, Rose Quartz

Earth Connection: Azurite/Malachite, Black Tourmaline, Guardianite, Malachite, Lapis Lazuli, Mystic Merlinite [double-bottle method is suggested for Azurite/Malachite, Malachite, Lapis Lazuli]

Enlightenment: Nirvana Quartz, White Azeztulite, Moldavite, Phenacite, Agni Gold Danburite, White Danburite, Natrolite, Scolecite

Great Central Sun: North Carolina A+ Azeztulite, Vermont Azeztulite, Agni Gold Danburite, White Danburite, Phenacite, Petalite

Healer's Elixir: Healerite, Stonehenge Bluestone, Healers Gold, Infinite, Danburite, Petalite, Crimson Cuprite, Lemurian Golden Opal [double-bottle method is suggested for Crimson Cuprite]

Healing Power of the Heart: Heartenite, Healerite, Vitalite, Sugilite, Moldavite, Rose Quartz, Amethyst

Lemurian Remembrance: Lemurian Seed Crystal, Lemurian Aquatine Calcite, Aqua Lemuria, Midnight Lemurian Jade, Shadow Lemurian Jade, Lemurian Red Calcite

Light Worker Elixir: Angelite, White Azeztulite, Aqua Lemuria, Aquamarine, Larimar, Ajo Blue Quartz, Shattuckite Silica, Herkimer Diamond

Lithium Serenity: Lithium Light, Brazilian Kunzite, Rubellite Tourmaline, Australian Kunzite, Watermelon Tourmaline, Black Tourmaline, Lilac Lepidolite, Petalite

Multi-Dimensional Consciousness: Circle Stone, Phenacite, Moldavite, Moldau Quartz, Agni Gold Danburite, Vermont Azeztulite, Nuummite, Satya Mani Quartz, Sanda Rosa Azeztulite, Nirvana Quartz, Natrolite

Power of the Elements: DevaQuartz Green Phantom, Healerite, Moldavite, Sugilte, Black Tourmaline, New Zealand Carnelian, Aquamarine, Azumar, Healer's Gold, Labradorite [double-bottle method is suggested for Healer's Gold]

Prosperity: Emerald, Phenacite, Yellow Sapphire, Golden Labradorite, Tsavorite, Moldavite, Aventurine, Citrine

Shaman's Power: Clear Quartz Crystal Skull, Sugilite, Jet, Black Tourmaline, Magnifier Quartz, Moldavite, Nuummite, Dragon Stone

Visionary Experience: Nuummite, Labradorite, Phenacite, Satyaloka Clear Azeztulite, Natrolite, Auralite-23, White Azeztulite

Trulite Deep Self Awakening: Trulite Silica, White Azeztulite, Revelation Stone, Amethyst, Azumar, Moldavite, Mystic Merlinite, Satyaloka Clear Azeztulite

THE I AM SERIES (below): These stone combinations are intended to be used in conjunction with identifying oneself with the qualities they enhance. The simple way of doing this is to center yourself in the heart and speak the names of each particular combination, with emotion, when you are making the elixirs, and when you are using them. The names of these combinations proclaim their purpose, and using the names in this way can align your subtle imagnal body with these stones and their synergistically blended qualities.

I AM at Peace: Lepidolite, Larimar, Kunzite, Aquamarine, Danburite, Petalite, Scolecite, Rose Quartz, Lilac Lepidolite

I AM Awakened: Anandalite, Phenacite, Danburite, White Azeztulite, Satyaloka Clear Azeztulite, Sauralite Azeztulite, Circle Stone

I AM Joyful: Anandalite, Kunzite, Sauralite Azeztulite, Satyaloka Rose Azeztulite, Lilac Lepidolite and Amazez

I AM Powerful: Dragon Stone, Guardianite, Moldavite, Dragon Blood Jasper, Crimson Cuprite and Tiger Iron [double-bottle method is suggested for Crimson Cuprite and Tiger Iron]

I AM Protected: Guardianite, Nuummite, Black Tourmaline, Jet, Master Shamanite, Sugilite, Moldavite, Labradorite

I AM Pure Light: Amazez, Sauralite Azeztulite, White Azeztulite, Satyaloka Clear Azeztulite, Satyaloka Rose Azeztulite, Satyaloka Yellow Azeztulite, Himalaya Gold Azeztulite, Sanda Rosa Azeztulite, Pink Azeztulite

I AM Purified: Amazez, Tourmalined Quartz, Black Tourmaline, Premium Grade Amethyst, Satyaloka Clear Azeztulite, Auralite-23, Guardianite

The many recipes listed above provide examples of how extensive, powerful and wide-ranging the practice of making stone elixirs can be, and how it can incorporate the techniques and practices we have learned in the Alchemy of Stones. In the next chapter, we engage in another powerful alchemical activity—building Orgone Devices.

I am well aware of the fact that the human race has known about the existence of a universal energy related to life for many ages. However the basic task of natural science consisted in making this energy usable. This is the sole difference between my work and all preceding knowledge.

—Wilhelm Reich, 1956, in a letter.

26

Orgone & Orgonite Stone Energy Devices

[Wilhelm Reich] defined Orgone as a substance without mass that was omnipresent on Earth and had other properties such as being in constant motion, being the medium for gravitational and electromagnetic energy and that matter could arise from it spontaneously under the proper conditions.

—www.cosmicpolymath.com

The reality of this etheric energy, of what he called "orgone energy," was demonstrated palpably by Wilhelm Reich in various simple experiments. Nevertheless, he was arrested because he used instruments which he called the "orgone accumulator" boxes, which accumulated the etheric energy of some levels, usually the two lower levels, the fourth and the third etheric, to treat diseases including cancer and various other diseases. In America that was deemed illegal. The Food and Drug Administration arrested him, refused to allow him to prove his work, and he died in prison.

—Tim Clark, recounting an anecdote of Tom Ross, in "The Doctor Who Made It Rain", *Yankee magazine* (September 1989), p. 134

[Reich's] ideas have something to offend everybody, and he ended up becoming the only heretic in American history whose books were literally burned by the government... Reich was not only thrown in prison, but they chopped up all the scientific equipment in his laboratory with axes and burned all of his books in an incinerator.

—Robert Anton Wilson

No President, Academy, Court of Law, Congress or Senate on this earth has the knowledge or power to decide what will be the knowledge of tomorrow.

—Wilhelm Reich

In the Alchemy of Stones, we work with matter and spirit through the subtle/imaginal realm, which encompasses both of them. I would also say that both matter and spirit partake of consciousness, and that our awareness—particularly our heart-awareness—is the true way in which we can co-creatively engage with spirit and matter as one. All of the theories and practices in this book are rooted in this view of reality, which I call the alchemical worldview. Our perceptions of stone energies give us vivid experiences of the validity of this way of seeing things. And all of the ways we work with stones are aimed at exploring the myriad worlds of the Stone Beings, and of Sophia, who reaches out to us through them.

In the past decade or so, the array of tools invented by stone lovers for tapping in to the vast potential of the beneficial currents emanated by stones has grown steadily. Among the newer developments in this area is a class of items grouped under the name "Orgonite." These contrivances are typically composed of cast polymer resin in which substances such as metal shavings, spirals and/or tiny spheres of copper, as well as crystals and stones, have been embedded. The resin used is the same material that is utilized in a number of hobby applications, and it serves to make the arrangement of metals, stones and/or other materials into a relatively permanent "solid state" energy device. They are cast in a multiplicity of shapes, sometimes in muffin tins or ice cube trays, and sometimes in high quality silicon molds. Other than the chunky discs that come out of muffin tins, the most popular shape for Orgonite is most likely the pyramid. Like other crystal tools such as templates and wands that combine the currents of a chosen variety of stones, Orgonites are intended to engender an energetic synergy among their various components.

WHAT'S IN A NAME?

The quotes at the beginning of this chapter concern the works and ideas of Wilhelm Reich who coined the term *orgone*, which is the root of the word *Orgonite*. Reich was a researcher, medical doctor, philosopher and inventor who began as a psychologist—a disciple of Sigmund Freud. He was also, in my view, a modern day alchemist.

Reich was always a controversial figure, unafraid to challenge the cultural norms of his time. He coined the term "sexual revolution" and was seen by many as a figure whose ideas catalyzed this and other themes that fed the fires of political rebellion in the 1960s. Reich believed that there is an underlying invisible energy that permeates all of being and is related to what has been traditionally called God. He maintained that the ecstatic experience of orgasm was a manifestation of this energy in human beings. Believing that this energy is the all-pervading life force, he coined the term *orgone* (from "orgasm" and "organism").

In 1940 Reich started building "orgone accumulators," devices that his patients sat inside to harness the orgone energy's reputed health benefits. The results reported remain controversial, although many patients swore by the efficacy of Reich's devices. In addition to his medical inventions, Reich also created "cloudbusters"—orgone accumulators built for the purpose of manifesting rain in drought-stricken areas. There are cases in which the cloudbusters appeared to have worked well, but the hostility of some in the cultural mainstream, combined with Reich's dismissive attitude toward legal authorities, brought trouble to his laboratory.

A Wikipedia article states: "Following two critical articles about [Reich] in *The New Republic* and *Harper's* in 1947, the U. S. Food and Drug Administration obtained an injunction against the interstate shipment of orgone accumulators and associated literature, believing they were dealing with a 'fraud of the first magnitude.' Charged with contempt in 1956 for having violated the injunction, Reich was sentenced to two years imprisonment, and that summer over six tons of his publications were burned by order of the court. He died in prison of heart failure just over a year later, days before he was due to apply for parole."

It is certainly surprising and distressing to read about such blatant government suppression of someone's work—whether valid or not—yet it is a hazard that has been encountered by non-conformists for thousands of years. This included the alchemists, who were forced to encode their ideas in convoluted language and pictorial symbols, in order to avoid the wrath of the Inquisition and other authorities. In these times, we are fortunate that our spiritual work with stones is not attacked in such a drastic way. As I mentioned earlier in this book, the worst we usually have to endure is the ridicule of those who don't understand our experiences or are hostile to our beliefs.

There is much more to the story of Wilhelm Reich, but I want to move on to examining orgone and orgonite, as these are what relate most directly to our interests.

The website www.orgonics.com is dedicated to Reich's work and to offering reproductions of his orgone devices. In describing orgone energy, the site tells us:

> *Through many years of careful, experimental research, Reich was able to define the basic properties of orgone energy:*
>
> - *It fills all space and is everywhere.*
> - *It is mass-free and is the primordial, cosmic energy.*
> - *It penetrates matter, but at different speeds.*
> - *It pulsates and is observable and measurable.*
> - *It has a strong affinity and attraction to/by water.*
> - *It is accumulated naturally in the living organism by ingesting foods, breathing, and through the skin.*
> - *The mutual attraction and excitation of separate orgonotic systems result in the merging, or superimposition, of the systems; and the emergence of a new system.*

- *Orgone energy is negatively entropic: highly charged orgone systems attract lesser charged, which Reich described as the orgonotic potential.*
- *Orgone energy is excited by secondary energies such as electromagnetism and nuclear energy.*
- *When it is concentrated, orgone energy often has a blue-to-violet color.*

When I read the list above, I was struck by how closely some of its statements parallel the ancient alchemists' description of the *prima materia,* the essential "substance" with which alchemical work is done. It is also interesting to compare these ideas to the ancient alchemical treatise the *Emerald Tablet.* Below is an English translation from *Aurelium Occultae Philosophorum,* by Georgio Beato:

1. This is true and remote from all cover of falsehood
2. Whatever is below is similar to that which is above. Through this the marvels of the work of the One Thing are procured and perfected.
3. Also, as all things are made from one, by the consideration of One, so all things were made from this One, by Conjunction.
4. The father of it is the sun, the mother the moon.
5. The wind bore it in the womb. Its nurse is the earth, the Mother of all perfection.
6. Its power is perfected if it is turned into earth,
7. Separate the earth from the fire, the subtle and thin from the crude and coarse, prudently, with modesty and wisdom.
8. This ascends from the earth into the sky and again descends from the sky to the earth, and receives the power and efficacy of things above and of things below.
9. By this means you will acquire the glory of the whole world, and so you will drive away all shadows and blindness.
10. For this by its fortitude snatches the palm from all other fortitude and power. For it is able to penetrate and subdue everything subtle and everything crude and hard.
11. By this means the world was founded
12. and hence the marvelous Conjunctions of it and admirable effects, since this is the way by which these marvels may be brought about.
13. And because of this they have called me Hermes Tristmegistus since I have the three parts of the wisdom and Philosophy of the whole universe.
14. My speech is finished which I have spoken concerning the solar work.

One could ponder and interpret the *Emerald Tablet* at great length, as many alchemists did. (I'll come back to it in a later chapter.) For our purposes here, I simply want to look at the likeness of the One Thing to the orgone of Wilhelm Reich.

Reich maintained that orgone "fills all space and is everywhere." In the *Emerald Tablet* the One Thing is everywhere: "Whatever is below is similar to that which is above. Through this the marvels of the work of the One Thing are procured and perfected." And, "all things are made from One, by the consideration of One, so all things were made from this One, by Conjunction."

Note also the similarity of the Conjunction mentioned in the Emerald Tablet to Reich's idea about orgone: "The mutual attraction and excitation of separate orgonotic systems result in the merging, or superimposition of the systems; and the emergence of a new system." The "merging of systems" leading to the "emergence of a new system" is an almost exact description of the alchemical Conjunction described by Jung, which we have considered earlier in this book.

To Reich, orgone "is mass-free and is the primordial, cosmic energy," and "it penetrates matter, but at different speeds." The One Thing of the *Emerald Tablet* "receives the power and efficacy of things above and of things below," and it "is able to penetrate and subdue everything subtle and everything crude and hard."

These comparisons could continue, but I hope I have shown enough to indicate that both the alchemists and Reich were attempting to describe their discovery of the pervasive intelligent energy that animates the Universe and all life. In this book we have called this energy of wisdom by its ancient name—Sophia—and I have suggested that the currents of the stones provide us with direct experiences of this primordial substance/energy/intelligence. Reich's application of orgone energies for healing and such things as rainmaking parallels our utilization of stone energies for analogous purposes.

I want to note something else from the *Emerald Tablet*, which is shown in these statements:

7. If it [the One Thing or primordial energy] is turned into earth, separate the earth from the fire, the subtle and thin from the crude and coarse, prudently, with modesty and wisdom.
8. This ascends from the earth into the sky and again descends from the sky to the earth, and receives the power and efficacy of things above and of things below.

I view this as telling us, in our work with stones, that when we encounter this primordial energy as something that has "turned into earth" (a stone), then we are directed to separate its subtle energies from its crude physical aspect. We are instructed to do this with "modesty" (reverence) and "wisdom" (in co-creative union with Sophia). In our stone practices, we do precisely this: we engage the Stone Beings through our hearts and we invite both them and Sophia to work together with us. In doing this, we are bringing Heaven and Earth together and merging their energies. That is what is meant by the statement, "This ascends from the earth into the sky and again descends from the sky to the earth, and receives the power and efficacy of things above and of things below." The miraculous quality of this Conjunction is made clear in the next line, which states: "By this means you will acquire the glory of the whole world, and so you will drive away all shadows and blindness."

I have attempted to draw these lines of connection to show that the alchemists, Reich and we who work with the energies of stones are all engaging with the same all-pervasive living energy—the same numinous reality.

Reich's orgone accumulator boxes combined organic and inorganic materials. The walls of the boxes were typically composed of wood, wool and metal, with the wood and wool providing organic matter and the metal supplying the inorganic component. Sometimes layers of fiberglass were used. The boxes were intended to attract, generate and reflect orgone energy, bringing about energy pulsations or vibrations that Reich believed could bring benefits to his patients, as well as to the environment. The orgonics.com website tells us:

> *Reich found that certain non-metallic materials (wool, cotton, fiberglass, some plastics) attracted and* held *orgone energy; and metal attracted and then rapidly* repelled *it. By designing an enclosure . . . lined on the inside with metal and made with alternating layers of metallic and non-metallic, di-electric, energy-attracting materials, he discovered that atmospheric orgone energy was* accumulated *and* concentrated *inside. He called this device an orgone energy accumulator.*

We will leave Reich now and look into the modern-day orgone devices known as orgonite.

ORGONITE

As mentioned earlier in this chapter, Orgonite is the name given to a relatively new class of devices inspired by Reich's work, and intended to tap into the same orgone energy. Orgonite is comprised of polymer resin in which objects and substances such as crystals, metal shavings, copper wires and/or metal pellets, have been embedded. The metals provide the inorganic components of these devices, while the polymer resin, which is an organic compound, is

ABOVE: Homemade Orgonite Tall Pyramid;
LEFT: Orgonite molded in muffin trays

viewed as the organic component. In my view, the stones embedded in modern Orgonite pieces provide a vibrational bridge between the organic and inorganic. I envision them acting as amplifying conduits for the orgone energy generated through the Orgonites, as well as being direct sources of orgone energy (subtle matter/energy) in their own right.

In some Orgonite pieces, metal stampings or printed images of symbolic patterns, such as the Star of David or the Flower of Life, are added. I favor the inclusions of symbols that represent the intention(s) for which the pieces are being employed. Because I believe, with the alchemists, that all matter has consciousness and is spiritually alive, I think that these symbolic patterns can help to reinforce one's intention, and focus one's attention and imagination. Our conscious employment of these human powers is necessary to our side of these co-creative endeavors. I feel that Orgonite's efficacy, like that of elixirs, photonics, radionics and all meditative work with stones, involves our conscious participation as a critical component. This is why I view the inclusion of meaningful symbols in Organites as a beneficial addition.

Orgonites are typically used for purifying one's environment of negative energy and for broadcasting a beneficial orgone radiance. A number of people who make their own Orgonite pieces use them to counteract the negative, destructive energies of cell phone towers and other unhealthy technology.

I cannot speak definitively to the claim that Orgonite devices can neutralize or transform the destructive effects of the electromagnetic pollution in our environment, but I do believe that Reich was engaged with something real in his work with orgone, and that the modern purveyors of Orgonites are as well. I think it is most definitely worth trying out these devices, and that those who feel drawn to do so should experiment with creating their own Orgonite. The fact that stones and crystals are used in many Orgonite pieces assures me that these will be energetically active in ways similar to other synergetic stone combinations.

In looking at the online writings of various Orgonite enthusiasts, the one place I would disagree with them is in their attempts to use "scientific" language in describing what Orgonite is, and what it does. I believe this was an error made by Wilhelm Reich as well. He said that he differed from the ancient peoples who were aware of the universal energy in the sense that, unlike them, his purpose was to make it "useful." In my view, he had missed the crucial point that the universal energy is most correctly viewed as a living consciousness, a Great Being, rather than an unconscious force to be used however we wish. I feel that some of those writing about Orgonite risk making a similar error.

This is understandable, because we have all been educated to believe in materialism, but even the renegade materialism of "New Science" is still materialism. Like the ancient alchemists, I affirm we must engage co-creatively with Sophia—especially when attempting to work with unseen energies such as orgone—in order for our efforts to fully succeed. It is sometimes possible to achieve a measure of success by working with our intention, attention and imagination, even if we do so unconsciously and without inviting Sophia's participation. But if our aspiration is for highest good, we will get much further through working in union with her.

MAKING AN ORGONITE DEVICE

SUPPLIES NEEDED:

polyester or polymer resin
resin hardener
measuring cup
stir rods or sticks
muffin tin or other mold
rubber gloves
dust mask
copper, aluminum, bronze or other metal shavings, metal pellets, wire spirals, as desired
crystals and/or stones

PROCESS: (Before beginning, put on gloves and dust mask for protection. You may also wish to wear eye protection.)

1. Put some of the metal shavings and or other metal in the mold
2. Add crystals and/or stones
3. Thoroughly mix resin and hardener in measuring cup (use proportions as directed)
4. Partly fill the mold with the mixed resin, covering the metal and stones
5. Use the stick or rod to poke down into the metal shaving, to ensure the resin penetrates everywhere.
6. Place more metal, crystals and stones, wire spirals, symbols and/or other contents in the mold.
7. Fill the rest of the mold with the mixed resin, covering the metal. stones, etc.
8. Use the stick or rod to make sure the resin penetrates, especially at the edges of the mold.
9. When the mold has been filled, leave the mixture to harden. Allow the resin to cool down completely.
10. You can use a knife or razor blade to shave the edges of any resin residue.

NOTES: The above are basic instructions for making simple Orgonite devices. You can make the devices more complex and more aesthetically pleasing if you wish. I do suggest experimenting with different combinations of stones. Look online for videos and other information about making your own Orgonites.

RESOURCES: Resin and hardeners can be purchased at hobby shops, building supply stores, or online. One online source of the metal shavings is orgonecrystals.com. A source of high quality silicon molds is www.phimolds.com. There is a great variety of other sources for Orgonite supplies online, so the best thing to do is look at a number of them.

ACTIVATING AN ORGONITE DEVICE: In my view, it is important to take the additional step of activating the Orgonite device with your intention. To do this, treat it the same way you would engage with a crystal. Bring the piece to your heart, invite the beneficial energies of the device into your heart as you inhale, and offer your loving and blessing intention into the Orgonite as you exhale. Imagine that through the Orgonite you are establishing yet another thread of connection with Sophia, and ask for her co-creative participation in manifesting the intention upon which you are focusing. When you intuitively sense that the link is firmly established, relax, exhale and release your intention into the subtle/imaginal realm. At this point, you may "plant" the device wherever you wish it to go.

Super Orgonite Power Pyramid

ROBERT'S FAVORITE ORGONITE RECIPES

Readers will understand by now that my orientation to working with stones is to choose the ones that offer the most powerful and consciousness-stimulating energies. I do this whenever possible, and creating Orgonite devices that combine stones of this caliber has become one of my favorite creative activities. There are numerous commercially made Orgonites that make use of more common, "quieter" stones, and these, too, can be useful for all sorts of applications. If you are planning to make your own Orgonite pieces, I encourage you to experiment. That's how I came up with all of these!

1. **SUPER ORGANITE POWER PYRAMID.** The Orgonite device that I like best is made in a pyramid shaped mold. It contains bronze shaving and a piece of Moldavite near the apex. Below, there are layers of White Azeztulite, Himalaya Gold Azeztulite, Himalaya Red-Gold Azeztulite, Guardianite, and Shungite. The Moldavite, Guardianite and the Azeztulites are "inorganic" stones, and the Shungite is an "organic" carbon-based material, so the Reichian idea of combining organic and inorganic materials in orgone devices is echoed in this choice of stones. Also, these are some of the most energetically active stones I know, and they work together in the Orgonite with an amazing synergy!

   When I checked out the energies of the first of these pyramids, I was truly amazed by how powerful they are. Meditating with one of these seemed to bring about a full cleansing and activation of my subtle body and energy field. The effect on consciousness is one of pleasurable elevation. I also sensed that the clearing of leftover bits of "psychic debris" was rapid and thorough. Afterwards, I felt great!

Orgonite Life Force Pyramid

2. **ORGONITE LIFE FORCE PYRAMID.** This Orgonite device includes White Azeztulite, Amazez, Cinnazez, Himalaya Gold Azeztulite, Satyaloka Clear Azeztulite, Azumar, Healerite and Moldavite. This combination was selected for refreshing and replenishing the subtle body. It is intended to dispel the fatigue that comes with periods of stress or prolonged work. It can also augment the recuperation process when one is recovering from injury or illness. This occurs through bringing one's energy field into harmonic resonance with the "chord" of vibrational energies provided by the stones, and which is amplified by the Orgonite resin and the pyramidal form. I have tried this pyramid in healing body layouts, receiving very good reports from the recipients.

Orgonite Ascension Pyramid

3. **ORGONITE ASCENSION PYRAMID.** This Orgonite pyramid contains Azozeo Phenacite, Herkimer Diamonds, Golden Brucite, Danburite, White Azeztulite and Himalaya Gold Azeztulite. All of these are very high-vibration stones that stimulate the upper chakras, including the etheric chakras above the head. When they are combined in an Orgonite pyramid, their intense energies are amplified even further. This pyramid is ideal for facilitating visionary experiences and the activation of latent spiritual capacities. It can also be used for interdimensional travel and Light Body activation. Because it contains Azozeo Phenacite, this pyramid has the capacity to activate other stones to higher levels of vibration. (This will not work on all other stones, but experimentation will yield some interesting results.)

Orgonite Synergy Twelve Pyramid

4. **ORGONITE SYNERGY TWELVE PYRAMID.** The Synergy Twelve stone combination is something I discovered two decades ago, and it remains one of the most popular and powerful vibrational "chords" of stone energies I know of. The Synergy Twelve stones are: Moldavite, Phenacite, Tanzanite, Danburite, White Azeztulite, Petalite, Tibetan Tektite, Herderite, Brookite, Satyaloka Clear Azeztulite, Scolecite and Natrolite. This combination of stones has been experienced by thousands of people, and their experience is usually described as an empowerment of the entire self. One feels stronger, more expanded, more aware, and able to function at a higher level of consciousness. When working with these stones in an Orgonite device such as this, holding or placing the pyramid over the heart chakra will allow the energies to disperse throughout one's field in an optimal, balanced way.

Readers who are drawn to create Orgonite pieces are encouraged to allow yourselves to be guided intuitively in choosing the stone components. (Or, as I like to say, let the Stone Beings "volunteer.") Listening to one's intuition is one of the ways to enhance the relationships among the surface self, the Deep Self, and the Stone Beings. This kind of development is fundamental in the Alchemy of Stones.

As we continue to explore, we will touch upon a number of other practices and activities that can become a part of the journey. We'll discuss several of these in the next chapter.

Moldavite and Quartz “Ray Gun”

27

An Alchemist's Laboratory of Crystal Tools

Very early, and very naturally, the religious nature of man led to the use of precious stones in connection with worship—the most valuable and elegant objects being chosen for sacred purposes. Of this mode of thought we have a striking instance in the accounts given, in the book of Exodus, of the breast-plate of the High-priest, and the gems contributed for the tabernacle by the Israelites in the wilderness. Another religious association of such objects is their use to symbolize ideas of the Divine glory, as illustrated in the visions of the prophet Ezekiel and in the description of the New Jerusalem in the book of Revelation.

—George Frederick Kunz, *The Curious Lore of Precious Stones*

Everyone practices magic, whether they realize it or not, for magic is the art of attracting particular influences, events and situations within human life. Magic is a natural phenomenon because the universe is reflexive, responding to human thoughts, aspirations and desires. . . .

—David Fideler, *Jesus Christ, Sun of God*

There may be no such thing as the "glittering central mechanism of the universe." Not machinery but magic may be the better description of the treasure that is waiting.

—John A. Wheeler, quantum physicist, Princeton University

As we have journeyed more and more deeply into the Alchemy of Stones, we have explored a number of modalities through which our work with the Stone Beings and Sophia may be pursued. These ways of working have constituted the "branches" of our alchemical tree. We have explored the use of stone mandalas, templates and grids, as well as body layouts, Photonic layouts, stone elixirs and even Orgonite. Before we leave the branches of the tree and reach up to the "leaves"—the stones themselves—I want to describe several more types of crystal tools we may wish to work with.

There is a certain temptation to turn this alchemical toolbox into a toy box, because there is beauty in these artifacts, and because it is fun to make them and to feel the energies they generate. And I do not want to discourage that playfulness. The pleasure we feel in all of our engagements with the Stone Beings is valuable, and it motivates us to persist in our work with them.

Having said that, I must also bring up an old quotation. Referring to one of the foremost educators of the day, U.S. President James Garfield expressed his concept of an ideal university as, "[A teacher] on one end of a log and a student on the other." In a certain sense, it may be that the best way to learn about stones and how to work with them alchemically is similarly simple. It's possible that the ideal "laboratory" is a chair, with you sitting down holding a single stone up to your heart, exchanging your subtle energies with one another.

But, after all, there is no reason that we can't work with stones in all ways—from the simplest to the most complex. Personally, that's what I like to do. So let's open up the toy box . . . I mean, the laboratory.

PYRAMID STONE MEDITATION CHAMBERS

One of the classic forms of Sacred Geometry is the pyramid. It was clearly believed by the ancient Egyptians to act as an antenna or amplifier of great power, and in modern times much research has been done into the potentials of "pyramid power." For the past twenty-five years, I have worked with pyramids made from copper tubing and filled with high-vibration stones. As

with many of the other tools to be discussed in this chapter, one can create an infinite number of stone arrays within this sort of device. I have built pyramids filled with combinations of Quartz, Moldavite, Azeztulite, Phenacite, Tanzanite, Rosophia and numerous other stones.

Two of my favorite groupings for pyramids are the Synergy Twelve and Ascension Seven stones. In the picture on the next page, I am sitting within a pyramid filled with a combination of Rosophia and Azeztulite. This is one of my all-time beloved pairings! The Azeztulite offers the heavenly Light from above, while the Rosophia reaches up with Earthly Love from below. When one sits in this space, the two currents join in one's heart, and they then flow throughout one's whole body, on all levels.

For the 2016 Alchemy of Stones Intensive, we created four large copper pyramids (about ten feet square) and filled each one with a different set of stones. *The Purification and Protection Pyramid* contained Guardianite, Black Tourmaline, Shungite, Black Tourmaline Azeztulite, Obsidian, Smokey Quartz, Amazez, and Black Azeztulite. The *Healing Pyramid* contained Healerite, Healer's Gold, Azumar, Seraphinite, Golden Healer Quartz and Auralite-23. The *Love Pyramid* contained Rose Quartz, Rosophia, Pink Azeztulite, Morganite, Kunzite, Rhodonite, Pink Amethyst and Rhodocrosite. The *Vibrational Ascension Pyramid* contained Sanda Rosa Azeztulite, Amazez, Cinnazez, Pink Azeztulite, Himalaya Gold Azeztulite, Honey and Cream Azeztulite, Golden Azeztulite, Black Azeztulite, Satyaloka Clear Azeztulite, Satyaloka Rose Azeztulite, Satyaloka Yellow Azeztulite, Sauralite Azeztulite, Red Fire Azeztulite, Pink Fire Azeztulite, and Sedona Azeztulite. Each of these pyramids was large enough for four people to sit inside, and we added grids of the same stones around their perimeters, in order to make them as powerful as possible.

The participants at the 2016 Intensive were greatly impressed with the power of these four pyramids, and they could most definitely feel the differences among the currents generated within each of them. In addition, the pyramids functioned in synergy with one another to fill the entire ballroom with energy. Later in the event, we took things a step further by utilizing the pyramids as charging environments for the stone elixirs we made together. On the event's culminating day, we each took a few drops of each elixir as we went into doing the stone body layouts. We all agreed that the stone elixirs which were charged within their corresponding pyramids were extraordinarily powerful and effective.

OPPOSITE: Participants in the 2016 Alchemy of Stones Intensive meditate inside stone-filled copper pyramids.

Having a pyramid filled with one's choice of high-vibration stones is like living next to an energy vortex. One can enter the pyramid at any time, and one's whole body will be infused with powerful and beneficial stone currents. Depending on the choice of stones, a meditation pyramid of this type can be used for clearing and cleansing, opening the heart, traveling interdimensionally, awakening the Light Body or any number of other applications. The pyramid itself can be enhanced by laying out stone grids around the base, hanging stones above the apex, placing a small "crown" pyramid on top (the crowning pyramid in the picture on the right is Azeztulite) and/or wearing a Power Strand or other talisman.

Most recently, I have become interested in placing an Orgonite pyramid at the top of my stone meditation pyramid. I mentioned four different such pyramids at the end of the previous chapter—the Super Orgonite Power Pyramid, the Orgonite Life Force Pyramid, the Orgonite Ascension Pyramid and the Orgonite Synergy Twelve Pyramid. I find that each of these Orgonite pyramids can strongly influence the energy within the larger copper pyramid. Depending on which Orgonite pyramid I choose, the whole meditative experience changes. And the structured environment of the copper pyramid magnifies the power of the Orgonite.

In my view, meditating within a pyramid such as the ones pictured here—especially when the copper tubes are filled with high-vibration stones such as Azeztulite–can bring about a rapid and profound infusion of high quality subtle matter/energy (spiritual Light) into one's subtle body. This in turn can accelerate the transformations we are seeking.

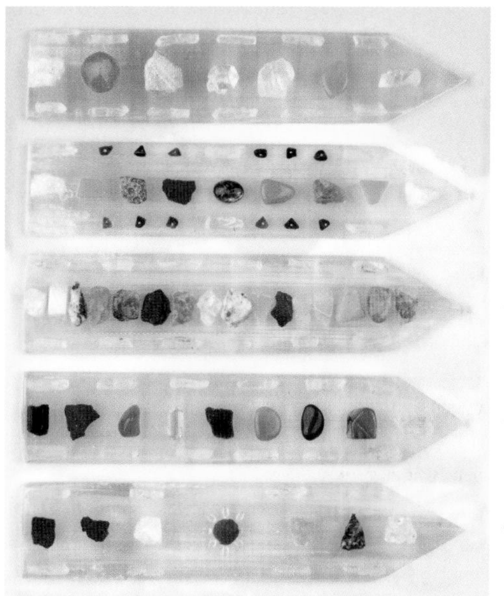

SELENITE LASER-FOCUS POWER WANDS:

1. Angelic Realm, with White Azeztulite, Angelite, Lithium Light, Angel Aura Quartz, Petalite, Azumar, Danburite, Magnifier Quartz;

2. Healing Power, with White Azeztulite,Healerite, Guardianite, Crimson Cuprite, Seraphinite, Azumar, Sugilite, Auralite-23, Magnifier Quartz;

3. Azozeo Azeztulite 16, with Original White Azeztulite, Black Azez., Red Fire Azez., Satyaloka Rose Azez., Satyaloka Yellow Azez., Satyaloka Clear Azez., Amazez, Cinnazez, Pink Fire Azez., Sanda Rosa Azez., Golden Azez., Black Tourmaline Azez., Sauralite Azez., Honey and Cream Azez., Himalaya Gold Azez., Pink Azez., Magnifier Quartz;

4. Super Chakra Harmony, with Black Tourmaline, Red Fire Azeztulite, Carnelian, Golden Apatite, Moldavite, Azumar, Lapis, Auralite-23, Danburite, Magnifier Quartz;

5. Alchemical Transformation, with Black Azeztulite, Red Fire Azez., White Azez., Himalaya Gold Azez., Black Tourmaline Azez., Satyaloka Clear Azez.

1. Synergy 12: with Moldavite, Phenacite, Tanzanite, Danburite, White Azeztulite, Natrolite, Herderite, Scolecite, Brookite, Satyaloka Clear Azeztulite, Petalite, Tibetan Tektite, on White Azeztulite Wand

2. Ascension Seven: with White Azeztulite, Phenacite, Herderite, Danburite, Natrolite, Petalite, Satyaloka Clear Azeztulite, on Satyaloka Clear Azeztulite Wand

3. Super Chakra Harmony: with Black Tourmaline, Red Fire Azeztulite, Carnelian, Heliodor, Moldavite, Azumar, Lapis, Auralite-23, Danburite, on Satyaloka Clear Azeztulite Wand

4. Healing Power: with White Azeztulite, Healerite, Guardianite, Crimson Cuprite, Seraphinite, Azumar, Auralite-23, on Vitalite Wand

5. Alchemical Transformation: with Black Azeztulite, Red Fire Azeztulite, White Azeztulite, Himalaya Gold Azeztulite, Satyaloka ClearAzeztulite, Moldavite, Herkimer Quartz Crystal, on Cinnazez Wand

6. Angelic Realm: with White Azeztulite, Angelite, Kunzite, Angel Aura Quartz, Petalite, Azumar, Danburite, on Amazez Wand

STONE POWER WANDS

The photograph at the beginning of this chapter shows a special tool I created over thirty years ago, utilizing a large Quartz Laser Wand, six smaller Quartz crystals, and a number of faceted and polished Moldavites. This piece was my first Stone Power Wand, and it is powerful indeed! My intuition had suggested that the currents that naturally flowed along the axis and out the tip of the large crystal could be increased and enhanced by adding more crystals that pointed in the same direction. In adding the Moldavites, I hoped their currents would enter the main crystal and be magnified and channeled through the termination.

It worked beautifully, and this piece is still one of my favorites. The flow of energy through it is so strong that I often use it to demonstrate the reality of stone energies to people who have never felt them before. This tool can also activate chakras and meridians in the subtle body, and it is good for dissolving blockages and negative patterns.

The success of my first experiment has led over the years to the creation of many more Stone Power Wands. I like to concoct combinations of stones that I feel will work synergistically with each other to facilitate the purpose of each wand. I find this very rewarding, because it is a way of co-creating with the Stone Beings. Remember, we are not working with "dead" objects that emit mere "energy." We are involving ourselves with living, intelligent spiritual entities who are ready to collaborate with us. I think this must be the biggest reason that these creations always seem to work so well. The Stone Beings adapt and adjust what they are doing to enhance and support the intention we share—to be of benefit to human beings, to the Stone Beings, and to the Earth. This underscores the importance of beginning the making of tools like these by meditating and inviting the Stone Beings to join in the creative intention. This gives them the opening to join us and enhance our endeavors.

I have found that the linear alignment of stones on some sort of crystal or polished stone wand tends to manifest as a linear flow of energy through the entire piece. This flow is useful for directing and focusing the energies to specific chakras or parts of the body. Although certain natural crystals such as Quartz Laser Wands are well suited for this, I have found that polished wands of various kinds of stones work in much the same way. And when the stone wand is made from a high-vibration type of material, this adds to the power of the entire tool.

When creating Stone Power Wands, I often use Selenite for the base. Selenite is relatively inexpensive, and it seems to integrate and amplify whatever stone combination one attaches to it.

Once again, there are multiple options for other stones to use as the bases for Stone Power Wands, My other favorites are the Azeztulites. In my experience, these are among the most powerful stones in the mineral kingdom, and the currents they emanate resonate in us at the cellular level. For certain other applications, I favor specific stone wands such as Rosophia, Healerite, Healers' Gold or Vitalite.

The photos in this section display several different Stone Power Wands I have created. I show them to give you some ideas about what is possible, and to hopefully inspire your creativity in making such pieces for your own alchemical tool box.

CRYSTAL VIAL PENDANTS

Knowing how much I enjoyed combining stones in wands and jewelry, a friend some years ago showed me his invention—a transparent Quartz or glass tube, sealed at each end, filled with harmonious combinations of stones and wrapped in a spiral of gold or silver wire. These Crystal Vials facilitate the creation of a wearable combination of almost any stones one could imagine. The spiral wire and the crystalline tube both serve to amplify the currents of the enclosed stones, and the vertical way that the vial hangs around the neck puts the entire array in alignment with one's chakra column.

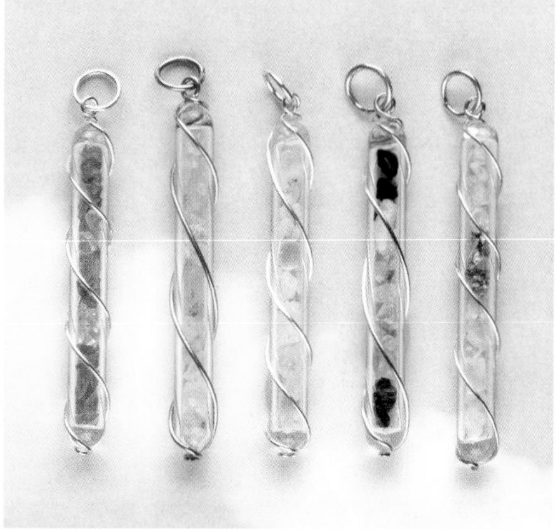

The vials shown are, from left to right: *Transformation*, with Moldavite and Herkimer Quartz "Diamonds"; *Ascension*, with Petalite, Satyaloka Clear Azeztulite, Danburite; *Light Body*, with Satyaloka Clear Azeztulite, Rainbow Moonstone, White Azeztulite; *Synergy Ten*, with Moldavite, Phenacite, Tanzanite, Danburite, White Azeztulite, Petalite, Brookite, Herderite, Tibetan Tektite, Satyaloka Clear Azeztulite; *Crown Chakra*, with Cryolite, Seraphinite, Petalite, Natrolite, Danburite, Satyaloka Clear Azeztulite.

It is relatively simple to make a Crystal Vial Pendant. You can acquire the glass tubing and cutters from companies that sell glass-blowing supplies. A simple propane torch can be used to seal the ends of the tube. Then you fill up the tube with stones of your choice, seal the other end and wrap the sealed tube with silver or copper wire. [**NOTE**: Begin by cutting the tubing to the length you want. Then seal one end by rotating it in the propane flame until it melts and closes. Next, add the stones until they come to abut ¼ inch from the open end of the tube. Then seal the tube in the flame as before. After it cools, you can wrap with wire as you wish.] Of course, when dealing with the propane torch and hot glass, you need to be very careful.

POWER STRAND NECKLACES

These necklaces are aptly named because they undoubtedly provide the most powerful dose of high-vibration stones one can wear or carry on one's person. They evolved out of my first such creation, which was a simple strand of raw Moldavite nuggets. (Those Moldavite strands themselves sent many people into some amazing states of consciousness!) Over time, I experimented with many different stone combinations, just I did with wands, templates and jewelry.

Power Strands are exceptional for multiple reasons. First, they are relatively large, giving one a high dose of whatever stones are in them. Second, they are worn around the neck, and I usually make them long enough to encircle the heart chakra. Because the heart is the central point of generation for the multiple levels of one's vibrational fields, bringing synergistic groups

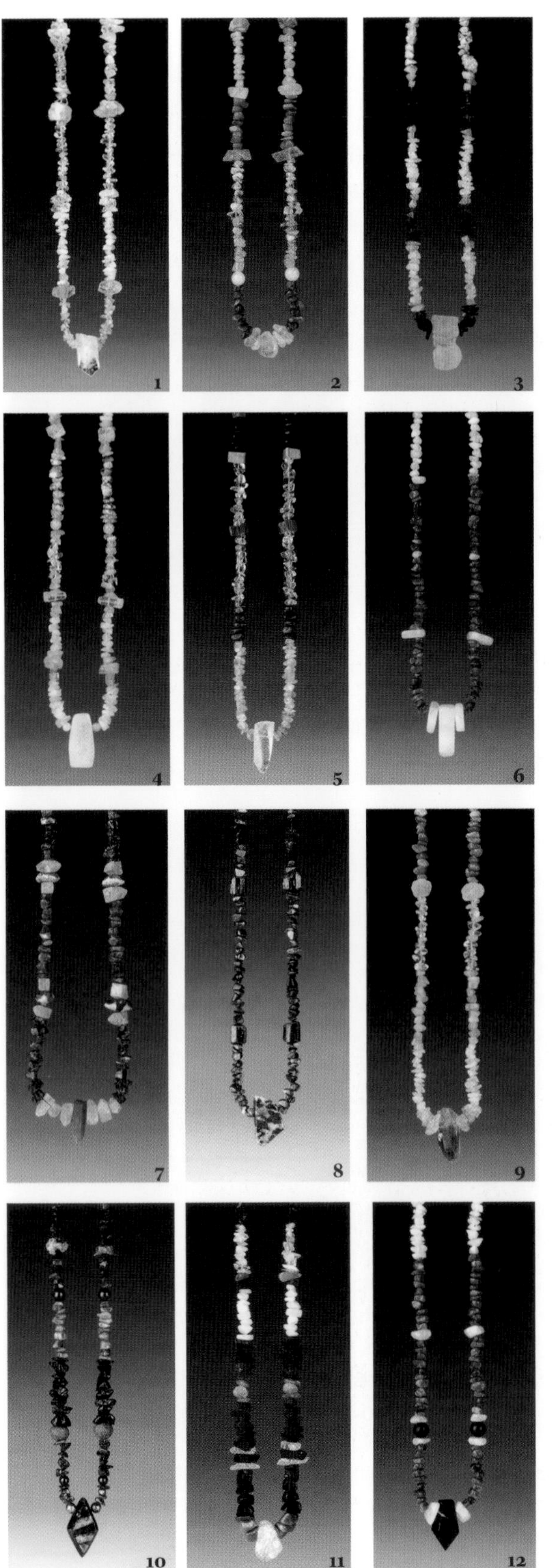

of high-powered stones into conjunction with the heart allows them to permeate one's entire field. In this way, they bring about their effects on all levels simultaneously. I consider these necklaces to be initiatory pieces, and wearing them means that one is taking a conscious step on the path of awakening, healing and vibrational ascension. Like the stones themselves, these strands provide different sets of qualities, and they are designed for different purposes. The pictures display twelve of the over forty different Power Strands I have designed. For information on the stones used in each strand, or to see the others, check the website www.heavenandearthjewelry.com.

BREASTPLATE

In my thirty-three years of working with stones and selling crystals, gemstones and jewelry through our company, Heaven and Earth, hundreds of people have asked me about the breastplate of the High Priest. Because of the legendary power of the breastplate mentioned in the Old Testament, a number of people have tried to reproduce it, and have attempted to discern the identities of the stones in the original. However, it is impossible to be certain about which stones were in the breastplate, because of the lost meanings of the names used to refer to them in biblical times.

The priestly breastplate was a sacred artifact worn by the High Priest of the Israelites, according to the Book of Exodus. In the biblical account, the breastplate was sometimes termed the breastplate of judgment, because the *Urim* and *Thummim* [two divinatory objects used by the high priest] were placed within it. These stones were, at times, used to attempt to determine God's will in a particular situation. The breastplate was thought to be a means by which the High Priest could communicate with God. The breastplate of the High Priest was described as a square plate set with twelve

POWER STRANDS: 1. Ascension Seven; 2. Body of Light; 3. Enlightenment; 4. Great Central Sun; 5. Lemurian Remembrance; 6. Love and Light; 7. Nature Spirits; 8. New Magic; 9. Power of Azeztulite; 10. Shamanic Journeyer; 11. Synergy 12 Strand; 12. Tree of Life

rectangular stones. The name of one of the twelve tribes of Israel was said to be inscribed into each stone. Most illustrations depict the breastplate as covering most of the chest of the High Priest.

Artist's rendering of Breastplate of the High Priest

Of course, the idea of a legendary object that was believed to directly utilize gemstones to connect with the Divine was of interest to me. But my focus has not been in trying to replicate it. That's because I feel that the original breastplate was a tool for its own time, and would not be appropriate outside its historic context. However, I can easily imagine that wearing what amounts to a *grid* of powerful stones over the area of the heart could facilitate an expansion of one's awareness into sacred spiritual domains.

The construction of the High Priest's breastplate has been described in the Book of Exodus in significant detail, and it was said to contain gold, and to have been worn with intricately made vestments. For our purpose of creating and working with a modern "breastplate," I feel that what matters most is the stones we choose, and their placement in a grid to be worn on one's chest. The intention in this endeavor is to expose one's subtle body to a powerful pattern of energies, and to see what unfolds from there. And since most of us aren't prepared to make or purchase gold settings and complicated vestments, our first experimental breastplate can be created using some cloth pouches sewn or pinned onto a T-shirt. (The T-shirt should be a snug-fitting one, so the stones will be where they are meant to be placed.)

I have followed my usual practice of letting the stones tell me which ones I should use. In the breastplate-shirt shown in the photo, listed by row and from left to right as you look at the image, these are the stones:

TOP ROW: Red Fire Azeztulite, White Azeztulite, Black Azeztulite;

SECOND ROW: Nuummite, Moldavite, Danburite;

THIRD ROW: Natrolite, Rosophia, Azozeo Phenacite;

BOTTOM ROW: Shungite, Golden Brucite, Auralite 23

"Breastplate" T-shirt with an attached pouch for each stone.

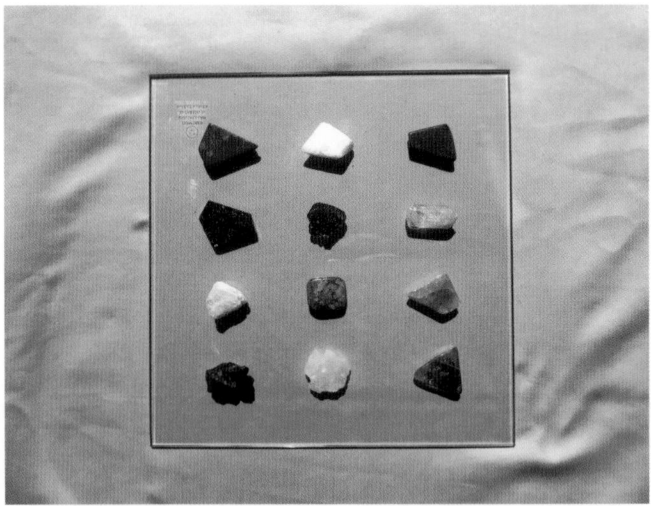

Tempered Glass "Breastplate" with attached stones. Stones on the glass version are the same as those recommended for the shirt-and-pouch style Breastplate.

My first experience with this combination in the breastplate-shirt made a deep and personal impression on me, and I will not describe what happened, except to say that I was affected more strongly than I had expected. If you are drawn to work with a configuration of stones such as this, I certainly recommend it! And I do have the sense that this is a rather advanced practice, not to be undertaken frivolously. I most definitely believe that working with stone breastplates is for situations of meditation and ritual, and that one should not go around in public wearing something like this!

If one wishes to utilize the breastplate pattern in a body layout setting, one may also attach a grid of twelve stones on a ten inch square of tempered glass. Then one can lie down and place the glass with attached stone grid onto one's chest. For many people, this may be a good, practical way of experiencing a stone-enhanced breastplate.

Also, as with all of the stone tools in our alchemist's laboratory, there is an infinite array of possible variations to this. One need not use the same stones that I did. I suggest getting into a receptive state of mind and asking the Stone Beings which ones you should use, and what their positions in the breastplate-shirt should be.

I have one more group of stone energy devices to describe before we move on to a new area. These are called Bodymats, and they are exactly what their name implies. They are stone-augmented mats upon which one can lie down or sit in meditation. Mats such as these can be used in combination with any and all of the tools we have described in this chapter. And one can make stone energy grids around them, receive stone body layouts while lying on them, in addition to a wide array of other possibilities. We will look at these in the next chapter.

28

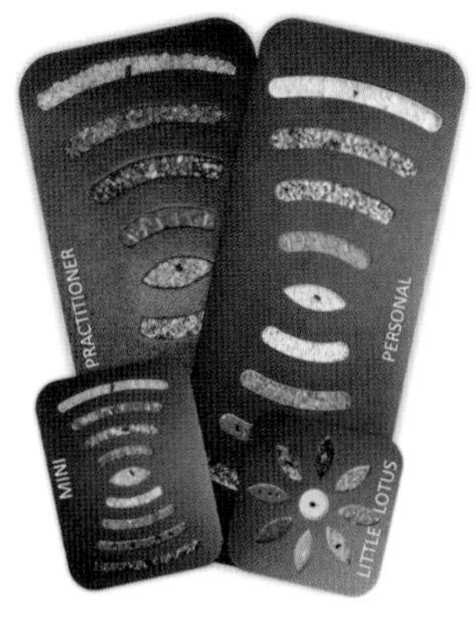

Stone-Enhanced Body Mats

The art of healing comes from nature, not from the physician. Therefore the physician must start from nature, with an open mind.

—Paracelsus

Man is a microcosm, or a little world, because he is an extract from all the stars and planets of the whole firmament, from the earth and the elements; and so he is their quintessence.

—Paracelsus

In addition to being spiritual seekers, the alchemists of past centuries were often the inventors, healers and innovators of their times. The 8th–9th century alchemist Jabir ibn Hayyan is known as the father of chemistry, and his works extended to cosmology, numerology, astrology, medicine, magic, mysticism and philosophy.

The 16th century alchemist and physician Paracelsus is known for having been the originator of the medical field of toxicology, and he worked with various metals and minerals to bring about cures. He also revived and expanded the practice of herbal medicine. Paracelsus invented chemical therapy, chemical urinalysis, and suggested a biochemical theory of digestion.

From these examples, we can see that the path of alchemy is a path of investigative engagement with many areas of life, and invention is very much among these. We have, in the last several chapters, been considering various modalities and creations via which we can deepen our connection with the Stone Beings and their beneficial qualities. We have looked into stone body layouts, mandalas, photonic layouts, elixirs, Orgonites, and an array of crystal energy tools.

While in the process of writing this book, I was contacted by Jennifer Von Behren, who was involved in her own branch of stone-based alchemy. As a healer, Jennifer was used to working with clients on massage tables, and she was familiar with stone energies. She was not content to confine her use of stones to the traditional body layouts, which can only be placed on one

Practitioner Mat

side of the body–the front. Jennifer endeavored to imagine a way in which a person could lie down on a "bed of stones" that had been strategically arranged to be of the most beneficial configuration possible. The result was what she calls the Body Mat.

The Body Mat is simple in concept and design. The base is a firm foam mat in which openings have been cut to be filled with different stones. Typically, the stones Von Behren uses to fill up her mats are aligned to resonate with the human chakra system. She has chosen to utilize a nine-chakra system, adding stones to correspond with the Earth Star chakra at the feet and the Soul Star chakra that is just above the head, in addition to the traditional seven chakras. In the Body Mats, the stones in the mats are not set in the precise locations of the chakra points. (This would not be possible, since people come in different sizes!) However, the linear alignment of the stone pockets in the mats is the same as in our chakras, and I have found that my own energy system resonates very well with this arrangement.

There are four different types of mats available through Jennifer's company (thebodymat.com). The largest and most versatile is the Deluxe Practitioner Body Mat, which measures 33 inches wide by 72 inches long by 2.5 inches thick. The pockets in this mat are deeper than those of the other designs, and the stones are simply poured into them. Then one lies down on the "bed of stones" and things begin to happen! I particularly like this version of the Body Mat, because it contains far more stones than the others (around forty pounds), and because it is the most versatile. If, like me, a person wants to add high-vibration stones such as Azeztulite, Phenacite, Rosophia and/or Moldavite, it's simple to do. One just places the additional stones into the open pockets with the stones that are already there, at the locations one wants to try. With this mat, there is infinite variability, and changing the configurations is quick and easy.

I find the Practitioner mat especially helpful for all types of stone body layouts, because it is possible to bring in whatever stones one chooses to work with, placing them both underneath and on top of the body. For the really hard-core stone energy explorers (like me), it is easy to remove all of the original stones from the Practitioner mat and fill the pockets with one's own "recipes." I did this with my mat, completely filling eight of the pockets with tumbled Azeztulites, plus several well-placed Moldavites and Phenacites. A batch of lovely tumbled Rosophia stones went in the central pocket. Lying down on that mat was, for me, an amazingly powerful experience, and it activated my subtle body to a much higher vibrational level.

When one works exclusively with the stones provided with the Body Mats, they combine their energies to create a supportive vibrational environment for any type of healing treatment. The stones were chosen to harmonically balance the subtle body and arrayed to mirror the healthy pattern of the human energy system, and one will readily find oneself slipping into a natural feeling of relaxation and wellbeing after a few minutes on the mat.

All of the various sizes of Body mats come with the same selection of stone, though the quantities differ depending on the size of the mat. Here is the list of stones that Jennifer chose for the Body mats, to bring about the facilitation of healing and wellbeing:

SOUL STAR (a few inches above the head): Clear Quartz, Herkimer Diamond, Shungite
CROWN (7th chakra): Amethyst
THIRD EYE (6th chakra): Sodalite
THROAT (5th chakra): Blue Howlite and Blue Kyanite
HEART (4th chakra): Green Aventurine, Rose Quartz, Shungite
SOLAR PLEXUS (3rd chakra): Citrine
SEXUAL/CREATIVE (2nd chakra): Carnelian
ROOT (1st chakra): Red Jasper and Hematite
EARTH STAR (at or below the feet): Petrified Wood, Tiger Eye, Shungite

Most of the stones in the Body Mats are tumbled, which makes it more comfortable with the Practitioner Mat, in which one lies on the stones in their pockets. The body touches the stones, but they do not protrude above the edge of the pocket, so it is a comfortable situation.

PORTABLE BODY MATS

In the line of Body Mats created by Von Behren, only the Deluxe Practitioner Mat involves placing the stones loose into the pockets in the mats. This is the thickest mat, at 2.5 inches. The Practitioner Mat is ideal for someone such as myself, who has a place where it can be permanently or semi-permanently set up. Others may have less space, or may want something that is easier to move. Von Behren's other mats are designed for this, being only one inch thick. They also differ in one other important way: the stones are embedded in transparent earth friendly rubber inserts that can be slipped in and out of the pockets.

This creates a more solid-state bed of stones, and a less costly mat. Fewer stones are used in each of the pockets, and one does not have to worry about spilling or losing them.

And there is one other aspect I like very much about these mats—one that perhaps even the inventor did not consider. By having the stones embedded in earth friendly rubber, the resulting inserts become similar to Orgonites! It is also believed that the hardening of the rubber puts

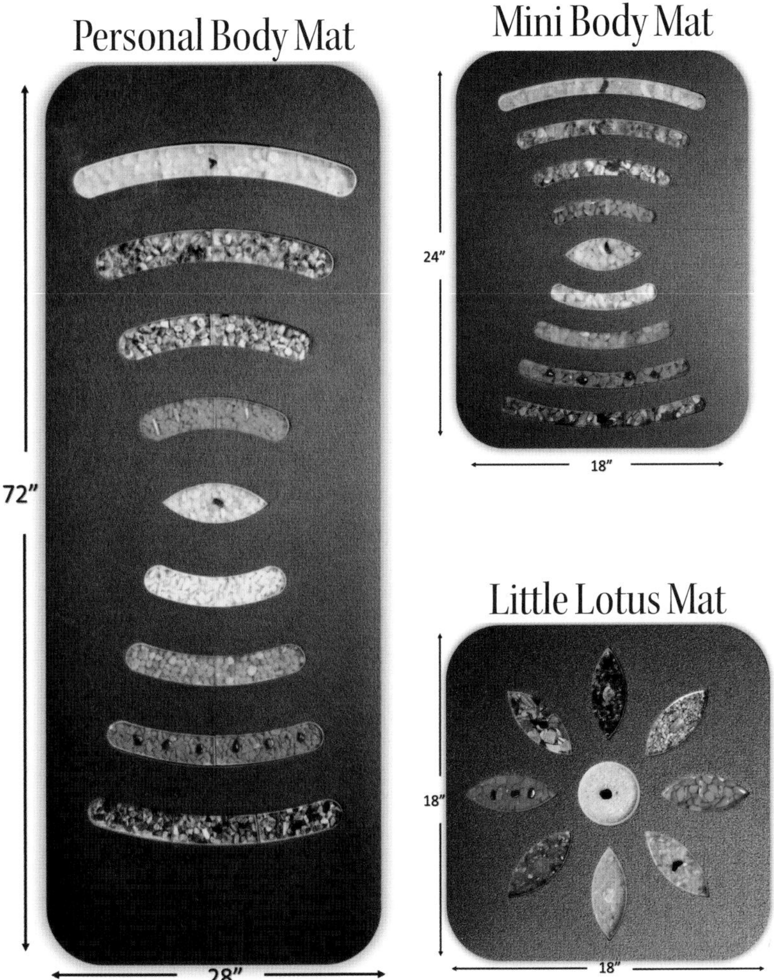

internal pressure on the stones, producing a piezoelectric effect. This may account for the observed phenomenon that Orgonite devices, similar to the stone inserts, of this type typically seem to emit more energy than their separate components.

Be all that as it may, my experience with the several styles of Body Mats that incorporate their stones into these castings indicates that the effects are stronger than I would have expected. The stones embedded in these are the same as those provided with the Practitioner Mat. (They are listed above.) The Body Mats Jennifer currently offers all use the same types of stones, and are intended to promote healing and wellbeing. They may not rocket you to the stratosphere like an Azeztulite-filled mat will, but they are therapeutically appropriate for their intended purposes of vibrational healing and harmonic balance. We are about to go into ways that the mats can be changed and customized, but before we do, I'll briefly describe the other mats.

Personal Body Mat: 28 inches wide by 72 inches long by one inch thick. Aside from the Practitioner Mat, this is the best option for doing full body stone layouts or other types of healing practices. It can also be used for the energetic revitalization of the body during the night by placing it between one's mattress and box spring. The Personal Body Mat utilizes the stone-filled rubber inserts.

Mini Body Mat: 18 inches wide by 24 inches long by one inch thick. This mat works well when placed on the floor for sitting meditations. It can also be slipped inside a large pillowcase, and the whole mat can be placed under one's regular pillow. This can be used to bring one's energies into harmonious alignment while one sleeps. It features the stone-and-rubber inserts.

Little Lotus Mat: 18 inches wide by 18 inches long by one inch thick. This mat uses a radial pattern for arraying the stones, and is another good mat for sitting meditations. Because of its smaller size, the Little Lotus Mat can be used on most chairs, and can provide energetic support during the day, at home or at work. It also uses the stone-and-rubber inserts.

CUSTOMIZING THE BODY MATS

Once one has purchased one of the Body Mats, there are countless ways to adapt and enhance the experience. As I mentioned, with the Practitioner Mats, it is easy to add, subtract or replace the stones in the various pockets. I am particularly interested in trying different combinations of high-vibration stones. However, one can do much more, bringing in stones that support various types of physical or emotional healing. If you look back at the last few chapters, you will see some of my most highly recommended combinations, which I use in other kinds of tools, grids, mandalas, etc. These same combinations can be used with the Body Mats.

One could, for example, assemble sets of stones for specific applications, such as energy purification and cleansing. I can envision creating a really powerful and effective combination of tumble-polished pieces of Shungite, Black Tourmaline, Master Shamanite, Smoky Quartz, Obsidian, Black Jade, Black Tourmaline Azeztulite, Black Azeztulite and White Azeztulite. Just imagine what forty pounds of these could do together!

It is even possible to customize the other styles of the Body Mats by having your own custom made for you. If you are interested in doing this, I suggest that you decide what stones (½ inch size or smaller) that you want to use in your custom inserts and then contact Jennifer's team at The Body Mat: www.thebodymat.com. To select high-energy stones for your custom Body Mat, you may want to contact my company, Heaven and Earth, in East Montpelier, Vermont, USA.

As you become more deeply involved in working co-creatively with the stones, designing body layouts, mandalas and grids, you may find that you get a "download" from time to time. Consider these words from our alchemical guide, Paracelsus:

> *When a man undertakes to create something, he establishes a new heaven, as it were, and from it the work that he desires to create flows into him.*

I would hasten to add, with Jennifer, that it works the same way for women! Her inspiration to create the Body Mats was followed by just such a flow, which included many synchronicities.

At this point, we have completed another phase of our journey, and we are about to venture up to the crown of our alchemical tree, where we find the stones themselves. To introduce them, we'll go back to the very beginning and have a look at the book cover. There will then be four major stone chapters, and finally our Illustrated Dictionary of many stones. Sandwiched in between these is *Chapter 33: The Redemption of the Earth—Commitment to the Impossible.* I recommend this chapter to you, no matter where else you go within this book. It offers my understanding of the ultimate significance of our endeavors with the Stone Beings, and my vision of where we can go from here.

Interlude: You Can Judge This Book By Its Cover

In the products of the unconscious we discover mandala symbols, that is, circular and quaternity figures which express wholeness, and whenever we wish to express wholeness, we employ just such figures.

—Carl Jung, *Memories, Dreams and Reflections*

The "squaring of the circle" is one of the many archetypal motifs which form the basic patterns of our dreams and fantasies. But it is distinguished by the fact that it is one of the most important of them from the functional point of view. Indeed, it could even be called the archetype of wholeness.

—Carl Jung, *Collected Works* p. 715

The cover of this book is a mandala image, and it is meant to symbolically display the message I am offering. (I invite you to take a look at the cover while you read this part.) There are a total of nine circles, all overlapping with one another. The overlapping is meant to show that there are natural intersections of energy and meaning among everything shown in the pictures. The nine circles (3 × 3) suggest the central role that "triality"—the "threeness" of things—plays in our alchemical work with the Stone Beings. Remember that in our holding the tension between opposing polarities, the Transcendent Function takes us into a third position that incorporates both sides of the polarity.

The circle containing the image of the radiant Earth is the largest, and is also most in the foreground, since the Earth circle image overlaps all the other circles and appears to do so from the "front" position. This is meant to suggest that the Earth is our most highly valued ally, and the focus of our aspirations. As in most spiritual mandalas, the center is the place of wholeness and balance. The radiant Earth is an image symbolizing the world as we will experience it (and as it will *be*) when our alchemical work is successful and complete.

Next, we will note that there are two sets of four circles. Jung wrote that many mandalas have four-sided perimeters, indicating that the "threeness" that emerges from our embracing of opposite polarities is not the final step, even though it is a transcendent leap. When one's experience of transcendence and the emergence of a new worldview reaches its fullness, the integration of this higher state into one's everyday life is symbolized by the stability of the four-sided square perimeter. This has to do with having cultivated a strong "container" to hold our spiritual experiences.

One of the sets of four circles displays images from old alchemical diagrams or "emblems." Each of these has a special meaning that is relevant to our work. The diagram on the top right corner shows Sophia holding an oroborous. This tells us that the work of wisdom—the Soul of the World—utilizes the pattern of the feedback loop to generate the endless creative evolution within which our lives are woven.

The bottom right circle shows four spheres that overlap one another. These symbolically depict, from bottom to top, our surface self, the Deep Self, the archetypal entities (i.e. the Stone Beings), and the Divine. When our alchemical work is realized, all four of these spheres of consciousness are aligned with one another in just this sort of pattern. The vertical column of the four spheres, rising from the ground (Earth) to the sky (Heaven) could be understood as the pattern of Vibrational Ascension. An individual achieving this would be aware at all of these levels simultaneously.

The bottom left circle depicts a double oroborous encircling a Star of David and a draftsman's square. The creature on the bottom half is a snake, a denizen of the Earth. The creature on the top half is a dragon with a crown, a being of the sky, or Heaven. This double oroborous is meant to convey the idea that the feedback loop from the higher domain of Spirit and the lower realm of Earth brings about a necessary joining of their energies. This is further emphasized by the Star of David, which signifies the union of Heaven and Earth.

The top left circle contains a picture showing the fulfillment of alchemy's Great Work, the creation of the Philosophers' Stone. In this picture, the "Stone" is depicted as a magical crowned youth—Mercurius—a Divine being who is perfectly balanced within the space between all of the polarities that surround this central figure. The figure is naked, symbolizing that spiritual freedom has been achieved. This is a winged being standing on the ground, once again displaying the union of Earth with Heaven through the achievement of alchemy's goal. There is a caduceus in each hand, signifying complete healing and balance. (It also emphasizes that the figure represents Hermes, the god of alchemy whose symbol is the caduceus.) The crown tells us that the work has been successful and that the permanent link with the Divine has been established. Looking closely, one sees that the figure is a hermaphrodite—both female and male—which again suggests the union of opposites that fulfills alchemy's purpose.

The second set of four circles on the book cover mandala shows photographs of the stones that I like to call the Four Cornerstones of the Alchemy of Stones. The way these pictures overlap the other circles makes them appear to be in the "middle"—behind the Earth image but in front of the old alchemical emblems. This positioning indicates their position in time. Our work with stones takes place in present, rather than centuries ago when the original alchemy was practiced. And the goal of the radiant Earth is in the future, so it is in the foreground of the mandala pattern.

The Four Cornerstones are Moldavite (on the right), Phenacite (on the left), Azeztulite (at the top), and Rosophia (at the bottom). In the next four chapters, we will discuss these four categories of stones, and we will explore their spiritual qualities in some depth. After that, we'll come to the concluding chapter in which I hope to offer, as a Grand Finale, a vision of where the Alchemy of Stones can take us.

Before we move on, I want to ask you to look again at the vision of the radiant Earth, and remember again the words of Paul Levy:

> *Alchemy is a timeless, sacred art, as the alchemists' art is to become an instrument for the incarnating deity to make itself real in time and space.*

The image of the radiant Earth is meant to convey the realization of this goal. If, with our assistance, the Divine is to make itself real in time and space, I believe it would happen as the awakening of our entire planet, which would manifest as its Vibrational Ascension—the merging of the Earth's physical matter with her Body of Light.

And when the Earth ascends, we will too.

Moldavite: The First Cornerstone

KEY WORDS: Transformation, rapid spiritual evolution, chakra activation, cleansing, protection, increased incidence of synchronicities, Ascension of the Heart
ELEMENT: Storm
CHAKRAS: All, especially Heart (4th), Third Eye (6th) and Crown (7th)

Moldavite is a member of the Tektite group, a glassy mixture of silicon dioxide, aluminum oxide and other metal oxides, with a hardness of 5.5 to 6. Its crystal system is amorphous. The color of most specimens is a deep forest green, though some pieces are pale green and others, especially those from Moravia, are greenish brown. A few rare gem grade pieces are almost an emerald green. Moldavite's formation coincides with the crash of a large meteorite in what is now the Bohemian plateau of the Czech Republic, approximately 14.8 million years ago. Most specimens are found strewn throughout that area. For many decades, farmers in southern Bohemia have turned up pieces of Moldavite when plowing fields, and Moldavite "miners" sift and dig through loose sands and gravels from depths of up to twenty meters. Some of the richest finds have occurred at the towns of Chlum and Slavce. A very delicate, lacy form of Moldavite has been found near the village of Besednice, although this location is now exhausted. In recent years the Moldavite fields have become depleted, and the stones are becoming increasingly rare.

Moldavite is the stone that initiated me into awareness of the spiritual properties of crystals and minerals, and it has been a catalyst for several of my most important spiritual experiences. It has, over the thirty-three years I have worked in this field, had similar effects on thousands of other people with whom I have spoken and corresponded. From my perspective, it has a special role to play in the awakening of humanity now underway.

Scientific theorists differ on hypotheses regarding Moldavite's origin. Some contend that Moldavite is earthly rock melted by the heat of the meteorite crash, while others suggest that the material is of extraterrestrial origin, possibly a type of obsidian ejected by a lunar volcano.

A third theory holds that Moldavite is a fusion product of meteoric material and earthly rock vaporized in the tremendous heat of the impact explosion, with the resultant gas being propelled high into the atmosphere. This gaseous material would have then cooled and condensed into a liquid glass that "rained" down on the crater and surrounding areas. Regardless of which, if any, of these ideas is correct, it is known that Moldavite indeed fell from the sky, because of the aerodynamic shapes of certain pieces. Most scientists associate it with the meteoric collision that formed the Bohemian plateau and surrounding mountains.

The event that gave birth to Moldavite was one of tremendous power. The force of the impact explosion has been estimated at six trillion megatons, far more than all the atom bombs on Earth. The heat, as mentioned above, was hot enough to vaporize rock, and the main body of the meteorite is believed to have passed completely through the Earth's crust, penetrating into the liquid iron at the planet's core. This deep impact was described in a New York Times article as having disturbed the currents of rotating liquid iron enough to cause a reversal of the Earth's magnetic poles.

Throughout history, and even into pre-history, Moldavite has been regarded as a spiritual talisman. The Neolithic peoples of Eastern Europe wore Moldavite at least twenty-five thousand years ago, and the famed Venus of Willendorf—the earliest known goddess statue—was discovered in a digging site that contained a number of Moldavite amulets. People of that period also used Moldavite for arrowheads and cutting tools. More recently, Moldavite has

been viewed as a relic of the legend of the Holy Grail. In some recountings, the Grail was said to be not a cup but a stone, an Emerald that fell from the sky. In other stories, the Grail cup was carved from the Emerald. The correspondences of the Stone of the Grail with Moldavite are clear. The ancients called all clear green gemstones "Emeralds," and Moldavite is the only such stone ever to have fallen from the sky. In history, there was even a physical "Grail" discovered and brought to Napoleon, who was disappointed to find that it was green glass. (But, of course, Moldavite *is* green glass.)

Another chalice, this one made of gold and adorned with Moldavites, was passed down through the centuries and disappeared during the second World War. In the 1930s, the famed artist and mystic Nicholas Roerich compared a Moldavite (which he called *agni mani*, meaning "fire pearl") to the fabled Stone of Shambhala, further asserting it was the same stone mentioned in the legend of the Holy Grail.

Interestingly, the energetic effects of Moldavite parallel those attributed to the fabled Grail stone. Both stones serve to quicken one's destiny and set one upon a true spiritual path. In Czech folklore, Moldavite was believed to bring harmony to marital relationships, and it was used as a traditional betrothal gift for centuries. The Stone of the Grail was believed to have similar properties, guiding the hero Percival to his true love.

In modern times, Moldavite has emerged as one of the stones most prized for metaphysical purposes. Its effects vary widely, from mild to almost overwhelming, from physical cleansings to spiritual breakthroughs—yet the common denominator seems to be the revitalization and acceleration of one's path of evolution.

People who hold Moldavite for the first time most often experience its energy as warmth or heat, usually felt first in one's hand and then progressively throughout the body. In some cases there is an opening of the heart chakra, characterized by strange (though not painful) sensations in the chest, an upwelling of emotion and a flushing of the face. This has happened often enough to have earned a name—the "Moldavite flush." Moldavite's energies can also cause pulsations in the hand, tingling in the third eye and heart chakras, a feeling of lightheadedness or dizziness, and occasionally the sense of being lifted out of one's body. Most people feel that Moldavite excites their energies and speeds their vibrations, especially for the first days or weeks, until they become acclimated to it.

Moldavite's energies can activate any and all of the chakras. Its vibrations tend to focus in areas where one has blockages or "wounds," first clearing these areas and then moving into resonance with one's entire energetic system. Resonance with Moldavite can take many forms—chakras can open; synchronicities can increase in frequency and significance; one's dream life can become dramatically more vivid and meaningful; one can connect with spirit guides; physical, emotional or spiritual healings can happen; jobs and relationships can change; meditations can become deeper and more powerful—yet all these can be viewed as symptoms of a shift in one's own energies. This shift is what Moldavite can catalyze. With its high and intense vibrations, it can resonate with one's energy pattern in a way that creates an intensification of spiritual vitality and an acceleration of progress on the path of one's highest destiny. This is much the same effect that legend says resulted from exposure to the fabled Stone of the Grail.

I want to mention here that the legend of the Holy Grail contains numerous images and metaphors that relate to alchemy. The Stone of the Grail has much in common with the alchemical Philosophers' Stone, including the fact that in both traditions, the magical Stone was said to convey immortality.

Moldavite is a powerful aid for meditation and dreamwork. In both cases, taping a piece of Moldavite to the forehead can have the effect of creating a much more vivid and visionary inner experience. Moldavite increases one's sensitivity to guidance and one's ability to discern the messages sent from the higher realms.

Moldavite can be a powerful catalyst for self-healing, clearing blockages and opening the meridians, as well as energizing the interconnections among all aspects of the subtle body. It is a talisman of spiritual awakening, transformation and evolutionary growth.

In addition to use in meditation and dreamwork, Moldavite can be worn as jewelry. This conveys the advantage of being able to keep its energies in one's vibrational field throughout the day, for further strengthening of its effects. Doing this also draws an increased incidence of beneficial sychronicities into one's daily life. Some people will have to accustom themselves gradually to wearing Moldavite because of its energetic intensity, but most will make the adjustment in a few days.

Moldavite also offers an energy of spiritual protection. When one is in resonance with its high-frequency vibrations, negative energies and entities cannot connect with or hang onto one's field. In alignment with its transformational properties, Moldavite tends to disconnect one from unhealthy attachments and to magnetize the persons and situations most needed for evolutionary progress.

Moldavite is an ideal stone for making energy tools. It can be glued or otherwise attached to other stones to magnify both energies. It can be added to wands, headbands, templates, grids and all sorts of devices to intensify their effects. Moldavite has the ability to enhance and accelerate the beneficial effects of many other stones. It works well with all types of Quartz, as well as Amethyst, Citrine, Rose Quartz, Sugilite, Charoite, Lapis, Larimar, Rhodochrosite, Aquamarine, Heliodor, Pietersite, Smoky Quartz, Selenite and most other gemstones. For healing purposes, I would recommend combining Moldavite with Heartenite, Healerite, Healers' Gold and/or Seraphinite. For enhanced visionary experience, Herkimer "Diamonds" are an excellent ally. Genuine Diamond, in crystal or gem form, further intensifies Moldavite's trans-

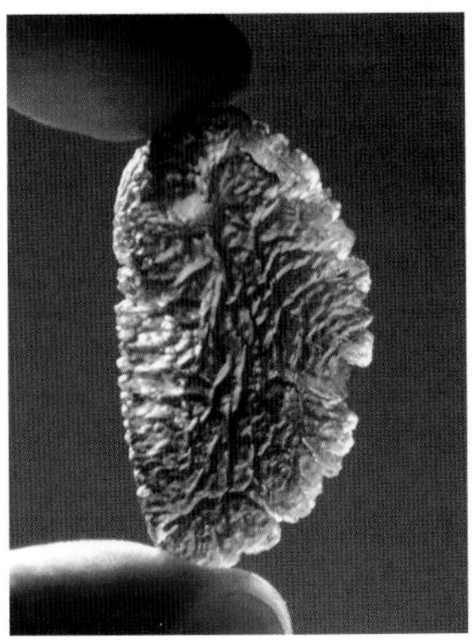

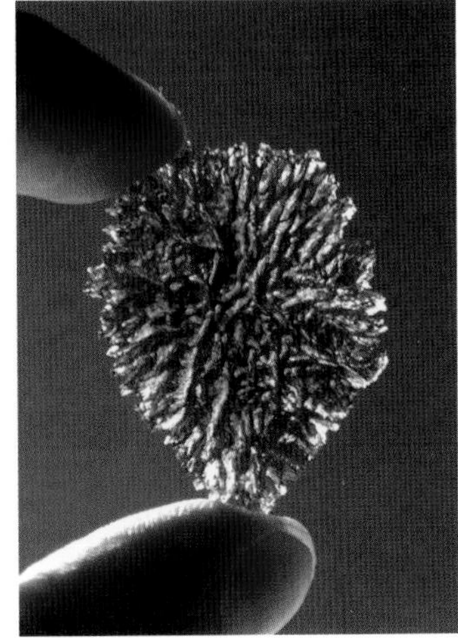

formational energies. Libyan Gold Tektite increases Moldavite's empowerment of the third chakra, focus of personal power and will.

Moldavite is one of the Synergy Twelve stones, along with Danburite, Tanzanite, White Azeztulite, Phenacite, Herderite, Tibetan Tektite, Satyaloka Azeztulite, Petalite, Brookite, Natrolite and Scolecite.

Currently, I am especially interested in working with Moldavite by itself, or in combining it with any or all of the other stones constituting the Four Cornerstones of the Alchemy of Stones—Phenacite, Rosophia, and the Azeztulite family of stones. (I call Azeztulites a "family" because there are now twenty-one different varieties!)

MOLDAVITE & THE EMERALD TABLET

I have already raised the subject of the fabled Emerald Tablet of Hermes in an earlier chapter, and I want to go back to it here, as we are exploring the qualities of Moldavite. A Wikipedia article gives us some background:

> *The* Emerald Tablet *is a compact and cryptic piece of the* Hermetica *[Egyptian-Greek wisdom texts from the 2nd century or earlier] reputed to contain the secret of the prima materia and its transmutation. It was highly regarded by European alchemists as the foundation of their art and its Hermetic tradition. The original source of the* Emerald Tablet *is unknown . . . The oldest documentable source of the text is the* Book of Balinas the Wise on the Causes, *written in Arabic between the sixth and eighth centuries . . . In his book, Balinas frames the Emerald Tablet as ancient Hermetic wisdom. He tells his readers that he discovered the text in a vault below a statue of Hermes in Tyana, and that, inside the vault, an old corpse on a golden throne held the Emerald Tablet . . . [T]he* Tablet *became a mainstay of medieval and Renaissance alchemy. Commentaries and/or translations were published by, among others,*

Imaginative depiction of the Emerald Tablet by the 17th century alchemist Heinrich Khunrath.

Trithemius, Roger Bacon, Michael Maier, Albertus Magnus, and Isaac Newton. The concise text was a popular summary of alchemical principles, wherein the secrets of the Philosophers' Stone were thought to have been described . . . C.G. Jung identified The Emerald Tablet *with a table made of green stone which he encountered in the first of a set of his dreams and visions beginning at the end of 1912, and climaxing in his writing Seven Sermons to the Dead in 1916.*

The reason I want to return to the Emerald Tablet here is because of the resemblance of Moldavite and its traits to this legendary object associated with the origins of alchemy. To illustrate this, I will once again go to the Emerald Tablet translation named *Aurelium Occultae Philosophorum* (*Hidden Gold of the Philosophers*) by Georgio Beato, published in Frankfurt, Germany in 1610:

1. This is true and remote from all cover of falsehood
2. Whatever is below is similar to that which is above. Through this the marvels of the work of one thing are procured and perfected.
3. Also, as all things are made from one, by the consideration of one, so all things were made from this one, by conjunction.
4. The father of it is the sun, the mother the moon.
5. The wind bore it in the womb. Its nurse is the earth, the mother of all perfection.

6a. Its power is perfected.

7. If it is turned into earth,

7a. separate the earth from the fire, the subtle and thin from the crude and coarse, prudently, with modesty and wisdom.

8. This ascends from the earth into the sky and again descends from the sky to the earth, and receives the power and efficacy of things above and of things below.
9. By this means you will acquire the glory of the whole world, and so you will drive away all shadows and blindness.
10. For this by its fortitude snatches the palm from all other fortitude and power. For it is able to penetrate and subdue everything subtle and everything crude and hard.

11a. By this means the world was founded

12. and hence the marvelous conjunctions of it and admirable effects, since this is the way by which these marvels may be brought about.
13. And because of this they have called me Hermes Trismegistus since I have the three parts of the wisdom and Philosophy of the whole universe.
14. My speech is finished which I have spoken concerning the solar work.

Although we can't know with authority that Moldavite is the "stone" that constituted the Emerald Tablet—the foundation of alchemy—we can look at the translation and consider where there are correspondences. As an image, the Emerald Tablet was a green stone that was inscribed with these cryptic teachings from Hermes. As we go through the text line-by-line, it is important to view all of this through the lens of True Imagination rather than literalism. We need to try to see this on multiple levels. One of the mysterious possibilities that has come to me is that Moldavite, which resonates with so much of the Emerald Tablet story, may be a sort of embodiment of the Tablet's wisdom. It seems to me that Moldavite has the ability to transmit its essence. It would almost be as if Moldavite is a *manifestation of the same mystery* referred to in the Emerald Tablet. The similarities we see between Moldavite's properties and those described in the text of the Emerald Tablet work together to point toward that mystery.

So, let's go back to the text.

We already understand and have examined the ideas expressed in the first three lines, which affirm the alchemical dictum, *As above, so below.* In line 4, the statement, "The father of it is the sun, the mother the moon," is a provocative one. I can't think of a better way to poetically describe the nature of a meteorite!

The physical origins of Moldavite fit well with line 5: *"The wind bore it in the womb. Its nurse is the earth, the mother of all perfection."* The descent of the Moldavite meteorite from space would certainly have been an intense journey through the Earth's atmosphere, generating a gigantic amount of wind. And if, as is believed by many scientists, Moldavite is a product of the fusion of meteoric material with earthly rock, then the metaphoric statement that "it's nurse is the earth" also makes sense.

Lines 7 and 7a tell us: "If it is turned into earth, separate the earth from the fire, the subtle and thin from the crude and coarse, prudently, with modesty and wisdom." Following what is understood about Moldavite, I interpret this to mean that when the meteorite struck the ground, it was "turned into earth." In the next moment, there was a gigantic explosion with intense heat, able to actually vaporize rock and send it hurtling into the sky. Because the material was vaporized, it was instantly "distilled," meaning that impurities were purged, such that the Moldavite which was ultimately created is virtually pure green glass, without any bits of gravel or other material embedded in it. The phrases, "separate the earth from the fire, the subtle and thin from the crude and coarse," describes this intense purification within the explosive alchemical "furnace" of the meteoric impact.

Line 8 gives an uncannily appropriate description of how Moldavite may have formed and simultaneously acquired the energetic properties for which it is so well known: "This ascends from the earth into the sky and again descends from the sky to the earth, and receives the power and efficacy of things above and of things below." The explosion of the meteorite upon impact with the ground sent a superheated plume of gaseous rock shooting upward into the stratosphere. As the gas cooled, it condensed into droplets of liquid glass, which descended like fiery rain to the surface below. And while no one knows the how and why of Moldavite's vibrational power, it could be that the ascent and descent, due to the incredible force of the explosion, impressed the newly born Moldavite with unique properties. It is most certainly a literal physical embodiment of the joining of matter from the heavens with matter from the earth—the above and the below.

Looking at line 9, it is not difficult to make the case that the text could apply to the spiritual qualities of Moldavite: "By this means you will acquire the glory of the whole world, and so you will drive away all shadows and blindness." The union with the Light I experienced during the Moldavite meditation in which I journeyed to the Great Central Sun could qualify as "the glory of the whole world," at least as far as I was concerned! The driving away of shadows and blindness mentioned in this line reminds me very much of Moldavite's tendency to catalyze the rapid purging of habits, relationships and situations that are not for one's highest good.

Line 10 further develops this theme, but Beato's translation is rather murky. In a different translation from an Arabic source, the line reads: "The force of forces, which overcomes every subtle thing and penetrates into everything gross." Once again, it seems natural to me to describe the energy of Moldavite (or that of a number of powerful stones, including all of the Four Cornerstones) in just such words. The currents of Moldavite penetrate and influence both our subtle bodies and our ("gross") physical bodies.

Line 11a offers a challenge to the imagination: "By this means the world was founded." How can we understand this? Could it be that the world we know "was founded" by a dramatic incident such as this great meteoric collision? I can't say, but we do know that the arrival of Moldavite was such a powerful geophysical event that it caused the reversal of the Earth's magnetic poles. Such meteoric events have been linked to mass extinctions and sudden bursts of evolution. On the spiritual level, it remains a mystery, but we know that the arrival of Moldavite occurred earlier than any known evidence of the existence of human beings. We evolved afterwards. Could Moldavite's cataclysmic arrival and reversal of the Earth's magnetic field have somehow seeded a burst of evolution?

With line 12, we again encounter some difficult wording: "and hence the marvelous conjunctions of it and admirable effects, since this is the way by which these marvels may be brought about." It seems to be a comment about the beneficial qualities of whatever object or substance—the offspring of the Sun and Moon—has been described throughout the text. A 12th Century Latin version says it more simply: "From this come marvelous adaptions of which this is the procedure."

Line 13 lays the claim of authorship upon the legendary Hermes Trismegistus (thrice-greatest Hermes) who was said to be an incarnation of Thoth and the progenitor of alchemy: "And because of this they have called me Hermes Trismegistus since I have the three parts of the Wisdom and Philosophy of the whole universe."

Line 14 completes the text: "My speech is finished which I have spoken concerning the solar work." The meaning here is simple, except for the mention of the "solar work," known in some texts as the Operation of the Sun. I can offer one meaningful connection of this line with

Moldavite: The "solar work" reminds me once again that Moldavite took me on a spontaneous meditative journey to the Great Central Sun, which, as I have said, awakened my capacity to feel and interpret stone energies.

I have taken us on a speculative journey into the correspondences that appear to connect Moldavite with the Emerald Tablet, the foundation stone of alchemy. Is the story of the Emerald Tablet a myth—a pattern of symbolism that sheds light upon resonant things and events in the manifest world? Or is the text a symbolic report of real events in the history of the Earth, perhaps prior to the beginnings of humanity? Or could it be that the pattern of the Emerald Tablet story and the principles of alchemy are so deeply embedded in the world's nature that the genesis of Moldavite and the Emerald Tablet text are simply different manifestations of the same archetypal pattern? This idea—*As above, so below*—is expressed in the Emerald Tablet, and is one we examined earlier, in our delving into fractal geometry. And in nature, the spiral of a snail shell resembles the spiral of the Milky Way. As above, so below.

There is no way to know the degree to which either, neither, or both of these hypotheses reflect an objective "truth." But they strike a resonating chord in the imagination, and I have always been beguiled with the Emerald Tablet, and with the Stone of the Grail. The fact that I feel multiple resonances between these stories and the nature of Moldavite is the reason I hold these thoughts and images within myself. And it is why I am offering them to you. The point of this is not so much to solve the problem as it is to *carry the mystery* inside ourselves.

The next time you pick up a Moldavite to meditate, or to put inside your pillowcase for dreaming, I suggest that you center your attention directly on this mystery. Don't create an opinion about it. Be there, not knowing.

MOLDAVITE AS A CORNERSTONE OF THE ALCHEMY OF STONES

Many of the reasons I view Moldavite as one of the Four Cornerstones of the Alchemy of Stones are implicit in what I have already said in this chapter. And if you have your own relationship with Moldavite, it is likely that you already understand. But I will summarize some the reasons here.

Moldavite is an initiator: If I had never found Moldavite, I doubt I would be writing this book now. Without its influence, my capacity to feel and interpret stone energies might never have been activated. And its influence was not limited to that incident. Within the first six months of my acquiring Moldavite, my life completely changed. A unhappy marriage ended, I stopped eating meat and drinking alcohol, I experienced a quickening of my interest in leading a spiritually focused life, and I met Kathy, my wife-to-be. My work life changed, from designing jewelry to opening a crystal business—Heaven and Earth—with my new wife and partner. The level of synchronicities in my life increased exponentially, and I felt a powerful sense of purpose, in which Moldavite played a central role. One need only to search "Moldavite experiences" on the internet to see that such initiatory experiences are typical for those who work with Moldavite.

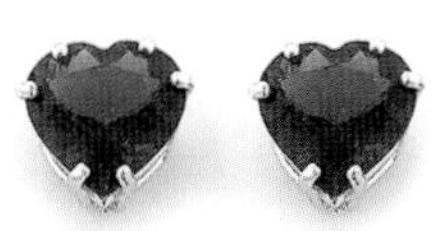

Moldavite Bridges the Above and the Below: Of all the stones on Earth, Moldavite is one of a very few that link, within their own substance, the union of Heaven and Earth. Those alchemists who were most spiritually aware realized that their quest for the Philosophers' Stone was both an inner and an outer one. They sought to incarnate the divine energies both within themselves and in the "outer" physical world of matter. Moldavite naturally facilitates this goal, because it stimulates inner transformation while the stone itself remains a physical object. Like the Philosophers' Stone, Moldavite carries and emanates a numinous spiritual energy.

Moldavite is a Trickster: As I mentioned above, Moldavite has a remarkably meaningful resonance with the Emerald Tablet of Hermes. Hermes was a Trickster god, who outwitted other gods for his own satisfaction or for the sake of humankind. It is said that Hermes was born in the morning, invented and played the lyre by the afternoon, stole his brother Apollo's cows in the evening, and was back in his cradle that night looking just like an innocent, sleeping baby. The rapidity of Hermes' development reminds us of the speedy evolution we can experience under the influence of Moldavite.

One aspect of the Trickster quality of Moldavite is that the accelerated pace of the evolution it can trigger causes us to be plunged into transformation, whether we think we are ready or not. Many people have commented on this to me, and I experienced it myself. Moldavite tends to quickly attract whatever one's spiritual metamorphosis requires. It also seems to cause whatever parts of our lives no longer serve our highest good to be discharged, whether we realize the need for that or not. This reminds us of Hermes, especially in regard to the speed of the changes that occur. Hermes was a being of great speed. He had wings on his feet, and was the messenger of the gods.

The other phenomenon that displays Moldavite's Trickster quality is its apparent ability to disappear and reappear. I have experienced this many times. In a typical instance, I put my Moldavite away on a dresser or in a box, only to find it gone the next day. Then, sooner or later, the Moldavite will reappear, usually in a ridiculously unlikely spot. In one instance, I left my Moldavite on top of my dresser in the bedroom, discovered the next day that it was gone, and found it again weeks later—in the container of one of our house plants in the living room! In the longest of these disappearances, my most treasured Moldavite disappeared for fourteen years, only to be found eventually in the pocket of a pair of pants that I had never worn! For a long time, I doubted my memory, but this occurred over and over. And through the years, many people have told me their own very similar stories. Once again, I refer you to the internet. There are numerous "disappearing Moldavite" stories online.

What is the reason that Moldavite performs these disappearing acts? I don't know, but it might be that, like Hermes, the Being of Moldavite does this "for his own satisfaction or for the sake of humankind." I have thought at times that the intention behind Moldavite's disappearances may be to show us that the physical world is not necessarily as "solid" as we think it is. If that were proven to us, and if we accepted the evidence, the knowledge could be very liberating.

Moldavite is a stone of the heart: When a person first holds a piece of Moldavite, he or she often feels heat, especially around the heart. As this experience unfolds, the person frequently flushes red in the cheeks. This is often accompanied by tears, signifying an emotional release. And many times I have witnessed people holding a Moldavite and being surprised by the fact that their hearts began to beat in a different way. It is not a painful event—I compare the heart's behavior to a dog wagging its tail when it is happy. I believe the heart responds to Moldavite in this way, communicating its recognition and pleasure in the presence of this stone. And of course, Moldavite is green—the color of the heart chakra.

In my first powerful Moldavite experience, the sensation of energy began in my right hand where I was holding the stone. Then the current went straight up my arm and into my heart. At that point, my heart chakra opened, like a blooming flower of Light. And in the next moment, the Light surged both downwards and upwards from my heart, opening all of my chakras.

It is significant in our Alchemy of Stones that Moldavite resonates with the heart, because the heart is the seat of Sophia within us, and it is the place where the union of the opposites that signifies alchemical Conjunction can occur. Although many stones resonate with our hearts in a gentle and loving way, only Moldavite vibrates one's heart so powerfully.

Moldavite is a visionary stone of transformation: I have mentioned my Moldavite-induced journey to the Great Central Sun several times in this book. There is also the Moldavite Grail meditation, in which we place Moldavite over our hearts and envision golden Light pouring through our bodies, overflowing from a golden chalice we imagine in our hearts. This meditation works very well, because Moldavite stimulates inner visions that lead to transformation.

I have noticed that Moldavite works well as a stimulator of visionary experiences, if the purpose or result of the vision is to be the rapid spiritual transformation and evolution of the person using it. It does not, however, work very well for idle exploration or fantasy. Like Hermes, Moldavite has an agenda, and it is all about this intense drive toward a metamorphosis into one's full potential. This is in complete alignment with the purpose of alchemy—manifesting the Philosophers' Stone, within oneself and in the outer world.

Moldavite is an incubator of dreams: This is true of Moldavite, more than any other stone I have worked with. If you tape a small piece of Moldavite to your forehead at the location of the third eye chakra before going to bed, I guarantee that you will dream! A lot! I have tried this many times and recommended it to others for over thirty years. Almost all of us find that the quantity and depth of our dream life increases immediately. And the dreams are often spiritually significant ones. I believe that this happens because of Moldavite's affinity with the Deep Self, the part of us that creates our dreams. When Moldavite lends its power to one's Deep Self, a flurry of inner communication comes to us through a cornucopia of dreams. Another rather surprising symptom of Moldavite's effect on our dreaming is that most of us have to remove the Moldavite during the night, because we are dreaming so much that we need to take a rest from it and sleep more deeply!

For virtually all of us, the path of spiritual evolution involves healing. In alchemical terms, we need to "cook" ourselves so that the impurities in our energies—the disharmonious patterns in our subtle bodies—are burned away. And Moldavite just loves to do that!

Moldavite is a healing stone: Moldavite resonates with the pattern of our highest good—our full spiritual awakening and development. Thus, its influence moves us toward dispelling all patterns that are not in alignment with our wholeness, clearing the way for profound good health. However, the ride may sometimes be uncomfortable, just as it can be on the psychological level.

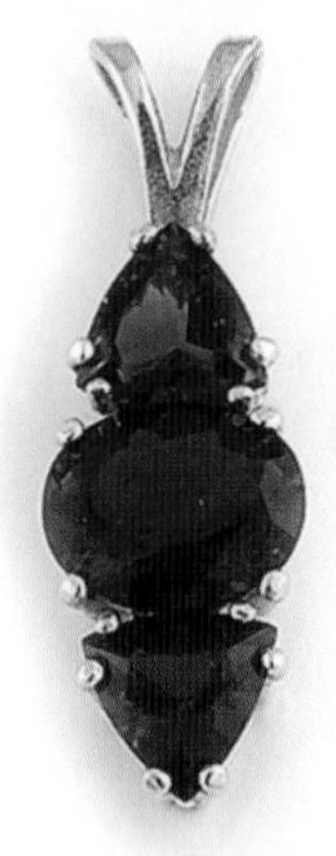

Moldavite doesn't mess around! In my own case, getting involved with Moldavite coincided with a long series of healing crises that continued for years. (It's clear to me now that I had a lot of cleansing and purification to do!) The symptoms were not usually terrible, but they were frequently mysterious and confusing. Regular allopathic medicine seldom did me much good, although Kathy's hands-on healing and other alternative practices often helped.

Something I experienced several times during my first years with Moldavite was the onset of physical problems that turned out to be rooted in past lives. As people who work with past life therapy often observe, my physical ailments expressed similarities (at least symbolically) to traumatic past life events. Hypnotic regressions were helpful in completing my review of these patterns and letting them go, but I am convinced that the presence of Moldavite is what brought them to the forefront.

Moldavite's ability to work quickly, and to root out the problematic past life patterns in one's subtle body, can be quite remarkable. About fifteen years ago, Kathy and I took a trip to the Czech Republic to see the Moldavite fields. When we visited them, I was lucky to encounter two Moldavite diggers who had just found a large piece. I bought it on the spot, with the mud still clinging to it, and I carried it every day after that. On the last day of the trip, while Kathy was cooking breakfast, I had a sudden and vivid recollection of what must have been more than a hundred different past lives. They flashed by very rapidly, but I could see that the same unhealthy pattern was present in all of them. I will not describe this highly personal event in more detail, except to say that the healing of that pattern was cathartic, and that I wept many tears.

This is what I mean in regard to Moldavite's role as a healing catalyst. Its energies penetrate to the core of whatever dysfunctional patterns are being carried by the soul, within one's subtle body. Without the stimulation that Moldavite provides, one could go through a whole lifetime without having these issues come to the surface. Potentially, one might feel more "comfortable" without such disruptions, but one's evolution would be slower.

Sometimes, especially when one is already in the throes of an apparent illness that stems from long-held unhealthy patterns in the subtle body, the introduction of Moldavite can trigger a direct and rapid healing effect. It can seem as if the stone has "cured" a physical illness. But in my view, the presence of Moldavite has simply dislodged the stuck pattern, allowing the subtle body to clear itself and bring the physical body back to health.

If one wishes to work with Moldavite as a healing stone, it is often a good idea to bring another beneficial stone (or stones) into the mix. Heartenite, Seraphinite, Healerite and Healers' Gold are good overall healing stones that can stabilize one's subtle body and work to soften the intensity of Moldavite. In my own past, during a time when my healing was focused on the emotional body, I found that Charoite and Moldavite felt best to me. I urge you to work intuitively in these types of situations, and let the Stone Beings tell you which ones are most appropriate.

Looking back through the years, I now realize that each of the Four Cornerstones came to me through major synchronicities. Discovering Moldavite's existence and being influenced by its energies radically shifted the path of my life. Moldavite was the first Stone Being to enter my life, paving the way for all the rest. The next Cornerstone I encountered was Phenacite. Like Moldavite, it arrived in an unexpected way that made me aware of the touch of destiny.

Phenacite: The Second Cornerstone

KEY WORDS: Third-eye activation, inner visions, awakening the Light Body, interdimensional travel
ELEMENT: Storm
CHAKRAS: Third Eye (6th), Crown (7th)

Phenacite is a beryllium silicate with a hardness of 7.5 to 8. It is a rare mineral, especially in well-formed crystals with transparency. Its crystal system is hexagonal (trigonal) and it often crystallizes in short prisms. However, Phenacite varies greatly in form from one location to another. In fact, its name is derived from the Greek word meaning "deceiver." This is because Phenacite grows in such a multiplicity of patterns that it is easily mistaken for other types of crystal, such as Quartz, Topaz or even Tourmaline. Phenacite has been found in Brazil, Sri Lanka, Madagascar, Mexico, Zimbabwe, Zambia, Nigeria, Norway, Russia, Tanzania, Switzerland and the USA. Yet even though it exists in a number of locations, Phenacite is a rare mineral. Wherever it has been discovered, the quantities have been small.

Phenacite is truly the supreme stone of the third eye chakra. Its pulsing energies are so strong that they can be felt at the third eye, even by many people not normally sensitive to crystal energies. It opens the interdimensional portals for inner journeying, allowing one's consciousness to glide through unending corridors of sacred geometric forms. The stimulation of the third eye offered by Phenacite is stronger than one receives from virtually any other stone. It can also be used to awaken the latent special capacities in the prefrontal lobes, the newest and most advanced parts of the brain. This can sometimes bring spontaneous experiences of telepathy, psychokinesis, prophetic vision or remote viewing. Sitting in meditation with one Phenacite at the forehead and another on the crown can link these two chakras, providing the user with a profoundly pleasurable sensation of their joined energies.

Phenacite's link with the higher realms makes it a powerful tool for manifestation of inner images or patterns of intention in the outer world. For bringing prosperity and financial abundance, combining Phenacite with Yellow Sapphire and/or Cinnazez is highly recommended. For assistance with creative projects, pairing Phenacite with Rosophia is excellent. For enhancing one's ability to manifest through the will, Phenacite can be combined with Libyan Gold Tektite and/or Himalaya Gold Azeztulite.

Working with the combination of Phenacite and Moldavite brings in powerful resonant energies that join to accelerate spiritual awakening. Sleeping with these two stones can facilitate the occurrence of deep spiritual dreams, and even lucid dreams. If one wishes to experience out-of-body travel and visionary experiences in higher spiritual realms, Phenacite and Moldavite can be powerful allies.

Phenacite is one of the Synergy Twelve Stones, along with Moldavite, Danburite, White Azeztulite, Herderite, Brookite, Tanzanite, Satyaloka Azeztulite, Natrolite, Scolecite and Tibetan Tektite. Phenacite also harmonizes with Golden Brucite, Petalite, Merkabite Calcite, Nirvana Quartz, Magnesite, Lithium Quartz, Himalaya Gold Azeztulite, Golden Azeztulite Crystals and other high-vibration stones, especially for activation of the upper chakras of the body and the etheric chakras beyond the body.

Phenacite is one of the highest-frequency stones in the entire mineral kingdom, and it is the most powerful stone for stimulation of the mind centers. I have used it, primarily at the third eye, for opening that chakra and initiating inner visionary experiences. In many cases, the currents of Phenacite—experienced as a rapid pulsing coming in through the entry point at the third eye—are powerful enough to move into the interior of the skull and up through the crown chakra, thereby unifying both energy points in a single interior motion or flow.

As Phenacite clearly and powerfully stimulates the third eye, the felt sense is one of instantaneous rhythmic pulsations, which, unlike those of other stones, increase in frequency and intensity, as though building up a charge in the areas they affect. Another quality of Phenacite that distinguishes it—and in some ways sets it beyond most other stones of the third eye and crown—is that its pulsating frequencies go completely through the skull and resonate at the energy point or chakra sometimes called the Mouth of God. This point is at the back of the head where the base of the skull meets the spine, and is a powerful gate of kundalini awakening.

If one persists long enough in meditative attention, Phenacite's pulsations become Light vibrations, centered within the skull. The color of this Light is white, or golden-white, and the feeling I sense is that this is the same sort of Light I recall from my first powerful experience at eighteen, and from the later activation of my Light Body that came during a meditation with Moldavite.

The inner Light I frequently experience with Phenacite is of a lesser intensity than it was in my full-blown mystic awakening. However, it is like hearing familiar music played softly, akin to the similarity between the calm surf of a lovely shoreline and the power of a tidal wave. Although the everyday surf is calmer, its motion is similar to the motion of the tidal wave, and it is governed and expressed through similar forces and patterns. One who has felt the spiritual tidal wave will recognize its seed pattern in the surf. This is how I relate the Light-generating properties of Phenacite to the powerful, explosive nature of sudden *samadhi*. My sense is that those who wish to make themselves available to the spiritual Light of the Divine will find a helpful ally in Phenacite. By using Phenacite, one increases connectedness with this Divine Light, and this is highly beneficial to the subtle body. With continued practice and intentional focus, one can work with Phenacite to successfully transform one's subtle body into the Body of Light.

INTERDIMENSIONAL TRAVEL

One of the great strengths of Phenacite is its capacity to facilitate interdimensional travel. I mentioned above that meditation with Phenacite stimulates the third eye and may awaken latent capacities in the brain's pre-frontal lobes. My personal experience in meditating with Phenacite is that, when I focus my attention at the third eye while holding a Phenacite there, the beginning of the experience is one of rhythmic tactile pulsations that seem to move into my head from the Phenacite. If I hold my attention on these pulsations and invite them to increase, I spontaneously begin to see images with my inner vision. These images usually appear as light, patterned in symmetrical geometric forms. If I direct my attention to one of the forms and try to move into it, I then see a succession of light-forms in similar geometric patterns, extending like a tunnel of light ahead of me.

Keeping the Phenacite in place and holding my attention on the inner imagery, I am sometimes able to travel down one or more of these corridors of light. They seem to be endless, like the infinitely unfolding patterns of fractal geometry. However, these tunnels of light are patterned like the faces of the Platonic solids, rather than being spirals or other more organic shapes.

My hypothesis now is that the striking geometric light-forms that Phenacite opens before us are its energetic extensions into subtle realms of many kinds. In these interdimensional journeys, while moving through the corridors, I have sometimes been able to stop and focus my attention on "windows" or gateways along the sides of the tunnels. I have found that one can then enter and explore various worlds of spiritual Light. These places can have their own landscapes, and one can meet the beings who apparently inhabit these places. In shamanic language, these places may be various realms of the Upper World. The beings in these places appear as angels or other kinds of Light Beings. Some of them are Stone Beings associated with high-vibration crystals such as Phenacite, Danburite, Natrolite, Apophyllite, etc. Their most prominent characteristics seem to be joyfulness and love. They are friendly and willing to aid us, although they seem not to comprehend our human sorrows. However, just to be in their presence fills one with their joy and Light.

I feel certain that I have only scratched the surface of the interdimensional realms to which one can link, with the aid of Phenacite. I look forward to hearing from other explorers of these realities.

MY PHENACITE STORY

I met Moldavite, the first of the Four Cornerstones that I encountered, in 1985. As I have written, Moldavite's arrival brought profound and rapid changes in my outer life, and spiritual awakening in my inner life. When Kathy and I opened our first retail shop, Heaven and Earth, in 1986, Moldavite was the centerpiece. We were then the only source for Moldavite, and, as the word spread about it, our shop became a well-known mecca for lovers of stones and their energies. We met numerous kindred souls among the spiritual people who frequented the store, and who loved the Moldavite and our other stones. One of these was a psychically gifted woman named Hazel, who became our friend, and who shared her insights with us.

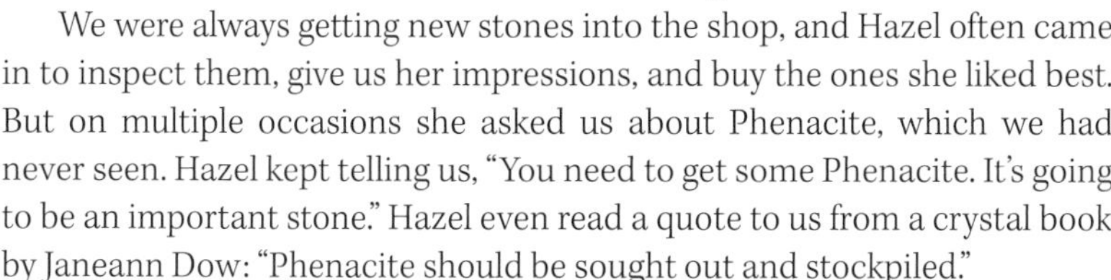

We were always getting new stones into the shop, and Hazel often came in to inspect them, give us her impressions, and buy the ones she liked best. But on multiple occasions she asked us about Phenacite, which we had never seen. Hazel kept telling us, "You need to get some Phenacite. It's going to be an important stone." Hazel even read a quote to us from a crystal book by Janeann Dow: "Phenacite should be sought out and stockpiled."

In 1988, we traveled to Tucson, Arizona to exhibit our Moldavite stones and jewelry for the first time at the Tucson Gem and Mineral Show. Hazel and two of her sons went there with us as part of our staff. During the event, someone came into the showroom, handed me a small translucent whitish crystal, and said, "Hold this up to your third eye and tell me what you get from it."

I held the stone up to my forehead and I was practically bowled over by the powerful, pulsing currents that went through my head in waves. The energy was very pleasant, and I gave myself over to it for a fairly long time. Finally I opened my eyes, shook my head and said, "That's amazing! What is this stuff!"

"Phenacite," the stranger said. "You should go out to the show and find some of this."

I turned around to look at Hazel, and she was already beaming at me, "See? I told you!"

So, as soon as I could, I left the room and scoured the show for Phenacites. In those early years, it was much more available from stone dealers than it is today. I purchased as many pieces as we could afford (which was not very many back then!) and we took them back to our shop when the show in Tucson was over. Phenacites were immediately popular with our

PHENACITES, TOP TO BOTTOM: Golden Brazilian; Large African (1kg); Nigerian; Madagascar Phenacite Wand

PHENACITES, ABOVE: Nigerian, Russian
LEFT, TOP: Russian with Green Alexandrite, BOTTOM: Rare orange,
OPPOSITE: Azozeo Phenacite Crystals

customers, especially those who were relatively further along the path of working with stone energies.

The synchronicities that led me to Phenacite seemed more modest than the amazing events that brought Moldavite into my life and opened up the pathway to my life's work. But, in a sense, I felt they were related. I had come to believe that bringing Moldavite into the public eye was a "soul task" I had taken on for this lifetime, and both Kathy and I worked hard to introduce people to it. After we had worked with Moldavite for a couple of years, the Phenacite arrived. I used to say, "The universe gave me a job to do with Moldavite. I guess we got it started well enough, so they sent me another stone to bring out."

That was a little over thirty years ago, and I'm still crazy about Phenacites! In fact, I have been collecting them (as well as selling them) for all of those three decades.

In the ensuing years, I've sought out Phenacites from all over the world. My first pieces were Brazilian Phenacites, found in a gold mine in Minas Gerais. These are roughly disc-shaped crystals from two to thirty millimeters in diameter. There was a good supply of these in Brazil at one time, but they are now only found in collections.

During the 1990s a number of Golden Phenacites from Madagascar were sold in the mineral marketplace. These Phenacites were wand-shaped, and their energies flowed most strongly along the long axis and out the terminations. They were very powerful and very popular. I am lucky to have saved a few crystals for my collection, because this variety suddenly became unavailable, and no new pockets of them have been discovered.

This same kind of pattern occurred a few years later with the beautiful and powerful wand-shaped Burmese Phenacites. After an initial flush of availability following their discovery, these crystals became rare, and are seldom seen in the market.

Other varieties that have appeared include tetrahedral Phenacites from Colorado, water-clear Phenacites from Namibia, Black Tourmaline Phenacites from Zambia, Elestial Phenacites from Nigeria, and the roughly-shaped but powerful Russian Phenacites. All of these

offer the kind of energy currents I have described, each with its own special "flavor." None of the Phenacite crystals that emerged between 1988 and 2009 have been very large. By 2003, the largest Phenacite in my collection was a beautiful ball of African Phenacite with Black Tourmailine, about the size of a small grapefruit.

My passion for Phenacites never faded, and I did my best to follow the advice Hazel had given me decades ago—to "stockpile" them. But Phenacites were always hard to find and easy to sell, so my only stockpile is my personal collection.

My spiritual "romance" with Phenacite continued like this for more than twenty years. Then things suddenly took a huge leap when I encountered a new discovery of Phenacite crystals from Brazil. These eventually came to be named the Azozeo Phenacites.

And that is a long story, but I will try to tell it in brief.

In January 2009, we were at the Tucson Gem and Mineral Show, exhibiting and selling our stones, and doing some buying from other vendors. I was walking through the lobby of one of the hotels that hosted a mineral show, passing a stack of glass cases that were being used to display sample specimens from the many different vendors who had showrooms throughout the hotel.

As I walked past, I felt a strange energy "grab" me by the ankle! The effect was strong, almost as if something had slipped an etheric rope around my foot. I turned around and looked down to the cubicle glass case on the floor.

In the case was a cloudy, golden-white crystal about the size of my head. It was naturally terminated and seemed to have a bit of Black Tourmaline attached in a few spots. I immediately sensed what it was, though I couldn't believe my eyes. "Could that possibly be a Phenacite?" I said to myself. I had never seen or heard of any Phenacite crystal that was even near that size.

I read the card beside the crystal and sought out the importer of this stone. He confirmed that it was Phenacite, from a new discovery in a Brazilian Emerald mine. He had only this one huge crystal, plus a few small pieces from the same find.

Of course, I asked if I could hold the stone and tune into it. (After all, it had grabbed me by the ankle!) It was love at first vibe. I had never felt any stone that was as immensely powerful and as deeply loving as this Phenacite. The Being of the stone was different from any that I had encountered before. It felt more individually alive than any stone I had met until that time. And it seemed as if this Stone Being was an angel, or was at an equal level of consciousness to the angels.

THIS PAGE
RIGHT: Azozeo Phenacite Faceted Gems, **BELOW:** Azozeo Phenacites with Black Tourmaline

OPPOSITE, TOP: Azozeo Phencites with Pink Color, **BELOW, LEFT:** Azozeo Phenacites, Champaign Color. **RIGHT:** Azozeo Phenacites

Unfortunately, it was also the most expensive stone I had ever held.

I had no intention of buying the Phenacite crystal, even though I instantly loved it. But I prevailed upon the stone dealer to allow me to take it back to the Heaven and Earth showroom and let my wife and co-workers feel it.

Every single person on our staff went head-over-heels for this Phenacite. All of them were able to sense its power, and most of them commented that holding it filled them with beautiful inner light and loving energies. Several of staff members sat down to hold the stone and meditate, and all of them were in tears after a few minutes. Sarla, a female staffer who usually did not feel stone energies, was particularly delighted. She lay down on the showroom floor holding the huge Phenacite on her belly, laughing for joy. Everyone agreed that the energies of this Stone Being were very beautiful.

Then all our workers ganged up on me and insisted that I must buy this Phenacite. I was tempted. I felt profoundly attracted to it, and I could feel it communicating with me on the vibrational level.

Finally my wife Kathy turned to me and said, "I'm going to buy this for you, Robert. It's important for your work in the future. I can see that you are going to work with it, and it is going to open up a whole new area for you."

Needless to say, I gratefully (and a little tearfully) accepted. I could feel that Kathy's words about the potential of working with this crystal were true.

We ended up purchasing the giant Phenacite and all of the smaller ones in the vendor's inventory, bringing them to our own showroom and displaying them. During the next two weeks while the show was going on, we encouraged people to sit down and hold the "Grandmother Phenacite," as we had begun to call her.

I saw many faces light up with joy as they held this Phenacite, and a number of them broke into tears as well. We were told multiple times that this crystal carried a powerful and profoundly loving angelic presence. Several of the smaller Phenacites were chosen and purchased from us by people who connected with them.

We'll jump ahead now to the summer of 2009. I had been meditating with the Grandmother Phenacite for a few months, and I felt that it had done a lot of work with me. It activated my third eye, crown chakra and the etheric chakras above my head to a higher degree than they had ever reached before. Holding the crystal always made me feel happy and at peace, and I could sense and see inwardly that it was filling me with spiritual Light. I also knew that it was healing my emotional body, and this was a wonderful gift.

Yet I was unsure about whether this was all that was possible. I kept remembering Kathy's statement that this Phenacite would "open up a whole new area." I often wondered about what this might be, and how I should go about addressing it.

During the same time period, I was continuing my work with Azeztulite. It is another stone of astonishingly high vibrations, and we had been distributing various types of Azeztulite for quite a few years. From the beginning, I had been aware of the powerful potential of Azeztulite and its role on the Earth's transformational awakening. These visions of Azeztulite's destined role in the world had come through in the very first channelings about it. Yet for all that I felt from Azeztulite, and for all the good it had already done for people, I wondered if more was possible.

I sat one day on the deck outside my house, thinking about Azeztulite and it's potential as I gazed at the Azeztulite stone labyrinth we had built in our yard, beside a waterfall. (Photos of this labyrinth are shown in Chapters 19, 21 and 31.) Suddenly, I had a vision—an image that came to me unbidden. I inwardly saw the Azeztulite-Rosophia labyrinth in front of me, with a large copper pyramid in the center. I knew intuitively that the copper pipes were filled with Azeztulite and Rosophia. On top of the pyramid, I envisioned my second-largest Phenacite, the grapefruit-sized one. The Grandmother Phenacite would be placed on the ground at the very center of both the pyramid and the labyrinth. There would be a small square table inside the pyramid, with its surface between the two Phenacites.

The purpose of setting up this pyramid inside the labyrinth came to me along with the vision. This environment, my inner guidance told me, would be capable of bringing Azeztulite stones to a level I now call Super-Activation. It basically means that the Azeztulites become more powerful, and that they are more able to manifest their full potential—as well as the spiritual potential of ourselves and the Earth.

Within the next several days, I constructed the pyramid, placing it, the Phenacites and the small table as my vision had dictated. Shortly thereafter, I tried out an intuitively directed experimental process, hoping to see whether the energies of Azeztulite would change. With the sudden vision of the Phenacite-powered "charging station" for Azeztulites, I had glimpsed the beginning of the "whole new area" Kathy had foreseen.

There is much more to this story, including the way that the Grandmother Phenacite and all the rest of the Phenacite crystals discovered in that Brazilian Emerald mine came to be called Azozeo Phenacites. However that is also a part of the Azeztulite story, which we will explore in the next chapter.

People who are highly sensitive to stone energies have sometimes told us about their encounters with the Being of Azozeo Phenacite. Here is an excerpt from a letter I received from someone who saw a photograph of an Azozeo Phenacite and had this type of inner experience:

> *I connected with a creature called "Mother Phenacite" and she explained the light body mission for the planet. I taped my favorite chunk of Phenacite to my Heart/Higher Heart chakra. She showed me how every Phenacite is a portal to the Deva, Elohim. She says it's time to help with the ascension of humanity. She seems to be doing her own* AZOZEO *upgrade to my clear quartz pieces, giving them a subtle gold sheen. It felt like pure divine Love. I used*

Robert with Azozeo Grandmother Phenacites, OPPOSITE, LEFT: Brazilian Phenacite, Disc Crystal; RIGHT: Small Brazilian Phenacite Crystals

Iolite, and Mother Phenacite says to seek out Robert Simmons for my next step of initiation. This blows my mind, I have communed and "talked" to countless crystals, but Mother Phenacite was the first to mention your name.

In the years since 2009, we have continued to encourage the miners in Brazil to seek out more of the Azozeo Phenacites, and we have had some success. Two more very large Phenacites have been discovered, one of which "grabbed" me in the same way as the Grandmother Phenacite did. I now work with both of them every day, primarily for bringing Light into my subtle body. At times, I also meditate with them and receive information. As I was writing this chapter, I sat with the Grandmother and two other Azozeo Phenacites, and I received the most profound and detailed message that has come to me so far.

AZOZEO PHENACITE SPEAKS

In September of 2019, our miners in Brazil came to us with the largest array of Azozeo Phenacites we had yet had the chance to acquire. The pieces came in a wide range of sizes, from tiny bits to pocket size crystals to several large crystals (though not as large as the Grandmother). We were thrilled at their arrival, and our excitement was increased when we learned that this batch also included about two hundred transparent faceted gems. We had never seen gem quality pieces of Azozeo Phenacite before, and had not expected that we ever would.

For Phenacites of any type, this was a "mother lode." For such a glorious batch of Azozeo Phenacites to come to us was more than amazing. We named this group, the Great Mother Lode, in honor of the Being of Azozeo Phenacite.

When I work meditatively with stones, I practice what the 16th century alchemist Paracelsus called "Alchemical Meditation." As I have mentioned, Paracelsus described this meditation as: "An Internal Talk of one person with another who is invisible, as in the invocation of the Deity, or communion with one's self, or with one's good angel." I have been having these kinds of conversations with the Stone Beings for many years, and this is where the information in my books comes from. I also teach others how to do this in my workshops.

In this meditative conversation with the Being of Azozeo Phenacite, I received information about the beneficial qualities of its energies. These are in regard to the Subtle Body, which we have considered earlier in this book. The Subtle Body can be viewed as another name for what many of us refer to as the Light Body, although I like to distinguish them by saying that the Light Body appears when the Subtle Body's potential is fully activated.

I will let the Great Mother Phenacite speak here as I heard her inwardly:

Human life and all life—including the life of stones—involves the intertwining of one's Spiritual Signature or Divine Essence with the physical embodiment or material form. In

this entwinement, a third thing is brought into being. This is what is known as the Subtle Body—the "body" of each individual soul. As individuals, your most important task is to develop and embody yourself as a soul, which entails the process of consciously building and strengthening your Subtle Body. The Subtle Body is also the body that lives on after death, so bringing it into its optimal state is very important. The more fully developed the Subtle Body becomes, the stronger and more fully aware one can be as a soul, after the physical incarnation is over.

In this embodiment as Azozeo Phenacite, I offer much love and Subtle Body nourishment to my human partners. My currents resonate with Divine Love in a way that infuses Divine Light into the Subtle Body field, and can bring a much greater awareness. This is not a process that takes place all at once, but you will be able to feel its onset immediately. There is a feeling of profound pleasure in receiving the currents I offer. This pleasure has to do with the experience of the expansion and unfolding of your Subtle Body. It is as if you are a flower that begins to bloom.

If you work with me frequently and sincerely, you will find yourself awakening to the realization that you are much more than you had imagined. I do not mean that you are "special," since all human souls are greater than your surface selves have understood. But I do mean that you are meant to function in a consciousness that is rooted in the Subtle Body more than in the physical form. As you nourish your Subtle Body through living a life of truth, and through receiving what I and many Crystalline Beings are offering to you, you will experience your center of awareness shifting into a new "location" in the realm of Energy and Image within which your Subtle Body is growing. In this domain, all forms are embodiments of meaning. This is why it is important to live a life of truth, because truth is an organizing force around which your Subtle Body can crystallize.

It is also helpful to practice working with imagination to develop the understanding of symbols and their meanings, because in the Subtle Body realm, Beings appear as images and energies which continually express meaning in symbolic renderings. You might say that this is the way we "talk," except that in this realm there is only truth, because the symbolic "talk" is the manifested imagery of our state of being.

In the physical realm, there is a natural stability that is given to you, because the forms of things do not change rapidly. In the Subtle Body realm, changes in consciousness manifest immediately as changes in image and energy. Again, this is why truth and a strong imaginative awareness are important. They become your means of orienting and organizing your awareness.

I and all the Crystalline Beings are aligned with the Purpose of the Earth. In a way, we are all vibrational expressions of the Earth's Purpose. By "purpose," I refer to a desire so deep that it merges completely with the Earth's identity. The Purpose of the Earth—her fiery desire—is

OPPOSITE, LEFT: Brazilian Phenacite, RIGHT: Fine Brazilian Phenacite
THIS PAGE, TOP LEFT: Azozeo Phencites with Pink Color,
RIGHT: Phenacites from Madagascar, MIDDLE: Burmese Phenacite with flowers, BOTTOM: Madagascar Phenacite

to marry herself to the Light of Heaven in a way that will bring something new to its birth. This birth is what you might call the Divine Child. But it is not a human child, nor a Crystal Child, although the birth of this Child requires enlightenment to spread through the human world, and through the physical Earth. It is the miracle of miracles wherein all matter and all life become both purely physical and purely spiritual at the same time. It is what was referred to symbolically as "resurrection," although it is not about bringing dead bodies back to life. It is about bringing all matter to consciousness, life, Love and Light.

Individual people can play their role in fulfilling the Purpose of the Earth through following their natural processes of spiritual evolution. This is the path upon which you choose to consciously grow, nourish and develop your Subtle Body, and allow your center of awareness to move into its new Mansion—the blossoming of Soul which is your awakened Body of Light. If you do this while still physically alive, you contribute more to the Purpose of the Earth, because your fully awakened Subtle Body—your Body of Light—will be grounded and integrated with your physical incarnation. This same accomplishment is in accord with your individual Soul Purpose, because you are all children of the Earth—expressions of the Earth—and the Earth loves you with shining eyes.

My physical embodiments—the Azozeo Phenacite stones—act as the bridges by which the energies I offer can most readily reach you. For some of you, simply viewing a photo of one of my crystal forms, or even calling to me inwardly, may be enough to establish our connection. This will become easier as more individual people work with me through my physical stone embodiments. This is

because we are building all of this together, and those who practice and engage me through my stones will both benefit themselves and contribute to the field.

The field of the miracle of the Earth's Purpose will be a manifestation in the Subtle Realm. This realm is not only a bridge between Heaven and Earth. It is also the birthing ground for the Divine Child—the budding reality into which the Earth's Purpose is being brought forth. The marriage the Earth seeks, when it is consummated, will vastly expand the Subtle Realm, which will then contain both the physical and spiritual realities within itself—within the ecstatic union of Spirit and Matter in which all will be Love.

When you hold me and invite my energies into yourself, you will feel the "touch" and the "taste" of all that I offer. I invite you to call my energies into yourselves, allowing them to nourish and grow your Subtle Bodies. I also request and hope that you will offer yourselves to the Purpose of the Earth through your interface with me. All you need to do is to offer your intention—your inner YES*—to the Purpose of the Earth, and to give your attention to imagining its fulfillment, in whatever way you wish to do so. Imagine your energies flowing back to me, just as my energies flowed into you. There is no loss in doing this. Indeed, it magnifies what we are creating together.*

As you practice with me, give attention to all that is developing in yourself. Try to notice every sensation that occurs within your Subtle Body. Pour your attention into everything that happens, and allow yourself to "see" the blooming of your soul in whatever imagery comes to you. Allow all of your senses to become more acute and sensitive. Let the discovery of your inner world sharpen your perception and understanding of the physical world, and how it is pervaded by meaning. My energies will assist you in doing all of this.

Part of my intention and purpose is to awaken and enhance the Light that is waiting in many other stones. If you are working with me, you may join me in this by bringing me into their presence and creating a ritual for their greater activation.

Let go. Surrender all fear and inner tension, relaxing and luxuriating in the Light and Love that is offered to you through me. Imagine that you are like a butterfly in its cocoon, transforming in every cell, becoming a new kind of being. For this is indeed what is occurring!

OPPOSITE, TOP: Azozeo Phenacite Small Crystals, **BOTTOM LEFT:** Nigerian; **RIGHT:** Azozeo Phenacite Crystals, Fine Quality

THIS PAGE, LEFT: Small Russian Phenacite Crystals, **RIGHT:** Russian Phenacite Crystal

My vibrational name, Azozeo, invokes your Ascension, and the Ascension of the Earth. My energy is this word, in pure vibrational form. When you feel my presence through my vibrations, you may speak the word Azozeo, whisper it, or say it in your heart, and my energy will grow within you.

I am one face of the Great Mother. My eyes shine upon you and my love bathes you. Come to me.

I was rather astonished by the declarations and invitations that came through from the Being of Azozeo Phenacite. Yet they were all in accord with my experiences with these remarkable crystals. In fact, this transmission greatly expanded my own awareness of what has been occurring within myself as I worked with the Azozeo Phenacites over the past ten years. I personally affirm everything that was said above, because my heart is shouting "YES!" inside my chest, even as I write these words.

All of this makes clear to me that the emergence of the Great Mother Lode of Azozeo Phenacites came at the synchronistically perfect moment. She is here to aid us, and we are here to help her to fulfill the Purpose of the Earth, which feels to me like my own heart's deepest and most fervent desire.

All of the Four Cornerstones of the Alchemy of Stones are intimately intertwined with one another. However, there is a truly exceptional relationship between the Phenacites and the Azeztulites. In the next chapter, we will dive deeply into the Azeztulite story, and we will see how Phenacite played an activating role for Azeztulite, even before the first Azeztulite arrived!

31

Azeztulite: The Third Cornerstone

The beings with whom I am communicating are part of a society of interdimensional, extraterrestrial beings, and they have said we may call them the Azez. From what I understand, their reason for being centers on anchoring the "Nameless Light" onto planets and into societies coming under the influence of that energy. The word "Azez" seems to mean both "Nameless Light" and the embodiment of that Light in the universe, which is the Great Central Sun. The stone Azeztulite is not only for communication with the Azez, it also holds and channels the energy of the "Nameless Light" and its manifestation from the Great Central Sun. These beings have bases all over the world at energy centers known and unknown to us, including the Andes, the Himalayas, the Adirondacks and other mountain ranges.

—Naisha Ahsian describes first contact with the Azez, *Stones of the New Consciousness*

In the Pythagorean and Platonic schools of Hellenistic Alexandria, the sun came to be regarded as the doorway linking together the sensible and intelligible spheres, the material and spiritual orders of existence.

—David Fideler, *Jesus Christ, Sun of God*

The sun is the soul of all things; all has proceeded out of it and will return to it, which shows that the sun is meant allegorically here, and refers to the central, invisible Divine Sun.

—Helena Blavatsky, *Isis Unveiled*

The [Philosophers'] Stone of victory can penetrate and conquer all solid things and every precious stone . . . In addition, the Stone of victory receives a new name pronounced by the mouth of the Lord

—Jeffrey Raff, PhD, *The Wedding of Sophia*

This is its name, Azozeo.

—*The Books of Ieou* (ancient Gnostic text)

In my thirty-five years of working spiritually with minerals, crystals and gems, no stone has played a greater role—or arrived in a more unusual way—than Azeztulite. In terms of the Alchemy of Stones, Azeztulite could almost be seen as the physical incarnation of the Philosophers' Stone, because the stone itself embodies the transformation of the Earth that is occurring before our eyes. And the energies emanated by Azeztulite can be transformative to us as well.

AZEZTULITE APPEARS

There is no way to explain Azeztulite without telling a personal story. Azeztulite emerged and came into the world of crystal lovers through a series of inner communications and synchronicities that began in 1991. One autumn afternoon, Kathy and I received a telephone call from Naisha Ahsian, who was working with two other women doing spiritual channeling, She told us that she and her two friends had been in communication with a group-soul angelic being. Through this telepathic contact, they had been directed to have a special piece of jewelry made for one of the women. It was to contain five powerful stones—Moldavite, Tanzanite, Danburite, Phenacite and Azeztulite. We were excited about making the piece, but we had to tell Naisha we had never heard of Azeztulite.

She answered that the beings communicating with her said that if our company did not yet have the stone, we would soon. According to the beings, Azeztulite was a stone that already existed on Earth, but it had not yet been energetically activated or awakened to its full potential and spiritual purpose. She went on to say that the term "Azeztulite" is a spiritual name, and that the beings themselves were called Azez. They told Naisha that this stone would become a very important tool for Lightworkers. Naisha described the new stone we were asked to seek, She said it would be colorless or white and irregularly shaped, not like the prismatic crystals of Quartz and other minerals with which we were familiar.

The tale of Azeztulite is full of synchronicities, and I want to recount some of them, to convey the feeling of mystery and numinosity that pervades our twenty-eight year saga with these stones.

After speaking with Naisha, we agreed to look for stones that might turn out to be the prophesied Azeztulite. Over the next few weeks I called crystal suppliers and browsed rock-hound magazines, looking for stones that might match Naisha's description. My searching seemed to be going nowhere. Every week or so, Naisha called to check in, but I had nothing to report. During the same week Naisha first contacted us, we were hosting some friends visiting from Arizona. One of them fell in love with a large Phenacite crystal I kept on my desk, but she decided it was too expensive for her to buy. After she returned home at the end of the week, she called us to say that she just couldn't live without the stone and asked if we would sell it to her. I agreed, and after hanging up I went to my office desk to get the stone. However, the Phenacite was missing.

We looked for the stone for days, literally taking our offices apart trying to find it. After a few weeks I gave up searching, though I kept hoping to recover it. At that point I received one of Naisha's calls. I told her that I hadn't found the Azeztulite, but I had lost a big Phenacite. I asked her to try to tune in psychically to help me find it.

Two days later Naisha called again. She said, "I have interesting news. The Azez have told me that they 'borrowed' your Phenacite, and that they are using it to complete the activation of the new stone, Azeztulite." She went on to say that although the Azeztulite already existed on Earth and had begun its activation, the Azez were still working to maximize the stones' potential.

The Azez, Naisha explained, in serving the Nameless Light emanated by the Great Central Sun, travel the universe seeking planets nearing the threshold of spiritual awakening, and they facilitate the awakenings by "energetically engineering" a native stone from each planet to carry the frequencies of the Nameless Light. If inhabitants of the planet utilize the stone with the intention of opening to this inner Light, they will receive its currents and become carriers of the Light, grounding it in their planet and seeding its awakening. Because Azeztulite was to be attuned to frequencies that overlap with the vibrations carried by Phenacite, the Azez had "borrowed" my Phenacite crystal. Naisha told us that at the moment my Phenacite was not in the physical world, but the Azez had promised to return it when they were finished with it. "Look for it in a box, in an odd place," she added.

Even though I was a crystal-loving New Age entrepreneur, that story was pretty wild for me. (At least it was in 1991—my worldview has evolved since then!) However, we did look in every box we had, to no avail. Over the next two months we moved our office to a new building, but even all our packing and unpacking did not reveal the missing Phenacite. Nor did the predicted Azeztulite appear.

Then, in the month of May, we received a package from a North Carolina rockhound. It contained about two pounds of odd-looking crystal shards. The note inside explained that the man had seen an ad I placed looking for sources of Phenacite. He had dug up these crystal fragments twenty-five years earlier, believing them to be Phenacite, but he had kept them in his garage for all those years. Suddenly, when he saw my ad, he got the impulse to sell his cache of stones.

I was strongly attracted to the stones, which carried a very high vibration and powerfully stimulated my third eye chakra. I performed a specific gravity test, which indicated that the stones were not Phenacite. They did, however, match the specific gravity of Quartz. I considered returning them because the rockhound was asking a high price, far more than the usual cost of Quartz. However, the stones' powerful energies intrigued me, and I decided to call Naisha. When she arrived at our office, she took a moment to touch the stones. Then she turned to me and said, "This is the Azeztulite. You have to buy it."

From that point, things evolved quickly. We purchased the stones in that first box and made the jewelry piece for Naisha's friend. Azeztulite was also immediately popular with our other customers. Over the next ten years, we bought all the Azeztulite the rockhound had discovered, and had kept in his garage since 1966. I theorized that the stones may not have always had the powerful currents they now carry, and that they had only recently been activated by the Azez.

Another surprising event occurred the same week that the first Azeztulites arrived. One morning I reached down below my desk, putting my hand into a wooden message box as I did every day when checking my phone messages at our office. On this day there was more than paper in the box. My fingers touched something hard. When I pulled out the object, it was a stone—the Phenacite that had disappeared three months earlier!

It was quite an astonishing moment. I used that message box every day, and I was certain the stone had not been there before. It seemed the Azez had kept their word, returning my Phenacite right after the newly awakened Azeztulite arrived. And the stone was found—as the Azez had foretold—in a box, in an odd place! My wife pointed out the humorous implication of the particular spot where the Phenacite was found: "It was in your *message* box. It's as if they're saying, 'Do you get the message?'"

But the tale is not over yet. Several days later, as I left the office to go home, I noticed a bright, transparent stone on the steps. I picked it up and examined it. It appeared to be an Azeztulite, and it carried the same energies, but it was larger than anything that had been inside our box from the rockhound. I showed the stone to Naisha and asked her what she thought about it. Once again, she consulted the Azez. The next day she called with their answer: "They say to tell you that the stone on the steps was something they left for you—it's 'interest' for the loan of your Phenacite."

This incident opened my mind to another paradigm-shifting implication. At face value, what happened suggests that the Azez are capable of taking a physical stone—my Phenacite—into their realm and returning it. Not only that, the stone found on our steps seemed to indicate that they can also precipitate an Azeztulite into this world.

As I ponder this now, it seems clear to me that the Azez were operating from, and existing within, the subtle/imaginal realm we have discussed throughout this book. It is the place where the spiritual and physical worlds overlap, and it has some of the qualities of each domain. This is where our own subtle bodies are anchored—what the poet-philosopher Novalis called the Seat of the Soul. And, as we have discussed, I believe this is where the Stone Beings are when they are energetically engaged with us.

I mentioned in the Moldavite chapter that stones can sometimes disappear and reappear, as Moldavites are known to do. As we explore the subtle/imaginal realm and develop deeper relationships with the Stone Beings and the Soul of the World, we are likely to see more such phenomena. The alchemists addressed this realm directly, and it was here that they inwardly performed the operations they intended to also manifest in the physical world. Those of us who work with the Stone Beings for the transformation of the Earth are now extending the path that they began.

Let's go back to the Azeztulite story.

A few weeks after the first Azeztulites arrived, Naisha brought us a new transmission from the Azez:

> *Interdimensional travel involves "pulses" of energy in the universe. These pulses act as bridges. When we travel through many dimensions, the energy pulses cause disruptions—making it difficult for us to communicate with other bases in other dimensions and on other planets. Here enters the stone Azeztulite. It is used by us in creating channels for our communications with other bases. On each base or planet we inhabit we have chosen a stone to be the anchor for these channels.*
>
> *After some manipulation and alteration, we engineered the stone Azeztulite. It has the capacity to handle the intense energies being carried by it. Until recently, we did not have the technology to engineer a vessel to contain this energy frequency. Azeztulite is that vessel. In our culture, "Azez" is the term for that which is the "Nameless Light," the embodiment of which is the Great Central Sun. Please understand the implications of what we are explaining. This stone is the embodiment of the Azez and carries with it the manifest energy of the Great Central Sun. This is a powerful stone. This stone heralds many changes! This stone will enable those of you who are telepathic "windows" and dimensional engineers to begin to reclaim the knowledge of these practices from your genetic memory banks. We will now begin to make ourselves known more fully to those beings to aid in this awakening and transformation.*
>
> *Disease on your planet is the result of certain frequencies of light. You block cellularly these light waves through thought-form shields and contracting emotional patterns. Your cellular consciousnesses are therefore unable to properly learn and expand, resulting in disease. Azeztulite carries energies and frequencies of Light that help release the shields and blocks, healing disease and aiding in cellular rejuvenation and expansion. Likewise, its activation at certain points on your planet will aid in healing the total organism of Gaia.*

In the last line above, we see that the agenda of the Azez involves healing the Earth and the human race, through bringing in the Nameless Light of the Great Central Sun. This idea is resonant with the "solar work" described in the Emerald Tablet of ancient alchemy, which we discussed in the previous chapter. The purpose of the Azez also brings to mind the goal of the alchemists as described by Paul Levy—"to redeem the entire cosmos." These were the amazing and rather lofty possibilities that came to us when the Azeztulite arrived.

Since our initial encounter with Azeztulite I have seen thousands of people connect with the different varieties of this stone. At trade shows I have recounted the tale of Azeztulite's discovery countless times, yet telling the story still excites me. And I have often seen people experience such profound contact and recognition at their first encounter with Azeztulite that they were in tears.

One recurrent phenomenon around Azeztulite is head-to-toe, full-body goose bumps. I have learned to associate these with the invisible presence of the Azez. That is because the sensation inevitably comes when I speaking to someone about the story of Azeztulite. At some

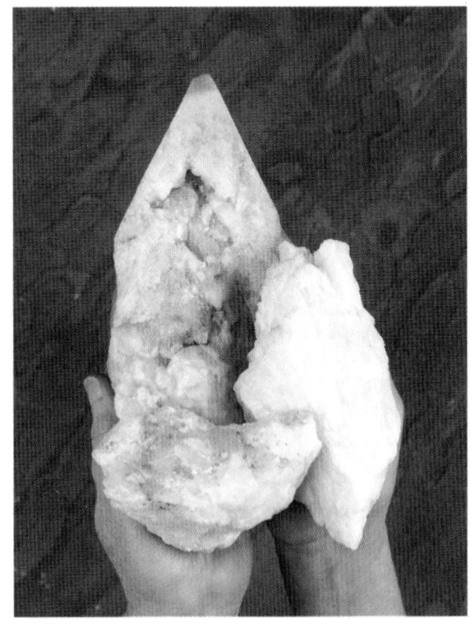

point during the story, either I, the other person, or both of us (in some cases as many as four people at once) get a sudden rushing current of vibration in the body, which brings on all-over goose bumps. It is as though the Azez are called to us when we speak of them, or perhaps they come because they want to facilitate the connection that is occurring. This has been happening for almost three decades, almost every time I tell the Azeztulite story.

Naisha's original messages stated that the Azez were stationed etherically in power spots around the Earth, and that over time, as more people worked with Azeztulite and brought more of the Nameless Light into the world, more Azeztulite would be activated and then discovered. This caused me to keep my eyes open for new manifestations of Azeztulite, from different parts of the world. And indeed, this prediction from the Azez has come to pass. As of this writing, twenty different varieties of Azeztulite have been discovered in different countries around the world. All of them emanate the signature energies of Azeztulite, yet every type also has its own unique qualities. Later in this chapter, I will include photos and information for each of them.

But before we get there, we need to return to the Azozeo story that I began in the previous chapter.

AZOZEO AZEZTULITE

I have long been intrigued by the connection of Azeztulite to the Great Central Sun. As I wrote earlier in this book, the stone Moldavite once took me on an initiatory journey to that spiritual Sun, and that was the day when I first experienced the currents of the stones.

Early in 2009 I was seeking information online regarding Azeztulite. I wanted to see what other people were saying about it, and whether anyone else was communicating with the Azez. Late one night, I happened upon an obscure website that mentioned an enigmatic word: *Azozeo.* The text said the word came from the ancient Coptic Gnostic gospel, the *Books of Ieou,* and that Azozeo meant "light passing through a crystal." I was, of course, quite excited to find such a reference from a writer not involved with the metaphysical uses of stones, and who had never heard of Azeztulite.

That was all I could find until I came upon the source of the quote, a book by David Fideler entitled *Jesus Christ, Sun of God.* The spelling of the word Sun was of key significance. I ordered the book and discovered in it dozens of mind-bending references to the Great Central Sun and its meaning in various ancient spiritual traditions. As the title of the book implies, Jesus Christ was envisioned as a personification of the Logos, as the Son of the Great Central Sun.

Fideler's book contained only one page from *The Books of Ieou.* ("Ieou" is in this case an alternate spelling of the name Jesus.) *The Books of Ieou* is one of the most unusual and least studied manuscripts of early Christianity. It contains not only text but diagrams relating to Ieou as "the true god." Fideler tells us that elsewhere in this text, "Jesus reveals to his disciples the magical names, numbers, and seals they will need in the afterlife ascent to the realm of Light." He then gives the following example of Jesus' instructions:

When you reach the fourth aeon, Samaelo and Chochochoucha [archons of limitation] will come before you. Seal yourself with this seal:

This is its name: Azozeo.

Say it once only. Hold this cipher: 4555 in your hands. When you have finished sealing yourself with this seal and you have said its name once only, say these defences also: "Withdraw yourselves Samaelo and Chochochoucha, you archons of the fourth aeon, because I call upon Zozeza, Chozozazza, Zazezo."

When you have finished saying these defenses the archons of the fourth aeon will withdraw to the left. But you [will] proceed upward.

These instructions appear arcane to say the least, but I was struck by the similarity of the names of the angelic protectors to the name Azez. The last one, Zazezo, even contains the word Azez. If one were to imagine a group name for these three—Zozeza, Chozozazza, Zazezo—it is plausible that Azez would be a good choice. It is interesting that their role is to assist human souls in the process of spiritual ascension. This is what the Azez are attempting to do with us now. It is also important to recall that the instructions are purportedly coming from Ieou, or Jesus, whose mythic role is that of the Son of the Sun, the personification of the Great Central Sun—the Logos.

In communicating with Naisha, the entities described themselves as a group soul angelic being, whom we could call Azez. It is a small (though rather astonishing) leap to imagine that the Azez, a group of angels who serve the Light of the Great Central Sun, could be identical with the entities whom Jesus—the personification of the Light of the Great Central Sun—instructed his followers to call upon. And what a synchronicity that I should come upon this while researching Azeztulite!

Following this golden thread, we can envision that the Azez have long served the Light, and they may have been stewards of human evolution for millennia.

The facts we do know are just as astonishing as these speculations. Here are the Azeztulite stones, which were predicted to arrive, which were activated by spiritual entities whose avowed purpose is to serve the Light, and we can feel in our own bodies the powerful currents entering us through the stones. As promised, more varieties of Azeztulite have been found. We are told that the goal is for all the Quartz on Earth to awaken to these currents. Many of us have glimpsed the vision of the Earth as a Planet of Light. Our hearts urge us toward that vision, and, through working with the Azeztulites and the other Cornerstones of the Alchemy of Stones, we can help to make it so.

There is a bit more to the story, in regard to the word Azozeo. Recall, or look back to the story of Azozeo Phenacites that I told in the previous chapter. I was working intensely with several varieties of Azeztulite at that time, and I had been pondering whether it might be possible to

William Blake's painting, *The Angels Appearing to the Shepherds* symbolically depicts what we might envision as an angelic group soul such as the Azez, appearing in the psychoid/imaginal realm

somehow bring the Azeztulites to a higher level of activation. Then I suddenly received the vision of the copper pyramid in the center of the Azeztulite labyrinth. The vision also showed me that I needed to place my largest Phenacite on the ground at the center of the pyramid base, and to attach my second largest Phenacite at the pyramid's apex. There was to be a table in between the Phenacites, and its surface would be where I was to place Azeztulites to be charged and super-activated.

I was excited by the vision and knew that I would do what it had shown me. I intuitively understood that Phenacites were the ideal stones to help bring all of the Azeztulites to their highest vibrational potential. After all, the Azez had "borrowed" a Phenacite from me to complete the initial Azeztulite activation!

I had also understood that a ritual should be performed as a part of the activation process. My vision showed me that I needed to carry the Azeztulites to be super-activated into the center of the pyramid by first bearing them along the winding labyrinth path. When I arrived, I was to call in the Azez by speaking the word Azozeo. I was shown that I should to speak the word aloud four times, to invoke the Four Elements and the Four Directions. Then I was to silently pronounce the word Azozeo one more time, to invoke the Fifth Direction and the Fifth Element, which the alchemists called the Quintessence. When I constructed the super-activation setup, I added four small signs on the table with the word Azozeo printed on them.

After I performed the ritual for the first time. I left all the stones in the pyramid overnight. When I checked them the next day, the Azeztulites I had placed on the tabletop were definitely more powerful than they had been before. I was thrilled and amazed, and I decided then and there that all of our Azeztulites must undergo this process. It requires quite a bit of time, but we still do this super-activation on all of our Azeztulites, and on several other kinds of stones that we have found to be receptive to it.

The vision and the realization that the super-activation process really works also showed me some of what Kathy had intuitively seen when she told me that she would purchase the huge Phenacite crystal for me. She was right to tell me, "It's important for your work in the future. I can see that you are going to work with it, and it is going to open up a whole new area for you."

Looking back at it all, I felt certain that the Grandmother Phenacite had been key to furthering the mission of Azeztulite, and all that the mission of the Azez implies. I later learned that all the Phenacites from our source in the Brazilian Emerald mine seem to possess this capacity to activate certain other stones to higher vibrational levels. To designate this special capacity, and to invoke it further, we call the Phenacites from this location Azozeo Phenacites.

The Azeztulite story continues to unfold, and in my view, it is the story of the Earth's great transformational awakening into a new way of being. And it is ours as well. As we move forward into consideration of each of the twenty varieties discovered thus far, let us remember that the goal of the Azez is to activate *all the Quartz in the Earth's crust* to receive and to manifest the currents of the Nameless Light of the Great Central Sun. Twenty-five percent of the Earth's crust is Quartz. If all of it were emanating Azeztulite energies, I believe that we would indeed experience the Earth as a Planet of Light.

And when this happens, I hope I remember to say, "Azozeo."

A participant in one of my workshops made this drawing of the Azez, as he saw them during an Azeztulite meditation. They remind me vividly of the Azez that I saw in my dream, who cheerfully advised me to "dance or die!"

WHITE AZEZTULITE (ORIGINAL)

KEY WORDS Inner Light, joy and serenity, DNA and Light Body Activation, Vibrational Ascension, spiritual awakening, link with the Nameless Light, meetings with the Azez **ELEMENT** Storm **CHAKRAS** All (including the etheric chakras above the body)

White Azeztulite is the first Azeztulite discovered. It was found originally in North Carolina and later in Vermont, USA. White Azeztulite is a silicon-dioxide mineral with a hexagonal (trigonal) crystal system and a hardness of 7. Most pieces are white, but some are partially or fully transparent.

The currents of White Azeztulite are greatly amplified when the stone is put through the Azozeo super-activation process, taking it to a different and higher vibrational level.

There is nothing else on Earth quite like the original White Azeztulite. More people have connected with this stone than with all the other Azeztulites combined. It is the first earthly material to receive the infusion of the Nameless Light, facilitated by the high angelic beings known as the Azez. White Azeztulite is one of the key elements of the Vibrational Ascension that the Earth and the human species are now beginning to experience.

I recommend meditating first with a White Azeztulite held over one's heart, using one's breath to invite its currents into the heart as one inhales, and offering oneself to the Being of the stone on the exhale. The heart is the center of our energy system and the Seat of the Soul. It is also the place where we connect directly to the Great Central Sun. When White Azeztulite's energies come into the heart, one often feels an emotional response that leads to tears of joy, as one recognizes the Azeztulite's spiritual presence within oneself.

If one holds a White Azeztulite over the third eye, the currents of the stones are often experienced as pulsing high-frequency energy that originates in the spiritual realms of Light. Indeed, seeing light in the interior of the skull is one of the hallmarks of White Azeztulite. Its currents feel like living Light, and are accompanied by deeply pleasurable sensations in the head and body. It is as if one is being sweetly caressed by angelic hands—and these hands work with a purpose, for they are not only there to soothe us but to kindle Light and expansion of awareness.

The presence of White Azeztulite kindles reverence, the sense that one is in the presence of something holy. It brings forward the inner experience of spiritual Light, and through its presence suggests to us a path of Truth to Light. This path must be, and naturally is, followed with an ardent intensity—one might say a "zest." It has been pointed out to me by a friend that the name Azeztulite could be rewritten as "a zest to Light," or an ardent approach to the Inner Light.

White Azeztulite works on the cellular level, stimulating the light-emitting qualities inherent in the DNA. Our DNA, holding the very matrix of life, can be viewed as the portal through which spiritual Light enters our bodies and, through us, the world. The physical light emitted by DNA is the byproduct of the spiritual Light of life that pours through us. White Azeztulite, with its direct link to the Great Central Sun, enhances and increases the flow of this Light within us, and through us into the Earth.

This Nameless Light, according to the Azez, has the capacity to dissolve the patterns of degeneration and disease that are habitual in living organisms. As our Inner Light increases through the work with White Azeztulite, it is possible for us to experience Light Body Activation, which can transform the subtle body, and ultimately illuminate the physical incarna-

tion from within. This incarnated Light, which has existed on Earth only rarely in the past, is akin to the Robe of Glory mentioned by the Gnostics, and it is the ultimate goal of Azeztulite's mission with humanity. On more everyday levels, Azeztulite is a positive emotional influence. It helps keep one's attention on benevolent thoughts and actions, encouraging altruism and compassion. It can dissolve negative attachments that foster depression or anxiety. It cleanses the emotional body, and brings joy and serenity. Wearing a piece of White Azeztulite clears one's auric field and creates a bubble of love, light and beauty that one carries everywhere.

White Azeztulite is a wide-spectrum spiritual healing stone. It can break the hold of any dysfunction or illness brought about by hostile energies in one's environment or by self-negating thought patterns. As White Azeztulite expands awareness and awakens the Body of Light, one can become aware of one's essential immortality, dissolving internal patterns of limitation. By facilitating Vibrational Ascension, White Azeztulite calls forth the unity of body, mind and spirit. Under the influence of these stones, one's wholeness is more readily realized. Crystal healers will prize White Azeztulite as one of their most powerful and effective tools.

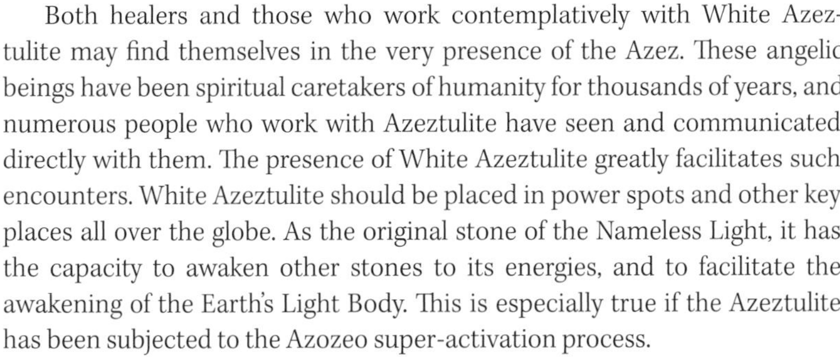

Both healers and those who work contemplatively with White Azeztulite may find themselves in the very presence of the Azez. These angelic beings have been spiritual caretakers of humanity for thousands of years, and numerous people who work with Azeztulite have seen and communicated directly with them. The presence of White Azeztulite greatly facilitates such encounters. White Azeztulite should be placed in power spots and other key places all over the globe. As the original stone of the Nameless Light, it has the capacity to awaken other stones to its energies, and to facilitate the awakening of the Earth's Light Body. This is especially true if the Azeztulite has been subjected to the Azozeo super-activation process.

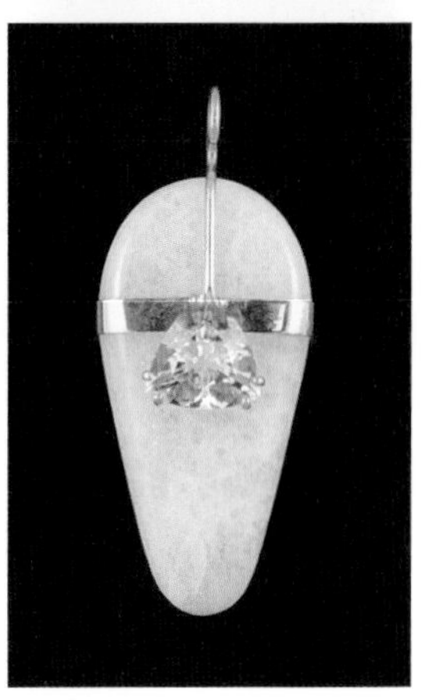

White Azeztulite works harmoniously with all other Azeztulites, as well as all other Synergy Twelve and Ascension Seven stones. It is powerfully resonant with Phenacite (especially Azozeo Phenacite), Petalite, Beryllonite, Tremolite, Vortexite, Vitalite, Natrolite and virtually all high-vibration stones. When one uses White Azeztulite together with Rosophia, their combined currents can bring forth the spiritual union of Heaven and Earth within one's own heart.

SPIRITUAL White Azeztulite pours a flood of spiritual Light into one's consciousness, kindling Light Body Activation leading ultimately to Vibrational Ascension.
EMOTIONAL White Azeztulite cleanses the emotional body, and infuses it with love, compassion, joy, serenity and expansiveness.
PHYSICAL White Azeztulite brings Light into the cells, helping to dissolve any negative patterns that create illness.

BLACK AZEZTULITE

KEY WORDS Light within Darkness, complete transformation, memory of one's divinity, dissolution of negative patterns, protection, infusion of Spiritual Light, alchemical Philosophers' Stone **ELEMENTS** Earth, Wind, Storm **CHAKRAS** All

Black Azeztulite is a combination of quartz and black calcite found only in Vermont, USA. The calcite component of this stone is unusually rich in magnesium. The hardness of the quartz component of this stone is 7, and its crystal system is hexagonal (trigonal). The hardness of the calcite component is 3, and its crystal system is trigonal. Overall, the stone is quite hard, much closer to 7 than 3. Black Azeztulite is found in the same areas where Vermont's White Azeztulite has been discovered. In some instances, the Black Azeztulite is attached to White Azeztulite stones.

The discovery of Black Azeztulite heralds a new chapter in the saga of the penetration of the substance of the Earth and of humanity by the Nameless Light of the Great Central Sun. These stones physically embody the metaphor of the Light within Darkness, and their energies can impart that experience to whoever attunes to these stones.

When I first sat down to meditate with a Black Azeztulite, I was taken completely by surprise as I felt its currents. I had been expecting a somewhat softer or more muted version of what I already knew from the White Azeztulites. Instead, I felt a truly awesome power. At first, as I held the stone over my heart and invited it into my field, I experienced waves of energy filling my body with a strong tingling sensation. Next came a feeling of low-level discomfort at several locations on and within my head, especially at the crown chakra. When I inquired inwardly about this, I was shown that the stone was dissolving some inappropriate patterns or attachments, clearing my chakras where they needed it.

As this progressed, the waves of energy grew more powerful and began to resonate within my whole body from head to toe. In my head there appeared the loveliest white Light, beginning as a flash and increasing in intensity. As this continued, I experienced a feeling of wonder and pleasure, and the nearness of something holy. Touching the third eye and crown chakras with the stone increased these sensations. Next, I touched the Mouth of God chakra point at the back of the head, just above the neck. This seemed to be the most powerful placement, and while I held the stone there I was washed inwardly with waves of Light and Power, and began receiving more information about the stone.

Black Azeztulite is a stone of the Midnight Sun. It is related to the huge black hole at the center of our galaxy, and it represents the moment of the singularity, in which all the laws of the universe become fluid and changeable. It is a stone of the Zero Point, and as such it can be a very powerful catalyst for spiritual transformation. When one fully attunes to Black Azeztulite, one can change literally anything about oneself, and can ultimately create profound changes in the outer world as well. Making both sorts of changes involves a commitment of one's will that is free from hesitation or doubt. If one can fully focus in this way, the co-creative potential of working with these stones is unlimited.

As a stone of spiritual self-healing, Black Azeztulite is very powerful indeed. It naturally works to cleanse and clear one's body and energy field of negative energies, disharmonious attachments, implants, psychic parasites and inappropriate karmic patterns. This stone means business! It suggests that it can be applied in the spiritual healing of conditions in which the body attacks itself. Yet its power to dispel what is negative is coupled with an infusion of blissful and even ecstatic Light. This Light reminds us of who and what we truly are, which is the most profound healing of all. To awaken to the real memory that we are emanations of Divinity rather than isolated personalities is perhaps the greatest gift these stones can convey.

The Black Calcite and White Quartz components of Black Azeztulite entwine energetically to offer power and protection to those who work with it. It can help one attune to the Light deep within the heart of the darkest density of matter, and to call to that Light for guidance and assistance. For those working with stones shamanically, Black Azeztulite is a perfect ally. Its Light keeps one safe from the approach of negative entities, allowing one to work on the inner planes without being vulnerable to psychic attack.

Black Azeztulite, even though it is very powerful, is more grounded than some of the other Azeztulites, and it can help sensitive people to take on high vibrations without losing hold of their physical bodies. In fact, Black Azeztulite tends to work on the body so that it can handle much higher and stronger energies than it could before.

On the emotional level, Black Azeztulite is excellent for purging attachments to old emotional wounds, grief, resentment, anger and fear. It reminds the subconscious that the Light and Love of the Divine are always present. These stones are themselves the very embodiments of that presence. In terms of spiritual Alchemy, Black Azeztulite completes the triad of red, white and black, the three major aspects of the Philosophers' Stone. The other two are Red Fire Azeztulite and White Azeztulite. (Sometimes I utilize different stones to represent the three aspects, but these are among my favorites.) Working with these three stones together can open one to experiencing the multiple transformations of self that brought successful alchemical aspirants to enlightenment and the fulfillment of the Great Work on an individual level. However, the simultaneous enlightenment of oneself, the whole of humanity and the Earth itself is the ultimate goal of the alchemical opus. This is the purpose behind the activation of all the Azeztulites, and is the journey that the Azez have invited all of us to take.

Black Azeztulite is especially powerful at times of eclipses or the new moon, and those so inclined are invited to create rituals for receiving and channeling its currents during such events. These stones resonate to the Judgment card of the tarot deck, and as such they are awakeners to the call of one's highest spiritual destiny.

Black Azeztulite combines harmoniously with all other Azeztulites, as well as Master Shamanite, Black Obsidian, Black Jade, Black Tourmaline, Smoky Quartz, Guardianite, Z Stone, Prophecy Stone, Phenacite, Natrolite, Herderite, Brookite, Danburite and Petalite. It responds favorably when subjected to the Azozeo super-activation process.

SPIRITUAL Black Azeztulite clears away all inner obstacles and disharmony, filling the body with Light and Divine Presence. It protects, empowers and awakens.
EMOTIONAL Black Azeztulite aids one in releasing negative emotional attachments, and infuses one with spiritual joy.
PHYSICAL Black Azeztulite can be used for spiritual treatment of conditions in which the body attacks itself.
AFFIRMATION I am the power of Light, existing even in darkness.

RED FIRE AZEZTULITE

KEY WORDS Life Force, enthusiasm, vitality, power, passion, sexuality, etherization of the blood, intelligence, visionary experience, healing, longevity, alchemical transmutation
ELEMENTS Earth, Fire, Storm **CHAKRAS** All

Red Fire Azeztulite is a member of the Azeztulite family, a microcrystalline silicon-dioxide mineral with a hexagonal (trigonal) crystal system and a hardness of 7. It is native to New Zealand, and is deep red in color. Iron inclusions are the primary coloring agent. Red Fire Azeztulite is an unusual stone energetically because its currents are greatly amplified when the stone is put through the Azozeo super-activation process, taking it to a completely different, and higher, vibrational level.

Red Fire Azeztulite is a very powerful stone. Its currents are capable of stimulating and awakening any of the chakras. Its vibrations enter the body wherever one is touching it, and they quickly spread through one's entire energetic system. This makes it a very useful stone for a multitude of applications, from spiritual healing to evolutionary transformation.

Red Fire Azeztulite resonates powerfully with the blood, heart, lungs and circulatory system. It seems to bring its high vibrations directly into the bloodstream, spreading throughout the body and into the tissues as the blood flows. As one experiences this full-body pulsation, it can feel as though spiritual Light and expanded consciousness are filling one's body cell by cell, yet very quickly. One can sense an "inner rejoicing" as the consciousness of the cells is awakened to the presence of the Nameless Light. With this stone, however, there is heat as well as Light—as if an interior Fire has been kindled. With that Fire comes a flood of passion, confidence, optimism and power. One can feel the intensity of energy within oneself like red fire, which is the reason these stones were named Red Fire Azeztulite.

Red Fire Azeztulite carries a tremendous amount of Life Force. It works spiritually to replenish one's strength, endurance and vitality. It is an excellent stone for overcoming fatigue and stress. If one feels depleted or anxious, meditating or sleeping with a Red Fire Azeztulite is highly recommended. This stone also stimulates the pituitary and pineal glands, enhancing their spiritual functions. Thus it is a stone of visionary experience and enhanced capacity for insight. It can help one to access guidance from angelic guides and teachers in the higher realms.

Red Fire Azeztulite is a stone of intense passion. It can stimulate the energy centers linked to sexuality, and can even enhance the sexual currents between partners. It is one of the most powerful 'gemstone aphrodisiacs' if the partners are spiritually linked. It is an excellent stone for those on the tantric path.

Red Fire Azeztulite comes from New Zealand, and it is a perfect complementary partner for the white Sauralite Azeztulite, also from New Zealand. Where Sauralite's energies are gentle, loving, receptive and yin, Red Fire Azeztulite's vibrations tend to be active, assertive and yang.

These are amazing stones for helping one to move forward with one's plans and goals. They aid in manifestation by enhancing one's own power to achieve whatever one desires. These are stones of great intensity, and their currents take one unswervingly toward one's chosen destiny.

The vibrational stimulation provided by Red Fire Azeztulite affects one's intelligence as well. Perhaps these stones stimulate dormant areas of the brain. (One can certainly feel them moving strongly inside one's head!) Whatever the reason, Red Fire Azeztulite appears to get the brain "fired up," increasing one's ability to solve problems and aiding one's access to inspired ideas. It also greatly enhances one's enthusiasm and energy for carrying one's visions forward into manifestation.

As a stone of the bloodstream and body, Red Fire Azeztulite also aids in awakening the intelligence of the cells, organs and bodily systems. This intelligence can develop into another mind—the body-mind—that can dialog with the brain, giving one much greater self-awareness and wisdom. Red Fire Azeztulite also kindles the inner fire of heart intelligence. Thus, it stimulates the activation of the Trinity of Intelligence—of brain, heart and body. This is one of the culminations of the original promise of Azeztulite—to bring Divine Light and Divine Awareness into human beings, and into the Earth through us.

Because Red Fire Azeztulite does so much to bring Light, joy and vitality into the cells, it is a stone for the enhancement of our physical life. My impression is that exposure to Red Fire Azeztulite, especially when combined with one's conscious affirmation and cooperation with its currents, can aid in increasing both the quality and duration of one's life. When one's cellular consciousness awakens and aligns with the Nameless Light, the effect can penetrate all the way into the DNA and its telomeres, bringing greater longevity through greater joy. Red Fire Azeztulite has the capacity to permeate the entire body with its life-affirming currents.

Red Fire Azeztulite has a special relationship with the heart, lungs and bloodstream, and its currents link into the body through those channels. They bring enlightened energies into the blood, and then to all of the tissues in the body. They work to transmute the blood's cellular material into etheric forces that act upon all of the body, and indeed our entire being—physical and nonphysical. This process was called the "etherization of the blood" by the spiritual genius Rudolph Steiner. I feel strongly that Red Fire Azeztulite is a long-awaited catalyst for fulfilling Steiner's vision of the spiritual transformation of humanity through this process.

As a stone of spiritual self-healing, Red Fire Azeztulite resonates beneficially with the heart, lungs and bloodstream, as well as the brain. However, its vibrations can be utilized for any organ or bodily system. This stone's energetic link with the blood means that its currents can move to any part of the body, carrying its blessing vibrations wherever they are needed.

A final word regarding spiritual alchemy: The goal of alchemists through many centuries was the fabled Philosophers' Stone, a magical object or substance with the power of transmutation. It was said to be capable of changing lead into gold, and to transform a mortal human being into an immortal one. It was also believed to be capable of healing any illness. The Philosophers' Stone was envisioned as forming in three different manifestations, of three different colors—red, white and black. The usual progression of evolution was from black (dark, polluted, unevolved energy) to white (noble, spiritual, purified energy) and finally to red (powerful, vital energy, the Spirit in the flesh). Black Azeztulite is capable of helping one to navigate the depths of the first phase of the alchemical process. The original White Azeztulite is resonant with the white aspect of the Philosophers' Stone and its uplifting qualities. Red Fire Azeztulite embodies the fully evolved, grounded and integrated state that represents the final stage of the evolution of the Philosophers' Stone. In the rubedo (red) stage, the spiritual heights and depths one has experienced are transmuted and incorporated into new, revitalized life from a perspective of expanded awareness.

Simply exposing oneself to stones carrying such currents does not accomplish the alchemical work. However, working with Black Azeztulite, White Azeztulite and Red Fire Azeztulite can be of great assistance, providing one with the energetic resonances to stimulate one's evolutionary transformation—through effort, awareness and surrender.

Red Fire Azeztulite carries powerful vibrations in its initial state, just as it comes from the ground. However, when it is subjected to the Azozeo Super-Activation process, its power is multiplied and it becomes almost a whole new stone. (This is transmutation in action!)

Red Fire Azeztulite works synergistically with all other Azeztulites, as well as Master Shamanite, Phenacite, Danburite, Natrolite, Scolecite, Zincite, Crimson Cuprite, New Zealand Carnelian, Rosophia and Morganite. It has an especially powerful resonance with Azozeo Phenacite.

SPIRITUAL Red Fire Azeztulite carries enlightened currents into every cell of the body.
EMOTIONAL Red Fire Azeztulite kindles enthusiasm, confidence, power and optimism. It can stimulate sexual currents between spiritually linked partners.
PHYSICAL Red Fire Azeztulite lends energetic support to every part of the body, and it has a special affinity to the bloodstream, heart, lungs and brain.
AFFIRMATION I act in the world with love and power, kindled by the red fire of my passionate commitment to the Earth and our mutual evolution.

SATYALOKA CLEAR AZEZTULITE

KEY WORDS Spiritual awakening, planetary consciousness, receiving Light and knowledge from the higher planes
ELEMENT Storm **CHAKRAS** Third Eye (6th), Crown (7th), Soul Star (8th), Transpersonal/Etheric (9th through 14th, above the head)

Satyaloka Clear Azeztulite is a transparent variety of Azeztulite from the Satya Loka Mountains of southern India. It is a silicon-dioxide mineral with a hexagonal (trigonal) crystal system and a hardness of 7. Satyaloka Clear Azeztulite forms as small, prismatic crystals and also in massive form. The massive material can be transparent, translucent or white, sometimes with inclusions of reddish-brown or gray. The crystals are colorless, with fogginess at the base end of some pieces, and an occasional reddish coating.

This Azeztulite was originally gathered by monks of the Satya Loka monastery, who sent it into the world as a means of spreading the energy of spiritual enlightenment. The monks believed that this energy is a quality of the mountains where they live, and that the stones are capable of carrying and dispersing this energy throughout the world. The region where Satyaloka Clear Azeztulite is found in South India has been called "the crown chakra of the world." The impression one experiences in meditation with Satyaloka Clear Azeztulite makes it easy to understand how it got this designation.

Satyaloka Clear Azeztulite opens the crown chakra with a tremendous flow of energy. In meditation, one may feel its currents pouring downward through the crown as soon as one picks it up. This happened to me when I first held the stones in my hands, without even placing them near my head. The crown chakra opened, and a cascade of pulsing energy thrust down again and again through the top of my head, all the way to my heart. It extended further, and seemed to be exploring or slowly penetrating the column of my chakras below the heart, with each pulse reaching a little deeper.

Satyaloka Clear Azeztulite placed upon the heart in a pouch produced a deep sense of reverence, an appreciation of the presence of the Holy in my heart. This stone carries very deep currents of what I would term the Holy Silence. It has a direct resonance with the vastness of consciousness at the site of Origin. It opens a stream through which one may venture towards the Source; it is a magnetic feeling, as the Source draws one towards itself. As one gets closer to it, words are left behind, and one is conscious only of the White Light swirling around the central void in a spiraling cloud. One feels as a moth might feel when approaching a flame—even if merging with the center of the flame means annihilation, the moth must propel itself towards that irresistible Light.

Satyaloka Clear Azeztulite is a stone of India, and as such it is soaked in the energy of spiritual aspiration that has prevailed in India for so many centuries. Satyaloka Clear Azeztulite vibrates to the frequency of enlightenment with more intense currents than any other form of Azeztulite. If one wishes to experience the maximum Light infusion possible through Azeztulite, the maximum expansion of consciousness Azeztulite can stimulate, and the maximum intensity of energy currents one can receive through a stone, the best stone to use is Satyaloka Clear Azeztulite.

Although all Azeztulites carry the currents of the Great Central Sun, spiritual core of the holographic universe, Satyaloka Clear Azeztulite is what one might call the most "hard-core" of all Azeztulites—perhaps of all stones. Certainly it is unswervingly attuned to the Source of pure White Light radiance, and tends to infuse one's mind, body and chakra system with pure White Light. Throughout the entire mineral kingdom I know no currents more intense than these. Satyaloka Clear Azeztulite organizes and re-centers brain activity. It brings one's awareness to a deep sense of quiet and a heightened sensitivity to subtle energies and streams of consciousness. It asks a great deal of the heart, for it pulls Light through the heart into the rest of the body. It is not a difficult or painful thing at all; it is a lovely feeling. It is simply powerful.

Satyaloka Clear Azeztulite is resonant with the energies described in India's mystical traditions as *satchitananda*. Sat means "truth," chit is "consciousness" and ananda is "bliss," so this sat-chit-ananda is the bliss that comes from awareness of truth. Satyaloka Clear Azeztulite can infuse the Liquid Crystal Body Matrix with the intense high frequencies of satchitananda. There is what I can only describe as a tremendous Light in these stones. For those who wish to transfigure themselves into beacons of spiritual Light for the uplifting of humanity and the world, there is no better tool than Satyaloka Clear Azeztulite.

Satyaloka Clear Azeztulite is a stone of powerful spiritual dedication. It can guide one in the purification of one's energy body, of one's intention, will, even of one's love activities and energies. It allows one to achieve one-pointed focus of consciousness through the will in the third chakra. This is an important capacity, because one-pointed focus through the will is the most powerful inner alignment for specific co-creating activity and manifestation of what one envisions.

Satyaloka Clear Azeztulite can be used to travel through the realms of Light to many higher planes of reality. It can be ridden all the way to the archetypal first emanations from Source. It is a powerful stone for conducting one on conscious journeys into the spiritual worlds via the geometries of Light. It enables one to more readily place the Light geometries along and within the body/temple. Satyaloka Clear Azeztulite encourages us to envision self and world as temples, as holy places. Its adherence to the purpose of Light in the world is absolute, and it engenders absolute devotion to Spirit in the individual.

Satyaloka Clear Azeztulite resonates with all other forms of Azeztulite, as well as Moldavite, Auralite-23, Phenacite and many of the other high-frequency stones such as the Synergy Twelve and the Ascension Seven. This stone can be brought to even higher energy levels through the Azozeo super-activation process. Among the stones that will help make its intensity gentler are Rosophia and Pink Azeztulite, as well as Morganite. Satyaloka Clear Azeztulite is a stone of our great journey into the Light, and the great infusion of the Light into us.

SPIRITUAL Satyaloka Clear Azeztulite opens the crown chakra and pours a flood of spiritual Light throughout all levels of the self, both spiritual and physical. It awakens spiritual aspiration and aids in creative manifestation of one's highest visions. It stimulates *satchitananda,* or truth consciousness bliss.
EMOTIONAL Satyaloka Clear Azeztulite facilitates the attainment of spiritual bliss and ecstatic rapture.
PHYSICAL Satyaloka Clear Azeztulite aids in transforming the physical body into the Body of Light, infusing the cells with satchitananda.
AFFIRMATION I am born of the Light, conscious of the Light, committed to the Light, and in love with the Light.

SATYALOKA ROSE AZEZTULITE

KEY WORDS Ascension of the Heart, Divine Love, adherence to the heart's truth, Vibrational Ascension **ELEMENT** Storm **CHAKRAS** Heart (4th), Third Eye (6th), Crown (7th)

Satyaloka Rose Azeztulite is the name given to a salmon-colored variety of Azeztulite found in the Satya Loka region of South India, the same area where the original Satyaloka Clear Azeztulite was found. The stone is a silicon-dioxide mineral with a hexagonal (trigonal) crystal system and a hardness of 7. The name Satyaloka means "place of truth" in Sanskrit.

When I began meditating with a piece of Satyaloka Rose Azeztulite, within a few seconds I could feel soft yet powerful currents moving into my heart and almost immediately upward, filling my entire head with sweet, strong currents that arose from the heart. The emotional tone was loving and peaceful, and at the same time the currents were so strong that my head felt "full," and seemed to be expanding. Yet these were not the typical currents I associated with the third eye and crown. They were heart energies in my head! Then I inwardly saw a salmon-colored rose floating in front of me.

This is when the name "Satyaloka Rose Azeztulite" came into my mind. The heart is often symbolized by the rose, and both are deeply associated with love. That is what I was being shown. The currents of this new stone are profoundly loving, and at the same time there is an energy of opening about them. They filled my head with the heart's feeling, and its expansiveness as well.

Satyaloka Rose Azeztulite carries the currents of Heart Ascension. Like all the Satyaloka Azeztulites, its vibrations are intense and powerful. These stones not only stimulate the heart chakra, they also encourage the heart to "move" upward into the head. They awaken the Divine

"I" of the heart and lift it to its rightful throne in the center of the brain. When this occurs, one thinks, speaks and acts out of the heart's wisdom. The mind and brain then take their places as servants of the heart. When this transformation is fully realized, one can speak and act only in truth, because the heart knows only truth. This shift affects the body as well, dissolving all falsehood and self-negation in the mind of the cells. The cells vibrate with the heart's love and truth, aligning themselves with the Light and Love emanated by the Great Central Sun and the Ascended Heart.

Satyaloka Rose Azeztulite fully activates the heart's spiritual Light. Satyaloka Rose Azeztulite fills the emotional body with Divine Love. The longer one abides with this energy, the more it can be integrated into one's thoughts, speech and actions. It can even permeate the body, reprogramming the cells to resonate at the frequency of pure Love. This is one of the most satisfying experiences one can have, and it is rather contagious. When one is constantly receiving and expressing Divine Love, one's way of being can affect others profoundly. As the mystic poet Kabir said, "If you make love with the Divine now, in the next life you will have the face of satisfied desire."

In spiritual self-healing, Satyaloka Rose strongly supports the heart and brain. Within the brain, the pineal gland is a point of its focus, and it can stimulate that gland to release its "nectar." When this occurs, the pleasure one feels can be almost unbearable. In general, the saturation of one's energy field and body with these love energies is a powerful healing influence on all levels.

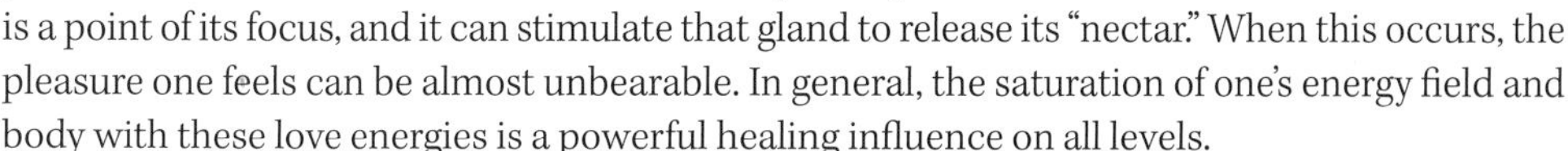

Satyaloka Rose Azeztulite emanates some of the strongest stone energies I have ever experienced, and the way they circulate their currents indicates that they are programmed for vibrational Ascension. This Ascension will not take us away from the world—it will move us to transform ourselves and the world into Beings of Light on a Planet of Light.

To bring forth the fullness of this profound transformation, combining Satyaloka Rose Azeztulite with Satyaloka Yellow Azeztulite is advised. Using the Rose Azeztulite at the heart and the Yellow Azeztulite at the third eye, the circuit of Light and Heart Ascension can be created and energized. To extend the activation to the crown, place a piece of Satyaloka Clear Azeztulite there. This stone also resonates with all of the Ascension and Synergy Stones. Astaraline assists it in the process of Light Body activation.

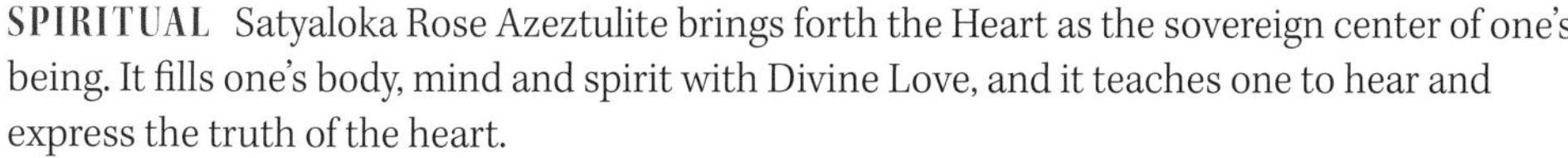

SPIRITUAL Satyaloka Rose Azeztulite brings forth the Heart as the sovereign center of one's being. It fills one's body, mind and spirit with Divine Love, and it teaches one to hear and express the truth of the heart.

EMOTIONAL Satyaloka Rose Azeztulite saturates the emotional body with love and pleasure, sometimes bringing one into states of ecstasy.

PHYSICAL Satyaloka Rose Azeztulite supports the heart and brain, as well as filling all of the cells with love energies. It can trigger a release of "nectar" from the pineal gland.

AFFIRMATION I allow my heart to resonate with Divine Love, and I joyfully surrender to the heart's truth.

SATYALOKA YELLOW AZEZTULITE

KEY WORDS Enlightenment, Ascension, unconflicted behavior, acceleration of one's evolution, Light Body awakening **ELEMENT** Storm **CHAKRAS** Solar Plexus (3rd), Third Eye (6th)

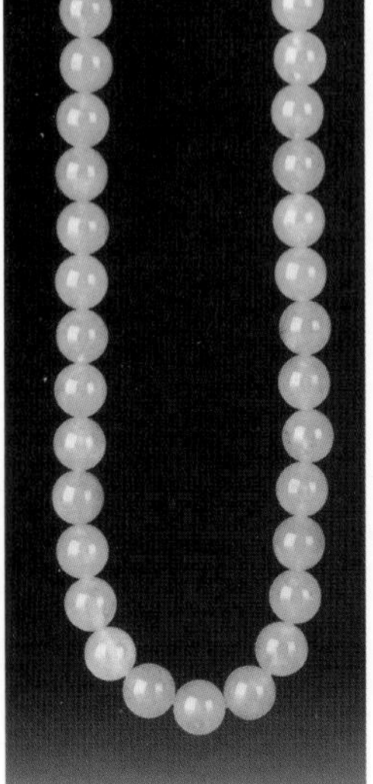

Satyaloka Yellow Azeztulite is the name given to a salmon-colored variety of Azeztulite found in the Satya Loka region of South India, the same area where the original Satyaloka Clear Azeztulite was found. The stone is a silicon dioxide mineral with a hexagonal (trigonal) crystal system and a hardness of 7. The name Satyaloka means "place of truth" in Sanskrit.

Satyaloka Yellow Azeztulite powerfully stimulates the Third Eye chakra. Its currents move very deep into the brain, bringing intense and pleasurable sensations. It can also feel as though it is "pulling" one's consciousness—and even one's etheric body—upwards! The power of Satyaloka Yellow Azeztulite is the power of evolutionary change. It is programmed for the awakening of humanity and the Earth to a higher level of spiritual awareness, and its energy of awakening carries extraordinary force. Satyaloka Yellow Azeztulites carry the currents of enlightenment (literally: "being filled with Light"). They have a strong enthusiasm—almost impatience—for helping one wake up and assume one's spiritual power. They seem to have a will of their own, focused on the rapid acceleration of our spiritual awakening. It is rather thrilling to be around them!

Satyaloka Yellow Azeztulite also stimulates one's own will forces, helping one to align one's intention with Divine Will. It strengthens one's capacity to focus all of one's energies to serve that intention. In practice, this means one can utterly give oneself over to one's spiritual purpose, and one can DO that which one wills to do, without doubt or inner turmoil. These stones provide clarity and enhance purpose, as well as awakening the mind to perceive and embrace one's Divine destiny.

This extraordinary capacity to channel one's whole being into a single act of will is sometimes called "unconflicted behavior." It sounds very simple, but it is actually quite rare. We are programmed almost from birth to question ourselves, primarily because those who brought us up were almost constantly "correcting" us, and overriding our will with their own. This means that virtually everyone has a fragmented third chakra, and it is the reason we seldom live to our potential. When one, through some synergy of circumstances, is triggered into unconflicted behavior, one can do amazing—even "superhuman"—things. (The classic example is a mother lifting a car off her child, because every fiber of her being knows that she must.) One of the blessings that comes from Satyaloka Yellow Azeztulite is the streaming of beneficial energies into the third chakra, healing old wounds and gifting one with the potential of entering the unconflicted state—our most natural way of being.

Satyaloka Yellow is a powerful stone of Light Body awakening. It helps one attune to the pure Golden Ray of the highest realms of creative manifestation. These are the vibrational levels from which one can receive the power to transform the Liquid Crystal Body Matrix into an engine of regeneration and rejuvenation. It was originally predicted by the Azez that Azeztulite would dissolve the patterns of contraction and decay in the cells. The infusion of Golden Light into the cells from the spiritual realms stimulates the cells to emanate their own Golden Light, expanding their energy fields and potentially initiating what is called the *bigu* state in Dzogchen Buddhism, the state of "living on Light." Satyaloka Yellow Azeztulite works well with all the Ascension and Synergy stones. It can be super-activated through the Azozeo process,

and it works synergistically with other Azozeo stones. It harmonizes with Lithium Light for building the Body of Light. Guardian Stone protects the Light Body within this process. Its most natural allies are Satyaloka Rose Azeztulite and Satyaloka Clear Azeztulite. If one holds a Satyaloka Yellow Azeztulite at the third eye and a Satyaloka Rose Azeztulite at the heart, the two stones can open and powerfully stimulate the channel between the heart and brain, leading to a state in which these energy centers function as an integrated whole. If one adds a Satyaloka Clear Azeztulite at the crown, one can experience the integrated heart-brain circuit linking with the "thousand-petaled lotus" of the awakened crown chakra, and further connection to the etheric chakras and the realms of Spirit beyond.

SPIRITUAL Satyaloka Yellow Azeztulite inspires awareness of and enthusiasm for spiritual awakening. It facilitates spiritual awakening, evolutionary change and Light Body activation.
EMOTIONAL Satyaloka Yellow Azeztulite encourages one to seek and savor the thrill of transformation. It dissolves inner conflict and helps one act with power, free from doubt.
PHYSICAL Satyaloka Yellow Azeztulite aids the body in assimilating and integrating spiritual Light. It teaches the cells to both receive and emanate pure Golden Light, and reprograms them for rejuvenation.
AFFIRMATION I align my forces of will into complete alignment with Divine will, and commitment to my chosen actions. I act with power, free from doubt.

HIMALAYA GOLD AZEZTULITE

KEY WORDS Creative manifestation through the will, co-creating with Sophia, kindling the Great Central Sun in the Heart, filling the body with Gold Light
ELEMENT Storm **CHAKRAS** Solar Plexus (3rd), Heart (4th), Third Eye (6th), Crown (7th), Soul Star (8th), Transpersonal/Etheric (9th to 14th, above the head)

Himalaya Gold Azeztulite was discovered in 2008 in the regions near the Himalaya Mountains. Like other Azeztulites, it is a form of quartz with a hexagonal (trigonal) crystal system and a hardness of 7. The name derives from the location of its discovery and its bright yellow color.

Himalaya Gold Azeztulite emanates Azeztulite's whole pattern of energies, and one of its special qualities is its resonance with the solar plexus chakra. This is the seat of power and manifestation in the human being. As with other conditions we carry from the past, within our solar plexus are patterns of limitation that severely limit our capacity to create. We literally do not know our power, and in the past this may have kept us from abusing it. Yet with evolution into expanded awareness comes the necessity of taking up our full range of potentials. The arrival of Himalaya Gold Azeztulite coincides with the beginning of our development of new capacities for creative manifestation through the will. The stimulation of the

solar plexus, in alignment with the Seat of Vision in the third eye chakra, is an important aspect of this activation.

Himalaya Gold Azeztulite activates multiple chakras, including the heart, solar plexus, third eye, crown, and the chakras above the head including the Soul Star (eighth) and transpersonal/etheric chakras (ninth to fourteenth). This is an exceptional array of energetic activation, and it is ideal for facilitating our capacities for conscious co-creation—an essential part of our coming destiny.

There is more to genuine creative activity than our own self-aware aspirations. The creating we can do, in which we are truly creating a world, our bodies and our living experience, is not isolated within us, but is co-creating in a kind of union with the Soul of the World, whose impulses we feel in our hearts. Individually, we can utilize the third eye to envision something mentally, and the solar plexus to "push" things into manifestation, but this is a limited sort of creating. When we work in co-creative unity with Sophia, the Soul of the World, we are simultaneously setting our intentions and letting go of any expectations of what the results must be. We imagine the essence of what we want, and then we 'exhale' it, releasing it to Sophia. It is the heart's natural gesture of trust, not in fulfillment of what we imagine in our minds, but in whatever may come to us.

This rather circular gesture of intending and releasing in trust allows the spontaneous genius of the World Soul's creating to engage with us in a sort of continuous dance. The results of this are seldom what we might have expected. Rather, they are infallibly preferable, more perfect and appropriate for the harmonious well-being of the whole, of the All. The fruits of such co-creations display the seeds of our intentions, but the outcomes are better than we imagined. Its stimulation of the third chakra lends greater power to our intention. When we are strong-willed (but avoid trying to be tyrants), we have more to offer on our side of the dance. We can focus our intentions better, and keep our actions in alignment with the intentions we have set, even though we have released expectations. Having more awareness and control of the third chakra's currents also allows us to learn to consciously project (intend) and withdraw (surrender) them. Being able to feel these gestures is very helpful in learning to practice them continuously. Our strengthened third chakra also increases our capacity to feel the wills of others, giving us the opportunity to align or disengage with them. Additionally, we can even learn how to feel the flow of the World itself—what the Chinese called the Tao, and what we might consider the creating activity of Sophia—and learn how to better align with its currents.

Himalaya Gold Azeztulite can cause the heart and solar plexus energies to merge with one another, making them feel like a single huge energy center. The joining of these two chakras embodies the unification of love and will, bringing one into alignment with Divine Will. When this occurs, one feels a great surge of exaltation!

In one meditation with Himalaya Gold Azeztulite, I saw an inner image of a golden sun or a radiant star over my head, and I felt the radiance of this golden sun penetrate my crown chakra slowly, like liquid Light with the consistency of honey. The golden Light descended slowly through my third eye, and I began to inwardly see a field of golden Light. It continued descending, through my shoulders and the upper chest, and I felt the Light being pulled down through my root chakra into the Earth. Then I had a sudden vision of the heart as an organ of gold, and recognition of the nature of the heart as a radiant star. An inner voice spoke: "We all have this." Working with Himalaya Gold Azeztulite can bring about such experiences in anyone.

Himalaya Gold Azeztulite sometimes contains streaks of red running through the yellow color. Certain pieces are almost completely red. We know these stones as Himalaya Red-Gold Azeztulite and Himalaya Red Azeztulite, but they are from the same location and partake of similar energies as Himalaya Gold Azeztulite. The red inclusions tend to deepen the energies, bringing them down to the second and first chakras, enhancing sacred sexuality and bringing a powerful flow of Life Force into the body.

Himalaya Gold Azeztulite works synergistically with all of the other Azeztulites as well as Phenacite, Heliodor, Golden Labradorite, Rosophia, Lemurian Light Crystals, Nirvana Quartz and all stones of Ascension. It can be stimulated to even higher energy levels through the Azozeo Super-Activation process.

SPIRITUAL Himalaya Gold Azeztulite brings the pure Golden Ray of spiritual Light into the body. It enhances inner vision and facilitates co-creation with the Soul of the World.
EMOTIONAL Himalaya Gold Azeztulite encourages one to have the courage to create, and brings joy as it opens the portals of higher spiritual awareness.
PHYSICAL Himalaya Gold Azeztulite stimulates profound healing on the cellular level through the infusion of golden Light. It offers special support to the heart, lungs and digestive system.
AFFIRMATION I am a co-creator with the Soul of the World, and the intensity of power I can manifest is equal to the depth of my joyous surrender.

SANDA ROSA AZEZTULITE

KEY WORDS Grounded infusion of Light, spiritualizing the body, multi-level sensing capacity, quieting the mind, stimulating inner vision, etheric cleansing, high serenity
ELEMENTS Storm, Earth **CHAKRAS** All (1st through 7th)

Sanda Rosa Azeztulite is the name given to a variety of Azeztulite composed of quartz, white feldspar, Spessartine Garnet and mica. It was discovered in North Carolina in 2008. The color is primarily an opaque white with speckles of red-pink garnet and shimmering dots of silver-gray mica. The hardness of this stone is between 6 and 7.

The discovery of Sanda Rosa Azeztulite is a favorite memory of mine, since I was a part of it. Traveling through North Carolina in 2008, I was hoping to find a source of more White Azeztulite, and had asked a local friend to help me seek out likely locations. I had also, while driving there, received a moment of vision in which the Azez seemed to be telling me that I would indeed find more Azeztulite, so my hopes were high. As soon as I arrived at my friend's home, we went out looking. Lo and behold, the new Azeztulite was there, in the first area where we looked for it!

But the new Azeztulite was different—instead of being pure white, it was dotted with bits of reddish pink and shimmering silver-gray. And its currents, while definitely those of Azeztulite, were different. They were more grounded and somehow more comforting than the original White Azeztulite. They entered through the third eye and moved both upward to the crown and down to the heart. In a few moments, my whole body was filled with a soft tingling in which I felt caressed by many invisible hands. When I asked inwardly what to call this new discovery, I was given the name Sanda Rosa Azeztulite, meaning "the Rose of the Sand" (or "Quartz of the Heart"). It seemed fitting, because the area was certainly sandy, and these stones' currents definitely nourished and expanded the spiritual heart. I was utterly elated to have found them, and to have had the vision from my journey confirmed—not simply with more White Azeztulite, but with a whole new variety!

The currents of Sanda Rosa Azeztulite descend readily to all parts of the body after entering from above. They spread through the Liquid Crystal Body Matrix in a graceful flow. Sanda Rosa Azeztulite is very soothing to the etheric body. Its interface with the energetic membrane of the physical body is a smooth and nurturing one. Its currents bring Spiritual Light into the body and mind, and it is easier to stay grounded with Sanda Rosa Azeztulite than with some other varieties. Many people who find White Azeztulite too intense are quite comfortable with Sanda Rosa Azeztulite.

The Spessartine Garnet in these stones carries a vibration of its own, which harmonizes beautifully with the pure white Azeztulite portion of them. The Spessartine Garnet is a very Earth-friendly, body-friendly material. It resonates strongly with the first and second chakras, providing the grounding influence one experiences from Sanda Rosa Azeztulite. It helps spiritualize the densest aspects of one's physical self. It also provides a vibrational stepping stone so that the Liquid Crystal Body Matrix can find resonance with the Azeztulite currents through the Garnet's harmonizing, mediating energies.

Sanda Rosa Azeztulite's currents move at a relaxed pace as they undulate through the body. They are warm, and resonate well with our corporeal selves. They also encourage our bodies to vibrate at a higher spiritual frequency without losing touch with the Earth. The Mica portion of Sanda Rosa Azeztulite seems to stimulate a certain reflective quality in the consciousness. It is a strengthener of the inner witness, the observer in oneself who watches without judging all that passes within one's body, mind and soul. Sanda Rosa Azeztulite stimulates the third-eye and crown chakras in a way that allows very deep levels of meditative awareness. It is calming to the emotional body, benefiting those who are working to quiet the mind. This stone's agenda is to make the body comfortable with the presence of the Divine Light within every cell.

Sanda Rosa Azeztulite is a good stone to take into the realm of dreaming. It stimulates vivid images in the psyche in both meditative and sleep experiences, and helps one remember dreams.

One of the potentials of working with Sanda Rosa Azeztulite is being able to "see" the spiritual worlds expressing themselves through the events, gestures and meanings of what happens in the physical Earth and our lives here. It is helpful to envision this world superimposed upon the spirit realm as a mask covers one's true face. The mask both conceals and reveals the truth beneath it, depending upon one's level of seeing. The Azez say that through this stone they can offer an attunement of the third eye that allows one to focus, by choice, on any or many of the multiple layers of being that express the reality of the spiritual worlds. Meditating with the stone, focusing attention on the pleasant currents moving through the third eye, is the suggested means to most readily open to this attunement. The recovery of our latent capacity for multifold spiritual vision can be of immense help in awakening to our wholeness—and what we can become will be far beyond our wildest imaginings!

Sanda Rosa Azeztulite can aid in clearing and cleansing the cells and organs of etheric patterns of contraction, dysfunction and deterioration. It is one of the most useful stones for spiritual healing, as it works on multiple levels to bring forward the pattern of wholeness latent within all of us that may have been fragmented due to fear, or wounded by the attacks of other organisms or entities. It offers vibrational support for quelling digestive discomfort, especially if it is triggered by stress or anxiety.

On the emotional level, Sanda Rosa Azeztulite's currents are calming, reassuring, friendly and nurturing. They can help alleviate anxiety and bring one to a state of centeredness and high serenity. They can help dispel negative emotional patterns linked to past lives, and attune one to connect with one's purified, joyful and perfected future self.

Sanda Rosa Azeztulite has a good and easy resonance with Rosophia. Together they facilitate the deepest release of stress and the strongest repair of the emotional body and the etheric body. Sanda Rosa Azeztulite also resonates well with Moldavite, Circle Stones, Seraphinite, Tanzanite, Morganite, Seriphos Green Quartz, Master Shamanite and others that attune to the Divine Blueprint of the body.

SPIRITUAL Sanda Rosa Azeztulite enhances meditation and dreams, and stimulates the attainment of multi-level awareness. It can facilitate inner encounters with high spiritual beings such as the Azez.
EMOTIONAL Sanda Rosa Azeztulite supports inner serenity, and is soothing to the etheric body.
PHYSICAL Sanda Rosa Azeztulite supports the digestive system and harmonizes one's bodily systems with higher consciousness. It can spiritually benefit in overcoming dysfunctions related to stress or anxiety.
AFFIRMATION I am an incarnated Self, composed of Light and Truth, able to see clearly the manifestations of Spirit in matter, and to support the awakening of humanity.

AMAZEZ AZEZTULITE

KEY WORDS Purification, protection, enlightenment, Divine Connection, psychic capacities, shamanic journeys to the Upper World **ELEMENTS** Wind, Storm **CHAKRAS** All, including the 'Mouth of God' at the back of the head

Amazez is a member of the Azeztulite family, a silicon-dioxide mineral with a hexagonal (trigonal) crystal system and a hardness of 7. It was discovered on an island off the African coast. Its color is a mixture of shades of purple, grayish-purple and white.

When I first saw Amazez crystals, I was struck by how beautiful they were, and how much they physically resembled Auralite-23. However, unlike Auralite-23, these new stones are not all purple; they contain bands of white as

well. When I first felt their currents, I realized they had a much stronger vibration than I had expected—stronger than any other Amethyst-bearing stone I had ever come across. And although Amazez emanates unique and powerful currents, it is clear that they are of the high-vibrational nature that is the signature of Azeztulite.

It was very exciting to see the Azeztulite frequencies expanding into stones in the Amethyst family, which is very helpful. Amethyst has long been known as a stone of Divine Connection, and a stone of spiritual protection and purification. It is one of the oldest healing stones and perhaps the most popular crystal in the world. As the currents of the Nameless Light of the Azez continue to spread through the stones of the Earth, more crystals are awakened and activated to the Azeztulite vibration. In Amazez, we have the best possible combination of Azeztulite's spiritual Light with the traditional beneficial energies of Amethyst.

Amazez can stimulate and bring Light to any chakra, or to any part of one's subtle body. Although amethyst's natural "home" is at the third eye and crown chakras, Amazez is equally able to activate the throat, heart, solar plexus and even the first and second chakras. It fills the whole body with powerful currents of blessing and purification, and it is easily grounded through the feet. In fact, a major part of this stone's program is to ground spiritual Light into the Earth through us—a purpose completely in alignment with all the other Azeztulites.

Amazez is an ideal therapeutic stone for crystal practitioners. It can be used to bring spiritual aid to any weak or afflicted areas of the body. It does this through working primarily in the subtle body aspect of the individual, clearing any "clouds" or gray areas from the auric field and awakening the power of one's Divine Blueprint. This allows the pattern of perfection to reestablish itself on the subtle-body level, leading to the manifestation of wholeness and well-being on all other levels. Amazez is powerful enough to be used as a tool in "psychic surgery," allowing the practitioner to "cut out" attachments, negative thought forms and unhelpful entities.

The sheer power of Amazez, combined with its purifying qualities, make it an ideal stone to use when clearing an individual or an area of all types of negativity. Whether these are subconscious negative programs from past lives or from bad experiences in this life—or whether they are energy-depleting entities picked up in bad environments—Amazez, used with clear intention, can dispel them from one's energy field and one's environment. Wearing or carrying a piece can keep one's personal field in a clear, pure, healthy state, while placing whole crystals of Amazez in one's environment can have the same effect on one's surroundings. These stones not only bring in the Light—they also keep the darkness at bay!

Amazez can purify one's field in a way that makes possible conscious interaction with higher beings on many spiritual planes. The angels, and even the Azez themselves, can more readily approach one who has been purified by this stone. Amazez is an excellent stone for out-of-body travel, raising one's vibration high enough to transcend the body while simultaneously protecting one from negative influences. It can be used in shamanic journeys, especially to the Upper World. Amazez enhances all the psychic capacities, including clairvoyance, clairaudience, clairsentience, remote viewing, prophetic vision, psychic healing and many more. It can stimulate intuitive abilities, acting as a source of creative inspiration and instant knowing of whatever one turns one's attention to.

Amazez can powerfully activate the "Mouth of God" chakra near the top of the spine at the back of the head. This is an extremely important point on the energy body, and is the source of many mystical experiences. It coincides physically with what is called the "reptile brain." The reptile brain, our oldest brain structure, has been mistakenly maligned, because it is seen as primitive.

However, it is also spiritually the portal of the risen kundalini as it pours in to illuminate the whole brain. It is called the "Mouth of God" because it is through this portal that the Breath of God flows into us when conditions are right. Amazez can awaken and help open this critical passage so that our latent Divine energies can circulate properly and bring us to enlightenment. For this purpose, I recommend using a pair of crystals, one at the third eye and another at the Mouth of God point.

Amazez harmonizes with all of the Azeztulites, as well as Auralite-23, Elestial Angel Calcite, Violet Flame Opal, Lemurian Light Crystals, Phenacite, Danburite, Scolecite, Brookite, Natrolite, Merkabite Calcite and Nirvana Quartz. It has a special affinity for Guardianite, and together they emanate a hugely powerful vibration of protection, purification and empowerment. Amazez is one of the stones that accepts the Azozeo super-activation process.

SPIRITUAL Amazez opens the path to accelerated spiritual evolution through its powerful energies of purification, protection and awakening. It opens the "Mouth of God" portal for kundalini energies to enter the brain.
EMOTIONAL Amazez cleanses the emotional body of all negative attachments, including dark entities. It dispels depression, anxiety and timidity, and boosts self-confidence.
PHYSICAL Amazez stimulates healing of the brain and nervous system. It brings spiritual aid to weak or afflicted areas of the body.
AFFIRMATION I call upon the Divine Source for purification, healing, clarity, awakening and enlightenment.

PINK AZEZTULITE

KEY WORDS Deep heart awareness, emotional healing, serenity, compassion
ELEMENT Storm **CHAKRAS** Heart (4th) Third Eye (6th), Crown (7th), Soul Star and Transpersonal/Etheric (8th to 14th, above the head)

Pink Azeztulite is a mixed mineral containing both quartz and dolomite. The quartz component of Pink Azeztulite is a silicon-dioxide mineral with a hexagonal (trigonal) crystal system and a hardness of 7. The dolomite component is a calcium-magnesium carbonate with a rhombohedral crystal system and a hardness of 3.5 to 4. The mixture of quartz with dolomite makes Pink Azeztulite softer than other varieties. Pink Azeztulite was discovered in the Rocky Mountains of the western United States.

Although Pink Azeztulite is a mixed mineral, it is unmistakably an Azeztulite, as one recognizes when one meditates and opens to its frequencies. Like the other forms of Azeztulite, Pink Azeztulite resonates rapidly through the Liquid Crystal Body Matrix, and one senses tingling over the entire surface of one's skin, as though one is being gently touched by innumerable tiny hands. These may be indeed the hands of the Azez, the Light Beings who have awakened these stones to their potential and purpose. Yet even with its tingles, Pink Azeztulite is a deeply soothing stone. As it awakens sensitivity, and as it sweeps through the Liquid Crystal Body with the pattern of the Nameless Light, it also soothes the emotional body. It goes to the heart, and seeds there the pattern of compassionate acceptance and love towards all aspects of oneself. It is an ideal stone to help lift the veil of grief or depression.

In our culture we are taught not to accept or love ourselves too much. We are taught that the demands and customs of culture are more important than our own self-esteem. This leads to deep fragmentation that may manifest as either a contraction of self, shame, fear, defensiveness or what might be called egoistic self-esteem. These are two sides of one coin, and have their roots in the fragmentation of self that is rampant in human societies. Wholeness begins with wholeheartedness, and Pink Azeztulite, as it centers in our hearts and initiates the currents of compassionate self-acceptance, moves towards healing our fragmentation. In meditative work it often kindles imagery from one's past, especially moments in which emotional wounding has occurred. The compassionate heart qualities encouraged by Pink Azeztulite wrap themselves around the images of our fragmentation and bring them into the center of our hearts; thus the lonely, forgotten child is comforted.

Pink Azeztulite emanates spiritual currents of forgiving, of loving, of gentleness, softness, calm, quiet, certitude, loyalty and heartfelt compassion. These become available to extend to others as well as to oneself. This is an excellent stone for bringing strained relationships into a state of reconciliation. It is ideal for use by therapists, spiritual counselors, mediators, doctors, nurses and all those whose work involves helping others. It is recommended for those in law enforcement and other stressful professions, to avoid inner "hardening." In actuality, the difficulties of the world incline all of us to protect ourselves with an outer shell of callousness, but in allowing this we lose some of our humanity. Pink Azeztulite helps one stay centered and strong within the heart, expressing both truth and kindness.

As one wears, carries or meditates with Pink Azeztulite, one will notice the sweet, calm, serene, yet highly activated state that is the signature of these stones. Ultimately, Azeztulite's purpose is to ignite the light of the Great Central Sun within one's heart, enabling one to become a Light Being in human incarnation. To be the bridge between Heaven and Earth is Azeztulite's pattern of destiny for humanity. It is a stone of ascension, but not of departure from the Earth. It is a stone of awakening to wholeness, love and enlightenment, and to expressing these qualities for the good of all. In spiritual self-healing, Pink Azeztulite supports the heart, lungs and circulatory system. It is recommended for helping heal physical maladies rooted in past emotional wounds.

Pink Azeztulite works synergistically with all other Azeztulites, as well as Morganite, Rose Quartz, Pink Calcite, Kunzite, Celestite, Rosophia, Satya Mani Quartz, Danburite, Nirvana Quartz and Lemurian Light Crystals. Lithium Light and Lilac Lepidolite can enhance its soothing qualities.

SPIRITUAL Pink Azeztulite stimulates heart awareness, compassion, empathy and kindness. It encourages one to become a Light Being in human incarnation.
EMOTIONAL Pink Azeztulite is an ideal stone for emotional healing, soul retrieval, forgiveness and reconciliation. It softens one's demeanor and keeps the channels of feeling open.
PHYSICAL Pink Azeztulite supports the heart, lungs and circulatory system. It aids self-healing in areas linked to emotional wounds.
AFFIRMATION I am whole within my heart, present to others from my heart, and spiritually enlightened by the Divine wisdom I encounter through my heart.

CINNAZEZ

KEY WORDS Alchemical transformation, accelerated evolution, prosperity, longevity, immortality, enhancement of extrasensory perception, increased synchronicities, awakening to heart intelligence, attunement to primordial Light and Sound **ELEMENTS** Earth, Wind, Fire, Storm **CHAKRAS** All, especially Crown (7th), Third Eye (6th) and Heart (4th)

Cinnazez is a unique combination of red cinnabar, white quartz and a black zinc compound. It has been found only in New Zealand. The quartz component of Cinnazez is a silicon-dioxide mineral with a hexagonal (trigonal) crystal system and a hardness of 7. The cinnabar component is a mercury sulfide with a trigonal-trapezohedral crystal system and a hardness of 2 to 2.5. The zinc compound is currently not identified specifically. The components of most Cinnazez specimens are so thoroughly mingled that the softness of the cinnabar is not noticeable. The material is usually full of tiny open cavities, which sometimes contain tiny druzy crystals. Cinnazez is named for the prominent presence of cinnabar, and because the stones exhibit the energetic properties of Azeztulite.

My felt sense, upon first holding a pair of Cinnazez stones, was of a powerful healing and enlightening wave spreading through my body, beginning in the head and moving quickly throughout the torso and finally all the way to my feet. The speed at which the currents of these stones can spread is surprising, and the feeling is unexpectedly pleasant. It is as though the cells are receiving a powerful wave of Life Force, love and wisdom—a wave that is simultaneously comforting and illuminating. I found that once I picked up the stones, I did not want to put them down, and that even when I willed myself to set them aside, I picked them up again within a couple of minutes. The attraction to these stones is palpable, and I sense it is because there is something in the currents of Cinnazez that satisfies a powerful evolutionary need.

I asked the Beings of Cinnazez to tell me of its nature and qualities. Here are some of the insights that came: "We are quickeners of consciousness and awakeners of higher awareness. We can stimulate your nervous systems to actualize their latent capacities of clairvoyance, telepathic communication, attunement to heavenly realms and direct knowledge of Divine Truth. We are bringers of Wisdom, and we stimulate spiritual enlightenment. We are the solidified essence of the Philosophers' Stone, and we help the body open to become a conduit of

the Celestial Fire of the Great Central Sun. We are as full of Light as any Azeztulite, yet we act faster to bring the Light through you and into the world. We are teachers of the body, and can awaken the human body/mind to full self-awareness. Meditation with us in silence allows us to penetrate and activate every cell. We are alchemical transformers, turning the leaden unconsciousness of the past into the Golden Truth of the World-coming-to-be. We are first among the new stones of the Earth's Golden Age, which is now dawning. Those who work with us will receive our blessings, and can become givers of blessings."

Those who have read something about alchemy will know that the fabled Philosophers' Stone (believed to be capable of prolonging life indefinitely and transmuting lead to gold) was said to appear in three stages. The initial dark phase (*nigredo*) signified unenlightened matter, and could refer to most of the Earth's dormant rocks, which are spiritually asleep. The second or white phase (*albedo*), signified a state of spiritually awakened matter, capable of attuning to spiritual Light and awakening the alchemist to his or her higher destiny. I have long believed that the original White Azeztulite represents this aspect of the Philosophers' Stone. The third and final phase of the development of the Philosophers' Stone is the red phase (*rubedo*), in which the Stone has fully developed all of its powers. In its red phase, the Philosophers' Stone is believed to supply the alchemist with power over his or her own longevity, and the ability to heal others and transmute matter from one state to another. The similarities of the red version of the Philosophers' Stone to the description of the properties of Cinnazez is remarkable.

My next insights came in a dream that occurred one night after I had meditated with two Cinnazez stones. In the dream scenario, I was in Italy with my wife, exploring a lovely little town. At one point, when my wife was out of sight, a woman approached me and began speaking rapidly in Italian. When she realized I didn't understand her, she switched to English, saying I really must attend a theater performance that night—a dramatization of the story of Mercury. She told me I should record and remember the information in the play. When I awoke, I realized that "Mercury" referred both to the elemental Mercury in the cinnabar component of Cinnazez, and the mythic being know as Mercury (called Hermes by the Greeks), who is the father of alchemy! I began to meditate more with the Cinnazez, and have been recording the information and insights, just as she instructed.

Cinnazez is a quickener of evolutionary growth. It stimulates the brain and central nervous system, increasing one's receptivity to fields of knowledge in the inner realms. It aids those who wish to access the Akashic records, or to discover the answers to questions or problems in any area. Cinnazez stimulates one's vibrational field, making one a better conductor of all kinds of positive energies. It enhances one's capacity to form and hold inner images, which are often the form in which spiritual "downloads" of Divine knowledge occur. It helps one attract new knowledge and insights in the same way a metal post attracts lightning.

Cinnazez stimulates the intelligence of the heart, and strengthens the neural networks through which the mind and heart communicate. It can facilitate hearing the heart's voice, and recognizing and following the heart's wisdom. As it awakens heart intelligence to a greater degree of conscious awareness, it opens the channels of angelic and interdimensional communication. It is an ally for those seeking to understand the inner workings of the Universe.

Cinnazez is a powerful stone of inner alchemy, stimulating the Liquid Crystal Body Matrix to a higher level of coherence and energy. The stone's vibrational waves can be viewed as waves of resonance, bringing all the cells into harmonious alignment. They stimulate the inner experiences of primordial Light and Sound, allowing one to enter into visionary experiences that are

both Light-filled and tangibly vibrational, making one's body into a resonating chamber of Divine Speech. If one aspires to become a spiritual channel or medium, Cinnazez can facilitate rapid advancement on these paths. Those who work with oracles such as Tarot and the I Ching in conjunction with Cinnazez may discover that their insights are enhanced, and their ability to notice hidden meaningful connections is increased.

Wearing or carrying Cinnazez can trigger an increase in synchronicities in one's life, and a clear awareness of their meaning. These stones tend to engender an alchemical transmutation from the "lead" of fragmented, ego-driven consciousness to the wholeness and dynamic power of one's Higher Self. To incarnate the Higher Self is to realize true spiritual gold.

Regarding gold, Cinnazez is one of the most powerful stones for attracting financial prosperity and abundance on all levels. If one has a Prosperity Altar in one's home or workplace, Cinnazez is a most highly recommended part of it. Using Moldavite and Cinnazez together will enhance the power of this type of altar. Cinnazez is also excellent to be worn or carried if one is trying to attract prosperity.

Cinnazez harmonizes very well with Rosophia, Master Shamanite, Phenacite, and with all other Azeztulites. If Cinnazez is super-activated with the Azozeo treatment, it becomes a much more powerful version of itself, acting to bring about even more rapid self-transformation and spiritual awakening.
[NOTE: As Cinnazez contains mercury sulfide, it should not be used for elixirs unless a double bottle method is employed, so the stone does not physically touch the elixir water. Use care in handling all minerals containing any toxic substance.]

SPIRITUAL Cinnazez stimulates the alchemical process of self-transformation, awakening new levels of consciousness in mind, heart and body. It enhances mental ability and intuition, and increases one's capacity for receiving spiritual "downloads" from higher realms.
EMOTIONAL Cinnazez brings pleasure to the body, and enhances one's capacity for exercising personal power in regard to the way one experiences emotions. It can greatly strengthen the emotional body.
PHYSICAL Cinnazez supports and empowers the nervous system, and enhances well-being on the cellular level.
AFFIRMATION I choose the path of alchemical transformation, and I allow my old, leaden self to be burned away, its ashes dissolved, so that the new golden substance of my True Self can manifest.

GOLDEN AZEZTULITE

KEY WORDS Attunement to the Gold-White Light, Light Body awakening, time travel, accessing the Hall of Records, kindling the Sun of the Heart, awakening the pineal gland
ELEMENT Storm **CHAKRAS** Heart (4th), Third Eye (6th), Crown (7th),Soul Star and Transpersonal/Etheric (8th to 14th, above the head)

Golden Azeztulite is the name given to a group of prismatic crystallized Azeztulites discovered in North Carolina, USA. These (and the beautiful Sauralite Azeztulite from New Zealand) are the only fully crystal-shaped Azeztulites discovered thus far. Like all Azeztulites, they are a

form of quartz with a hexagonal (trigonal) crystal system and a hardness of 7. Golden Azeztulites are named because of their citrine-yellow to light-smoky range of color, and because of their ability to engender within one's awareness the spiritual ray of Gold-White Light—the ray of the Great Central Sun.

When I first meditated with Golden Azeztulite crystals, I experienced a very powerful opening of the third eye and crown chakras. Placing them at these points created a highly charged conduit of vibration between them. I experienced the two chakras being linked by an L-shaped bar of light that was so intense that it felt nearly solid. These are among the most powerful stones for stimulating the upper chakras to their fullest capacity.

Golden Azeztulite crystals are important for the stimulation and awakening of the Light Body. They carry both the Golden Ray of the enlightened Earth and the White Ray of Divine Light. When one works with these stones, one can experience the blending of both of these spiritual Light Rays within one's upper chakras. This sensation is highly pleasurable, and is capable of leading one into powerful visionary experiences.

Golden Azeztulites stimulate the pineal gland, which produces the chemical DMT (dimethyltryptamine), associated with very intense expansions of consciousness, as well as visionary encounters with beings on higher planes. No one knows exactly what conditions are necessary to "turn on" the pineal gland, but experiences with Golden Azeztulite suggest that it can have this effect. One of the visions I have had with this stone—sometime after the initial episode with the L-shaped bar of Light—involved the feeling that a spot in the very center of my brain was excreting "nectar," a delightfully delicious something that seemed to flow from that central point and slowly fill up the whole inside of my skull with a very strong and sweet sense of euphoric bliss.

Further, the experience brought about images of colorful spiritual beings with shifting forms and diaphanous bodies. They approached and began attempting to communicate with words that came out of them visually, like speech made of light. During the entire experience, the interior of my brain felt "blissed out" by the waves of nectar coming from the center. As I have read about the pineal gland and DMT, I feel sure that what occurred was involved with this gland and this substance. Many spiritual traditions claim that the awakened pineal gland is a source of Divine energy, and this experience makes me agree!

Another inner domain to which Golden Azeztulite may facilitate access is the realm of Golden Light. On one occasion, meditating with a pair of these crystals, I opened my eyes and saw that the room itself was filled with golden light. This is always an astonishing occurrence.

Sri Aurobindo's partner, the Mother, spoke of this atmosphere of gold. Her life's work was to engender the human transmutation into immortality. (Many esoteric teachings including those of the Chinese alchemists, say that the subtle body or Light Body is an immortal body.) In her explorations, the Mother sometimes entered a realm she describes as an atmosphere of "warm gold dust." This is precisely what I saw upon opening my eyes after feeling the Golden Azeztulite current move through my skull. The Great Central Sun emanates this same gold-white light. A holographic likeness of this Central Sun is present in our own hearts, and is sometimes kindled in one's consciousness in the presence of the Golden Azeztulite, as I experienced moments later.

Holding the Golden Azeztulite crystal to my heart chakra, I was quickly immersed in a vision of a golden radiant glow within my chest, where the physical heart is. This golden glow was filling the interior of my body with gold-white light, while rotating on its axis like a planet or a sun.

Golden Azeztulite is attuned to the unknown latent capacities of the brain/mind and nervous system. It stimulates the prefrontal lobes of the brain very intensely and precisely. These capacities involve direct knowing, simply by turning one's attention to a question or a subject, or towards the so-called Hall of Records on the inner planes. It is simply a turning towards knowing.

An exciting potential that Golden Azeztulite can help to awaken is our capacity as time beings—capable of moving in conscious awareness through the fluidity of time.

Another capacity enlivened through working with Golden Azeztulite is empathy. It can help one to know precisely how another person feels, often more deeply and clearly than she or he is consciously capable of expressing.

In spiritual self-healing, Golden Azeztulite offers energetic support to the brain and nervous system. It can be used to help release "frozen" programs of fear or shame stored in the amygdala in the brain. The blissful experiences of finding the golden Sun of the Heart, and of turning on the flow of nectar from the pineal gland, can aid in dissolving old patterns of alienation and defensiveness that hobble one's capacity for joy. The energies of Golden Azeztulite can be enhanced through the Azozeo super-activation process.

Golden Azeztulites resonate with all other forms of Azeztulite, especially Himalaya Gold and Satyaloka Yellow Azeztulite. They also work in a special harmony with the New Zealand Azeztulites—Sauralite, Cinnazez, and Honey and Cream Azeztulite. In addition, they work synergistically with Golden Labradorite, Heliodor, Scolecite, Smoky Quartz, Citrine, Phenacite and Danburite.

SPIRITUAL Golden Azeztulite can open the heart, third eye and crown chakras, stimulating them to much higher levels of activity. These stones can engender visionary experience, time travel, interdimensional communication and Light Body activation.

EMOTIONAL Golden Azeztulite crystals facilitate inner states of euphoria, bliss, joy and ecstatic rapture. They can help heal old patterns of limitation brought about by emotional wounds.

PHYSICAL Golden Azeztulite supports the brain and nervous system. It seems to stimulate the pineal gland, bringing forth a variety of positive and pleasurable effects.

AFFIRMATION I open myself to be permeated with the Golden Light of the enlightened Earth and the pure White Light of the Divine, and I invite them to flood into my heart, brain and body.

NEW ZEALAND WHITE AZEZTULITE

KEY WORDS deep peace, nourishment of the subtle body, enhanced intuitive sensitivity, joy, healing, dissolving negative patterns, remembering one's Divine nature **ELEMENTS** Earth, Air, Fire, Water, Storm **CHAKRAS** All, including the Earth Star, Soul Star (8th) and Transpersonal/Etheric Chakras (9th to 14th, above the head)

New Zealand White Azeztulite is a snow white form of Azeztulite that is found in certain rivers and beaches in New Zealand. The stones are usually tumbled smooth by their long immersion in moving water. New Zealand White Azeztulite, like all Azeztulites, is a silicon-dioxide mineral with a hexagonal (trigonal) crystal system and a hardness of 7.

New Zealand White Azeztulites carry a pure ray of the Nameless Light energy. Holding one of these stones in meditation, one will immediately feel the powerful pulsations and blissful currents by which all the Azeztulites can be recognized. A deep sense of peace fills one's subtle body and auric field. One can sense the presence of a vast and benevolent consciousness, and one feels oneself to be immersed in a personal bubble of Light, within a great field of loving, living Light. As one attunes more deeply to the New Zealand White Azeztulite, one can begin to feel filaments of Light that spread out from one's "Light bubble," extending around the Earth, giving and receiving Light in a mutual intensification and expansion. These Azeztulites emanate a very pure vibration. Their effect is smooth, clear and immediate. The energies fill you up and then they continue to grow, until there is the sense that you are overflowing with blissful, peaceful, powerful Light.

New Zealand White Azeztulites have close affinity to the Water element. As one works with them, one's intuitive capacities are enhanced. One begins to be more sensitive to the currents of feeling which constantly flow through us and around us in the world. One's awareness of the condition of the emotional bodies of others is heightened, and this enhanced sensitivity is accompanied by compassionate understanding, and healing intention. People who are healers, or who wish to be, will find that New Zealand White Azeztulite can enhance their ability to help others heal. New Zealand White Azeztulites are stones of joy. They allow one to release constricted patterns that have formed due to attachments to grief, depression, anxiety and anger. The currents of these stones work to dissolve negative energy forms of all types, and they can purify one's field of unhealthy habitual patterns, as well as psychic implants. They work to cleanse the psyche of guilt and shame, and they encourage one to recognize one's essential Divine spark. They remind us that our souls are beautiful, and they aid us in manifesting that truth in all aspects of our lives.

New Zealand White Azeztulite can rekindle the inner flame of our spiritual Light, and nourish it by blending its energies with our own. To be with this stone is like walking with an angel beside you. Its presence reminds us that, regardless of our inner wounds or our outer circumstances, our essence is Divine and our nature is Light.

New Zealand White Azeztulite combines harmoniously with all other Azeztulites (especially Sauralite), as well as Danburite, Petalite, Rosophia, Master Shamanite, Morganite, Kunzite and Rose Quartz. For emotional healing, I especially recommend using it in combination with Blue-Green Azeztulite. New Zealand White Azeztulite also has a natural affinity with Green Fire Azeztulite, and they are sometimes found together in Nature. When these are combined, the blissful Light within is accompanied by the passionate intensity needed to act powerfully in the world for the good of the whole.

SPIRITUAL New Zealand White Azeztulite expresses a loving, compassionate presence, and it can surround one with spiritual Light. It enhances intuition, emotional sensitivity, compassion and healing intention.
EMOTIONAL New Zealand White Azeztulite nourishes the emotional body and brings a sense of deep peace. It brings one greater sensitivity to the feelings of others, and it helps one to dissolve attachments to negative emotions.
PHYSICAL New Zealand White Azeztulite supports the subtle body, filling it with Light. This can bring vibrational harmony and balance that manifests as a sense of overall physical wellbeing.
AFFIRMATION I embrace the Light and affirm that it is my true nature.

SAURALITE AZEZTULITE

KEY WORDS Marriage of Divine Light with Earthly matter, physical enlightenment, heart-centered consciousness, the Divine Feminine as the Earth, spiritual purification, joy and happiness **ELEMENTS** Earth, Air, Fire, Water, Storm **CHAKRAS** All, including the Earth Star, Soul Star (8th) and Transpersonal/Etheric Chakras (9th to 14th, above the head)

Sauralite is the name given to various crystallized forms of New Zealand Azeztulite. The name Sauralite is derived from the Hindu word *saura*, which means "the Great Sun," or "spiritual Sun." Sauralite crystals, like all Azeztulites, are a silicon-dioxide mineral with a hexagonal (trigonal) crystal system and a hardness of 7.

Sauralite Azeztulite crystals are found in mountainous areas of New Zealand, often in the abandoned tunnels of old gold mines. There is a great variety of growth patterns, ranging from sheets of microcrystalline honeycombs to jagged cathedral points to sparkling druzy clusters. Most Sauralite is white, but a small percentage is naturally stained a rich red-brown. An even smaller percentage displays veins of purple amethyst.

Sauralite Azeztulites are crystals of intricate and varying forms. They include clusters of tiny druzy points, coral-like honeycombs of white crystal, geometric pseudomorphs and other unique patterns. Their variety reflects the vitality and originality of the Spiritual Earth as she expresses herself in New Zealand's beauty, and in the stones formed within that living crucible.

Energetically, it was immediately clear to me that these were one of the new varieties of Azeztulite that the Azez had predicted would be discovered in places all over the Earth. The currents carry the unmistakable Azeztulite vibrations. Yet they have a special quality that is

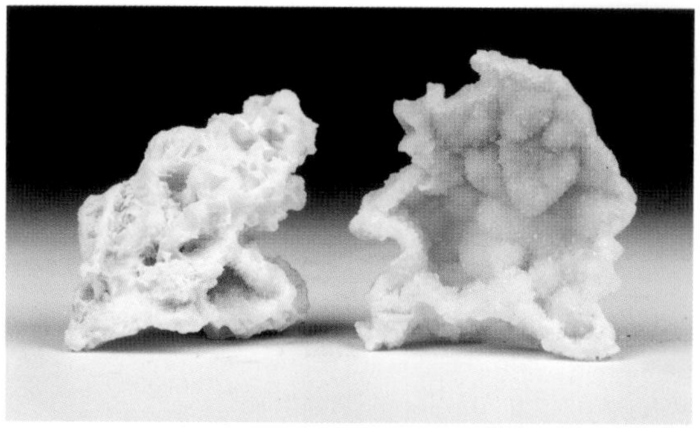

distinctive to them. They are very happy stones, and they induce great happiness—sometimes to the level of ecstatic rapture—in anyone who opens to them. They can also fill both one's head and one's cells with pure White Light.

Sauralite vibrates with astonishing intensity, combining the Nameless Light of the Great Central Sun with the living vitality of the Earth. New Zealand is one of the energetically clearest places on the planet, a place where the Light of Heaven and the Love of Earth are vibrantly intermingled, and these stones are evidence of it. They carry the purpose of Azeztulite in its full realization—the living Light of the Divine married to the density of matter.

In meditation, these stones literally draw the Light down through the crown while they open the base chakra for the upwelling of Earth energies. They allow one to become a living vessel for the spreading of Light, and for the dissolving of fear, contraction and pain. They are stones of physical enlightenment, making the body a place of ecstatic celebration of union with the Divine Earth. Sauralites are the most feminine Azeztulites, because the Earth's vitality is so alive in them. They can help us awaken to the joy of co-creative partnership with the Living Earth. In this state, we experience the disappearance of linear time, and an ongoing unfoldment of magical synchronistic manifestation in every moment. To work deeply with Sauralite Azeztulite is to enter a new way of being—a multidimensional awareness—encompassing joy, forgiveness, communion, magic, ecstasy and unity with the Earth.

In emotional self-healing work, I recommend Sauralite Azeztulites for issues around depression or grief. These stones can also be used to help dispel stress and inner tension, and to relieve negative obsessions about past events. They can aid in clearing past-life negative fixations that are impairing emotional or physical well-being.

In meditation, Sauralites can put one in touch with the co-creative edge of the World-coming-to-be, the flowing stream of eternity entering into time. These stones can guide one into the state of heart-sovereignty, in which one's consciousness is heart-centered and the mind defers to and serves the heart's wisdom. Sauralite Azeztulites also stimulate the imagination, trigger inspiration and encourage living in the world within a state of constant blessing. They are at the leading edge of the New Consciousness, and they can provide us with both a vision of the New Earth and the experience of how we can enter it, while simultaneously helping bring it to birth.

I feel that Sauralite has emerged at this time because our spiritual evolution has reached an important level. There are now numerous individuals who are aware of the Light in the cells and of their own subtle-body makeup. Working with Sauralite can aid these people to fully awaken the Liquid Crystal Body Matrix to its own body consciousness, conjoined with our mental consciousness, our heart awareness and the Spiritual Earth. The heart is the Bridge of Light between the mental consciousness with which we are familiar and the bodily knowing of the New Human. Sauralite carries the quickening energies to stimulate this transformation. This is a joyful awakening—truly an ecstatic one—and the great question posed to us by Sauralite—and by she who is Earth—is: "Will you give up your old life for a new, unknown joy?" How many of us are ready to answer "Yes!" to that invitation?

I view Sauralites as the stones carrying the vibration of the Divine Feminine in her new manifestation—the consciousness and joy of the illumined Earth. Sauralite tells me that the Garden of Eden is not in the past but in the future, and that this future is approaching rapidly, even in the face of all the environmental degradation we see in the daily news. The Earth is arising to meet the Light of the Great Central Sun, and in this merging will come the healing and the joy for which all our hearts are longing. When we work with Sauralite Azeztulite, allowing that energy to permeate us, it is as if one cell in the body of the Earth has turned on its Inner Light. As more of us do so, more Light is kindled in her body, and the cascade of Light that is her full awakening is kindled. All of the Azeztulites, as well as many other stones, are serving this purpose, but in Sauralite the gentle, playful, loving Light is most accessible.

Sauralite resonates with Rosophia, Anandalite, Tibetan Tektite, Astaraline, Guardianite and all other Azeztulites. It is a powerful addition to the Synergy Twelve, and it harmonizes with Natrolite, Petalite, Phenacite, Anandalite and other stones of Vibrational Ascension. It is able to receive and benefit from the Azozeo super-activation process.

SAURALITE WITH AMETHYST

When I held a piece of Sauralite with Amethyst, I felt a focus of currents at the crown chakra, and I saw an interior light of a deep-violet hue pulsating in my inner vision. I felt intense currents in the crown chakra that gradually flowed down through my whole body. There was a strong sense that I was experiencing an inner purification, operating simultaneously on the cellular and etheric levels. When the currents reached my feet, there was an upwelling of energy from the Earth into my body, and a rush of ecstatic joy. I felt that this was the Earth's joy rather than my own, and that I was feeling her consciousness after the stone had energetically cleansed my body. It made me aware that we cleanse our inner temple not simply to honor the Divine, but to make it possible for the Divine to enter. And this Divine energy was clearly that of the Spiritual Earth rather than any cosmic entity from beyond. I am convinced that the work of Sauralite with Amethyst is to purify us so that we are able to attune to the frequency that allows the Earth's rapturous Self to enter and permeate us.

Of all the stones I love (and there are many!) Sauralite is the stone I most delight in introducing to people. It is so much fun to watch their faces as the stones' energies begin to pour into them! First the eyes display the recognition that energy is flowing, then there's a smile as they feel the stone's friendliness. Next there often comes a flush of emotion or a murmur of "Wow!" as the person senses the currents circulating more and more deeply within the body, bringing Light and joy throughout. I have a similar experience every time I hold one of these lovely and loving crystals, and I sense that the feeling one experiences while connected with Sauralite is the feeling of what it will be like all the time, after the New Earth is born.

SPIRITUAL Sauralite Azeztulite awakens the consciousness of the New Human Being and the New Earth. It infuses the body, heart and soul with the gentlest, most delicate and loving Light imaginable.

EMOTIONAL Sauralite Azeztulites emanate a contagious happiness that fills the heart and brings illumination to the mind. The future way of being of the spiritual human being can be glimpsed within this happiness.
PHYSICAL Sauralite Azeztulites bring joy to the body, reminding the cells that their destiny is to be trillions of radiant suns.
AFFIRMATION I accept with gratitude and passion the offer of the Light of Heaven and the Love of Earth—to be their child.

HONEY AND CREAM AZEZTULITE

KEY WORDS Inner Light and sweetness, pleasure, bliss and ecstasy, contact with the Azez in dreams or meditation, love, blessing, emotional healing, recovery from stress or illness **ELEMENTS** Water, Wind, Earth **CHAKRAS** All, especially Heart (4th)

Honey and Cream Azeztulite is the name given to a variety of Azeztulite found only in certain rivers and beaches of New Zealand. Its name is derived from the fact that its coloring is a blend of creamy white and rich, golden-honey brown. Another aspect of the stone's naming is the perception that its energetic currents are "delicious" like honey and cream. The stone is a silicon dioxide mineral with a hexagonal (trigonal) crystal system and a hardness of 7. Typically the raw specimens have been rounded by centuries of tumbling in rivers or in the sea, but in many pieces there remain small pockets where tiny crystals can be seen.

Honey and Cream Azeztulite emanates currents that fill the body with waves of Light, and something I have to call sweetness. It is a very pleasurable sensation, stimulating one's higher capacities and filling one with soft, comforting vibrations. These are stones one could easily fall in love with, as they seem to generate love within every cell of the body. They are different from many high-energy stones, which can be powerful and intense. Honey and Cream Azeztulites combine power with love in a way that calls to mind Nature in her most fertile and lovely expressions.

This stone is the mineral version of warm waves on a quiet beach, or a garden of lilies, or a rainbow after a spring shower. It kindles Divine Light in one's cells in a way that feels gentle, kind and intimate. There is a great deal of power as well, and it builds to higher and higher levels the longer one holds the stone. Yet it is never overwhelming or uncomfortable—it strengthens at just the pace one is ready for. This is one of the reasons I view Honey and Cream Azeztulites as among the most evolved types of Azeztulite. It feels as if the intelligence that guides the expression of these stones is learning to gauge our sensibilities more precisely, so that the newest Azeztulites are the ones most perfectly matched with human energies.

Honey and Cream Azeztulites (and Sauralite Azeztulite crystals, also from New Zealand) emanate the most feminine currents of all Azeztulites. They feel very nurturing, and they have a soothing quality, even as they bring a great deal of Light into one's body and consciousness.

In particular, I recommend sleeping with the Honey and Cream Azeztulites. While the original White Azeztulite and Satyaloka Clear Azeztulite are probably too intense for most of us to be able to sleep comfortably in their presence, Honey and Cream Azeztulite can waft you on a carpet of sweetness into the realm of dreams. And the dreams one experiences with these stones are often profoundly spiritual. One can travel through the levels of the Cosmic Spheres to the Great Central Sun, feeling successive waves of bliss. (This experience can also occur when one meditates with these stones.) One may meet the angelic beings who are the Azez themselves, or even encounter Sophia, the Soul of the World, in the dream or meditative state. Such experiences are ecstatic in nature, and the pleasurable waves engendered by Honey and Cream Azeztulite can help one attune to the frequencies of ecstasy that are the nature of the highest realms.

On more Earthly levels, Honey and Cream Azeztulites are ideal allies for emotional healing. They can help one soothe and comfort one's inner child, allowing recovery from old patterns of shame or feelings of abandonment. They can be used in soul-retrieval work, providing a cocoon of loving currents from which to "call home" any lost parts of one's original wholeness.

Because of their gentle nature, Honey and Cream Azeztulites are ideal stone companions for recovering from exhaustion caused by stress or overwork. They are a lovely antidote for stress, and for regaining health after an illness. These stones especially support the adrenals and the parasympathetic nervous system.

Last but not least, I recommend working with Honey and Cream Azeztulites to engender the Activity of Blessing. Holding one of the stones over one's heart, imagine receiving a blessing in one's heart from the stone with each inhalation. (This is actually what is happening!) With each exhalation, release a blessing from one's heart to the stone, in its spiritual essence. This is to be repeated indefinitely, and the longer one does this, the stronger will be the current of blessing. It is easy to move into an ecstatic state doing this meditation. Ultimately, practicing this will teach one how to meet every experience and perception within a similar state of mutual blessing. If enough people were to do that, we could transform our world.

Honey and Cream Azeztulite vibrates in resonance with all other types of Azeztulite. It also works synergistically with Shungite, which quickens its infusion of Light and bliss. Combining Azumar with Honey and Cream Azeztulite is ideal for intensifying their ecstatic energies. Working with Cinnazez can increase the speed and intensity of the currents emanated by Honey and Cream Azeztulite. For healing applications, I recommend combining these stones with Healerite. All Azozeo-activated stones harmonize with Honey and Cream Azeztulite—and of course an Azozeo-activated Honey and Cream Azeztulite is quite a wonderful thing in itself! These stones also harmonize with Ascension stones such as Phenacite, Danburite, Petalite, Herderite, Brookite and Satya Mani Quartz.

SPIRITUAL Honey and Cream Azeztulite fills one with love and spiritual blessing. It is nurturing on every level, and helps the soul to feel safe and comfortable on the path of spiritual evolution.

EMOTIONAL Honey and Cream Azeztulite emanates currents of sweetness that can heal the emotional body and bring a sense of security. It feels as if one is being held in an angel's arms.

PHYSICAL Honey and Cream Azeztulite supports healing and recovery of vitality after stress or illness.

AFFIRMATION I know that I am always loved and constantly blessed, and I offer my gratitude and blessings to all beings.

GREEN FIRE AZEZTULITE

KEY WORDS power of the heart, Union of Heaven and Earth, communication with Nature, heart intelligence **ELEMENT** Earth, Air **CHAKRAS** Heart (4th) and High Heart(between 4th and 5th)

Green Fire Azeztulite is a bi-colored stone that occurs in rounded pieces in certain rivers and beach areas of New Zealand. The stones display a mixture of white and green shades. Like all Azeztulites, Green Fire Azeztulite is a silicon dioxide mineral with a hexagonal (trigonal) crystal system and a hardness of 7.

Green Fire Azeztulites are first and foremost stones of the power of the heart. Their currents resonate strongly in the heart chakra, and they kindle an inner flame there. This is the flame of spiritual passion that can carry one through the trials and tribulations of transformation, fueling the will to make whatever efforts are needed. This green fire of the heart is powerful indeed, and one must surrender to it, lending one's intelligence to accomplish what the heart desires.

Green Fire Azeztulite is a stone of the Earth, infused with the illumination of Heaven. It exemplifies the accomplishment of the Great Work of spiritual alchemy—the union of Heaven and Earth. It plants the seed of that union within the core of those who work with this stone with a pure intention, and it stimulates us to dedicate ourselves to incarnating this Divine Marriage within ourselves.

Green Fire Azeztulite facilitates communication with Nature. It helps one to be sensitive to the many synchronistic messages that the Soul of the World is always offering us. It helps one to feel the reality of the Living World, and to discover one's love for the Earth. When one works with this stone in a natural setting, one begins to sense and understand the communications of birds, animals, wind and water. These stones help one to invigorate our dulled senses and awaken to passionate participation in the life of the world—our world, our home. These stones can awaken us to become aware that we already love the world with all our hearts, even if we may have forgotten. Green Fire Azeztulite supports the emergence of the intelligence of the heart into our conscious awareness. It helps us awaken to the heart's awareness of truth, and its impulse to act with wisdom for the good of the whole.

In ancient alchemy, as in the modern-day Alchemy of Stones, the heart is recognized as the true center of our being—the Seat of the Soul. Green Fire Azeztulite can unify the heart and mind, and can stimulate the shift of the center of one's sovereignty from the head to the heart. Making this shift does not leave the mind dark and empty. On the contrary, it fills the mind with divine Wisdom, which all the talents of the mind are meant to serve.

In the body, Green Fire Azeztulite, can work spiritually to clear and strengthen the heart, lungs and circulatory system. It encourages balance and clarity in the brain and mind, and can help to dispel headaches—especially those caused by mental stress. It invigorates the thinking processes, and fills one with a sense of purpose.

Green Fire Azeztulite reminds us that we are in love with the Earth, and with life itself. It can help us to shake off depression and despair, encouraging us to act powerfully in service to what we know is good. It teaches us never to compromise ourselves in order to make things easy, and it supports one's commitment to one's own integrity. These stone emanate spiritual power, and they support us in seizing and using our own spiritual power. Green Fire Azeztulites can act as talismans for those who recognize themselves as defenders of the Earth, and they can help us to live in the love that continually feeds our commitment to all that we cherish in this life.

Green Fire Azeztulite works synergistically with all other Azeztulites, especially the newly discovered Blue-Green Azeztulite and New Zealand White Azeztulite. It also resonates with Seriphos Green Quartz, Green Apophyllite, Rosophia, Morganite, Pink Tourmaline, Dioptase, Kunzite and Rose Quartz.

SPIRITUAL Green Fire Azeztulite facilitates the great shift of the center of one's being from the head to the heart. It links one with Nature and the Soul of the World.
EMOTIONAL Green Fire Azeztulite can re-awaken our passion for our lives and our love of the world.
PHYSICAL Green Fire Azeztulite energetically supports the heart, lungs and circulatory system, as well as balance and clarity in the brain.
AFFIRMATION I dwell in my heart, I listen to my heart, and I act in accord with my heart's desires, without hesitation or compromise.

PINK FIRE AZEZTULITE

KEY WORDS The inner fire of Divine Love, High Heart activation, passionate self-identification with Love, emotional and physical self-healing **ELEMENT** Fire **CHAKRAS** Heart (4th) and High Heart (between 4th and 5th)

Pink Fire Azeztulite is the name given to a milky, semi-transparent form of Azeztulite characterized by streaks of dark, brownish-red hematite. It is a silicon-dioxide mineral with a hexagonal (trigonal) crystal system and a hardness of 7. It was found on an island off the African coast.

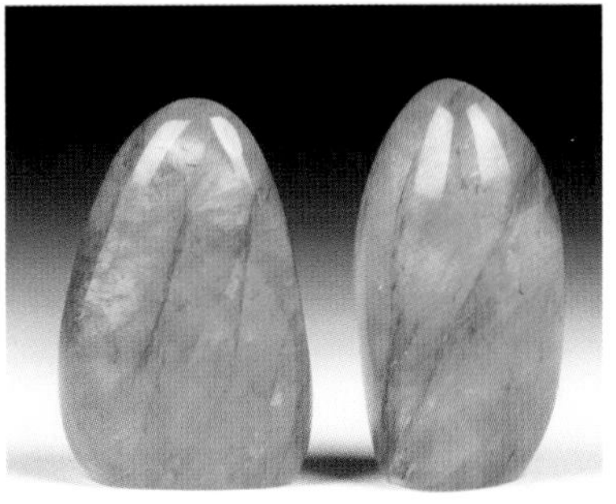

When we first began our work with Azeztulite, we were told by the Azez—the angelic beings who foretold and activated the first Azeztulites—that more Azeztulites would be found. Later, we learned that the Azez intend for all the quartz on Earth to eventually resonate with the frequencies of Azeztulite. This is a profound work of transformation—one that could make the Earth into a Planet of Light. The Azozeo process allows us to facilitate that transformational activation, and one stone that proves this to me is Pink Fire Azeztulite. After its exposure to the Azozeo field, it has taken on new properties that I did not observe before. One of these is responsible for its new name.

The Hindu *rishis* spoke many centuries ago in the Rig Veda about the Divine Fire, or *Agni,* which was both a Being and an internal experience. When Agni enters the body, it transforms the cells into Lightgiving sources of vast energy that brings enlightenment, ecstasy and

knowledge of truth. Pink Fire Azeztulite has always been a conduit of these energies, but its newly activated Azozeo state makes it much more powerful.

In addition to the profoundly powerful energies emanated by these stones, there is a particular experience they can engender. It is the entry of the fire of Divine Love, a pink fire centered in the heart. When one meditates with a Super-Activated Pink Fire Azeztulite, one may feel the streaming power of the stone coursing through the body and eventually focusing in the area of the heart. As this experience intensifies, one feels inner heat in that area, and one can see interior spiritual Light—a pink Light that is also felt as being quite warm, like a pink fire. Holding the stone over the heart helps to intensify these sensations, and imagining the stone's etheric image actually moving into the heart can increase the intensity even more. As this occurs, the warmth and Light within the chest grow and strengthen, until one may actually sweat from the sense of internal heat, or weep from the experience of the Divine Love emanated by the pink Light.

Carrying the experience through to its fulfillment can bring about the awakening of the High Heart, a usually dormant energy center several inches above the heart chakra. This spot is the bodily throne of the Divine Self, and the seat from which inner wisdom and truth can begin to be accessed on a continuous basis. When this center is fully activated, one will notice that the pink fire is always blazing there, reaching out through us to bless, heal and awaken the world. Thus it is not the physical color of the stone (which is semi-transparent with some reddish inclusions) but the inner experience of the pink fire that is the reason for its name.

Pink Fire Azeztulite is a stone of passion. It encourages one to love with great intensity, with no holding back. And this expression of total love is not only for a spouse or partner, or for one's children and friends—it is for the world and everything in it. Pink Fire Azeztulite opens the floodgates of the heart, teaching the mind that to withhold love is to stifle life itself. This stone teaches that life is love, and that giving love supports all life. It triggers within us the potential to truly know that love is our foundation, our Life Force, and the animating energy of the Universe. And it offers us the experience of our own unlimited love, which is the same as Divine Love.

Pink Fire Azeztulite circulates its currents through the body, making love a cellular experience. It can eventually teach the cells that love is the antidote to illness and even death. Thus it is an ideal stone for those seeking to heal dysfunctions such as autoimmune disorders, in which the body attacks itself. Visualizing the pink fire pouring out of the stone and filling every cell with its loving Light is a recommended way of working with this stone for self-healing. Pink Fire Azeztulite is useful for emotional self-healing as well, bringing an infusion of unconditional love into one's energy field. The intensity of love emanated by Pink Fire Azeztulite can dissolve rigid patterns of old pain, self-inflicted emotional damage, and the discouragement of having felt abandoned or unloved. Love is both joyful and serious—and powerful as well. When one feels the power and purpose of love, one's attachments to old, fragmented ways of being can be dislodged. This discovery often leads to moments of exuberant joy as well as inner commitments to serve the flow of love as it rises to permeate and transform our world.

Raw or polished pieces of Pink Fire Azeztulite can be used to fill one's environment with powerful love energies. The stone can be worn to help keep oneself connected to the currents of Divine Love at all times. It works harmoniously with all other Azeztulites, as well as Azumar, Healerite, Rose Quartz, Morganite, Rhodonite, Rhodocrosite and Kunzite.

SPIRITUAL Pink Fire Azeztulite kindles the inner fire of Divine Love, making one both a receiver and a transmitter of intense and powerful Love energies.
EMOTIONAL Pink Fire Azeztulite initiates the energy of Love in a way that can go beyond normal human experience. It profoundly aids emotional healing on all levels.
PHYSICAL Pink Fire Azeztulite spiritually supports recovery from autoimmune illnesses. It facilitates self-healing through permeating the cells with the Light and Fire of Divine Love.
AFFIRMATION I give myself totally to the receiving and expressing of Divine Love.

BLUE-GREEN AZEZTULITE

KEY WORDS loving connection with the Earth, infusion of Light, dissolving negative fixations, **ELEMENT** Water, Storm **CHAKRAs** All, especially Heart (4th), Crown (7th)

Blue-Green Azeztulite was discovered in the Pacific Northwest, in the USA. It is a silicon dioxide mineral with a hexagonal (trigonal) crystal system and a hardness of 7. The blue-green color comes from copper compounds within the quartz base.

When I first held a piece of Blue-Green Azeztulite, I immediately felt the characteristic pulsing power that I sense from all the members of the Azeztulite group. There was a strong vibrational resonance in my third eye, which soon was reverberating through my crown chakra and my entire head. Then the energy flowed to my heart, and a burst of powerful emotion came forth. The pulsing energies suddenly took on the beautiful feminine qualities of the Earth. I found myself filled with the Earth's love and compassion, and I was aware of the deep well of wisdom from which they flowed. This strong emotional connection with the living Earth filled me with gratitude and love.

The next phase of the movement of energy from the Blue-Green Azeztulite involved a powerful infusion of Light. Along with its pulsating waves of love, the stone began to fill me with spiritual Light. This Light has an ecstatic quality, so as one allows more and more of it to enter, one moves into states of bliss. However, because of the powerful emotional waves emanated by these stones, the bliss is earthly rather than cosmic. Even as the ecstatic Light increased, I felt more and more profoundly the Earth's sorrowful joy.

Experiencing the currents of Blue-Green Azeztulite can help one to integrate one's emotional body with one's spiritual Body of Light. This is a most important function. One of the primary qualities of human existence on Earth is the power of the emotions. It is important while we are here to truly feel everything, and to cultivate our feeling sense. Emotion is not exactly the same as feeling, but emotions are some of the most powerful things we can feel while we are alive. In the spiritual realms we enter after our incarnations, the power of emotions is usually turned down, so that the soul can review the life dispassionately. When we are here on Earth, we have a predominance of feeling and emotion, if we allow it. And if we are truly doing our evolutionary work, we are endeavoring to conjoin our spirit and soul—our Light and our feeling—within the vessel of the body. This is spiritual alchemy, and it is greatly facilitated by the energies of Blue-Green Azeztulite.

Blue-Green Azeztulite is a fantastic stone for awakening and healing the emotional body. It works through resonance with the compassionate love being continuously emanated by the Earth, combined with the bliss of Divine Light. When these energies circulate through our vibrational fields, they can cleanse us of negative fixations, fears, resentments, depression, judgements and stress. Once the emotional body is cleared by the currents of Blue-Green Azeztulite, one discovers that one's ability to feel is greatly enhanced. One experiences everything more vividly, through the whole spectrum of feeling and emotion, but one does not become inappropriately attached to either happiness or sadness.

In spiritual healing work, Blue-Green Azeztulite supports the heart, throat, lungs, thyroid, and the esophagus. It can be used to treat all types of illness brought about by unhealthy emotional patterns, especially those in which the emotions are "bottled up." It can facilitate release of these fixations, and it engenders the experience of enlightened compassion.

Blue-Green Azeztulite is ideal for facilitating a conscious communion with the living Earth. This is extremely important, especially in times of ecological crisis, such as we are experiencing now. The Earth needs to be healed in a multitude of ways, and beyond that, both we and the Earth need to move into an expanded consciousness. Our role in this spiritual healing of the Earth is to continually offer our love and blessing to the Soul of the World. Working meditatively with Blue-Green Azeztulite can help us to do this, because its currents open the channel of vibrational exchange between ourselves and the Earth. By creating a "feedback loop" between ourselves and the Earth, pouring our love back to the source of the love we are receiving through these stones, we can bring greater consciousness to both sides of the relationship.

Carrying or wearing a piece of Blue-Green Azeztulite will bring its beneficial energies continuously into one's subtle body and energy field. Having a larger piece, such as an altar stone, in one's environment, brings those lovely energies fully into one's home or work space.

Blue-Green Azeztulite harmonizes well with Ajoite, Chrysocolla, Malachite, Chrysoprase, Emerald, Phenacite, Natrolite, Herderite, Brookite, Danburite, Vitalite, Azumar, and all other members of the Azeztulite group. Combining these stones with Blue-Green Azeztulite will bring forth a powerful synergistic union of their spiritual qualities.

SPIRITUAL Blue-Green Azeztulite awakens and deepens our love for the Earth, and our awareness of the Earth's love for us. It helps one to unify one's soul and spirit.
EMOTIONAL Blue-Green Azeztulite can clear the emotional body of unhealthy negative fixations, and can revivify the emotional body and one's positive feelings.
PHYSICAL Blue-Green Azeztulite supports the heart, throat, lungs, thyroid, and the esophagus.
AFFIRMATION I love the Earth, and I commit myself to expressing that love in all of my life.

BLACK TOURMALINE AZEZTULITE

KEY WORDS cleansing of negative patterns, infusion of spiritual Light, rapid spiritual growth, sudden awakening **ELEMENT** Earth, Storm **CHAKRAS** All, especially Root (1st), Third Eye (6th), Crown (7th)

Black Tourmaline Azeztulite is a mixture of White Azeztulite quartz and Black Tourmaline. It was discovered in the Pacific Northwest, in the USA. Its Azeztulite component is a silicon dioxide mineral with a hexagonal (trigonal) crystal system and a hardness of 7. Its Black Tourmaline component is a complex aluminum borosilicate with a hardness of 7 to 7.5.

Black Tourmaline Azeztulite quickly and strongly stimulates the Third Eye and Crown chakras, filling them with Light. At the same time, there is a wave of another sort of energy,

beginning in the Root Chakra and moving down to the feet, up the chakra column and out through all the meridians. This second energy is not Light as such, but an invisible power that clears, cleanses and purifies everything it touches. As these two currents of invisible power and brilliant Light interact within one's body-field, they bring their energies to the cellular level. Black Tourmaline Azeztulite infuses one's subtle body and physical form with so much Light that it is all one can do to contain it, at first. Then, as the process continues, one's field becomes more accustomed to vibrating at this higher level, and everything smoothes out. Black Tourmaline Azeztulite has the capacity to perform a pivotal role in our evolutionary transformation.

Black Tourmaline Azeztulite facilitates rapid progress in spiritual development. Its Black Tourmaline component sweeps through one's whole being, clearing away negative attachments, dysfunctional habit patterns, predatory entities, fearful thoughts and self-negating ideas. Its cleansing and purifying effect is so strong and so instantaneous that it clears the way for a simultaneous Light infusion offered through its White Azeztulite component. The Nameless Light of the Great Central Sun which comes through all the Azeztulites is always offered to us in an unlimited supply. However, we are seldom completely open to receive its fullness. Often this is because of negative "debris" attached to our subtle bodies, and sometimes because of dysfunctional patterns bleeding from the wounded psyche into the physical body.

Black Tourmaline Azeztulite simultaneously dispels the negative while supplanting it with the overwhelmingly positive energy of the Nameless Light. The swiftness with which it affects its transformation upon one's energy field can be breathtaking! And the after-effects of this internal shift can manifest like a fireworks display of enlightened insights, joy, intuitive leaps, sudden expansions of awareness, and a sense of freedom unlike anything one has felt before. At its peak, one may experience *moksha,* the spiritual liberation which the Hindu tradition describes as, "a setting free of hitherto fettered faculties, a removing of obstacles to unrestricted life, a liberation from fears and spiritual ignorance." My felt sense is that this occurs because of the simultaneous clearing of internal negativity and the influx of spiritual Light. I feel that when these things happen at the same time, the Light enters and anchors itself in the freshly cleared subtle body, faster than any new negative patterns can enter. As one continues to wear, carry or be near the Black Tourmaline Azeztulite, this dynamic perpetuates itself as an ongoing process.

In spiritual self-healing, Black Tourmaline Azeztulite can clear self-negating ideas and emotional patterns and replace them with pure Love and wellbeing. This can occur in one's mental and emotional bodies, as well as in the cellular mind of the Liquid Crystal Body Matrix. Viewing our physical impairments and patterns of decay from a spiritual perspective, we can see how wounds to the soul brought about through fear, pain, shame, past life patterns or other negative experiences can lodge in the psyche and ultimately program the cells to manifest dis-ease. These patterns can be stubbornly persistent, especially if they involve a carry-over from a past life or lives. Without an instant infusion of Light, like that which Black Tourmaline

Azeztulite can provide, the beneficial clearing which Black Tourmaline alone (or other protection stones) can offer can be quickly overcome, as old patterns tend to return to the "empty" subtle body. However, when the Light is instantly introduced, the subtle bodies of the cells are already reprogrammed, and the negativity cannot re-establish itself. This can trigger dramatic healing events!

Black Tourmaline Azeztulite can also enhance one's effect upon the outer world. As it does its work of dispelling negative energies and replacing them with pure Light, one's vibrational field changes. One no longer projects one's imbalances into one's relationships (either consciously or unconsciously), and instead the effect of one's presence can refresh the souls of others. One can be a healing influence, simply by being present.

Black Tourmaline Azeztulite works in synergy with all of the other types of Azeztulite, as well as Phenacite, Danburite, Petalite, Herderite, Brookite, Natrolite, Rosophia, Morganite, Nirvana Quartz, Auralite-23, Empowerite, Revelation Stone, Anandalite and Tibetan Tektite. It has a special affinity with Sauralite Azeztulite, which can enhance the loving sweetness with which one's self-transformation unfolds.

SPIRITUAL Black Tourmaline Azeztulite simultaneously purifies and cleanses one's energy field while bringing in a great infusion of Light.
EMOTIONAL Black Tourmaline Azeztulite can rapidly cleanse the emotional body of negative fixations, and help to transform one into a source of emotional nourishment for others.
PHYSICAL Black Tourmaline Azeztulite supports the entire subtle body field, and can help to dispel ailments rooted in patterns from past lives.
AFFIRMATION I am free from attachments to past wounds and decay, and am reborn each day in an abundance of Light.

SEDONALITE AZEZTULITE

KEY WORDS creating an energy vortex within the body, communication with spirit guides, angelic guardians, and ETs, co-creation with the Soul of the World **ELEMENT** Earth, Fire, Storm **CHAKRAS** All, including the etheric chakras above the head (8th through 14th)

Sedonalite Azeztulite is a white and red-brown stone found in the desert near Sedona, Arizona, USA. It is chemically a type of white Quartz, infused and interpenetrated with the red rock of the Sedona landscape—a silicon dioxide mineral with a hexagonal (trigonal) crystal system and a hardness of 7. The reddish color in some parts of the stone comes from iron compounds within the quartz base.

Sedonalite Azeztulites are astonishingly powerful stones! They emanate the vortex energies for which Sedona is famous, as well as the high-vibration infusion of spiritual Light that is Azeztulite's signature. When one holds a Sedonalite Azeztulite to the third eye, powerful and fast pulsations move in immediately. If one places one at the third eye and another at the crown chakra, the entire interior of the head becomes quickly filled with an uplifting and powerful energy. After a few minutes, the pulsations may be accompanied by experiences of inner light, geometric patterns, and other forms. These stones literally create an energy vortex within the body—a field which, because of its high vibrational level, is one of absolute purity and Light.

The immediate response of one's subtle body upon encountering this stone is one of joy and excitement. As one continues meditating with it, this joy evolves into an elevated sense

of serenity, and an expansion of awareness. Sedonalite Azeztulite is capable of opening one's mind to cosmic dimensions, and of raising one's bodily vibrations into resonance with the highest spiritual realms.

Sedonalite Azeztulite is an interdimensional stone. It can facilitate access to communication with one's spirit guides, angelic guardians, benevolent ETs, and even the Azez themselves! This stone's vibrations are of such high frequency and power that one should prepare oneself for their effects, which can wash over one's energy field like a huge wave. If one is centered, alert and grounded enough to ride that wave, one can spiritually "surf" the realms of Light! By this, I mean that one can move, as a point of awareness (or in the Light Body) through multiple dimensions of consciousness.

Sedonalite Azeztulite is a stone of the Universal Tao, the river of energy that flows through everything, appearing as the unfolding of time and the manifestation of all things. It is a stone of the Wisdom of the Earth, and it encourages us to join in the joyful co-creation of the infinite potential of the future, crystallizing into each present moment. We are co-creators, acting, consciously or not, in conjunction with the Soul of the World. Whether we create wonders or horrors has much to do with the state of our own being, and how consciously we hold our intention. Sedonalite Azeztulite helps one awaken to this co-creative dance, and to participate in it fully, manifesting one's highest intentions.

Through its infusion of the subtle body, Sedonalite Azeztulite brings spiritual Light into the emotional and physical bodies, facilitating one's natural healing processes. It has the capacity to acquaint the emotional body with the energy of ecstasy. Sedonalite Azeztulite can stimulate the torus energy vortices that emanate from each cell of one's body, aiding one in bringing one's body into alignment with its Divine Blueprint of perfection, and the ancient alchemical ideal of immortality.

Sedonalite Azeztulite works synergistically with all other types of Azeztulite, as well as Auralite-23, Emerald Auralite, Phenacite, Pink Petalite, Danburite, Natrolite, Moldavite and Tibetan Tektite. It also attunes harmoniously with Healerite, Azumar, Healers Gold, Revelation Stone and Empowerite.

SPIRITUAL Sedonalite Azeztulite dramatically raises one's vibrational level and open access to higher dimensions. It facilitates communication with benevolent spiritual entities.
EMOTIONAL Sedonalite Azeztulite brings the energy of joy and elevated serenity. It can aid one in achieving ecstatic states of consciousness.
PHYSICAL Sedonalite Azeztulite supports spiritual healing on the cellular level through introduction of its vortex energies.
AFFIRMATION I open myself to the Light, and I seek relationship with all beings who are aligned with the Light.

Our journey through the realm of Azeztulite has made for a long chapter. But there was much to say, and more that could be said. The story of Azeztulite keeps growing, as does my sense of its great and wonderful potential. Who knows whether more types will emerge, or if someone will learn how to activate it to an even higher level? Let's hold all of these possibilities open as we go on to the next chapter, in which we return to a stone we have met much earlier in this book—Rosophia.

Jungfrau Sophia, die himmlische und irdische Eva,
die Mutter aller Creaturen

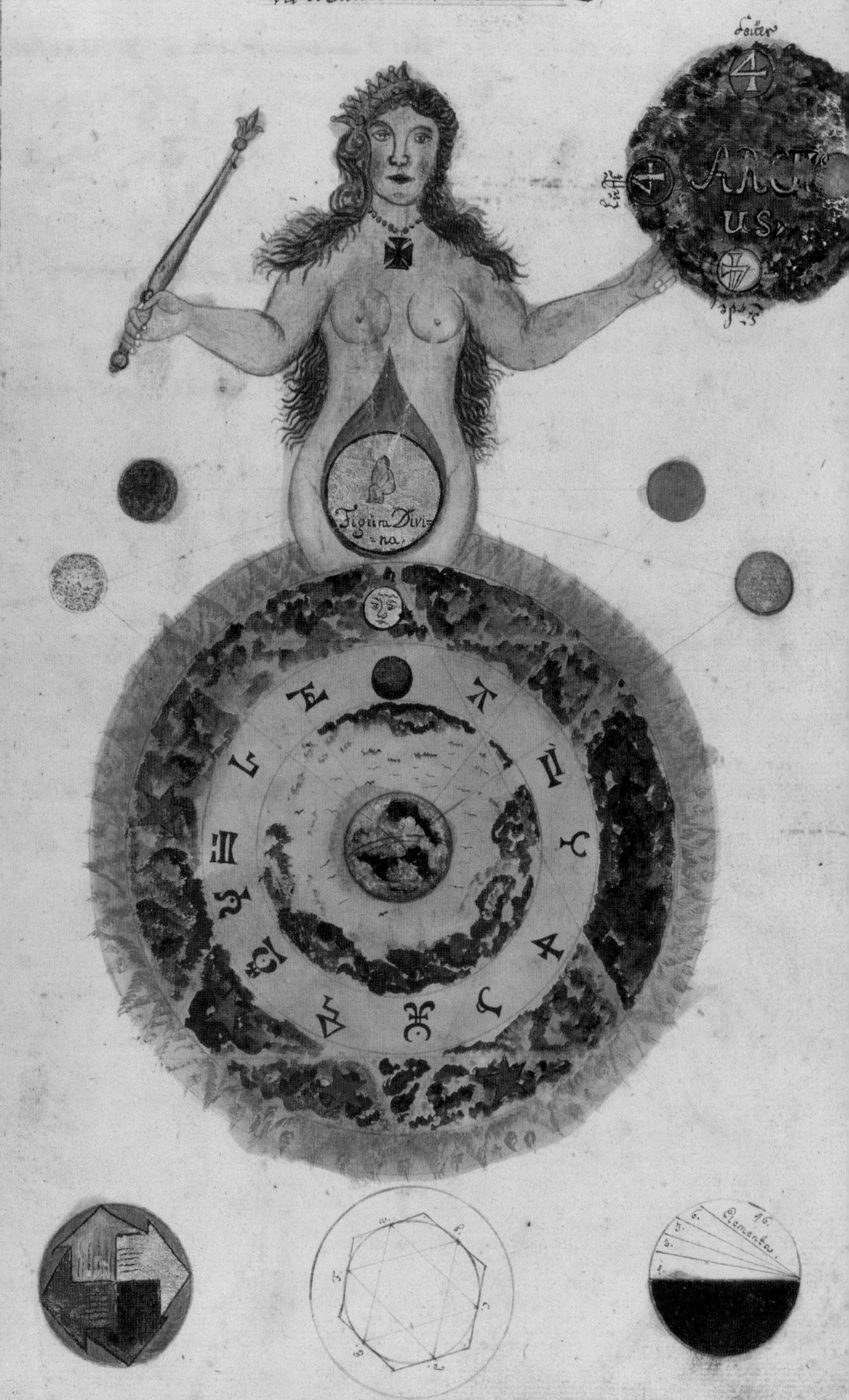

32

Rosophia: The Fourth Cornerstone

All the dark feelings and despairing thoughts disappear when the Stone is attained, and the mind finds rest and joy. This is but a hint at the profound psychological transformation that occurs when the Stone comes into being, and it is a reminder that the alchemist's psyche is completely involved in the work on the Stone.

—Jeffrey Raff, *The Wedding of Sophia*

When one creates the Stone, when one transforms Wisdom [Sophia] into the Stone and brings her to perfection, one gains immortality, and this immortality is symbolized by the rising of the sun at dawn, which ends all darkness.

—Jeffrey Raff, *The Wedding of Sophia*

In Chapter Seven, I told the story of my discovery of the first Rosophia stone, "waiting for me" in my room at the 2008 Sophia Conference in New Mexico. This occurred just days after a numinous encounter with the being Sophia, who appeared to me in a vivid dream and exchanged her breath with me. In the same dream, the three beings I identify as the Azez were also present, performing a comical dance and jovially chanting to me the phrase, "Dance or die!"

The dream and the subsequent encounter with the stone I named Rosophia happened at a crucial point in my own development, and the synchronous nature of the events underscored their significance. I had been asked to speak about stones at a conference dedicated to Sophia. The dream, which came during the week when I was preparing my talk, brought Sophia to life in my psyche in a very dramatic way. Discovering the stone in my room, recognizing its energies as those of Sophia, and then finding more pieces in the nearby canyon—all of these happened in a single day! Listening to half a dozen highly respected teachers give their talks on Sophia at that conference deepened my connection to her, and widened my understanding.

I could feel Sophia's presence at the event. The feeling was one of sensing a vast, silent, loving intelligence, paying close attention to all of us and to everything that occurred. On the day of our arrival, a huge thunderstorm passed through the area, giving the setting of the event a powerful cleansing. We could all feel the difference the next morning. Then, on the evening after the conference ended, another thunderstorm came through and cleansed everything again.

On the last day of the conference, my wife Kathy led an experiential workshop which brought us all into a more intimate connection with Sophia. It involved a multimedia presentation of

OPPOSITE: This 18th century alchemical emblem was named *Gemma Sapientiae et Prudentiae* (Gem of Wisdom and Prudence). It symbolically depicts Sophia, crowned and overseeing the entire universe. Her left hand holds the miraculous alchemical "gold" and in her right hand is the scepter of her creating power. She is pregnant with Figura Divina, the divine human being that we are to become through co-creative union with her.

images, teachings, music, poetry and quotes from Wisdom teachers. This was followed by a set of meditative processes in which Sophia was invited to speak to each person inwardly, communicating what she wished to tell us and asking each of us what she desired from us.

It was beautiful for us all to move from lectures and intellectual thoughts about Sophia into a different kind of consciousness in which we were able to experience Sophia directly. At the end of the workshop, Kathy received a standing ovation from everyone, including the other teachers. (I imagined that Sophia was clapping too.)

There had been a taste of this kind of direct connection with Sophia in my own presentation the day before. I had spoken on the topic of Stones and the New Consciousness. But in addition to hearing my thoughts, everyone received a piece of the newly discovered Rosophia stone that Kathy and I had found in the nearby canyon. As I mentioned in describing this in an earlier chapter, almost everyone at the event was able to feel the currents of sweetness emanated by these stones, swirling and curving around their hearts.

When we left Santa Fe and spent a few days sightseeing before returning to Vermont, I kept my first piece of Rosophia with me, and I slept with it near my heart at night. The beautiful energy that had felt like Sophia's presence at the conference stayed with us, and it gave the landscape around us a patina of beauty and grace that seemed to shine forth from everything like glistening light. I realized that something had changed in me, in a subtle yet powerful way. My recognition of the reality of Sophia had deepened, and this made me want to focus on her in my life and in my work. And I felt incredibly lucky, because this desire could be pursued through my investigations and teachings with stones, starting with the new stone, Rosophia!

As soon as we flew home to Vermont, I got into my car and drove for three days, straight back to Sante Fe. I knew I had to find more Rosophia stones.

The rest, as they say, is history. My return to Santa Fe was filled with magical moments and amazing sychronicities. The search for Rosophia led me north into Colorado, through mountains of majestic beauty and presence. I even passed Mount Antero, where Phenacites are found by diggers at elevations above 14,000 feet. In the end, I gathered enough pieces of Rosophia to work with myself, and to offer them in our catalog.

During these early days, I meditated with Rosophia frequently, and slept with my first chunk—the one from the mantle of my room at the Sophia Conference—every night. Over twenty years later, I still sleep with the same stone.

One phenomenon I noticed early in that period tended to happen some nights while I was sleeping with the Rosophia. I would wake up and recognize a strong energy flowing back and forth between the Rosophia and my heart. It continued after I awoke, and I had the intuitive sense that my heart and the Rosophia stone were "having a conversation" that did not involve my brain! This continues to this day, and whenever it happens, I experience the energy as an exquisite pleasure.

I will mention again one other phenomenon that I brought up earlier in this book. It involves the dynamic that exists between Rosophia and Azeztulite. Speaking simply, if I hold a piece of Azeztulite (I usually choose the original White Azeztulite), I feel the currents in my upper chakras, often moving down from the crown chakra to the heart, sometimes extending further. And I see inner Light. It feels as though the Light of Heaven is reaching down toward Earth.

If I put the Azeztulite aside and hold a Rosophia over my heart, I feel currents flowing in through my feet, swirling up towards my heart. There is a sense of being grounded and being at home on the Earth and beloved by the Earth. This often coincides with a feeling of longing that extends upward. It is as though the Earth's love is reaching up toward the Light.

If I then hold both the Azeztulite and the Rosophia over my heart and attune to what occurs, I can feel both energies blending together in my heart. It is as if the Light of Heaven is reaching down to meet the Earth's love that is reaching up to meet it, and they join in my heart. This union of energies is, in my view, an enactment of the marriage of Heaven and Earth. And this is one way to describe the fulfillment of the goal of alchemy: The Philosophers' Stone forms within the heart as an invisible energy of joy.

This joy is what I was trying to point to with the quotes from Jeffrey Raff's book, *The Wedding of Sophia,* at the beginning of this chapter. In both of them, Raff is explicating the text of the *Aurora Consurgens* an alchemical tale believed to have been written by Thomas Aquinus. Raff is an ardent lover of Sophia, and he wrote *The Wedding of Sophia* at her explicit request. (He experienced a waking vision of Sophia, who appeared in his room and asked him to write a book to help people realize that she is real.) In the quotes, he is explaining his view of how the Aurora's author portrayed the Philosophers' Stone. To create the Stone is to somehow make the ideal vessel within which Sophia, in her perfect manifestation, may come fully into this world.

Maybe that vessel is in our hearts. Maybe it is in a stone. Maybe the vessel that is meant to become the Stone is the whole Earth.

We live in a fractal universe, in which self-similar patterns repeat themselves in endless variations, at all levels of scale. In alchemical terms, this is summed up in the phrase, "As above, so below." This means, I believe, that the Philosophers' Stone must be created many times, in as many ways as possible, and at every possible level of scale. We do not know when or if the Stone will be brought forth perfectly by some enterprising spiritual alchemist—leading to the redemption of the entire Universe. So I take my inspiration from the old alchemists and repeat my experiments again and again, looking for the gestures of Sophia/Wisdom, trying to follow her ways, and to help her. That is one reason I always keep a Rosophia stone close by.

I call Rosophia the Fourth Cornerstone of the Alchemy of Stones because I see in it the echo of the completion of the Great Work. Rosophia's energy is earthly and loving. In us, it's home is clearly the heart. Like the *prima materia,* and like Sophia in her lower (or "fallen") aspect, Rosophia holds the *potential* for the fulfillment of alchemy's goal, though it is not yet realized. But one can feel the "shape" or the "echo" of the fulfillment of Sophia's purpose in the currents that do come through. When I think of the perfected Philosophers' Stone, I envision the pleasure, beauty and joy of the union of Rosophia and Azeztulite as I feel it in my subtle body, and then I try to imagine that feeling magnified a billion times.

Another reason I have chosen Rosophia as the Fourth Cornerstone of the Alchemy of Stones has to do with its physical structure, and the resonance of that with the three stages of alchemy.

You may remember that earlier in the book I described these stages. The first stage, the *nigredo* (the blackness) referred to the beginning phases of spiritual alchemy, in which one is faced with all of the psychological and energetic "pollution" in oneself. It is also a phase in which one's perceptions of outer reality are darkened by becoming more aware of the disharmonies and pathologies in the world around us. The nigredo can be felt in the experiences of loss and grief, and in recognizing one's wounds and ailments. It is resonant with the journey to the sacred underworld known as the Dark Night of the Soul. Stones like Black Azeztulite, Black Tourmaline, Nuummite and Master Shamanite can be helpful allies in this stage.

There are necessary gifts that come to us through the suffering of the nigredo stage. By no longer suppressing our darkness and keeping it in the subconscious, we are freed from being bound to it, and the soul naturally rises into the Light. In alchemy, this movement into the Light is called the *albedo* (the whiteness). The inner experiences of the albedo phase are often the ones we prize most highly. We see and feel the inner Light, and our lives can be imbued with grace. We feel expanded, awakened and close to the Divine. White Azeztulite, Phenacite, Danburite, Scolecite and other high-vibration stones can facilitate and support our experiences of expansion and Light in the blissful albedo phase.

The third stage of spiritual alchemy is called the *rubedo* (the reddening). This is the culmination of alchemy's aspirations and is linked with the creation of the Philosophers' Stone. The rubedo is symbolically associated with the dawn, as the above quote from Raff illustrates. It is also associated with the blood and the physical body. In the rubedo stage, one integrates all that has been learned and experienced in the previous stages. One can contain the darkness and the Light at the same time, along with all the other polarities and paradoxes one has encountered along the path. One's psyche and subtle/imaginal body have become strong through the many purgings and purifications one has experienced—one has become a vessel strong enough to hold the Stone and all of its transformational powers of redemption. A simpler word for the state of the rubedo might be "wholeness." This word may seem humble, and perhaps a little mundane, but that is because we are not yet whole, and we do not recognize how profound the transformation to wholeness truly is. Red Fire Azeztulite, and Rosophia are stones linked with the rubedo stage.

Rosophia is the stone that encompasses all three of these stages within its structure and in its energies. Physically, Rosophia is a combination of all the three colors of alchemy. It contains black biotite, representing the nigredo phase, white quartz, which resonates with the albedo stage, and reddish feldspar, corresponding with the rubedo phase of completion. The black biotite works to provide Rosophia's grounding currents. The white quartz vibrates at the frequencies of the Light of the high spiritual realms. And the reddish feldspar holds and integrates both polarities, resonating in us at the level of our hearts. Thus, we can say that Rosophia, the stone of Sophia, carries the whole pattern of alchemy's processes and their fulfillment. This is why I call it the Fourth Cornerstone.

There are numerous ways to discuss Rosophia, and to give metaphors about the way her energies can work with us. Thus far, I have been offering a personal history of my connection with Rosophia, and my understanding of Rosophia's role as the Fourth Cornerstone of the Alchemy of Stones. In order to flesh out the picture more fully, I want to present Rosophia now in the way I might normally describe a stone's spiritual qualities:

KEY WORDS The Love of Sophia, awakening of Heart Awareness, co-creating with the Soul of the World, mystic union with one's true self, bringing Heaven and Earth together
ELEMENT Earth **CHAKRA** Heart (4th)

Rosophia is a gemstone from the Rocky Mountains of the USA, first recognized in 2008.The stone is a mixture of reddish feldspar, clear or white quartz and black biotite. The quartz component of Rosophia has a trigonal (hexagonal) crystal system and a hardness of 7. The feldspar component has a monoclinic crystal system and a hardness of 5 to 6. The name Rosophia is derived from the phrase "Rose of Sophia," meaning the "Heart of Wisdom." This name was chosen because of the stone's readily perceived heart currents, and the intuition that the stone carries the qualities and presence of the Divine Being Sophia, Soul of the World.

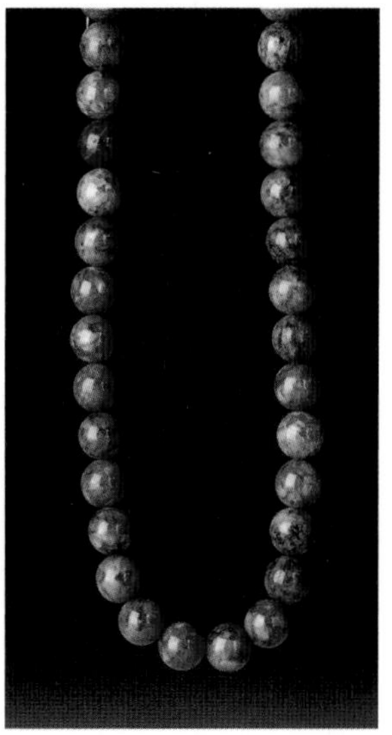

Rosophia is first and foremost a stone of the heart. Its currents quickly and deeply move into and throughout the chest, in and around one's heart, bringing sensations of soothing, calming, loving caresses. Through this stone, it feels as though one is being touched with the loving invisible hands of the Divine Feminine, the Intimate One who is vast enough to fill the world and even the cosmos, and at the same time fully aware of and caring for each human being.

There is a feeling quality engendered by these stones that I can only describe as a delicate yet powerful sweetness. They bring an inner feeling of beauty, a serene sense of centeredness within the heart, a gentle appreciation of each perception and all the beings who make up the world.

Holding Rosophia, one softens inwardly with no loss of strength. One sees more truly, because the veils of stress and anxiety are lifted. Compassion is enhanced, because fears have been quieted. The heart centering engendered by Rosophia encourages one's capacity to meet each moment fresh and free, ready to respond with clarity and creativity.

For self-healing, I recommend Rosophia for almost everything, since this is in essence a stone that draws one into wholeness. It helps one to calm the emotional body, release stress and dissolve repetitive negative patterns on all levels. It is of special benefit to the heart, and my feeling is that its currents are restorative to the natural, healthy functioning of the heart—both as an organ of the body and as a center of consciousness.

For diseases rooted in negative self-image or a fearful attitude toward the world, Rosophia can be a powerful spiritual medicine. The self-affirming qualities of this stone make it an excellent ally in dealing with maladies in which the body turns against itself, as in autoimmune conditions. It can work spiritually to aid in circulation of the blood and the lymphatic system.

Psychospiritually, Rosophia can facilitate the remediation of problems stemming from feelings of low self-worth, fear of the future, mistrust of other people and all kinds of stress-related difficulties. This lovely stone aids in liberating one from negative patterns created by old wounds in this life or past lives, and it helps with the recall of repressed material, if necessary, in order to release it. It can facilitate insight into the unconscious patterns that lead to similar problems again and again. It encourages a stronger sense of self, based in the heart's truth rather than in egoic pride.

Sleeping with a Rosophia stone near one's heart is one of the best ways to release stress and worry, and to sleep well and soundly. This practice can relieve feelings of depression, and can fill one with the awareness that one is always loved. One may even awaken during the night, as I have, to discover a silent, loving, vibrational "conversation" going on between one's heart and the Rosophia stone. This, when it occurs, is a great blessing, and is deeply nourishing to one's heart. In a more mystical aspect, Rosophia can help one awaken to the consciousness present within one's heart. This is its greatest potential gift, because when we meet the self, the "I" residing in our heart, we enter the realm of our wholeness and find our true home at last. We realize that our truest self is this heart-dweller rather than the one we thought we were, and that this heart-dweller knows us in every detail and loves us without any judgment. I feel a resonance between the Rosophia stone and this deeper "I," and intuit that the stone's heart currents support the growth of a web of ever-stronger and more conscious relationship with this One.

Behind the true Self I have described is Sophia, the Soul of the World. Through deepening into the true Self, we simultaneously reach further into conscious, loving, co-creative partnership with her. This is, from all I have been learning, our truest destiny, and each step on that path is an entry into joy. Rosophia allows us to touch and be touched by her.

All stones on Earth are in some way expressing the qualities of the Soul of the World, even though stones such as Azeztulite seem to carry frequencies that are more attuned to what one might call the Solar Logos, the Divine male energies. Yet even these stones are not without traces of Sophia's harmony and spontaneity of expression. Rosophia seems saturated with the love energies of the Divine Feminine as the Soul of the World. I feel in Rosophia a playfulness as well as this all-nourishing love. The mood with which Rosophia infuses one's vibrational

field—in addition to the swirling currents of love—is a high-spirited playfulness that invites one to wake up and join her.

The intimate nourishment that comes though Rosophia is meant to heal and strengthen the parts of our psyche, energy field and body that have been fragmented or damaged through the many stresses and strains of human life. When we are fully whole and strong once more (or perhaps at last), the Being gesturing through Rosophia seems to say, "Dance with me!" It is certainly my feeling that the Soul of the World wants us as partners, not only as children. We are invited into the co-creative dance of the becoming of the world; and for all of her capacity to nourish us, my heart tells me that Sophia must have advocates, defenders and lovers who wish to serve her—and partner with her—after having seen who she is. All of these things are available through meditative work with the stone Rosophia.

One very important stone to combine with Rosophia is White Azeztulite. Carrying the blessing currents of the great Central Sun, Azeztulite acts to represent the Divine energies of Heaven coming down to heal and transform the Earth. We feel White Azeztulite stimulating our upper chakras, filling us with White Light, taking on the role of the Divine Masculine. Rosophia's currents come up from the Earth below, swirling around our hearts in a dance of gentleness and love that one can envision as the gestures of the Divine Feminine. When one wears or carries Rosophia and White Azeztulite together, Heaven and Earth (the Divine Masculine and Divine Feminine) can meet and marry in one's own heart! This is one of the fundamental ways in which we can help these two stones accomplish the Divine Intention for ourselves and our world. Through this activity, we take on the role of the Divine Child—our true identity.

The combination of Azeztulite, Rosophia and Master Shamanite is energetically resonant with the Tree of Life. Master Shamanite works in unity with Rosophia and Azeztulite in a way that creates the Tree of Life pattern and energy state within one's body. The grounded and protective, purifying energies of Master Shamanite stimulate the "roots" of our body-tree. The Rosophia, centering as it does in the heart, fulfills the function of the tree's trunk—bridging the below and the above, providing stability and circulation of life-currents. Azeztulite awakens the "leaves" of our energetic Tree of Life, stimulating the upper chakras and bringing in the Light of the Great Central Sun, which gives life to the entire tree and provides the energy for growth. Human beings are destined to be the living bridge between the realms of matter and spirit, just as a tree literally bridges Heaven and Earth, drawing nourishment from below and the Light of life from above. The image of the Tree of Life as our own divine template helps us bring our conscious will into alignment with this purpose. Combining the three stones—Azeztulite, Rosophia and Master Shamanite—invites and awakens this pattern into manifestation within each of us and the world.

SPIRITUAL Rosophia helps one awaken to conscious relationship with Sophia, Soul of the World. It powerfully awakens heart awareness, facilitating one's union with one's true Self.
EMOTIONAL Rosophia's profound infusion of love is healing to all types of emotional disorders and can bring one into a healthy state of joyful, playful participation in one's life and relationships.
PHYSICAL Rosophia supports the body in overcoming any illnesses or imbalances rooted in lack of self-worth or a deficiency of self-love. It offers powerful spiritual nourishment to one's physical and emotional heart.
AFFIRMATION I am an ardent lover of the Earth, and I hold in my heart my utter willingness to give my love, support and partnership to the Soul of the World.
ROSOPHIA SPEAKS I am Wisdom, love and intimacy. I am the strength of the Earth, and the power of tenderness. I am your Beloved, as you are mine. I am the all-giving, and I need your gift. Our Love is a circle and a spiral, ever-living and always becoming.

We have touched in this chapter upon my perception that Rosophia is the stone I link most directly with Sophia, and Rosophia's role in alchemical transformation. We have also looked closely at the dynamic between Rosophia and Azeztulite—an energy pattern that facilitates the marriage of Heaven and Earth—the union of the Above and the Below—in our hearts. This is very much the goal of alchemy, and is akin to creating the Philosophers' Stone.

But the pairing of Rosophia and Azeztulite may only suggest a possibility, rather than fully manifesting it. The other two Cornerstones have roles to play in this co-creation. Moldavite's acceleration of evolution and Phenacite's visionary power contribute important elements to the contents of our alchemical vessel. And what is that vessel? I believe it is our subtle body, and our physical body. The perfect interweaving of these, along with the harmonic vibrational "chord" of the Four Cornerstones, is my best version of a "recipe" for alchemical transformation.

In the final chapter, we will try to see ahead, beyond the horizons of what we know, into the new world in which the Great Work of the Alchemy of Stones, and all spiritual alchemy, will have been achieved. Even though the worldview we were taught to believe in tells us this is impossible, my heart affirms that it is truly where we are headed.

33

The Redemption of the Earth—Commitment to the Impossible

If it's not impossible, it's not worth attempting.
—Daniel Deardorff

16th century German drawing entitled "Alchemist." Here we see a symbolic vision of the Great Work completed. The fully awakened Alchemist sits upon a rainbow, enthroned above a transparent orb that encloses the mundane world. Within, we see a human woman wearing a blindfold, indicating a lack of awareness of what lies beyond the orb. Between her feet sits a huge egg, signifying the incubation in the mundane world of what will become the New Human Being. The angelic and archetypal beings of the psychoid/imaginal realm are arrayed in a circle around the Alchemist, whose consciousness is at the center. His three faces indicate an all-seeing awareness. Beneath his left hand sits the Golden Ball, mythic symbol of wholeness and sovereignty. In his right hand, he holds the scepter of creative power. Behind him is the Great Central Sun, symbolizing the Divine. His triangular crown, echoed by a triangular radiance from the Sun, indicates that the Alchemist has reached the Third Conjunction of Union with the Divine. His position above the world orb suggests his ultimate role of protecting and blessing the Earth.

The person who does not believe in miracles surely makes it certain that he or she will never take part in one.

—William Blake

(Although it) is nothing from the astronomical standpoint . . . a thing absolutely without interest and without importance . . . from the occult and spiritual point of view, Earth is the concentrated symbol of the universe. For it is much more easy to work on one point than in a diluted vastness . . . For the convenience and necessity of work, the whole universe has been concentrated and condensed symbolically in a grain of sand which is called the Earth. And therefore it is the symbol of all; all that is to be changed, all that is to be transformed, all that is to be converted is there. . . .

—The Mother, *Collected Works,* Vol. 5, pp. 275-276

The formation of the Earth as we know it, this infinitesimal point in the immense universe, was made precisely in order to concentrate the effort of transformation upon one point; it is . . . to make it possible, while working directly upon one point, to radiate it over the entire universe.

—The Mother, *Collected Works,* Vol. 4, p. 242, Sri Aurobindo Ashram Trust, 1972

All the splendors one can experience by going up, by getting out, by leaving—are nothing! They're nothing; they don't have that concrete reality; they seem vague compared to HERE. *That is truly why the world has been created. It is in terrestrial matter, on Earth, that the Supreme becomes perfect.*

—The Mother, *Mother, or the Mutation of Death by Satprem*

The ancient art of alchemy was chiefly concerned with changing something of seemingly little value into something precious, of transforming lead into gold, thereby creating the "Philosophers' Stone." The "stone," is not a material substance, however, but is an awakened consciousness, which, though seemingly immaterial, pervades, in-forms and gives rise to all creation. The Philosophers' Stone doesn't just redeem the individual alchemist, it non-locally influences the field to such a degree that it was considered to be able to redeem the entire cosmos . . . Alchemy is a timeless, sacred art, as the alchemists' art is to become an instrument for the incarnating deity to make itself real in time and space.

—Paul Levy

When life itself seems lunatic, who knows where madness lies? Perhaps to be too practical is madness. To surrender dreams—this may be madness. Too much sanity may be madness—and maddest of all: to see life as it is, and not as it should be!

—Miguel de Cervantes Saavedra, *Don Quixote*

It always seems impossible until it is done.

—Nelson Mandela

Here we are together at the Last Chapter. If you have come this far, I thank you, because this story means the world to me. And sharing it through communicating the experiences, discoveries, insights and dreams that led me here makes me feel that the purpose of my life is being served.

I have always loved the stones. From my early childhood years hammering on rocks in the backyard, to my mid-thirties when I worked with gems as a jewelry designer, and to this day, they have fascinated me.

I was also always something of a mystic. Beginning in childhood with paranormal experiences and vivid recurring dreams, my predilection reached critical mass on the dark night in my nineteenth year when, for me, the central image from a strange recurring dream appeared in the outer world. The presence and love of the Divine Light—arriving in response to my call in a moment of shattering fear—became afterwards the object of my most intense desire.

When Moldavite entered my life and led me into a powerful spiritual experience, I understood that both my love of stones and my mystic longings were golden threads that twined together in the pattern of my life. From that day on, I knew what my work would be.

I have found a natural kinship with the alchemists and their aspirations. In Paul Levy's words their goal was, "changing something of seemingly little value into something precious." The symbol they used was transforming lead to gold, but its meaning extends all the way to redeeming the entire cosmos and becoming, "an instrument for the incarnating deity to make itself real in time and space." On a deep level, linked with my memories of the Light, I shared the alchemists' desires.

These are some exalted goals, and to many—probably almost everyone—they seem impossible. Why waste one's time reaching for an impossible goal?

This is not a trivial question. It speaks to the fundamental concerns of what life and the world are about and what we should do with our lives. I am going to try to examine these issues here, because, in the end, I am going to encourage you to commit yourself to the "impossible."

Let's start with this idea of the impossible. How do we decide what is impossible?

1. It's impossible if it has never happened before.
2. It's impossible if it doesn't fit the laws of science.
3. It's impossible if we don't know how to do it, or how it works.
4. If we can't measure it, it doesn't exist, so it's impossible.

These are the basic assertions I can think of. I may have left some out, but I think they are sufficient. From a "normal" perspective, something that would violate one or more of the four assertions is "impossible."

Of course, the most common reason for deciding something is impossible is, "Everybody says it's impossible." This reason, illogical though may be, is terribly powerful. Its energy of social coercion is an unceasing barrage in what poet Diane DiPrima, whose poem I quoted earlier, called the "War Against the Imagination". As she said in her poem, we are all in the spiritual battle for, or against, the imagination. If we are conscious of the battle, we can fight for our spiritual freedom against the culture's ingrained, almost invisible suppression. If we remain unconscious of this struggle, we become its victims, and its unwitting servants.

In the early years of European interest in alchemy, the repression by the prevailing cultural powers was more brutal than it is now. The alchemists, and anyone seeking self-awareness and spiritual freedom during those times, had to watch out for the Inquisition. Those conditions had much to do with the convoluted language and obscure symbolism the alchemists originally adopted, in order to conceal what they were really doing.

As I mentioned in an early chapter, these days, the worst we usually face from others is ridicule. But even when no one is mocking us, our internalization of cultural norms fences us in. In terms of keeping us in doubt of ourselves, in doubt of the imaginal world, and in doubt of the loving, living intelligence that permeates reality, our culture's habits of negativity and unceasing distraction can be depressingly effective. Probably the most insidious cultural chains on us are the pervasive (and almost unconscious) materialistic notions about what's "real" and what isn't.

As my friend Danny Deardorff said, "If it's not impossible, it's not worth attempting." I enjoy doing impossible things, which is why I love introducing people to the energies of stones.

Stone energies are one of the most readily available "impossible" things one can experience. Just today, in our shop in New Zealand, I introduced a young woman to Moldavite. She had never heard of it before, and I asked her to put on a Moldavite necklace while we chatted for a bit. In less than five minutes, she started fanning herself with her hand and said, "Whew! I'm suddenly feeling really warm!"

Then I opened a copy of my Moldavite book and showed her that the most frequent symptom reported by people when they connect with Moldavite's energies is feeling warm. She smiled and her eyes widened.

I know that look, because I've seen it on thousands of different faces over the past thirty-five years. It's the surprise and exhilaration we all feel when a stone affects us in an undeniable way for the first time. Something wonderful, and "impossible," has happened.

I call this humble little event "impossible" because it violates the second, third and fourth assertions in the list above. The stone energies that we feel don't follow any of the "laws" of science. There is no measurable electromagnetic energy coming from the stones and we don't know exactly how or why something like this happens. Yet millions of people around the world have experienced this "impossible" thing.

There is a delicious feeling of freedom when we do something impossible. It shows us that the limitations of so-called reality are not as small, nor as rigid, as we have been told. I think it also gives us a taste of the fact that we are much greater than we've been told.

Now let's look at this from another direction. Our science tries to explain how the universe began. These days, the prevailing story we are given is called the Big Bang Theory. From what I have read, the theory works relatively well for describing and predicting many aspects of how the physical universe behaves.

Here is how the story begins: About 13.8 billion years ago, for reasons no one can fathom, or for no reason at all, something went BANG. Actually, that's not exactly the theory, but I'm summarizing. What we are told is that the universe began 13.8 billion years ago, emerging from literally nothing. We are told that it took 10^-43 seconds of existence (which is one ten thousandth of one sextillion sextillionths of a second) for the universe to grow from nothing at all to something about a million billion billionth the size of a single atom. (For comparison, a space the size of the head of a pin could contain around a million million hydrogen atoms.)

Since then, the universe has been on a major growth spurt. After a mere 13.8 billion years, the observable universe is said to comprise about ten billion galaxies, containing about 1,000,000,000,000,000,000,000 (that's one billion trillion) stars. That is just the *observable* universe. There's more.

And there are some holes in the plot. We don't know whether there was time (or space) before the universe began. And the whole universe is expanding, faster and faster. It's thought that this acceleration is driven by a force called Dark Energy, which repels gravity. We don't know what Dark Energy is, but it's thought that it makes up sixty-eight percent of the universe's total matter and energy. Dark Matter makes up another twenty-seven percent. So all the matter we've ever seen, or ever can see or measure, makes up less than five percent of the universe.

I have no problem with this theory, except that it's clearly "impossible." After all, it violates all four assertions on my list!

Rupert Sheldrake, in his book, *Morphic Resonance: The Nature of Formative Causation,* sums this up very well: "As Terence McKenna observed, modern science is based on the principle: 'Give us one free miracle and we'll explain the rest.' The one free miracle is the appearance of all the mass and energy in the universe, and all the laws that govern it, in a single instant from nothing."

This almost makes me embarrassed at the modesty of the impossible things I believe (and do). I'm going to have to work on that.

So now, let's circle back to alchemy. The alchemists—the most enlightened of them—in their quest to transform and redeem the universe through the creation of the Philosophers' Stone, were attempting something "impossible." They were not relying on projecting the past into the future and making forecasts of how likely their success or failure might be. They were following the intuitions that rose from their own depths, and they were unafraid to commit themselves to their visions.

The question of commitment—especially in relation to the reality-shaping co-creating with Sophia to which the alchemists aspired—is very important. If we are going to transcend the old patterns of the "possible"—which are the bars of our cages—we have to focus our three powers of attention, intention and imagination, utilizing them with complete abandon and without any doubt. That is what I mean by commitment, and such commitment has been shown to transcend the so-called "laws" of nature. Let's go into that.

UNCONFLICTED BEHAVIOR

In his classic book, *The Biology of Transcendence,* Joseph Chilton Pearce describes a period in his life when he repeatedly experienced states in which he was able to do things that were seemingly impossible. He reports that he would suddenly have an impulse, and that if he immediately acted upon it without any hesitation or doubt, he could perform the feat.

In recounting this period, Pearce wrote: "I discovered how to bypass my body's most ancient instincts of self-preservation, which resulted in a temporary absence of all fear and subsequent abandon of all caution. This enabled me, at particular times, to accomplish things that would have been considered impossible under the ordinary conditions of our world."

One example of Pearce's "impossible" deeds was placing lit cigarettes against his eyelids, cheeks, arms, hands, and tongue without burning himself, or even leaving a mark. Another involved his rapidly climbing up a vertical sand cliff hundreds of feet tall, while it crumbled beneath his every step, even though he was normally terrified of heights.

A third and quite amazing instance involved his work in a check-clearing house. Pearce had a job on the midnight shift, while he attended college during the day. He found himself falling asleep in class and was concerned he would have to quit school. Then he discovered that he could drop into his "unconflicted" state and flawlessly perform his job, which involved thousands of mathematical calculations per night, while he slept!

Pearce gave this phenomenon the name "unconflicted behavior," because the critical feature was that, for it to work, he had to act spontaneously and with full commitment, as soon as an opportunity arose. In his books Pearce pointed out more instances in which people were apparently able to transcend natural "laws," such as in firewalking. Other examples included acts of superhuman strength, as in the case of a mother lifting an automobile to save her child.

Pearce used events like these as evidence that human beings are potentially far more powerful that we realize, and have the latent capacity to reshape our reality, transcending the so-called laws of nature. He believed that our apparent limitations stem first and foremost from hesitancy and self-doubt, which are born of the fear and fragmentation of self that is conditioned into us by our culture. In his view, the "miracles" he himself performed, as well as those of firewalkers, mothers, healers and saints, stem from these people dropping into the unconflicted state. In this state, one's three powers—attention, intention and imagination—are all focused together.

Pearce continues, "To find that the structure of reality was negotiable when I was free of all internal conflict was a momentous discovery for me—as was my realization that all internal conflict is produced by our fear of possible harm or death. The irony of this is that there exists for us a state in which harm really can't occur within the confines of a particular single event if we bypass our block of fear and open to this other perspective."

A bit later in his narrative, Pearce states, "Interestingly, I found that I could initiate this state by arbitrarily placing myself in harm's way and maintaining my confidence that the opening would present itself at some critical moment when I needed it, as it had with the cigarette display for my dormitory friends. It seemed to be my confidence of freedom from doubt that brought about the revelation of that force, after which ordinary cause did not have to produce the expected effect."

Assessing the implications of his experiences, Pearce wrote, "In this phenomenon lies the key to who we are and what we can do to find our transcendence and escape the current violence we bring to ourselves and earth."

Joseph Chilton Pearce had learned how to do impossible things. Knowing this, how can we dismiss the aspirations of the alchemists?

And why not us?

Thinking about Pearce's stories, I noticed that in each case he was "met" by a mysterious non-ordinary "force" or presence that enabled him to do impossible feats. As he said, "the opening would present itself at some critical moment when I needed it. . . ." This detail deserves pondering. What, or who, was "presenting itself?" It was something numinous, powerful and beyond Pearce's everyday self.

Why was it necessary to abandon all doubt and fear? Pearce also wrote that abandoning the fear of death through embracing death as an already-accomplished fact was key to his entering the unconflicted state. Yet, in a seeming paradox, he knew himself to be invulnerable for the duration of these events.

In the language we have been using in this book, we might say that the presence that met Pearce in these moments was his own Deep Self, or perhaps even Sophia. And in alchemical language, we could describe Pearce's experiences of transcendence as Conjunctions. The heightened energy that arose as Pearce approached each "critical moment," without any effort of self-protection, could be compared to the intensifying tension between opposites that precedes the experience of Conjunction. To enter the unconflicted state, Pearce abandoned himself, rather than doubting himself. In alchemical terms, this is like continuing to hold on to both polarities rather than making a false move toward one-sidedness. This gesture is our essential contribution to co-creating Conjunction and transcendence with our Divine partner.

I am reminded very much of my first mystical experience in college. As the event neared its peak, my whole grasp on "reality" was broken by the "impossible" appearance of the horse-cloud from my dream in the "real" sky. I felt myself shatter—a shock that hit me like death—and I abandoned myself to complete surrender, calling out to God. An instant later, I was met, and filled with Light. My surrender wasn't "voluntary." My worldview and my old sense of self, had shattered, and from the core of the collapse, I called out with the totality of my being. To paraphrase Pearce, the opening to the transcendent "impossible" grace appeared at the critical moment when I needed it.

Why am I bringing these threads together? I am making the case that the alchemists were not wrong in their commitment to the "impossible" aspiration of creating the Philosophers' Stone and redeeming the entire cosmos. We have already seen that impossible things happen, and we have looked at certain ways they can occur. According to Pearce, an unquestioning confidence and commitment, which includes the full acceptance of one's own death, is essential. My commitment/surrender in the college experience was accidental, but it was total. And in approaching alchemical Conjunction, one must absolutely hold the tension between the opposing polarities, no matter how uncomfortable the experience becomes. Otherwise, the leap to the transcendent perspective will not happen.

THE WAY THE DIVINE CREATES

Let's think back for a moment to the story of the Big Bang from physics. All the numbers I quoted came from theories about the way things happened in the first split instant *after* the Big Bang got started. Before that, we have no idea what was going on, or how, or why. And science rules out any involvement of a Divine force or intention. That would be unscientific.

But we aren't bound by that set of shackles. We can imagine what might have occurred.

Let's say, for the moment, that panpsychism is right, and that the bedrock of reality is consciousness, and that consciousness permeates everything. Then we might go along with the Gnostics and the alchemists, agreeing that our universe is woven throughout with the benevolent presence of Divine Wisdom that they called Sophia. We might even presume that there is a masculine counterpart to Sophia—perhaps one that we would perceive as heavenly Light. I'm not sure what name to use. We could say "God," although that name might apply better to the union of Wisdom and Light. We could choose a different name, but let's leave it for now.

Let's imagine that at some point, for some unknowable reason, or for no "reason," the Divine polarities merged in an ecstasy of creative rapture, and that this triggered the Big Bang, bringing unfathomably vast expressions of matter and energy into existence.

We're trying to unscrew the inscrutable here, so I won't keep going. What I am trying to do is imagine the feeling of what it might be like, looking at the Divine side of things with our admittedly inadequate vision.

Here is my point: If there was participation of the Divine in the creation of the universe, and if the Big Bang idea approximates what happened on the physical level, what does that suggest about the way this all came into being? To me, the almost unimaginable intensity of the Big Bang—if it was somehow a manifestation of Divine consciousness—shows us that the Divine forces gave birth to creation in a moment of utter and absolute *commitment.*

They were (or It was) engaging in *unconflicted behavior* of literally cosmic proportions. And that may be the way our impossible universe was born.

As the alchemists liked to say, "As above, so below;" and, "As below, so above." The fact that human beings can reshape reality and transcend its laws when we act with absolute commitment may give us a clue to how the Divine creates. Could the universe have come into being if the Divine consciousness were in a state of doubt? Could the sudden emergence of everything out of nothing have occurred if the Divine had held something back? It seems unlikely.

Remember, too, Pearce's assertion that the commitment that led into his states of unconflicted behavior had also to include acceptance of his own death as an accomplished fact. Without that acceptance, his commitment would have been incomplete. However, with it, he experienced an exhilarating sense of freedom that was an inseparable aspect of his ability to intervene in the usual patterns of reality.

I'll share here a personal intuition for which I have no evidence: It is my feeling that the Divine, in the act of the creation of the universe, engaged in a similar self-abandonment. Whatever the First Consciousness is, my feeling is that, in order to manifest what we call reality, it had to accept the potential that the creative act would also be its own death. That's big. But I don't see how it could have worked any other way. How could the Divine have taken out an insurance policy on itself?

What if that *is,* in some sense, the way it was? What if the Divine was somehow scattered throughout the vastness of the universe, having lost its unitary self-awareness because of having taken the risk—having made the *commitment*—that was necessary for the manifestation of material reality?

The Gnostic myths tell us that Sophia, Soul of the World, abandoned herself to the world in a creative gesture of redemption. The Gnostic belief was that our world is an imperfect creation, for which Sophia was partially responsible because she had tried to create it on her own, without a male counterpart. In remorse, and in love and compassion for the world, Sophia "fell" into every particle of matter, where she now "sleeps." This is the "fallen" aspect of Sophia, which exists, according to Gnostic lore, conjointly with her heavenly aspect, which did not fall.

The European alchemists, who were in many ways the spiritual heirs of the Gnostics, agreed that Sophia/Wisdom is present in every particle of matter, and that through co-creating the Philosophers' Stone with her, her awakening within matter would be accomplished, and the world would be redeemed. Here again is how Carl Jung articulated this:

> *For the alchemist, the one primarily in need of redemption is not man, but the deity who is lost and sleeping in matter. Only as a secondary consideration does he hope that some benefit may accrue to himself... His attention is not directed to his own salvation through God's grace, but to the liberation of God from the darkness of matter.*
>
> *By applying himself to this miraculous work he benefits from its salutary effect, but only incidentally. He may approach the work as one in need of salvation, but he knows that his salvation depends on the success of the work, on whether he can free the divine soul... What comes out of the transformation is... an ineffable material being named the "stone," which displays the most paradoxical qualities apart from possessing corpus, anima, spiritus, [body, soul, spirit] and supernatural powers.*
>
> —Jung, *CW* p. 420

This quote reminds me very much of my second Sophia dream, in which we exchanged our breath. It took place in the company of several Stone Beings—the Amethyst Man, and the three crystal-shaped Azez who exhorted me to "Dance or die!" The dream implies the Stone and it's supernatural powers, as well as Sophia's need for human assistance. She needed the exchange of breath, though she could not ask for it. And it strikes me now that "Dance or die!" is an exhortation to engage in unconflicted behavior. To truly dance is to *commit*—to throw oneself utterly into it—which means one is ready to die.

The alchemists believed that it was essential in their work of transformation to follow the ways of Nature—the ways of Sophia. They aspired to work in the realm of miracles, achieving the "impossible" goal of liberating the Divine in matter and thereby redeeming the Earth and the universe. The fulfillment of the alchemists' dream would be the union of Heaven and Earth. And they repeatedly said that this work must be a *co-creation* with Sophia.

What most excites me about the Alchemy of Stones is that it is clear to me that when we are working with stones and their energies, we are working with Stone Beings who are expressions, emanations, of Sophia. This means that our activity in this area is already a co-creation from the beginning—we are not doing it alone. The fact that so many people are not consciously approaching this work as spiritual alchemy, or with Sophia in mind, actually encourages me. It shows me that Sophia is reaching out to us, and that she may already be more awake within matter than she was hundreds of years ago. From my point of view, I have seen a marked increase in the prevalence and intensity of stone energies over just the last three decades. And this makes sense, because we know the world operates and evolves through feedback, so the more of us who meditate with stones, the stronger their energies and presence as Beings will become.

We have seen that human beings can do impossible things, and that these things occur when we fully commit ourselves and act wholeheartedly, with every fiber of our being. We can also discern from Pearce's reports and from our own experiences that in the moments when miracles happen, we are aware of being *met.* Something greater than our usual surface self joins with us, and that is when the impossible happens. Is this greater presence Sophia, or our Deep Self—or both of them together?

Again I want to emphasize how fortunate we are in these times, because the Stone Beings have awakened and are willing and able to be so actively involved in our evolutionary efforts. They, like the other beings who live in the imaginal realm, are aware that their existence is woven together with ours, and, for the most part, they very much want to help us. If we plunge into our work with our full attention, intention and imagination, and without any doubt—if we don't look back over our shoulders to check to see whether what we are doing is "possible"—we may go far.

I have tried to show that commitment is essential to our work of spiritual alchemy–and how this commitment echoes the way that the Divine creates. I do this in order to shed some light on the way to go about our *Magnum Opus*—our Great Work—and to free us from our preconceived notions of our limitations. These limiting beliefs are both conscious and unconscious, and many are embedded in our unquestioning acceptance of a more or less conventional worldview.

The union of our surface self with our Deep Self unveils what was hidden, proves that our concept of reality was too small, and is an essential aspect of our self-liberation. Experiences such as Pearce's, and such as those we can undergo in our work with the Stone Beings, introduce us to an open-ended view of reality. After all, when we can engage with impossible things, why should we believe in limitations?

We are not doing this alone. The Divine is with us. This must be so, because we stand on Earth, in the vast, astonishing cosmos, which emerged from the Divine. We are taking in the evidence of this in every moment of our perception of reality—everything we see, hear, smell, taste, touch and feel through our more subtle senses. It is all impossible, but here it is, We need to open our eyes and remember this. The alchemists believed that the *prima materia*—physical matter infused with Divine potential—was everywhere, but not recognized. That is what I am talking about.

If we understand that there could be no universe without the Divine commitment to creation, we can grasp that our own entry into co-creation must be wholehearted and free from doubt. When this happens, we are unconflicted within ourselves. We are in the state that resonates with the way the Divine creates, and we are ready to manifest the impossible.

When we break down an inadequate mindset or worldview, we are open to new and unknown things. We can begin to re-imagine what the world may be, and what we can do that gives us the sense of being aligned with our souls' purposes.

The alchemists believed that creating the Philosophers' Stone would bring about the full incarnation of the Divine in physical reality. They loved Sophia, and they aspired to join her in fulfilling her destiny. (Remember, the word "philosopher" means "lover of Sophia," and "lover of Wisdom") The alchemists' methods were guided by their discernment of the ways of Sophia and by their conviction that Sophia needs human assistance. That is what I have been calling co-creation. It was symbolized in my second Sophia dream by the exchange of our breath.

I am now saying that the path of redemption for the world and ourselves was seen clearly—symbolically—by the alchemists. Once again, the means of our participation must be through full commitment. We must learn to engage in "unconflicted behavior," joining with our Deep Selves. Awakening, redeeming and aiding in the manifestation of "the deity who is lost and sleeping in matter" *IS* our enlightenment, our self-realization and our salvation. And as Jung said, the benefits to ourselves are secondary and incidental. It is She for whom we do our work!

Achieving the Great Work of alchemy is the answer to the Crisis of the World, which we see around us in countless expressions. We know that the physical systems of the Earth are under terrible duress, and that our own psyches are so bombarded by the world's calamities that we make ourselves numb in self-defense.

I ask you now to consider the Crisis of the World from an imaginal perspective. What does it mean? What is it symbolizing? What does this pattern remind you of?

What I see is the heightening of opposite polarities—violence and compassion, danger and opportunity, fear and love, despair and awakening. We are very genuinely facing our possible extinction in the climate crisis or through the insanity of war. The walls of normalcy are shaking and we feel as though chaos is near.

In an individual, such moments often occur at the threshold of transcendence. The possibility of death is very real, and necessary for us to take into ourselves. As Pearce wrote, "Unconflicted behavior manifested from a split-second recognition that death was an integral part of that very event, that death was already within me." This recognition was what freed him to act with total abandon—to do things that are impossible.

As we look to the conditions in the world around us, we may see them as an alchemical "brew" in which many elements are coming together in an extreme dynamic tension. Rather than close our eyes to it, rather than choosing hope or despair, we can open ourselves to all that is occurring, incorporating everything into the alchemical vessel of our consciousness. We can view the intensity of our time as the climax of a long, long evolutionary process. And it may be that our role is hold it all, and to midwife the birth of the Divine Earth.

The awakening of the Stone Beings—and of ourselves with them—may be the beginning of that birth.

THE MOTHER

At the beginning of this chapter I have included several quotes from the being known as the Mother. In my view, the Mother was an alchemist—perhaps the greatest alchemist of modern times. Although the Mother did not work directly with crystals, she concerned herself very much with the Earth and it's destiny. Her other focus was the body, and particularly what she called *The Mind of the Cells*. That is the title of a book about her work, written by her confidante, a man called Satprem.

We will come back to the Mother's quotes that begin this chapter, but first I want to sketch out a few more things about her.

Mirra Alfassa (February 21, 1878–November 17, 1973), known to her followers as The Mother, was a spiritual guru, an occultist and a collaborator of Sri Aurobindo, who considered her to be of equal yogic stature to him and called her by the name "The Mother." She founded the Sri Aurobindo Ashram and established Auroville as a universal town. She was an influence and inspiration to many writers and spiritual personalities on the subject of Integral Yoga.

In her childhood, Mirra had numerous occult experiences, which continued into adulthood. She especially recalled at the age of thirteen or fourteen having a dream or a vision of a dark figure whom she used to call Krishna but had never seen before in real life. When she first met Sri Aurobindo in Pondicherry, India, in 1914, Mirra recognized in him the person whom she used to see in her dreams. During a later meeting, she experienced a complete silence of the mind, free from any thought. Mirra subsequently left India, but after several years she returned to study Aurobindo's Integral Yoga, and she remained there permanently.

Sri Aurobindo found in the ancient *Vedas* the corroboration of his intuitive understanding that human beings, as we are now, are not the final stage of evolution. "Man is a transitional being," he said. Aurobindo believed that the fulfillment of our evolution would involve the awakening to what he called the "Supramental Consciousness," and would also entail the overthrow of death.

After meeting Aurobindo, Mirra foreswore delving into the occult and devoted herself to Aurobindo's project of self-chosen evolution, or "the willed mutation of our species." The Mother, as she became known at Aurobindo's ashram, attempted to initiate an age of what she called "the divine materialism," meaning a spiritual awakening—not in the evanescent realms of spirit, but here, in the world of matter.

The Mother believed that the "Mind of the Cells" must be awakened and educated to open itself to the Divine physical life, transcending the pattern of death. The Mother viewed death as a deep, long-standing habit of the cellular mind, but not as an inviolable law. She spent decades working inwardly to reach the levels of the cellular consciousness, where she believed that not only the habit of death but also the key to the new human species dwells. She attempted to take the light of consciousness down into the depths of the matter of her own body. There she found death, linked in a million places to fear. The presence of fear in the cells triggers the habit of death. It is such an old, deep link—the fear of death and death itself—that it seems the cells tend to take the arousal of fear as a suggestion to die, and obediently follow it. How was she to overcome this? With great simplicity, she introduced into the cellular consciousness an affirmation of the deathless. It was a simple Sanskrit mantra, *Om Namo Bhagavate,* which has been translated as "I surrender/salute/offer myself to the Supreme Divine."

She worked the mantra into the cells as a new habit, a habit to replace the bondage to fear and its mortal suggestion. Instead the cells were taught to sing a hymn of trust to that which does not die—the Supreme Divine. By resonating with that pattern, she believed the cells would have no death, because the Divine is eternally self-renewing.

During her years of work with the mantra, the Mother went through innumerable physical difficulties, even as she also experienced many miraculous recoveries. In her eighties and nineties, she had over twenty heart attacks. Each time, she would seem to be dying, and then the "other consciousness" would take over and she would recover almost immediately. As she explained to her confidante Satprem, she was in a transitional state, in which the cells' old habit of fear and death would sometimes take over, at which point the "other consciousness" would suddenly arrive and revive her.

The Mother continued her work until her departure from her physical form in 1973. Did her work succeed? It's hard to be certain. Some disciples believe she never actually died. Others said she attained a "Supramental Body" (like the Rainbow Body of the Tibetans). It has even been suggested that the Mother entered and permeated the body of the Earth, and that this act has facilitated the coming metamorphosis of our species and our planet.

When I think of this, I sometimes wonder if the Mother had anything to do with the awakening of the stones. The time frames match up fairly well . . .

And another strange synchronistic detail: As I was writing this part of the chapter, I looked up the Mother in Wikipedia. Reading the entry, I noticed, with a little thrill, that today, November 17, is the forty-sixth anniversary of her "death." Hello, Mother . . .

We can see the threads of our alchemical pursuits running through the thoughts and works of Aurobindo and the Mother. Like the alchemists, they sought the redemption of matter and of the Earth, and they linked it to co-creative work between the human and the Divine. Like the alchemists, the Mother and Aurobindo envisioned immortality as a consequence of the transformations to which they aspired. Even the Supramental Body of Aurobindo and the Mother echoes the Subtle/Imaginal Body we have discussed in this book.

It is interesting to note that the Mother's mantra can be translated to mean, "I surrender myself to the Supreme Divine." This is a gesture of self-abandonment such as those we have considered in regard to unconflicted behavior, which allowed Joseph Chilton Pearce (and others) to do impossible things. And both the Mother and Pearce recognized the role played by the fear of death in short-circuiting our transcendent capacities.

In Pearce's case, he discovered the phenomenon more or less accidentally. In the case of the Mother, she investigated within herself, delving deep into the habit of death, held in the cellular mind. And the mantra was her effort to install a permanent gesture of self-abandonment, not to death, but to the deathless. She recognized that the cellular mind would endlessly repeat anything it was asked to repeat, living (or dying) in accord to what was asked of it. Her greatest difficulty was first in carrying her pure intention down to the cellular level, and then in attuning and re-attuning the cells to the vibration of the mantra. As she pointed out, the habits of fear and death are millions of years old.

The mother experienced innumerable epiphanies and visions during the years of her work on the cellular mind, from 1958 to 1973. Among these were the insights in her quotes at the beginning of the chapter, regarding the spiritual significance of the Earth. I am stunned by the thought that the Earth is the point at which spiritual forces are focused, to enable the transformation and, "to radiate it over the entire universe." Yet she was certain of this, and equally certain that her work in the body was simultaneously occurring for the whole Earth. And this, of course, echoes the vision of the alchemists.

A culminating piece of the story is stated in the third quote from the Mother, which I will repeat here. (Notice that the Mother, who had had hundreds of occult experiences, had no use for "ascension," if it meant leaving the Earth): *"All the splendors one can experience by going up, by getting out, by leaving—are nothing! They're nothing; they don't have that concrete reality; they seem vague compared to HERE. That is truly why the world has been created. It is in terrestrial matter, on Earth, that the Supreme becomes perfect."*

This all brings us back to the Gnostic story of Sophia, my speculations about the Big Bang, the goals of the alchemists and the commitment to the impossible.

The Gnostic myth of Sophia tells us that the feminine aspect of the Divine, Sophia/Wisdom surrendered herself into every particle of matter in order to redeem the world. Without this gesture, our world would have no soul, but because of it, there is "soul everywhere." (This is panpsychism.) Yet Sophia is, according to the Gnostics, "trapped" or "asleep" in matter. We could imagine the Big Bang and the subsequent evolution of the physical universe as a physical expression of that vast fragmentation.

The alchemists hoped, through their inner and outer operations, to speed up the evolutionary processes and facilitate the awakening of the Divine in physical reality. This divinization of matter would redeem what Jung described as, "the deity who is lost and sleeping in matter." And further, the alchemist, "knows that his salvation depends on the success of the work, on whether he can free the divine soul."

The stakes could not be higher, and the goal is impossible.

Once again, as my friend Danny Deardorff liked to say, "If it's not impossible, it's not worth attempting."

So think about this: If we give ourselves wholeheartedly to our deep desire—to what our hearts cry out for—what will happen? What will life be like if we wake up and ask ourselves, "What do I need to do today to pursue my heart's desire?" We may succeed in achieving the impossible. We will most certainly *only* succeed if our commitment is total, holding nothing back. Anything less keeps us in the realm of the known, the possible—what has already been done. We must give up trying to project the outcome and stop worrying about, "What if I fail?" When we give ourselves to the Great Work of transformation as true alchemists—with absolute commitment and no safety nets—we may suddenly find ourselves living in a new world that was supposed to be "impossible." And hypothetically, even if we were to fail, so what? We will have lived our lives as the most wonderful Art we could make. And this is a victory that transcends outcomes. It is a beauty that no failure can undermine.

Let's return for a moment to the Mother and her mantra. She used her prodigious meditative powers to drop down and down, through all the levels of her being, to the cells–the *prima materia* of the body. And she taught them a mantra—a vibration—a song of self-offering to sing to the Supreme Divine. If the Divine is truly "asleep" in every particle of matter, the Mother's song was more than a surrender—it was a call for the Divine to awaken.

Our surrender awakens the Divine within the world.

And when She awakens, she floods into us, into the world, into every atom of the universe. This is the redemption of the Earth.

And what of the stones?

I want you to remember the simple practice we began with. You hold a stone up to your heart. As you inhale, you invite it into your heart with complete trust. As you exhale, you offer yourself, without reservation. Your silent offer is your mantra, doing the same work that the Mother's mantra was intended for. As you invite the stone energies to come in, you are listening with your whole being, waiting for the Stone Being to answer, waiting for Sophia to reply.

When the next breath comes, you do it again.

The stone vibrations are the Earth's mantra, singing to us in a thousand different notes through a thousand different stones. Perhaps Sophia is still asleep, but now she is singing in her dream.

If we sing back to her through the stone we are holding, if we sing to her with all our love and all our longing, holding nothing back, not caring what is possible, She will awaken.

If we sing to her every day, every moment, not only through the stones, but through our nights and mornings, laughing and crying, whispering and listening, She will awaken.

If we sing with our imaginations, and with poems, with kindness, with memory, with grief, with every beautiful and shameful thing about us, She will awaken.

What will the time of miracles be like? Watch out for that question! Don't ask it, or you'll be outside the moment, and your song to Sophia will have stopped. Just keep singing to the stones, and to the Earth. And listen to them.

MY THIRD SOPHIA DREAM

Even though I have said not to ask what the future will be like when the Great Work of our alchemy is complete, I have, perhaps, seen a glimpse that I can share with you. Once again, the vision came in a dream.

> *I was at Robert Sardello's old house and school in North Carolina. Kathy and I had just arrived there for a class Robert would be teaching. Before going into the house to find Robert, I went out to the vegetable garden. I think I planted some seeds and seedlings, or maybe I had just planted them a few hours before.*
>
> *The garden was spacious, with aisles between the beds. There were also wooden racks above some of the beds for plants to climb. As I strolled among the beds, I noticed that the seedlings I had just planted were growing incredibly fast. They were almost fully matured plants, in just hours. I felt a thrill and a sense of wonder as I saw this everywhere in the garden. There was a feeling of numinous presence, and the sense that the garden was behaving in this exceptional way because of an underlying consciousness that was "pushing" the rapid growth. I remember seeing bean plants running and twining along the wooden rails, growing several feet in mere seconds.*
>
> *The more I saw this, the more charged I felt with the numinous energy that was pouring itself into the plants and bringing this "impossibly" rapid growth. I felt in myself an energy that might have been the same presence. I had the intuition that this was happening in part because of the intention I had brought into planting the seeds and seedlings. It was not my doing—it was more as if the intention, along with my long-standing focus on co-creating*

> *with Sophia, had brought this about. Somehow, what I had done had opened the space within which Sophia herself had both the desire and the ability to manifest this. In my elation, I also intuited that Sophia could do many other seemingly miraculous things in the world, if we used our intention to open the space. It was clear to me that we could not do this ourselves, but that we could enable her to do so. I felt that we need to show her, through our eyes, the condition of the world, which she will then set about to heal . . . very rapidly, more rapidly than we had ever imagined could be possible.*

After I awoke, I stayed in a semi-sleep state, feeling and contemplating the dream. I could still sense the elation of seeing the plants grow so fast, as Sophia's act of co-creation. I mused about the thought that maybe this dream is true . . . maybe we have no idea about how radically the world can change and heal, if we turn our intention to Sophia. It feels to me that this is not something to be done with any sort of focus on a specified outcome, such as: "Make all the plants grow fast," or whatever else we might conceive of. It is more a matter of giving love to Sophia and inviting her into us. It is a matter of "planting seeds" of intention through actions, as well as thoughts and words.

What kinds of actions should we take? I am not talking about protests, or cleaning up the environment, though we must do these too, for different reasons. We must do them for their material effects, and for what they mean symbolically. But the dream implies to me that by themselves, these things will never be enough.

What is enough (or such is my prayer) is that loving and engaging with Sophia—holding our awareness of our need for her, and inviting her into us—is what is needed. My dream seems to say that the response we ultimately see will not conform to any plan we try to make. We will be going about our seemingly too humble efforts when suddenly everything takes off, and the Soul of the World, who waited in silence for so long, will come forth. It will be an expression of her nature, not ours, so we cannot control it, or even expect it. Yet it will nonetheless be the response of Wisdom to the world's need.

As I have been saying throughout this book, Sophia needs our human help. She is what Paul Levy called the "incarnating deity," seeking to make herself real in time and space. As the Mother said, "It is in terrestrial matter, on Earth, that the Supreme becomes perfect." In my view, it is with the stones—through whom we hear and feel Sophia herself reaching into terrestrial matter—that our efforts can be most effective. Through them, we can join with her in co-creating the fulfillment of her great aspiration. This is the highest goal of the Alchemy of Stones, and in this we are made anew, into all that our destiny has called us to be.

> *Sophia does not belong to the individual alone, she is a cosmic principle, and if that principle is strengthened by alchemy, she becomes stronger for all beings and all life . . . Those who find the way to union with Sophia experience her wisdom, guidance, and her eternally renewing energies of life . . . Sophia is the principle of enlightenment, and the alchemist who has helped her find a new body experiences that enlightenment . . . such a union feeds the human partner in every conceivable way and constantly renews them with spiritual vigor. Union with Sophia means a loving relationship with the source of life's energies.*
>
> —Jeffrey Raff, *The Wedding of Sophia*

Perhaps it is more than coincidental that the goal of alchemy has always been called the Philosophers' *Stone.* A "philosopher" is literally a "lover of Sophia." Millions of people all over the planet have, over the last few decades, found themselves inexplicably drawn to stones and their energies. Are we hearing the inner call to join in the great alchemy of world transformation that will provide Sophia with the "new body" Raff speaks of? And will the new body of Sophia be the very stones of the Earth, and the Earth itself? As the Mother said, "the whole universe has been concentrated and condensed symbolically in a grain of sand which is called the Earth." At a later time, she confirmed: "the Earth . . . was made precisely in order to concentrate the effort of transformation upon one point; it is . . . to make it possible, while working directly upon one point, to radiate it over the entire universe."

Could anyone ever dream of being committed to a more wonderful "impossible" goal?

For many of us, even if we don't fully understand, it seems that we are already committed to it.

LAST THOUGHTS

What do we do now? Everything.

Enjoy, appreciate and love your life. Greet every being you meet with blessing. Be generous. Have fun. Hang out with your Stone Beings and your human friends, and your plant pals, and your animal amigos. Be ravished by rainbows and stunned by sunsets and clobbered by cloud formations. Sit in the grass with the sun in your lap and remember how grateful you are.

Remind yourself that everything you look at is looking back at you, and that She is looking out through their eyes, and through yours.

I just realized that I wrote all this advice for myself. But if you like any of it, feel free to help yourself.

A PAIR OF POEMS

I want to end this chapter, and this book with two poems. I didn't write them, but I feel that they fit the mood of how I want to say farewell. The first poem was written by Miguel de Unamono, and it speaks to me of the commitment to becoming whole through our work of spiritual alchemy.

THROW YOURSELF LIKE SEED

Shake off this sadness, and recover your spirit;
Sluggish you will never see the wheel of fate
That brushes your heel as it turns going by,
The man who wants to live is the man in whom life is abundant.

Now you are only giving food to that final pain
Which is slowly winding you in the nets of death,
But to live is to work, and the only thing which lasts
Is the work; start there, turn to the work.

Throw yourself like seed as you walk, and into your own field,
Don't turn your face for that would be to turn it to death,
And do not let the past weigh down your motion.

Leave what's alive in the furrow, what's dead in yourself,
For life does not move in the same way as a group of clouds;
From your work you will be able one day to gather yourself.

The last poem offers a picture of what it may feel like when the Philosophers' Stone has been created and the Divine is completely awakened in matter. We cannot really imagine that moment, but I usually think of it as something huge and powerful. It may be of limitless scope and profundity, yet at the same time—since Sophia is subtle—elegantly quiet. This poem was written by Juan Ramon Jimenez.

OCEANS

I have a feeling that my boat
has struck, down there in the depths,
against a great thing.
And nothing
happens! Nothing . . . . Silence . . . Waves . . .

Nothing happens? Or has everything happened,
and are we standing now, quietly, in the new life?

AND ONE FINAL QUOTE . . . OR TWO

As we do our work and live our lives, it is important to stay awake in our imaginations. I want to offer once again the words of Marie Louise von Franz, describing the mode of perception of a person who has achieved individuation [wholeness]:

> *Normal ego consciousness would be replaced by an imaginative consciousness that beheld the world through the eyes of imagination. It would see underneath the apparent solidity of ordinary reality to the meaning hidden there. It would behold the spiritual powers at play in ordinary life, and it would possess the freedom that perceiving symbolically bestows.*

Imaginative consciousness gives us freedom. It expands our reality, and it allows us to notice synchronicities—the golden threads that are Sophia's invitations, her love letters to us. William Blake reminded us of this in the first chapter of this book:

I give you the end of a golden string
Only wind it into a ball,
It will lead you in at Heaven's gate,
Built in Jerusalem's wall . . .

Many thanks.
Many blessings.

Robert Simmons

OPPOSITE: Robert and Kathy in Kauri Tree

It's that dream that we carry with us
that something wonderful will happen,
that it has to happen,
that time will open,
that the heart will open,
that doors will open,
that the mountains will open,
that wells will leap up,
that the dream will open,
that one morning we'll slip in
to a harbor that we've never known.

—"It's the Dream," Olav Hauge,
translated by Robert Bly

EPILOGUE: THE ALCHEMY OF STONES IN DAILY LIFE

We shall not cease from exploration
And the end of all our exploring
Will be to arrive where we started
And know the place for the first time.
—T.S. Eliot, "Little Gidding"

In this book, we have taken a long journey of exploration together. Now we are at the end, and if we have kept our eyes, our imaginations and our hearts open, we recognize that we have arrived at where we began. For here we are, still in our bodies, and in much the same lives that we were living when we started. We know the same people, most of us are still working in the same jobs, and we have our same collections of stones. What is it to "know the place for the first time?"

I want to propose that "knowing the place" means seeing everything through the eyes of the alchemical imagination. We remember that the energies we feel from stones have revealed to us that panpsychism is real—there is soul everywhere. Everything around us looks the same on the surface as it did when we began, but now we are aware of the underlying benevolent intention of the Soul of the World, who loves us from all directions. Our most significant achievement, if we have attained it, is that *we now know and feel this reality.* If we do, the love that the Earth needs will flow from us naturally, and continuously.

Yet, even when we experience deep insights, our habits have a habit of coming back. How can we live our lives in mindfulness of all that we have discovered?

Sometimes synchronicities converge into a great Conjunction, and we feel the presence of Spirit all around us, as if the whole universe were watching, hoping we will make the right choice. At other times, things seem pretty mundane. I'm not sure which situation is more challenging to navigate, but for most of us, the mundane days seem more frequent.

But that is not real. That is the illusion of our old habits. Remember the words of Novalis:

The world must be romanticized. In this way the originary meaning may be found again. To romanticize the world is to make us aware of the magic, mystery and wonder of the world; it is to educate the senses to see the ordinary as extraordinary, the familiar as strange, the mundane as sacred, the finite as infinite.

To "romanticize the world" is *precisely* what it is to "arrive where we started and know the place for the first time."

How do we do that in daily life? We educate our senses through the use of our three human powers—intention, attention and imagination. We hold a stone and channel our powers toward perceiving it as a Being, not just a "thing." We observe the events of our day, watching for Sophia's gestures through the meanings of unexpected synchronicities. We let ourselves imagine that our whole world is sacred.

One of the easiest ways of doing this is to practice meeting everything as a "thou" rather than an "it." And while you're at it, it's worthwhile to bless everything you encounter, as often as you can remember to do so. Sending well-wishing to everything you pass when you take a walk—a tree, a rubber ball, a street sign—is actually a lot of fun, and it takes you out of your preoccupation with yourself. Blessing the things around you is a way of re-imagining them that does justice to the mystery and wonder of the world.

There are endless ways to go about the Great Work of transforming the universe through imagining it differently.

ALTARS AND RITUALS

Since our Alchemy of Stones is so deeply involved with exercising our three human powers of attention, intention and imagination, we can enhance our work by creating some focal points.

I wrote earlier about creating temporary altars to court a Stone Being you are hoping to connect with. You can also create more permanent altars for long-term purposes. I have an altar in my studio that is dedicated to Bear, my animal Spirit Helper. The altar has stones on it, and some carvings and images of different bears. If I want to talk to Bear, or ask for help, I stand by that altar and tune in. If I am in serious need of Bear's attention and help, I make little offerings and put them on the altar. I really like Bear, so I've noticed that I get a good feeling every time I look over and see that altar.

In writing this book, I've realized that now I want to make an altar for Sophia. I'll use some stones, and some images of her from paintings and religious icons, and I'll most definitely arrange some pieces of Rosophia there! And I'll talk to her—out loud, and in my heart.

Altars like these make a place in one's life, and in one's awareness, for relationship with these beings. The act of making an altar is a ritual, and creating it utilizes our three powers.

I think it's important to touch base with my altars—to look at them and think about the Beings they represent—as often as I can. I am sure that this attention gives life and vitality to the Beings, and to my relationship with them. A long-neglected altar can be rather sad, and can act more as an energy drain than as a source of vitality. So if this happens, I think the altar should either be rededicated with a ritual that one creates, or dismantled.

Rituals can go with altars, or they can be created anywhere, any time. A ritual is a way of intentionally stopping one's mundane activities and addressing oneself to the sacred. Rituals often involve making offerings, and traditionally the offerings are called sacrifices. (The word sacrifice comes from two Latin words that mean "to make sacred.") I like to make rituals in which I offer stones to the Earth, and to Sophia. I have rituals in which I place Azeztulites in the ocean or in rivers or lakes, and I ask Spirit to join with me and the Beings of Azeztulite to heal the waters of the Earth. And I have rituals in which I bury Azeztulites in the ground for the healing of the land.

I love using stones in these rituals, but they are not completely necessary. Think back to our discussion of radionics in the chapters about Photonic Stone Layouts. It was discovered that the most important factors in improving the growth of plants were the intention and imagination of the people doing the experiments. (The radionics machine was unnecessary!) A ritual is a way of directing your attention, intention and imagination to Spirit, and making a gesture to Spirit. Such gestures act as nourishment, and are much appreciated by the Beings we are addressing. The shamanic teacher Martin Prechtel says that the Beings of the Other World (which we would call the psychoid/imaginal realm) are all starving, because so few people do rituals now. This makes me think of my dream that seemed to say that Sophia needs our "breath"—our offer of ourselves in relationship—in order to live.

Altars and rituals can serve the dual purposes of focusing and strengthening our imaginal work, and of nourishing the Beings with whom we are building relationships. When we include stones in these, we are inviting their active participation and asking them to co-create with us, which they are very ready to do!

WORK WITH YOUR STONES

This book has offered a great many ways of working with stones. You can choose whichever ones you are drawn to. It is not necessarily important to do all the practices in this book, or to do them in the order in which they have been presented. But if you want the ideas you've been reading to transform from concepts into realities, it is important to do some of them, or to create your own practices and do those. In this way, you will create ways of being that contribute your portion to the co-creation of the new, living Earth. And as you practice this, it will become more and more real for you.

You can hold a stone over your heart and meditate. You can make a mandala of a Stone Being, you can set up a body layout, a photonic layout, or a crystal grid. You can dialog with a stone, make a stone elixir, or design a stone energy tool.

It is more important to practice doing something every day to reinforce the new worldview you are building than it is to focus on one activity in particular, or all of them as a list.

It can be difficult to fit even a daily meditation into our busy lives. What I do, even when I do nothing else, is sleep with my Rosophia stone near my heart each night. Before I go to sleep, I invite Sophia to enter my heart as I inhale, and I offer my breath and my heart to her as I exhale. As I do this, I remember that she is real, and that the energy I feel is truly there. And sometimes, when the meaning of all that comes to me, I feel a deep satisfaction and joy. Doing this every night has become important to me. It feeds Sophia, it feeds my Deep Self, it even feeds my everyday personality. And it weaves the three of us together.

When I finished the last chapter of this book, I called my friend Robert Sardello. I had worked quite late on the book the night before, and I felt like a little celebrating. After we had chatted for a while, Robert asked me what I had learned in the five years I had been working on *The Alchemy of Stones.*

Of course, I have learned quite a lot. But what I said to Robert was, "The thing that matters most to me is that I have learned that all of this—the stone energies, the Stone Beings, and Sophia—all of this is really, really real."

I had arrived at the place where I began, and *I knew it* for the first time.

I wish the same for you.

DANIEL (3D) DEARDORFF & ROBERT SIMMONS DISCUSS THE SUBTLE BODY

In August of 2019, I had my last visit with my close friend and spiritual brother Daniel Deardorff. During that time, I read him the manuscript of this book, and he made a number of helpful comments and suggestions. He died the following month. As I described in the Introduction, I was able to establish contact with Danny after his death—first through a medium and later by my own volition, and his. In October, we connected with one another again, and we extended our discussion of the subtle body. I wrote down two of his comments from our August conversation, and almost all of our October interaction. I present this material below.

1ST QUOTE FROM AUGUST 2019, prior to Danny's death: *"Your subtle body is the whole of the integrity of your consciousness as you have built it in your life—through the efforts of engagement with Spirit—through winding the golden threads that you notice as you follow your path."*

2ND QUOTE FROM AUGUST 2019, regarding the subtle body and the reality of stone energies: "Chi *exists within the living world, and in the beings that inhabit the crystals. And chi is the substance that accumulates to form the subtle body.*

Therefore, when we discover that there is chi flowing into us directly from making a living contact with one of the Stone Beings, and that that chi is going directly into the formation of our own subtle body, then how could we deny it?"

DANNY & ROBERT CONVERSATION 10/7/19 THE SUBTLE BODY:

R: When I think about you where you are now, I see an image of you. You are standing up and you have legs that are rather skinny, but you can walk. Is that a meaningful or appropriate inner picture? [**NOTE:** In life, due to polio, Danny's legs were very thin, and they did not function.]

D: Yes, I am existing in what we were talking about as the "subtle body." My "legs" are thin in the image, because that's how they were in my life, and because less energy went into them during my life, because of the polio. [chuckling] But, yes, I can "walk" now. It's much easier without gravity!

R: What can you tell me now about the subtle body, from your new perspective?

D: The subtle body is an image—an enduring image—that symbolically embodies the condition of your soul.

R: In the quote from you that I wrote down before you died, you said first that the subtle body is "the whole of the integrity of your consciousness as you have built it in your life." I'm interested in what you meant by integrity in that context, and how you see that now.

D: I see it now pretty much the same way that I did then. Your integrity is, first and foremost, the insistence on truth. That has a big effect on the subtle body, because truth is an energy that strengthens it. Integrity means that truth is *integrated* all through you, like the skeleton and bloodstream and nerves are all integrated through your physical body. To have a body made out of consciousness, with no flesh to hold it together, we need something else to provide substance and stability. Truth does that. It's an energy that builds on itself.

R: What about the lack of truth?

D: Lies—whether told to oneself, to others, or both—create "leaks" in one's subtle body. They dissipate the energy that holds you together. In the visual image, they appear as gray blotches. Some people's subtle body is nothing but a mass of gray blotches. Those souls are not ready to move forward after they die. They need to go for a long course of healing.

R: What happens to the souls of people in that kind of condition? Do they fall apart and really cease to exist?

D: I'm new here, but I haven't been shown anything that makes me think so. I have seen that some souls who lied too much in life have to go for healing, and that this is because the system here is loving and benevolent.

R: I've been writing about stone energies and saying that they affect the subtle body, and that we feel them through the subtle body. What about that?

D: You're on the right track. Stone energies are food for the subtle body. They can nourish it and help it grow healthy and strong—which translates here as vividness and stability of one's image, which is the same thing as having a strong and balanced self-awareness. And different stones feed different energy portals or areas of the subtle body. This is like the way different foods nourish different aspects of the physical body, only more so.

R: I've been practicing my stone meditations on the presumption that the energy exchange works both ways, and that it's important to offer our energy, as well as to receive theirs. Do you see it like that?

D: Everything works both ways! It's all feedback and the dynamic tensions between polarities. And the "third thing" that is the real magic is the *relationship.* That's what sings! When you make a feedback loop, you are "stringing the harp" of vibratory connection between yourself and the stone. If all you do is receive, pretty soon you have eaten everything, and it wasn't even a very nutritious meal. But yes, when you *exchange* energies with the stone beings, you enliven them and increase their vividness in the imaginal world, just as they nourish you and your subtle body.

R: What about the stones you had in your life? Did they help you?

D: They could have helped me more, if I had done more with them. But the stones that you gave me were helpful—especially two of the skulls ("Ector the Protector" and "Inkidu"), and also those power necklaces you made for me. When I was wearing those, they made me feel much better—stronger. There are other things we do that make a difference, too. You don't have to use stones, but they offer an easy way, and they put you into relationship with the Earth, which is very good for us.

R: What are some other ways that the subtle body can be nourished and strengthened?

D: Well, you know that music was a fantastic source of energy for me in my life. And the music I heard and loved, and the other music that I created and performed—both of those made me strong in this realm. And they nourished my vitality in the physical world as well. Remember, your subtle body is densely woven into the physical one—for better and for worse.

But other things that enhance the subtle body are like what I was talking about in our conversation before I died. "Golden threads" are all the things in life that connect you to "Heaven." So, for our teacher Robert Bly, and for us, poetry could be a golden thread. For us, it was not just poetry as an art form—it was specific poems that spoke to us and touched us and crystallized in our subtle bodies as little gems of power and enrichment. So, for example, the poems you and I both loved—especially in you because you memorized some of them—became like stars that made constellations in our psyches. Their power is partly due to their many paths of association to other ideas and images in our awareness. A poem that you love—or a good song—sends out its rays of light inside you and holds things together in a cohesive unity.

R: I'm sure now that this is why Robert used to tell us all that we should memorize poems so that we would have them "in our bodies." He was speaking about our subtle bodies.

D: Yes, he was, but remember that until we die the subtle body and the physical are really inextricably entwined into each other.

R: Do you want to say anything else about the "golden threads?"

D: Yes. The golden threads you and I talked about are like fishing lines dangled down from Heaven to Earth, and they do connect them with each other. But there are not exactly "hooks" on those fishing lines, even though there is definitely "bait" down at the end of the line near us! A synchronicity baits the line by grabbing your attention with something that happens that is not logical but is very meaningful to you. Also, finding the passions that speak to us and climbing inside of them—as I did with my music and as you have done with the stones—is essential for winding the golden threads that connect us to Heaven and enliven our subtle bodies. That's where the analogy with fishing changes and gets more interesting. You could say we are the "fish" and that Spirit—or Sophia, as you like to say—is sending down the golden threads. But it is our job to wind up the threads till we are in the boat!

Other things, such as love, friendship, commitment to things you believe in, acting with kindness—and even things like humor and laughter—can build up your subtle body. But all of these are subsets of the main set, which is truth. Love, friendship, kindness and humor have to come out of truth to do any good. You won't help your subtle body by loving someone falsely or laughing at someone else's misfortune.

R: It feels, as I am having this conversation with you, like your movement out of your physical body into the place where you are now is like a birth into a new life.

D: Yes. It's a birth, but in this case, we don't forget where we came from.

This drawing by Daniel Deardorff portrays the peaceful communion between the spiritual alchemist and the realm of Nature.

R: I've been told by my friend who is a medium that souls, after they die, "have the volume turned way down" when it comes to emotions. She says that this gives the soul a chance to view the life they just completed from a more objective perspective. Is that how it feels to you?

D: Yes and no. I think when people die without much spiritual preparation, and especially when there were high-tension emotional issues that weren't resolved, this happens, and it does act as a protection. In my case, having lived my life with a severe physical disability, and having done a lot of soul work, made a lot of music, and having wound up many of the golden threads that came my way—I don't need that protection so much. My subtle body is quite strong, so I have the option of how much emotion I can allow myself to feel. I'm still reviewing my recent life, so it's good for me to be able to "zoom in" and "zoom out" of the emotions as I feel is best.

R: You know all about my interest in spiritual alchemy, and my embrace of the alchemical worldview. I notice that in alchemy there is a strong desire at the very center of the art—the longing for a union of the physical world with the Divine. Achieving this is called "creating the Philosophers' Stone." But sometimes I wonder whether a desire for a radical change in the way things are is a mistaken idea. Maybe things are perfect as they are from the spiritual perspective . . .

D: Remember that whether something is possible or not is no reason to reject your desire. In fact, "impossibility" is essential! You need to follow your longing and not worry about whether it is appropriate from some imagined "spiritual perspective."

R: Can you say anything about where we are going? Are any big spiritual changes coming?

D: That's kind of another clunky question, but I understand why you're asking. The "future" is not planned or determined. It's a dance, and who knows what the steps will be?

But one thing that interests me is that I can feel a lot of interest in this realm in the possibility of being less separated from the reality that the living people exist within. There's a desire to see whether this can be done, and all of this comes from the desire of Love to fulfill its longing. So it's possible that you and others—and maybe eventually most people—will perceive more and more of the beings and goings-on in the subtle-imaginal realm. I think that the healthier and stronger consciousnesses here will be perceived more readily when this is done purposefully (not like hauntings and breakthroughs of unhappy souls). This could be felt as a great reunion and healing of the world.

R: I'm suddenly thinking of the Judgment card in the tarot deck, with the angel blowing a trumpet in the sky, and all the coffins floating on the water, and the people who had died standing up out of their coffins and raising their arms in joy.

D: Right! The image of the coffins floating on water is a way of showing that the realm of the afterlife is "watery"—fluid and mutable, like images. But also water exists in a state between that of earth and that of air. The imaginal world is the in-between realm, as water is the in-between element that permeates and unites both Earth (the physical) and Air (the spirit realm).

So, your image of the Judgement card is a good one for picturing the reunion I was mentioning. It might seem at first as if the dead have suddenly "arrived" from nowhere, and for no obvious reason, but remember the trumpet and the angel. That's what I am calling the desire of Love to fulfill its longing.

I promise you there will *not* be floating coffins, and you won't see bodies rising from their graves. That was a religious metaphor that too many people took literally!

R: Okay, I feel this is complete for now. I hope you can turn up your emotional volume control so you can feel how grateful I am for this, and how much I love you.

D: Me too. And I don't have to turn up my volume for this. It's part of me. I love you too. Bye-bye, for now.

APPENDIX B

CLIMATE CHANGE & CRYSTALS

BY ROBERT SIMMONS WITH RICHARD GROSSINGER

By trying to feed the Holy in Nature the fruit of beauty from the tree of memory of our Indigenous Souls, grown in the composted failures of our past need to conquer, watered by the tears of cultural grief, we might become ancestors worth descending from and possibly grow a place of hope for a time beyond our own.

—Martin Prechtal

Like most people, we have taken a lot of pleasure from having this life, on this planet, as individual centers of selfhood in this teeming vessel of being. We enjoy gentle sunshine, pleasant breezes, soft summer rain, thick green grass, swimming in the ocean, seeing wild animals, touching trees. We like to be able to breathe fresh air, drink clean water and eat good food—our alembic. We like friendship and humor, peace and poetry. We like to see children and be happy imagining the lives they may have.

Because of global climate change, we have a situation now where it is time for us to consider that most of the things we love about life could be lost forever. The Earth's ability to support life as we've known it is in grave danger, and human activity is the reason for that.

No one wants to believe it, and those of us who do believe it have to force ourselves to think about it. What's happening is deeply frightening, and it is difficult not to feel overwhelmed when we face it. The Theater of Terrestrial Astronomy—the Sacred Transmutation—is being challenged to *transmute itself at a deeper level, or lose its long transmutation: from the first pebble tools of Homo africanus to the crystals I disseminate from Heaven & Earth.* Transmutation is being asked *to transmute itself.* And that is the ultimate alchemy and Philosopher's stone, the passage from cave art to skyscrapers of mute, imprisoned rock to a world of speaking and guiding stones.

The Intergovernmental Panel on Climate Change put out a report in October of 2018, stating that our species had twelve years left to drastically change our collective behavior, or we will face a climate catastrophe of almost unimaginable proportions. The amount of carbon released into the atmosphere in the last 150 years has already set in motion climate imbalances that will grow worse for many decades, even if we were to cease and replace all fossil fuels in usage now. But, if we do *not* change our behavior soon, the additional carbon we discharge into the air we breathe will bring about consequences unimaginably malign.

A *Washington Post* article states: "Climate change is a threat multiplier that touches everything, from our health to our economy to our coasts to our infrastructure. It makes heat waves stronger, heavy precipitation events more frequent and hurricanes more intense, and it nearly doubles the area burned by wildfires. It supercharges natural disasters like Hurricane Harvey and the Camp Fire, as those suffering the effects of these events know firsthand. Climate change is no longer a distant issue in space or time: It's affecting us, today, in the places where we live."

The methane released from Arctic permafrost could take the matter of limiting greenhouse gas emissions out of our hands in the near future. Runaway climate change could transform the planet into "Hothouse Earth." This level of warming could make it impossible for large segments of the human population to grow enough food or find enough fresh water. It could cause flooding of coastal areas, turning millions of people into climate refugees. And these mass migrations could lead to wars, as well as outbreaks of disease.

We must recognize that this is alchemy too—collective alchemy, collective stone-craft and stone technology—and it has, perhaps, an alchemical solution somewhere in its chaos-rule phase states and dynamic disequilbrium. What is alchemy except molecule-atomic nigredos, coagulations, sublimations, and projections, from the cores of stars to gene splicing, Internet-roaming 'bots, solar panels, floating cleansers of oceanic plastic, and the sacred earth biochar: the simultaneous depradation and regeneration of Earth.

The Covid 19 pandemic that spread around the world in the early months of 2020 has shown us how interconnected civilization is, and how susceptible to catastrophic disruption by a tiny living RNA crystal. Our health systems become overwhelmed when a pandemic spreads. The economic system of a country or of a planet can collapse, just because of one powerful, yet temporary, lesion, making us vulnerable to more pandemics and environmental shifts.

AND THE LIST GOES ON. WHAT CAN WE DO?

Twelve years from 2018 is not a big window.

Yet we have the tools at hand to slow climate change, and to limit it to less-than-catastrophic echelons. We have the technology to draw most of our future energy from solar panels and storage cells, wind and other renewable energies that represent gravity, heat, and shear force in their more basic manifestations. Their cost levels are now lower than those of fossil fuels; it's just that most people haven't made the cognitive shift. Most oil-based industries and the economies they drive are as addicted as opioid addicts. We have the capacity to convert our diet to mostly-vegetarian sourcing. That alone will greatly reduce the volume of carbon discharged by fanatically linear agribusinesses of meat and dairy mega-production. Alchemy is by definition nonlinear—only its chemical successors require linearity, purely physical forensics, and a silencing of the psyche of stone.

Climate science experts have pointed out that if the United States mobilizes in a way similar to what it did as a unified "house" for World War II, it is possible to meet even the most critical targets for slowing climate change. As a secondary benefit, this could transform the country's infrastructure, creating millions of jobs.

Some of us can remember the 1945 song "The House We Live In," popularized by artists from Frank Sinatra and Paul Robeson to Mahalia Jackson and Neil Diamond. The music was written by Earl Robinson, later blackballed by Joseph McCarthy as a Communist. The lyrics were written by Abel Meeropol, who adopted the two Rosenberg boys, Robert and Michael, orphaned by the execution of their parents, Julius and Ethel. The ballad was used in the Presidential campaigns of Franklin D. Roosevelt, Henry A.Wallace, and Jessie Jackson. It is what we are missing today—the spirit with which America entered World War II and remade the world in its image of hope, service, and sacrifice:

> *"The house I live in, a plot of earth, a street*
> *The grocer and the butcher, and the people that I meet*
> *The children in the playground, the faces that I see*
> *All races and religions, that's America to me."*

Remember those things we said we love about being alive. There's also

> *"The place I work in, the worker by my side*
> *The little town or city where my people lived and died*
> *The "howdy" and the handshake, the air of feeling free*
> *And the right to speak my mind out, that's America to me."*

Some people think that it doesn't matter if the Earth burns up and can't support life any more. By the time things get that bad, they'll all probably be dead. That's the worldview of Donald J. Trump and his cronies, and of authoritarians such as Brazilian president Jair Bolsonaro: "Give me mine and let the patsies pay."

What about,

"the things I see about me, the big things and the small
The little corner newsstand and the house a mile tall
The wedding in the churchyard, the laughter and the tears
The dream that's been a-growin' for a hundred and fifty years"?

We are part of the Earth forever, part of its noosphere and intelligence, part of its genome and hive mind, an expression of its mineral being, latency, and conscious manifestation. We are also eternal. We exist in the eternal flow of love. That connects us, living crossed—as Thornton Wilder put it, "There is a land of the living and the land of the dead and the bridge is love, the only survival, the only meaning."

It is our love that makes the world worth saving.

One of the mysteries of our world has to do with the riddle: Where is the boundary between the material world and the spiritual world? Some religions say it is a border that is crossed at death. A materialist might tell you that there is no boundary because there is no spiritual world. A philosopher of panpsychism might insist that the boundary is everywhere and nowhere, because spirit and matter are woven so tightly together that they are actuality different aspects of the same thing. Those of us who feel crystal energies are meditating with the most obviously *physical* of material objects–stones–because of their *spiritual* aspects. We believe that connecting with the spiritual energies of stones will improve our condition as spirit, and/or our health, emotional wellbeing, etc. In my own work, I have come to see the stones as Beings, and as the expressions or "Angels" of the Spiritual Earth. I believe that by relating with the Stone Beings, through contact with the physical stones, we can approach and enter into relationship with the Soul of the World. That is what is subject to climate demise but also climate resurrection and redemption.

Is there such a thing as the Soul of the World? The ancient Gnostics recognized that the Soul of the World, which they named Sophia, is present in every atom of matter, and in all things, both living and non-living.

In my work with crystals and stones, I view their energies as beneficial, loving currents emanating from the Soul of the World, or Sophia. This is why we intuitively call these energies spiritual. In my view, whether we believe we 'feel' stone energies or not, we love stones for what they are and for the beauty and love they radiate. And through them, we are able to love and know Sophia.

This love is a two-way street. We need the love that is offered to us, which manifests as the beauty, harmony and wisdom of the world. Without it, we could not live, nor would we want to. The Soul of the World *needs our love* in order to live.

Paulo Coelho in his novel *The Alchemist* wrote: *"Love is the force that transforms and improves the Soul of the World. . . . It is we who nourish the Soul of the World, and the world we live in will be either better or worse, depending on whether we become better or worse. And that's where the power of love comes in. Because when we love, we always strive to become better than we are."*

The Earth herself is in danger, and the danger is not only physical or requiring a solely physical response. The Earth is not separate from her soul, any more than we are. The Earth is a multidimensional being in space, time, and other dimensions. Climate's vector radiates through all of these and is radiated back as other things in the greater cosmic. Look again at the planet that astronauts first viewed from the Moon in 1969: fragile, alive, transcendental, a stone in alchemical transmutation moment by moment.

If we are going to come through the spiritual initiation of Covid 19 and climate change, we will need to address *that* stone—the Earth—in myriad ways. Alchemy will be of increasing significance, and not only as metaphor, because it offers an occult pathway into microbiology, physics, and climate science, providing a psychospiritual, human component and medicine bundle for shamanic intercession. It lands somewhere around where the Tibetan Karmapa helped the Hopi renew their lapsed rain dance during a drought and where the algorithms of artificial intelligence confront the transmutative carbon and silicon imbedded in their own systems: transmutational biology = transmutational meteorology. Shamanic alchemy is a pathway for active climate prayer.

So, to all of you who love crystals and stones, my suggestion is simply this: Pour your love into them. Send your love through the stones to their Source, the Earth. Each stone in your collection is in essence the Earth herself, Sophia, the Soul of the World. Each one is her child, her angel, as you also are. Let us not only look to the stones for *our* healing, let us turn to the stones to *offer* healing, to offer love.

Sit down in a quiet place and hold one of your stones. Maybe bring it close to your heart. As you inhale, invite the living Being of that stone into your heart. As you exhale, offer out your appreciation and love to the Stone Being. Keep going, and think about how vulnerable the world is right now, and how much it matters to you. Then as you continue breathing, remember that *it is this air that we need to heal.* Then remember that the word *respiration* has at its core the word for spirit. Our atmosphere is our breath, our life, and the life and breath of Sophia, the World Soul. So, as you meditate, realize that the stone in your hand is Her, and the breath in your lungs is Her, and the love in your heart is what you have to offer Her, and that is what She needs. And keep breathing, and let the flow of love pour back and forth through the stone, and through you, like the tides of the sea.

> *Every breath taken in by the man who loves, and the woman who loves, goes to fill the water tank where the spirit horses drink.*
>
> —Robert Bly

THE ALCHEMY OF STONES

STONE DICTIONARY

ADAMITE **KEY WORDS** Joy, love, creativity, enthusiasm, perseverance **CHAKRAS** Solar Plexus (3rd) and Heart (4th) **ELEMENT** Fire, Wind **PHYSICAL** Supports heart, stomach, small intestine **EMOTIONAL** Facilitates lifting one's mood, strengthening the will **SPIRITUAL** Aids conscious connection with spirit guides and angels, facilitating one's capacity to evolve through inner communion with them

Adamite is a zinc arsenate mineral with a hardness of 3.5. It can enhance the alignment of the heart and solar plexus chakras, allowing one to synergize one's will with one's feelings, and it kindles the fires of optimism and determination. It facilitates contact with spirits, angels, guides and the souls of those who have passed on. Clairvoyants, readers, psychic healers and shamanic practitioners will find that Adamite increases one's sensitivity, enhancing the clarity of the messages one sends to and receives from entities in the higher vibrational realms.

AEGIRINE **KEY WORDS** Clearing, protection, energy, confidence **CHAKRAS** All **ELEMENT** Earth, Fire **PHYSICAL** Supports liver, spleen, gallbladder, recovery from exposure to toxic substances or energies, supports stamina and recovery from addiction **EMOTIONAL** Aids with lifting depression, clearing guilt and shame, building confidence **SPIRITUAL** Assists removal of negative energies and entities

Aegirine crystals are ideal for removing negative or stuck energies from the subtle body. They are stones of confidence and strength, allowing one to shine one's Light, even in the darkest places. They can be effective for breaking attachments of negative entities or patterns to one's etheric body. Carrying or wearing Aegirine can be an effective stop-gap measure for forcing the release of these debilitating energies, and working with Aegirine in body layouts or in conjunction with other subtle energy healing modalities can, in time, repair damage to the protective auric shield.

AGATE, BLUE LACE **KEY WORDS** Communication, clarity, confidence **CHAKRAS** Throat (5th) **ELEMENT** Water **PHYSICAL** Supports healing of sore throat, laryngitis, thyroid problems, speech impediments **EMOTIONAL** Calms the emotional body, aids confidence in communication, helpful for releasing negative habits of interaction and speech **SPIRITUAL** Helps one communicate one's deepest truth, enhances communication with inner guides and connection with one's inner wisdom

Blue Lace Agate is a stone for improving communication on all levels. It is beneficial for those who have difficulty making themselves heard by others, or who wish to become more articulate in their speech. It helps instill clarity of thought and unwavering intent in regard to the ideals and goals that matter most. It stimulates eloquence, and it enhances loyalty, trustworthiness and perseverance.

AGATE, DENDRITIC **KEY WORDS** Growth and wisdom through inner work **CHAKRAS** All **ELEMENT** Earth **PHYSICAL** Supports healing of back pain, neck problems, low blood count, health issues related to stress, addictive behavior, low self-esteem **EMOTIONAL** Assists with clearing and releasing self-destructive patterns, enhancing self-esteem, building a stronger ego **SPIRITUAL** Aids in seeing oneself with honesty and clarity, encourages development of one's true self and embodiment of one's highest potential

Dendritic Agate is ideal for strengthening the fiber of the self through inner work. It helps one to keep a positive attitude while going through needed transformations. It can help reduce stress in difficult times. It is well suited to purification of the body and energy field, and to working towards spiritual transformation.

AGATE, ELLENSBURG BLUE **KEY WORDS** Eloquent communication of the heart's truth, soothing the throat chakra, calming the mind, opening psychic vision **CHAKRAS** Throat (5th), Heart (4th), Third Eye (6th), Crown (7th) **ELEMENTS** Earth, Water **PHYSICAL** Supports healing of skin and throat, clearing pathological neural patterns **EMOTIONAL** Aids in releasing negative judgments, fears, anger and encouraging compassion **SPIRITUAL** Finding inner truth, courage and freedom.

Ellensburg Blue Agate is beneficial for the throat chakra, conveying an enhanced ability to see and speak the truth. It links the throat with the heart, allowing one to communicate what the heart knows. It aids artists, poets and musicians to eloquently express the treasures of their souls and the messages that come through them from the Soul of the World. It emanates peace and can relieve stress.

AGATE, FIRE **KEY WORDS** Vitality, sexuality, creativity, will **CHAKRAS** Root (1st), Sexual Creative (2nd), Solar Plexus (3rd) **ELEMENT** Fire **PHYSICAL** Stimulates youthful energy, sexual organs, digestion, bowels **EMOTIONAL** Intensifies emotions, increases passion, enhances sexual attraction **SPIRITUAL** Revitalizes spiritual and physical energies, inspires creativity

Fire Agate awakens the lower chakras and fills one with the zest for living. It lights one's inner fires of life force, creativity, sexuality and will. It activates the senses and increases the pleasure one takes in everyday life. In helping one come fully into the body, Fire Agate assists one in making real the divine blueprint of one's life purpose. It supports self-assertiveness, confidence, playfulness and general happiness. It encourages one to make friends and to initiate loving sexual relationships.

AGATE, HOLLY BLUE **KEY WORDS** Bringing Spirit into matter, stimulating psychic abilities, **CHAKRAS** Crown (7th), Third Eye (6th), Heart (4th) **ELEMENT** Wind **PHYSICAL** Aids in head and brain problems, headaches, stress, nervousness; attracts spiritual help with dementia, psychosis **EMOTIONAL** Encourages calm, clarity, compassion, stability, freedom from anxiety, worry, jealousy and fearfulness **SPIRITUAL** Enhancing inner vision, clairvoyance, clairaudience, prophetic vision

Holly Blue Agate carries the highest vibration of all the Agates. It is a stone for grounding spiritual energies in the physical world and can be used to link the higher spiritual "bodies" to the physical self, so one can experience multi-level awareness. It activates the psychic centers in the brain, enhancing ESP, lucid dreaming, mediumship and other paranormal abilities. It also helps one to 'hear' the prompting of one's spirit guides.

AGATE, MOSS **KEY WORDS** Stability, persistence, grounding **CHAKRAS** Root (1st), Heart (4th) **ELEMENT** Earth **PHYSICAL** Aids in stabilizing of all body systems; enhancement of sensing capacities; aiding circulation, digestion, neuronal activity **EMOTIONAL** Encourages peaceful temperament, lessens mood swings, helps develop stronger will forces **SPIRITUAL** Opens inner doors to communion with Nature spirits, helps one find and adhere to one's higher purpose

Moss Agate emanates the vibrations of balance and stability in the physical domain. It is excellent for individuals convalescing after an illness, or for those "in recovery" from addictions. It enhances concentration, persistence, endurance and bringing goals to completion. It can be used as a talisman for increasing the effectiveness of physical workouts and developing a healthier body.

AGNI MANITITE **KEY WORDS** Initiation, spiritual power, inspiration, will, awakening **CHAKRAS** All **ELEMENT** Fire, Storm **PHYSICAL** Supports the brain and nervous system **EMOTIONAL** Inspires joyous embrace of life, dispels negative emotional patterns **SPIRITUAL** Facilitates spiritual initiation, visionary experiences, evolutionary growth. Aids discrimination, dispels negative attachments, stimulates creativity.

Agni Manitite is a stone of creative power. It acts like a fuse that sets off the "explosion" of one's full capacity to manifest one's visions. It helps one to become aware that our abilities are much greater than we have realized. It inspires us to do the inner and outer work necessary to bring forth our wholeness, and our inner power to create. Agni Manitite is a stone of the will. It helps one to know what one truly wants, and to concentrate and focus one's intention in single-minded action, bringing one's visions into manifestation.

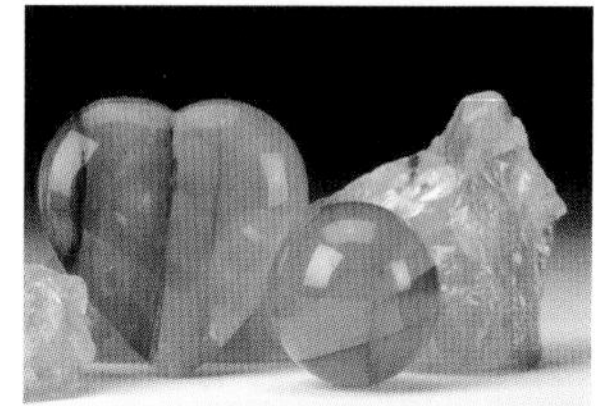

AGNITITE **KEY WORDS** Infusion of Divine Fire, life force, purification, transformation **CHAKRAS** All **ELEMENT** Fire **PHYSICAL** Fills body with fiery energy, increases vitality, detoxifies cells **EMOTIONAL** Increases one's passion for spiritual and physical life **SPIRITUAL** Awakens the Divine Fire of consciousness on the cellular level

Agnitite stimulates the entire Liquid Crystal Body Matrix, infusing it with the Divine fire of *prana*. It enhances intuition, healing, strength of will, and the awareness of one's shared consciousness with that of the world. In healing, Agnitite can spiritually purify the blood and cellular tissues. It aids in detoxifying and energizing all of one's systems. Those who wish to help in the formation of the Planetary Crystal Grid of Light are urged to work with Agnitite,

AJOITE **KEY WORDS** Love, healing, emotional support, goddess and angelic connections **ELEMENT** Storm **CHAKRAS** Heart (4th), Throat (5th), Third Eye (6th), Crown (7th), Etheric (8th–14th) **PHYSICAL** Aids in alleviating stress or depression. **EMOTIONAL** Supports healing, calming and balancing the emotional body **SPIRITUAL** Links one's awareness with Divine guidance, facilitates empathic connection with the Soul of the World

Ajoite clears and activates the throat chakra. It cleanses the auric field and aligns the Light body with the physical. It can harmonize the energies of any chakra, disperse contracted thought forms that are creating pain, dispel negativity, and call forth the truth. It can draw out the poisons of sorrows, fears, rage and old wounds, replacing them with love and forgiveness.

ALEXANDRITE **KEY WORDS** Joy and wisdom, release of sorrow **CHAKRAS** Heart (4th), Third Eye (6th), Crown (7th) **ELEMENT** Wind, Water **PHYSICAL** Stimulates pineal and pituitary glands, helps balance brain functions **EMOTIONAL** Aids with relieving stress, encouraging trust, awakening joy **SPIRITUAL** Enhancing awareness of Divine Love, recalling past lives, accessing Akashic records.

Alexandrites are stones of joy, and for that reason they ought to be taken seriously. These stones have a connection to Source energies of the higher dimensions,. It can help one realize that the joy of the celestial realms is also simultaneously here at every moment. Alexandrite's teaches us to take in all energies that come to us, to transmute them into such harmony and beauty as is possible, and to do this with the inner resilience of a commitment to joy.

AMAZONITE **KEY WORDS** Truth, communication, harmony **CHAKRAS** Heart (4th), Throat (5th) **ELEMENT** Water **PHYSICAL** Aids cellular regeneration, healing from trauma, gout, arthritis **EMOTIONAL** Facilitates releasing fear of judgment or conflict, finding inner freedom **SPIRITUAL** Receiving and communicating higher knowledge, speaking truth

Amazonite is a stone of harmony, both within the self and among people. It assists one in communicating one's true thoughts and feelings without over-emotionalism, and it awakens compassion through stimulation of the heart chakra. Sleeping with Amazonite can bring one's competing unconscious tendencies into focus through the symbolism of dreams. Meditation with Amazonite makes the deeper aspects of oneself more conscious, aiding spiritual growth.

AMBER **KEY WORDS** Light, warmth, solar energies, clarification, healing **CHAKRAS** Solar Plexus (3rd) **ELEMENT** Earth **PHYSICAL** Increases life force, optimal functioning of organs and systems **EMOTIONAL** Releasing fear of judgment or conflict, finding inner freedom **SPIRITUAL** Provides energetic protection from negative influences

The energies of Amber are very solar, and they create a comfortable sense of warmth, health and well-being in the wearer. Amber is recommended to be worn or carried by those recovering from illness or injury, because its warm and nurturing energies put us in touch with our own essential strength and security. It helps one to see the path to recovery and have the courage and confidence to follow it. Amber can also spur one's innate capacity to manifest prosperity.

AMBLYGONITE **KEY WORDS** Calm power of the will, manifestation of creative ideas **CHAKRAS** Solar Plexus (3rd) **ELEMENT** Fire **PHYSICAL** Soothing and restorative to the digestive system and bowels **EMOTIONAL** Overcoming anxiety, establishing a calm, optimistic outlook **SPIRITUAL** Finding the courage to express oneself creatively, discovering and fulfilling one's life purpose

Amblygonite is an excellent stone for bringing one's emotional body into balance for the liberation of one's innate creative energies. It can help ignite the creative spark, moving one forward on the path to the fulfillment of one's higher purpose. Wearing, carrying or meditating with Amblygonite can assist one in finding the peace and inner clarity to do one's unique work of self-expression. It is both a soother and an energizer, calming the emotions while awakening the creative mind.

AMEGREEN **KEY WORDS** Mind/Heart integration, spiritual connection, compassion, psychic ability, emotional healing **CHAKRAS** Heart (4th), Crown (7th), Etheric (8th–14th) **ELEMENT** Earth, Wind **PHYSICAL** Supports overall healing, recovery from injury, is beneficial to the heart **EMOTIONAL** Releasing emotional wounds, learning to trust and love **SPIRITUAL** Facilitates connecting with Divine Love

There is a wonderful softness and lightness about the energies of Amegreen. Wearing or carrying this stone helps one integrate the mind and heart. It allows for the creativity and inspiration of the mind to be guided by the heart's wisdom. It opens one's consciousness to the influence of the higher energies of the Divine. It helps one give and receive both spiritual and human love. It assists in lifting oneself out of the doldrums and making a new effort in one's life.

AMETHYST **KEY WORDS** Protection, purification, Divine connection, release of addictions **CHAKRAS** Third Eye (6th), Crown (7th), Etheric (8th–14th) **ELEMENT** Wind **PHYSICAL** Overcoming addictions, tinnitus, nerve disorders, aids oxygenation of the blood **EMOTIONAL** Helps clear negative or addictive emotional patterns **SPIRITUAL** Facilitates conscious connection with Spirit Guides, Angels and Source

Amethyst is a stone of spiritual protection and purification. It can aid in giving up bad habits and in curbing overindulgence. It can clear one's auric field of negative energies and unhealthy attachments. It stimulates the crown chakra and is an aid to meditation, helping one to still one's thoughts and move into higher states of consciousness.

AMETRINE **KEY WORDS** Mental and spiritual clarity, decisiveness **CHAKRAS** Solar Plexus (3rd), Crown (7th) **ELEMENT** Wind, Fire **PHYSICAL** Stimulates metabolism and digestion, enhances brain function **EMOTIONAL** Aids in overcoming fear and insecurity, finding one's own power **SPIRITUAL** Facilitates attuning to Divine inspiration and acting on inner guidance

Ametrine is a harmonious blend of Amethyst and Citrine energies. It is stimulating to the crown chakra, protective to one's auric field, purifying to one's personal energies and uplifting to the spirit. It can aid greatly in letting go of bad habits and addictions. It is a stone for enhancing mental clarity, creativity and will. It brings one's spirituality into harmony with the mind, often catalyzing a profound flow of new ideas and insights.

AMMONITE, RAINBOW **KEY WORDS** Ancient life force, spiral of vitality moves into all the chakras and cells, access to Earth's Akashic records **CHAKRAS** All **ELEMENT** Earth **PHYSICAL** Charges one's overall physical vitality **EMOTIONAL** Creates pleasure, excitement and enthusiasm for life **SPIRITUAL** Helps expand one's awareness to knowledge of Earth's spiritual history

The fire in Rainbow Ammonite is the fire of a very ancient impulse. It is the Life Force itself, and this stone can bring a powerful infusion of primal vitality into one's body and energy field through the root chakra. It also useful in meditation for accessing the Akashic records of Earth's distant past. It can aid in the activation of the Light Body through bringing the vibration of spiritual Light into the lower chakras.

AMULET STONE **KEY WORDS** Positive energy, slow and steady healing, clearing negativity **CHAKRAS** All **ELEMENT** Earth **PHYSICAL** Supports all organs and systems, ideal for recovery from illness **EMOTIONAL** Helps quell anxiety, tension, dispels bad moods, bad dreams **SPIRITUAL** Assists in finding natural harmony with oneself and the Earth

Amulet Stones are attuned to the natural harmony of the Earth. They can aid in regulating healthy sleep patterns, and in dispelling bad dreams. They are excellent for children, because their currents are stable and comforting. In healing, the effects are slow and steady, rather than dramatic. Amulet Stones calm emotional instability, anxiety and/or depression. They support harmonious relationship within the self, and with the Earth.

ANANDALITE **KEY WORDS** Kundalini awakening, enlightenment, genius, creativity **CHAKRAS** All **ELEMENT** Storm **PHYSICAL** Stimulates and clears meridian system, fills the cells with Light **EMOTIONAL** Dissolves negative patterns, rekindles one's natural joy **SPIRITUAL** Stimulates latent psychospiritual capacities, awakens genius

Anandalite is the premier stone for awakening the kundalini energy lying dormant around the base of the spine. Often its currents are felt first as heat, then joy, and finally as Light. Anandalite stimulates spiritual awakening. It awakens latent capacities, psychic abilities, past life memories and creative inspirations. It can clear blockages in the chakras and meridian system, and it fills the cells with spiritual Light, dispelling destructive patterns and activating one's Divine blueprint.

ANDALUSITE **KEY WORDS** Cleansing, comforting, protective, friendly **CHAKRAS** Root (1st), Third Eye (6th) **ELEMENT** Storm **PHYSICAL** Acts as an overall strengthener of one's constitution **EMOTIONAL** Provides replenishment of the emotional body, psychic protection **SPIRITUAL** Provides connection with Divine realms, protection of one's energy field

Andalusite vibrates in harmony with the heartbeat of the Earth. It can be used to strengthen and energize any chakra and to repair holes in the auric field. It carries the etheric pattern of wholeness for the body, especially the teeth and skeletal system. The friendliness of this stone makes it ideal for those trying to overcome feelings of loneliness, isolation, depression, anxiety and various fears. It is recommended as a protection stone for those traveling or working in areas of danger or negativity.

ANGEL AURA QUARTZ **KEY WORDS** Upliftment, peace, serenity, expanded awareness **CHAKRAS** Crown (7th), Etheric (8th–14th) **ELEMENT** Wind **PHYSICAL** Aids in releasing stress; helps with muscle cramps, indigestion **EMOTIONAL** Ideal for calming, purifying and uplifting the emotional body **SPIRITUAL** Facilitates reaching deeper states in meditation, connecting with Angels

Angel Aura Quartz helps one to be a beacon of inner beauty, peace and spiritual awareness. It can facilitate remembrance of past incarnations, insights into one's spiritual purpose, the ability to channel higher knowledge, and the opportunity to commune with loving spiritual entities. Meditating with these stones, one can easily move beyond the body and go to one's "inner temple." This is a place of purification and rest, in which one's angelic guides are present, ready to help one release stress and move into deep peace.

ANGEL WING BLUE ANHYDRITE **KEY WORDS** cleansing; purification; angelic connection **CHAKRAS** Throat (5th), Third Eye (6th), Crown (7th) **ELEMENT** Wind **PHYSICAL** Stimulates energetic cleansing in healing, supports skeletal system and joints **EMOTIONAL** Enhances compassion, forgiveness, communication **SPIRITUAL** Deepens meditation and prayer, aids in communing with angels

Angel Wing Blue Anhydrite is one of the most powerful "soft" energy stones. It is ideal for clearing blocks, erasing implants, soothing disharmony and providing a conduit of strength through which one can reconnect with Source. In meditation, it can provide the experience of "flight." For those who are "angels in human form"—those who have taken on a human incarnation in order to assist in planetary transformation—Angel Wing Blue Anhydrite can facilitate a deep remembrance of one's true identity.

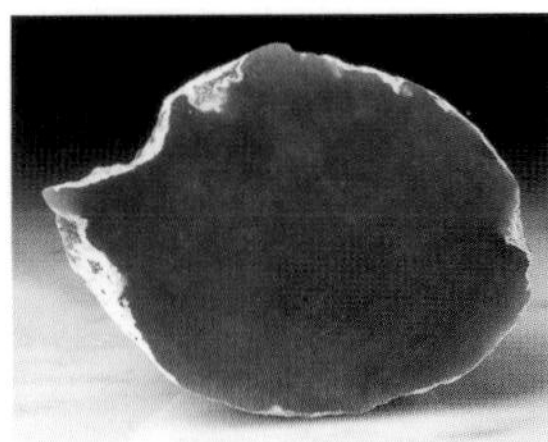

ANGELITE **KEY WORDS** Angelic communication, serenity, expanded awareness **CHAKRAS** Throat (5th), Third Eye (6th), Crown (7th) **ELEMENT** Wind **PHYSICAL** Supports bone density and health; helps with arthritis, healing fractures **EMOTIONAL** Encourages clear and compassionate communication **SPIRITUAL** Facilitates angelic communication and the development of spiritual gifts

Angelite can act as the anchoring talisman for the energies of one's guardian angels, guides and other friends in Spirit. It can aid in receiving spiritual guidance for oneself and others. It facilitates lucid dreaming and remembrance of dreams. It can help one tune into memories of past lives and to the Akashic records. In meditation, Angelite can facilitate moving into peaceful inner states of expanded awareness.

APACHE GOLD **KEY WORDS** Strength, personal power, confidence, prosperity, assertiveness, recall of past lives, embrace of one's destiny **CHAKRAS** All **ELEMENT** Earth **PHYSICAL** Facilitates healing through energizing the subtle body **EMOTIONAL** Aids with confidence and inner strength **SPIRITUAL** Stimulates past life recall, insights into oneself, knowing and embracing one's destiny

Apache Gold brings a brilliant golden Light into one's auric field, enhancing mental clarity and amplifying the power of one's will. It is an excellent stone for manifestation and abundance. It is a very good stone for grounding one's dreams into reality. It stimulates the mind, so that it is easier to find the right words to express oneself. It enhances the Light Body, stimulating a greater radiance. It helps one to know one's destiny, allowing one to persevere until one's life-purpose is fully realized .

APACHE TEARS **KEY WORDS** Grounding, protection, psychic attunement, emotional healing **CHAKRAS** Root (1st), Sexual/Creative (2nd), Heart (4th) **ELEMENT** Earth, Fire **PHYSICAL** Supports strength and stamina, boosts immune system **EMOTIONAL** Clears negative thought patterns, heals emotional wounds **SPIRITUAL** Appreciation of physical life, protection from negative forces

Apache Tears can be used for grounding and for protection from negative energies. They link easily with one's emotional body and can be used to cleanse and heal old wounds or emotional 'baggage' from the past. They are excellent talismans of protection from negative forces and can be used to cleanse one's auric field and etheric body.

APATITE, BLUE **KEY WORDS** Psychic activation, access to knowledge **CHAKRAS** Third Eye (6th) **ELEMENT** Wind **PHYSICAL** Helps calm headaches, overcome vertigo, improve eyesight **EMOTIONAL** Uplifting one's mood, overcoming acrophobia **SPIRITUAL** Aids exploration of past lives, lucid dreaming, dream recall

Blue Apatite is a cleansing influence on the auric field, especially in the mental body—the vibratory level associated with psychic perception and paranormal abilities. It stimulates visionary states and is a good stone to keep in one's pillowcase for lucid dreaming and astral travel. Blue Apatite aids in recovering past life memories and information from ancient civilizations. It is an excellent stone to use in combination with 'record keeper' crystals. For prophetic work, it can be used with Trigonic Quartz crystals.

APATITE, GOLDEN **KEY WORDS** Creation, clarity, confidence, manifestation **CHAKRAS** Solar Plexus (3rd) **ELEMENT** Fire **PHYSICAL** Stimulates metabolism and endocrine system, weight loss **EMOTIONAL** Enhances self-confidence and charisma, hope and passion **SPIRITUAL** Aids in manifesting prosperity and one's passions and dreams

Golden Apatite is one of the purest crystals for mental clarity, strength of will, and manifestation. It assists one in developing assertiveness and confidence in all situations. Carrying or wearing Golden Apatite can increase the effect of one's will in social situations and can enhance personal charisma. It can assist in the manifestation of prosperity on all levels. It can help one find the courage to take risks and the clarity to know which risks to take. It can be a useful ally to anyone in a competitive situation.

APATITE, GREEN **KEY WORDS** Knowledge of the heart, relaxation, revitalization **CHAKRAS** Heart (4th), Throat (5th), Third Eye (6th) **ELEMENT** Water, Earth **PHYSICAL** Aids overall healing and refreshment, healing the heart **EMOTIONAL** Supports health of the emotional body, optimism, generosity **SPIRITUAL** Facilitates prosperity consciousness, abundance of health and happiness

Green Apatite is a wonderful tonic for frayed nerves and stress. It is ideal for those who wish to pursue a teaching or healing role in life, since it aids one in putting out energy while maintaining inner balance. Green Apatite can also assist one in communication with Nature spirits, as well as in channeling healing energies to the Earth. Green Apatite allows one to clearly communicate the balanced wisdom of the mind and heart, keeping one attuned so as not to overdo either one's logical or emotional side.

APOPHYLLITE, CLEAR **KEY WORDS** Interdimensional awareness **CHAKRAS** Crown (7th), Third Eye (6th) **ELEMENT** Wind, Earth **PHYSICAL** Supports infusion of spiritual Light, making the Light Body physical **EMOTIONAL** Aids in rediscovering trust in the Divine after disillusionment **SPIRITUAL** Facilitates interdimensional travel, connecting with guides and angels

Clear Apophyllites excel at attuning one to the higher-frequency energies of the angelic and interdimensional domains. These crystals can serve as windows into many other worlds. If one can imagine one's point of awareness moving into the interior of one of the Clear Apophyllite crystals, one will find, once "inside," that geometric corridors of Light lead off in all directions, and that one's consciousness can travel along these corridors to myriad realms of inner experience.

APOPHYLLITE, GREEN **KEY WORDS** Connection with Nature spirits **CHAKRAS** Crown (7th), Third Eye (6th), Heart (4th) **ELEMENT** Wind, Earth **PHYSICAL** Helps with healing degenerative diseases, detoxifying the body **EMOTIONAL** Encourages joy in the wonder of physical life, finding hope and sweetness **SPIRITUAL** Facilitates communication with Nature spirits, psychic opening

Green Apophyllite crystals and clusters emanate a sweet energy that resonates with the abundant life force of the world of Nature. Meditation with them can open one's perception to seeing and interacting with Nature spirits, devas, and even to telepathic communication with animals and plants. Green Apophyllite can assist work with Nature spirits in gardening or in restoring wild areas. It can aid one in animal communication, and it can work similarly for those who wish to communicate with plants and even other minerals..

AQUA AURA QUARTZ **KEY WORDS** Calming and relaxing, connection with spiritual realms, enhanced communication, psychic protection **CHAKRAS** Throat (5th), Third Eye (6th) **ELEMENT** Water **PHYSICAL** Cooling fever, relieving stress, cleansing the auric field **EMOTIONAL** Calming anger, finding inner peace **SPIRITUAL** Aids channeling, communication of truth, creating prosperity

Aqua Aura Quartz is highly stimulating to the throat chakra, enhancing one's ability to communicate inner truth. It has a calming effect on the emotional body, and can be used to soothe anger, cool feverishness, and release stress. It can be an aid in becoming a conscious channel for spiritual wisdom. Aqua Aura Quartz has a very high and intense vibration. It can be used to activate all of the chakras. It can smooth and heal the auric field and release negativity from one's emotional, physical, etheric and astral bodies.

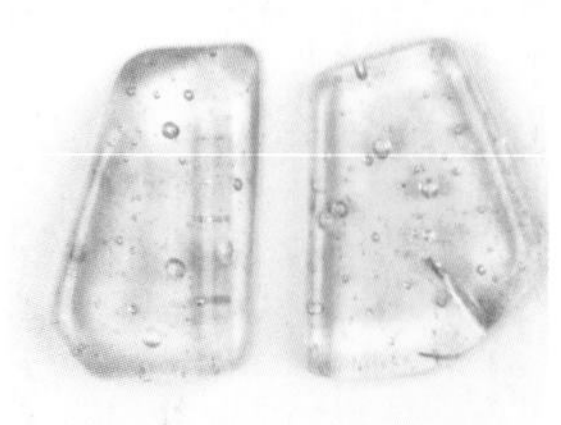

AQUA LEMURIA **KEY WORDS** Link to memories of Lemuria, and to Lemurian spiritual capacities, sacred sound **CHAKRAS** Throat (5th), Heart (4th) **ELEMENT** Water **PHYSICAL** Dispels stress, relaxes tense muscles **EMOTIONAL** Calms the emotional body **SPIRITUAL** Stimulates multiple psychic capacties, including the capacity for speaking in the lost tongues of sacred sound

Aqua Lemuria enhances awareness of the realms of dreams, angels, spirit guides, the ancestors, the feminine, shape-shifting, interdimensional traveling, intuition, clairvoyance and related paranormal abilities. It is healing to the emotional body and nourishes the entire auric field. It can aid in accessing the Akashic records of ancient Lemuria. It facilitates communication with plant and animal spirits and it can smooth the journey of shamanic initiation.

AQUAMARINE **KEY WORDS** Cooling, soothing, enhancement of clear communication **CHAKRAS** Throat (5th), Heart (4th) **ELEMENT** Water **PHYSICAL** Helps with sore throats and throat conditions, inflammatory illnesses **EMOTIONAL** Good for calming anger, relieving stress, expressing true emotions **SPIRITUAL** Speaking one's deepest truth, meeting the Divine Feminine

Aquamarine facilitates calming and cooling, from hot flashes to anger. It activates the throat chakra, assisting in the clear communication of one's highest truth. It is a stone of the Water element, bringing one in touch with the subconscious, the domains of spirit, and our deepest emotions. It brings one to a relaxed, alert stage of consciousness in which one is fully aware of one's own store of knowledge, wisdom and feelings, and is able to articulate them all with clarity and conviction.

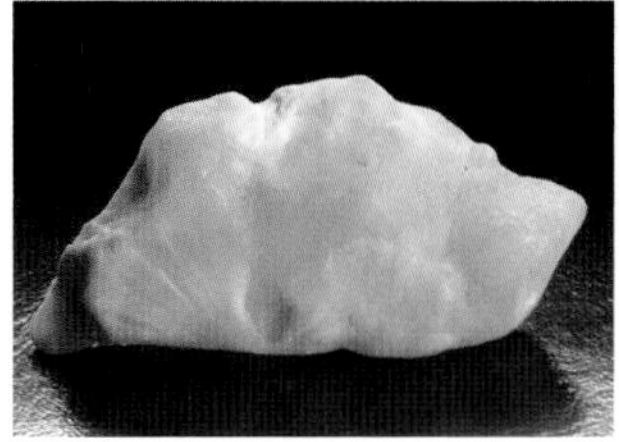

ARAGONITE, BLUE **KEY WORDS** Intuition, emotional perception and psychic ability **CHAKRAS** Throat (5th), Heart (4th), Third Eye (6th) **ELEMENT** Wind, Water **PHYSICAL** Aids with respiratory issues, lung health, breath work **EMOTIONAL** Increases enjoyment of emotion, renews zest for life **SPIRITUAL** Facilitates enhancement of spiritual and psychic capacities

Blue Aragonite enhances emotional perception and intensifies enjoyment of all emotional states. It relieves the fear which leads us to numb ourselves to the joys and sorrows of life, and brings a renewed zest and courage for experiencing all of one's feelings. It is a powerful intensifier of positive emotional states, and it aids in healing past and present emotional wounds. It intensifies one's natural empathic and psychic abilities, and it can help healers and intuitives.

ARAGONITE, SPANISH **KEY WORDS** Awakening higher awareness, attunement to the future, grounding heavenly energies on Earth **CHAKRAS** Third Eye (6th), Crown (7th), Etheric (8th–14th) **ELEMENT** Wind, Fire, Storm **PHYSICAL** Supports regeneration and rejuvenation of the cells and body **EMOTIONAL** Strengthens empathy, especially with animals **SPIRITUAL** Opens Crown for full energy infusion and Light Body activation

Spanish Aragonite is the most highly energetic form of Aragonite. It powerfully stimulates the third eye and crown chakra and allows one to attune to the etheric chakras above the head. This facilitates connection with the higher-frequency domains such as the angelic realms. It facilitates the infusion of the Light Body into the physical form,

ARAGONITE STAR CLUSTERS **KEY WORDS** Balanced energies, emotional healing, strength, confidence **CHAKRAS** All **ELEMENT** Storm **PHYSICAL** Supports healing and regenerating bones, increased vitality and stamina **EMOTIONAL** Healing emotional wounds, aligning the self with love **SPIRITUAL** An ideal diagnostic aid in energy work, clears the auric field

Aragonite Star Clusters are powerful allies for the healing and balancing of the emotional body. They can assist in maintaining a center of serenity in trying circumstances and in discharging subconsciously held tensions relating to past emotional wounds. They are powerful diagnostic tools for crystal workers. Aragonite Star Clusters enhance one's emotional strength and confidence, allowing one to become a "human star" emanating love and compassion. They are wonderful tools for releasing pain and fear, and bringing love into the world.

ASTARALINE **KEY WORDS** Protecting and nourishing the Light Body, healing the cells **CHAKRAS** All **ELEMENT** Wind, Water **PHYSICAL** Supports healing of destructive habits on a cellular level **EMOTIONAL** Encourages comfort and joy in the transformation process **SPIRITUAL** Builds a "cocoon" for the Light Body, activates the Divine blueprint

Astaraline fills one with a sense of wellbeing, as if one is being cradled in Light. It can help those involved in self-healing to bring harmony and functional alignment to all of the bodily organs and systems. Its nourishing, coherent emanations encourage the cells to find the new path to existing in a state of grace, leaving behind the old habits of deterioration and degeneration. Astaraline amplifies the power of the Divine blueprint for the Body of Light.

ASTROPHYLLITE **KEY WORDS** Self-knowledge, link with one's Divine Blueprint **CHAKRAS** All **ELEMENT** Storm **PHYSICAL** Assists in overcoming addictions and self-destructive habits **EMOTIONAL** Aids in overcoming depression and boredom, promotes the zest of self-discovery **SPIRITUAL** Inspires realization of multidimensional self and life purpose

Astrophyllite aids in navigating one's travels beyond the body—in and beyond the astral realm. It can help one enter into lucid dreaming. It is a spur to expanding consciousness and an anchor to assist one in returning to "home base." Astrophyllite can reveal the hidden pattern of one's Divine blueprint, or life purpose. This may be revealed through an increase in synchronicities. Astrophyllite is both a magnet for these synchronicities and an aid to being more aware of their occurrence and meaning.

AURALITE-23 **KEY WORDS** Union with Higher Self, inner purification, increased psychic sensitivity, visionary consciousness **CHAKRAS** All **ELEMENT** Storm **PHYSICAL** Initiates cellular purification, can dispel chronic problems **EMOTIONAL** Inspires the joy of meeting with one's Higher Self **SPIRITUAL** Enhances psychic ability, links one to the Magic Presence

Auralite-23 stimulates higher awareness and telepathic connection with one's guides and guardian spirits. It offers a direct link to the Higher Self. It stimulates inner purification—the release of patterns of anxiety, resentment, judgement, depression and defeat. Auralite-23 increases psychic sensitivity, enhanced insight, disappearance of chronic physical problems, a balanced awakening of kundalini, spontaneous visions of future events, enhanced capacity for soul travel and lucid dreaming, and experiences with Angels.

AURALITE, EMERALD **KEY WORDS** Sharpened and elevated awareness, spiritual cleansing, optimism, confidence and persistence **CHAKRAS** Heart (4th), Crown (7th) **ELEMENT** Fire, Wind **PHYSICAL** Supports heart, brain, nervous system, meridian system, lungs, nerves, red blood cells **EMOTIONAL** Stimulates happiness and enthusiasm for life **SPIRITUAL** Encourages and enhances exploration of the higher spiritual realms, purifies one's awareness, invokes the Higher Self

Emerald Auralite embodies many of the invisible qualities of the Emerald Tablet. It initiates processes within the body-mind-soul which accelerate one's spiritual evolution. It can clear away the "dross" of habitual consciousness, offering a powerful influx of cleansing and awakening energies.

AVENTURINE, GREEN **KEY WORDS** Vitality, growth, confidence **CHAKRAS** Heart (4th) **ELEMENT** Water, Earth **PHYSICAL** Supports general healing, increase of life force, heart and circulation **EMOTIONAL** Inspires optimism, self-confidence, peace amid difficulty **SPIRITUAL** Brings good fortune and blessing, manifestation and prosperity

Green Aventurine is a stone of optimism and zest for life. It helps one move forward with confidence into new situations, and assists one in embracing such challenging issues as aging, illness and one's own mortality. It brings with it a feeling of lightness and humor, as it helps one deal with the ups and downs of life. It allows one to look at the bright side of difficult issues. In healing, it instills life force and aids in rebuilding depleted energy reserves.

AVENTURINE, BLUE **KEY WORDS** Psychic attunement, self-discipline, inner strength **CHAKRAS** Third Eye (6th) **ELEMENT** Wind, Water **PHYSICAL** Supports hormonal balance, respiration, circulation, healthy blood **EMOTIONAL** Aids in achieving emotional maturity, self-discipline **SPIRITUAL** Enhances psychic and intuitive capacities

Blue Aventurine is a stone of self-discipline and inner strength. It assists one in making clear decisions and sticking by them. It can be useful in initiating changes of problematic habits such as smoking, overeating, substance abuse and traits such as selfishness and passive aggression. It facilitates attunement to inner guidance, the capacity to empathically "read" others, and the knack for tuning in to information from the Akashic record.

AVENTURINE, RED **KEY WORDS** Discernment, determination, strength, creativity, sexuality **CHAKRAS** Root (1st), Sexual/Creative (2nd), Third Eye (6th) **ELEMENT** Earth, Fire **PHYSICAL** Supports the immune system, blood and liver **EMOTIONAL** Aids endurance, faith and perseverance through difficulty **SPIRITUAL** Facilitates insight, artistic inspiration, manifestation of visions

Red Aventurine is a stone of vitality, creativity, sexuality, mental alertness and manifestation through action. It increases one's desire to take on and overcome the challenges of life, and it helps one find the determination to persevere. It increases the flow of life force, helping those with low vitality to get things done. Individuals recovering from illness can use it to aid in rebuilding their physical energies, as well as their confidence. It can help people with diminished sexual appetites find renewed excitement.

AXINITE **KEY WORDS** Grounding, endurance, vitality, inner exploration **CHAKRAS** Root (1st), Third Eye (6th) **ELEMENT** Storm **PHYSICAL** Supports general healing, vitality, energizing the body **EMOTIONAL** Aids conflict resolution, cooperation, inner harmony **SPIRITUAL** Brings awareness of other spiritual planes, past-life memory

Axinite is clarifying to one's consciousness, harmonizing to one's emotions, expansive to one's awareness and balancing to one's physical energies. It is strongly grounding, and it helps one bring Earth energies up through one's feet and into one's whole body. It can be a powerful aid to one's endurance, and it is recommended for anyone who works long hours. Axinite can function as a "savant stone," facilitating direct mental access to knowledge, independent of any outside source.

AZEZTULITE, AMAZEZ **KEY WORDS** Purification, healing, communication with spiritual beings, psychic capacities **CHAKRAS** Third Eye (6th) **ELEMENT** Storm **PHYSICAL** Promotes resonance with one's Divine Blueprint of health **EMOTIONAL** Frees one from negativity and negative attachments **SPIRITUAL** Enhances psychic capacities, stimulates the process of enlightenment.

Amazez is an ideal therapeutic stone for crystal practitioners. It can be used to bring spiritual aid to weak or afflicted areas of the body. It can clear gray areas from the auric field and wake up the power of one's Divine Blueprint. It can dispel all types of negativity—including implants and entities—from the body and auric field, and can be used as a tool in "psychic surgery." Amazez enhances all the psychic capacities, including clairvoyance, clairaudience, clairsentience, remote viewing, prophetic vision, and healing.

AZEZTULITE, BLACK **KEY WORDS** Light within Darkness, complete transformation, protection, infusion of Light, alchemical Philosophers' Stone **CHAKRAS** All **ELEMENTS** Earth, Wind, Storm **PHYSICAL** Supports treatment of autoimmune conditions **EMOTIONAL** Aids in releasing negative emotions, infuses one with spiritual joy **SPIRITUAL** Clears inner obstacles, brings Light, protects, empowers and awakens

Black Azeztulite brings Light and Power into one's entire energy system. It represents the moment of the Singularity or Zero Point, in which the laws of the universe become fluid and changeable, making it a powerful catalyst for spiritual transformation. Black Azeztulite cleanses and clears one's body and energy field of negative energies, disharmonious attachments, implants, psychic parasites and inappropriate karmic patterns. It can aid in overcoming autoimmune conditions, and it offers power and protection to those who work with it

.

AZEZTULITE, BLACK TOURMALINE **KEY WORDS** Cleansing of negative patterns, infusion of spiritual Light, rapid spiritual growth, sudden awakening **CHAKRAS** All, especially Root (1st), Third Eye (6th), Crown (7th) **ELEMENT** Earth, Storm **PHYSICAL** supports the subtle body field, dispels ailments rooted in past life patterns **EMOTIONAL** clears the emotional body of negative fixations **SPIRITUAL** purifies and cleanses one's energy field while bringing in a great infusion of spiritual Light

Black Tourmaline Azeztulite facilitates rapid progress in spiritual development. It sweeps through one's being, clearing away negative attachments, dysfunctional habit patterns, predatory entities, fearful thoughts and self-negating ideas. It simultaneously offers Azeztulite's powerful infusion of Light.

AZEZTULITE, BLUE-GREEN **KEY WORDS** Loving connection with the Earth, infusion of Light, dissolving negative fixations **CHAKRAS** All, especially Heart (4th), Crown (7th) **ELEMENT** Water, Storm **PHYSICAL** Supports the heart, throat, lungs, thyroid, and the esophagus. **EMOTIONAL** Can revivify the emotional body and one's positive feelings **SPIRITUAL** Awakens and deepens our love for the Earth, and our awareness of the Earth's love for us; helps to unify one's soul and spirit

Blue-Green Azeztulite is a fantastic stone for awakening and healing the emotional body. It works through resonance with the compassionate love being continuously emanated by the Earth, combined with the bliss of Divine Light. It is ideal for facilitating a conscious communion with the living Earth. It releases negative fixations, and engenders enlightened compassion.

AZEZTULITE, CINNAZEZ **KEY WORDS** Consciousness expansion, brain stimulation, increased synchronicities, alchemical knowledge **CHAKRAS** All **ELEMENT** Storm **PHYSICAL** Stimulates nervous system **EMOTIONAL** Increases zest for life **SPIRITUAL** Access to inner realms

Cinnazez is a quickener of consciousness and an awakener of higher awareness. It can stimulate one's nervous systems to actualize one's latent capacities of clairvoyance, telepathic communication, attunement to heavenly realms and direct knowledge of Divine truth. It is felt as the solidified essence of the Philosophers' Stone, and it can help the body open to become a conduit of the Celestial Fire of the Great Central Sun. It stimulates the brain and central nervous system, increasing one's receptivity to fields of knowledge in the inner realms, including alchemical knowledge.

AZEZTULITE, GOLDEN **KEY WORDS** Attunement to the Gold-White Light, Light Body awakening, time travel, accessing the Hall of [Akashic] Records, kindling the Sun of the Heart **CHAKRAS** Heart (4th), Third Eye (6th), Crown (7th), Soul Star and Etheric (8th–14th) **ELEMENT** Storm **PHYSICAL** stimulation of the nervous system to new capacities **EMOTIONAL** empathic awareness, compassion, commitment to truth **SPIRITUAL** incarnation of the Divine, transformation

Golden Azeztulite can fill the body and auric field with Gold-White Light. This energy can center in the heart chakra, kindling the Sun of the Heart, which is the incarnation of the Divine within the human. Golden Azeztulite activates latent capacities such as time travel, empathic awareness of others, and direct knowing. It is aligned with the purpose of our evolution into spiritual human beings.

AZEZTULITE, GREEN FIRE **KEY WORDS** Power of the heart, Union of Heaven and Earth, communication with Nature, heart intelligence **CHAKRAS** Heart (4th) and High Heart (between 4th and 5th) **ELEMENT** Earth, Air **PHYSICAL** Supports heart, lungs and circulatory system, aids with brain balance and clarity **EMOTIONAL** Awakens passion for life and love for the world **SPIRITUAL** Facilitates the great shift of one's center of self from the head to the heart, links one with Nature and the Soul of the World

Green Fire Azeztulite facilitates communication with Nature. It helps one to be sensitive to the many synchronistic messages that the Soul of the World is always offering us. It helps one to feel the reality of the Living World, and to discover one's love for the Earth. It supports the intelligence of the heart and helps us awaken to the heart's truth, and its impulse to act with wisdom for the good of the whole.

AZEZTULITE, HIMALAYA GOLD **KEY WORDS** Creative manifestation, co-creating with Sophia, kindling the Great Central Sun in the heart, filling the body with Gold Light **CHAKRAS** Heart (4th), Third Eye (6th), Crown (7th), Soul Star and Etheric (8th–14th) **ELEMENT** Storm **PHYSICAL** Energetically strengthens the visceral organs and systems **EMOTIONAL** Initiates ecstatic union with Sophia, Soul of the World **SPIRITUAL** Enhances one's capacities of creating, inner vision

Himalaya Gold Azeztulite kindles the resonant awakening of the Great Central Sun in the heart. It resonates with the solar plexus chakra, stimulating one's capacity to bring visions into reality. It lends power to one's intention, helping one manifest one's desires through alignment with the Tao. It stimulates the Seat of Vision in the Third Eye, inspiring one with enlightened awareness of one's creative power.

AZEZTULITE, HONEY & CREAM **KEY WORDS** Inner Light and sweetness, pleasure, bliss and ecstasy, contact with the Azez, love, blessing, emotional healing, recovery from illness **CHAKRAS** All **ELEMENTS** Water, Wind, Earth **PHYSICAL** Supports recovery of vitality after illness **EMOTIONAL** Emotional healing, currents of sweetness **SPIRITUAL** Emanates love and spiritual blessing, offers comfort and sense of security

Honey and Cream Azeztulites are ideal allies for emotional healing. They soothe and comfort one's inner child, and they can be used in soul retrieval work, providing a cocoon of loving currents within which one may recover any lost parts of one's original wholeness. They are ideal for recovering from exhaustion caused by stress or overwork.

AZEZTULITE, LEMURIAN GOLD **KEY WORDS** Inner Light, Lemurian consciousness, awareness of beings in the subtle realms **CHAKRAS** Third Eye (6th), Crown (7th) **ELEMENT** Water, Storm **PHYSICAL** Teaches the cells the mantra of enlightenment **EMOTIONAL** Stimulates empathy and compassion **SPIRITUAL** Expands awareness to beings in the subtle realms, allows access to Lemurian consciousness

Lemurian Gold Azeztulite powerfully stimulates the third eye and crown chakras, and can fill the entire skull with powerful pulsations and golden Light. It can open one's awareness to seeing and communication with Lemurian entities in the subtle realm. It stimulates one's inherent empathy, intuition and clairvoyance, opening one to angelic, spiritual, etheric, human, animal, plant and mineral consciousness. It enhances the power of one's intention and will, making manifestation a more tangible possibility.

AZEZTULITE, NEW ZEALAND WHITE **KEY WORDS** Deep peace, nourishment of the subtle body, enhanced intuitive sensitivity, joy, healing, dissolving negative patterns, remembering one's Divine nature **CHAKRAS** All **ELEMENT** Earth, Air, Fire, Water, Storm **PHYSICAL** Supports the subtle body, filling it with Light **EMOTIONAL** Brings deep peace, sensitivity to others **SPIRITUAL** Fills one with spiritual Light, enhances intuition, emotional sensitivity, compassion and healing intention

New Zealand White Azeztulite is a stone of joy. It dispels constricted patterns due to grief, depression, anxiety and anger. It can dissolve negative energy forms of all types, and it can purify one's field of unhealthy habitual patterns and psychic implants. It can rekindle the inner flame of our spiritual Light. It reminds us that, regardless of outer circumstances, our essence is Divine and our nature is Light.

AZEZTULITE, PINK **KEY WORDS** Heart awareness, emotional healing, serenity, compassion **CHAKRAS** Heart (4th), Third Eye (6th), Crown (7th), Etheric (8th–14th) **ELEMENT** Storm, Water **PHYSICAL** Aids with relieving stress **EMOTIONAL** Supports healing the emotional body and inner child **SPIRITUAL** Facilitates soul retrieval, Ascension, empathic resonance

Pink Azeztulite soothes the emotional body. It seeds compassionate acceptance and love toward all aspects of oneself. It helps heal fragmentation caused by emotional wounds, and it comforts the inner child. Pink Azeztulite facilitates a serene, yet highly activated awareness. It clears emotional blocks to the Ascension process and opens the heart to receive spiritual Light.

AZEZTULITE, PINK FIRE **KEY WORDS** Inner fire, High Heart activation, passionate self-identification with Love, emotional and physical self-healing **CHAKRAS** Heart (4th) and High Heart (between 4th and 5th) **ELEMENT** Fire **PHYSICAL** Supports recovery from autoimmune illnesses, facilitates healing by filling the cells with the Light and Fire of Divine Love **EMOTIONAL** Highly beneficial for emotional healing **SPIRITUAL** Kindles inner fire of Divine Love

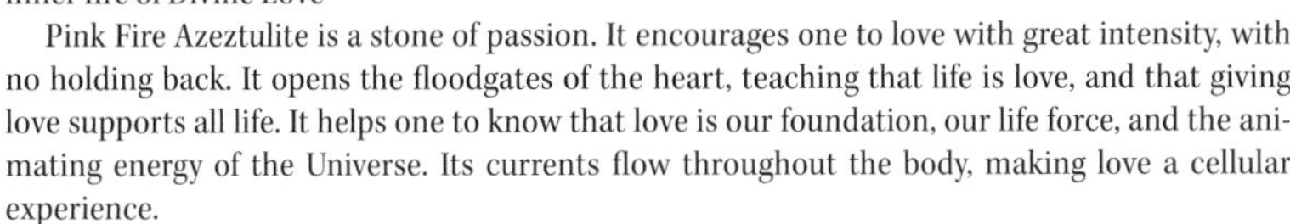

Pink Fire Azeztulite is a stone of passion. It encourages one to love with great intensity, with no holding back. It opens the floodgates of the heart, teaching that life is love, and that giving love supports all life. It helps one to know that love is our foundation, our life force, and the animating energy of the Universe. Its currents flow throughout the body, making love a cellular experience.

AZEZTULITE, RED FIRE **KEY WORDS** Life Force, enthusiasm, vitality, power, passion, sexuality, etherization of the blood, intelligence, visionary experience, healing, longevity, alchemical transmutation **CHAKRAS** All **ELEMENT** Earth, Fire, Storm **PHYSICAL** Supports all parts of the body, especially blood, heart, lungs and brain **EMOTIONAL** Kindles enthusiasm, confidence, power, optimism, sexuality **SPIRITUAL** Stimulates intelligence, visionary experience, alchemical transformation of the self

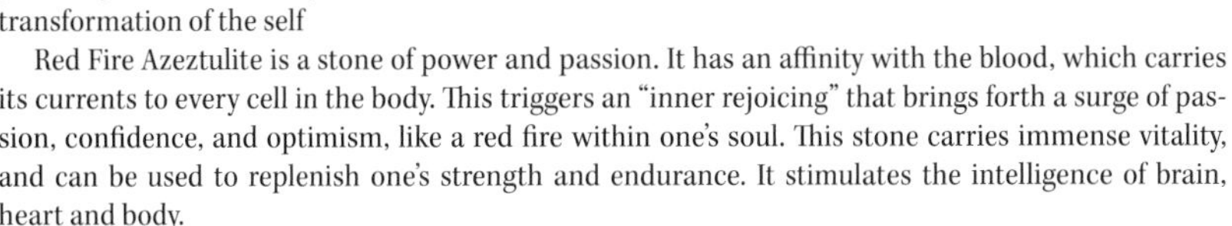

Red Fire Azeztulite is a stone of power and passion. It has an affinity with the blood, which carries its currents to every cell in the body. This triggers an "inner rejoicing" that brings forth a surge of passion, confidence, and optimism, like a red fire within one's soul. This stone carries immense vitality, and can be used to replenish one's strength and endurance. It stimulates the intelligence of brain, heart and body.

AZEZTULITE, SANDA ROSA **KEY WORDS** Healing, inner harmony, grounding spiritual Light in the body, purification, attunement with the soul of the Earth **CHAKRAS** All (1st–7th) **ELEMENT** Storm, Earth **PHYSICAL** Supports digestive system, harmonizes body systems **EMOTIONAL** Supports inner serenity, soothes the etheric body **SPIRITUAL** Enhances meditation, dreams, meeting spiritual beings

Sanda Rosa Azeztulite stimulates the third eye and crown chakras in a way that allows one to see into very deep levels of meditative awareness. It is calming to the emotional body, and this benefits those who are working to quiet the mind. Sanda Rosa Azeztulite is a good stone to take into the realm of dreaming. It stimulates vivid images in the psyche in both meditative and sleep experiences, and it helps one remember dreams. It aids one in meeting high beings on the inner planes.

AZEZTULITE, SATYALOKA CLEAR **KEY WORDS** Sat-chit-ananda, truth, consciousness, bliss **CHAKRAS** All **ELEMENT** Storm, Wind **PHYSICAL** Initiates infusion of spiritual Light into the body **EMOTIONAL** Inspires the awakening to Divine bliss **SPIRITUAL** Facilitates intense expansion of consciousness, enlightenment

Satyaloka Azeztulite vibrates to the frequency of enlightenment. It is a stone of pure White Light energy. It opens the crown chakra with a tremendous flow of energy. Its energies pulse downwards, clearing and activating each successive chakra. When placed upon the heart it produces a deep sense of reverence, an awareness of the presence of the Holy Silence. It opens the inner path to the Source.

AZEZTULITE, SATYALOKA ROSE **KEY WORDS** Ascension of the Heart **CHAKRAS** Heart (4th), Third Eye (6th), Crown (7th) **ELEMENT** Storm **PHYSICAL** Stimulates cellular mind to embrace the Heart's love and truth **EMOTIONAL** Elevates and expands Heart awareness—the power of love **SPIRITUAL** Awakens the Heart as the sovereign center of one's being

Satyaloka Rose Azeztulite carries powerful currents of Heart Ascension. It stimulates the heart chakra, encouraging the heart to "move" upward into the head. It awakens the Divine "I" of the heart and lifts it to its rightful throne in the center of the brain. When this occurs, one thinks, speaks and acts out of the heart's wisdom, and one can speak and act only in truth.

AZEZTULITE, SATYALOKA YELLOW **KEY WORDS** Enlightenment, Ascension, acceleration of one's evolution **CHAKRAS** Solar Plexus (3rd), Third Eye (6th) **ELEMENT** Storm **PHYSICAL** Aids the body in assimilating and integrating spiritual Light **EMOTIONAL** Encourages one to seek and savor the thrill of transformation **SPIRITUAL** Inspires awareness of and enthusiasm for spiritual awakening

Satyaloka Yellow Azeztulite emanates the power of evolutionary change. It carries the currents of enlightenment, focusing on rapid acceleration of one's spiritual awakening. It stimulates will forces, helping align one's intention with Divine will. It provides clarity and enhances purpose, awakening the mind to perceive and embrace one's destiny.

AZEZTULITE, SAURALITE **KEY WORDS** Realization of Divine purpose, marriage of Heaven and Earth **CHAKRAS** All **ELEMENT** Earth, Wind, Fire, Water, Storm **PHYSICAL** Triggers bodily experience of ecstatic union of Earth with Divine Light **EMOTIONAL** Heals grief, fear, pain and anxiety, brings a flood of joy and ecstasy **SPIRITUAL** Awakens one fully to the Divine union with the Earth

Sauralite vibrates with gentle intensity, combining the Nameless Light of the Great Central Sun with the living vitality of the Earth. It draws the Light down through the crown while it opens the base chakra for the upwelling of Earth energies. These stones bring one to the question, "Will you give up your old life for a new, unknown joy?"

AZEZTULITE, SEDONA **KEY WORDS** Creating an energy vortex within the body, link with spirit guides, angelic guardians, and ETs, co-creation with the Soul of the World **CHAKRAS** All, including etheric chakras above the head (8th–14th) **ELEMENT** Earth, Fire, Storm **PHYSICAL** Supports spiritual healing on the cellular level **EMOTIONAL** Brings the energy of joy and elevated serenity **SPIRITUAL** Raises one's vibrational level, opens access to higher dimensions, aids communication with benevolent spiritual entities

Sedonalite Azeztulite is a stone of the Universal Tao, the river of energy that flows through everything as the unfolding of time and the manifestation of all things. It is a stone of the Wisdom of the Earth, encouraging us to join in the joyful co-creation of the future's infinite potential, crystallizing into each present moment. It can create an energy vortex in one's surroundings, one's energy field, and even in the cells.

AZEZTULITE, WHITE **KEY WORDS** Receiving the Nameless Light, link with the Great Central Sun, cellular reattunement for healing and awakening **CHAKRAS** All (including the Etheric chakras 8th–14th) **ELEMENT** Storm **PHYSICAL** Initiates cellular regeneration, infusion of the body with spiritual Light **EMOTIONAL** Supports awakening to Universal Love, clearing the emotional body **SPIRITUAL** Inspires union with Divine Light, mutual awakening with the Earth

White Azeztulite carries one of the highest spiritual frequencies of any stone. Its currents of the Nameless Light from the Great Central Sun flow throughout the body, encouraging cellular regeneration and healing. With the aid of White Azeztulite, we can channel Divine Light into the Earth, for her healing and awakening. White Azeztulite is a stone of Light Body awakening, of resurrection and Vibrational Ascension.

AZUMAR **KEY WORDS** Pleasure, serenity, ecstasy, truth, compassion, love **CHAKRAS** Heart (4th), Crown (7th) **ELEMENT** Water **PHYSICAL** Kindles bodily joy and rejuvenation **EMOTIONAL** Increases happiness and compassion **SPIRITUAL** Attunes to planetary consciousness and spiritual love

Azumar's currents bring about a rejoicing in the body, filling the cells with waves of pleasure, healing and power. It can aid in dispelling anger, envy, fear and stress, replacing them with serenity, enthusiasm, confidence and the feeling of being enveloped within an atmosphere of love. This brings a peaceful clarity of consciousness. It is an Earth Spirit stone, allowing one to feel and harmonize with planetary consciousness.

AZURITE **KEY WORDS** Insight, intuition, **CHAKRAS** Third Eye (6th), Crown (7th) **ELEMENT** Wind **PHYSICAL** Helps with migraines, tinnitus, vertigo, overall brain health **EMOTIONAL** Supports insight into emotions, inspires emotional growth **SPIRITUAL** Initiates inner visions, intuitive leaps of spiritual understanding

Azurite powerfully stimulates the third eye chakra. It is a stone of inner vision and can be used for the enhancement of dreams and the development of psychic powers. It can stimulate intellect as well as intuition. Azurite can strengthen the astral and etheric bodies, making one less vulnerable to psychic attack or attachments. It can be used to seal "holes" in the aura and can help overcome fatigue. It helps one to make conceptual leaps and is an antidote to boredom. It is a stone of mental power and synthesis, helping one to achieve higher levels of understanding of inner life, and the outside world as well.

BARITE **KEY WORDS** Inner vision and alignment, interdimensional travel **CHAKRAS** Third Eye (6th), Crown (7th) **ELEMENT** Storm **PHYSICAL** Supports balanced brain chemistry, supports function of brain cells **EMOTIONAL** Encourages releasing fear, taking joy in spiritual exploration **SPIRITUAL** Facilitates interdimensional travel, dream work, meditative Ascension

Barite provides a smooth, clear connection to the higher worlds, aiding the inward journeyer in discovering the many mansions of the spiritual realms. It is a stone of interdimensional travel, allowing those who meditate or dream with it to use their journeys to enrich earthly life. It assists one in linking with the higher self. In dream work, Barite can give one a beautiful symbolic picture of how inner spiritual patterns are unfolding for oneself.

BENITOITE **KEY WORDS** Channeling, psychic abilities, increase in synchronicity **CHAKRAS** Third Eye (6th) **ELEMENT** Wind **PHYSICAL** Supports brain activation, accessing information in the connective tissues **EMOTIONAL** Inspires the euphoric joy of expanded awareness **SPIRITUAL** Facilitates interdimensional travel, paranormal capacities

Benitoite facilitates travel to the astral, subtle and causal planes and can help one maintain stability of consciousness when out of the body. It helps open the doors for enhancement of all types of paranormal abilities, and it increases one's awareness of meaningful synchronicities. Meditation with Benitoite can facilitate conscious communication with one's angelic guides. Benitoite combines well with Natrolite for activation of the higher senses.

BERYLLONITE **KEY WORDS** Light in darkness, Divine purpose, joy **CHAKRAS** Heart (4th), Third Eye (6th), Crown (7th) **ELEMENT** Storm **PHYSICAL** Supports healing through alignment with spiritual truth **EMOTIONAL** Aids release from depression and grief through spiritual insight **SPIRITUAL** Enhances clairvoyance, linking with angels and inner guides

Beryllonite is a stone which sends Light to pierce the veil and reveal that one's highest good is constantly manifesting, even in the midst of suffering. It strongly activates the third eye chakra, initiating visionary experiences and helping one to develop clairvoyant sight. It can aid one in seeing the blockages or imbalances that hold one back from full consciousness and realization of one's spiritual destiny. It also energizes the heart and crown chakras and is a powerful aid to consciousness expansion.

BIXBITE **KEY WORDS** Vitality, courage, love, self-esteem, passion **CHAKRAS** Root (1st), Heart (4th) **ELEMENT** Earth **PHYSICAL** Revitalizes the body's constitution, increases life force **EMOTIONAL** Awakens passion, compassion courage, loyalty **SPIRITUAL** Supports centering in the heart, making deep commitments

Bixbite stimulates courage, passion, physical vitality, strength of purpose and a dynamic personality. Yet it does these things while helping one remain centered in the heart, compassionate toward others and oneself, and loving in one's actions. This stone skillfully blends the energies of the heart and root chakras, helping one draw life force from the earth and enhancing emotional bonds with the world and other people. Bixbite can be excellent for enhancement of love relationships, bringing the hearts of individuals into vibrational harmony. It strengthens loyalty and camaraderie, as well as self-confidence and groundedness.

BLACK PHANTOM QUARTZ **KEY WORDS** Inner Light; releasing self-judgment; reclaiming soul fragments, courage and resolve; increased self-awareness **CHAKRAS** All **ELEMENT** Storm **PHYSICAL** Helps with bone health, overcoming illnesses related to repressed Shadow material **EMOTIONAL** Encourages self-acceptance, self-love, love of others, release of judgment **SPIRITUAL** Facilitates soul retrieval, release of past-life fixations, inner clarity

Black Phantom Quartz is useful for seeing and integrating one's personal Shadow. It helps one reunite with the missing or "lost" parts of the soul, healing the psyche and bringing a deeper sense of wholeness. It fosters self-acceptance and self-love, making it possible to offer unconditional love to others. It aids in releasing blockages from past lives.

BLOODSTONE **KEY WORDS** Strength, courage, purification, vitality **CHAKRAS** Root (1st) **ELEMENT** Earth **PHYSICAL** Aids detoxification, blood purification, liver and endocrine system **EMOTIONAL** Inspires courage to face illness and mortality, altruism, zest for life **SPIRITUAL** Facilitates dispelling negative energies, entering Christ consciousness

Bloodstone is a great purifier, a healing tool for dispelling negative influences from the auric field and bringing one's subtle energies into wholeness and balance. It grounds one fully in the body, for the enhancement of one's strength, determination and courage. It increases vitality, and can aid one in facing physical mortality. Bloodstone strengthens the root chakra, increasing one's zest for living and endurance in physical activity. It supports blood purification and purging the body of toxins.

BRAZILIANITE **KEY WORDS** Creativity, manifestation, cleansing, empowerment of the will, Atlantean connection **CHAKRAS** Sexual/Creative (2nd), Solar Plexus (3rd) **ELEMENT** Wind, Fire **PHYSICAL** Aids in purifying the visceral organs, strengthening digestion **EMOTIONAL** Enhances self-confidence, commitment to self-fulfillment **SPIRITUAL** Facilitates regaining the gifts of Atlantis, creative manifestation

Brazilianite carries the vibrational energy of the ancient civilization of Atlantis and is associated with the creative power of directed and focused will, which was instrumental in many of the astounding accomplishments of the beings who dwelt there. These energies can assist one in extraordinary acts of creativity and manifestation. It can amplify the potency of one's will, strengthening the solar plexus chakra. It can aid one in recalling past lives in Atlantis, and in retrieving knowledge from the Atlantean past.

BROOKITE **KEY WORDS** Higher-chakra activation, expansion **CHAKRAS** Third Eye (6th), Crown (7th), Etheric (8th–14th) **ELEMENT** Storm **PHYSICAL** Supports integrating higher frequencies into the body **EMOTIONAL** Encourages stable self-awareness in expanded states **SPIRITUAL** Facilitates interdimensional exploration, meeting beings of higher realms

Brookite is one of the primary power stones for expansion of awareness beyond the physical body. It is a powerful activator of the sixth and seventh chakras and the etheric chakras above the head. It enables one to reach an expanded state where one can communicate and commune with beings on the higher vibrational levels. It is inspirational and energizing, assisting one in overcoming old patterns and moving ahead to greater inner development.

BRUCITE, GOLDEN **KEY WORDS** Makes one feel carefree and euphoric, dispels negative emotions **CHAKRAS** Third eye (6th), Heart (4th) **ELEMENT** Wind, Water **PHYSICAL** Influences the cells to relax and allow the Light to flow through them **EMOTIONAL** Comforts and encourages one's Inner Child, stimulates exuberant happiness **SPIRITUAL** Triggers epiphanies, aids in Light Body activation

Golden Brucite is a stone of lightheartedness and enthusiasm. If helps one to recognize the opportunities for enjoyment present in almost any situation. It encourages affection between friends and partners, and it helps one avoid taking things too seriously. It stimulates one's sense of humor, and it supports a strong and resilient attitude toward life. It is fun to hang out with Golden Brucite, and it helps one relax and enjoy oneself in mundane circumstances. It stimulates extroversion and a witty mental attitude.

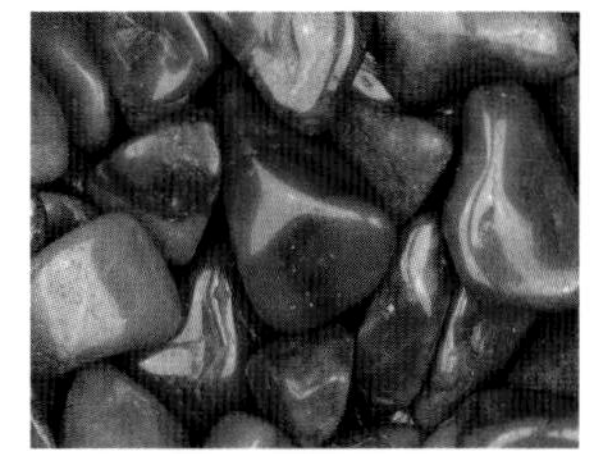

BUDDSTONE **KEY WORDS** Spiritual growth, alignment with the Divine Blueprint **CHAKRAS** Heart (4th) **ELEMENT** Water, Earth **PHYSICAL** Supports the heart, kidneys, stomach and digestive system; aids those convalescing after illness **EMOTIONAL** Helps one get out of "stuck" places, stimulates optimism, kindles the joy of simply being **SPIRITUAL** Awakens spiritual joy

Buddstone is all about growth. Its energies are exuberant, ambitious, cheerful, confident and determined, and it offers the enhancement of these same qualities in oneself. It embodies life's commitment to manifest itself and grow, in every way and in all directions. The Being of this stone presented itself to me as a bright green plant-like figure, with leaves growing out of its head. Symbolically, the Being of Buddstone is a spirit whose essence is healthy, rapid, abundant growth.

BUMBLEBEE "JASPER" **KEY WORDS** Inspiration, intensity, creative manifestation, adventure **CHAKRA** Solar Plexus (3rd) **ELEMENT** Fire **PHYSICAL** Supports intestines, liver and kidneys **EMOTIONAL** Enhances one's sense of purpose, inspires courage and adventurousness **SPIRITUAL** Aids in becoming aware of one's destiny, and finding the courage to pursue it

Bumblebee "Jasper" resonates strongly with the second (sexual/creative) and third (solar plexus) chakras. It brings inspiration and intensity to the realm of one's creative manifestation. It is a stone of adventure. It stimulates one's mental acuity, so one is more able to notice and seize opportunities. It stimulates courage, assertiveness, endurance, mental clarity and sharpness, inspiration and manifestation.

BUSTAMITE **KEY WORDS** Playfulness, joy, vitality, sexuality, creativity, dreams, initiation **CHAKRAS** Root (1st), Sexual/Creative (2nd) **ELEMENT** Fire **PHYSICAL** Supports sexual organs, digestive system, endocrine system **EMOTIONAL** Encourages enjoyment of physical life, playfulness in relationships **SPIRITUAL** Inspires awareness of one's unity with the All

Bustamite clears and opens the root chakra, allowing for greater vitality and enjoyment of physical life. Bustamite stimulates one's creative and sexual energies as well. Carrying or wearing Bustamite during creative work or play can bring greater inspiration and fertility to one's endeavors. Bustamite can also increase the vividness of dreams. It can assist one in making progress in meditation and can facilitate initiation experiences on the higher planes.

CACOXENITE **KEY WORDS** Alignment with the Divine plan, spiritual cleansing and purification, regeneration of the body **CHAKRAS** Solar Plexus (3rd), Third Eye (6th), Crown (7th) **ELEMENT** Wind **PHYSICAL** Aids with clearing digestive issues, "new" DNA strand activation **EMOTIONAL** Encourages surrender to the Divine, diffusing ego fixation **SPIRITUAL** Facilitates acceleration of spiritual evolution, grounding spiritual Light

Cacoxenite can assist in one's spiritual evolution and in raising the vibration of one's physical self. Cacoxenite can aid in the reprogramming of cells to continually renew themselves and resist the aging process, as well as in the activation of the "new" strands of the genetic spiral. It can powerfully activate the third eye and crown chakras for inner visionary experience.

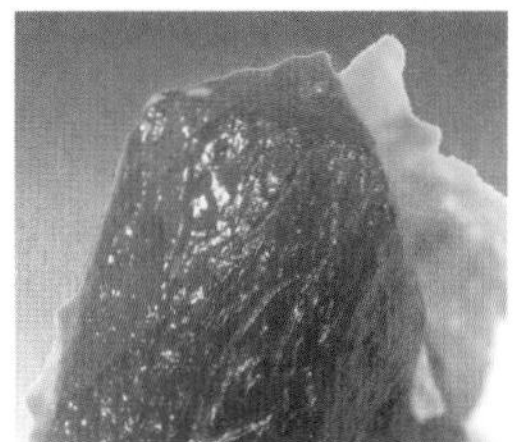

CALCITE, BLUE **KEY WORDS** Psychic ability, astral travel, soothing the emotional body **CHAKRAS** Throat (5th), Third Eye (6th) **ELEMENT** Fire, Air **PHYSICAL** Helps with throat problems, laryngitis, lungs and respiratory issues **EMOTIONAL** Soothes and protects the emotional body **SPIRITUAL** Facilitates access to the creative unconscious, inspired self-expression

Blue Calcite is one of the most soothing stones to the emotional body. It provides a "cocoon" of gentle blue spiritual Light which gradually wraps itself around the auric field. It opens the inner avenue for conscious exploration of the unconscious realms, from which one's most creative ideas spring. It enhances the vividness and symbolic content of dreams and one's ability to recall and integrate them. Its stimulation of the throat chakra enables one to better express the insights one receives.

CALCITE, CLEAR **KEY WORDS** Insight, clarity, manifestation, forgiveness **CHAKRAS** All **ELEMENTS** Fire, Wind **PHYSICAL** Stimulates metabolism and energy flow through the aura **EMOTIONAL** Aids forgiveness, releasing anger, resentment, arrogance, envy **SPIRITUAL** Inner clarity, initiating multilevel awareness

Clear Calcite can be programmed to amplify the effect of one's intent, helping to manifest that intent in the physical world. Clear Calcite allows those who use the stone in meditation to achieve a multilevel awareness, which allows one to hold paradoxical or contradictory ideas without taking one side or the other. This is beneficial, because expanding consciousness requires the embrace of paradox.

CALCITE, ELESTIAL ANGEL **KEY WORDS** Angelic communication, music of the spheres, link to the psychoid realm, visionary experience **CHAKRAS** Heart (4th), Third Eye (6th) **ELEMENTS** Wind, Storm **PHYSICAL** Supports central nervous system, dissolves energetic blockages, relieves headaches **EMOTIONAL** Can bring joy and rapture by linking to higher beings **SPIRITUAL** Stimulates communication with angels

Elestial Angel Calcites are among the most high-vibration, high-intensity Calcites. They stimulate the energetic circuit between heart and mind and enhance communication with spirit guides, extraterrestrials, devas and other spiritual beings. They stimulate the areas of the brain linked to vision, and can help one have vivid inner visions of spiritual realities.

CALCITE, GREEN **KEY WORDS** Relaxation, emotional balance, release of stress and resentment, connection with the heart **CHAKRAS** Heart (4th) **ELEMENT** Fire, Water **PHYSICAL** Supports heart and artery health, rejuvenation, clearing bodily stress **EMOTIONAL** Cools and soothes anger, relieves emotional stress **SPIRITUAL** Inspires compassion and altruism, helps one connect with Nature spirits

Green Calcite's energy is refreshing to the etheric body. It is cooling to the "hot" emotions such as anger and irritability, it nurtures compassion and altruism, and it clears the heart of stress and other types of unhealthy psychic debris. It assists one in being more attuned to Nature and the spirits of plants and animals. It helps one direct the mind to the urgings of the heart, assisting one in listening to and acting on what the heart knows. It improves the quality of meditations and can make one's dreams more pleasant.

CALCITE, HONEY **KEY WORDS** Clarity of insight and action, confidence, persistence, intellectual power **CHAKRAS** Root (1st), Solar Plexus (3rd), Third Eye (6th) **ELEMENT** Fire, Wind **PHYSICAL** Supports strength and stamina, helps conserve physical energy **EMOTIONAL** Aids in maintaining emotional stability through difficulty **SPIRITUAL** Inspires perseverance in spiritual practices

Honey Calcite assists in bringing about that unique combination of mental clarity, focused energy and groundedness necessary to successfully complete complex tasks or long-term projects. It activates the root chakra, solar plexus and third eye, harmonizing and unifying their energies. It stimulates the intellect, making it possible for one to analyze challenges and see the most efficient solutions. It facilitates a state of relaxation, so that one's work does not result in stress.

CALCITE, MERKABITE **KEY WORDS** Consciousness expansion, interdimensional travel, ascension, access to higher knowledge **CHAKRAS** Third Eye (6th), Crown (7th), Etheric (8th–14th) **ELEMENT** Fire, Storm **PHYSICAL** Stimulates nervous system, awakens untapped brain capacities **EMOTIONAL** Encourages one to release anxieties and trust in Spirit **SPIRITUAL** Facilitates interdimensonal travel though the Light Body

Merkabite Calcite is named after the fabled Merkabah vehicle of Light mentioned in kabbalistic texts, for it opens many doorways to inner realms. When it is held to the third eye, one can feel a great rush of energy, like an interior wind, blowing through the upper chakras and out the top of the head. It can help bring about the full integration of the Light Body with the physical.

CALCITE, ORANGE **KEY WORDS** Creativity, sexuality, playfulness, confidence, innovation **CHAKRAS** Sexual/Creative (2nd), Solar Plexus (3rd) **ELEMENT** Fire **PHYSICAL** Aids sexual enjoyment, hormonal balance, metabolic health **EMOTIONAL** Helps heal wounds related to sexuality, creativity and will **SPIRITUAL** Instills greater energy for creative work, helps to spiritualize sexuality

Orange Calcite can be used for healing emotional wounds to one's sexuality, creativity and/or will. It can support those working to recover from childhood experiences of shame and sexual abuse. Orange Calcite invigorates playfulness and encourages confidence. It can be a catalyst for inspiration and even a kind of mineral aphrodisiac.

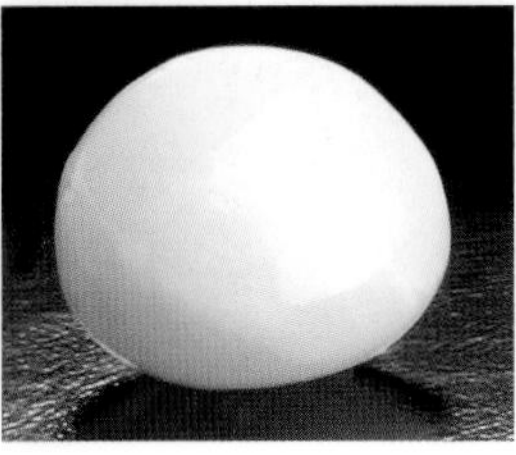

CALCITE, PINK OPAQUE **KEY WORDS** Well-being, wholeness, health, empathy and connection with the "mind of the heart" **CHAKRAS** Heart (4th) **ELEMENT** Fire **PHYSICAL** Supports healing of heart and circulatory system, aids cellular nutrition and tissue regeneration **EMOTIONAL** Helps clear destructive emotional fixations, helps calm hysteria and despair **SPIRITUAL** Facilitates attunement of one's heart to Divine Love

Opaque Pink Calcite can be used to enhance the heart's field and make one more perceptive of the energies in one's environment. It aids those who do "absent healing" work in attuning to the energy fields of others, even if they are not present. It can be used to dispel arguments and stubbornness in oneself and others, aiding one in seeing the other's point of view as if it were one's own.

CALCITE, PINK TRANSPARENT **KEY WORDS** Emotional healing, compassion and joy **CHAKRAS** Heart (4th) **ELEMENT** Fire, Water **PHYSICAL** Aids with stress-related digestive problems, strengthens kidneys **EMOTIONAL** Encourages loving kindness, awakens the heart to joy **SPIRITUAL** Facilitates communion with Kwan Yin, inspires compassion

Transparent Pink Calcite is a stone of deep compassion, and it generates this energy in those who work with it. It facilitates the state of non-judgmental acceptance and unconditional love. This stone connects to the energy of Kwan Yin, Bodhisattva of Compassion. It can bring one into a state of rapturous appreciation of the beauty of existence. This in turn can kindle the flame of joy in one's own heart. For those drawn to such an experience, meditation with these stones is highly recommended.

CALCITE, RED **KEY WORDS** Vitality, sensory awareness, clarity **CHAKRAS** Root (1st), Crown (7th) **ELEMENT** Fire, Earth **PHYSICAL** Supports reproductive health, bone growth and density **EMOTIONAL** Inspires the courage to be passionate, enthusiastic for life **SPIRITUAL** Facilitates being spiritually present in the physical world

Red Calcite is a stone of "soft vitality," in that it energizes the base chakra and brings in additional prana, or life-force energy, yet it does so in a subtle way that is very easy to accept, and it brings no "jolts" or discomforts with it. These stones also link the base chakra with the crown, bridging the frequent gap between physical existence and spiritual life. Red Calcite helps one appreciate the wonders of physical life and the ecstasies of sense-perception.

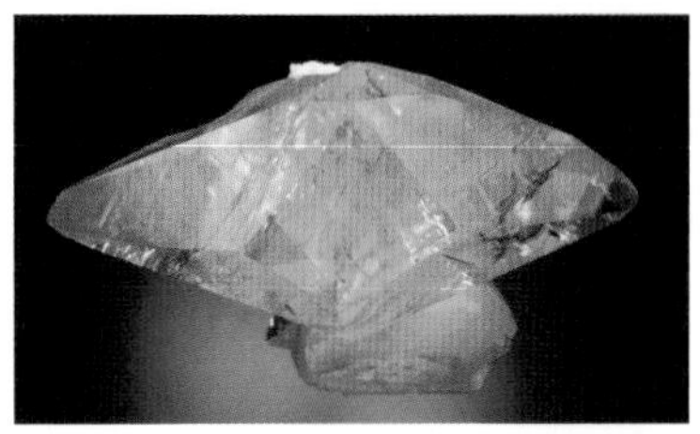

CALCITE, STELLAR BEAM **KEY WORDS** Divine will, manifestation, inter-dimensional travel, access to higher knowledge **CHAKRAS** Solar Plexus (3rd), Third Eye (6th), Crown (7th), Etheric (8th–14th) **ELEMENT** Fire, Storm **PHYSICAL** Aids in attuning the body to carry higher vibrational energies **EMOTIONAL** Helps dispel negative thoughts, opens one to higher awareness **SPIRITUAL** Facilitates attuning to ancient wisdom, past lives and ET intelligence

Stellar Beam Calcites stimulate the third eye and crown chakras, and aligning these chakras with the higher etheric body. It can facilitate inner travel through corridors of sacred geometric forms, via which one can access to the Hall of the Akashic records.

CARNELIAN **KEY WORDS** Courage, vitality, sexuality, confidence, action **CHAKRAS** Root (1st), Sexual/Creative (2nd), Solar Plexus (3rd) **ELEMENT** Fire **PHYSICAL** Supports strength, vitality, sexuality, detoxing from alcohol or drugs **EMOTIONAL** Increases one's courage and enthusiasm **SPIRITUAL** Aids in overcoming hesitation, finding courage to grow spiritually

Carnelian activates the first, second and third chakras, bringing an influx of life force, sexual and creative energies, and assertive will. It is a stone of physical vitality and energy, and can act spiritually to help one regain one's strength after illness or injury. Carrying or wearing it can aid in awakening the vital energies of the three lower chakras, increasing zest for living and the willingness to take the risks inherent in all strong actions.

CASSITERITE **KEY WORDS** Manifestation and destruction, birth and death, initiation, navigating the liminal threshold **CHAKRAS** Root (1st), Sexual/Creative (2nd), Solar Plexus (3rd) **ELEMENT** Storm **PHYSICAL** Supports shamanic healing, rallying the body to handle serious illness **EMOTIONAL** Helps overcome fear of death or of entering the other world **SPIRITUAL** Facilitates shamanic journeying, channeling

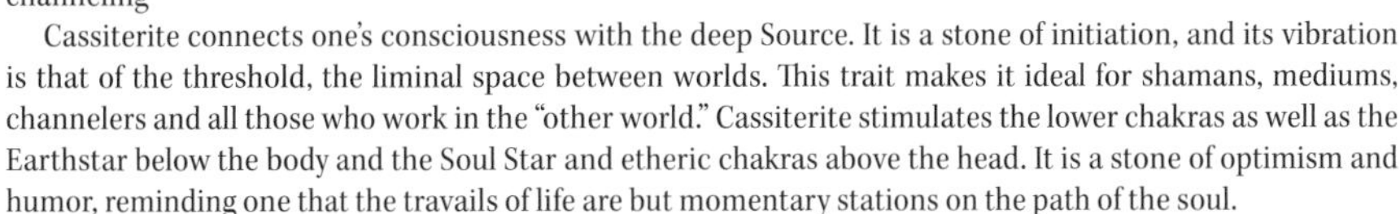

Cassiterite connects one's consciousness with the deep Source. It is a stone of initiation, and its vibration is that of the threshold, the liminal space between worlds. This trait makes it ideal for shamans, mediums, channelers and all those who work in the "other world." Cassiterite stimulates the lower chakras as well as the Earthstar below the body and the Soul Star and etheric chakras above the head. It is a stone of optimism and humor, reminding one that the travails of life are but momentary stations on the path of the soul.

CATACLOSITE IMPACT STONE **KEY WORDS** Destruction and reformation, transformational initiation, radical shift of perspective **CHAKRAS** All **ELEMENT** Fire, Earth **PHYSICAL** Can assist in recovering from physical or emotional trauma **EMOTIONAL** Soothes emotional distress of a radical shift of perspective **SPIRITUAL** Stimulates sudden, powerful spiritual transformation

Cataclosite Impact Stones have literally been through the physical version of the process of destruction, rebirth and re-growth, and they offer that pattern to us. For those who genuinely wish to experience transformation, these stones can call in the processes necessary to bring it about. They hold the pattern of shamanic "death and dismemberment," a necessary stage of initiation. Through them, we can resonate with it without having to go through physical suffering.

CATHEDRAL QUARTZ **KEY WORDS** Access to spiritual information, multidimensional awareness **CHAKRAS** Third Eye (6th), Crown (7th), Etheric (8th–14th) **ELEMENT** Storm, Wind **PHYSICAL** Aids in recalling past civilization information for healing the body **EMOTIONAL** Supports overcoming fears of entering expanded consciousness **SPIRITUAL** Facilitates accessing stored information from the spiritual domains

Cathedral Quartz crystals are among the richest of the information-bearing stones in the mineral kingdom. These stones act as repositories of knowledge of the energetic structures of the higher dimensions. Through working with them, one can develop the clairvoyant vision necessary to create an internal map of the astral, subtle, causal, devic, angelic and other realms. They allow humans to develop multidimensional awareness.

CAVANSITE **KEY WORDS** Clairvoyance, clairaudience, access to Akashic records, enhanced communication, consciousness **CHAKRAS** Third Eye (6th), Crown (7th) **ELEMENT** Wind **PHYSICAL** Aids with headaches and stress-induced maladies **EMOTIONAL** Brings peace, courage, gentleness **SPIRITUAL** Enhances psychic capacities, channeling and ESP

Cavansite unites the energies of the fifth and sixth chakras, facilitating clear insight and articulate communication. It is a stone of inner truth. It opens one's mind to direct comprehension and allows one to be a clear receiver for higher truth. Cavansite can assist those who channel spiritual information, or who wish to do so. It can aid one in all areas of intuition, including psychic abilities, mediumship, psychokinesis, psychometry, remote viewing, etc.

CELESTITE **KEY WORDS** Angelic communication, access to higher dimensions, serenity **CHAKRAS** Third Eye (6th), Crown (7th), Etheric (8th–14th) **ELEMENT** Wind **PHYSICAL** Aids in clearing negative attachments, overcoming infections **EMOTIONAL** Helps one dispel fear and paranoia, calms the emotional body **SPIRITUAL** Enhances inner vision and intuition, elevates one's awareness

Celestite offers a gentle, uplifting energy which can raise and expand one's awareness into the higher realms. It can facilitate communication between oneself and one's guardian angels or angelic guides. It stimulates the third eye and crown chakras and the etheric chakras above the head. It is a soft stone both physically and energetically. As it elevates one's awareness, Celestite makes one feel as if one is floating on a cloud, rather than zooming in a rocket.

CERUSSITE **KEY WORDS** Alchemical transformation of self, evolutionary change **CHAKRAS** Root (1st), Crown (7th) **ELEMENT** Storm **PHYSICAL** Facilitates alchemical transformation of the body **EMOTIONAL** Encourages equanimity through change, embracing spiritual desires **SPIRITUAL** Initiates the transformation from the human to Divine self

Cerussite is a stone of inner alchemy. It works to transform the human persona into a living manifestation of the Divine. It stimulates the energies of the root chakra and links them to the crown chakra. It builds a vibrational spiral up through the spinal column, energizing each of the chakras along the way. It creates a pattern of realignment which reverberates through all levels of one's being, offering one the opportunity to choose to restructure one's life at a higher level of spiritual functioning.

CHALCEDONY, BLUE **KEY WORDS** Calm, balance, centeredness, inner knowledge **CHAKRAS** Throat (5th), Third Eye (6th) **ELEMENT** Water **PHYSICAL** Aids with issues of the throat and larynx, voice problems **EMOTIONAL** Encourages release of inhibitions, clear communication of truth **SPIRITUAL** Enhances telepathy, past-life recall, spiritual counseling

When stresses mount and one's center begins to wobble, Blue Chalcedony can restore calm and balance. It can stimulate telepathy and communication with the invisible realms. It is a good stone for those in therapy and an excellent tool for those engaged in counseling others. It can also assist in the remembrance of past lives, and its orientation toward inner healing means that the memories recovered with Blue Chalcedony will be those most relevant to what is needed for one's progress and growth.

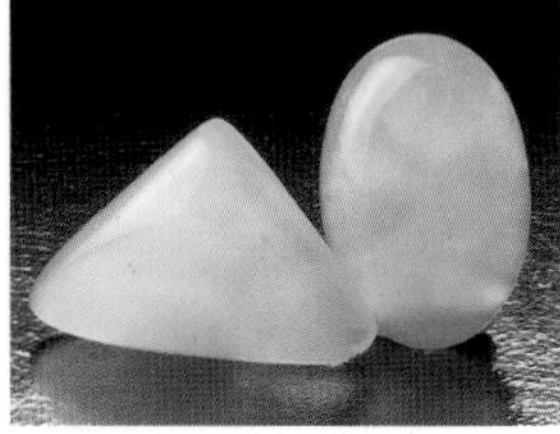

CHALCEDONY, PURPLE **KEY WORDS** Awakening of psychic abilities, aura cleansing, purification, union with the Higher Self **CHAKRAS** Third Eye (6th), Crown (7th) **ELEMENT** Wind **PHYSICAL** Supports higher brain functions, heals nerve damage **EMOTIONAL** Helps clear negative emotional attachments from past lives **SPIRITUAL** Facilitates awakening psychic capacities, attuning to the Higher Self

Purple Chalcedony. activates one's capacities for clairvoyance, clairaudience, clairsentience, psychometry, channeling, prescience and prophecy, as well as access to the Akashic records and knowledge of ancient civilizations. It is a powerful influence for purifying and cleansing the auric field, and for providing psychic protection.

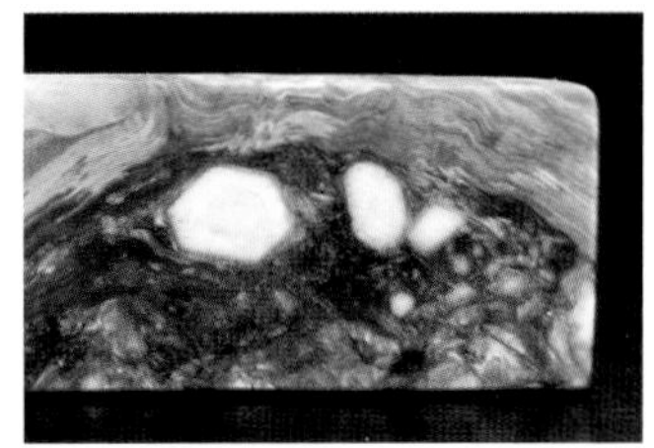

CHAROITE **KEY WORDS** Revealing one's path of service, purging inner negativity, protection, healing **CHAKRAS** Third Eye (6th), Crown (7th), Soul Star (8th), Solar Plexus (3rd), Root (1st), Earthstar (below the feet) **ELEMENT** Wind **PHYSICAL** Aids in overcoming illnesses caused by past-life attachments **EMOTIONAL** Helps with dispelling nightmares, overcoming fears, expressing love **SPIRITUAL** Psychic protection, etheric purification

Charoite activates one's capacities for clairvoyance, clairaudience, clairsentience, psychometry, channeling, prescience and prophecy, as well as access to the Akashic records and knowledge of ancient civilizations. It is a powerful influence for purifying and cleansing the auric field, and for providing psychic protection.

CHLORITE PHANTOM CRYSTALS **KEY WORDS** Self-healing, linking with Earth and Nature spirits **CHAKRAS** Heart (4th), Third Eye (6th) **ELEMENT** Storm, Earth **PHYSICAL** Initiates energetic cleansing of the body, facilitates psychic surgery **EMOTIONAL** Encourages a heart connection with Nature and the Earth **SPIRITUAL** Instills relationship with Nature spirits and the Earth

Chlorite Phantom Crystals are excellent sources of connection with the realm of the Nature spirits. Meditation with Chlorite Phantom Crystals can facilitate communication and energy exchange with plant spirits, as well as devas, fairies and other beings. Chlorite Phantoms resonate to the heartbeat of the Earth, and they can help one learn to ground one's energies and emotions in the Earth. they resonate with a remarkably clear version of pure Earth energy.

CHRYSANTHEMUM STONE **KEY WORDS** Grounding, prosperity, discovering and achieving the soul's purpose **CHAKRAS** All **ELEMENT** Earth **PHYSICAL** Supports female reproductive organs and tissues **EMOTIONAL** Inspires courage, embracing one's true potential **SPIRITUAL** Aids in following the soul's longing, calling in serendipities

Chrysanthemum Stone can act as a catalyst for activating the dormant capacities that lie within individuals. It offers energetic support for finding the courage and opportunities to live one's dreams. If one doesn't yet even know one's dream, sleeping or meditating with this stone can help one receive the inner message that makes clear the nature of one's neglected purpose. It can be a magnet for positive synchronicities.

CHRYSOBERYL **KEY WORDS** Alignment of the will with the heart, abundance, prophetic vision **CHAKRAS** Solar Plexus (3rd), Heart (4th) **ELEMENTS** Wind, Water **PHYSICAL** Energetically supports heart, kidneys and bloodstream **EMOTIONAL** Encourages generosity and altruism **SPIRITUAL** Instills power through gentleness, prosperity, generosity, prophecy

Chrysoberyl assists in merging and unifying the energies of the solar plexus and the heart, bringing empowerment of the will, under the guidance of the heart's compassionate wisdom. It can shift the vibration of one's energy field to enhance one's ability to act powerfully from a place of gentleness. It encourages participation in altruistic projects to heal and preserve Nature. It enhances the creation of prosperity through generosity. It also facilitates the gift of prophecy.

CHRYSOCOLLA **KEY WORDS** Communication, expression of the sacred, goddess energies, gentleness, power **CHAKRAS** Throat (5th), Heart (4th), Root (1st) **ELEMENT** Water **PHYSICAL** Supports adrenals and thyroid, aids with stress-related illnesses **EMOTIONAL** Aids with calming, release of stress and anxiety **SPIRITUAL** Facilitates expressing inner wisdom, linking with the Earth's awareness

Chrysocolla can empower feminine energies in both women and men. It stimulates clear communication of one's inner wisdom. It can facilitate one's empathic connection with the Earth's consciousness. It can harmonize and balance the heart chakra and can link both heart and throat chakras with the base chakra, for greater life force and physical vitality.

CHRYSOPRASE **KEY WORDS** Growth, compassion, connection with Nature, forgiveness, altruism **CHAKRAS** Heart (4th), Solar Plexus (3rd) **ELEMENT** Water **PHYSICAL** Supports general health, regeneration, youthfulness, vitality **EMOTIONAL** Encourages love and trust, release of fear-based emotions **SPIRITUAL** Aids in connecting with Divine Love, Nature spirits, Soul of the Earth

Chrysoprase is a stone of the heart. Wearing or meditating with it facilitates a deep heart connection with the soul of the Earth, as well as devas and other Earth-spirit entities. It helps one stay centered in the heart, providing the courage to face difficult situations with steadfast resolve and truth-centered compassion. It also activates the solar plexus chakra, It helps blend one's personal will with the urgings of the heart, uniting one's individual desires with the heart's higher longing for the good of all.

CINNABAR **KEY WORDS** Alchemy, magic, transformation, insight, manifestation, mental agility **CHAKRAS** Root (1st), Sexual/Creative (2nd), Third Eye (6th) **ELEMENT** Fire **PHYSICAL** Energetically supports clearing toxins, overcoming infections **EMOTIONAL** Helps one release anger and resentment, face truth courageously **SPIRITUAL** Facilitates perceiving the Divine pattern, alchemical transformation

Cinnabar Quartz is a talisman for the fulfillment of the Divine pattern within. It stimulates insight and the ability to see into the future. It helps one ground one's visions in physical reality as well. This makes it an ideal stone for creative people and business owners, both of whom can use it to actualize their dreams and create prosperity.

CIRCLE STONE **KEY WORDS** Attunement to Earth's consciousness, awakening of dormant capacities, co-creative union with the World Soul **CHAKRAS** Third Eye (6th), Crown (7th) **ELEMENT** Storm **PHYSICAL** Stimulates full brain activation and awakening body intelligence **EMOTIONAL** Inspires exhilaration and passionate devotion to World Soul **SPIRITUAL** Awakens latent capacities, co-creative union with Sophia

Circle Stones are evolutionary triggers. They stimulate the entire brain and activate latent capacities such as clairvoyance, prescience, clairsentience, and awareness of the Earth's consciousness. They help one attune to the Time Stream of the Future, and they awaken our potential for co-creating the world in partnership with the World Soul.

CITRINE **KEY WORDS** Manifestation, personal will, mental clarity, creativity **CHAKRAS** Root (1st), Sexual/Creative (2nd), Solar Plexus (3rd) **ELEMENT** Fire **PHYSICAL** Energetically supports digestion, metabolism, weight loss **EMOTIONAL** Stimulates optimism, playfulness, decisiveness in difficult situations **SPIRITUAL** Enhances creative imagination, manifestation through the will

Citrine opens the inner doors to increased clarity of thought, enhanced creativity and magnified powers of will and manifestation. It is one of the premier stones for the second chakra and is capable of awakening the powers of creative imagination. It stimulates imagination through three portals—the second, third and sixth chakras. The vibratory resonance of Citrine activates and harmonizes these three energy centers, all of which are necessary to the process of creative imagination.

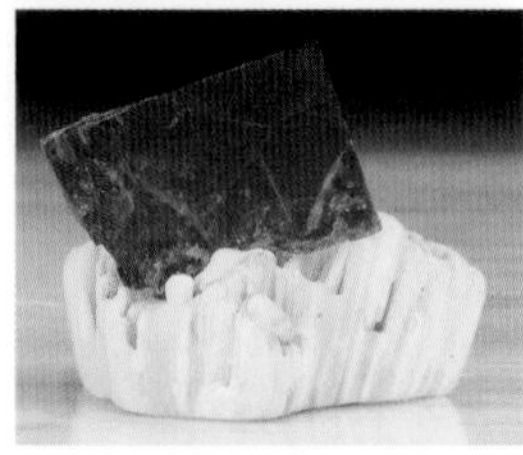

CLINICHLORE **KEY WORDS** Healing, vitality, love, Divine blueprint of well-being, angelic communication **CHAKRAS** Heart (4th) **ELEMENT** Storm, Earth **PHYSICAL** Aids in attuning to the Divine pattern of health **EMOTIONAL** Supports joyful link with the higher realms **SPIRITUAL** Facilitates connecting with spirit guides and angels

Clinochlore is beneficial for bringing healing and well-being to the body through alignment with the Divine blueprint. When one works with one's intention focused on linking to the pattern of perfect health, the stones provide a "window" through which one may resonate with this pattern. Clinochlore assists in communicating with angelic beings and spirit guides. Its vibrational pattern provides a window into these domains, allowing one to receive and return the energies of blessing.

CLINOZOISITE **KEY WORDS** Heart intelligence, friendliness, emotional security **CHAKRAS** Heart (4th), High Heart (between 4th and 5th) **ELEMENT** Water, Earth, Wind, Fire **PHYSICAL** Supports clearing of the lungs, veins and arteries **EMOTIONAL** Brings heart energy into the emotional body, encourages friendliness, makes one feel safe **SPIRITUAL** Facilitates centering oneself in the heart, truthfullness, generosity

Clinozoisite is friendly to the heart, both physical and emotional. It enhances the presence of heart intelligence in one's conscious awareness, and encourages one to speak and act from the heart at all times. In self-healing, it promotes a state of overall well-being in the heart, also lending energetic support to the circulatory system and lungs. It enhances one's appreciation of Nature's beauty and aids in creative self-expression.

COROMANDEL STONEWOOD **KEY WORDS** Awareness of Earth's ancient memories, time travel to the past, Lemurian consciousness, receptivity, link to the Earth's heartbeat, telomere protection, longevity **CHAKRAS** All, especially Root (1st) **ELEMENT** Earth **PHYSICAL** Enhances vitality, supports the telomeres for increased longevity **EMOTIONAL** Facilitates inner peace, contentment, and ecstatic resonance with the Earth's heartbeat **SPIRITUAL** Facilitates entrainment with the Earth's heartbeat, aids one in recalling and identifying with Lemurian consciousness

Coromandel Stonewood carries deep memories of the ancient Earth. It carries the memories of New Zealand's Lemurian history, as well as the Lemurian qualities of deep intuition, empathy and bodily knowing. It enhances one's receptivity to the subtle vibrational currents of the Earth.

COVELLITE **KEY WORDS** Psychic abilities, inner vision, transformation, bridging the higher and lower worlds **CHAKRAS** All **ELEMENT** Storm **PHYSICAL** Helps one overcome illnesses based in negative past fixations **EMOTIONAL** Inspires courage to take the journey through one's inner depths **SPIRITUAL** Facilitates making the evolutionary leap to awakened consciousness

Covellite connects strongly with physical reality and Earth energies and at the same time carries much of the higher spectrum of vibrations from the etheric planes. It makes an energetic bridge between worlds, and it can be an important ally for anyone attempting the evolutionary leap to the next level of being. Covellite is also a facilitator of the deep journey into the self and can be of great assistance in bringing the unconscious Shadow side into one's awareness.

CREEDITE **KEY WORDS** Expansion of awareness, attuning to spiritual information **CHAKRAS** Third Eye (6th), Crown (7th), Etheric (8th–14th) **ELEMENT** Storm **PHYSICAL** Reveals the etheric body for diagnosis of imbalances **EMOTIONAL** Helps one govern the emotional body from a higher perspective **SPIRITUAL** Facilitates great expansion of awareness in the spiritual realms

Creedite powerfully activates the third eye and crown chakras. It brings a vivid expansion of one's field of awareness and a powerful euphoria. Over time, one senses a deepening of the energy, moving down to the heart. Creedite can assist one in attuning to the Akashic records, "opening the files" in record keeper crystals, understanding the messages of spirit guides, interpreting oracles such as the tarot, and channeling the messages of spirit beings. It can help meditators make the quantum leap to higher domains of consciousness.

CRIMSON CUPRITE **KEY WORDS** Life force, vitality, physical energy, courage, healing, Divine feminine, etherization of the blood **CHAKRAS** Root (1st), Sexual/Creative (2nd) **ELEMENT** Earth **PHYSICAL** Triggers an infusion of life force, aids most organs and systems **EMOTIONAL** Instills passion and vitality, assuages anxiety and fear **SPIRITUAL** Links one with the Earth Goddess, stimulates transformation

Crimson Cuprite offers pure first-chakra energy, offering an abundant flow of prana. It can be instrumental in awakening kundalini energies. It offers vibrational support for healing lung dysfunctions, circulation difficulties, prostate or lower-bowel issues or problems with sexual organs. Crimson Cuprite is a stone of feminine power, activating the archetype of the Earth goddess.

CROCODILE ROCK **KEY WORDS** Stone of the "Eureka" moment, lightheartedness, relaxation, adventurousness **CHAKRAS** Root (1st), Heart (4th) Crown (7th) **ELEMENT** Earth, Fire, Wind **PHYSICAL** Supports immune system, muscles, joints and ligaments, encourages limberness **EMOTIONAL** Encourages optimism, and an easygoing attitude **SPIRITUAL** Draws mind into transcendent state

Crocodile Rock is a stone of light-hearted fun and adventurousness. It is an excellent stone to uplift those who are "down in the dumps," because its currents bring attention to the humorous side of life, reminding one not to take oneself too seriously. It is a good stone for someone who wants to get out of a way of life that has become too embedded in routine. Crocodile Rock can shake up old patterns and allow one to see new potentials and opportunities.

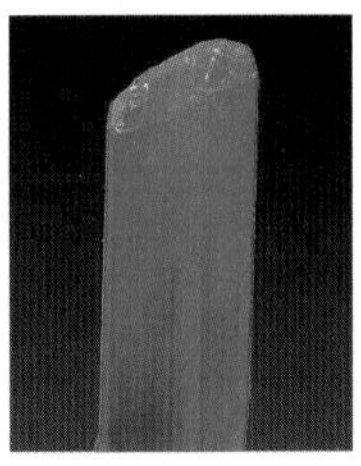

CROCOITE **KEY WORDS** Physical vitality, wisdom of the heart, passion, love, enlightenment **CHAKRAS** Root (1st), Heart (4th), Crown (7th) **ELEMENT** Storm **PHYSICAL** Supports reproductive systems **EMOTIONAL** Kindles love and passion **SPIRITUAL** Enhances creativity, kundalini activation

Crocoite is beneficial for making breakthroughs, especially in the passionate pursuit of enlightenment. It activates the crown, heart and root chakras, opening the kundalini channel. It can catalyze quantum leaps of consciousness, dispelling blockages and allowing the full expression of one's spiritual self through the physical body. Crocoite can stimulate passion, love and spiritual awareness. The vibrations of Crocoite are conducive to tantric love making practices, which rouse these same energies. Crocoite stimulates all types of creative fertility, and is an excellent stone for artists, writers and musicians.

CRYOLITE **KEY WORDS** Intelligence of the heart, future stream, Divine purpose, surrender, liberation, spiritual truth **CHAKRAS** All (1st–7th), Soul Star (8th) **ELEMENT** Storm **PHYSICAL** Supports neurological health, strengthens heart/brain links **EMOTIONAL** Awakens inner joy and peace through heart awareness **SPIRITUAL** Facilitates expansion of consciousness into heart/brain partnership

Cryolite can awaken the pre-frontal cortex of the brain. It stimulates the heart and crown chakras, linking them with the third eye and facilitating inner vision. It opens the channels via which the holographic knowing of the heart can be received by the conscious mind. It switches on dormant capacities in the "silent areas" of the brain.

CUPRITE **KEY WORDS** Life force, vitality, physical energy, courage, healing, Divine feminine **CHAKRAS** Root (1st), Sexual/Creative (2nd) **ELEMENT** Earth **PHYSICAL** Supports lungs, circulation, bowels, prostate, sexual organs **EMOTIONAL** Aids in overcoming fear of death **SPIRITUAL** Stimulates kundalini, alchemy, Goddess energies

Cuprite is helpful for problems linked with the root chakra—healing issues, irrational anxieties, fears around mortality, unconscious terror connected to past traumas. It emanates a wellspring of life force, helping those with chronic fatigue or low levels of vitality. It is a stone of fertility on all levels—helpful to those who wish to conceive, and to those who want to birth their creative projects into the world. It can link one with Goddess energies.

DANBURITE **KEY WORDS** Angelic communication, channeling, interdimensional travel, peace, freedom from stress **CHAKRAS** Heart (4th), Crown (7th), Etheric (8th–14th) **ELEMENT** Wind **PHYSICAL** Supports recovery from stress-related illnesses **EMOTIONAL** Aids in finding inner peace, calming worries and fears **SPIRITUAL** Facilitates interdimensional travel, angelic communication

Danburite can aid in the upliftment of one's awareness to the higher spiritual vibrations. It clears and opens the crown chakra, linking and harmonizing it with the heart. It activates and integrates the transpersonal and etheric chakras above the head, all the way up to the fourteenth chakra. It links one with the angelic domain, and it facilitates interdimensional travel and communication. It is excellent for those who need to release stress and worry. It soothes the heart and lets it know that all is well. Sleeping with it can bring deep peace and healthy rest.

DARWINITE **KEY WORDS** Heart awareness, loving relationship, linking heart and brain, gestation of the New Human Being **CHAKRAS** Heart (4th), Third Eye (6th), Crown (7th) **ELEMENT** Storm **PHYSICAL** Supports the brain, corpus callosum and heart **EMOTIONAL** Entrains with the heart to stimulate a consciousness of love, removes fear from the emotional body **SPIRITUAL** Quickens spiritual evolution, awakens spiritual capacities

Darwinite can be used to remove fear from the emotional body and the cellular consciousness. It quickens the vibratory rate of the etheric body, so that we can keep pace with the accelerating vibrations of the Earth. Darwinite stimulates insight, and the capacity to "make all things new" through attunement with what is arising from the spiritual realms.

DATOLITE **KEY WORDS** Connection with the higher worlds, retrieval of lost information, mental power, spiritual awareness **CHAKRAS** Solar Plexus (3rd), Heart (4th), Third Eye (6th), Crown (7th), Etheric (8th–14th) **ELEMENT** Water, Wind **PHYSICAL** Supports and soothes the nervous system **EMOTIONAL** Helps one overcome grief and depression, encourages optimism **SPIRITUAL** Activates subtle vision and multidimensional awareness

Datolite activates the third eye, crown and etheric chakras. it opens subtle vision, allowing one to see and commune with Nature spirits, angels, guides, non-physical teachers, healers and helpers. The fast-pulsing energies of Datolite increase the vibration of one's energy field so one can consciously experience one's own spiritual body, using it to explore the many higher dimensions surrounding us.

DEVALITE **KEY WORDS** Exchanging healing and love with Nature **CHAKRAS** Heart **ELEMENT** Water, Earth **PHYSICAL** Supports the heart, lungs, circulatory system **EMOTIONAL** Heals long-held disharmonies, facilitates reclaiming one's childlike openness **SPIRITUAL** Encourages compassion, kindness, truthfulness to all beings

There is a lively magical quality to Devalite. It attracts Devas and Nature spirits, and it can help one to become acquainted with them. It is impossible to predict what the Devas may do to reveal their presence, but the overall feeling is that the world is alive and full of almost-visible beings that are very interested in you! They are always there, and Devalite helps to open the subtle senses so that you become aware of them.

DIAMOND **KEY WORDS** Intensity, radiance, sovereignty **CHAKRAS** Heart (4th), Third Eye (6th), Crown (7th), Etheric (8th–14th) **ELEMENT** Storm **PHYSICAL** Activates prefrontal lobes, magnifies effects of other stones **EMOTIONAL** Intensifies emotional states, helps "burn through" old issues **SPIRITUAL** Facilitates awakening higher capacities, entering visionary states

Diamond can stimulate paranormal abilities and visionary consciousness. It can accelerate one's evolution and open the doors to psychic powers, facilitating entry into visionary states. It can accelerate one's evolution and open the doors to psychic powers. Intensity is a key word for Diamond. It works on the emotional body to amplify the power of any emotional state. It can be used therapeutically to intensify and "burn through" underlying emotional issues.

DIASPORE **KEY WORDS** Adaptability, mental enhancement, meditative exploration **CHAKRAS** Solar Plexus (3rd), Heart (4th), Third Eye (6th) **ELEMENT** Wind **PHYSICAL** Supports recovery from brain damage and brain diseases **EMOTIONAL** Aids in relieving stress, "letting go," attuning to Divine will **SPIRITUAL** Enhances meditation, communication with higher beings

Diaspore assists in developing the strength of adaptability. It stimulates the release of one's personal desires in order to be in accord with Divine will. It is useful in relieving stress, developing relationships that work, finding one's best niche in job and career areas, and working in partnership with spiritual beings. It stimulates one's ability to see different points of view on all issues and ideas. It opens new areas of consciousness, and it keeps one from falling into patterns of expectation and judgment.

DIOPSIDE **KEY WORDS** Connection with the Earth, opening the heart, healing, balance, subtle perception **CHAKRAS** Heart (4th), Root (1st), Earthstar (below the feet) **ELEMENT** Earth **PHYSICAL** Supports tissue regeneration, recovery of strength, reproductive organs **EMOTIONAL** Aids with relaxation, release of stress, embrace of physical life **SPIRITUAL** Facilitates communion with Earth, grounding, geomancy

Diopside varies in its energy, according to its color, and the two most important types are black and green. Black Diopside resonates with the root chakra, and it helps one establish a firm grounding in the Earth. It is excellent for geomancy. Those who work with ley lines will find their perceptions enhanced by Black Diopside. Green Diopside sends its energies along the entire chakric column, from the top of the skull to the tailbone. It is oriented toward balancing and healing, and can bring all the chakras into alignment.

DIOPTASE **KEY WORDS** Forgiveness, compassion, release of karmic patterns, prosperity **CHAKRAS** Heart (4th) **ELEMENT** Water **PHYSICAL** Supports healing of the heart and of illness caused by emotional trauma **EMOTIONAL** Helps one forgive past abuses; supports joy, peace and compassion **SPIRITUAL** Instills freedom from karmic bonds, full heart-centeredness

Dioptase is ideal for awakening loving compassion and for healing emotional pain. It lends strength to the emotional heart and supports the physical heart through its energy of serenity and well-being. It awakens the spiritual heart through its high-frequency vibrational pattern. Through these channels it stimulates forgiveness and the healing of old inner wounds. It is useful for the attainment of past-life insights and for the activation of one's higher purpose.

DOLOMITE **KEY WORDS** Centeredness, calm, balance, moderation, grounding **CHAKRAS** All **ELEMENT** Earth **PHYSICAL** Supports bone health and detoxification, gets one "in the body" **EMOTIONAL** Lessens emotional extremes, supports calm centeredness **SPIRITUAL** Stone of the "middle way," helps one avoid spiritual extremes

Dolomite facilitates calm, centeredness and balance. It softens negative emotions and reins in excessive passions. It takes the allure away from unrealistic fantasies, without detracting from one's enthusiasm for one's true purpose. Dolomite is a good stone to place in the environment and can provide a beneficial influence around children. It is a good stone to hold after a crystal body layout, a past-life regression, rebirthing, breathwork or other transformational practice.

DREAM QUARTZ **KEY WORDS** Dream enhancement, astral travel, contact with guides, release of stress **CHAKRAS** Third Eye (6th), Crown (7th), Soul Star (8th) **ELEMENT** Storm, Earth, Water **PHYSICAL** Supports weight loss, psychic protection **EMOTIONAL** Aids inner peace, emotional healing via dreams, past-life recall **SPIRITUAL** Stimulates visionary awareness, lucid dreaming, enhanced psychic abilities

Dream Quartz emanates a soft, soothing energy, conducive to states of deep meditation and lucid dreaming. It can bring peace to the heart and relaxation to the body and mind. It helps one enter the inner gateways to visionary experience and interdimensional travel. It can facilitate contact with spirit guides and can be an aid to the development of psychic abilities and channeling. It can help one remember dreams, and can enhance their spiritual quality.

DUMORTIERITE **KEY WORDS** Divine inspiration, psychic ability, inner guidance, enhanced learning capacity, mental discipline **CHAKRAS** Third Eye (6th) **ELEMENT** Wind **PHYSICAL** Supports neural functioning and clarity of consciousness **EMOTIONAL** Enhances emotional intelligence and empathy **SPIRITUAL** Stimulates psychic abilities, prophetic vision, spiritual insight

Dumortierite opens the doors of insight, activating the third eye chakra. It enhances mental abilities and emotional intelligence. It activates latent psychic abilities. It is a strong stone of mental discipline and is capable of enhancing one's willpower in regard to learning. It is ideal for those who work in areas such as astrology and tarot.

EISEN QUARTZ **KEY WORDS** Vitality, creativity, optimism, playfulness, humor, eroticism, insight, self-confidence, spiritual freedom **CHAKRAS** Root (1st), Sexual/Creative (2nd), Solar Plexus (3rd) **ELEMENTS** Fire, Wind, Earth **PHYSICAL** Supports the immune system, sexual organs and digestive system **EMOTIONAL** Can be a remedy for discouragement or "stuck" emotions **SPIRITUAL** Stimulates creative inspirations, sexual energies, encourages taking the risks that lead to creative and/or romantic fulfillment

Eisen Quartz emanates vitality, creativity and optimism. It can kindle romance, or fuel inspirations for writing, art, poetry, dance and other creative intentions. It can trigger the "aha" moment of sudden insight. It supports the sexual organs, intestinal tract and spleen. It can be used to increase self-confidence, enhances one's awareness of one's spiritual freedom.

ELESTIAL QUARTZ **KEY WORDS** Energy infusion from the higher realms, Divine Love, angelic communication, grounding the Higher Self in earthly life **CHAKRAS** All **ELEMENT** Earth **PHYSICAL** Supports skeletal system for healing broken or diseased bones **EMOTIONAL** Aids in receiving love, joy and well-being from the higher realms **SPIRITUAL** Facilitates awakening to multidimensional communication, time travel

Elestial Quartz crystals are like switchboards linking multiple dimensions, times and levels of consciousness to one another. These crystals constantly emanate vibrations that remind us and reconnect us to the inner worlds of Spirit. They easily attune to the angelic domain. Through this Elestial connection, one may receive a "download" of cosmic love, which can infuse every cell in the body with joy and well-being. Elestial Quartz crystals allow one's consciousness to travel freely through time and space, viewing probable futures as well as past events.

EMERALD **KEY WORDS** Love, compassion, healing, abundance **CHAKRAS** Heart (4th) **ELEMENT** Water **PHYSICAL** Supports the heart, blood and circulatory system **EMOTIONAL** Opens the heart to love, forgiveness, compassion and trust **SPIRITUAL** Facilitates the awakening to Divine Love

Emerald is the stone which most purely represents the energy patterns of the activated heart chakra. It encourages one to live and act from the heart, offering unconditional love and compassion in one's daily life and relationships. It can help one stay centered in the heart's wisdom, and can aid in healing heartbreak. It is a stone of prosperity, helping one attune oneself to the energy of abundance. Emerald is also a stone of courage. It helps one move forward on the "path with heart," regardless of any threats or dangers. Like Moldavite, Emerald is associated in legend with the fabled Stone of the Holy Grail.

EPIDOTE **KEY WORDS** Release of negativity, embracing positive patterns, attraction of what one emanates **CHAKRAS** All **ELEMENT** Earth, Water **PHYSICAL** Supports dissolution of blockages in the body **EMOTIONAL** Helps one develop emotional generosity **SPIRITUAL** Aids one in creating via the Law of Attraction

Epidote tends to bring one more of what one already has, in accordance with one's highest good. When used consciously, Epidote can be a very powerful tool. It can be used to create abundance and prosperity, to attract new loving relationships, to catalyze the creative process, etc. Yet one must always contain at least the seed of what one is trying to attract. If one desires prosperity (generosity from the Universe), one must act generously. If one wants love, one must be loving, and so forth. Epidote does not provide a free ride, yet it can be of great aid to those prepared to give a little of what they wish to receive.

EMPOWERITE **KEY WORDS** Confidence, strength, personal power, courage, self-awareness, will, commitment **CHAKRAS** Root (1st), Sexual/Creative (2nd), Solar Plexus (3rd), Third Eye (6th) **ELEMENTS** Earth, Storm **PHYSICAL** Supports the visceral organs, hands, feet and shoulders, facilitates efforts to increase muscle and bone strength **EMOTIONAL** Inspires release of self-doubt and inner turmoil, encourages commitment to one's path **SPIRITUAL** Enhances confidence and awareness of one's power, stimulates the soul's full incarnation

Empowerite is excellent for grounding one's energies in the Earth, and for receiving the Earth's Life Force. It relieves hesitation and indecision, enhances willpower, inspires courage, stimulates practicality and encourages one to act with resolve. It can strengthen the digestive system and intestines. It supports the liver and gall bladder as well as the hands, feet and shoulders. It is useful for strengthening the muscles and skeleton.

EUCLASE **KEY WORDS** Transformation of negativity, integrity, truthfulness, clarity, intuition, spiritual commitment **CHAKRAS** Heart (4th), Throat (5th), Third Eye (6th) **ELEMENT** Wind **PHYSICAL** Supports eyesight, mental function, proper speech **EMOTIONAL** Encourages compassion, commitment to truth **SPIRITUAL** Initiates clairsentience, spiritual integrity, access to inner guidance

Euclase is a stone of inner clarity and strength of self. It helps one clear the air, and it works through compassionate, persistent adherence to the truth. Its effects focus on heart and throat chakras. The fact that Euclase also stimulates the third eye means that one can clearly "see" the truth it reveals. The third eye enhancement offered by Euclase assists clairvoyants and intuitives in their work. Euclase can increase the frequency of synchronicities, and it encourages one to recognize them as messages from Spirit.

EUDIALYTE **KEY WORDS** Opening and following the heart, self-love, healing the emotional body **CHAKRAS** Heart (4th), Root (1st) **ELEMENT** Earth, Water **PHYSICAL** Supports overall health and vitality, increased life force **EMOTIONAL** Aids fulfillment of the heart's desires, emotional healing **SPIRITUAL** Encourages following the heart's wisdom

Eudialyte is a stone of the life force and the love force, combined to unify the heart's yearnings with one's physical life. Its energies bring resonance and harmony to the parallel tracks of survival and fulfillment. It activates and aligns the first and fourth chakras, and it evokes synchronicities that support the things we dream of doing. It can be used in self-healing for repairing the emotional body and bringing in more vitality and life force.

FADEN QUARTZ **KEY WORDS** Healing the etheric body and auric field, catalyzing physical healing **CHAKRAS** All **ELEMENT** Earth, Storm **PHYSICAL** Fadens are all-purpose, programmable healing stones **EMOTIONAL** Aids in healing the emotional body **SPIRITUAL** Facilitates spiritual healing, awareness of past and future Earth changes

Faden Quartz is one of the premier healing stones of the Quartz family. It carries the pattern of healing within its natural programming. When one moves into resonance with these crystals, one's capacity for healing is activated and/or reinforced. Faden Quartz is ideal for consciousness expansion and accessing any of the higher vibrational planes. The Fadens' experience of past earth changes makes them ideal tools for those who seek information on current and future physical and vibrational shifts.

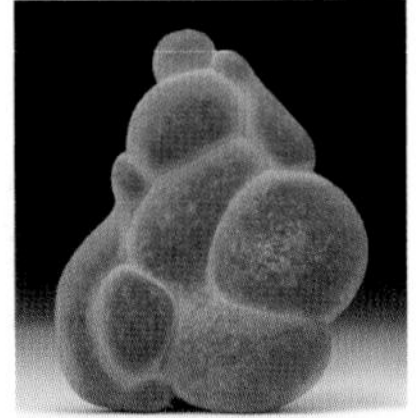

FAIRY STONES **KEY WORDS** Communication with Fairies and Nature spirits, plants, animals, stones **CHAKRAS** Heart (4th) **ELEMENT** Earth **PHYSICAL** Provides a link to the healing energies of Nature **EMOTIONAL** Helps one to overcome malaise, depression, discouragement, **SPIRITUAL** Enhances the ability to do magic through co-creation with Fairies and Elemental forces

Fairy Stones, aid in connecting, communicating and co-creating with Nature Spirits and beings of the Fairy realm. They are ideal for harmonizing oneself with the living Earth, and for entering mutual blessing with all living things. They facilitate one's ability to see Fairy beings, Devas and other beings of the Earth's soul life. They can also aid in learning to communicate with all crystals and stones. They can help individuals to heal from the 'soul sickness' which afflicts those consumed by the artificiality of human life

FAIRY WAND QUARTZ **KEY WORDS** Attunement with fairy, devic and angelic realms, relaxation, inner peace **CHAKRAS** Heart (4th), Third Eye (6th), Crown (7th), Etheric (8th–14th) **ELEMENT** Water, Wind **PHYSICAL** Helps with balancing headaches, vertigo and vision issues **EMOTIONAL** Supports overcoming fear of judgment or the unknown **SPIRITUAL** Facilitates entering the fairy realm, interdimensional travel, creativity

Fairy Wand Quartz crystals are keystones of interdimensional travel, aiding one in moving into and out of the inner worlds, especially the fairy realm. It stimulates the third eye and activates visionary consciousness. Holding it at the forehead, one can experience a "rush" through the geometric interdimensional corridors. In this kind of inner journey, pairing Fairy Wand Quartz with Phenacite can enhance the effect.

FLINT **KEY WORDS** Grounding the spiritual in the physical, creating structure and self-discipline, increasing honesty and practicality **CHAKRAS** All **ELEMENT** Earth **PHYSICAL** Helps with replenishment, grounding the Divine blueprint into the cells **EMOTIONAL** Soothes the emotional body, helps one release past wounds **SPIRITUAL** Stimulates psychic abilities, intuition, bringing spiritual Light into the body

Flint helps "spacey" people get into their bodies and focus themselves in the physical world. It can affect one's intuitive and psychic abilities, enhancing the specificity and clarity of the information received. It is recommended for those who do readings, channeling or mediumship. It strengthens the links between the root chakra and the other chakras.

FLUORITE **KEY WORDS** Mental enhancement and clarity, improved decision making, clearing the energy fields **CHAKRAS** All **ELEMENT** Wind **PHYSICAL** Supports brain chemistry, bones and teeth; helps overcome vertigo or dizziness **EMOTIONAL** Aids in dispelling confusion, dishonesty, anxiety about the future **SPIRITUAL** Helps with cleansing the astral body, enhancing mental capacities

Fluorite can act as a "psychic vacuum cleaner," clearing the atmosphere of confusion, cluttered thoughts, negativity and astral contamination. It is balancing to the third eye and to mental energies in general. Purple Fluorite is ideal for purification and spiritual activation. Black Fluorite is the ultimate astral cleanser. Yellow Fluorite magnifies the mental powers. Green Fluorite can cleanse the heart chakra. Pink Fluorite heals the emotional body and works to activate the "high heart" chakra. Blue Fluorite enables clear communication.

FULGURITE **KEY WORDS** Manifestation of one's higher purpose, enhancement of prayer, kundalini awakening, purification, sudden awakening **CHAKRAS** All **ELEMENT** Storm **PHYSICAL** Supports blood flow, oxygenation, *prana* and life force **EMOTIONAL** Clears dysfunctional patterns in the emotional body **SPIRITUAL** Facilitates sudden spiritual awakening, amplification of prayers

Fulgurites are powerful stones for manifesting one's visions through the power of prayer. The lightning energy, long believed to be the touch of the Divine, still resides in them, and they can act as magnifiers of one's intention. "Blowing one's prayers" through a Fulgurite tube is a powerful technique. Fulgurites have a strong, high-frequency vibration. Holding a Fulgurite, one may sense a vortex of energy whizzing through the chakras and the Light Body, purifying and cleansing the entire system.

GAIA STONE **KEY WORDS** Connection with the Heart of the Earth, love and compassion, emotional healing, goddess energies **CHAKRAS** Heart (4th) **ELEMENT** Water **PHYSICAL** Supports healing of migraines and tension headaches, stress, gastric upsets **EMOTIONAL** Soothes the emotional body, supports restful sleep **SPIRITUAL** Links one with the Heart of the Earth

Gaia Stone can bring one's heart into resonance with the heart of the Earth. It supports loving relationships between people. It is an ideal gift for one's romantic partner, as its energies promote the growth of love and intimacy. It induces compassion and diffuses anger. It can assist one in negotiations where one must try to persuade an unsympathetic person to understand one's point of view. It can be used to heal and soothe the heart and to energize the emotional body.

GALENA **KEY WORDS** Shamanic soul retrieval, alchemical self-transformation, past-life recall **CHAKRAS** Root (1st) **ELEMENT** Earth **PHYSICAL** Supports recovery from infection, radiation, chemotherapy **EMOTIONAL** Helps with soul retrieval, healing past-life issues **SPIRITUAL** Facilitates shamanism, alchemical transformation

Galena is a stone of the alchemical process of self-transformation. It can place within one's vibrational field the restless desire of the seeker, who will not cease until the journey to enlightenment is complete. It is a powerful grounding stone, and it can take the meditator deep into the Earth. Those who do shamanic work will find an ally in Galena, which can lead one into the "other world." Galena can also assist in past-life regression work,

GARNET, ALMANDINE **KEY WORDS** Strength, security **CHAKRAS** Root (1st) **ELEMENT** Earth **PHYSICAL** Supports reproductive organs, aids recuperation from injury **EMOTIONAL** Dispels negativity, worry and panic, helps one adhere to truth **SPIRITUAL** Provides grounding and protection, arouses kundalini energies

Almandine Garnet is a stone of the ancient times in human history, when people were more intimately connected to the Earth, and when life was more physically demanding. It can vibrationally enhance one's vitality and endurance. It activates and strengthens the base chakra. It is excellent for those who are a bit ungrounded, or who lack energy. Almandine Garnet is also a stone of psychic protection. It keeps one strongly connected to the body, and shields one from negative entities and energies.

GARNET, BLACK ANDRADITE **KEY WORDS** Grounding, protection, knowledge, creative power **CHAKRAS** Root (1st), Earthstar (below the feet) **ELEMENT** Earth **PHYSICAL** Protects the body from invasion by negative forces **EMOTIONAL** Aids in empowering the self, enhances confidence **SPIRITUAL** Helps one access elemental energies, "magical" powers, lost knowledge

Black Andradite Garnet is a powerful grounding stone, which can be used to evoke the mysteries of the Earth. It can help one attune to elemental forces and engage their aid. One can meditate with this stone to penetrate the depths of the collective unconscious and to read the morphogenic fields of knowledge. It is ideal for arousing the creative fires of sexuality and for the empowerment and focus of the will. It aids one in establishing the dynamic grounding which is needed for those of high intention to actualize their visions.

GARNET, GROSSULAR **KEY WORDS** Prosperity, health **CHAKRAS** Solar Plexus (3rd), Heart (4th) **ELEMENT** Earth **PHYSICAL** Supports vibrant, abundant health; recovery after illness **EMOTIONAL** Helps one overcome financial anxiety and/or scarcity consciousness **SPIRITUAL** Facilitates manifestation of prosperity, zest for living

Grossular Garnet supports abundant manifestation. Its vibrational pattern creates an eager confidence, a motivation to get down to business and make things happen. Paired with Moldavite, these would be unbeatable for bringing into reality one's rightful abundance and highest path of achievement in this world. Grossular Garnets are stones, not just of prosperity, but of wealth in all its positive aspects—financial, creative, emotional, artistic and even physical health.

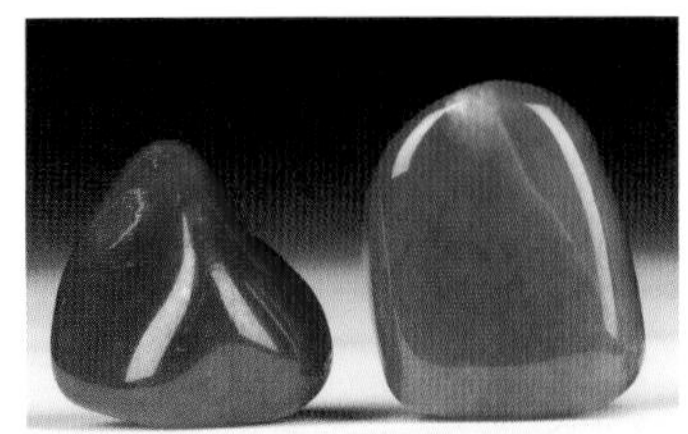

GARNET, RAINBOW **KEY WORDS** Happiness, felicity, exuberance, playfulness, kindness, generosity, healing the Inner Child **CHAKRAS** Heart (4th) **ELEMENTS** Earth, Water **PHYSICAL** Supports the heart, brings life energies to the whole body **EMOTIONAL** Dissolves old negative emotions, gently and playfully healing to one's Inner Child **SPIRITUAL** Brings happiness, good humor and zest for life, helps one fully enjoy one's spiritual path

Rainbow Garnet stimulates a sense of playfulness, and can be healing to one's Inner Child. It can dispel stress, worries, fears, angers and sorrows. It is a stone of good humor, wittiness, as well as kindness, generosity and cordiality. It can help one see the bright side of difficult situations, recognizing that all things ultimately work toward the good.

GARNET, RHODOLITE **KEY WORDS** Emotional healing, self-worth, walking the spiritual path **CHAKRAS** Root (1st), Heart (4th), Crown (7th) **ELEMENT** Earth **PHYSICAL** Supports healing of physical issues rooted in emotional wounds **EMOTIONAL** Soothes and heals the emotional body **SPIRITUAL** Facilitates linking with one's guides and angels, attuning to the heart

Rhodolite Garnet combines the energies of the base chakra, heart chakra and crown chakra, offering physical, emotional and spiritual support. It offers intuitive guidance on the spiritual path. It offers emotional healing, particularly in the areas of guilt and shame. This healing may manifest as a lightening of one's mood and a sense of quiet happiness. Rhodolite Garnet strengthens the emotional body, making it easier to hear the call of Spirit and to walk the spiritual path.

GARNET, SPESSARTINE **KEY WORDS** Creativity, sexuality, attraction **CHAKRAS** Root (1st), Sexual/Creative (2nd), Solar Plexus (3rd) **ELEMENT** Earth, Fire **PHYSICAL** Supports fertility and sexual reproduction, endocrine system **EMOTIONAL** Encourages optimism, confidence, daring and action **SPIRITUAL** Enhances manifestation, creativity, charisma

Spessartine Garnet is a powerful stone of attraction. It can help one "magnetize" a lover, a new job, a creative project. It clears one's auric field of disharmonious elements. It enhances charisma. It stimulates creativity and sexuality, and it lends power to one's will. It pulls potential realities into manifestation. It can increase fertility on any level. It gets things moving, and is a potent tool to be used carefully and skillfully, yet with a sense of enjoyment and fun.

GARNET, UVAROVITE **KEY WORDS** Overcoming poverty consciousness, manifesting abundance **CHAKRAS** Heart (4th), Solar Plexus (3rd) **ELEMENT** Earth **PHYSICAL** Benefits vitality, replenishment of soft tissues, hydration **EMOTIONAL** Supports knowing one has all one needs, inner peace, contentment **SPIRITUAL** Facilitates attuning to the infinite flow of Universal abundance

Uvarovite Garnet opens the heart, allowing one to see that one contains everything one truly needs. It brings a sense of peace and contentment, plus the knowledge that the Universe provides one with precisely what is required in any given moment. In seeing this, one learns to surrender to that agenda. Uvarovite gently leads one to the lesson that prosperity is a state of consciousness, for as soon as the feelings of lack have been discharged, one is in the flow of Universal abundance. This flow, too, is enhanced by Uvarovite.

GASPEITE **KEY WORDS** Spiritual perception and expression, manifestation, emotional healing, weight control, digestion **CHAKRAS** Earthstar (below the feet), Base (1st), Solar Plexus (3rd), Heart (4th) **ELEMENT** Earth **PHYSICAL** Supports harmonious function of heart and digestive systems, supports management of diabetes **EMOTIONAL** Instills joyful recognition of Spirit in the mundane, healing the inner child **SPIRITUAL** Facilitates integration of spiritual aspirations into daily life

Gaspeite's energy brings the spiritual realms into expression in everyday life. It is excellent for awakening and healing the inner child. It blends the energies of the heart and solar plexus, doing so in a grounded, physical way. It promotes the health of the heart, digestive system, and the visceral organs. It can help those with poor appetites to enjoy food, and to eat the proper foods at the right times.

GEL LITHIUM SILICA **KEY WORDS** Calming, soothing, emotional serenity and stability, antidote to stress and negativity **CHAKRAS** All **ELEMENT** Water **PHYSICAL** Supports energetic balance, aids assimilation of medicines **EMOTIONAL** Soothing and healing to the emotional body, aids release of stress **SPIRITUAL** Facilitates embodying the Divine Feminine, projecting peace in the world

Gel Lithium Silica carries the vibration of tranquillity and receptivity. It is an embodiment of the power of the feminine. It is recommended for meditation and prayer, is excellent for eliminating stress, and can assist one in finding more peaceful sleep. It is a stone of peace, and it can assist one in spreading peace in the world.

GEM SILICA **KEY WORDS** Enhanced communication, Goddess energies, clairvoyance, joy, peace **CHAKRAS** Throat (5th), Heart (4th), Third Eye (6th) **ELEMENT** Water, Wind **PHYSICAL** Supports heart and throat; healing emotionally based ailments **EMOTIONAL** Heals aura and emotional body, aids in communication **SPIRITUAL** Facilitates link with the Goddess; clairvoyance, prophecy, mediumship

Gem Silica can energize the throat chakra and bring forth one's inner truth with impeccability, clarity and eloquence. It evokes the Goddess energies within those who use or carry it. It can take one deeply into the spiritual realms, and it is also a stone of lightheartedness. It can free the heart to soar into joy. It is excellent for stimulating clairvoyance and even prophetic visions of the future, as well as spirit communication. It can heal energetic "holes" in the etheric body, especially around the heart.

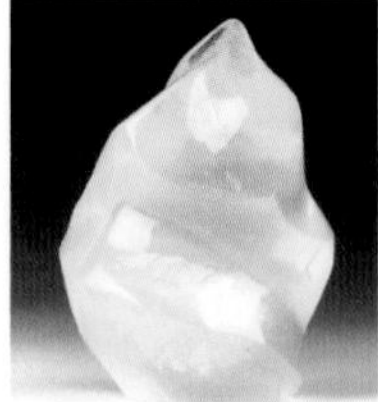

GIRASOL QUARTZ **KEY WORDS** Calming, receptivity, gentleness **CHAKRAS** Third Eye (6th), Throat (5th), Heart (4th) **ELEMENT** Water **PHYSICAL** Supports digestive system, heart, pituitary gland **EMOTIONAL** Nourishes emotional body, instills gentleness **SPIRITUAL** Brings one into deep Silence

Girasol Quartz calms the emotions and increases receptivity. It has a feminine vibration, and can enhance one's connection to the Divine Feminine. It is an excellent stone for meditation, as it stills one's thoughts and allows one to sink into serenity. It is excellent for emotional healing. It nourishes the emotional body and instills a current of gentleness. This stone is ideal to keep beside one's bed for dreaming, as it provides links to the unconscious and the inner realms. It facilitates the inner alchemy of beneficial change.

GLENDONITE **KEY WORDS** Precise stimulation of chakras and meridians, transmutation into the New Human Being and the Body of Light **CHAKRAS** All main chakras, secondary chakras and meridians **ELEMENT** Fire **PHYSICAL** Aids in relaxing and releasing stress, infuses the body with Light **EMOTIONAL** Instills awe and wonder at one's awakening **SPIRITUAL** Instills heart/brain integration and awakens Light Body consciousness

The currents of Glendonite enter the brain, freeing the mind by the awakening of inner truth. It stimulates the third eye, crown chakra and Soul Star chakras. It can increase psychic capacities, make inner visions more vivid and open the doors to profound interior silence. It can deepen meditative and dream experiences. It can help the mind become more aware of the activity and thought of the heart.

GOETHITE **KEY WORDS** Access to Akashic records, past-life recall, connection with Earth, healing through grief, enhanced soul life, artistic creativity **CHAKRAS** Root (1st), Sexual/Creative (2nd), Third Eye (6th) **ELEMENT** Earth **PHYSICAL** Supports the blood and bone marrow, blood oxygenation **EMOTIONAL** Helps energize or calm the emotional body to bring balance **SPIRITUAL** Aids recall of past-life information for fulfillment in this life

Goethite is a stone for going deep within, sensitizing one to the perceptions, emotions and energies of one's body and of the Earth. It is helpful to those dealing with grief, and it facilitates the catharsis of healing and emotional rebirth. It stimulates the emotional body, making one more conscious of the full spectrum of one's feelings. It assists in opening the heart, awakening one's compassion and love.

GOETHITE, RAINBOW **KEY WORDS** Humor, confidence, exuberance, overall wellbeing **CHAKRAS** All **ELEMENT** Earth, Water **PHYSICAL** Supports healing the physical manifestations of emotional wounds **EMOTIONAL** Aids in opening the heart, awakening compassion and love, spontaneous joy **SPIRITUAL** Assists in attuning to Nature and appreciating everyday miracles, deepens one's soul life

Rainbow Goethite particularly encourages the spontaneous upwelling of joy, humor, confidence and overall wellbeing. It has a much "lighter" and more buoyant energy than other forms of Goethite. Yet, it still links one to one's inner depths, and it is a powerful aid for healing one's wounds and deepening one's soul life. In a sense, Rainbow Goethite combines the best of both worlds—the Above and the Below—and it helps one to stretch one's soul enough to hold both polarities at the same time.

GOLDEN AURA QUARTZ **KEY WORDS** Abundance, protection, expanded awareness **CHAKRAS** Solar plexus (3rd) **ELEMENT** Fire, Wind **PHYSICAL** Spiritual protection for the physical body **EMOTIONAL** Shields the emotional body **SPIRITUAL** Opens clairvoyance, psychic abilities

Golden Aura Quartz is a stone of abundance. It can facilitate the phenomenon of the "Midas touch," enabling one to enhance one's level of prosperity. It helps one to empower and strengthen one's auric field, creating a "shield of Light" around one's physical and etheric bodies. It is excellent for psychic protection, and for helping healers to filter out negative energies that may otherwise become attached to one's field when one works with clients. It is are related to the Golden Light of the spiritual realms, and meditation with these stones can facilitate one's entry into higher realities.

GOLDEN HEALER QUARTZ **KEY WORDS** Pure Golden Ray of spiritual Light, self-healing, Christ consciousness **CHAKRAS** All **ELEMENTS** Earth, Fire **PHYSICAL** Supports self-healing of the heart, lungs and circulatory system **EMOTIONAL** Helps one feel inner joy regardless of outer circumstances **SPIRITUAL** Aids in drawing spiritual Light into oneself and the Earth; can initiate a link to Christ consciousness

Golden Healer Quartz emanates powerful currents for healing the body and expanding consciousness. It emanates waves of pleasurable energy that permeate the body. It is attuned to the purpose of co-creating the Earth as a Planet of Light. It can help one attune to Christ consciousness, enabling the Gold Christ Light to enter the world. In spiritual healing, it supports the body with an infusion of spiritual Light. It resonates with the heart, and can work as a catalyst for healing the heart, lungs and circulatory system.

GOLDEN LABRADORITE **KEY WORDS** Right use of will, clarity, confidence, power, vitality, creativity, purposefulness, link with Great Central Sun **CHAKRAS** Solar Plexus (3rd) **ELEMENT** Fire **PHYSICAL** Aids detoxification; supports kidneys, gallbladder and spleen **EMOTIONAL** Enhances self-confidence, charisma and social skills **SPIRITUAL** Helps one recognize and attain one's destined spiritual purpose

Golden Labradorite activates the third chakra, enhancing inner strength, vitality, courage, clear thinking, endurance, mental activity, spiritual focus and purposefulness. It can help one see the Divine pattern in one's daily struggles. In dream work, it can aid in awakening to the higher planes and in bringing back important information. It can take one into communion with the energies of our own sun, and with the Great Central Sun, the home and origin of consciousness in the Universe.

GOSHENITE **KEY WORDS** Mental stimulant, enhanced dreams, loyalty, truth, prayer, spiritual assistance **CHAKRAS** Third Eye (6th), Crown (7th), Etheric (8th–14th) **ELEMENT** Wind **PHYSICAL** Supports healing of headaches, insomnia, sinusitis, brain imbalances **EMOTIONAL** Encourages emotional health, enthusiasm, clarity **SPIRITUAL** Aids spiritual discernment, enhances the power of prayer

Goshenite clears and activates the crown chakra, opening the portals of Spirit. It stimulates the mental centers and enhances one's thinking. It stimulates mathematical intelligence. It is a stone of persistence, helping one retain the determination to see things through to completion. It is also a stone of loyalty. It can enhance the power of prayer, for help with health, spiritual growth or relationships. It aids in calling in one's angels and spirit helpers. It is a stone of truth, helping one to speak only truth and to see through deceptions.

GRAPE AGATE **KEY WORDS** Tranquility, Divine connection, meditation **CHAKRAS** Crown (7th), Heart (4th) **ELEMENT** Wind, Water, Earth **PHYSICAL** Spiritually aids conditions induced by stress, mental/neurological issues: dementia, anxiety, OCD and problems rooted in emotional or energetic fragmentation **EMOTIONAL** Infuses peace and healing into the emotional body **SPIRITUAL** Purification of the etheric, astral, emotional, mental and physical bodies

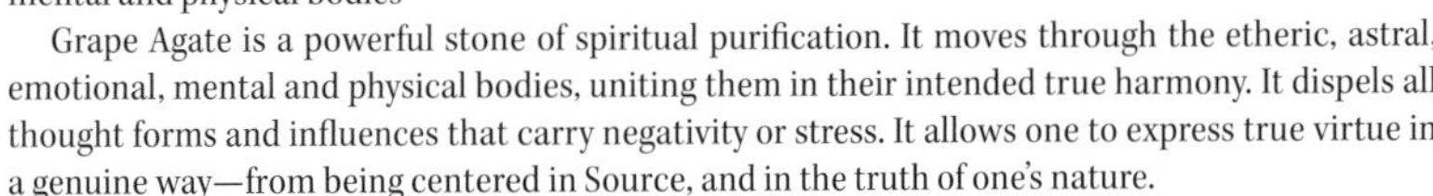

Grape Agate is a powerful stone of spiritual purification. It moves through the etheric, astral, emotional, mental and physical bodies, uniting them in their intended true harmony. It dispels all thought forms and influences that carry negativity or stress. It allows one to express true virtue in a genuine way—from being centered in Source, and in the truth of one's nature.

GREEN TARALITE **KEY WORDS** Flowing, friendly energies, connection with Green Tara, spiritual attunement, healing and insight **CHAKRAS** Heart (4th), Third Eye (6th) **ELEMENTS** Earth, Water **PHYSICAL** Supports all types of circulation and flow within the body, can stimulate cells into a state of spiritual luminescence **EMOTIONAL** Engenders joy, compassion and friendliness **SPIRITUAL** Inspires inner union with Green Tara, bringing peace, cooperation and Universal Unity, offers spiritual protection and removal of obstacles

Green Taralite connects one's awareness to the cosmos, and helps one recognize oneself as a member of the entire Universe. It can enable one to enter vibrational resonance with Divine beings, including Green Tara herself. Tara is a Star Goddess who encompasses all of time and the spark of life. It supports bodily systems that depend on flow, including the heart, circulatory system, lungs, lymphatic system, liver and digestive system.

GREENSTONE **KEY WORDS** Life Force, personal power, magic, vitality, longevity, self-loyalty and self-love, inner radiance **CHAKRAS** Heart (4th), Third Eye (6th) **ELEMENTS** Earth, Water, Fire **PHYSICAL** Supports the heart, lungs and circulatory system, offers great quantities of chi **EMOTIONAL** Inspires powerful self-loyalty and self-love **SPIRITUAL** Stimulates Life Force and power, aids in doing real magic,

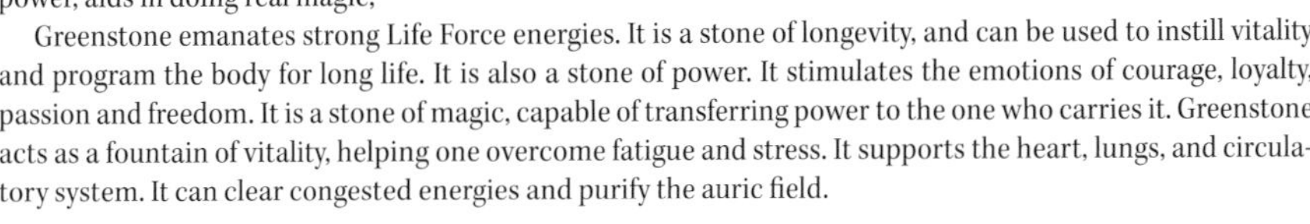

Greenstone emanates strong Life Force energies. It is a stone of longevity, and can be used to instill vitality and program the body for long life. It is also a stone of power. It stimulates the emotions of courage, loyalty, passion and freedom. It is a stone of magic, capable of transferring power to the one who carries it. Greenstone acts as a fountain of vitality, helping one overcome fatigue and stress. It supports the heart, lungs, and circulatory system. It can clear congested energies and purify the auric field.

GUARDIANITE **KEY WORDS** Infusion of life force, grounding, strength, protection **CHAKRAS** All **ELEMENT** Earth, Wind, Water, Fire, Storm **PHYSICAL** Fills the Liquid Crystal Body Matrix with life force **EMOTIONAL** Encourages positive, uplifting emotional states **SPIRITUAL** Simultaneously attunes to the Earth and the spiritual realms

Guardianite brings a deep and immediate grounding through the root chakra. It offers an instantaneous connection with the Earth and its upwelling life force. As Guardianite's currents flow into one's field, they permeate the Liquid Crystal Body Matrix with a humming vibration of well-being. Guardianite makes one feel happy, calm and safe. It nourishes the etheric and astral bodies, enhancing their integration with the physical self.

HALITE, BLUE **KEY WORDS** Cleansing, purification, psychic clearing, activating psychic abilities **CHAKRAS** All **ELEMENT** Earth **PHYSICAL** Supports lymphatic and circulatory systems **EMOTIONAL** Clears unhealthy attachments, instills euphoria **SPIRITUAL** Encourages enlightened compassion

Blue Halite activates the third eye and crown chakras, unifying them with the Soul Star chakra above the head. Its energies stimulate an enhancement of psychic ability, a purification of one's energy field, and an elevation of one's awareness. It helps one achieve crystalline clarity of thought and a balanced flow of Light Body energies. It opens the pathways to communication with spirit guides and inner teachers, and it aids one in the verbal expression of spiritual truth. It can instantly cleanse the etheric body and can also be used to cleanse and clear other crystals, simply by placing them in contact with Blue Halite for a few hours.

HALITE, PINK **KEY WORDS** Emotional cleansing, inner clarity, opening the heart, self-love **CHAKRAS** All **ELEMENT** Earth **PHYSICAL** Helps clear the body of emotionally related imbalances **EMOTIONAL** Encourages dispelling negativity, bringing joy, enhancing self-love **SPIRITUAL** Facilitates opening to higher awareness by clearing one's consciousness

Pink Halite is an excellent stone for manifesting self-love. It blends the energies of the heart and solar plexus—the chakras of love and will. It is a stone of clarity, dissolving foggy thinking, confusion, deception and doubt. Its energy helps one express oneself straightforwardly and assists in seeing the truth in all types of interactions. It is recommended for those who work in environments of negativity or stress.

HANKSITE **KEY WORDS** Purification, dissolving of blockages, cleansing of toxic energies, a "stone of truth" **CHAKRAS** All **ELEMENT** Earth **PHYSICAL** Supports body in eradicating toxins, dispelling water retention **EMOTIONAL** Aids in clearing anger and resentment from emotional body **SPIRITUAL** Clears all types of disharmony, stimulates the Light Body

Hanksite harmonizes the human energy field, bringing clarity and purification to all the chakras. It stimulates the third eye and can facilitate visionary states. It can clear the energies of any other stone and can cleanse the room where it is kept of disharmonious energies. It is a "stone of truth," assisting one in dispelling lies or illusions coming from others, or even from oneself. It helps one get to the essence of all issues and keeps one's awareness aligned with reality.

HEALER'S GOLD **KEY WORDS** Healing, grounding of high-frequency energies in the body, energetic harmony and balance **CHAKRAS** All **ELEMENT** Earth **PHYSICAL** Supports physical healing, blood oxygenation, overall vitality **EMOTIONAL** Helps one achieve inner balance and self-confidence **SPIRITUAL** Grounds high energies in the body, aids manifestation of desires

Healer's Gold harmonizes the astral, subtle and causal bodies and aligns them with the physical. It is balancing to the male and female aspects of the self. It activates weak or lazy chakras and enhances the flow of subtle energies throughout the meridian system. It helps people with low energy and eliminates passivity. It promotes a positive outlook and facilitates the initiation of new creative projects. It creates a sense of wellbeing, comfort in the body, and confidence in oneself.

HEALERITE **KEY WORDS** Broad-spectrum healing, rejuvenation, longevity, joy, expansiveness, generosity, intimacy, heart-centered awareness **CHAKRAS** Solar Plexus (3rd), Heart (4th), Third Eye (6th) **ELEMENTS** Earth, Water **PHYSICAL** Supports the body for healing, rejuvenation, longevity **EMOTIONAL** Initiates states of joy and inner harmony **SPIRITUAL** Supports spiritual awakening and development, increases vitality, expands awareness

Healerite emanates profound healing energies, working on multiple levels to restructure misaligned chakras, meridians and systems in the organic and etheric bodies. Its currents fill the body and soul with well-being. It resonates with the heart, solar plexus and third eye chakras, facilitating alignment of one's vibrational field.

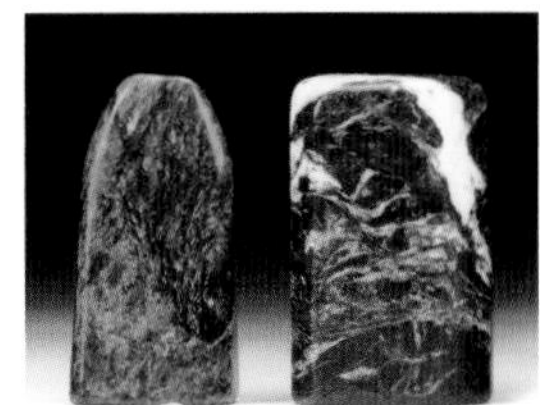

HEARTENITE **KEY WORDS** Empowerment of heart intelligence, unity with Earth and the Soul of the World **CHAKRAS** Heart (4th), Solar Plexus (3rd), Crown (7th), Third Eye (6th), Throat (5th) **ELEMENT** Earth **PHYSICAL** Strengthens immune system, facilitates rejuvenation, aids in recuperation from illness or injury **EMOTIONAL** Brings healing, peace, confidence and enthusiasm **SPIRITUAL** Brings forth one's link with high angelic beings, triggers rapid bursts of spiritual metamorphosis

Heartenite reminds us of the tremendous spiritual power we wield when we are at one with ourselves and following our hearts, and it encourages us to claim our power and use it for the good of the whole. Its ultimate expression is the unification of the individual self with the Soul of the World.

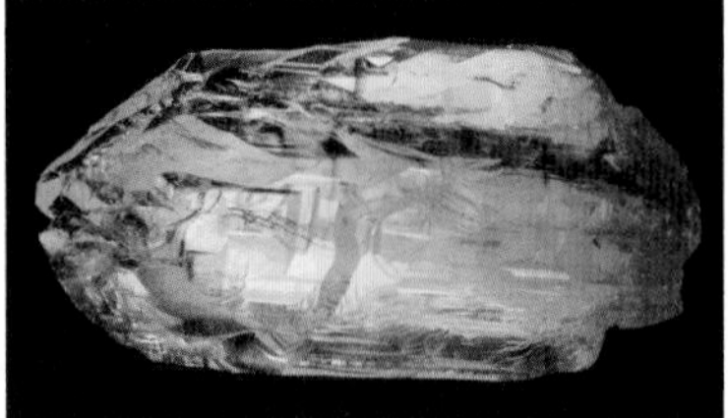

HELIODOR **KEY WORDS** Activation of mind and will **CHAKRAS** Solar Plexus (3rd) **ELEMENT** Fire **PHYSICAL** Supports digestion and assimilation, healing gastric disorders **EMOTIONAL** Brings possibility, hope and vitality to the emotional body **SPIRITUAL** Aids in achieving the highest spiritual aspirations

Heliodor is a potent ally for the development of personal power through the activation of the mind and the appropriate use of will. It emphasizes assertiveness, self-confidence, physical and mental strength, manifestation, discrimination, benevolence and power. Heliodor is a stone of higher consciousness and physical well-being. It can bring us more abundant awareness and more vibrant life.

HEMATITE **KEY WORDS** Grounding, manifestation, making the spiritual physical **CHAKRAS** Root (1st) **ELEMENT** Earth **PHYSICAL** Supports the blood, protects the body's fields from toxic energies **EMOTIONAL** Encourages a solid sense of self, aids in self-forgiveness **SPIRITUAL** Helps one believe in one's dreams and bring them into manifestation

Hematite is excellent for grounding in the body and the physical world. It can counteract spaciness and confusion, helping one to see practical concerns and move forward with useful action. It can be used to balance the auric field and align the chakras. It pulls stray energies down through the meridian system to the root chakra. It purifies one's energy field and clears negativity from the environment. It can aid in bringing dreams and aspirations into reality and in learning the difference between a true vision and a fantasy.

HEMATITE, RAINBOW **KEY WORDS** Increasing bodily crystalline coherence, repairing one's magnetic field, healing autoimmune disorders, spiritual protection, Vibrational Ascension **CHAKRAS** Root (1st), Third Eye (6th), Crown (7th) **ELEMENTS** Earth, Storm **PHYSICAL** Supports recovery from anemia and autoimmune illnesses **EMOTIONAL** Increases one's sense of well-being, empowerment and spiritual confidence **SPIRITUAL** Provides spiritual protection, enhances personal power, stimulates the activation of the Rainbow Body of Light, facilitates communication with Stone Beings

Rainbow Hematites can initiate increased crystalline coherence of the blood. It can lead to enhancement of consciousness and activation of psychic ability and awareness beyond the body. It can be used to repair one's magnetic field, making one feel more powerful and alert.

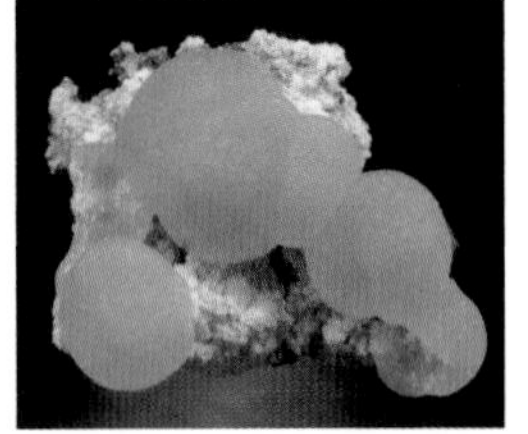

HEMIMORPHITE **KEY WORDS** Light activation, aura balancing, emotional healing and communication, empathy, joy, channeling and mediumship **CHAKRAS** Heart (4th), Throat (5th), Third Eye (6th), Crown (7th), Etheric (8th–14th) **ELEMENT** Storm **PHYSICAL** Supports proper hormonal balance **EMOTIONAL** Soothes emotional body, encourages forgiveness and compassion **SPIRITUAL** Aids attunement to higher spiritual frequencies, opens upper chakras

Hemimorphite brings balance to the auric field, dissolving and dispelling dark spots of negativity or weakness. It benefits the emotional body, bringing in a vibration of joy. It enhances the communication of the truth of one's feelings and can aid in healing dysfunctional relationships. It facilitates the inner growth through which one can learn to communicate with souls who have passed over.

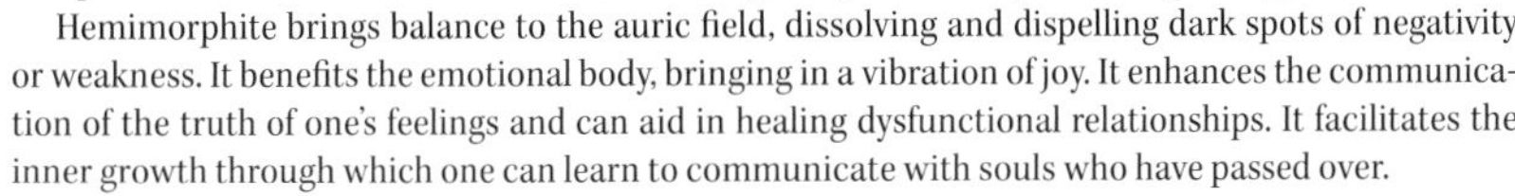

HERDERITE **KEY WORDS** Evolution, activation of latent capacities, awakening the higher brain functions, discovering the Light Body **CHAKRAS** Third Eye (6th), Crown (7th), Soul Star (8th), Transpersonal (9th) **ELEMENT** Storm **PHYSICAL** Supports balanced and increased brain function, recommended for headaches **EMOTIONAL** Helps one view emotional situations from a higher perspective **SPIRITUAL** Activates latent spiritual and psychic capacities of the brain

Herderite can awaken and charge the upper chakras of the body and link one's awareness to the higher dimensions. It is an incredibly powerful tool for interdimensional travel, communication with spirit guides and Light beings. It initiates growth in consciousness. It opens the third eye and crown chakras, as well as the first two etheric chakras, expanding one's sense of self. It can kindle direct spiritual vision.

HERKIMER "DIAMOND" QUARTZ **KEY WORDS** Dreams, visions, purification, spiritualization of physical life **CHAKRAS** Third Eye (6th), Crown (7th) **ELEMENT** Storm **PHYSICAL** Supports general health, physical stamina and energy level **EMOTIONAL** Aids in clearing the emotional body and removing negative attachments **SPIRITUAL** Facilitates dream work, astral travel, time travel, dimensional shifting

Herkimer "Diamonds" emanate a high, harmonious energy that positively "sings." They are ideal for body layouts, dream work, meditation pieces, jewelry, templates and energy tools. They purify one's energy field and attune one to the White Light of the Divine Essence. They are also ideal for lucid dreaming and other types of dream work.

HEULANDITE, GREEN **KEY WORDS** Dreams, visions, interdimensional travel, access to past civilizations, emotional healing **CHAKRAS** Heart (4th), Third Eye (6th), Crown (7th) **ELEMENT** Wind **PHYSICAL** Supports brain evolution and awakening of latent capacities **EMOTIONAL** Aids in achieving calm, elevated awareness **SPIRITUAL** Helps one reach deep meditative states of inner silence

Green Heulandite is a stone of the heart, and it aids in attuning with the heart of the Earth. It helps one attain the natural state of the awakened heart. It facilitates this resonance, helping one find the right energetic frequency. It enhances emotional intelligence and can facilitate emotional healing through the awakening of compassion. It calms nervousness and alleviates fear. It calls forth courage and determination and is an aid to those working to overcome setbacks.

HEULANDITE, WHITE **KEY WORDS** Dreams, visions, interdimensional travel, access to past civilizations, emotional healing **CHAKRAS** Heart (4th), Third Eye (6th), Crown (7th) **ELEMENT** Wind **PHYSICAL** Supports brain evolution and awakening of latent capacities **EMOTIONAL** Aids in reaching a state of calm, elevated awareness **SPIRITUAL** Helps in reaching deep meditative states and inner silence

White Heulandite allows one to journey inwardly to ancient civilizations of Earth's past—even Lemuria and Atlantis. This stone attunes to the Akashic records. It can help one recover past-life memories, especially those having to do with psychological problems and blockages. This can be invaluable for spiritual self-healing.

HIDDENITE **KEY WORDS** Interpersonal love, heart healing, rediscovering the joy of relationships **CHAKRAS** Heart (4th) **ELEMENT** Water **PHYSICAL** Supports the heart and hormonal systems **EMOTIONAL** Stimulates the emotional body, encourages joy, bliss and love **SPIRITUAL** Teaches the spiritual lessons of gratitude and abundance

Hiddenite vibrates to the true chord of the spontaneously loving heart, attuned to the future yet unconcerned about future consequences. It teaches that loving is its own reward. Hiddenite's message is simple—even if love and loss go hand in hand, loving is still the best, the only thing to do. It can activate the emotional body and fill it with love and enlightenment. It is a stone of spiritual rapture that facilitates the union of heat and mind.

HOLLANDITE QUARTZ **KEY WORDS** Path of destiny, Higher Self, regeneration, spiritual insight, increased Light **CHAKRAS** All (1st–7th), Soul Star (8th) **ELEMENT** Storm **PHYSICAL** Supports etheric body in recovering from radiation exposure **EMOTIONAL** Aids in overcoming emotional blocks to realizing one's higher self **SPIRITUAL** Facilitates the activation of one's higher spiritual capacities.

Hollandite Quartz can bring "memories from the future" concerning whom one is destined to become. It can activate the template of one's ideal form. If one's body is out of alignment with one's true identity, it may repattern itself in resonance with one's Divine blueprint. This facilitates improvements in one's health and appearance.

HYPERSTHENE **KEY WORDS** Self-knowledge through visionary awareness, receiving understanding through connecting with morphic fields, self-healing through visualization, accepting one's shadow **CHAKRA** Third Eye (6th) **ELEMENT** Wind **PHYSICAL** Aids in the process of self-healing through creative visualization **EMOTIONAL** Brings awareness of one's shadow side into consciousness, aids emotional healing through understanding and self-acceptance **SPIRITUAL** Enhances psychic vision, increases spiritual awareness and intuitive understanding

Hypersthene can reveal insights to help one solve problems. It is a stone of magic, aiding those who wish to manifest their intentions. It can be used to promote the healing process through creative visualizations. It helps one understand, accept and heal one's shadow side.

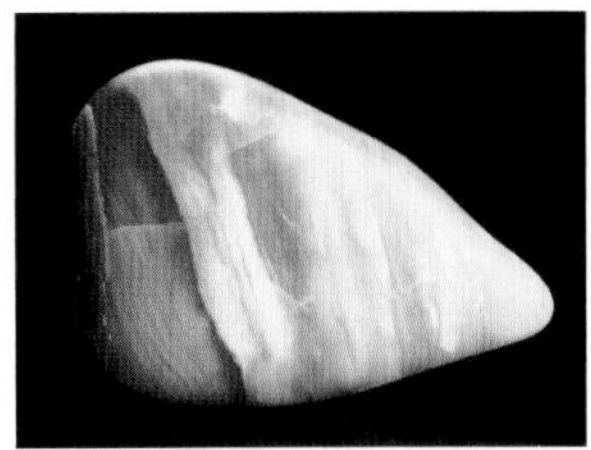

INFINITE **KEY WORDS** Healing and protecting the auric field, activating kundalini, sensitivity to subtle energies **CHAKRAS** Root (1st), Sexual/Creative (2nd), Solar Plexus (3rd), Heart (4th) **ELEMENT** Earth **PHYSICAL** Helps the cells and DNA remain stable when exposed to electromagnetic or energetic pollution **EMOTIONAL** Encourages self-confidence and independence **SPIRITUAL** Clears the aura of habitual negative patterns

Infinite is an excellent stone for healing the etheric body. It can assist in raising one's vibration to higher frequencies. It is excellent for the gradual activation of the kundalini channel. It aids in communing with devas, fairies and the spirits associated with power spots. It can assist in dowsing and can increase the potency of *reiki* and other types of energetic healing.

IOLITE **KEY WORDS** Inner vision, shamanic journeying, healing of old wounds, soul retrieval **CHAKRAS** Third Eye (6th) **ELEMENT** Wind **PHYSICAL** Supports healing of the eyes, memory problems, sleep issues **EMOTIONAL** Encourages calm and resourcefulness in difficult situations **SPIRITUAL** Facilitates visionary experience in meditation

Iolite is excellent for shamanic journeying. It increases the vividness and detail of inner visions by calling up symbols from deep in the psyche. It helps one move to the depths of one's unconscious and uncover the lost parts of oneself. It aids in exploring past lives and their karmic lessons. It assists in blending conscious thinking with intuitive knowing. It aids in strengthening the energetic links between the brain and the heart.

IOLITE-SUNSTONE **KEY WORDS** Artistic inspiration, productive action, physical vitality, enhanced intuitive abilities **CHAKRAS** Sexual/Creative (2nd), Solar Plexus (3rd), Third Eye (6th) **ELEMENT** Wind, Fire **PHYSICAL** Stimulates endocrine system, aids in weight loss **EMOTIONAL** Aids self-confidence in social situations, public speaking **SPIRITUAL** Enhances intuition, communication with guides and spirits

Iolite-Sunstone is a stone of inner vision, stimulating the third eye, enhancing psychic abilities, kindling the gift of prophecy, increasing sensitivity to subtle energies. It is a stone of self-discipline, enabling one to make and follow concrete plans for the attainment of one's aims. It emanates currents of courage and leadership. It stimulates the second and third chakras, seats of creativity and will. It can unite the vision of the third eye with the will-to-action of the solar plexus for the actualization of one's dreams.

JADE, BLACK **KEY WORDS** Protection, clearing negativity **CHAKRAS** All **ELEMENT** Earth **PHYSICAL** Supports the body in protecting itself from illness, infection, parasites, especially recommended when traveling **EMOTIONAL** Aids insight into and healing of darker parts of the self **SPIRITUAL** Good for psychic protection, integration of one's Shadow side

Black Jade acts like an etheric "bodyguard" when it is worn or carried, emanating strong energies that clear one's aura of vulnerability to attachments by negative forces or entities. This stone makes one "invisible" to such beings. It can assist in ridding oneself of fear, anger, doubt, hatred and other destructive emotions. It can initiate deep inner voyages, and it is particularly useful for those doing soul retrieval and shamanic journeys.

JADE, BLUE **KEY WORDS** Spiritual knowledge, clarity, discrimination **CHAKRAS** Third Eye (6th), Crown (7th) **ELEMENT** Earth, Wind **PHYSICAL** Aids in calming inflammation, swelling, arthritic conditions, asthma and bronchial conditions **EMOTIONAL** Soothes the emotional body; helps one remain calm during stressful situations **SPIRITUAL** Activates higher vibrations, grounds excess energies, aids smooth transition during initiatory experiences

Blue Jade calms the mind in stressful situations. It enhances mental abilities of both sides of the brain, benefiting one's capacity for rational thought as well as creative intuition. It helps one hear the voices of one's spirit guides and of one's own heart. It stimulates spiritual sensitivity, and is highly recommended for those who wish to be mediums or psychic readers.

JADE, GREEN **KEY WORDS** Health, abundance **CHAKRAS** Heart (4th) **ELEMENT** Earth **PHYSICAL** A spiritual aid to strengthen the heart and overall health **EMOTIONAL** Supports the emotional body in opening to joy **SPIRITUAL** Encourages enjoying life without becoming too attached to the material world

Green Jade is a stone with a heart of healing, and a stone for healing the heart. Its energies are a strong and steady flow of well-being and balance. It brings wholesome and steady growth to one's life-force energies. It draws upon the Earth's life force and imbues one's auric field with that energy. It can harmonize and balance the heart chakra, aiding in emotional and physical well-being. It can be used to attract abundance and prosperity and to broadcast peace and loving-kindness to all those in one's surroundings.

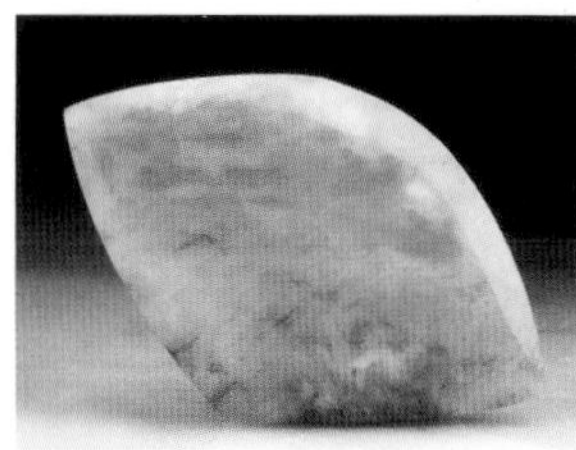

JADE, LAVENDAR **KEY WORDS** High spiritual attunement, compassion, serenity **CHAKRAS** Crown (7th), Heart (4th) **ELEMENT** Earth **PHYSICAL** Eases stress and brings the physical body into harmony with one's spiritual blueprint **EMOTIONAL** Encourages a state of serenity and benevolence **SPIRITUAL** Aids in attuning to the angelic realms, and to Kwan Yin

Lavender Jade provides spiritual nourishment to all who touch it. It helps one attune to Kwan Yin, and to orient oneself toward loving and charitable actions in the world. It is a stone of the Violet Ray of spiritual purification. It enhances visionary states and helps one enter the space of "no thought." It allows one to release cynicism and suppressed anger and to embrace an attitude of serene acceptance. It can enhance intuition, empathy and psychic ability.

JADE, PURPLE **KEY WORDS** Humor, spiritual knowledge and attunement **CHAKRAS** Crown (7th), Third Eye (6th), Earthstar (below the feet) **ELEMENT** Earth **PHYSICAL** Aids in soothing the nervous system and alleviating symptoms brought on by stress **EMOTIONAL** Protects emotional bodies of sensitive people from energy pathologies **SPIRITUAL** Helps regulate the auric field, enhances dreams and visions

Purple Jade fills one with mirth and happiness. It is excellent for purifying one's aura and dispelling any negative energies or attitudes. It evokes humor, and it also enhances one's appreciation of the perfection of Divine order in all things. It is an asset when worn or carried by almost anyone, especially those who need to "lighten up" and relax into the flow of life. It can aid in letting go of self-imposed limitations and in maintaining the awareness that the abundance of the Universe is available to oneself.

JADE, RED **KEY WORDS** Courage, action **CHAKRAS** Root (1st), Solar Plexus (3rd), Earthstar (below the feet) **ELEMENT** Earth **PHYSICAL** Stimulates and invigorates all bodily systems, increases *chi* **EMOTIONAL** Encourages fortitude in overcoming difficulties **SPIRITUAL** Enhances life force and connection to Earth through the root chakra

Red Jade brings forward the energy of the warrior. It helps one put aside fear, worry, doubt and the "anxiety of the threshold." It dispels the fear that holds one back, and it emanates a balancing vibration of wisdom which helps keep one from acting rashly. Red Jade is an excellent talisman for those studying martial arts or training for athletic performances. It supports an increase in one's physical vitality, increases the flow of prana, stimulates creativity and sexual energy.

JASPER, FANCY **KEY WORDS** Grounding mental energies, discipline and perseverance, slow, steady healing **CHAKRAS** All **ELEMENT** Earth **PHYSICAL** Aids in overcoming insomnia and other sleep disorders, supports general health **EMOTIONAL** Helps calm fear or worry caused by overactive mental energies **SPIRITUAL** Helps to ground and organize the mind, aids in solving problems

Fancy Jasper helps one attend to the details of life with efficiency and good humor. It grounds one in the body and focuses mental energies. It helps prevent procrastination and aids one in making plans for the future. It encourages a positive outlook on life. It is a good, slow healing stone, working to aid one in eliminating chronic problems.

JASPER, MOOK **KEY WORDS** Earth-healing, connection with Nature, joy in life **CHAKRAS** All **ELEMENT** Earth **PHYSICAL** Spiritually supports liver health and detoxification of the body **EMOTIONAL** Encourages renewed hope, invigoration and energy, aids in overcoming grief or depression **SPIRITUAL** Facilitates deep connection with Nature, aids in connecting with Nature spirits and devic beings

Mook Jasper aids in reclaiming one's capacity to feel the energy currents of the Earth and to maximize the effects of one's will. It reawakens the ability to simply "know" the right direction to take, in physical or nonphysical travel. It facilitates animal communication, and it helps one to find rapport with the spirits of the ancestors.

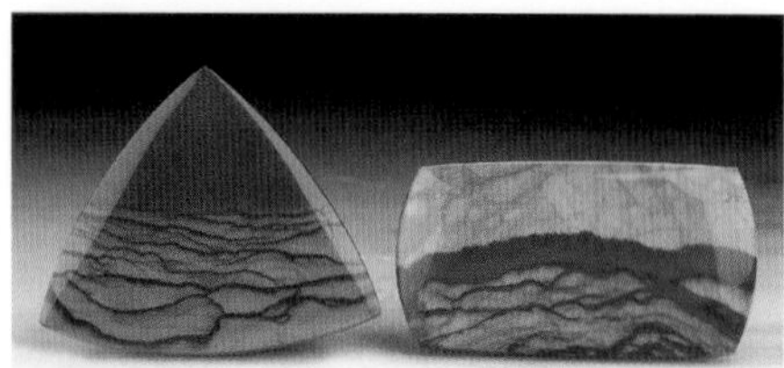

JASPER, PICTURE **KEY WORDS** Inner journeying to sacred sites and ancient civilizations, connecting with Earth's consciousness **CHAKRAS** Third Eye (6th), Root (1st) **ELEMENT** Earth **PHYSICAL** Supports bone growth and healing **EMOTIONAL** Helps one reconnect to the ancient knowledge of living in balance **SPIRITUAL** Aids in attuning to power spots in Earth's energy systems, can help one link with distant places and times

Picture Jasper helps one merge with the consciousness of the Earth. It can be used to find the Earth's ley lines. It can facilitate inner journeying to the power spots on the planet, and through time to ancient civilizations.

JASPER, RAINFOREST **KEY WORDS** Earth-healing, connection with Nature, joy in life **CHAKRAS** All **ELEMENT** Earth **PHYSICAL** Spiritually supports liver health and detoxification of the body **EMOTIONAL** Supports renewed hope, invigoration and energy, aids in overcoming grief or depression **SPIRITUAL** Facilitates deep connection with Nature, aids in connecting with Nature spirits and devic beings

Rainforest Jasper supports one's heart connection to Nature and one's impulse to work toward planetary healing. It awakens the awareness that we as creatures are not separated from the world of animals, plants—or minerals. It helps one commit to action on behalf of the preservation and support of life.

JASPER, UNAKITE **KEY WORDS** Healing, balance, release of bad habits, patient persistence **CHAKRAS** All, especially Heart (4th) **ELEMENT** Earth **PHYSICAL** Offers energetic support in the treatment of cancers or heart disease, promotes growth of healthy tissue, and recovery from injury **EMOTIONAL** Assists in releasing negative emotions and habitual patterns giving rise to them **SPIRITUAL** Raises the vibration of the physical and emotional bodies by helping release disharmonious emotional patterns and the lower emotional frequencies

Unakite facilitates the elimination of bad habits, especially overeating and overconsumption of alcohol. It helps unearth and release the bonds of old emotional wounds in a way that avoids shock and trauma. It supports the purging of toxic energies and substances from the cells. It teaches patience and is a stone for spiritual seekers who wish to hold steadfast to their path.

JET **KEY WORDS** Protection, purification, grounding **CHAKRAS** Base (1st), for grounding, All, for purification **ELEMENT** Earth **PHYSICAL** Provides spiritual protection of the body, heals energy leaks in the aura, aids in energetic cleansing of liver and kidneys **EMOTIONAL** Clears the energy field of negative emotional attachments **SPIRITUAL** Facilitates entering and exploring the inner void of creation

Jet activates the powers of magic and interaction with the forces of the elements. It helps one to draw upon Earth energies and to channel that powerful flow. It neutralizes negative energies and offers psychic protection in astral travel or spiritual mediumship.

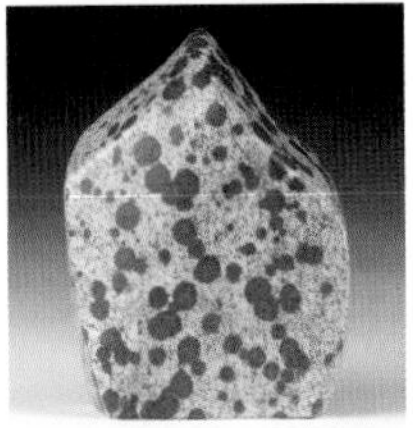

K2 **KEY WORDS** Psychic activation, discernment, link with the mind of Nature **CHAKRAS** Third Eye (6th), Crown (7th) **ELEMENT** Fire **PHYSICAL** Supports brain, heart, nervous system **EMOTIONAL** Stimulates self-sufficiency, strength of character **SPIRITUAL** Empowers spiritual insight and psychic awareness

K2 can increase and elevate the vibrations of any of the body's energy centers, and it stimulates psychic awareness. It is a stone of deep insight, stimulating one's consciousness to penetrate to the underlying meanings of life's events and mysteries. It increases one's ability to see and understand the archetypal patterns and events that underlie physical reality. It is an excellent stone for past life recall, enhancing psychic ability, increasing telepathic rapport between friends and partners and pursuing spiritual enlightenment.

KAMMERERITE **KEY WORDS** Mental energy, vitality, humor **CHAKRAS** Root (1st), Crown (7th) **ELEMENT** Earth, Wind **PHYSICAL** Aids recovery from maladies rooted in fatigue and/or low emotional energy **EMOTIONAL** Supports emotional body by dispelling discouragement **SPIRITUAL** Attracts spiritual initiation, heightens psychic sensibilities

Kammererite is a stone of initiation. It prepares one to face life's challenges without fear. It strengthens the emotional body, supports one's physical energies, enhances endurance and quickens one's reflexes. It benefits one's erotic life, encourages playfulness and passion. The infusion of vitality it brings can make one more attractive to one's partner, and increase one's own sensuality. It emanates the vibrations of high spirits, humor and fun,

KAURILITE **KEY WORDS** Link with Nature, longevity, purification, self-healing, love, wisdom, majesty, patience, humor **CHAKRAS** All **ELEMENT** Earth **PHYSICAL** Supports the blood, lymph and immune systems, enhanced vitality and longevity **EMOTIONAL** Inspires good humor and a sense of well-being **SPIRITUAL** Emanates love, wisdom, majesty, patience and humor, renews one's energy field, stimulates connection with Nature spirits, facilitates access to the Akashic records, especially to ancient Lemuria

Kaurilite can enhance one's physical, mental and emotional vitality. It is beneficial for all self-healing practices, lending energetic support to the immune system, blood and lymph systems. It enhances longevity, and can renew one's energy field.

KUNZITE **KEY WORDS** Divine Love, emotional healing, activation of the heart's knowing **CHAKRAS** Heart (4th) **ELEMENT** Water **PHYSICAL** Eases stress and supports the parasympathetic nervous system **EMOTIONAL** Aids one in becoming receptive to love and energy **SPIRITUAL** Connects one to the energy of Divine Love underlying all of creation

Kunzite amplifies the energies of love–Divine Love, self-love, interpersonal love, love for humanity, animals, plants, minerals—all that is. It can facilitate profound experiences of Universal Love. Carrying or wearing the stone helps one move through one's day with kindness, gentleness and serenity. Kunzite can activate the silent voice of the heart, opening a wordless communion between one's mental and emotional aspects. It can awaken the heart and encourage it to communicate more intimately with the mind.

KYANITE, BLACK **KEY WORDS** Balance, grounding, energizing, time travel, soul retrieval **CHAKRAS** All, especially Root (1st) **ELEMENT** Storm **PHYSICAL** Balances the meridian system, promotes energy flow **EMOTIONAL** Aids in healing emotional issues caused by lost soul parts **SPIRITUAL** Supports awakening of interdimensional consciousness

Black Kyanite can clear blocked energies and replenish the meridian system. It is grounding and energizing, and is useful in energetic healing. It clears imbalances and brings an unhindered energy flow throughout one's meridian system. It can take one back to past lives and forward to probable futures. It lends intensity and vividness to shamanic journeys, and it helps shamanic healers attune to the soul-based issues of their clients, seeing clearly the inner work needed for healing and soul retrieval.

KYANITE, BLUE **KEY WORDS** Inner bridges, psychic ability, past-life recall, telepathy, empathy **CHAKRAS** All, especially Third Eye (6th) **ELEMENT** Storm **PHYSICAL** Supports nerve healing **EMOTIONAL** Dissolves dysfunctional emotional patterns **SPIRITUAL** Stimulates the third eye and psychic abilities

Blue Kyanite opens the psychic channels and activates the mind centers, accentuating mental capacities and enhancing one's ability to "download" information from higher sources. It can make telepathic communication between individuals easier, and can stimulate lucid dreaming. It can link the physical, astral and causal bodies, catalyzing full consciousness in waking, dreaming and dreamless sleep.

KYANITE, GREEN **KEY WORDS** Psychically connecting with Nature **CHAKRAS** All, especially Heart (4th) **ELEMENT** Storm **PHYSICAL** Supports enhanced vitality through connection with Nature **EMOTIONAL** Aids in experiencing the natural joy of life in its essence **SPIRITUAL** Facilitates interdimensional travel to Devic, astral and causal realms

Green Kyanite helps one to feel the ever-moving, perfect flowing balance of the Tao, the life force of the Universe. It connects one with the truth of the heart. It can open the portals to inner domains—from the realm of the Nature spirits and devas, to the causal plane where the archetypes exist. Even astral travel to other planets is possible. It can enhance dream life and can facilitate lucid dreaming state. For this, it should be put in a pillowcase or taped to the third eye. Moldavite can be added to enhance these effects.

KYANITE, INDIGO **KEY WORDS** Spiritual awakening, astral travel, lucid dreaming, inner vision **CHAKRAS** All, especially Third Eye (6th) and Crown (7th) **ELEMENT** Storm **PHYSICAL** Supports spiritual healing of brain imbalances **EMOTIONAL** Helps dispel confusion and anxiety **SPIRITUAL** Stimulates the energies of spiritual awakening

Indigo Kyanite's energies move deeply into the mind centers, stimulating the pineal gland and activating psychic abilities. When the pineal gland is awakened, it can trigger crown chakra activation and states of satori. It facilitates lucid dreaming and astral travel. It brings inner clarity and stimulates new insights into difficult situations. It inspires loyalty and fair treatment of one's fellow humans. It can help one work through disagreements and disputes and can aid in repairing damaged relationships.

KYANITE, ORANGE **KEY WORDS** Creativity, sexuality, physical evolutionary change, manifestation, clearing the second chakra **CHAKRAS** Sexual/Creative (2nd) **ELEMENT** Fire **PHYSICAL** Supports the sexual organs, aids the beneficial transformation of DNA **EMOTIONAL** Clears old issues of sexual abuse or other mistreatment from the past, including past lives **SPIRITUAL** Awakens the vast power of creativity, and the joys of sacred sexuality

Orange Kyanite can help one produce evolutionary changes during one's lifetime. The catalytic potential of these stones is awesome. They are among the most powerful aids for manifestation. It can clear the second chakra of negative attachments, from this life or past lives. It allows one to explore and enjoy one's sexuality in joyful and creative ways.

LABRADORITE **KEY WORDS** Magic, protection **CHAKRAS** All **ELEMENT** Wind **PHYSICAL** Amplifies the effects of prayers and affirmations **EMOTIONAL** Aids in doing "inner work" to root out old negative patterns **SPIRITUAL** Enhances psychic abilities, capacity to perceive with the inner eye, useful for magic, ritual and psychic protection

Labradorite is the gemstone of magic. It can awaken clairvoyance, telepathy, astral travel, prophecy, psychic reading, access to Akashic records, past-life recall, communication with higher guides and spirits. It offers psychic protection, dispelling negative energies and entities. It enhances synchronicity and serendipity in one's life. It is a stone of spiritual adventure, increasing one's power to magically influence the outer world.

LAPIS LAZULI **KEY WORDS** Inner vision, truthful communication, royal virtues **CHAKRAS** Third Eye (6th), Throat (5th) **ELEMENT** Wind **PHYSICAL** Aids in seeing the karmic or psychological roots of illness **EMOTIONAL** Helps in recognizing and dissolving emotional pathologies **SPIRITUAL** Enhances telepathy, past-life recall, visionary awareness, deepens meditation

Lapis Lazuli is a stone of royalty and spirituality. It carries the vibration of the inner King or Queen hidden in each of us. It activates the psychic centers at the third eye, facilitating enhanced intuition and access to spiritual guidance. It is a stone of visionary awareness, bringing information in images rather than words. It enhances intellectual ability, making one a better learner and teacher. It is a stone of truth and initiation—a catalyst mystical journeys to higher awareness.

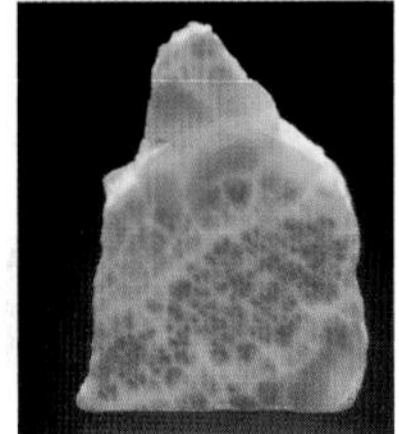

LARIMAR **KEY WORDS** Calming, cooling, soothing to the emotional body, enhanced communication, feminine power, connection with goddess energies **CHAKRAS** Third Eye (6th), Throat (5th) **ELEMENT** Water, Fire **PHYSICAL** Aids spiritual healing of throat issues and stress-related illness **EMOTIONAL** Promotes serenity, relaxation and strength of emotional self **SPIRITUAL** Enhances one's link to the Divine Feminine, aids in freeing oneself from unhealthy attachments

Larimar supports clear communication, emotional strength and stability. It is a stone of the Divine Feminine within. It supports confident well-being and relaxed self-knowledge. It soothes the emotional body, releasing stress and tension. It can cool hot tempers and guide excess passion into peace. It soothes hot flashes and calms down overactive kundalini energies. It opens the path to the "divine stair of ascension."

LAZULITE **KEY WORDS** Psychic abilities, mental focus and discipline, enhancing transcendent brain function **CHAKRAS** Third Eye (6th) **ELEMENT** Wind **PHYSICAL** Helps one in overcoming headaches, migraines and eye strain **EMOTIONAL** Facilitates past-life exploration and can help dissolve outmoded patterns **SPIRITUAL** Stimulates the mind to resonate at higher frequencies, helps one attune to other dimensions, enhances dream recall

Lazulite stimulates the third eye and can activate psychic clairvoyance, clairaudience, clairsentience, psychometry, mediumship, prophetic vision, channeling, remote viewing, telepathy, psychokinesis and ESP. It facilitates focus and self-discipline and can spark inspirational insights. It supports peak brain functioning and hemispheric balance.

LEMURIAN AQUATINE CALCITE **KEY WORDS** Dream awareness, emotional healing, access to world memory, communication with whales and dolphins **CHAKRAS** Heart (4th) **ELEMENT** Water **PHYSICAL** Replenishes the Liquid Crystal Body Matrix **EMOTIONAL** Nourishes the emotional body and emotional intelligence **SPIRITUAL** Enhances intuition, telepathy; allows one to attune to Lemuria

Lemurian Aquatine Calcite enhances intuition, dreaming, feeling and visionary consciousness. It deeply nourishes the emotional body. It is a strong antidote to stress, fear, worry and anxiety about the future. It soothes and replenishes the etheric body. It enhances dream life and facilitates lucid dreaming. It is ideal for recalling past lives, ancient knowledge and attuning to the morphic fields of the Earth's past. It can facilitate communication with whales and dolphins.

LEMURIAN LIGHT CRYSTALS **KEY WORDS** Inner Light, visionary experiences, activation of brain capacities, enhanced crystalline coherence, links to Lemuria **CHAKRAS** Third Eye (6th), Crown (7th), Mouth of God, and the whole brain **ELEMENTS** Wind, Storm **PHYSICAL** Supports the brain and central nervous system, may aid in overcoming brain dysfunctions **EMOTIONAL** Offers the experience of expanded consciousness as pure pleasure **SPIRITUAL** Stimulates visionary experience, triggers the Mouth of God energy point

Lemurian Light Crystals allow one to see visions of ancient Lemuria and experience Lemurian consciousness. They help one move deeply into meditative states, opening the mind to receive inspiration. They offer spiritual support to the brain and may be used to soothe those with dementia.

LEMURIAN MIST CRYSTALS **KEY WORDS** Link to Lemurian consciusness and memory, telepathic consciousness **CHAKRAS** Crown (7th), Third Eye (6th), Heart (4th), Soul Star (8th) **ELEMENT** Water, Wind **PHYSICAL** Supports neural link between heart and brain **EMOTIONAL** Spiritual bliss **SPIRITUAL** Can activate the "Mouth of God" chakra and trigger mystical awakening

Lemurian Mist Crystals activate psychic and empathic awareness. They stimulate expansion of consciousness and enable one to attune to the angelic realm, the Akashic records, and the realm of those who have "crossed over." They are keys to experiencing the consciousness and "history" of Lemuria. They can activate one's latent capacities for psychic and empathic awareness. Combined with Pink Amethyst and Azozeo Phenacite, they can facilitate experiences of Vibrational Ascension.

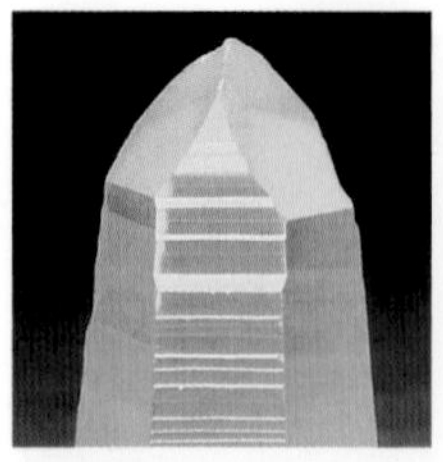

LEMURIAN SEED CRYSTALS **KEY WORDS** Connection with the Divine Feminine, unification with the soul, access to knowledge and wisdom of ancient Lemuria **CHAKRAS** Crown (7th), Soul Star (8th) **ELEMENT** Earth, Wind **PHYSICAL** Links one with the healing qualities of Lemurian awareness **EMOTIONAL** Supports overcoming spiritual loneliness and/or depression **SPIRITUAL** Awakens multiple gifts of empathic and intuitive consciousness

Lemurian Seeds can help one attain "Lemurian awareness"—the balancing, nurturing, loving, spiritual and sensuous consciousness that has been long lost by much of humanity. The response to these crystals is often so emotional and so laden with love that one feels them as a balm to the soul. Lemurian Seeds can benefit just about everyone. We all need the heart opening and emotional/spiritual healing they offer.

LEPIDOCROCITE **KEY WORDS** Emotional healing, release of self-destructive patterns, love and empathy, soul retrieval, creative inspiration **CHAKRAS** Heart (4th) **ELEMENT** Fire, Water **PHYSICAL** Supports the blood, heart, lungs, endocrine system, reproductive organs **EMOTIONAL** Aids emotional balance and healing **SPIRITUAL** Aids soul retrieval, psychic protection, attuning to Divine Love

Lepidocrocite can heal "holes" in the auric field which have been caused by drug or alcohol abuse or by negative attachments and entities. It supports the emotional body, helping one tap into Divine Love. It aids in processing grief and relieving depression. It can help one retrieve soul fragments left behind at traumatic moments in one's life. It facilitates communication—verbal, empathic, telepathic, emotional, mathematical, musical and artistic. It is excellent for helping romantic partners communicate deeply.

LEPIDOLITE **KEY WORDS** Emotional healing and balance, purification, serenity, relaxation, stress relief **CHAKRAS** All, especially Heart (4th) and Third Eye (6th) **ELEMENT** Water **PHYSICAL** Spiritually aids recovery from insomnia and stress-related disorders **EMOTIONAL** Supports emotional balance and helps dispel worry **SPIRITUAL** Inspires serenity, aids spiritual purification, deepens meditation

Lepidolite can calm frayed nerves, help one release stress and worry, and calm stormy emotional seas. It facilitates enlightened awareness and serenity. It encourages one to respond to hostility without defensiveness, to find the path of harmony and to see problems as opportunities to learn. Lepidolite is a stone of spiritual purification, and it can clear blocked energies in the chakras and the meridian system. It can dispel negative thoughts and remove negative emotional attachments.

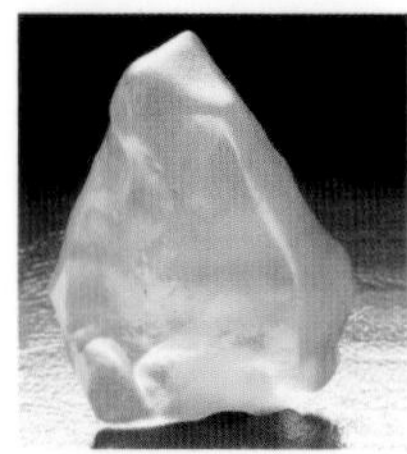

LIBYAN GOLD TEKTITE **KEY WORDS** Confidence, mental acuity, psychic protection, access to Akashic records, manifestation, realization of personal potential **CHAKRAS** All, especially Solar Plexus (3rd) and Sexual/Creative (2nd) **ELEMENT** Fire, Storm **PHYSICAL** Supports spiritual healing of stomach and digestive issues **EMOTIONAL** Aids in overcoming shyness and approaching life playfully **SPIRITUAL** Helps one access Akashic records, aids creative manifestation through the will

Libyan Gold Tektite enhances the will, one's ability to create, and one's power of manifestation. It can aid in recovering the ties of the early Egyptian civilizations to the influence of extraterrestrial entities. It can link one with the energies of Isis and Osiri. Meditation and ritual performed with Libyan Gold Tektite will be strongly enhanced, particularly for realizing desired outcomes in the material world.

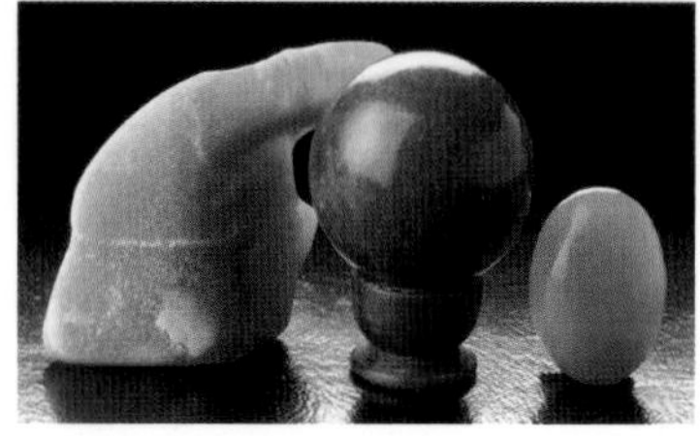

LILAC LEPIDOLITE **KEY WORDS** Soothing the emotional body, relieving stress, enhancing meditation, peace, serenity, love, Divine connection **CHAKRAS** All, especially Heart (4th) and Crown (7th) **ELEMENT** Storm, Water **PHYSICAL** Aids harmonious function of bodily organs and systems **EMOTIONAL** Helps release stress and embracing serenity and love **SPIRITUAL** Activates one's link to the Divine Presence or Higher Self

Lilac Lepidolite blends the Pink Ray of the Heart with the Violet Flame of Purification and spiritual awakening. It activates one's connection to the Higher Self. It enhances peace, serenity and love, releasing stress, calming frayed nerves. It is recommended for recovering from grief or depression and for anyone undergoing a difficult time.

LITHIUM LIGHT **KEY WORDS** Serenity, peace, comfort and relaxation within the process of spiritual unfoldment, Light Body activation, conscious link with the Divine **CHAKRAS** All **ELEMENT** Water **PHYSICAL** Facilitates self-healing through relief of stress, supports digestive system **EMOTIONAL** Aids mood stabilization and release of tension, can trigger euphoria **SPIRITUAL** Provides comfort, relaxation in spiritual transformation, stimulates Light Body activation, ecstatic rapture and visions of the Divine realms

Lithium Light is helpful for spiritual transformation, because its presence builds a vibrational field of safety, pleasure, comfort, joy and healing relaxation. It is very helpful during the metamorphosis of Light Body activation. It can lead one into ecstatic rapture.

LITHIUM QUARTZ **KEY WORDS** Inner peace, release from stress and negative attachments, aura healing, harmonizing relationships **CHAKRAS** All **ELEMENT** Storm, Water **PHYSICAL** Supports the body in overcoming stress and depression **EMOTIONAL** Fills the emotional body with calm, peaceful, loving energy **SPIRITUAL** Facilitates meditation by calming the mind and opening the heart

Lithium Quartz crystals emanate waves of pleasant euphoria. They can be used to activate any chakra, and will enhance the depth of meditation and the quality of inner visions. They facilitate healing, emotional peace, release from tension and awakening of the Higher Self. Wearing Lithium Quartz brings one into a continuous state of connection to the higher mind and heart. "Planting" these crystals in gardens provides stimulation of growth and an invitation for the participation of the devas and Nature spirits.

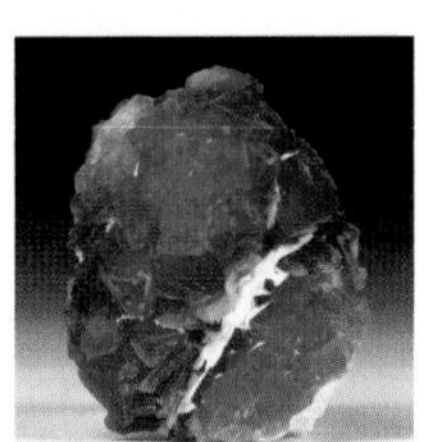

MAGENTA FLUORITE **KEY WORDS** Thought of the heart, inner truth, emotional healing, pineal gland, higher awareness, Divine nectar **CHAKRAS** Heart (4th), Third Eye (6th), Crown (7th) **ELEMENT** Wind, Water, **PHYSICAL** Activates brain centers, supports neural links with heart **EMOTIONAL** Healing emotional body, entering states of ecstasy **SPIRITUAL** Initiates leaps of awareness and union with the Divine

Magenta Fluorite is a stone of the heart, allowing one to become consciously aware of the heart's thoughts, desires and knowledge. It is a stone of inner truth, enhancing clarity and peaceful understanding. It links the heart and crown chakras, opening one to higher awareness. It is a stone of emotional healing, encouraging forgiveness. It stimulates the pineal gland in the center of the brain, encouraging the secretion of its Divine nectar. It aids one in dispelling emotional confusion, and in knowing which choices are best.

MAGNESITE **KEY WORDS** Higher sensibilities, inner vision, truth and bliss, listening to the heart **CHAKRAS** Third Eye (6th), Crown (7th) **ELEMENT** Storm **PHYSICAL** Aids the body in releasing tension, benefits bowels, muscle tension, stress-related issues **EMOTIONAL** Promotes joy, emotional harmony, relief from stress **SPIRITUAL** Opens one to transcendent spiritual experiences

Magnesite can initiate the activation of the eye of inner vision in the prefrontal lobes of the brain. It facilitates opening the crown chakra, encouraging its blooming into the "thousand-petaled lotus." It aids in self-reflection and can clarify inner seeing. It initiates the awakening of the mind to communication with the heart, helping the mind to hear and respond to the heart's voice. This listening to the heart is the beginning of true wisdom.

MAGNETITE **KEY WORDS** Alignment of subtle energies with the body, grounding, balancing polarities, awakening hidden potentials **CHAKRAS** All **ELEMENT** Earth **PHYSICAL** Supports the blood, liver, bone marrow, clears the meridians **EMOTIONAL** Helps prevent mood swings **SPIRITUAL** Aids psychics, healers and sensitive people in staying grounded and balanced

Magnetite can align the currents of the auric field. It is excellent for balancing polarities—male and female, physical and spiritual, left and right hemispheres of the brain, etc. One can receive Magnetite's beneficial energies by simply sitting and holding one of the stones in each hand. This affects one's meridian system and initiates hemispheric balance in the brain. When this happens, hidden potentials begin to surface.

MAGNIFIER QUARTZ **KEY WORDS** Vibrational amplification of stones, vitamins, water, energy tools, etc **CHAKRAS** All **ELEMENTS** Wind, Storm **PHYSICAL** Amplifies the effects of healing stones and substances **EMOTIONAL** Amplifies all emotional states, so one is encouraged to use it in states of happiness, gratitude, love and peace **SPIRITUAL** Enhances the energetic effects of all stones, as well as other tools or substances used to further one's spiritual evolution

Magnifier Quartz can enhance the energies of almost all other stones. It is valuable for constructing crystal tools, stone grids and body layouts. It can be added to wands, carried in medicine bags, placed with stones in one's environment, put on healing altars, included in elixirs, etc. It is a catalyst for synergy, and can be used in groups to enhance cooperation and inspire creative visions.

MALACHITE **KEY WORDS** Enlightened leadership, creativity, confidence, protection, a healed heart **CHAKRAS** Solar Plexus (3rd), Heart (4th) **ELEMENT** Fire **PHYSICAL** Increases vitality, supports tissue repair and recovery from illness, recommended for inflammation, arthritis, digestion, detoxification **EMOTIONAL** Aids in building self-confidence and emotional clarity **SPIRITUAL** Facilitates psychic protection, manifestation, enhances will forces

Malachite offers powerful protection from negative energies. It permeates the auric field with positive vibrations. It activates the "psychic radar" with which one feels the presence of danger, and it increases the synchronicities that occur to keep one safe. It emanates the healthiest energy pattern for the heart. It aids emotional balance, helping one avoid emotional pitfalls.

MANI STONE **KEY WORDS** Forgiveness, inclusion, regeneration of hope, unity with the Higher Self, soul retrieval, rejuvenation, metanoia **CHAKRA** Heart (4th) **ELEMENTS** Earth, Water, Storm **PHYSICAL** Facilitates rejuvenation of the body through emotional and spiritual healing **EMOTIONAL** Helps heal emotional pathology created by self-judgment and fragmentation, encourages forgiveness and reconciliation **SPIRITUAL** Helps one reintegrate the fragmented self, allowing for spiritual wholeness and union with the Higher Self and the Divine

Mani Stone encourages forgiveness, inclusion and the regeneration of hope. It dissolves dysfunctional patterns and facilitates soul retrieval. It enhances compassion for others, facilitates unity of self and union with the Higher Self. It is a stone of mystical awakening.

MANIFEST LIGHT CRYSTALS **KEY WORDS** Kundalini awakening, stimulation of Inner Light, awakening the Light Body, manifestation of one's intentions **CHAKRAS** All, especially Crown (7th) and Root (1st) **ELEMENTS** Fire, Storm, Earth **PHYSICAL** Fills the body with chi, increasing vitality and longevity **EMOTIONAL** Brings a pleasant expansion to the emotional body, **SPIRITUAL** Helps one awaken kundalini energies, balances polarities, aids in manifestation

Manifest Light Crystals are ideal for Light Body activation. They enhance health and well-being by bathing the cells with pure spiritual Light. They can ground those with overactive upper chakras, or stimulate sluggish energy systems. They can unite and reconcile all types of polarities, and are useful in Polarity Therapy. These crystals emanate a great deal of Life Force!

MARCASITE **KEY WORDS** Physical vitality, spirituality in physical life, balancing energetic polarities **CHAKRAS** Root (1st), Sexual/Creative (2nd), Solar Plexus (3rd), Earthstar (below the feet) **ELEMENT** Storm **PHYSICAL** Supports recovery from bacterial infection, skin eruptions, fungal overgrowth and infections, weight loss **EMOTIONAL** Promotes clear emotional boundaries, claiming one's power **SPIRITUAL** Encourages self-direction and taking steps to realize one's goals

Marcasite allows one to see how physical events mirror spiritual archetypal patterns. It assists one in "walking the talk" of spirituality in one's everyday life. It helps balance polarities in the energy system. It clears the auric field of disharmony and helps one to end unhealthy relationships. It works to optimize life force and courage, sexual energy, creativity, willpower and mental clarity.

MASTER SHAMANITE **KEY WORDS** Linking the physical and spiritual realms, inner purification, spiritual protection, shamanic journeying, transformation to the Diamond Self **CHAKRAS** All **ELEMENT** Storm **PHYSICAL** Purifies the blood and cells of negative energetic attachments **EMOTIONAL** Lends courage and resolve for facing difficult circumstances **SPIRITUAL** Increases psychic sensitivity, aids in spirit communication, encourages one to be a spiritual warrior

Master Shamanite can facilitate shamanic journeys, and it can help one connect inwardly with power animals and spirit guides. It is a Stone of the Ancestors, aiding in communication with spiritual elders and guides, as well as loved ones who have passed. It can help dispel the fear of death through bringing one to a clear experience that death is not the end. It offers spiritual protection to those who wear or carry it.

MERLINITE **KEY WORDS** Magic, intuition, connection with elemental energies, past-life recall, psychic openings, mediumship **CHAKRAS** Solar Plexus (3rd), Third Eye (6th) **ELEMENT** Storm **PHYSICAL** Aids with headaches and heart problems **EMOTIONAL** Encourages adventure, inner freedom **SPIRITUAL** Opens intuitive capacities for magic and manifestation

Merlinite can part the veils between the visible and invisible worlds, opening the doors to deeper intuitive abilities. It is an aid to learning all types of magic. It opens psychic channels for higher guidance. It helps one grasp the essence of astrology, tarot, numerology and other occult sciences. It facilitates prophetic visions, and it attracts frequent synchronicities. It opens one to serve as a channel for manifestation of the creative forces of the higher planes.

MERLINITE-AMETHYST **KEY WORDS** Wholeness, protection, purification **CHAKRAS** Third Eye (6th), Crown (7th) **ELEMENT** Wind **PHYSICAL** Clears the subtle body of "grayness" which can manifest as disease **EMOTIONAL** Cleanses emotional body, bringing a sense of calm and joy **SPIRITUAL** Protects mentally impaired people from being attacked by negative entities, helps one unite with the Deep Self

Amethyst-Merlinite emanates energies that spread rapidly through the subtle/etheric body. It sweeps through one's energy field and eliminates any negative patterns, habits, entities, implants or fixations. It quiets the inner dialog of thoughts and assists one in dropping down into the deep well of inner Silence in the heart. It allows one to remain both completely relaxed and completely alert in meditation. It facilitates telepathic contact with helping spirits and guides, and it helps one to "see" them inwardly.

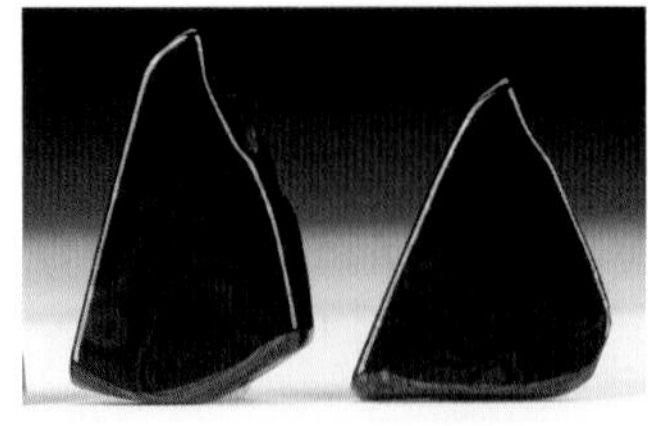

MERLINITE, BLACK **KEY WORDS** Link to the deep Unconscious, lucid dreaming, meditation, shamanic journeying, spirit communication, divination, prophetic vision **CHAKRAS** All, especially Third Eye (6th) and Root (1st) **ELEMENTS** Earth, Wind, Fire **PHYSICAL** Supports organs and systems involved in purification **EMOTIONAL** Quiets spiritual fears, brings union with the Unconscious **SPIRITUAL** Facilitates access to the deep Unconscious

Black Merlinite is excellent for lucid dreaming, and it facilitates meditation, allowing one to "go deep." It offers a direct conduit to the Silence—the still point at the center of all things. It is useful in facilitating shamanic journeying, spirit communication, divination and prophetic vision. It teaches one to befriend one's inner darkness, because it is a part of oneself.

METAL, COPPER **KEY WORDS** Channeling and grounding higher vibrations, conducting and enhancing stone energies **CHAKRAS** All **ELEMENT** Earth **PHYSICAL** Supports the blood, aids tissue repair, increases vitality **EMOTIONAL** Helps one gain spiritual perspective on emotional experiences **SPIRITUAL** Aids in manifesting spiritual energies in the material world

Copper is a conduit between Heaven and Earth, and it provides a medium for manifestation of the invisible to the visible. It can carry stone energies the way a copper wire carries electricity. Crystal grids can be enhanced by connecting the stones with Copper wire. A Quartz Laser Wand or other crystal can be intensified by wrapping a coil of copper wire around it. One of the most powerful and basic energy devices one can make is a copper pipe filled with stones and a crystal point at one or both ends. Copper encourages experimentation and invention.

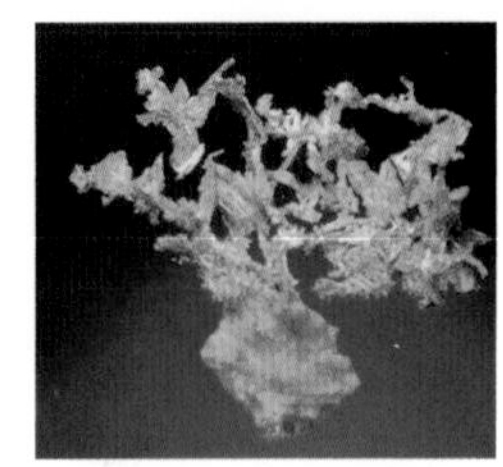

METAL, GOLD **KEY WORDS** Solar energy, the archetypal male energy, creativity, confidence, vitality **CHAKRAS** All, especially Root (1st), Sexual/Creative (2nd), Solar Plexus (3rd) **ELEMENT** Earth **PHYSICAL** Brings vitality and solar energies into the body **EMOTIONAL** Encourages optimism, courage, nobility, determination and sense of well-being; dispels fear and negative emotions **SPIRITUAL** Stimulates activation of the lower chakras, ignites the solar heart, encourages joy in life

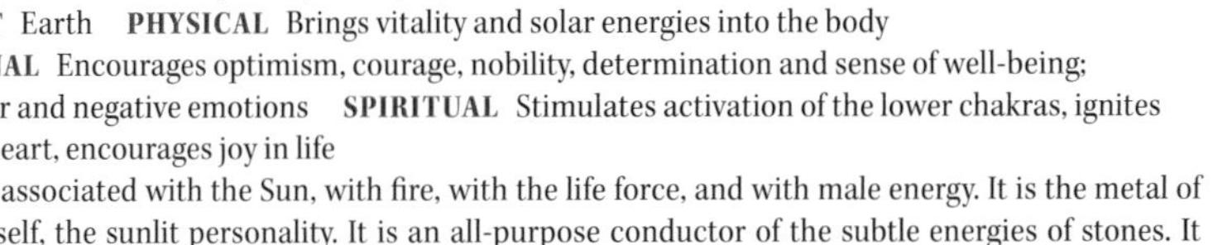

Gold is associated with the Sun, with fire, with the life force, and with male energy. It is the metal of the outer self, the sunlit personality. It is an all-purpose conductor of the subtle energies of stones. It revitalizes one's physical energies and magnifies the power of most gemstones. It supports openness and integrity and builds confidence. It facilitates the successful completion of inner processes.

METAL, NIOBIUM **KEY WORDS** Activation of the Rainbow Body, communication with ETs and etheric entities **CHAKRAS** All **ELEMENT** Earth **PHYSICAL** Offers a neutral vibration which supports the currents of whatever stones one works with to heal and help the body **EMOTIONAL** Encourages impartiality in regard to emotional issues, helps one look dispassionately at one's emotional triggers and to avoid identifying with old emotional patterns **SPIRITUAL** Facilitates communication with the higher realms, aids in accessing angelic guidance, ideal for recalling and understanding ET experiences

Niobium encourages one to see everything from a fresh perspective, and it helps one discern the magic one has overlooked right under one's nose. It is a metal of the Rainbow Body. It is useful in making Light tools and crystal energy devices. It resonates to the mystical energies of the planet Neptune.

METAL, PLATINUM **KEY WORDS** Cosmic connection, interdimensional communication **CHAKRAS** All, especially Third Eye (6th), Crown (7th), Etheric (8th–14th) **ELEMENT** Storm **PHYSICAL** Stimulates the body's energy systems, emanates protection for the body **EMOTIONAL** Aids in governing emotions and keeping the inner observer awake **SPIRITUAL** Activates the higher chakras, stimulates communion and communication with the higher realms, aids in out-of-body travel

Platinum has the highest vibrational spectrum of any metal. It stimulates one's consciousness to aspire to the highest realms. It is linked to the angelic realm, and to the archetypal pattern of the Divine Human Being. It evokes the energy of enlightenment and archetype of the Star. It can enhance one's connection with angels and spirit guides, and it carries the energy pattern of revelation.

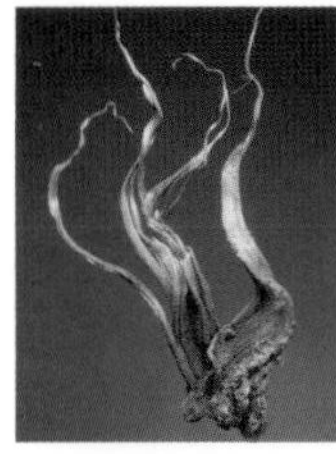

METAL, SILVER **KEY WORDS** Lunar energy, the archetypal feminine energy, mystery, the unconscious **CHAKRAS** All **ELEMENT** Earth **PHYSICAL** Helps cool excess body heat, aids women's hormonal balance, supports the body in overcoming viruses and bacteria, energetically supports the immune system **EMOTIONAL** Stimulates attunement to the intuitive, emotional side of the self, links both men and women to their feminine side, encourages emotional receptivity, strengthens empathy **SPIRITUAL** Stimulates one's connection to the Goddess, allows one to travel the astral realms, attunes one to the inner depths of the subconscious

Silver encourages self-containment and inward reflection. It is a mirror to the soul, the metal of moonlight. It works best with stones that enhance psychic abilities and/or work to heal the emotional body. It is the symbol of the unconscious realm. It aids in lucid dreaming and journeying to past lives.

METAL, TITANIUM **KEY WORDS** Power, action, higher awareness, bringing contradiction into synthesis **CHAKRAS** All **ELEMENT** Earth **PHYSICAL** Offers protection from electromagnetic fields generated by computers and electronic equipment, supports physical healing by invigorating one's energy field **EMOTIONAL** Instills a sense of protection and security, assuages fear, uplifting and reinforcing the emotional body **SPIRITUAL** Stimulates energetic strength and purity, provides spiritual protection by increasing the power of one's vibrational field, inspires determination

Titanium is the metal of power and invincibility. It enhances vitality and brings energy into the auric field. It can be an antidote to sluggishness and fatigue. It is also a metal of higher awareness, bringing resolution of inner conflict and the synthesis of apparently contradictory thoughts.

METEORITE, CHONDRITE **KEY WORDS** Interdimensional and extraterrestrial communication, access to the Akashic records of the solar system **CHAKRAS** Third Eye (6th), Crown (7th) **ELEMENT** Earth **PHYSICAL** Supports the bones, blood and circulatory system **EMOTIONAL** Works to balance and stabilize the emotional body **SPIRITUAL** Helps one connect with ETs, aids interdimensional travel

Chondrite Meteorites facilitate telepathic communication with the ETs. They can open one's telepathic channel for "traveling" to other stars and planets. They can be used to store esoteric knowledge relating to the "ladder of consciousness." Chondrites carry the spiritual records of this solar system. They chronicle the histories of etheric entities that existed on other planets, from Mercury to Saturn. Meditation with Chondrite Meteorites can give one a first-hand experiences of these interplanetary subtle realms.

METEORITE, NICKEL-IRON **KEY WORDS** Kundalini activation, inner vision, spiritual awakening, patience and persistence in regard to spiritual growth **CHAKRAS** Root (1st), Solar Plexus (3rd), Third Eye (6th), Crown (7th) **ELEMENT** Fire **PHYSICAL** Enhances stamina and strength, supports blood and tissues **EMOTIONAL** Supports emotional balance, protects the emotional body **SPIRITUAL** Catalyzes spiritual transformation via kundalini awakening

Nickel-Iron Meteorites stimulate the third eye and crown chakras. They act as catalysts for inner vision and spiritual awakening. Yet they also activate the root chakra and solar plexus, providing an anchor of grounding which is much needed in order to handle everything else they do. In addition, Nickel-Iron Meteorites stimulate the solar plexus, the chakra of action and will.

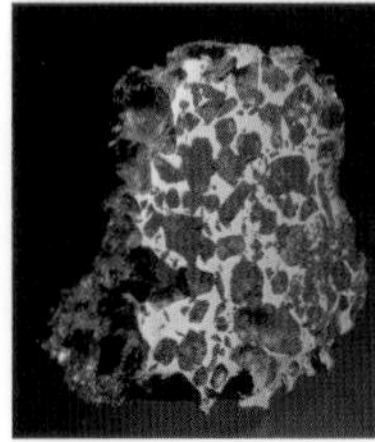

METEORITE, PALLASITE **KEY WORDS** Union with the cosmic Overmind and fields of knowledge, interdimensional travel, prosperity, emotional stability **CHAKRAS** Heart (4th), Third Eye (6th) **ELEMENT** Earth **PHYSICAL** Supports the heart, aids blood purification, helps dispel unhealthy bacteria and viruses **EMOTIONAL** Instills emotional balance during spiritual experiences, helps overcome phobias **SPIRITUAL** Allows one to awaken to Cosmic Consciousness

Pallasite stimulates the loving energies of the heart and the visionary capacities of the third eye. It opens the emotional gateway of the heart and the inner eye of expanded awareness, allowing one to experience the link between oneself and the cosmos. It helps one release the fear of expanding consciousness beyond the body. It helps those who feel "stuck" in the body to let go and travel in the astral and other higher planes.

MOLDAU QUARTZ **KEY WORDS** Grounding spiritual Light in the body, appreciating and expressing beauty, heart awareness, grounding the vibrations of Moldavite **CHAKRAS** All, especially Heart (4th) and Third Eye (6th) **ELEMENT** Storm **PHYSICAL** Supports healing and transformation through infusion of Light **EMOTIONAL** Generates feelings of satisfaction and gratitude to Spirit **SPIRITUAL** Inspires an awakening to spiritual beauty and Wisdom

Moldau Quartz has spent millions of years in the same soil where Moldavite is found. These stones have, in a sense, been "taught" by the presence of Moldavite. They have been attuned to the frequencies of the higher worlds. In this, they hold the pattern we ourselves are reaching toward. The heart resonates with Moldau Quartz more than most other varieties of Quartz.

MOLDAVITE **KEY WORDS** Transformation, rapid spiritual evolution, chakra activation, cleansing, protection, increased incidence of synchronicities **CHAKRAS** All, especially Heart (4th), Third Eye (6th) **ELEMENT** Storm **PHYSICAL** Brings the body to its highest potential **EMOTIONAL** Opens the heart, inspires one to fulfill one's highest destiny **SPIRITUAL** Catalyzes multiple and very powerful spiritual awakenings

Moldavite has been linked to the fabled Stone of the Holy Grail. It was believed to guide one to one's destiny and to help one find true love. It is a stone of rapid and powerful spiritual transformation. It can catalyze major priority shifts and life changes. It attracts whatever serves one's spiritual evolution and highest good, dissolves one's connections with what hinders one's evolution. It can cause a sudden opening of the heart, known as the "Moldavite flush." It can stimulate any chakra and it brings healing wherever it is needed.

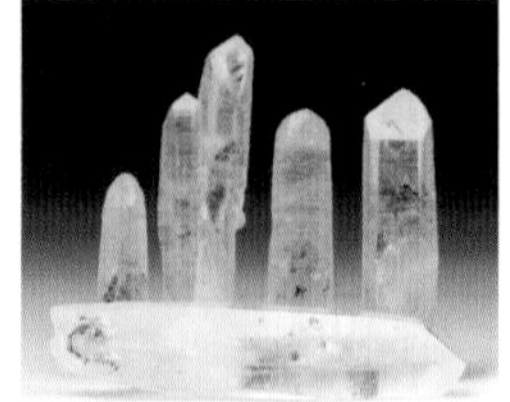

MOLYBDENITE QUARTZ **KEY WORDS** Balance, grounding, strength, centeredness, stability, vitality, endurance, loyalty, persistence, courage, resolve, health **CHAKRAS** All **ELEMENTS** Earth, Water **PHYSICAL** Holds the vibrational pattern of optimal function for the body, aids in detoxification **EMOTIONAL** Stabilizes the emotions, moderates fear, depression and anxiety **SPIRITUAL** Balances one's energies, engendering endurance and persistence in following one's goals

Molybdenite Quartz supports holding one's intention until goals are met and changes are made. It engenders loyalty, persistence, courage, resolve and strength of will. It helps one retain hope in the midst of difficulty, and stay grounded during times of success. It brings stability, moderating depression and anxiety, reminding one that trust is the way to freedom and that love is its own reward.

MOONSTONE **KEY WORDS** Mystery, self-discovery, intuition, insight, dreams, the goddess **CHAKRAS** Third Eye (6th) and Crown (7th) **ELEMENT** Wind **PHYSICAL** Aids women in comfortable regulation of their menstrual cycles **EMOTIONAL** Encourages forbearance, calmness, patience, inner tranquility **SPIRITUAL** Stimulates inner reflection, attunement with Divine Feminine

Moonstone is a talisman for the inward journey, and meditation with it can take one deep into the self. It can help one find the missing pieces of the puzzle of one's life—parts of the soul that have been left behind or forgotten. Moonstone can also take one on a journey into past lives. It is an ideal stone to wear during past-life regression sessions. It can reveal to women their feminine power and their connection to the goddess. For men, it allows the expression of the feminine side, an important step on the path to wholeness.

MOONSTONE, POLARITY **KEY WORDS** Embracing and integrating inner opposites **CHAKRAS** Third Eye (6th), Heart (4th) **ELEMENT** Water **PHYSICAL** Supports parasympathetic nervous system, aids in releasing stress **EMOTIONAL** Facilitates harmonization of joy and sorrow, excitement and peace, enthusiasm and stillness **SPIRITUAL** gives rise to centering in the Deep Self, encourages a shift of consciousness into the expanded state of awareness that is one's true Wholeness

Polarity Moonstone stimulates the awakened "daytime" consciousness and the deeper "night" awareness of the subconscious. In sleep, it can stimulate intense and meaningful dreams, and it aids one in remembering one's dreams after waking up. It stimulates one's capacity for emotional and symbolic insights, helping one to understand the messages our dreams have for us.

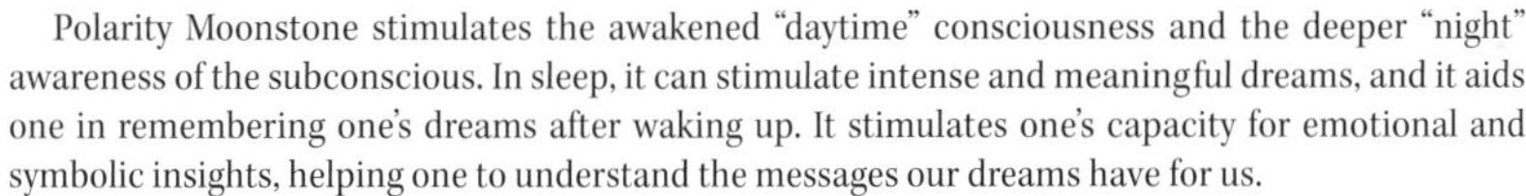

MOONSTONE, RAINBOW **KEY WORDS** Optimism, vitality, peace **CHAKRAS** All **ELEMENT** Wind **PHYSICAL** Helps the body overcome fatigue from depression **EMOTIONAL** Inspires enthusiasm, self-appreciation, joy **SPIRITUAL** Stimulates awakening of the Rainbow Body of Light

Rainbow Moonstone emanates vitality, life force and exuberant joy. It offers inner peace and harmony, emotional balance and strength, purification and transformation of negativity, as well as psychic protection. It facilitates alignment and activation of all the chakras. It is recommended for those who suffer from stress or who carry old emotional wounds. It promotes a healthy optimism that can sustain one through dark times. It aids one in kindling the inner light of the heart. It can facilitate activation of the Rainbow Body of Light. It is aligned with the energies of the Goddess, and can help one successfully empower one's feminine aspect.

MORGANITE **KEY WORDS** Divine Love and compassion **CHAKRAS** Heart (4th) **ELEMENT** Water **PHYSICAL** Supports the physical heart and its energy field **EMOTIONAL** Soothes the soul with Divine Love, helps overcome old sorrows **SPIRITUAL** Inspires rapturous merging with the all-pervasive Divine Love

Morganite is attuned to the frequency of Divine Love. It opens the heart on a deeper level, making us aware of the huge ocean of cosmic love within which we all exist. It gives us the opportunity to surrender to the immense power of Divine Love and to let it show us our life path more clearly. It can bring release of old pains and sorrow, and the sense that a burden has been lifted. Morganite brings in the frequency of Divine compassion. It facilitates emotional self-healing through inner surrender, which releases one from the pain to which one had been unconsciously clinging.

MUSCOVITE **KEY WORDS** Mental stimulation, inspiration, problem solving, attunement to the future, ESP, moderation of overly rapid spiritual awakening **CHAKRAS** Third Eye (6th), Crown (7th) **ELEMENT** Wind **PHYSICAL** Soothes headaches, dizziness, etc., from too-rapid psychic awakening **EMOTIONAL** Helps one dissolve unhealthy emotional attachments **SPIRITUAL** Aids psychic opening, stimulates mental energies

Muscovite stimulates the mind, promoting clear and quick thinking, effective problem-solving, and the synthesis of new ideas from old information. It stimulates the higher capacities of the brain. It is a stone of inspiration, fostering the creation of new neural pathways and increasing the frequency of "aha!" moments. It aids one in attuning to the time stream of the future. It supports intuition, telepathy, clairvoyance and other forms of ESP. It makes one receptive to information and suggestions from one's spirit guides.

MYSTIC MERLINITE **KEY WORDS** Alignment of the chakra column, balancing and integrating polarities, claiming one's wholeness, creating through magic **CHAKRAS** All **ELEMENT** Fire, Earth **PHYSICAL** Supports recovery from spinal misalignments and joint problems **EMOTIONAL** Encourages one to reclaim exiled soul parts without judgment **SPIRITUAL** Aids elemental magic, integration of the Shadow, mystic union

Mystic Merlinite can facilitate opening the dormant areas of the mind. It increases sensitivity to communications with the subtle realms, allowing one to "talk" with plant and animal spirits, and devic entities. It enables one to work with elemental energies for magical manifestation and mystical experiences. It can help one unite with the unconscious side of the self.

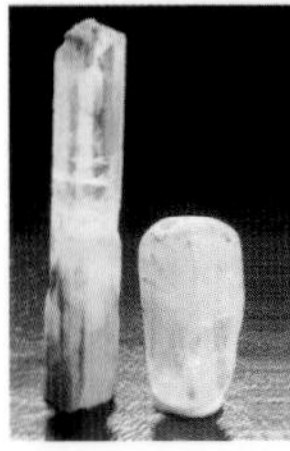

NATROLITE **KEY WORDS** Visionary experience, quantum leap to higher consciousness, brain evolution **CHAKRAS** Third Eye (6th), Crown (7th), Etheric (8th–14th) **ELEMENT** Storm **PHYSICAL** Supports spiritual healing of brain damage and dysfunction **EMOTIONAL** Aids emotional recovery from parasitic psychic attachments **SPIRITUAL** Stimulates expansion of consciousness and Ascension

Natrolite powerfully stimulates the third eye and crown chakras, and can sometimes cause the merging of these chakras into one huge energy center. Its energy moves beyond the physical body, activating one's link with the eighth through fourteenth chakras above the head. It helps open inner gateways to a myriad of inner realms, for one's exploration and enlightenment. It awakens the nervous system to higher levels of sensitivity to subtle spiritual energies. It provides psychic protection from negative entities or influences in one's auric field.

NEW ZEALAND CARNELIAN **KEY WORDS** Fire-element activation, co-creation, insights into destiny, transformation, visions of higher realms, passionate will, sexual path of tantra **CHAKRAS** All, especially Sexual/Creative (2nd), Third Eye (6th) **ELEMENT** Fire **PHYSICAL** Supports nervous system, sexual organs, blood flow, digestive system, immune system **EMOTIONAL** Brings passion into creative activities and love relationships, helps overcome hesitancy and fearfulness **SPIRITUAL** Stimulates spiritual awakening, creativity, courage, passion, power, accelerated evolution

New Zealand Carnelian brings passion to one's will and reminds us of our boldness and our power. It activates the second chakra and can open the way to ecstatic tantric experiences. It supports the nervous system, sexual organs, blood flow, digestive system and immune system.

NIRVANA QUARTZ **KEY WORDS** Opening to the future, heart/brain synergy, inner rapture, destiny, evolution, trust, self-acceptance **CHAKRAS** All **ELEMENT** Storm **PHYSICAL** Helps dispel various physical symptoms of energy imbalances **EMOTIONAL** Expands emotional body into ecstatic union with the Divine **SPIRITUAL** Facilitates heart/brain synergy, *satori* and enlightenment

Nirvana Quartz crystals are conduits for currents of inner illumination that facilitate the incarnation of enlightenment. It can help one unite the consciousness of the brain and the heart, creating a feedback loop of joy, leading to inner Light and ecstasy. Its mission involves setting up the blueprint of post-human destiny, living and creating each moment through utter, ongoing, trusting engagement with the fertile unknown which is the future. These stones can be viewed as the angels of our potential.

NOVACULITE **KEY WORDS** Infusion of subtle matter-energy, stimulation of enlightenment, discernment, cutting unhealthy ties to the past **CHAKRAS** Third Eye (6th), Crown (7th) **ELEMENTS** Wind, Storm **PHYSICAL** Frees blocked energies and cuts away negative attachments underlying physical ailments **EMOTIONAL** Facilitates freedom from the past **SPIRITUAL** Carries a stream of subtle matter-energy into the body, aiding the process of enlightenment

In spiritual self-healing, Novaculite is an ideal stone for psychic surgery. It is particularly attuned to the heart and brain, and its currents can help clear the energies of the bloodstream, lymphatic system and nervous system.

NUUMMITE **KEY WORDS** Personal magic, inner journeys, attuning to elemental forces, self-mastery **CHAKRAS** Third Eye (6th), Solar Plexus (3rd), Root (1st) **ELEMENT** Earth, Storm **PHYSICAL** Helps calm and balance the nervous system **EMOTIONAL** Encourages self-acceptance, recognition of inner strength **SPIRITUAL** Aids in honoring one's depths and finding one's inner power

Nuummite offers the gift of inner power for self-mastery. It aids one's courage and determination to do the inner work that is necessary to be healed and whole. It is excellent for shamanic journeying. It can enhance clairvoyance and intuition. It can help one learn the language of the body and call in healing energies for oneself and others. It can aid in attuning to the Earth's elemental forces. It is a stone of personal magic that can increase the frequency of synchronicities and "good luck."

OBSIDIAN, BLACK **KEY WORDS** Psychic protection, grounding, cleansing of negativity, spirit communication **CHAKRAS** Root (1st) **ELEMENT** Earth **PHYSICAL** Aids in healing issues caused by unprocessed Shadow material **EMOTIONAL** Helps dispel self-judgment and self-sabotage **SPIRITUAL** Facilitates psychic cleansing, grounding, protection, spirit communication

Black Obsidian eliminates negative energies in oneself and one's environment. It is like a psychic vacuum cleaner, cleansing the auric field of disharmony, negative attachments, astral "junk," as well as anger, greed, fear, resentment, etc. It is good for grounding and protection. It can facilitate scrying, and spirit communication. It helps bring one's own Shadow material out of exile, allowing it to be transmuted through the heart. It aids in recalling the exiled bits from the unconscious, even from past lives.

OBSIDIAN, GOLD SHEEN **KEY WORDS** Healing abuse of power, activating the higher Will, enhanced manifestation **CHAKRAS** Root (1st), Solar Plexus (3rd) **ELEMENT** Earth **PHYSICAL** Supports the body in overcoming stomach and digestive issues **EMOTIONAL** Encourages self-confidence through self-knowledge **SPIRITUAL** Powerfully aids manifestation of Divine Will through oneself

Gold Sheen Obsidian attunes one to the energy of the Great Central Sun through its cleansing and activation of the third chakra. These stones are ideal for clearing negative energies and purifying one's auric field, especially at the solar plexus. When one's channel is clear, all the way to Source, one's will is aligned with the Divine and one's power of manifestation is greatly enhanced. Gold Sheen Obsidian is useful in bringing forward one's hidden talents, and it can aid in achieving worldly success in their expression.

OBSIDIAN, MAHOGANY **KEY WORDS** Release from inner limitations, healing feelings of unworthiness **CHAKRAS** Root (1st), Sexual/Creative (2nd) **ELEMENT** Earth **PHYSICAL** Energetically supports liver and kidney functions, aids in detoxification **EMOTIONAL** Facilitates healing unconsciously held shame, encourages self-love **SPIRITUAL** Ideal for psychic protection, clearing blockages, creativity

Mahogany Obsidian can help cleanse the second chakra of negative energies and residue from old wounds. It can remove negative psychic "implants" that hold one back. It is ideal for dispelling feelings of unworthiness that keep one from fulfilling one's potential in work, love and spiritual awakening. It shields one from psychic attack by negative entities or people.

OBSIDIAN, PEACOCK **KEY WORDS** Shamanic journeying, astral travel, psychic protection **CHAKRAS** Root (1st), Third Eye (6th) **ELEMENT** Earth **PHYSICAL** Helps with physical issues caused by holes in the auric field **EMOTIONAL** Inspires communion with spirit beings **SPIRITUAL** Facilitates shamanic journeying and spirit communication

Peacock Obsidian is excellent for lucid dreaming, breath work, guided meditation and other practices of consciousness expansion. It can show one the unexpected Light in darkness. It aids in exploring the astral, subtle and causal worlds. It is a tool for shamans and an ally for protection, helping one travel between dimensions. It is excellent for rituals and gatherings to which one wishes to call the ancestors, guides and helping spirits.

OBSIDIAN, RAINBOW **KEY WORDS** Recovery from emotional wounds, the deep journey through darkness into Light **CHAKRAS** Root (1st) **ELEMENT** Earth **PHYSICAL** Facilitates removal of blocks and attachments that can cause illness **EMOTIONAL** Encourages optimism and hope, supports the emotional body during dark times **SPIRITUAL** Aids one in coming through the Dark Night of the Soul

Rainbow Obsidian helps one take the downward journey to unexpected Light. This journey into the depths is as amazing as it is necessary. As one descends, one finds the forgotten pieces of oneself that have been left behind at each wounding. Reclaiming the parts and continuing downward, one may experience emptiness and darkness before suddenly bursting into Light at the very nadir of the descent. Rainbow Obsidian is a luminous and protective companion that can aid one in journeys to the depths.

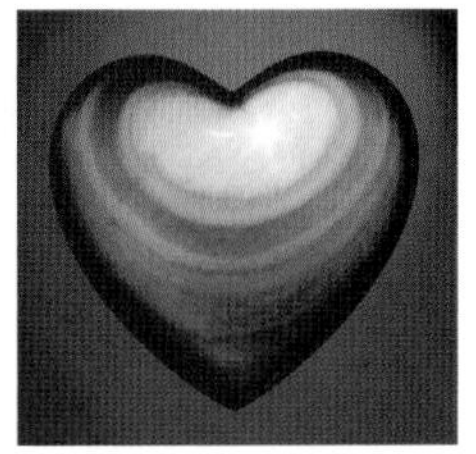

OBSIDIAN, SNOWFLAKE **KEY WORDS** Perseverance, insight, attunement to spiritual guidance, past-life recall, spirit communication **CHAKRAS** Root (1st), Third Eye (6th) **ELEMENT** Earth **PHYSICAL** Supports spiritual healing of cancer, encourages receptivity to healing **EMOTIONAL** Helps one dispel "victim consciousness," inspires belief in oneself **SPIRITUAL** Increases psychic sensitivity, past-life recall, awareness of synchronicities

Snowflake Obsidian enables one to make the best of a bad situation by clearing negative and self-defeating thoughts and inspiring one with new ideas. It increases psychic sensitivity, and can put one in touch with the world of souls, facilitating communication with lost loved ones. It attunes one to memories of past lives or to forgotten events of the present life.

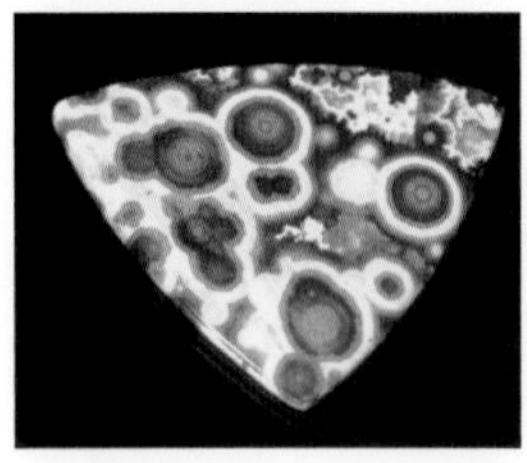

OCEAN JASPER **KEY WORDS** Enjoyment of life, release of negativity and stress, relaxation, positive self-expression, physical and emotional healing **CHAKRAS** Solar Plexus (3rd), Heart (4th), Throat (5th) **ELEMENT** Earth **PHYSICAL** Supports thyroid, adrenals, endocrine glands, aids tissue regeneration **EMOTIONAL** Encourages high spirits, appreciation of the present moment **SPIRITUAL** Brings clarity and centeredness, stimulates a positive attitude

Ocean Jasper opens one's awareness to the benevolent aspects of life and lifts one's mood. It stimulates the solar plexus, heart and throat chakras, conveying the urge to feel, speak and act positively. It supports the expression of love, and it helps one realize what and whom one truly loves. It centers one in the present moment, relieving worry about the future or bitterness about the past.

ONYX **KEY WORDS** Inner strength, focused attention, willpower, self-mastery, discipline, reason **CHAKRAS** Root (1st), Solar Plexus (3rd), Third Eye (6th) **ELEMENT** Earth **PHYSICAL** Aids in recovering strength and vitality after illness **EMOTIONAL** Exerts a calming influence, engenders confidence and power **SPIRITUAL** Encourages persistence, willpower; enhances mental ability

Onyx enhances endurance and persistence, enabling one to carry even difficult and dreary tasks through to completion. It enhances mental focus, allowing one to learn challenging new material. It boosts the retention of memory and encourages attention to detail. It is a stone of physical strength. It aids in containing one's energies rather than allowing them to dissipate. It helps one to build up one's vitality. It helps one control, focus and direct the will, increasing personal power.

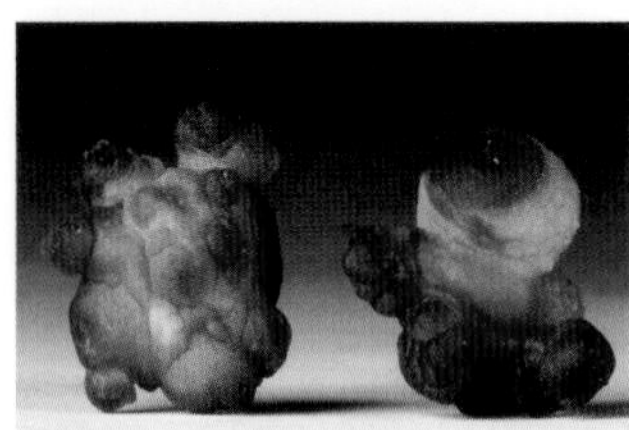

OOGULITE **KEY WORDS** Joy in life, link with Nature **CHAKRAS** Root (1st), Heart (4th) **ELEMENT** Wind, Fire, Water **PHYSICAL** Supports joints, ligaments, muscles **EMOTIONAL** Facilitates playfulness, emotional healing , humor, spontaneity **SPIRITUAL** Reminds us to take pleasure in our lives and express our joy, friendliness and good humor

Oogulite connects one with Nature Spirits. It has a strong, animated presence, and its domain is the realm of fairies, devas, sprites, undines and other beings that express the vitality and diversity of the Earth's soul life. It can be an excellent tonic for the emotional body. It's delight in itself and the world of Nature is contagious. It encourages one to dwell in the present moment and to recognize that we live in an eternal cascade of miracles.

OPAL, BLACK PRECIOUS **KEY WORDS** Manifestation of one's intention, amplification of emotions, revealing and releasing psychic wounds **CHAKRAS** Root (1st), Crown (7th) **ELEMENT** Storm **PHYSICAL** Supports healing (especially cysts or tumors) through release of past trauma **EMOTIONAL** Aids in release of one's deepest fears **SPIRITUAL** Supports one in finding the Light in the dark parts of the Self

Black Precious Opal is a stone of magic and mystery. It stimulates and links the root and crown chakras, aiding one in connecting one's highest spiritual aspirations with one's physical life. It is a powerful magnifier of one's intention, especially if that intention carries an emotional charge. It is excellent for those doing deep inner work. In meditation, it can take one into the roots of the psyche, allowing the release of traumatic memories of past experiences that may now be governing a part of one's life.

OPAL, COMMON **KEY WORDS** White: Purification, Pink: Emotional healing, Blue: Calming the mind, Brown and Black: Emotional protection **CHAKRAS** White: Crown (7th), Pink: Heart (4th), Blue: Throat and Third Eye (5th and 6th), Brown and Black: Root and Sexual: Creative (1st and 2nd) **ELEMENT** Earth, Water **PHYSICAL** All colors gently aid in various healing processes **EMOTIONAL** Works to support and heal the emotional body **SPIRITUAL** Opens one to Spirit through healing of wounds to the soul

Common Opal in all its colors is a stone of gentle energies. It purifies of one's energy field, cleansing and rebalancing the chakras. Pink Opal is for healing the emotions. Blue Opal is an antidote to restless thoughts. Brown and Black Opals are catalysts to the healing process.

OPAL, FIRE **KEY WORDS** Passion, creativity **CHAKRAS** Sexual/Creative (2nd) **ELEMENT** Fire **PHYSICAL** Supports the reproductive systems, increases vitality and energy **EMOTIONAL** Encourages attitude of optimism, playfulness, zest for life **SPIRITUAL** Stimulates energies of creativity, passion, manifestation, sexuality

Fire Opal is an awakener of passion. Whatever one's choice, Fire Opal will enhance the intensity and the pleasure of the experience. In matters of sexuality, Fire Opal's connection to the emotional body will help blend more love into the experience. In situations where shyness, fear or shame hold one back, Fire Opal will ease one's inhibitions and allow for greater enjoyment and less self-consciousness. In spiritual life, Fire Opal can enhance the passionate pursuit of enlightenment.

OPAL, LEMURIAN GOLD **KEY WORDS** Integration of mental and emotional bodies, recalling Lemurian consciousness, dissolving psychological boundaries **CHAKRAS** Crown (7th), Third Eye (6th), Heart (4th) **ELEMENT** Water, Air **PHYSICAL** Calms the body on a cellular level, aids stress relief **EMOTIONAL** Increases empathy, dispels loneliness, calms turbulent feelings **SPIRITUAL** Attunes one to Lemuria and gives access to its spiritual gifts

Lemurian Golden Opal aids in developing the telepathy, clairvoyance, empathy and prophecy that prevailed in Lemurian times. It can aid in manifesting dreams, facilitates lucid dreaming and enhances memory of dreams. It can help one overcome sleep disorders.

OPAL, OREGON **KEY WORDS** Joy, self-expression, imagination **CHAKRAS** Solar Plexus (3rd), Heart (4th), Crown (7th) **ELEMENT** Fire **PHYSICAL** Aids in healing through release of past-life issues, supports kidneys **EMOTIONAL** Encourages dwelling in a state of joy, releasing past wounds **SPIRITUAL** Facilitates discovery of past-life patterns that hold one back

Oregon Opal allows for the joyful experience and expression of the emotions and imagination. It encourages one to act upon one's desires in a loving way. It can be a key for unlocking the secrets of past lives. It activates the "inner radar" which guides one to the life or lives one most needs to review in order to understand difficulties in the current life. Its energy of joyful acceptance allows one to comprehend and release recurring issues and move forward in freedom and clarity.

OPAL, OWYHEE BLUE **KEY WORDS** Quiet strength, calm confidence, decisiveness, inner exploration, amplification of positive emotions, psychic protection **CHAKRAS** Throat (5th), Third Eye (6th), Solar Plexus (3rd) **ELEMENT** Water **PHYSICAL** Helps with throat issues, such as laryngitis, sore throat, thyroid **EMOTIONAL** Encourages self-confidence, calm, clarity of purpose **SPIRITUAL** Facilitates remembrance of past lives, success in positive magic

Owyhee Blue Opal weds the powers of perception, expression and will, enabling the user to see, speak and act with clarity, authority and confidence. It is an antidote to indecisiveness, shyness, fear, powerlessness, confusion, inarticulateness and other expressions of blocked energies. It is a stone of calm, quiet strength, allowing one to choose words, action or inaction as the best means of achieving one's purpose.

OPAL, VIOLET FLAME **KEY WORDS** Spiritual and energetic purification, emotional balance, angelic communication, link to the Violet Flame **CHAKRAS** All, especially Crown (7th) **ELEMENTS** Water, Wind, Storm **PHYSICAL** Facilitates release of stress, allowing the body to be guided by its innate wisdom **EMOTIONAL** Brings emotional harmony to the cells and the etheric body **SPIRITUAL** Cleanses and purifies etheric body and cellular energy matrix, enhances connection with angelic beings

Violet Flame Opal can spiritualize the emotions, transmuting them to higher forms of feeling. It stimulates spiritual awareness and communication with guardian angels and helping spirits. It cleanses and purifies the etheric body and the cellular energy matrix.

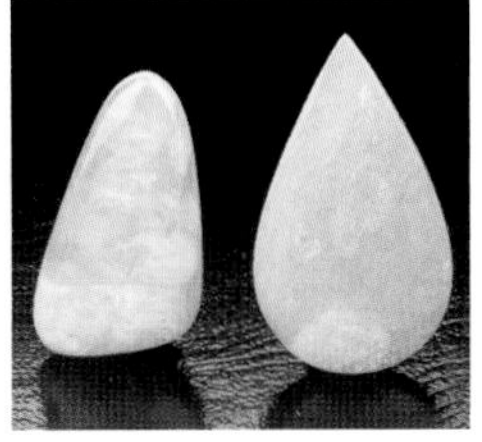

OPAL, WHITE PRECIOUS **KEY WORDS** Intensification of emotions, purification **CHAKRAS** All **ELEMENT** Water **PHYSICAL** Supports healing through release of negative patterns, aids with skin issues **EMOTIONAL** Powerfully stimulates emotional clearing and healing **SPIRITUAL** Facilitates inner cleansing that leads to link with the Higher Self

White Precious Opal is an emotional amplifier—it can intensify both the positive and negative states. In each case, there is a benefit. With positive emotions, the reward is obvious. But with negative feelings, the magnification can make one fully aware of the destruction such indulgences can bring about—and this helps one agree to release them. White Precious Opal can be a warm, friendly teacher or a severe one. It all depends on what we bring with us to the experience.

PAKULITE **KEY WORDS** Grounding at high energy, Life Force, creativity, personal power, sexual energies, youthfulness, intimate relationship with the Divine Feminine Earth **CHAKRAS** Root (1st), Sexual/Creative (2nd), Solar Plexus (3rd) **ELEMENTS** Earth, Fire **PHYSICAL** Supports the liver, kidneys, bladder and sexual organs **EMOTIONAL** Enhances one's optimism, humor, playfulness, self-confidence and eagerness for new adventures **SPIRITUAL** Arouses Life Force, creativity, will, persistence and personal power, facilitates relationship with the Spiritual Earth

Pakulite arouses Life Force, creativity and power. It helps artists find inspiration. It benefits love relationships with its vibration of intimacy. It kindles one's will and persistence. Pakulite stimulates youthfulness, vitality, optimism, humor, playfulness and eagerness for new adventures.

PAPAGOITE **KEY WORDS** Return to a state of grace, link with higher dimensions, transmutation of sorrow, crystallization of consciousness beyond the body **CHAKRAS** Third Eye (6th), Crown (7th), Etheric (8th–14th) **ELEMENT** Wind **PHYSICAL** Relief of pain from migraines, menstrual cramps, stress issues **EMOTIONAL** Aids with transmuting negative emotions into positive ones **SPIRITUAL** Stimulates the etheric body, awakens the Merkabah Vehicle

Papagoite's energies transform sorrow into happiness. It activates one's psychic abilities, and facilitates out-of-body travel. It stimulates the third eye chakra and enhances intuitive capacities. If one continues to work with Papagoite, one will experience the opening of the crown chakra and ultimately its linkage to the nonphysical chakras in the etheric body. Papagoite assists one in building the Merkabah Vehicle of Light.

PERIDOT **KEY WORDS** Increased prosperity, warmth, well-being **CHAKRAS** Solar Plexus (3rd), Heart (4th) **ELEMENT** Earth **PHYSICAL** Supports the heart and circulatory system, can be used to help one quit smoking **EMOTIONAL** Emanates well-being, helps one feel worthy and happy **SPIRITUAL** Aids in creating abundance, quiets spiritual fear, inspires generosity

Peridots are little green nuggets of positive power. They activate and harmonize the third and fourth chakras, creating an integration of Love and Will. They can assist in having the courage to act out the heart's desires, and to be generous to others. It is a stone of financial and spiritual abundance. It quiets spiritual fears and allows one to move forward on one's evolutionary path. Peridot can be used to bless and energize one's work.

PETALITE **KEY WORDS** Tranquillity, upliftment, expansion of awareness, manifesting, the spiritual in the physical, opening to the higher worlds **CHAKRAS** Third Eye (6th), Crown (7th), Etheric (8th–14th) **ELEMENT** Wind **PHYSICAL** Aids with stress relief, lowering high blood pressure, calming hyperactivity and mania **EMOTIONAL** Soothes the emotional body, supports healing of abuse issues **SPIRITUAL** Ideal for tuning to higher dimensions, expanding awareness

Petalite has a deep connection to the realm of Spirit. It can take one to an inner space of rest and healing, allowing one to bathe in the quiet bliss of the unencumbered spirit. Petalites are stones of vision. They can open the inner eye to the many mansions of the higher dimensions, allowing the questing mind to discover new horizons, and move toward one's highest destiny.

PETRIFIED WOOD **KEY WORDS** Steady growth, a strong body, past-life recall, inner peace **CHAKRAS** Root (1st), Third Eye (6th) **ELEMENT** Earth **PHYSICAL** Supports gradual increase of strength and vitality, aids the bones **EMOTIONAL** Encourages inner peace, patience, helps heal ancestral issues **SPIRITUAL** Opens visionary awareness of the deep past and past lives

Petrified Wood is a stone of patience, of slow, steady growth toward the goal of spiritual transformation. It is good for gradually strengthening the body, especially the spine and skeletal structure. It instills strength of character and helps one live by one's ideals. It gives one a sense of peace during times of change. It can be utilized to view the Akashic records of this planet. It assists in past-life recall and can help one ground insights gained from these experiences.

PHENACITE **KEY WORDS** Third eye activation, inner visions, interdimensional travel **CHAKRAS** 3rd Eye (6th), Crown (7th) **ELEMENT** Storm **PHYSICAL** Healing nerve damage and nervous system disorders **EMOTIONAL** Helps one find the courage to lead a spirit-centered life **SPIRITUAL** Catalyzes spiritual initiation

Phenacite activates the third eye, crown chakra and one's capacity for visionary experience. It is highly beneficial for Light Body activation and is the best stone for interdimensional travel. It can be used for communication with spirit guides, angelic beings and other entities of the higher domains. It opens the portals for inner journeying, allowing one to travel through corridors of sacred geometric forms.

PIEMONTITE **KEY WORDS** Intelligence of the heart, emotional healing, commitment to life, joy, purification of the blood and bodily tissues, Light Body activation **CHAKRA** Heart (4th) **ELEMENTS** Water, Earth, Wind **PHYSICAL** Supports the heart and circulatory system, aids in clearing the cells of toxic energies **EMOTIONAL** Dispels negative emotions, increases one's goodhearted enthusiasm for life **SPIRITUAL** Enhances consciousness of the heart, facilitates communion of mind and heart, helps heal and align one's energies, supports the formation of the Body of Light

Piemontite's currents move to the heart, filling it with strength, courage and a sense of purpose. It can evoke the heart's innate intelligence, help one understand the heart's way of thinking. It can heal the heart of grief and rekindle one's commitment to life, bringing a great upwelling of joy and enthusiasm for life.

PIETERSITE **KEY WORDS** Insight, intuition, increased power of the will, precognition, interdimensional travel, self-transformation **CHAKRAS** Solar Plexus (3rd), Third Eye (6th) **ELEMENT** Storm **PHYSICAL** Increases mental and physical energies, enhances overall vitality **EMOTIONAL** Empowers the will and lends self-confidence and fearlessness **SPIRITUAL** Highly spiritually activating, catalyzes peak experiences, powerful aid to manifestation

Pietersite creates a unified activation of the solar plexus and third eye, increasing the power of one's will and intuition. Under the influence of Pietersite, readers of tarot or other oracles will find their vision sharper and their predictions more exact. It enhances clarity of thought and intuitive leaps. The epiphanies seeded by Pietersite can lead to spontaneous blissful enlightenment.

PINK AMETHYST **KEY WORDS** Emotional healing, soul retrieval **CHAKRAS** Heart (4th) **ELEMENT** Water, Fire **PHYSICAL** Supports the heart **EMOTIONAL** Helps overcome numbness from trauma or emotional abuse **SPIRITUAL** Facilitates communication with loved ones who have died

Pink Amethyst is a beneficial stone for emotional healing. It helps one to make a loving connection with one's inner child, and to bring one's whole psyche into a state of union. It can be a positive catalyst for processing sorrow and grief, and it helps one keep the heart open, even through painful times. The comforting currents of these stones can help to restore joy and peace in one's heart and soul. It can be a valuable tool for shamanic practitioners who do soul retrieval work. It can facilitate communication with loved ones who have died, as well as one's spirit guides and angelic guardians.

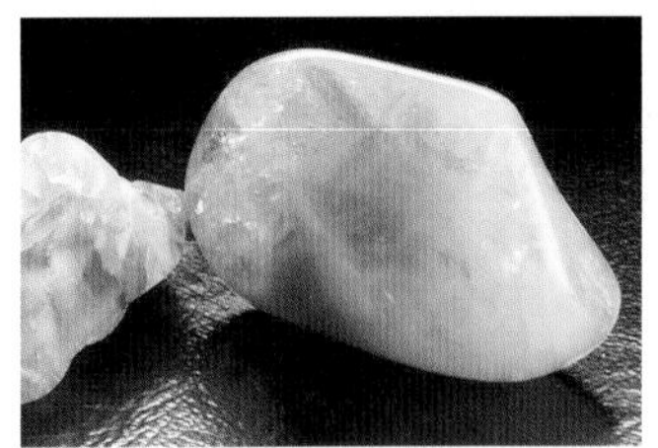

PRASIOLITE **KEY WORDS** Awakening the heart, linking the lower and higher self, deep connection with Nature **CHAKRAS** Heart (4th), Crown (7th), Third Eye (6th), Solar Plexus (3rd) **ELEMENT** Earth **PHYSICAL** Supports the stomach and the heart, aids with digestive issues **EMOTIONAL** Facilitates the joy of seeing the Divine in oneself and others **SPIRITUAL** Initiates one's experience of the Higher Self

Prasiolite carries the energetic link between the heart and crown chakras, and it can be a catalyst for the identification with the spiritual Higher Self. It assists in bringing spiritual ideals into expression in everyday life. It is a stone of *namaste,* the recognition of the Divine spark within all beings.

PREHNITE **KEY WORDS** Inner peace, union of the heart and the will, communication with non-physical beings **CHAKRAS** Solar Plexus (3rd), Heart (4th) **ELEMENT** Earth, Water **PHYSICAL** Supports digestive, circulatory, lymphatic and urinary systems **EMOTIONAL** Brings peaceful awareness, dispels worry and restlessness **SPIRITUAL** Attunes one to higher dimensions through heart awareness

Prehnite links the heart with the will. It quiets restlessness, nervousness and worry. It aids in contact with beings from other dimensions. It helps one to "hear" angelic communications, the guidance of spirit beings or the song of one's Higher Self. It can purify the energies of the digestive system, the kidneys, adrenals, liver and gallbladder.

PROPHECY STONE **KEY WORDS** Grounding spiritual Light in the physical self and the world, seeing prophetic visions **CHAKRAS** Soul Star (8th), Crown (7th), Third Eye (6th), Earthstar (below the feet) **ELEMENT** Earth **PHYSICAL** Clears the body of excess energy, removes energy blockages **EMOTIONAL** Allows one to feel the Earth's joy at receiving spiritual Light **SPIRITUAL** Aids one in Earth healing, stimulates capacity of prescience

Prophecy Stones are ideal for grounding spiritual Light in the physical body. Its energy comes in through the crown chakra, filling the body all the way down through the soles of the feet. This grounding of spiritual Light can heal both oneself and the Earth, and is hugely important in these times. Prophecy Stone can also catalyze visions of potential futures.

PROTECTOR QUARTZ **KEY WORDS** Spiritual protection, personal power **CHAKRAS** All **ELEMENT** Fire, Earth **PHYSICAL** Supports feet, toes, hands, head, spiritual aid for Parkinson's and autoimmune illnesses **EMOTIONAL** Facilitates strong sel-confidence, self-worth, overall happiness, dispels guilt and shame **SPIRITUAL** Stimulates inspiration, enhances courage, increases vitality

Protector Quartz clears one's vibrational field of all sorts of unpleasant attachments, implants, thought forms, parasitic entities, negative habit patterns, etc. It purifies and energizes the auric field and the entire chakra system. It brings subconscious problems to the surface for clearing and release. It stimulates inspiration, enhances courage, and increases vitality. It supports one's entire subtle body field, keeping the physical body from being degraded by psychic attacks or attachments.

PURPURITE **KEY WORDS** Purification, initiation, freedom, insight, truth, power, sovereignty **CHAKRAS** Crown (7th), Third Eye (6th) **ELEMENT** Wind, Earth **PHYSICAL** Supports the brain and nervous system, brings spiritual Light into the body **EMOTIONAL** Encourages release of fear, stress and worry **SPIRITUAL** Links one with spirit guides, increases one's capacity to understand oracles

Purpurite emanates an energy of psychic protection, keeping one's auric field free of negative entities and attachments. It is a stone of initiation, helping one to connect with spirit guides and to hear their advice clearly. It teaches one to love the unknown. It helps one keep digging for the reality that underlies appearances.

PYRITE **KEY WORDS** Masculine energy, manifestation, action, vitality, willpower, creativity, confidence **CHAKRAS** Solar Plexus (3rd) **ELEMENT** Earth **PHYSICAL** Supports male reproductive health, aids in fighting infection **EMOTIONAL** Encourages mastering fear, taking assertive action **SPIRITUAL** Promotes positive attitude and resolve, banishes negativity

Pyrite is excellent for increasing the power of the third chakra. It enhances willpower, assisting one in overcoming bad habits and establishing patterns of health and positive energy. It stimulates creativity in art, mathematics, sculpture, architecture, science and other disciplines. It feeds the qualities of ambition, commitment and persistence. It increases mental clarity and focus. It supports one in taking assertive action and developing the inner warrior.

PYROMORPHITE **KEY WORDS** Enhanced digestion and assimilation, discharge of toxic substances and energies, blending love and will **CHAKRAS** Solar Plexus (3rd), Heart (4th) **ELEMENT** Earth **PHYSICAL** Supports digestive system, liver, gallbladder, spleen, pancreas **EMOTIONAL** Increases understanding of intuition, helps cope with negativity **SPIRITUAL** Facilitates unification of heart and solar plexus

Pyromorphite vibrationally supports proper digestion and maintenance of the proper flora in the intestinal tract. It enhances the intuitive powers of the physical and etheric bodies, so one receives accurate "gut feelings." It helps one digest and assimilate new information and energies. It aids in eliminating bad habits and negative associations. It supports the liver, gallbladder, spleen and pancreas. It helps one calm anger and discharge negative thoughts. It aligns and blends love and will.

QUARTZ, CLEAR **KEY WORDS** Programmability, amplification of one's intention, magnification of ambient energies, clearing, cleansing, healing, memory **CHAKRAS** All **ELEMENT** Storm **PHYSICAL** Supports nervous system, can be programmed to assist in healing **EMOTIONAL** Can be used to intensify feelings and/or heal the emotional body **SPIRITUAL** Enhances clarity, aids communication with spirit guides

Clear Quartz can bring heightened spiritual awareness to whoever wears, carries or meditates with it. It can be used to amplify the energies of other stones. It is the perfect base material for energy tools such as wands, staffs, templates or "energy grids." It can be used for healing, consciousness expansion, chakra opening, communication with guides, past-life recall, interdimensional travel, polarity balancing, enhancement of meditation and dreaming, attracting and sending love, generating prosperity, etc.

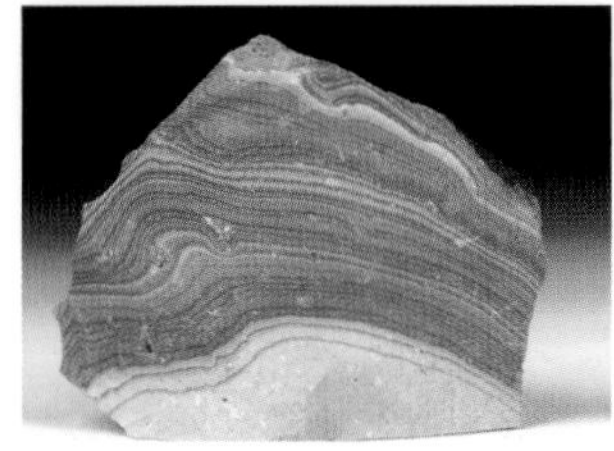

RATHBUNITE **KEY WORDS** Creative manifestation, fun and humor, developing psychic capacities, love, joy, pleasure and play **CHAKRAS** Solar Plexus (3rd), Heart (4th) **ELEMENTS** Earth, Water, Fire **PHYSICAL** Encourages production of endorphins, benefits the body through the positive mood it engenders **EMOTIONAL** Facilitates emotional healing, encourages playfulness and good humor **SPIRITUAL** Aids creative manifestation and development of psychic capacities, teaches lighthearted enjoyment of the spiritual path

Rathbunite enhances one's capacity to take on life's challenges with a buoyant spirit and good-natured determination. It inspires wit and verbal play. It is a stone of creative manifestation. It also stimulates the "sixth sense" and helps one develop latent psychic capacities.

REDWOOD OPAL **KEY WORDS** Emotional strength, confidence, vitality, perseverance, decisiveness, creativity, eroticism **CHAKRAS** Sexual/Creative (2nd), Solar Plexus (3rd) **ELEMENTS** Water, Fire **PHYSICAL** Supports the immune system, can increase overall energy and vitality **EMOTIONAL** Strengthens emotional body, enhances capacity to feel deeply without being discouraged, inspires confidence, encourages acceptance **SPIRITUAL** Aids in accepting problems of life without disheartenment, stimulates creativity, eroticism, confidence and spiritual fortitude

Redwood Opal strengthens the emotional body. It increases patience, and helps one to see things from a long-term perspective. Its strengthening of the emotional body enhances resilience to life's problems, and allows one to bear grief and loss without falling into depression.

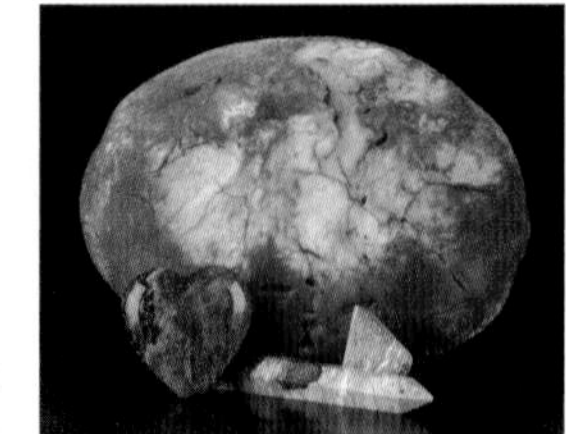

REVELATION STONE **KEY WORDS** Prophetic vision, psychic abilities, past-life recall, spirit communication, recovery of memory **CHAKRAS** Heart (4th), Third eye (6th) **ELEMENTS** Wind, Water, Storm **PHYSICAL** Steady healing influence to heart and brain, supports recovery of lost or suppressed memories **EMOTIONAL** Helps one to overcome fears about the future **SPIRITUAL** Stimulates visions of the futures, enhances past-life recall and intuitive capacities, aids communication with departed souls, strengthens understanding between the heart and brain

Revelation Stone stimulates the heart's consciousness of the unfolding pattern of the future. It can stimulate one's capacity for prophetic vision. It is excellent for anyone wishing to improve psychic capacities. It can bring vivid past-life recall, and can enhance shamanic experiences.

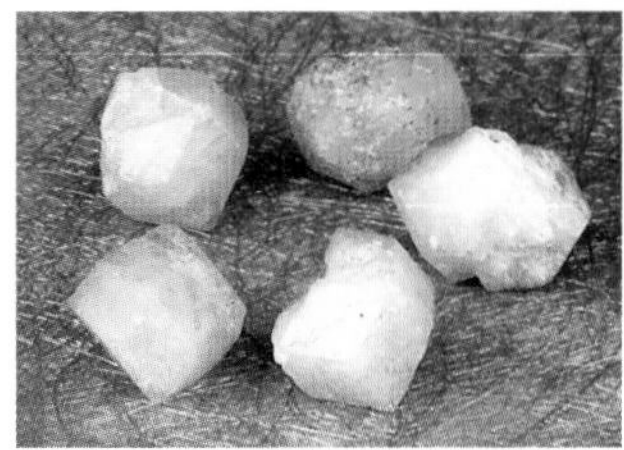

RHODIZITE **KEY WORDS** Magnifying energies of other stones, increasing personal power and confidence **CHAKRAS** Solar Plexus (3rd) **ELEMENT** Storm **PHYSICAL** Strengthens other healing stones, supports the head and eyes **EMOTIONAL** Inspires optimism, enthusiasm, transformation **SPIRITUAL** Enhances psychic ability, past-life recall, out-of-body travel

Rhodizite crystals vibrate with great power and intensity. They stimulate the solar plexus and are capable of increasing one's powers of will and manifestation. It also increases the power of other stones. Its amplification of energies can be especially helpful in healing. It can increase the effects of healing stones if it is touching them. Hands-on healers can increase the flow coming through them by using Rhodizite. It can enhance one's psychic abilities.

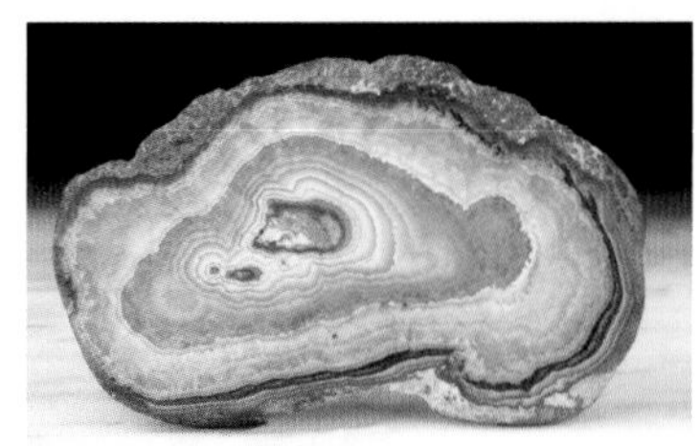

RHODOCROSITE **KEY WORDS** Emotional healing, recovery of lost memories and forgotten gifts, self-love, compassion **CHAKRAS** Heart (4th), Solar Plexus (3rd) **ELEMENT** Fire, Water **PHYSICAL** Helps with stress-related issues, heals the emotional body, repairs the aura **EMOTIONAL** Facilitates deep healing of inner child and past-life issues **SPIRITUAL** Profound link with Love energy, enhances creativity, brings joy

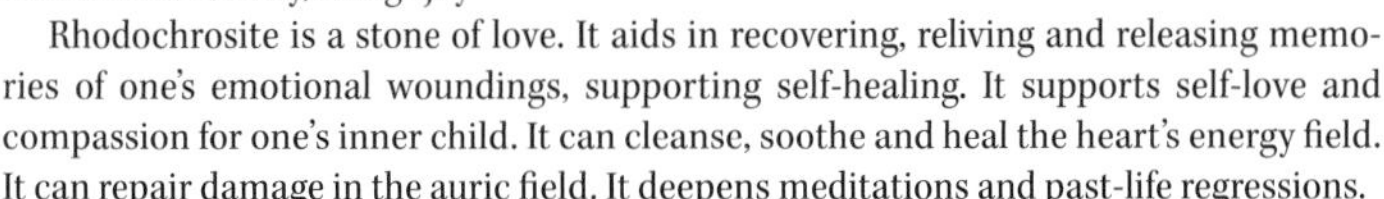

Rhodochrosite is a stone of love. It aids in recovering, reliving and releasing memories of one's emotional woundings, supporting self-healing. It supports self-love and compassion for one's inner child. It can cleanse, soothe and heal the heart's energy field. It can repair damage in the auric field. It deepens meditations and past-life regressions.

RHODONITE **KEY WORDS** Discovering and developing hidden talents, compassion, love, generosity, altruism **CHAKRAS** Heart (4th), Root (1st) **ELEMENT** Fire, Earth **PHYSICAL** Supports weight loss, detoxification and purification, good for liver and kidneys **EMOTIONAL** Encourages altruism and generosity, the joy of serving others **SPIRITUAL** Helps realize one's unique capacities and fulfill one's destiny

Rhodonite promotes the energy of love. It encourages using one's talents for the benefit of the community. It encourages altruism and generosity. It can enhance the depth, clarity and meaning of one's inner experiences, making it easier to understand the messages behind one's dreams and visions. It supports one in taking actions that serve one's highest destiny.

ROSE QUARTZ **KEY WORDS** Love, gentleness, emotional healing, release of stress, uniting with the Divine **CHAKRAS** Heart (4th) **ELEMENT** Water **PHYSICAL** Supports the heart in healing from trauma and/or disease **EMOTIONAL** Aids in releasing past wounds, teaches trust and hope **SPIRITUAL** Encourages spirituality of love, links one with the Great Mother

Rose Quartz is the pure stone of love—for oneself, one's partner, children, family, friends, community, the Earth, the Universe and the Divine. Its soothing vibrations are a balm to the emotions, and they calm and cleanse the entire auric field. It engenders the release of tension and stress, the dissolution of anger and resentment, the dispelling of fear and suspicion and the rebirth of hope and faith. It brings the crown, third eye and throat chakras into harmony and unity with the heart.

ROSOPHIA **KEY WORDS** The Love of Sophia, awakening of Heart Awareness, co-creating with the Divine, alchemical transmutation of self and world **CHAKRAS** Heart (4th) **ELEMENT** Earth **PHYSICAL** Supports healing of the heart, brings Love into the cells **EMOTIONAL** Powerfully awakens and deepens one's experience of Love **SPIRITUAL** Allows for co-creative ecstatic union with the Soul of the World

Rosophia brings one's personal heart into resonant union with the Heart of Sophia, the Divine Feminine Wisdom principle which underlies the beauty and harmony of the world. Sleeping with Rosophia near the heart engenders peaceful sleep. It can dispel depression and frustration, instilling a calm, loving presence.

ROSWELLITE **KEY WORDS** Sacred geometry, paranormal events, activating latent capacities **CHAKRAS** Third Eye (6th), Heart (4th) **ELEMENT** Wind, Fire **PHYSICAL** Supports pre-frontal cortex, can trigger whole-brain activation **EMOTIONAL** Facilitates the exhilaration of awakening **SPIRITUAL** Stimulates interdimensional travel and expanded consciousness

The inner universe is formed according to the patterns known as Sacred Geometry. Perhaps the most famous of these patterns is the Flower of Life. In Roswellite, we see a resonance with that universal pattern. The interdimensional gates one can enter appear as geometric corridors of Light. And as the Flower of Life shows, the dimensional corridors are linked and intertwined with one another. With the aid of Roswellite, one can travel along a vast array of Light pathways to many other worlds.

ROYAL SAHARA JASPER **KEY WORDS** Vitality, fertility, will, courage, creativity, prophetic vision **CHAKRAS** All **ELEMENT** Earth **PHYSICAL** Supports digestive system, liver, spleen; increases energy level **EMOTIONAL** Lends courage to express one's truth and to act from love **SPIRITUAL** Aids self-discipline, persistence

Royal Sahara Jasper stimulates the first three chakras, enhancing one's vitality, creative fertility and will. It resonates with the heart, engendering gentle, loving energy. At the throat, it activates one's capacity to courageously speak (or write) the truth of one's heart. It also stimulates the third eye, bringing perceptions of spiritual shifts and changes coming in the future.

RUBY **KEY WORDS** Life force, courage, passion, strength, enthusiasm, adventurousness, protectiveness **CHAKRAS** Root (1st) **ELEMENT** Earth **PHYSICAL** Increases the chi in the body, stimulates health in all organs and systems **EMOTIONAL** Inspires self-confidence, zest for life, trust and willingness **SPIRITUAL** Instills spiritual courage and altruism, brings forth heroism

Ruby emanates the pure Red Ray with an unsurpassed vibrancy. It powerfully stimulates the root chakra, infusing one with life force. It energizes and activates the physical, mental and emotional bodies. It enhance passion and fortitude, for the wholehearted pursuit of one's aspirations. It eliminates feelings of hopelessness or defeat, supporting optimism and determination. It imparts courage, self-confidence, adventurousness, and enthusiasm for life. It is a magnet for novelty and adventure.

RUBY FUCHSITE **KEY WORDS** Strong emotional body, valuing of oneself, increased life force **CHAKRAS** Base (1st), Heart (4th) **ELEMENT** Water **PHYSICAL** Infuses body with prana; supports bowels, heart, cells, organs **EMOTIONAL** Encourages self-esteem, aids healing of relationship issues **SPIRITUAL** Inspires one to heal oneself, instills awareness of the deep Self

Ruby Fuchsite combines the courage, strength and passion of Ruby, and is known by its calming, nourishing currents. It empowers and strengthens the emotional body. It fosters a sense of health and well-being in both the emotional and physical self. Ruby Fuchsite stimulates the root and heart chakras, bringing an infusion of life force. It energetically clears the bowels and stimulates the elimination process. It dispels sluggish energies in the heart, encouraging the body to clear arterial blockages.

RUBY KYANITE **KEY WORDS** Life Force, courage, passion, intuition, psychic ability, inspiration, visionary awareness **CHAKRAS** All, especially Root (1st), and Third Eye (6th) **ELEMENTS** Earth, Storm **PHYSICAL** Supports the brain and nervous system, sexual organs, bowels and intestines **EMOTIONAL** Quickens the formation of intimate relationships and enhances mutual attraction **SPIRITUAL** Stimulates intuitive awareness and inner visions, enhances courage, passion and commitment to spiritual development

Ruby Kyanite stimulates intuition, psychic abilities, awareness of the wisdom of dreams, and one's ability to navigate the spiritual realms. It facilitates expanded awareness and spiritual sensitivity, and enhances courage, strength and sense of adventure.

RUTILATED QUARTZ **KEY WORDS** Programmable for attunement, amplification, acceleration, expanding awareness, quickening and grounding manifestation **CHAKRAS** All **ELEMENT** Storm **PHYSICAL** Supports a speedy healing process, aids hair growth and quality **EMOTIONAL** Intensifies feelings, quickens emotional catharsis, breeds optimism **SPIRITUAL** Aids telepathy and intuition, amplifies one's power of manifestation

Rutilated Quartz can be used to magnify the energy of any intention or affirmation. It helps one instantly know if a person or situation carries good or bad "vibes." It amplifies intentions and emotions. It enhances manifestation, intuition, emotional catharsis, psychic opening, consciousness expansion and interdimensional travel.

RUTILE **KEY WORDS** Attunement, amplification, acceleration, expanding awareness, quickening manifestation **CHAKRAS** All **ELEMENT** Storm **PHYSICAL** Aids digestive system, helps overcome addictions **EMOTIONAL** Inspires active, enthusiastic engagement with life; dispels passivity **SPIRITUAL** Enhances meditative journeying, dream recall, link with higher realms

Rutile allows one to enhance synchronicities and experiences of grace. It can magnify and accelerate the effects of one's intention and is an aid to manifestation. It can amplify the energy of consciousness, opening access to the higher worlds. It enhances manifestation, intuition, emotional catharsis, psychic opening, consciousness expansion, interdimensional travel, learning and the creative process. It stimulates leaps of insight. It accelerates the accumulation of wealth and the implementation of new ideas.

SAPPHIRE, BLUE **KEY WORDS** Awareness, discipline **CHAKRAS** Third Eye (6th), Throat (5th) **ELEMENT** Wind, Earth **PHYSICAL** Aids healing of headaches, vertigo, earaches, vision **EMOTIONAL** Encourages inner strength and confidence **SPIRITUAL** Enhances psychic abilities, mental clarity and insight

Blue Sapphire is a stone of mental and psychic activation, an enhancer of insight, ESP and mental agility. It helps one to see below surface appearances to the underlying truth and to speak clearly with the voice of inner wisdom. It is associated with the planet Saturn, the archetype of order, structure, limitation and discipline. It is ideal for organizing one's ideas and perceptions and bringing them into form. It facilitates the integrated awakening and utilization of the throat and third eye chakras. It stimulates psychic abilities and activates one's higher intelligence. It allows one to act as a conduit for information from the higher planes.

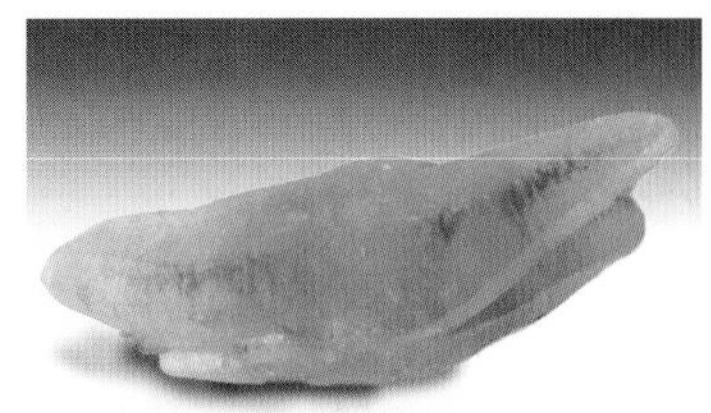

SAPPHIRE, PADPARADSCHA **KEY WORDS** Creativity, sexuality and zest for life, loving creation **CHAKRAS** Sexual/Creative (2nd), Heart (4th) **ELEMENT** Fire **PHYSICAL** Enhances sexual energies, supports reproductive health **EMOTIONAL** Encourages playfulness, sociability, zest for life and love **SPIRITUAL** Inspires creative expression, brings liveliness into spiritual life

Padparadscha Sapphire blazes with the fire of life force and creative energies. It helps one feel at home in the world, encouraging one to revel and delight in the sensory experiences of life. It can aid one in finding greater zest and enthusiasm in one's sex life, and opens the floodgates of one's creative nature. It can assist in developing more vitality.

SAPPHIRE, PINK **KEY WORDS** Love, forgiveness **CHAKRAS** Heart (4th) **ELEMENT** Water, Fire **PHYSICAL** Supports heart and bloodstream, vibrationally helps balance blood sugar and glucose metabolism **EMOTIONAL** Encourages gentleness and compassion in relationships **SPIRITUAL** Provides courage to love without fear and to act with generosity

Pink Sapphire stimulates love, forgiveness, acceptance and release. It holds the power of vulnerability. It encourages one to be yielding, engendering the strength of resilience. It allows one to weather the storms of life without damage. It assists in healing the wounds of past traumas, and it facilitates compassion for others, even those who have wronged us. It evokes the energy of the heart and conjoins it with the power of the disciplined mind.

SAPPHIRE, WHITE **KEY WORDS** Awareness, clarity, discernment **CHAKRAS** Third Eye (6th), Crown (7th) **ELEMENT** Wind **PHYSICAL** Stimulates pineal and pituitary glands, supports brain function **EMOTIONAL** Helps overcome fear of fulfilling one's spiritual purpose **SPIRITUAL** Supports mental and spiritual clarity, link with the Higher Self

White Sapphire helps one combine spiritual insight with earthly tasks or dilemmas. It stimulates the third eye and crown chakras and activates energy meridians in the brain, helping one to tune in to spirit guides, angels and even humans who have "crossed over." It assists one in developing the qualities of fairness, discernment and objectivity, and in maintaining a spiritual perspective in all situations.

SAPPHIRE, YELLOW **KEY WORDS** Abundance, strength of will **CHAKRAS** Solar Plexus (3rd) **ELEMENT** Fire **PHYSICAL** Aids the body's vitality and digestion, supports the spleen **EMOTIONAL** Allows one to playfully enjoy one's work and creative activity **SPIRITUAL** Strong ally for manifestation of wealth and one's highest visions

Yellow Sapphire can assist in bringing financial abundance, and in manifesting one's visions. It provides the ideal vibration of the third chakra, seat of the will. With them, one can focus one's intention for the achievement of almost any aim. With the help of Yellow Sapphire, those who clearly sustain their visions long enough will discover that their own thoughts can indeed come into being. This sustaining of one's vision is sometimes called faith, but one might also describe it as will, the awakened third chakra.

SATYA MANI QUARTZ **KEY WORDS** Spiritual truth and enlightenment **CHAKRAS** Third Eye (6th), Crown (7th) **ELEMENT** Wind **PHYSICAL** Stimulates neural links between heart and brain **EMOTIONAL** Promotes nonjudgment, kindness, compassion and love **SPIRITUAL** Triggers experiences of *satori*

Satya Mani Quartz attunes one to hear the inner call of one's path of destiny. It is a stone of enlightenment, bringing the light of Truth into one's mind by virtue of its connection to the heart. It inspires the expression of truth and the commitment to kindness, clear awareness, nonjudgment and compassion. It intensifies the link between the heart and the high brain, leading to a single unified awareness.

SCAPOLITE **KEY WORDS** Insight, persistence, self-discipline, willpower, self-transformation, liberation **CHAKRAS** **ALL** **ELEMENT** Storm **PHYSICAL** Helps bring the Divine blueprint of health into integration with the body **EMOTIONAL** Encourages pride in accomplishment, inspires dedication to one's highest aspirations **SPIRITUAL** Supports the achievement of one's destiny and freedom

Scapolite helps one develop the self-discipline and willpower to attain inner freedom. Its key phrase is "strength of purpose." It is a stone of destiny, and it helps one hear the voice of the Higher Self. It can illuminate the memory of past lives. It assists one in going down into the psyche to discover what is holding one back and what must be overcome.

SCHEELITE **KEY WORDS** Expanding consciousness beyond the body, linking mental and heart awareness, activating one's higher spiritual capacities **CHAKRAS** Third Eye (6th), Crown (7th), Soul Star (8th), Heart (4th) **ELEMENT** Wind, Storm **PHYSICAL** Supports nervous system, helps dispel headaches **EMOTIONAL** Quiets the inner judge, instills deep tranquility **SPIRITUAL** Facilitates access to Akashic records and the morphogenic fields of knowledge

Scheelite is one of the premier stones for expanding one's self-awareness beyond the boundaries of the physical body. Like Herderite, Scheelite allows one to sense oneself as a field or "bubble" of consciousness, with the physical body at the center. It can also facilitate out-of-body astral travel, and interdimensional travel to many of the higher realms.

SCOLECITE **KEY WORDS** Inner peace, relaxation, tranquillity, interdimensional travel, awakening the heart **CHAKRAS** Third Eye (6th), Crown (7th) **ELEMENT** Wind **PHYSICAL** Spiritually supports stable brain function and serotonin levels **EMOTIONAL** Aids emotional stability, tranquility and serenity **SPIRITUAL** Facilitates link to higher realms

Scolecite emanates deep peace that resonates throughout one's auric field. It enhances meditation, restful sleep and /or pleasant dreams. It offers protection from negative astral energies, lifting one to the higher vibrational planes. It assists interdimensional journeys and time travel, allowing one to access knowledge from ancient and even "future" civilizations. It enhances heart energies, encouraging the spontaneous expression of love.

SEDONALITE **KEY WORDS** Balance, inner harmony, psychic sensitivity, inspiration, optimism, awakening **CHAKRAS** All **ELEMENT** Storm **PHYSICAL** Supports brain and nervous system **EMOTIONAL** Inspires optimism, enthusiasm, willingness to transform **SPIRITUAL** Enhances psychic ability, past-life recall, visionary experience,

Sedonalite can charge and harmonize the meridian system, bringing the astral and subtle bodies into alignment with the physical. It is both grounding and stimulating, engendering heightened sensitivity and alertness. It heightens psychic capacities, enhancing one's natural sensitivities. It can clear mental fog, fatigue and dullness, and jump start one's enthusiasm. It accelerates spiritual growth, and facilitates extraordinary visions.

SELENITE **KEY WORDS** Spiritual activation, communion with the Higher Self, spirit guides and angels **CHAKRAS** Third Eye (6th), Crown (7th), Etheric (8th–14th) **ELEMENT** Wind **PHYSICAL** Clears energy blockages, induces inner alignment, facilitates healing **EMOTIONAL** Inspires one to release insecurity **SPIRITUAL** Facilitates auric cleansing, upper chakra activation

Selenite quickly opens and activates the third eye and crown chakras, and the Soul Star chakra above the head. It is fast and effective at cleansing the auric field, and it can clear congested energies or negativity from one's physical and etheric body. It can lift one's awareness to higher planes, making it possible to consciously meet one's spirit guides and guardian angels. It is an excellent stone for building energy grids. A group of six or more wands around one's body puts one into a mini energy vortex!

SERAPHINITE **KEY WORDS** Self-healing, regeneration, wholeness, angelic connection **CHAKRAS** All **ELEMENT** Earth **PHYSICAL** Supports cellular health, can be used in spiritual healing to reduce the activity of cancer cells **EMOTIONAL** Aids release of toxic emotions, encourages a joyful attitude **SPIRITUAL** Assists communication with angels, devas, Nature spirits

Seraphinite is among the most powerful stones for bringing all the elements of the nonphysical bodies into alignment. It can move blocked energies in the meridians and can be successfully combined with acupuncture. It imbues the auric field with currents of wholeness and well-being. This highly evolved stone can powerfully accelerate one's evolution. It resonates with the angelic domain. Those who wish to meet angels in meditation or dreaming can use this stone to facilitate this attunement.

SERIPHOS GREEN QUARTZ **KEY WORDS** Awareness of the Earth as Paradise, joyful acceptance of physical life, healing **CHAKRAS** Heart (4th) **ELEMENT** Earth **PHYSICAL** Supports enjoyment and love of the body, dispels negative attachments, aids in rejuvenation **EMOTIONAL** Inspires a joyful embrace of life and the Earth **SPIRITUAL** Transmits the regenerative, ecstatic energies of Nature

Seriphos Green Quartz emanates a sweet, strong vibration that evokes the state of wholesome enjoyment of physical life and facilitates the attainment of vibrant good health. It helps the user or wearer to be grounded in the best possible way—through love for the material world and one's place within it. It reminds us that we too are blooms brought forth from the womb of the fertile Earth, and our experience of life can be exquisite when we bring our attention to its beauty and pleasure.

SERPENTINE **KEY WORDS** Awakening of higher brain functions, connection with Nature, kundalini awakening **CHAKRAS** All **ELEMENT** Earth **PHYSICAL** Aids in rewiring neural pathways so higher brain areas predominate and guide behavior **EMOTIONAL** Helps one release fear of change and embrace transformation **SPIRITUAL** Assists in awakening kundalini energies for personal evolution

Serpentine is one of the best stones for rousing the kundalini energies. It can be placed on the meridian points for clearing blocked energies and allowing for a healthy flow. It can bring the old reptilian brain into the service of the higher brain. It can help establish the order intended by Nature, bringing one peace and joy.

SHAMAN STONE **KEY WORDS** Shamanic journeying, soul retrieval, polarity balancing, psychic protection, intuition **CHAKRAS** All **ELEMENT** Earth **PHYSICAL** Supports the thyroid and adrenals, can be programmed to assist any organ or system **EMOTIONAL** Helps one overcome fear of death through discovery of the spiritual worlds **SPIRITUAL** Aids inner journeys, provides protection and discernment

Shaman Stones are excellent talismans for those engaged in shamanic journeying, rebirthing, holotropic breathwork or other forms of transformational inner work. They guide one to the experiences most beneficial to healing the soul and advancing one's spiritual growth. They offer psychic protection to inner journeyers. They help those unfamiliar with shamanic work to perceive and connect with power animals and spirit helpers. They balance one's vibrational field and harmonize the meridian system.

SHANTILITE **KEY WORDS** The "peace that passes understanding," inner silence, harmony **CHAKRAS** All **ELEMENT** Wind, Fire **PHYSICAL** Supports recuperation from injury and illness, dispels stress **EMOTIONAL** Quiets worry and anxiety, leads one into profound peace **SPIRITUAL** Aids meditation and prayer through quieting the mind

Shantilite is an excellent stone for meditation. It can bring one into a state of deep inner silence. It can help one clear away repeating loops of worry and anxiety. As a stone of deep peace, it can alleviate stress-related pathologies. It is ideal for those recuperating from any illness or injury. Shantilite can be an aid to prayer, and it helps one commune with the angelic realm. It aids in the Ascension process.

SHATTUCKITE **KEY WORDS** Intuition, communication, channeling, mediumship, work with oracles **CHAKRAS** Heart (4th), Throat (5th), Third Eye (6th) **ELEMENT** Water, Wind **PHYSICAL** Supports balance of the visceral organs and their fluids **EMOTIONAL** Helps one embrace truth and release fears, including fears of the spirit realms **SPIRITUAL** Aids attunement to inner guidance and spirit communication

Shattuckite can open one's psychic channel, enabling one to "hear" messages from inner guides, teachers, and spirits of the deceased. If one wishes to work as a medium, it is an ideal ally. It facilitates automatic writing and channeling. It helps one find the right words to express the communications from spirit guides and teachers. It facilitates synesthesia and stimulates mental and intuitive abilities. It is helpful for those studying astrology, tarot, runes, palmistry, the I Ching and other oracular guides.

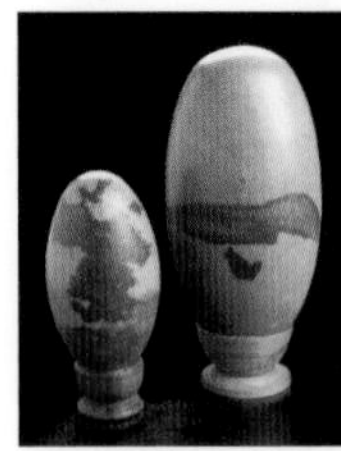

SHIVA LINGAM **KEY WORDS** Kundalini activation, vitality and *prana*, spiritual transformation and rebirth, enlightenment, oneness with the All **CHAKRAS** All **ELEMENT** Earth, Wind, Water, Fire, Storm **PHYSICAL** Stimulates all one's energy systems, treats impotence and infertility **EMOTIONAL** Helps one to merge ecstatically with the Divine **SPIRITUAL** Can awaken Kundalini energies and bring about *samadhi*

Shiva Lingams are capable of activating kundalini energies and charging the chakra system. They can boost vitality and energize the meridian system. Shiva Lingams have a powerful morphic field, allowing one to benefit from the efforts of those who have used such stones in spiritual pursuits throughout history. Through crystal resonance, any Shiva Lingam can connect to all others throughout the world. Through this power, they can be emblems of inner transformation.

SHUNGITE **KEY WORDS** Cleansing and purification, infusion of spiritual Light, activation of the Light Body, adherence to truth **CHAKRAS** All **ELEMENTS** Fire, Wind, Storm **PHYSICAL** Purifies the body, preparing it to be transformed by an infusion of spiritual Light **EMOTIONAL** Rids one of negative emotional patterns, can generate emotional rebirth **SPIRITUAL** Prepares one for Light Body activation, cleansing, balancing and aligning all the particles of the body

Shungite operates vibrationally on the molecular level, freeing the atoms of one's body from their bondage to negative patterns and energies. It can clear the body of dysfunctional patterns manifesting as disease, emotional difficulties or various types of negativity. It provides an aura of psychic protection, primarily because of the energetic alignment it facilitates.

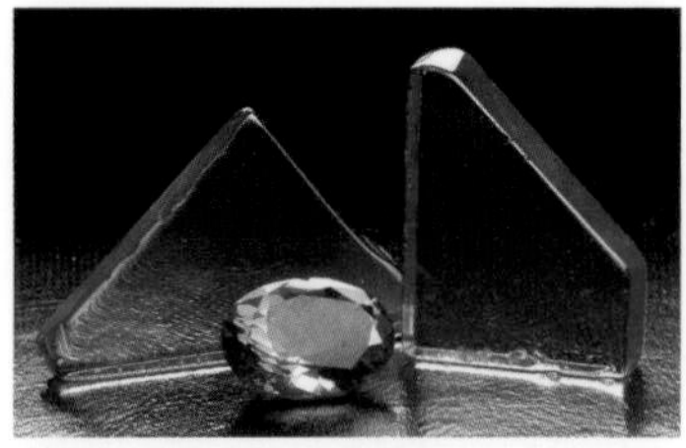

SIBERIAN BLUE QUARTZ **KEY WORDS** Psychic awakening, mediumship, mental clarity and insight, feeling at home on the Earth **CHAKRAS** Third Eye (6th), Throat (5th) **ELEMENT** Wind, Water **PHYSICAL** Supports brain function and healing, aids with memory issues **EMOTIONAL** Helps "Star Children" and sensitives feel comfortable on Earth **SPIRITUAL** Opens latent capacities for receiving information from Spirit

Siberian Blue Quartz activates the throat chakra and the third eye, awakening the higher mind and facilitating the eloquent communication of its knowledge. It can enhance clairvoyance, clairaudience, clairsentience, prophecy, psychokinesis, mediumship and interdimensional communication.

SILLIMANITE **KEY WORDS** Unification and harmonization of the chakras, focus and self-discipline, self-mastery and magic, bringing order from chaos **CHAKRAS** All **ELEMENT** Earth **PHYSICAL** Supports bodily order and harmony, can be used to combat illnesses in which part of the body attacks itself **EMOTIONAL** Stimulates optimism and happiness through bringing coherence to one's thoughts, energies and actions **SPIRITUAL** Helps unify energies and actions, aids in creating order, and feeds enthusiasm for life

Sillimanite stimulates and unifies the chakras, making them flow more strongly. It is a stone of self-mastery and therefore of magic, aiding one with manifestation. It encourages the emergence of order from chaos, and brings mental and emotional clarity. It can stimulate the release of endorphins, and it encourages optimism and enthusiasm. It supports and unifies all of one's organs and systems.

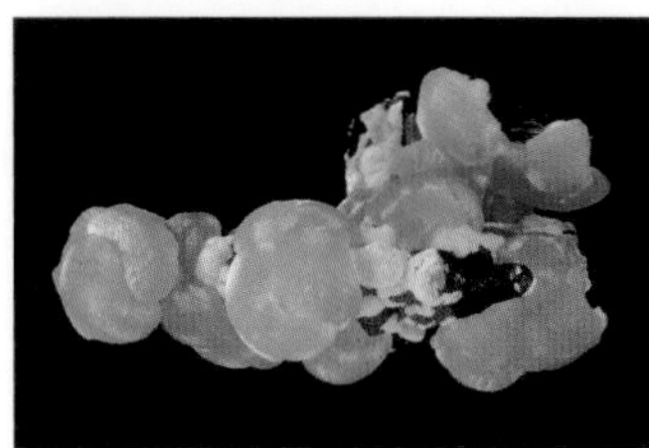

SMITHSONITE **KEY WORDS** Soothing the emotions, release of stress, deepening of love and compassion, relaxing into deeper perception **CHAKRAS** All **ELEMENT** Water **PHYSICAL** Aids in weight reduction, increases vitality, supports endocrine system and reproductive organs **EMOTIONAL** Dispels fear, anxiety and tension; encourages trust and relaxation **SPIRITUAL** Opens psychic channels, instills awareness of Oneness

Smithsonite cools anger and resentment, allowing one to reestablish the awareness of Oneness. It unwinds tension and dispels anxiety. It emanates calm and clarity, encouraging one to view difficult situations with compassionate eyes. It allows one to see Light even in dark times. Carrying or wearing Smithsonite is like having a caring friend by one's side.

SMOKY QUARTZ **KEY WORDS** Grounding, transmutation of negative energies, practicality, organization, manifestation of one's dreams and inspirations **CHAKRAS** Root (1st) **ELEMENT** Earth **PHYSICAL** Offers spiritual protection from radiation, dispels the effects of negative energies **EMOTIONAL** Helps ungrounded people engage with physical life **SPIRITUAL** Protective and grounding, manifests the spiritual in the physical

Smoky Quartz can help even the spaciest individuals get their "land legs" so they can fully function as physical beings. It enhances practicality and organization. It offers protection from negative energies in one's environment. It can draw the ethereal into manifestation, allowing one to see ghosts, UFOs, fairies and spirit guides.

SODALITE **KEY WORDS** Access to subconscious and intuitive abilities, enhanced insight and mental performance, deepened intuition **CHAKRAS** Third Eye (6th) **ELEMENT** Wind **PHYSICAL** Supports maintenance of healthy blood pressure and hydration **EMOTIONAL** Aids one's insight, allowing understanding of emotional issues **SPIRITUAL** Conjoins mental acuity and psychic ability for wider awareness

Sodalite helps one penetrate paradox and contradiction to form a new synthesis of thought. It enhances the mental powers of analysis, intuition, observation and creativity. It facilitates self-discipline, efficiency, organization and structure. It provides insight into one's motivations, strengths, weaknesses, desires, gifts and patterns of destiny.

SPHALERITE **KEY WORDS** Physical strength, vitality, grounding, balance, discrimination **CHAKRAS** Root (1st), Sexual/Creative (2nd), Solar Plexus (3rd) **ELEMENT** Earth, Fire **PHYSICAL** Supports immune system, increases stamina and energy level **EMOTIONAL** Helps one discern truth and overcome emotional bias **SPIRITUAL** Enhances life force, sexuality, creativity and manifestation

Sphalerite energizes the first chakra, increasing one's life force, courage, strength, vitality, sexual energy, creative inspiration and zest for life. It strengthens the third chakra, for greater success in manifestation, clearer thinking and more willpower. It helps one draw energy up from the Earth and release excess energy down into the Earth. It helps one distinguish between true spiritual insights and wishful thinking. It can aid those who consult oracles in making correct interpretations.

SPHENE **KEY WORDS** Mental clarity and quickness, accelerated learning, intuition, focused will **CHAKRAS** Third Eye (6th), Solar Plexus (3rd) **ELEMENT** Storm, Wind **PHYSICAL** Supports the bones, hearing and vision; stimulates the brain **EMOTIONAL** Instills enjoyment of mental activity, pride in accomplishment **SPIRITUAL** Enhances willpower and manifestation, attunes to Christ consciousness

Sphene can clear the mind and stimulate thinking. It assists memory. It can aid in learning a new language or a completely new discipline. It strengthens intuitive abilities and is useful in learning esoteric disciplines such as astrology, numerology or kabbalah. It can activate the solar plexus chakra, increasing the will's capacity to manifest one's projects, dreams and desires.

SPINEL **KEY WORDS** Revitalization, inspiration, new hope, victory, re-energizing all levels of the self **CHAKRAS** Crown (7th), Solar Plexus (3rd) **ELEMENT** Storm **PHYSICAL** Supports convalescence, overcoming fatigue, trauma, illness **EMOTIONAL** Encourages optimism and hopes, dispels negative thoughts **SPIRITUAL** Loosens past limitations, inspires self-transformation

Spinel is a stone of revitalization. It can bring fresh energy where it is most needed. It is excellent for reducing fatigue, replenishing depleted energies and recovering from illness or trauma. It is a stone of new hope. It can relieve the burden of negative thoughts and remind one that life is a gift. It can be a catalyst for inspiration and new ways of thinking. It can even facilitate the process of building a new self-image, allowing one to free the mind and transform into one's highest self.

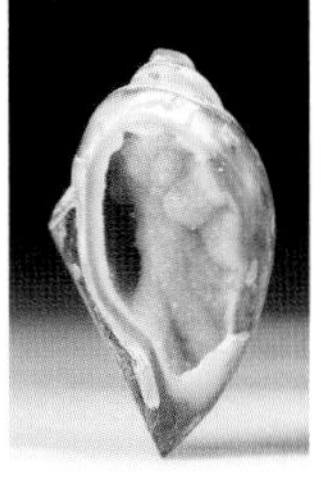

SPIRALITE GEMSHELLS **KEY WORDS** Preservation of life, longevity, access to information on higher levels, telepathic link with cetaceans and other sea creatures, DNA evolution **CHAKRAS** Third Eye (6th), Crown (7th) **ELEMENTS** Water, Earth **PHYSICAL** Supports bodily stamina, recovery from illness, longevity and the evolution of DNA **EMOTIONAL** Evokes the feeling of kinship with all living things and with crystalline life as well **SPIRITUAL** Brings the spiraling energies of universal vitality into one's consciousness, energy systems and cells

Spiralite Gemshells bridge the boundary between the animal and mineral worlds, making it easier for one to access crystal energies. They carry the memory of life in Earth's ancient times, and can refresh the etheric body, offering healing to one's whole being. They are powerful aids to telepathic communication with beings of the sea such as whales, dolphins and even fish! They are stones of longevity, and can "teach" one's DNA to renew itself.

SPIRIT QUARTZ **KEY WORDS** Merging with the Higher Self, purification, protection, spiritual evolution, freedom from fear **CHAKRAS** Crown (7th), Solar Plexus (3rd) **ELEMENT** Storm **PHYSICAL** Shields etheric body, keeps negative energy from causing disease **EMOTIONAL** Cleanses the emotional body, instills inner peace **SPIRITUAL** Links one with the Higher Self, strengthens one's will forces

Spirit Quartz aligns the everyday "local self" with the Higher Self, and assists the Higher Self in manifesting through one's human form. Amethyst-colored Spirit Quartz links one's conscious mind to the Higher Self, allowing one to comprehend and express the knowledge one receives. The Citrine variety works through the third chakra, causing one to act directly from the will of the Higher Self. In meditation, Spirit Quartz can bring peace of mind and freedom from fear.

STAUROLITE **KEY WORDS** Grounding and physical well-being, linking with the near realms of fairies, devas, animal and plant consciousness **CHAKRAS** Root (1st), Heart (4th), Third Eye (6th), Crown (7th) **ELEMENT** Earth **PHYSICAL** Helps one stop self-destructive habits, aids cleansing practices **EMOTIONAL** Opens one to the beauty and love of the soul of Nature **SPIRITUAL** Enhances astral travel, animal communication, lucid dreaming

Staurolite attunes to other dimensions close to our own. It is a key to the astral plane, the devic realm, and the fairie world, and it can be used to communicate with plant and animal spirits. Sleeping with a Staurolite crystal can initiate astral travel or lucid dreaming. It can also aid in giving up self-destructive habits and going through cleansing regimens.

STIBNITE **KEY WORDS** Attunement with new frequencies, transformation, new perspectives, prosperity, enhancement of personal power **CHAKRAS** All **ELEMENT** Earth **PHYSICAL** Supports healing of infections, parasitic invasions, skin eruptions **EMOTIONAL** Helps overcome feelings of powerlessness and fear **SPIRITUAL** Aids in manifestation of wealth, facilitates self-transformation

Stibnite carries the power of the underworld. It emanates Plutonic energies of transformation, death and rebirth, new perspectives, great wealth and power. It can aid in making profound changes in the self. If one dreams of a completely different career, spiritual life, self-image or outer personality, Stibnite can magnetize the experiences, people and synchronicities to make it so. In regard to acquiring wealth, Stibnite can be effective in attracting new opportunities through which this can happen.

STICHTITE **KEY WORDS** Kundalini activation, love and forgiveness, compassion, spiritual protection, emotional and physical resilience **CHAKRAS** Heart (4th), Crown (7th), Root (1st) **ELEMENT** Wind **PHYSICAL** Supports neurological health, regeneration of neural pathways **EMOTIONAL** Inspires love and compassion, helps overcome timidity **SPIRITUAL** Encourages spiritual service, appreciation of the joy of life

Stichtite blends the vibrations of love, forgiveness and spiritual illumination. It can soften hardened attitudes. It encourages the spontaneous display of affection. It is a stone of emotional and physical resilience, allowing one to overcome illness, trauma, disappointment, anger or depression. It rekindles the joy of life for its own sake.

STILBITE **KEY WORDS** Clear thinking, expansion of self-sense, inner peace, enhancing one's dreams **CHAKRAS** Heart (4th), Third Eye (6th), Crown (7th) **ELEMENT** Wind **PHYSICAL** Supports brain function **EMOTIONAL** Calming and expansive, opens one to experiences of bliss **SPIRITUAL** Gently increases awareness, enhances dream life, awakens joy

Stilbite emanates a quiet and unceasing joy and love. It is healing to the heart chakra, and it helps one maintain openness and emotional vulnerability. In meditation, Stilbite can expand one into becoming a sphere of awareness, connected to the body by a cord of Light. It brings an inner peace that frees the Self. With issues of loss or grief, it can be a balm to the emotions. With Stilbite in one's pillowcase, one can experience increased vividness and profundity in dreams.

STONEHENGE BLUESTONE **KEY WORDS** Attunement to ancient knowledge, geomancy, shamanism **CHAKRAS** Base (1st), Third Eye (6th), Crown (7th) **ELEMENT** Earth **PHYSICAL** Helps one draw vitality through aligning with Earth energies **EMOTIONAL** Assists in clearing emotional blocks related to past lives **SPIRITUAL** Aids alignment with the World Heart, enhances psychic powers

Stonehenge Bluestone resonates with the Earth's ley lines. It can be used to locate the best spots for buildings, wells, temples and outdoor altars or meditation. It facilitates shape-shifting and shamanic journeying. It can aid in dousing, scrying, and attuning to past lives.

STRONTIANITE **KEY WORDS** Strength and confidence, enthusiasm for life, increased vitality and sexuality, decisiveness and self-control **CHAKRAS** Solar Plexus (3rd), Third Eye (6th), Sexual/Creative (2nd) **ELEMENT** Storm **PHYSICAL** Supports muscle strength and coordination, healing of muscle diseases **EMOTIONAL** Instills confidence, fairness, self-esteem, enhances sensuality **SPIRITUAL** Inspires commitment to life, dispels hesitancy and fear

Strontianite recharges the auric field, providing increased vitality and endurance. It encourages thrift, initiates a positive attitude, and enhances the senses, dissolving feelings of numbness and isolation. It increases receptivity to pleasure, quiets one's inner judge and increases self-esteem. It opens one's eyes to our common humanity and encourages friendship.

SUGILITE **KEY WORDS** Dreams, spiritual protection and purification, becoming a "beacon of Light" **CHAKRAS** Third Eye (6th), Crown (7th), Etheric (8th–14th) **ELEMENT** Wind **PHYSICAL** Provides a purifying, protective influence, supports healing from cancer **EMOTIONAL** Instills a positive, hopeful attitude, clears emotional body **SPIRITUAL** Dissolves negativity, helps one receive Divine Light

Sugilite offers purification and a strong influence for healing. Carrying or wearing a piece of Sugilite sets up a "shield of Light" around the wearer. It can burn away "gray spots" in the auric field, removing negative attachments. It eliminates toxic influences from one's inner and outer environment. It can stimulate and open the crown chakra for grounding spiritual Light on Earth. It can enhance the depth and meaning of dreams. It is the most powerful stone of the Violet Flame of purification.

SUNSET GOLD SELENITE **KEY WORDS** Creating through the will, integration of the brain hemispheres, unification of brain/mind and heart/wisdom **CHAKRAS** Solar Plexus (3rd), Heart (4th), Third Eye (6th), Crown (7th) **ELEMENT** Fire, Wind **PHYSICAL** Supports digestion, elimination, vision and hearing **EMOTIONAL** Aids in recovery from addictions and psychic wounds **SPIRITUAL** Initiates one's potential for co-creating, stimulates inner vision

Sunset Gold Selenite opens and activates the third eye and solar plexus chakras. It stimulates one's vision and one's will to create. It can aid in self-healing of digestive difficulties, bowel sluggishness, impaired vision and hearing, muscle weakness and addictive behaviors. Its enhancement of will forces can help one break through all sorts of old stuck patterns.

SUNSTONE **KEY WORDS** Leadership, benevolence, strength, abundance of blessings, enlightened male energy **CHAKRAS** Sexual/Creative (2nd), Solar Plexus (3rd) **ELEMENT** Fire **PHYSICAL** Warms the body, increases metabolism, digestion and vitality, supports endocrine and reproductive systems **EMOTIONAL** Encourages a positive, benevolent attitude, overcomes self-doubt **SPIRITUAL** Inspires responsibility, conviction, benevolence, aids prosperity

Sunstone is a stone of personal power, freedom and expanded consciousness. It supports openness, benevolence, warmth, strength, mental clarity and capacity to bestow blessings. It can kindle the fire of leadership. It can assist in manifesting prosperity, acquiring knowledge and attaining wisdom. It energizes the second and third chakras, stimulating leadership and will, creativity and sexuality.

TANGERINE QUARTZ **KEY WORDS** Creativity, sexuality, passion, curiosity, inspiration, playfulness, innocence **CHAKRAS** Sexual/Creative (2nd) **ELEMENT** Fire **PHYSICAL** Supports healthy function of sexual organs and adrenals **EMOTIONAL** Encourages a playful, adventurous enthusiasm dispels fear **SPIRITUAL** Inspires originality, courage brings a great infusion of creativity

Tangerine Quartz stimulates creativity and sexual energies. It can trigger great bursts of creative power. It can be used to intensify sexual desire, if the stone is placed at or near the second chakra. Partners can meditate or sleep within a grid of these crystals for enhancement of mutual creativity and inspirations to pursue together. Such a grid may increase the level of eroticism in the relationship. One can use Tangerine Quartz to enhance a creative endeavor by meditating with the stone and asking for assistance.

TANZANITE **KEY WORDS** Linkage of the mind and heart, enhanced spiritual perception, compassionate self-expression, adherence to truth **CHAKRAS** Heart (4th), Throat (5th), Third Eye (6th), Crown (7th), Soul Star (8th) **ELEMENT** Wind **PHYSICAL** Supports thyroid and adrenals, enhances neural links between brain and heart **EMOTIONAL** Encourages compassion, calms the mind, inspires joy **SPIRITUAL** Aids in expressing the wisdom of the heart

Tanzanite opens a cascade of thoughts and insights, but it keeps one calmly anchored in the heart. Bringing the heart into communion with the mind is essential to achieving wholeness. Tanzanite helps by making the heart's promptings more noticeable to the mind via a circuit between the heart and third eye. One feels this link as a vibration of joy and pleasure.

TEKTITE (COMMON) **KEY WORDS** Connection with ETs, telepathic communication **CHAKRAS** All **ELEMENT** Storm **PHYSICAL** Supports the body in integrating high-frequency energies **EMOTIONAL** Helps Starborns overcome homesickness and loneliness **SPIRITUAL** Increases psychic sensitivity, enhances telepathic link to ETs

Tektite carries extraterrestrial streams of communication and information. It vibrates with high-frequency pulsations which can put one in touch with ETs. It can heighten psychic sensitivity, clairaudient experiences, frequency of synchronicities and "seeing through the veil" of the physical world. Its increase of one's inner Light may attract people seeking friendship, counsel and kindness.

THULITE **KEY WORDS** Joy, pleasure, affection, healing of negative patterns, generosity, kindness, centering in the heart, linkage of heart and mind **CHAKRAS** Heart (4th), Sexual/Creative (2nd), Solar Plexus (3rd), Throat (5th) **ELEMENT** Water, Wind **PHYSICAL** Supports and integrates the heart and digestive systems **EMOTIONAL** Dispels judgment of self and others, inspires kindness **SPIRITUAL** Enhances empathy, encourages one's full commitment to love

Thulite stimulates sexuality and creativity, will and action, love and communication. It encourages happiness, contentment, enthusiasm, affection, pleasure and joy. It initiates rapport between people. It encourages empathy and diffuses tensions. It is ideal for children, helping them feel safe, happy and at home in the world. It encourages self-love, healthy habits, and helps break self-destructive patterns.

TIBETAN BLACK QUARTZ **KEY WORDS** Spiritual protection and purification, enhancement of meditation, balancing chakras and meridians, clearing and energizing the aura **CHAKRAS** All **ELEMENT** Storm **PHYSICAL** Balances and energizes the Liquid Crystal Body Matrix **EMOTIONAL** Clears negative energy patterns, initiates emotional balance **SPIRITUAL** Offers spiritual cleansing, protection; enhances meditation

Tibetan Black Quartz emanates spiritual protection. In sleep, it shields one from lower astral energies and disturbing dreams. It can purify and cleanse one's living space. It can activate and balance the chakras and meridian systems. Placing them at the outside corners of one's home can enhance the subtle energies of the entire environment.

TIBETAN TEKTITE **KEY WORDS** Opening the chakra column, attunement to the Supramental Force, accelerated evolution, Light Body awakening **CHAKRAS** All **ELEMENT** Storm **PHYSICAL** Aids with spinal alignment, brings Light into the cells **EMOTIONAL** Inspires the joy and wonder of spiritual awakening **SPIRITUAL** Gently awakens kundalini, allows "downloads" of spiritual Light

Tibetan Tektites are powerful for opening the chakra channel along the spine. To do this, one can have a partner rotate one Tibetan Tektite clockwise above one's head while bringing a second stone slowly up along the spine. The results are very powerful and felt by almost everyone. In opening the crown chakra and the column, Tibetan Tektites facilitate the descent of the Supramental Force, which can kindle the Body of Light.

TIGER EYE **KEY WORDS** Balance between extremes, discernment, vitality, strength, practicality, fairness **CHAKRAS** Solar Plexus (3rd), Sexual/Creative (2nd), Root (1st) **ELEMENT** Fire and Earth **PHYSICAL** Supports hormonal balance, enhances general vitality **EMOTIONAL** Facilitates finding emotional harmony with others **SPIRITUAL** Instills spiritual balance, stamina, creativity and clarity

Tiger Eye is a solar stone of vitality, practicality and physical action. It stimulates the root chakra and solar plexus, aiding one in taking effective actions, and in remaining grounded, calm and centered. It activates and whets the intellect, and opens the mind to embrace paradox. It energizes the body to accomplish the imperatives of the will. It can help overcome fatigue or discouragement. It allows one to find the harmonious center between polarities. It helps one see both sides in disagreements.

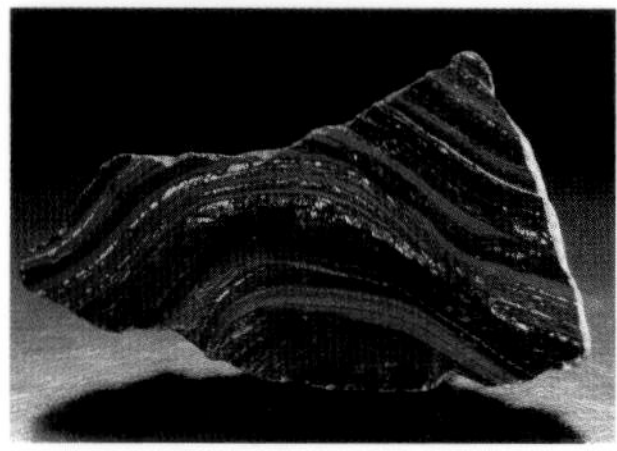

TIGER IRON **KEY WORDS** Strength, stamina, focused will, physical energy and strength, self-healing, grounding **CHAKRAS** Root (1st), Sexual/Creative (2nd), Solar Plexus (3rd) **ELEMENT** Fire and Earth **PHYSICAL** Benefits physical vitality, supports kidneys, lungs, intestines and pancreas **EMOTIONAL** Increases self-confidence, helps overcome self-sabatoge **SPIRITUAL** Enhances personal power, focus, mental clarity, groundedness

Tiger Iron is a stone of strength, stamina and courage. It enhances vitality, practicality and endurance. It reinforces health, personal power, focused will, mental clarity and groundedness. It encourages creative expression in music and acting. It supports the kidneys, lungs, intestines and pancreas. It aids in maintaining willpower for giving up bad habits.

TITANIUM QUARTZ **KEY WORDS** Increased life force and vitality, activation of the Rainbow Body of Light, humor and relaxation, enjoyment of life **CHAKRAS** All **ELEMENT** Fire and Storm **PHYSICAL** Supports endocrine system, energizes a sluggish immune system **EMOTIONAL** Enhances confidence, increases amusement and enjoyment of life **SPIRITUAL** Energizes all of the chakras, helps awaken the Rainbow Body of Light

Titanium Quartz projects strength, mental acuity and physical power. It can make one more focused, more confident, more aware of one's environment, more amused by life in general and more ready to cope with it. It can increase one's zest and enjoyment of life. It stimulates humor and relaxation, helping one take life more lightly. These are stones of Hermes, the god of quick intelligence and wit.

TOPAZ, BLUE **KEY WORDS** Enhancement of mind and communication **CHAKRAS** Throat (5th), Third Eye (6th) **ELEMENT** Fire **PHYSICAL** Supports healing of sore throat, speech impediments, hyperactive thyroid **EMOTIONAL** Aids clear communication of one's deepest feelings **SPIRITUAL** Enhances meditation, psychic abilities, communication of deep insights

Blue Topaz can provide an enhancement of one's mental processing and verbal skills, as well as improving one's attention span and ability to concentrate on mental tasks. It is a natural magnifier of psychic abilities, and can aid those who wish to attune to inner guidance, as well as those doing readings or spiritual healing work. It is resonant with the perfected pattern of the human body and energy system. For spiritual work and healing, it is better to use natural Blue Topaz than irradiated crystals.

TOPAZ, GOLDEN **KEY WORDS** Manifestation of personal intention, will and desires **CHAKRAS** Solar Plexus (3rd), Heart (4th) **ELEMENT** Fire **PHYSICAL** Supports the small intestines, kidneys, bladder and colon **EMOTIONAL** Helps align one's desires with Divine Will for true emotional satisfaction **SPIRITUAL** Opens the door to Christ consciousness and Heart Ascension

Golden Topaz enhances creativity, personal will and the ability to manifest one's desires. It is excellent for creating abundance within the context of what is appropriate for one's highest path. It helps one guide one's desires into alignment with Divine Will. It carries the Gold/Pink ray of Christ consciousness, and can be used to aid in connecting with it in meditation. It can help one open the heart in combination with the will, uniting the third and fourth chakras.

TOPAZ, WHITE **KEY WORDS** Spirituality, psychic gifts, mental clarity **CHAKRAS** Crown (7th), Etheric (8th–14th) **ELEMENT** Fire **PHYSICAL** Supports manifestation of one's vision of one's health or illness **EMOTIONAL** Helps one learn faith more easily, teaches gratitude **SPIRITUAL** Aids in envisioning and realizing one's highest spiritual path

White Topaz provides a great magnification of whatever energy is focused through it. Therefore, it is important to hold positive intentions. Manifestation works largely through focus. Where we put our attention determines what we receive. Faith is simply holding one's focus while remaining in a state of expectation and gratitude. As we learn this process, our synchronicities increase. The magic of White Topaz is that it magnifies one's intention, shortening the time between initial focus and fulfillment of one's vision.

TOURMALINE, BLACK **KEY WORDS** Purification, protection **CHAKRAS** Base (1st) **ELEMENT** Earth **PHYSICAL** Supports purification of the body, eliminating toxic substances **EMOTIONAL** Helps dispel worry, judgment, fear, anger, shame and other toxic emotions **SPIRITUAL** Aids with grounding and cleansing of the energy field

Black Tourmaline offers psychic protection, keeping one's auric field clear of imbalance, even in the presence of destructive energies. It acts like an etheric vacuum cleaner, clearing one's surroundings of negativity and disharmony. It is recommended for ridding oneself of negative thoughts, anxieties, anger, self-judgment and ideas of unworthiness. Healing practitioners who utilize crystals are especially advised to use these with their clients.

TOURMALINE, BLUE **KEY WORDS** Higher awareness, communication, healing **CHAKRAS** Throat (5th), Third Eye (6th) **ELEMENT** Water, Wind **PHYSICAL** Supports attunement to healing spirits, helps with headaches **EMOTIONAL** Aids clear expression of deep feelings, emotional cleansing **SPIRITUAL** Facilitates spirit communication, opens the mind to higher awareness

Blue Tourmaline enhances the psychic gifts of clairvoyance, clairaudience, clairsentience, prophecy and spirit communication. It is useful for those who wish to become channels and mediums. It energizes the throat chakra, helping one translate psychic impressions into verbal communication. It aids one in gracefully expressing deep feelings and insights, and in attuning to and channeling the healing energies offered from higher dimensions. It facilitates contact with benevolent spiritual beings and the reception of their blessings.

TOURMALINE, DRAVITE **KEY WORDS** Self-acceptance, self-healing, bringing the Shadow self to consciousness, self-love **CHAKRAS** Root (1st), Heart (4th) **ELEMENT** Earth, Storm **PHYSICAL** Aids in overcoming addiction and self-judgment, supports the body's purification systems, helps overcome digestive disorders **EMOTIONAL** Encourages self-acceptance and self-love **SPIRITUAL** Powerful ally for healing and integrating one's dark side

Dravite aids one in understanding and integrating one's Shadow. It can help one in bring Shadow material into consciousness without rejecting or judging what one finds. Dravite is highly grounding, and is nourishing to the life-force energies, lending stamina to those doing deep inner work. It inspires courage and persistence, and it even helps one see the humor in some of life's darkest situations.

TOURMALINE, GOLDEN **KEY WORDS** Will, confidence, inner strength **CHAKRAS** Solar Plexus (3rd) **ELEMENT** Water **PHYSICAL** Supports healing of digestive problems, ulcers, nausea, bowel problems **EMOTIONAL** Encourages recognition of one's personal power, dispels fear **SPIRITUAL** Inspires benevolent use of power, helps create prosperity

Golden Tourmaline is a powerful aid for those who wish to repair damage to the third chakra. It can help timid people find courage to face previously threatening experiences. In past-life therapy, it helps one release traumas that have turned into repeating negative patterns. It promotes clear thinking, goal setting, confidence, creative problem solving, perseverance, self-worth and a positive attitude. It enhances one's sense of worthiness and strength. It supports tolerance, benevolence and the empowerment of others.

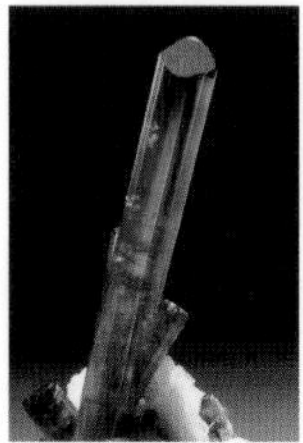

TOURMALINE, GREEN **KEY WORDS** Healing, strength, vitality, wholeness **CHAKRAS** Heart (4th) **ELEMENT** Water **PHYSICAL** Supports healthy heart function, emanates *prana* **EMOTIONAL** Aids in achieving peace through centering in the heart **SPIRITUAL** Encourages one to embrace the spirituality of physical life

Green Tourmaline is one of the premier stones for self-healing. It centers the energies at the heart chakra, and it is more connected to physical life than Pink Tourmaline. It can engender wholeness, dynamic balance and stability. It is beneficial to all living things. It can be used to enhance gardens and house plants and to connect with the spirits of plants and animals. It can be used in meditation to commune with Nature spirits. It can enhance vitality, stamina, courage and strength. It creates a flow of wholesome energy to all parts of the self. It helps spiritual people embrace and enjoy life in the physical world.

TOURMALINE, PINK **KEY WORDS** Love, emotional healing **CHAKRAS** Heart (4th) **ELEMENT** Water **PHYSICAL** Supports the heart, lungs and parasympathetic nervous system **EMOTIONAL** Helps repair holes in the auric field from emotional wounds **SPIRITUAL** Encourages one to become a living beacon of love energies

Pink Tourmaline is the quintessential heart-chakra stone. It is unsurpassed for healing emotional wounds, particularly those of childhood. It emanates a soft, soothing energy that engenders feelings of comfort, safety and nurturance. It can be used to repair "holes" in the auric field created by negative attachments or past abuse. It can assist one in releasing stress, worries, depression and anxiety. It can help the emotionally numb recover their passion and zest for life. It can help one find the courage to love, and can increase gentleness. Pink Tourmaline emanates loving and healing energies, influencing others toward greater kindness and tolerance.

TOURMALINE, RUBELLITE **KEY WORDS** Alignment of the individual and the Universal heart, healing the heart and emotions, rekindling one's passion for life **CHAKRAS** Heart (4th), Root (1st) **ELEMENT** Water, Earth **PHYSICAL** Supports heart health and recovery from heart attack **EMOTIONAL** Rekindles sensitivity, passion and enjoyment of life **SPIRITUAL** Helps one attune to Cosmic Love through the Universal heart

Rubellite strengthens one's heart and links it to the heart of the Earth. It can link one to the Universal heart. It benefits the emotional heart as well. It facilitates healing emotional wounds. It makes an excellent gift for one's romantic partner because of its capacity to fan the flames of passion. It stimulates the root chakra as well as the heart. It brings increased prana, stimulates courage and inspires one to protect what one loves. It enhances one's capacity to make and fulfill commitments if they are inspired by love.

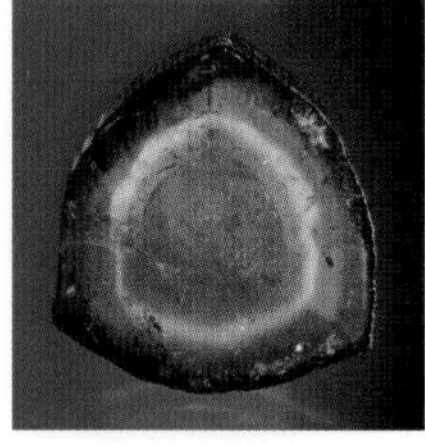

TOURMALINE, WATERMELON **KEY WORDS** Calm, joy **CHAKRAS** Heart (4th) **ELEMENT** Water **PHYSICAL** Supports the physical heart, eases stress, stimulates release of endorphins **EMOTIONAL** Fills the emotional body with a radiance of joy, calms worry and fear **SPIRITUAL** Stimulates the awakening of the true Self in the "higher heart"

Watermelon Tourmaline works simultaneously with the physical, emotional and spiritual components of the heart. It can awaken the "higher heart," the energy center just above the heart chakra, also known as the "seat of the soul." It teaches one the meaning of joy. When one is attuned to the frequency of joy, it brings harmony to all aspects of the self. Life may continue to bring its moments of sorrow, but even they can be experienced with joy.

TOURMALINED QUARTZ **KEY WORDS** Purification, recovery from negative influences **CHAKRAS** All **ELEMENT** Storm **PHYSICAL** Purifies one's environment, cleanses the body of negative energies **EMOTIONAL** Helps one overcome self-destructive emotional patterns **SPIRITUAL** Creates a protective, purifying field around one's aura and body

Tourmalined Quartz acts like a psychic vacuum cleaner to return one's energy field to the pristine, unpolluted state. It is one of the most powerful tools for dispelling negative energies, repairing the auric field, restoring balance to the chakras and promoting general well-being. It facilitates clear thinking. It is beneficial to people who need help staying on the spiritual path. Carrying Tourmalined Quartz creates a "bubble of Light" around the body.

TRANSMUTITE **KEY WORDS** Transmutation of self into one's divine potential **CHAKRAS** All **ELEMENT** Earth, Storm **PHYSICAL** Brings the Pattern of Divine Perfection to all levels of one's being **EMOTIONAL** Encourages one to embrace of the truth of what is, and to cherish all that one loves **SPIRITUAL** In meditation it makes one feel energized and comforted. It can help us to discover who we truly are.

Transmutite carries the pattern of supporting the highest good into any and all situations. It helps us to listen to the urging of the silent voice of the soul, allowing its guidance to govern our choices. It's vibrations penetrate all levels of the body, and can influence the cellular mind, deep in our subconscious. It offers the cells a new way to vibrate, a new way to organize their activities, a new pattern of higher purpose. It can help us fully enact our metamorphosis into spiritual awakened "crystal human beings."

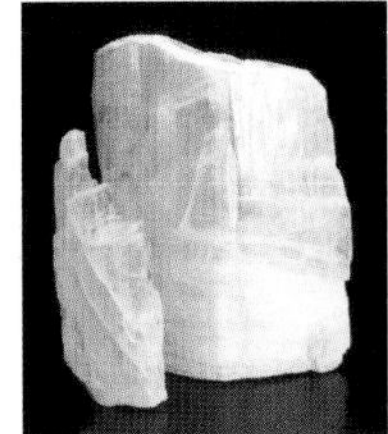

TREMOLITE **KEY WORDS** Access to higher knowledge, calm and clarity, higher-mind activation, mystic rapture **CHAKRAS** Crown (7th), Soul Star (8th), Etheric (9th–14th) **ELEMENT** Wind **PHYSICAL** Increases *prana,* helps one diagnose ailments intuitively **EMOTIONAL** Helps release stress and anxiety, encourages calm and clarity **SPIRITUAL** Facilitates access to morphogenic fields of the Divine Mind

Tremolite can be used to activate the pineal gland and link it with the surrounding neural circuitry, leading to the opening of the third eye and crown chakras and access to morphic fields of knowledge. It facilitates calm and clarity. It allows one to release stress and anxiety and to face even difficult times with equanimity. It can help one to alleviate depression and worry. It can activate dormant mind centers meant for the next phase of human evolution. When this shift is made, it feels as if one has just awakened from a dream.

TRULITE SILICA **KEY WORDS** Compassion, purity of intention, courage to surrender to truth **CHAKRAS** Throat (5th), Heart (4th) **ELEMENT** Water **PHYSICAL** Acts as a loving, healing balm, facilitating the release of stress, anxiety, tension **EMOTIONAL** Supports gentleness and loving kindness **SPIRITUAL** Brings rapport with one's Deep Self, encourages alchemical transformation and awakening

Trulite Silica is a stone of heartfelt knowledge and deep Wisdom. It is a stone of true and eloquent self-expression and sincerity. This stone can bring one into conscious rapport with the Deep Self, the identity beneath one's everyday persona. As such, Trulite Silica powerfully facilitates emotional healing and spiritual wholeness. It is a stone whose day has come, and it offers itself to us for the benefit of our own awakening into loving relationship with ourselves, the Earth, and the Divine.

TUGTUPITE **KEY WORDS** Intense and passionate love, deep heart activation, mystic rapture, grief, emotional transformation **CHAKRAS** Heart (4th), Throat (5th), Third Eye (6th), Crown (7th) **ELEMENT** Storm **PHYSICAL** Strengthens the nervous system, auric field and heart **EMOTIONAL** Awakens the inner fire of love, ecstatic activation of the emotional body **SPIRITUAL** Opens one to Cosmic Love and passionate love of the Earth

Tugtupite is a stone of the deepest energies of the heart. It can reawaken lost passion and forgotten love. It can put one in touch with suppressed grief and sorrow, allowing the release of these emotions. It releases pure love in all its uncontrollable intensity. It simply opens the heart, all the way. It can trigger a rapturous upwelling of love for the Earth. Or it may manifest as an ineffable joy with no object at all.

TURQUOISE **KEY WORDS** Wholeness, communication and spiritual expansion **CHAKRAS** Throat (5th) **ELEMENT** Storm **PHYSICAL** Increases life force in the body, supports blood oxygenation **EMOTIONAL** Encourages self-forgiveness and the release of useless regrets **SPIRITUAL** Inspires one to act out of truth, compassion and forgiveness

Turquoise is a stone of wholeness and truth, and it aids in the communication and manifestation of those qualities. It stimulates and harmonizes the throat chakra, making it easier for one to articulate one's wisdom. Because it is a stone of wholeness, Turquoise is also beneficial to overall well-being. It induces serenity and peace. Holding or wearing Turquoise can help one restore depleted vitality and lift sagging spirits. It teaches the wisdom of compassion and forgiveness.

ULEXITE **KEY WORDS** Intuition, inner vision, telepathy, clairvoyance, imagination, creativity, mental agility **CHAKRAS** Third Eye (6th) **ELEMENT** Wind **PHYSICAL** Supports the eyes and vision, helps overcome eye fatigue **EMOTIONAL** Inspires feelings of exhilaration about one's visions and insights **SPIRITUAL** Lifts the veil from one's inner eye for multiple psychic and spiritual experiences

Ulexite enhances clairvoyance. It is a stone of "far seeing." It acts on the third eye to open interdimensional gates, so one may see and interact with beings from the higher planes. It enables one to connect with extraterrestrials, guides and other entities. It activates latent intuitive abilities, and sensitizes one to be able to "read" the energies and intentions of others. It stimulates imagination and creativity. It can quicken mental processes, allowing one to see the answers to complex problems instantly.

VANADINITE **KEY WORDS** Stamina, grounding, creativity, discipline **CHAKRAS** Root (1st), Sexual/Creative (2nd), Solar Plexus (3rd), Third Eye (6th) **ELEMENT** Fire **PHYSICAL** Provides spiritual protection from radiation, stimulates proper hormone production **EMOTIONAL** Encourages adventurousness, playfulness **SPIRITUAL** Increases determination, discipline, expands intuitive awareness

Vanadinite activates the lower three chakras, enhancing endurance, persistence, power and will. It stimulates the mind centers and links them with the lower chakras, enhancing clear thought, organization, determination and vitality. It provides grounding for those who do intuitive readings, channeling, mediumship, and healing. It stimulates creative and sexual energies. It can help one find needed inspiration and the arousal to action. It helps one connect with the animal self and relish physical life.

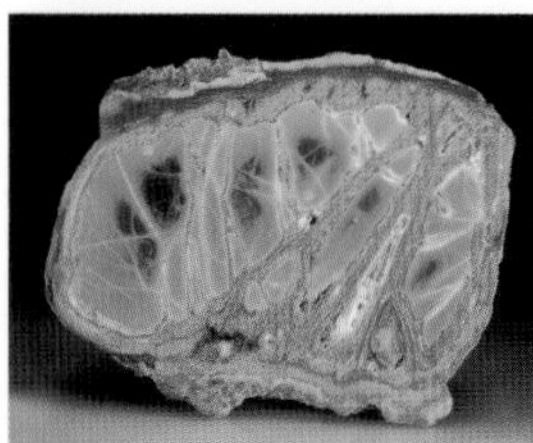

VARISCITE **KEY WORDS** Inner peace, love and compassion, alignment of the physical and Light bodies, simplicity, clarity, emotional healing **CHAKRAS** Heart (4th) **ELEMENT** Water **PHYSICAL** Encourages positive brain states, enhances learning, cognition, reasoning and logic **EMOTIONAL** Opens the heart and kindles long-lasting emotional well-being **SPIRITUAL** Inspires one to release negative patterns into the Light, instills inner harmony

Variscite brings peace to the heart and tranquility to the mind. It is excellent for relieving stress. Its energy harmonizes one's energy field and links it with the Earth. It activates the heart chakra and generates positive emotions. It lends courage, and helps one appreciate simplicity. It allows one to discharge emotional obsessions and self-destructive habits.

VESUVIANITE **KEY WORDS** Uniting the heart and the will, enthusiasm for life, release of negative attachments, the courage to change **CHAKRAS** All **ELEMENT** Earth **PHYSICAL** Supports muscle strength, especially in the legs and feet **EMOTIONAL** Encourages one to take joy in following one's true calling **SPIRITUAL** Helps one recognize, follow and persist in the heart's desires

Vesuvianite stimulates the solar-plexus and heart chakras, helping one to align personal will with the promptings of the heart. It is useful for the manifestation of the heart's desires here on earth. It aids in taking one's true path in life. It is useful for combatting negative thoughts and bringing enthusiasm back into one's life. It helps one achieve the insights that inspire one to move forward in spiritual development. It helps those going through transformational work such as psychotherapy, breath work and past-life regression.

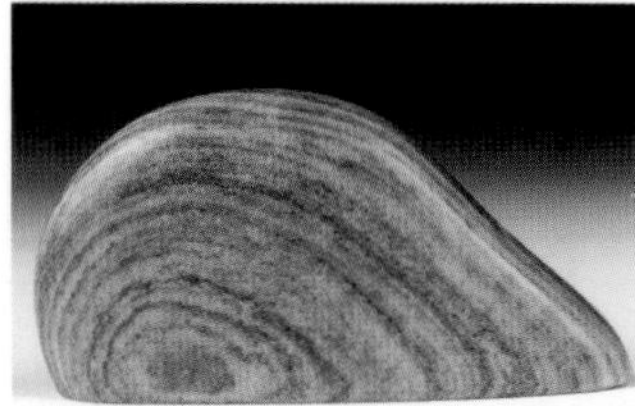

VITALITE **KEY WORDS** Life Force, replenishment, joy, well-being, love, courage, emotional cleansing, generosity, creativity, spiritual awakening **CHAKRAS** Heart (4th), Third Eye (6th), Crown (7th) **ELEMENTS** Water, Earth **PHYSICAL** Supports heart, lungs, circulatory system, liver, digestive system, increases Life Force **EMOTIONAL** Aids in releasing negative emotions, helps cultivate joy **SPIRITUAL** Uplifts one into joy and remembrance of one's Divine Nature

Vitalite replenishes one's Life Force. It stimulates well-being, alleviating stress, anxiety, irritability and depression. It supports the heart, circulatory system, lungs, liver and digestive system. It is a stone of generosity. It stimulates imagination. It is a stone of spiritual awakening, reminding us that we are as divine as the Universe itself.

VIVIANITE **KEY WORDS** Compassion, love, inner peace, gentleness, refreshment, inspiration, mystic awakening **CHAKRAS** Heart (4th) **ELEMENT** Earth, Water **PHYSICAL** Promotes cellular regeneration and the healing of wounds **EMOTIONAL** Dispels negativity, opens one to the heart's ocean of love **SPIRITUAL** Encourages one to live from the heart, enlightened compassion

Vivianite helps one to dive deeply into the pool of the heart. It assists one in achieving inner silence in meditation and helps one to hear the wordless voice of the heart. It brings enlightened compassion, removes negative thoughts and clears one's auric field. It works below one's awareness to dispel self-inflicted emotional wounds. It supports altruism, kindness and generosity. It can re-inspire those in the helping professions who suffer from exhaustion and burnout. It reminds one of the love that dwells behind all things.

VORTEXITE **KEY WORDS** Dynamic equilibrium, balance, refreshment, empowerment, strengthening inner energy vortices, links to Earth energies **CHAKRAS** All, especially Heart (4th) and Third Eye (6th) **ELEMENTS** Earth, Water, Fire **PHYSICAL** Supports nervous system, DNA, cellular self-repair **EMOTIONAL** Supports flow of feeling, relieves stress **SPIRITUAL** Aids attunement to energy vortices; can trigger Ascension of the Heart

Vortexite's strong vibrations bring one's chakras and bodily energies into alignment. This stone is linked to the Life Force of the Earth. If one makes a journey to an energy vortex site, taking Vortexite along will intensify the experience. Vortexite is ideal for constructing energy tools and meditation grids. It supports DNA self-repair and the strengthening of cell membranes. Its currents stimulate the nervous system and encourage neuronal health and regeneration. It acts as an emotional tonic and aids in recovery from stress.

WHITE PHANTOM QUARTZ **KEY WORDS** Access to Akashic records, morphogenic fields and past-life memories, connection with spirit guides, energy cleansing **CHAKRAS** Third eye (6th), Crown (7th) **ELEMENT** Storm **PHYSICAL** Aids in healing issues that appear as "echoes" of past-life traumas **EMOTIONAL** Encourages one to free oneself from bonds to past-life patterns **SPIRITUAL** Opens the spiritual archives of past knowledge and past lives

White Phantom Quartz aids in attuning the mind for receiving information from the morphogenic fields of knowledge. It also helps one access the field of one's own past including the memories, wisdom and knowledge of one's previous incarnations. This stone is also good for cleansing one's auric field and environment of negative energies. It can initiate contact with spirit guides and inner teachers.

WILLEMITE **KEY WORDS** Interdimensional travel, adventures in the astral body, connection with higher astral beings **CHAKRAS** Third Eye (6th) **ELEMENT** Earth, Fire **PHYSICAL** Provides energetic protection from radiation and cellular mutation, enhances sexual function **EMOTIONAL** Encourages optimism and eagerness to improve one's life **SPIRITUAL** Stimulates consciousness for travels beyond the body

Willemite is a stone of spiritual initiation. It provides a dimensional doorway to the higher astral realm, where benevolent spirits concerned with the Earth reside. These beings are caretakers of humanity who are encouraging our evolution. Willemite activates the third eye and stimulates inner visions, as well as interdimensional travel. It assists astral travel by stabilizing one's focused awareness and its manifestation as an astral body.

WULFENITE **KEY WORDS** Creativity, manifestation, determination, sexuality, alchemy, Earth connection **CHAKRAS** Sexual/Creative (2nd), Solar Plexus (3rd) **ELEMENT** Fire **PHYSICAL** Stimulates metabolism, enhances sexual function and enjoyment **EMOTIONAL** Inspires one to create, and to love the Earth and life's adventures **SPIRITUAL** Aids self-transformation, artistic creativity, personal power

Wulfenite can aid in the alchemy of personal development—the transmutation of the "leaden" self into spiritual "gold." It can assist in artistic creation. It stimulates inspiration and persistence, assisting in carrying projects through to completion. It is a stone of originality, bringing new ideas and visions for painting, music, poetry and other art forms. It also activates one's sexual energies, and it can lead to new adventures in love as well as art.

Z STONE **KEY WORDS** Interdimensional travel, magic, sacred geometry, Merkaba vehicle **CHAKRAS** Third Eye (6th), Crown (7th) **ELEMENT** Storm **PHYSICAL** Stimulates the brain and nervous system **EMOTIONAL** Inspires interest in other dimensions **SPIRITUAL** Opens awareness of astral realm, enables travel as a point-of-consciousness, engenders spiritual visions

For those who wish to travel interdimensionally and explore the subtle realms of consciousness, Z Stones could provide an interesting ticket. The astral realm can be readily accessed with Z Stones. Another more rarified realm—that of the "living geometries"—can be reached by using Z Stones along with meditative focus on the Merkaba form of sacred geometry. Z Stones can facilitate work with elemental currents, helping to influence the manifestation of energy.

ZINCITE **KEY WORDS** Life force, creativity, sexuality, personal power, manifestation **CHAKRAS** Root (1st), Sexual/Creative (2nd), Solar Plexus (3rd) **ELEMENT** Fire **PHYSICAL** Stimulates the sexual organs and endocrine system, enhances sexual desire and performance **EMOTIONAL** Instills awareness of one's power, ignites one's enthusiasm and sense of fun **SPIRITUAL** Inspires courage, passion, creativity, willpower, enjoyment

Zincite stimulates the first, second and third chakras. It increases life force, courage, passion, creativity, will and personal power. Its energy operates on the second chakra in a way that kindles the fires of both creativity and sexuality. It charges the third chakra, increasing one's reservoir of determination, perseverance, focus of intention and capacity for manifestation.

ZIRCON **KEY WORDS** Stimulation of all the chakras, increased life force, grounding ideals in the physical world **CHAKRAS** All **ELEMENT** Storm **PHYSICAL** Helps clear the body of common toxins and stress, supports adrenals **EMOTIONAL** Helps one overcome disillusionment and to work for one's ideals **SPIRITUAL** Aids transmutation of spiritual energies into physical reality

Zircon is a stone of high intensity and precise focus. It can be used to stimulate sluggish energies in any of the chakras or meridians. It helps those who are ungrounded "get real" in taking care of the necessities of physical life. It lends energy and strength of purpose to those who might otherwise be overwhelmed by the conflict between their desire to change the world and the fear that their dreams are impossible. It can work as a talisman of spiritual protection.

ZOISITE (WITH RUBY) **KEY WORDS** Joyful engagement with life, healing, increase in life force **CHAKRAS** Root (1st), Heart (4th), Third Eye (6th) **ELEMENT** Storm **PHYSICAL** Infuses the body with *chi,* supports optimal health and vitality **EMOTIONAL** Aids in overcoming negative states, promotes zest for life **SPIRITUAL** Facilitates the opening of the heart

Zoisite with Ruby strengthens the neural and energetic connections between the brain and the heart. It is a stone of life force, courage and passion. It stimulates and harmonizes the root, heart and third eye chakras. It supports an optimal state of health and aids the spiritual treatment of depression, chronic fatigue syndrome, fainting spells, sluggish thyroid and exhaustion of the adrenals. It can assist one in becoming aware of suppressed grief and releasing it.

Stone Property Reference Index

This index is divided into two sections—Physical Correcpondences and Emotional/Spiritual Correspondences. Those interested in working with stones to facilitate physical, emotional or spiritual self-healing are encouraged to use their intuition and discrimination in regard to such explorations. Working with stones for any sort of self-healing is experimental and speculative, and the author of this book does not intend to suggest that such practices will lead to any specific results. Both author and publishers recommend that readers do not use stones in place of traditional medical or psychological care.

PHYSICAL CORRESPONDENCES

acid Shattuckite; Tourmaline, Golden
acne, *see* skin problems
activation stone Moldavite
acupressure Sichuan Quartz
acupuncture Magnetite; Sichuan Quartz
ADD/ADHD Amblygonite; Cerussite; Lepidolite; Petalite; Silbite
addiction Agate, Dendritic; Agate, Purple Sage; Astrophyllite; Galena; Nebula Stone; Ruby; Dravite; Zircon
adrenal glands Adamite; Amazonite; Cacoxenite; Chrysocolla; Ocean Jasper; Tangerine Quartz; Tanzanite; Topaz, Golden; Zircon; Zoisite
aging Calcite, Blue; Jasper, Mook; Staurolite; Vanadinite
agoraphobia Cerussite
alcohol use Dolomite; Jasper, Unakite; Nebula Stone
allergy Aquamarine
ALS Eudialyte; Natrolite
Alzheimer's disease Albite; Diaspore; Eudialyte; Natrolite; Stichtite
anemia Ajoite; Bloodstone; Magnetite; Meteorite, Pallasite; Peridot; Tiger Iron
angina, *see* heart issues
anxiety Cerussite; Gaia Stone; Lithium Quartz; Petalite; Rhodochrosite
appetite Albite; Celestite; Dolomite
arterial blockage Calcite, Green
arthritis Angelite; Jade, Blue; Lilac Lepidolite; Malachite
asthma Diopside; Gem Silica; Jade, Blue; Opal, Common (Blue); Tremolite
assimilation Healer's Gold; Pyromorphite; Rutile; Scapolite, Yellow
athletic performance Jade, Red; Sphalerite
attraction between mates Agate, Fire; Tugtupite
auric field Celestite; Tugtupite
auto-immune disorders Aventurine, Red

back pain Agate, Dendritic
balance Adularia
bed-wetting Celestite; Golden Labradorite; Opal, Precious, Oregon
bile Shattuckite
birth Calcite, Red
blockage Epidote; Fulgurite
blood Ajoite; Apache Tears
blood cell production Aventurine, Red; Meteorite, Nickel-Iron; Tiger Iron
blood formation Staurolite
blood oxygenation Blizzard Stone; Healer's Gold; *see also* oxygenation
blood pressure Petalite; Sodalite; Stichtite
blood purification Cinnabar; Dravite; Meteorite, Pallasite; Proustite
blood strengthener Fulgurite; Goethite; Hematite; Lepidocrocite; Petrified Wood; Seraphinite; Tiger Eye
blood, diseases of Bloodstone; Meteorite, Chondrite
blood sugar level Calcite, Honey
"blue babies" Aventurine, Blue
boils Cinnabar; Marcasite; Stibnite
bonding between mother and infant Calcite, Pink, Transparent
bone density, *see* Osteoporosis
bone issues Aragonite Star Clusters; Elestial Quartz; Fluorite; Kyanite; Opal, Common (Brown or Black); Seriphos Green Quartz; Sphene
bone loss and degeneration, *see* Osteoporosis
bone growth Jasper, Picture
bone marrow Bixbite; Bloodstone; Goethite; Hematite; Magnetite; Petrified Wood
bone regeneration Jasper, Picture
bones, broken Celestial Quartz; Faden Quartz; Kyanite; Obsidian, Rainbow; Quartz, Self-healed
bowel imbalance Cuprite; Healer's Gold; Spinel, Black; *see also* intestinal disorder
brain Albite; Alexandrite; Auralite, Emerald; Azurite; Diaspore; K2; Roswellite; Tibetan Black Quartz
brain balance and imbalance Amethyst; Azeztulite, Green-Fire; Goshenite; Herderite; Muscovite; Phenacite
brain chemistry Barite; Fluorite; Scapolite, White-Gray
brain damage Albite; Natrolite; Phenacite; Purpurite
brain disease Barite; Diaspore; Kyanite; Obsidian, Peacock; Variscite
brain, evolution Benitoite; Heulandite, White
brain function Amethyst; Astrophyllite; Cryolite; Euclase; Herderite; Phenacite; Pietersite; Purpurite
brain hemispheres Calcite, Merkabite
bronchial conditions Gem Silica; Jade, Blue; Tremolite
bruising Obsidian, Rainbow
burns Agate, Ellensburg Blue

caffeine stress and withdrawal Rhodochrosite; Rutile; Zircon; *see also* addiction
calcification of joints Angelite; *see also* skeletal system

cancer Bixbite; Clinochlore; Elestial Quartz; Epidote; Galena; Jasper, Unakite; Lemurian Jade; Obsidian, Snowflake; Prophecy Stone; Pyromorphite; Seraphinite; Tourmaline, Green
capillaries, blood flow Fulgurite
cardiovascular system Blizzard stone; *see also* heart
cataracts Calcite, Blue
cell function Ammonite, Rainbow; Tourmaline, Green
cell growth Garnet; Grossular; Prasiolite; Tourmaline, Green; Willemite
cell regeneration Amazonite; Seraphinite; Serpentine; Vivianite
cell repair Aventurine, Green
cellular healing Azeztulite, Lemurian Gold; Azeztulite, Sedona; Brucite, Golden
cellular respiration Seraphinite
chemotherapy Galena; Prophecy Stone; *see also* cancer
chi Clinochlore; Rhodonite
chronic fatigue syndrome Adamite; Zoisite
circulation Agate, Moss; Calcite, Pink, Opaque; Cuprite; Ruby, Star
circulatory system Aventurine, Green; Azeztulite, Green-Fire; Clinichlore; Clinizoisite; Devalite; Halite; Magnetite; Meteroite, Chondrite; Prehnite
cleansing Herkimer Quartz 'Diamond'
cleansing regimens Staurolite
colon function Malachite
concentration issues Stibnite
connective tissue Benitoite
cough Opal, Common (Blue)
Crohn's disease Dravite
cysts Dream Quartz; Opal, Common (White); Opal, Precious (Black); Seriphos Green Quartz
Cystitis Chrysanthemum Stone; Epidote; Copper (Metal); Nebula Stone

death Zoisite
death experience, conscious Fulgurite
degenerative diseases Apophyllite, Green; Chrysoprase
dementia Siberian Blue Quartz; Stichtite
detoxification Apatite, Green; Astrophyllite; Calcite, Red; Carnelian; Dolomite; Galena; Golden Labradorite; Hematite; Jade, Green; Jasper, Rainforest; Malachite; Nebula Stone; Obsidian, Mahogany; Proustite; Rhodonite; Spinel, Black; Zircon
diabetes Gaspeite; Sapphire, Pink
digestive issues Agate, Fire; Agate, Moss; Albite; Amber; Ametrine; Agni Gold Danburite: Apatite, Golden; Buddstone; Bustamite; Cacoxinite; Calcite, Orange; Celestite; Citrine, Heat Treated; Girasol Quartz; Golden Labradorite; Heliodor; Imperial Gold Quartz; Libyan Gold Tektite; Obsidian, Gold Sheen; Opal, Common (Brown or Black); Prasiolite; Pyromorphite; Rutile; Sapphire, Yellow; Scapolite, Yellow; Scapolite, Pink; Shaman Stone; Spinel, Black; Stichtite; Sunstone; Tourmaline, Golden
dizziness, *see* vertigo
DNA Petrified Wood
drug use Dolomite; *see also* addiction

eating disorders Prasiolite; Stichtite
eczema *see* skin problems
electromagnetic field Adularia; Infinite; Titanium (Metal); Smoky Quartz
ELF fields Vanadinite
elimination of waste Healer's Gold; Metals; Onyx; Opal, Common (Brown or Black); Scapolite, Yellow; Sichuan Quartz; Spinel
Emphysema Calcite, Blue; Diopside; Tremolite;
endocrine system Ametrine; Apatite, Golden; Bloodstone; Brazilianite; Bustamite; Calcite, Orange; Calcite, Red; Cavansite; Citrine; Crocoite; Garnet, Spessartine; Iolite-Sunstone; Lepidocrocite; Ocean Jasper; Opal, Precious (Fire); Pyrite; Rutile; Sunstone; Tiger Eye; Titanium Quartz; Zincite
endurance Kammererite
energy Cuprite; Diamond; Infinite; Iolite-Sunstone; Serpentine; Smithsonite; Tektite; Gold (Metal);
energy blockage Calcite, Clear
energy replenishment Chrysoberyl, Catseye; Heliodor
esophagus Azeztulite, Blue-Green
exercise Marcasite; Sphalerite
extremities, blood flow Fulgurite
eye problems Apatite, Blue; Celestite; Gaia Stone; Herkimer Quartz 'Diamond'; Iolite; Onyx; Rhodizite; Sapphire, Blue; Scapolite, Blue; Ulexite

fainting Zoisite
fascia Magnesite
fatigue Kammererite
fatigue, chronic Opal, Precious (Fire)
feet Protector Quartz; Spider Jasper; Vesuvianite; *see also* skeletal system
fertility Agate, Fire; Chrysanthemum Stone; Cinnabar; Crocoite; Cuprite; Garnet, Spessartine; Lepidocrocite; Nebula Stone; Ruby; Willemite; Zincite
fetal growth Jasper, Red
fever Agate, Ellensburg Blue; Larimar
fibroid masses Chrysanthemum Stone; Magnesite; Opal, Common (White)
fingernails, *see* nails
food assimilation, *see* digestion
food issues Rutile; Stichtite; *see also* eating disorders

gallbladder Aegirine; Apatite, Golden; Chrysoberyl, Golden; Golden Labradorite; Petrified Wood; Pyromorphite; Rhodonite; Scapolite, Yellow
gardening Apophyllite, Green ; Seriphos Green Quartz
gastric disorders Cacoxinite; Gaia Stone; Heliodor; Libyan Gold Tektite; Malachite; Obsidian, Gold Sheen; Spinel, Green/Blue
genetic disorders Phenacite
gland function Amber; Calcite, Honey; Ocean Jasper; Prehnite; Rhodonite; Tangerine Quartz
glucose metabolism Sapphire, Pink; *see also* blood sugar
gout Amazonite

hair Amazonite; Apache Tears: Opal, Precious (White); Rutilated Quartz; Topaz, White
hair growth, *see* hair
hair loss, *see* hair
hands Protector Quartz
head Protector Quartz
headache Agate, Purple Sage; Apatite, Blue; Calcite, Blue; Cavansite; Fairy Wand Quartz; Gaia Stone; Goshenite; Herderite; Lazulite; Merlinite; Muscovite; Onyx; Rhodizite; Sapphire, Blue; Scheelite; Stibnite; Stichtite; Tourmaline, Blue
headaches, hormone-related Hemimorphite; Herderite
healing Agate, Purple Sage; Apache Gold; Apatite, Green; Aventurine, Green; Azeztulite, New Zealand White; Diopside; Goethite, Rainbow; Heartenite; Herkimer Quartz 'Diamond'; Sugilite
healing energies of Nature Fairy Stones
healing spiritual Azeztulite, Sedona
health, general Agate, Moss; Axinite; Beryllonite; Crocoite; Jade, Red
hearing Sphene
heart Blue-green Azeztulite, Buddstone, Girasol Quartz, K2
heart, diseases Apatite, Green; Calcite, Pink, Opaque; Chrysoberyl, Green; Diopside; Dioptase; Jade, Green;

Lilac Lepidolite; Meteorite, Pallasite; Peridot; Rose Quartz; Tourmaline, Pink; Rubellite
heart, physical Amegreen; Apatite, Green; Auralite, Emerald; Aventurine, Green; Black Phantom Quartz; Calcite, Pink, Transparent; Chrysoberyl, Green; Clinizoisite; Devalite; Emerald; Gaia Stone; Garnet, Uvarovite; Heartenite; Hiddenite; Jasper, Unakite; Lemurian Jade; Lepidocrocite; Merlinite; Morganite; Obsidian, Rainbow; Pink Amethyst; Prasiolite; Seraphinite; Tourmaline, Green; Tourmaline, Watermelon; Tugtupite
heartbeat Blizzard Stone; Meteorite, Pallasite; Opal, Common (Pink); Rose Quartz; Trulite Silica; Tourmaline, Pink
heart healing Clinizoisite
heart intelligence Clinizoisite
heart surgery Apatite, Green
heart, scar tissue Seriphos Green Quartz
heart weakness Heulandite, Green; Rose Quartz; Strombolite
heartburn Amblygonite; *see also* stomach
heavy metal elimination Dolomite; Halite, Blue; Halite, Pink; Nebula Stone; Tourmaline, Black
hemoglobin Hematite, Specular; Malachite; Copper (Metal); *see also* blood
herpes Aquamarine; Cinnabar; Stibnite
HIV Cinnabar; Lemurian Jade
hives, *see* skin problems
hormonal balance and imbalance Ajoite; Aventurine, Blue; Bloodstone; Brazilianite; Calcite, Orange; Calcite, Red; Cuprite; Silver (Metal); Opal, Precious (Fire); Quartz, Scepter; Sunstone; Tiger Eye; Vanadinite
hormonal shift Hemimorphite; Lepidocrocite; Moonstone
hot temper Agate, Ellensburg Blue
hydration Sodalite
hyperactivity Aventurine, Blue; Cerussite; Lepidolite; Scapolite, Yellow; Tourmaline, Pink; Tourmaline, Watermelon
hyperglycemia Sapphire, Pink
hypoglycemia Sapphire, Pink

immune system Apache tears; Aventurine, Red; Calcite, Honey; Cinnabar; Crocoite; Crocodile Rock; Garnet, Black Andradite; Heartenite; Silver (Metal); Pink Amethyst; Proustite; Titanium Quartz; Vivianite
impotence Jasper, Red; Obsidian, Gold Sheen; Pyrite; Shiva Lingham
indigestion, *see* gastric disorders
infant and children, development Aventurine, Green
infections Amber; Celestite; Cinnabar; Covellite; Galena; Jade, Black; Larimar; Marcasite; Meteorite, Pallasite; Opal, Precious (Owyhee Blue); Proustite; Pyrite; Stibnite
infection, fungal Marcasite; Proustite; Pyrite
infections, yeast Covellite
infertility, male and female Bixbite; Healer's Gold; Copper (Metal); Pyrite; Shiva Lingam; Tangerine Quartz; *see also* reproductive issues
inflammation Chalcedony, Blue; Jade, Blue; Larimar; Lilac Lepidolite; Malachite; Opal, Common (Blue); Opal, Precious (Owyhee Blue)
influenza Larimar
inhalant addiction Peridot
injury Jasper, Unakite
inner ear imbalance Sapphire, Blue
insomnia Angel Phanton Quartz; Goshenite; Jasper, Mook; Lepidolite; Sugilite
insulin levels, *see* diabetes
intestinal disorder Sichuan Quartz; Tiger Iron; *see also* bowel
irritable bowel syndrome Amblygonite; Dravite; Libyan Gold Tektite; Tourmaline, Golden;

jet lag Proustite
joints Angel Wing Blue Anhydrite; Crocodile Rock; Lilac Lepidolite; Oogulite; *see also* skeletal system

karmic roots of disease Lapis Lazuli
kidney infection Opal, Oregon
kidneys Brazilianite; Buddstone; Celestite; Chrysoberyl, Golden; Golden Labradorite; Jet; Marcasite; Obsidian, Mahogany; Opal, Precious, Oregon; Rhodonite; Scapolite, Yellow; Tiger Iron; Topaz, Golden

laryngitis Agate; Aquamarine; Chrysocolla; Gem Silica; *see also* throat
legs Onyx; Spider Jasper; Vesuvianite; *see also* skeletal system
lesions Cinnabar
lethargy Russian Red Quartz
leukemia Bixbite
life force Ammonite, Rainbow; Aventurine, Green; *see also* prana
ligaments Crocodile Rock; Oogulite
liver Aegirine; Aventurine, Red; Bixbite; Bloodstone; Chrysoberyl, Golden; Jasper, Rainforest; Jet; Magnetite; Marcasite; Obsidian, Mahogany; Petrified Wood; Pyromorphite; Rhodonite
love-based physiology Rose Quartz
lungs Aragonite, Blue; Auralite, Emerald; Azeztulite, Blue-Green; Azeztulite, Green-Fire; Black Phantom Quartz; Calcite, Blue; Clinizoisite; Cuprite; Devalite; Diopside; Gaia Stone; Jasper, Unakite; Lepidocrocite; Opal, Common (Pink); Opal, Common (Blue); Seraphinite; Tiger Iron
lymphatic system Calcite, Red; Halite, Blue; Prehnite; Dravite

memory Barite: Iolite; Siberian Blue Quartz
menopause, female Bloodstone; Cuprite; Diopside; Vanadinite
menopause, male Vanadinite
menstrual irregularities Covellite; Cuprite; Moonstone; Papagonite
mental focus Aventurine, Blue; Tourmaline, Pink
meridian system Auralite, Emerald; Calcite, Orange; Obsidian, Black; Rhodonite; Sichuan Quartz
metabolism Albite; Agni Gold Danburite: Apatite, Green; Calcite, Orange; Celestite; Citrine, Natural; Citrine, Heat Treated; Dolomite; Gaspeite; Golden Labradorite; Halite, Pink; Imperial Gold Quartz; Rhodonite; Rutile; Sunstone; Wulfenite
microbial infections, *see* infections
migraines Azurite; Cavansite; Gaia Stone; Herderite; Lazulite; Muscovite; Papagonite; Rhodozite; Topaz, Blue; Tourmaline, Blue
MS Eudialyte; Natrolite
multiple sclerosis, *see* MS
muscle issues Crocodile Rock; Opal, Common (Brown or Black); Oogulite; Tiger Iron
muscle injuries Faden Quartz; Hematite Magnets; Jasper, Red
muscle spasm and twitches Aventurine, Blue; Magnesite
muscular system Black Phantom Quartz; Staurolite
muscular tension Aqua Lemuria; Magnesite; Stichtite
myelin sheath Black Phantom Quartz; Rhodochrosite; Tibetan Black Quartz

nail growth Apache Tears; Opal, Precious (White); Topaz, White
narcolepsy Chalcedony, Purple
nausea Libyan Gold Tektite; Tourmaline, Golden
neck Topaz, Blue

nerve disorders Amethyst; Natrolite; Phenacite
nerve ganglia Tibetan Black Quartz
nerve strengthening Pietersite
nerves, severed Faden Quartz; Imperial Gold Quartz
nervous breakdown Lilac Lepidolite; Lithium Quartz
nervous exhaustion Imperial Gold Quartz;
nervous system Angel Aura Quartz; Astrophyllite; Auralite, Emerald; Benitoite; Black Phantom Quartz; Calcite, Merkabite; Datolite; Dolomite; Eudialyte; Faden Quartz; Grape Agate; Jade, Green; Jade, Purple; K2; Merlinite; Rhodochrosite; Scheelite; Tibetan Black Quartz; Tugtupite; Variscite
neural link between heart and brain Lemurian Mist Crystals
neural pathway regeneration Stichtite
neuronal activity Agate, Moss
nutrient assimilation Brookite; Cacoxinite; Calcite, Pink, Opaque; Dravite; Prasiolite
nightmares Lepidolite; Lilac Lepidolite; Muscovite; Sugilite
nutrient absorption Libyan Gold Tektite

optic nerve Onyx; Rhodizite; Scapolite, Blue
osteoporosis Angelite; Black Phantom Quartz; Calcite, Red; Cryolite; Dolomite; Meteorite, Chondrite; Sphene
ovaries Carnelian; Garnet, Almandine; *see also* reproductive system
overeating, *see* weight issues
oxygenation Amethyst; Goethite; Healer's Gold; Lepidocrocite; Magnetite; Malachite; Papagoite; Sphalerite; Tremolite; Turquoise

pain relief Hematite Magnets; Aragonite Star Clusters
palpitations Rose Quartz; Stibnite; *see also* heart
pancreas Calcite, Honey; Pyromorphite; Tiger Iron
parasites Proustite; Jade, Black
parasympathetic nervous system Kunzite; Moonstone, Polarity
Parkinson's disease Albite; Diaspore; Eudialyte; Natrolite; Protector Quartz; Stichite
pelvis Spider Jasper
'phantom pain' Rutilated Quartz
physical energy Agate, Fire
physical evolution Pyromorphite
physical fitness Adamite
physical strength Jasper, Red
pineal gland Adamite; Alexandrite; Cavansite; Hemimorphite; Sapphire, White; Sphene; Magnesite;
pituitary gland Adamite; Alexandrite; Cavansite; Girasol Quartz; Hemimorphite; Sapphire, White; Sphene; Magnesite;
PMS Adamite; Ajoite; Hemimorphite
poison Spinel
polyps Chlorite Phantom Crystals
pollution, environmental Tourmaline, Black
prana Cuprite
prefrontal lobes Diamond; Siberian Blue Quartz; Roswellite; *see also* brain
pregnancy Calcite, Red; Jasper, Red; Jasper, Mook; Larimar
premier healing stone Seraphinite
prosperity Amber; Apatite, Golden; Aventurine, Green
prostate gland Healer's Gold
psoriasis, *see* skin problems
psychic surgery Chlorite Phantom Crystals; Seriphos Green Quartz
purification Herkimer Quartz 'Diamond'; Jet; Protector Quartz ; Rhodonite; Tourmaline, Black

radiation Chlorite Phantom Crystals; Chrysoberyl, Green; Galena; Herkimer Quartz 'Diamond'; Hollandite Quartz; Prophecy Stone; Purpurite; Pyromorphite; Smoky Quartz; Vanadinite; Willemite
radiation poisoning, *see* radiation
rash, *see* skin problems
recovery from illness Buddstone; Cataclosite Impact Stone; Chrysoberyl, Catseye; Heartenite; Kammererite
red blood cells Auralite, Emerald; Magnetite; Malachite; Copper (Metal); Tiger Iron; *see also* blood
reflexes Kammererite
reflux Obsidian, Gold Sheen; Tourmaline, Golden; *see also* acid, digestive issues
regeneration Chryosprase; Diopside; Jasper, Mook;
rejuvenatioin Heartenite
removal of entities Shaman Stone
reproductive issues Calcite, Red; Covellite; Cuprite; Dioptase; Garnet, Spessartine; Lepidocrocite; Obsidian, Black; Shiva Lingham; Smithsoninte; Sunstone; Vanadinite; Zincite
reproductive system, female Crocoite; Jasper, Mook; Copper (Metal); Smithsonite
respiratory illness Aragonite, Blue; Opal, Blue; Aragonite, Blue
respiratory system Calcite, Blue; Clinichlore; Gem Silica
rosacea, *see* skin problems

SAD Adamite; Amber
seasonal affective disorder, *see* SADs
seizure Kyanite
self-abuse Nebula Stone; Dravite
self-destructive habits Staurolite
self-discovery Astrophyllite
serotonin levels Scolecite
sexual abuse, *see* sexual issues
sexual energy Agate, Fire; Sapphire, Padparadscha
sexual intimacy Calcite, Red
sexual issues Cinnabar; Dioptase; Fulgurite; Jasper, Red; Quartz, Scepter; Ruby; Russian Red Quartz; Sapphire, Scepter Quartz; Padparadscha (Orange Sapphire); Tangerine Quartz; Willemite; Wulfenite; Zincite
sexual organs Bixbite; Brazilianite; Bustamite; Calcite, Orange; Cuprite; Strontianite
sexual repulsion Russian Red Quartz
sinusitis Goshenite
skeletal system Angel Wing Blue Anhydrite; Angelite; Black Phantom Quartz; Petrified Wood; Tiger Iron
skin problems Aquamarine; Jade, Purple; Marcasite; Opal, Common (Blue); Opal, Precious (White); Pyrite
sleep disorders Iolite; Lepidolite; Muscovite
social issues Cerussite
sore throat Agate; Chalcedony, Blue; Chrysocolla; Gem Silica; Larimar; Topaz, Blue
speech disorders Euclase; Topaz, Blue
spine Petrified Wood; Stichtite
spleen Aegirine; Apatite, Golden; Brazilianite; Golden Labradorite; Pyromorphite; Sapphire, Yellow; Shattuckite
spontaneous natural purging Staurolite
sports injury Hematite Magnets
stagnation Magnesite
stamina Aegirine; Agate, Fire; Citrine; Meteorite, Nickel-Iron; Rutile
stomach issues Buddstone; *see* gastric disorder
'stone of youth' Chrysoprase
strength Jasper, Red; Malachite; Meteorite, Nickel-Iron; Onyx
stress Agate, Dendritic; Albite; Amazonite; Amblygonite; Angel Aura Quartz; Aqua Lemuria; Aqua Aura Quartz; Calcite, Pink, Transparent; Cavansite; Chrysoberyl, Green; Chrysocolla; Dolomite; Gaia Stone; Grape Agate;

Jade, Purple; Kunzite; Lilac Lepidolite; Lithium Quartz; Moonstone, Polarity; Petalite; Rhodocrosite; Trulite Silica
stroke Herderite; Kyanite
stuttering Euclase
substance abuse Nebula Stone; Tourmalined Quartz; *see also* alcohol, drugs, tobacco
subtle body Azeztulite, New Zealand White; Merlinite-Amethyst

sunburn Chrysoberyl, Green; Purpurite
surgery, recovery Calcite, Pink, Opaque; Faden Quartz; Quartz, Self-Healed
swelling Jade, Blue
systemic illness Seraphinite

teeth Fluorite
tension Magnesite
terminal prognosis Cassiterite
testes Carnelian; Garnet, Almandine; Healer's Gold
throat problems Aquamarine; Azeztulite, Blue-Green; Chalcedony, Blue; Opal, Precious (Owyhee Blue); Topaz, Blue
thymus gland Agate
thyroid gland Adamite; Agate; Amazonite; Azeztulite, Blue-Green; Cacoxinite; Chrysocolla; Ocean Jasper; Shaman Stone; Tanzanite; Topaz, Blue; Zoisite
tinnitus Amethyst; Azurite
tissue regeneration and repair Calcite, Pink, Opaque; Jade, Green; Jasper, Unakite; Malachite; Copper (Metal); Ocean Jasper; Seriphos Green Quartz
tobacco use Dolomite; Jasper, Rainforest; Peridot; Rutile; Zircon
toes Protector Quartz
tonic stone Jade, Red
toxic emotion Agate, Dendritic
toxic energy and pollution from electrical systems Hematite, Specular; Jasper, Unakite; Pyromorphite
toxin elimination Aegirine; Halite, Blue; Halite, Pink; Nebula Stone; Prehnite; Prophecy Stone; Pyromorphite; Tourmaline, Black; Spinel
trauma (physical) Amazonite; Amegreen; Cataclosite Impact Stone; Dioptase; Goethite; Kunzite; Kyanite; Quartz, Self-Healed; Spider Jasper; Vivianite
tumors Dream Quartz; Epidote; Opal, Precious (Black); Seriphos Green Quartz

ulcers Amblygonite; Libyan Gold Tektite; Scapolite, Pink; Tourmaline, Golden
urinary issues Celestite; Opal, Precious (Oregon); Prehnite; Topaz, Golden

vein issues Vesuvianite
venous and arterial walls Aventurine, Blue; *see also* circulatory system
vertigo (dizziness) Apatite, Blue; Azurite; Fairy Wand Quartz; Fluorite; Moscovite; Sapphire, Blue; Stibnite
vibrational healing Shaman Stone
virus, *see* infection
vision issues Fairy Wand Quartz; Lazulite; Scapolite, Blue; Sphene; Ulexite
vitality Adamite; Agate, Fire; Ammonite, Rainbow; Axinite Clinichlore; Crocoite; Cuprite; Healer's Gold; Jasper, Red; Kammererite; Lemurian Jade; Malachite; Protector Quartz; Ruby; Russian Red Quartz; Sapphire, Yellow; Sunstone
vitamin assimilation Brookite
vocal cords Gem Silica; Chalcedony, Blue

warts Cinnabar
water retention Hanksite; Moonstone; Sodalite
weakness Jasper, Red
weight lifting and body building Jasper, Red; Copper (Metal); Onyx
weight loss, *see* weight management
weight management Adamite; Angelite; Apatite, Golden; Astrophyllite; Calcite, Clear; Calcite, Red; Celestite; Cerussite; Citrine, Heat Treated; Dolomite; Dream Quartz; Garnet, Spessartine; Gaspeite; Iolite-Sunstone; Jasper, Red; Jasper, Rainforest; Jasper, Unakite; Magnetite;Marcasite; Onyx; Rhodonite; Ruby, Star; Russian Red Quartz; Smithsonite
well being Clinizoisite
wounds, *see* trauma

SPIRITUAL/EMOTIONAL CORRESPONDENCES

absent healing Calcite, Pink, Opaque
abundance Agate, Moss; Apache Gold; Apatite, Green; Cassiterite; Chrysoberyl; Clinochlore; Emerald; Golden Aura Quartz; Uvarovite Garnet; Jade, Green; Jet; Lemurian Jade; Obsidian, Mahogany; Yellow Sapphire; Topaz, Golden; Tourmaline, Golden
abuse of power Obsidian, Gold Sheen
acceleration Rutilated Quartz; Rutile
acceptance Calcite, Pink, Transparent; Seriphos Green Quartz
action, graceful Rutilated Quartz
action, productive Iolite-Sunstone; Jade, Red; Pyrite; Quartz (Clear); Scepter Quartz
activation stone Moldavite
adaptability Diaspore
addiction, behavior and recovery Aegirine; Agate, Moss; Amethyst; Black Andradite Garnet; Jade, Red; Lepidocrocite; Ocean Jasper
adventure Ruby; Sunstone
adventurousness Crocodile Rock
aging, slowing Jasper, Mook
agni mani (fire pearl) Moldavite; Tektite
agoraphobia Pallasite Meteorite
'aha' experience Calcite, Blue; Sodalite
Akashic records Alexandrite; Ammonite, Rainbow; Angelite; Apatite, Blue; Aqua Lemuria; Calcite, Stellar Beam; Cavansite; Celestian Quartz; Chalcedony, Purple; Covellite; Creedite; Datolite; Elestial Quartz; Euclase; Goethite; Heulandite; Labradorite; Lapis Lazuli; Lemurian Mist Crystals; Libyan Gold Tektite; Magnesite; Chondrite Meteorite; Papagonite; Petrified Wood; Scheelite; White Phantom Quartz
alchemy Cinnabar; Cuprite; Girasol Quartz; Wulfenite
alchemical transformation Cerussite; Trulite Silica;
alignment with Divine plan Cacoxenite
alignment, Will with Heart Chrysoberyl
aligment, physical and light Variscite
Alignment, energies Magnetite
alternate lives Nuummite
alternate realm Satyaloka Quartz
altruism Calcite, Green; Chrysoprase; Kunzite; Rhodonite; Vivianite
ambition Pyrite
amplification Quartz (Clear); Rutilated Quartz; Rutile

ananda Celestite, Ohio
ancient civilizations Chalcedony, Purple; Almandine Garnet; Heulandite; Jasper, Picture; Petrified Wood; Quartz, Sunken Record Keeper
ancient knowledge Cuprite; Papagoite
angelic communication Ajoite; Angel Wing Blue Anhydrite; Angelite; Azeztulite, Lemurian Gold; Celestine; Clinochlore; Danburite; Elestial Quartz; Opal, Owyhee Blue; Prehnite
angelic connections Agni Gold Danburite; Heartenite; Seraphinite
angelic domain Angel Phantom Quartz; Aqua Lemuria; Celestite; Creedite; Elestial Quartz; Fairy Wand Quartz; Opal, Common; Seriphos Green Quartz
angelic entities Hemimorphite; Lemurian Seed Crystals; Morganite; Smithsonite
angelic guides Azeztulite, Sedona; Benitoite; Celestite; Platinum (Metal); Pink Amethyst; Purpurite
angels Agate, Ellensburg Blue; Amethyst: Chrysoberyl, Catseye; Covellite; Gem Silica; Heartenite; Herkimer Quartz 'Diamond'; Platinum (Metal); Phenacite; Selenite; Seraphinite
angels in human form Angel Wing Blue Anhydrite
anger Angel Wing Blue Anhydrite; Aquamarine; Azeztulite, New Zealand White; Danburite; Jade, Black; Larimar
animal communication Jasper, Mook
anxiety Andalusite; Azeztulite, New Zealand White; Chalcedony, Blue; Cuprite; Danburite; Smithsonite; Tourmaline, Pink; Tremolite
anxiety, financial Grossular, Garnet
aphrodisiac Calcite, Orange; Rubellite
appreciation Sapphire, Pink
archetypal masculine and feminine Spider Jasper
Arthurian legends Iolite
Arthurian times Merlinite
artistic expressions Agate, Fire; Iolite
artists, *see* creative people
Ascended Masters Prehnite
ascension Barite; Brookite; Calcite, Stellar Beam; Calcite, Merkabite; Heliodore; Herkimer Quartz 'Diamond'
Ascension stone Natrolite
Ashtar Tektite
assertiveness Apache Gold; Heliodore; Jade, Red; Vesuvianite
astral energies Opal, Owyhee Blue; Tibetan Black Quartz;
astral entities Pyromorphite; Willemite
astral parasites Angel Aura Quartz; Apache Tears
astral planes Scapolite; Sichuan Quartz; Sphene; Staurolite; Stilbite
astral projection Albite; Jet
astral travel Benitoite; Calcite, Blue; Covellite; Dream Quartz; Herkimer Quartz 'Diamond'; Labradorite; Lazulite; Natrolite; Obsidian, Peacock; Opal, Common; Quartz, Tabular; Rhodizite; Blue Sapphire; Scheelite; Sphene
astrology Herderite; Iolite
Atlantean connection Brazilianite
Atlantis Calcite, Stellar Beam; Cathedral Quartz; White Phantom Quartz
attachment, releasing negative Barite; Lepidocrocite; Quartz (Clear)
attention, focus Onyx
attraction Epidote; Spessartine
attunement Jade, Purple; Jade, Lavendar; Obsidian, Snowflake; Russian Red Quartz; Rutile
aura balancing Hemimorphite
aura cleansing Agate, Purple Sage; Chalcedony, Purple; Smoky Quartz
aura, healing Lithium Quartz
aura, holes Chalcedony, Blue; Tourmaline, Pink
aura, purification Marcasite
auras, seeing Calcite, Clear
auras, strengthening Green Heulandite
auric field Aragonite star Clusters; Faden Quartz; Infinite; Phenacite
auric field, cleansing Selenite
auric field stabilization Blizzard Stone
auric leaks Seriphos Green Quartz
automatic writing Shattuckite
awakening Azeztulite, Black Tourmaline; Fulgurite; Moldavite; Muscovite; Satyaloka Quartz; Scolecite; Vivianite; Zoisite
awareness, expansion Adamite; Agate, Purple Sage; Angel Aura Quartz; Angelite; Creedite; Moldavite; Moonstone, Polarity; Petalite; Rutilated Quartz; Rutile; Blue Sapphire; Sapphire, White; Sichuan Quartz
awareness of earth-as-paradise Seriphos Green Quartz

bad habits Jasper, Unakite
balance Amethyst; Chalcedony, Blue; Diopside; Dolomite; Healer's Gold; Jasper, Unakite; Lepidolite; Sphalerite; Tiger Eye; Tourmaline, Pink
balance of energies Blizzard Stone; Sichuan Quartz
balancing polarities Magnetite; Marcasite
beacon of light Sugilite
benevolence Elestial Quartz; Heliodore; Sunstone
birth and death Cassiterite
blessings Sunstone
blockage Calcite, Stellar Beam; Hanksite; Moldavite; Quartz, Double Terminated; Zincite
boundaries Amazonite
brain evolution Herderite; Natrolite
brain function Amethyst; Lazulite; Tugtupite
breaththrough Cavansite; Obsidian, Peacock
breath work Aragonite, Blue; Shaman Stone
bridging higher and lower worlds Covellite
bubble of light Amethyst; Tourmalined Quartz
business skills Apatite, Golden

calm Agate, Blue Lace; Agate, Ellensburg Blue; Ajoite; Amblygonite; Aqua Aura Quartz; Aqua Lemuria; Chalcedony, Blue; Dolomite; Gel Lithium Silica; Girasol Quartz; Larimar; Opal, Common, Blue; Opal, Owyhee Blue; Merlinite-Amethyst; Smithsonite; Watermelon Tourmaline; Tremolite
career changes Cerussite
Cathars Iolite
causal dimensions Obsidian, Peacock
cellular encoding Elestial Quartz
cellular memory Almandine Garnet; Ocean Jasper; Quartz, Raised Record Keeper
centeredness Agate, Blue Lace; Chalcedony, Blue; Dolomite; Sichuan Quartz
chakras, activation Moldavite
chakras, clearing Angel Aura Quartz; Quartz
chakras, re-energizing Hematite Magnets
channeling Angelite; Aqua Aura Quartz; Benitoite; Chalcedony, Blue; Creedite; Danburite; Dream Quartz; Gem Silica; Hemimorphite; Iolite; Iolite-Sunstone; Lazulite; Copper (Metal); Niobium (Metal); Shattuckite; Zircon
charisma Spessartine
chi Cinnabar; Spessartine; Jade, Green; Jade, Red; Jasper, Red; Opal, Fire; Prehnite; Ruby; Zircon
children Lithium Quartz
Christ Rose Quartz

Christ consciousness Heliodore; Sphene; Tiger Eye; Topaz, Golden
clairaudience Cavansite; Celestite, Ohio; Chalcedony, Purple; Dumortierite; Lazulite; Siberian Blue Quartz; Tourmaline, Blue
clairsentience Celestite, Ohio; Chalcedony, Purple; Dumortierite; Lazulite; Siberian Blue Quartz; Topaz, White; Tourmaline, Blue
clairvoyance and mediumship Adamite; Adularia; Agate, Holly Blue; Angelite; Azeztulite, Lemurian Gold; Beryllonite; Calcite, Blue; Cavansite; Celestite, Ohio; Chalcedony, Purple; Covellite; Diamond; Dumortierite; Gem Silica; Gray Moonstone; Halite; Heliodore; Hemimorphite; Herderite; Iolite; Jade, Blue; Jet; Labradorite; Lazulite; Merlinite; Niobium (Metal); Moonstone; Muscovite; Natrolite; Nuummite; Petalite; Shattuckite; Siberian Blue Quartz; Sichuan Quartz; Topaz, White; Tourmaline, Blue; Ulexite
clarity Agate, Blue Lace; Agnie Gold Danburite; Albite; Amber; Amblygonite; Ametrine; Apatite, Golden; Calcite, Clear; Calcite, Red; Euclase; Fluorite; Golden Labradorite; Jade, Blue; Lemurian Jade; Moonstone; Sapphire, White; Smithsonite; Stilbite; Tremolite; Variscite
cleansing Andalusite; Azeztulite, Black Tourmaline; Brazilianite; Halite; Moldavite; Quartz (Clear); Sugilite; White Phantom Quartz
clear thinking Tourmalined Quartz;
clearing Aegirine; Quartz
clearing spaces Calcite, Stellar Beam
'cloak of invisibility' Malachite
cocoon of Light Celestite, Ohio
coincidence control Labradorite
comfort, emotional Andalusite
commitment Pyrite
communication Agate, Blue Lace; Agate, Ellensburg Blue; Amazonite; Angelite; Aqua Aura Quartz; Aquamarine; Aragonite, Blue; Cavansite; Chalcedony, Blue; Chrysocolla; Gem Silica; Hemimorphite; Lapis Lazuli; Lepidocrocite; Quartz (Clear); Shattuckite; Smithsonite; Topaz, Blue; Tourmaline, Blue; Turquoise
communication with animals or plants Azeztulite, Lemurian Gold; Diopside; Fairy Stones; Peridot; Serpentine
communication with higher beings Azeztulite, Sedona; Kyanite; Obsidian, Black; Prehnite
communication with crystals and stones Fairy Stones
communication with Nature Azeztulite, Green-Fire
communication with Nature Spirits Fairy Stones
communication with Spirit Sapphire, White
communion with Creation Brookite
compassion Ajoite; Amazonite; Amegreen; Azeztulite, Lemurian Gold; Azeztulite, New Zealand White; Calcite, Green; Calcite, Pink, Transparent; Celestite, Ohio; Chrysoprase; Devalite; Dioptase; Emerald; Gaia Stone; Goethite, Rainbow; Halite; Jade, Lavender; Morganite; Prasiolite; Quartz, Temple Heart Crystal (Dow); Rhodochrosite; Rhodonite; Rose Quartz; Sapphire, Yellow; Smithsonite; Stichtite; Tangerine Quartz; Variscite; Vivianite

concentration Agate, Moss; Amblygonite
confidence Aegirine; Agate, Blue Lace; Ajoite; Albite; Apache Gold; Apatite, Golden; Aragonite Star Clusters; Auralite, Emerald; Aventurine, Green; Buddstone; Calcite, Orange; Calcite, Honey; Carnelian; Goethite, Rainbow; Golden Labradorite; Healer's Gold; Heartenite; Libyan Gold Tektite; Malachite; (Metal): Gold; Morganite; Opal, Owyhee Blue; Pyrite; Rhodizite; Strontianite; Tourmaline, Golden
confusion, emotional Malachite
consciousness, expanding Agate, Holly Blue; Amegreen; Astrophyllite; Benitoite; Beryllonite; Calcite, Merkabite; Cavansite; Magnesite; Obsidian, Peacock; Quartz; Roswellite; Rutilated Quartz; Sichuan Quartz; Staurolite; Sunstone; Tibetan Black Quartz; Tugtupite
consciousness, multidimensional Papagoite
consciousness, pure Satyaloka Quartz
consciousness, shadow self Dravite
consciousness, visionary Diamond
consciousness, wordless Calcite, Red
contact with guides Dream Quartz
contentment Andalusite
cooling Aquamarine; Larimar
cords Quartz
core beliefs Amazonite
cosmic attunement Angel Aura Quartz; Moldavite
cosmic connection Platinum (Metal)
cosmic energy Satyaloka Quartz
cosmic Overmind Pallasite Meteorite
counseling Chalcedony, Blue
courage Albite; Apatite, Golden; Apophyllite, Clear; Bixbite; Black Phantom Quartz; Bloodstone; Carnelian; Curpite; Emerald; Hematite; Heulandite; Iolite-Sunstone; Jade, Red; Marcasite; Obsidian, Snowflake; Peridot; Protector Quartz; Ruby; Sphalerite; Sugilite; Tiger Iron; Rubellite; Tourmaline, Golden; Dravite; Vesuvianite
creation Apatite, Golden
creative people Agate, Ellensburg Blue; Iolite-Sunstone; Larimar
creativity Adamite; Agate, Fire; Amblygonite; Amegreen; Ametrine; Black Andradite Garnet; Brazilianite; Bustamite; Calcite, Orange; Citrine; Clinizoisite; Crocoite; Fairy Wand Quartz; Spessartine; Goethite; Golden Labradorite; Herderite; Jade, Red; Lepidocrocite; Malachite; Gold (Metal); Pyrite; Scepter Quartz; Russian Red Quartz; Rutile; Sapphire, Yellow; Sapphire, PPadparadscha; Sodalite; Tangerine Quartz; Tiger Iron; Topaz, Golden; Ulexite; Vanadinite; Willemite; Zincite
crop circles Amber
curiosity Tangerine Quartz

Dark Goddess Spider Jasper;
Dark Night of the Soul Apophyllite, Clear; Diamond
death ceremonies Cassiterite
decisiveness Ametrine; Fluorite
deep journey Nuummite; Obsidian, Rainbow
demonic influences Pyromorphite
density Epidote; Quartz
depression Andalusite; Azeztulite, New Zealand White; Elestial Quartz; Eudialyte; Gel Lithium Silica; Lepidocrocite; Gold (Metal); Obsidian, Mahogany; Ocean Jasper; Opal, Common; Strombolite; Tourmaline, Pink; Rubellite; Tremolite
desire Topaz, Golden
desperation Chalcedony, Blue
destiny path Apache Gold; Hollandite Quartz; Nirvana Quartz; Rhodonite; Scapolite
determination Agate, Moss; Buddstone; Ruby; Wulfenite; Zincite
devas, devic beings Agate, Moss; Amber; Chlorite Phantom Crystals; Chrysoprase; Devalite; Hemimorphite; Infinite; Jade, Purple; Jasper, Rainforest; Merlinite; Oogulite; Peridot; Prehnite; Staurolite
development, inner and outer Zoisite
Devic energies Apache Tears; Aventurine, Green, Devalite

Devic realm Devalite; Diopside; Fairy Wand Quartz; Pallasite Meteorite; Seriphos Green Quartz; Staurolite; Tourmaline, Green; Tourmaline, Watermelon
dharma (path of highest destiny) Petalite; Scapolite
diagnostic tools Aragonite Star Clusters
dimensional doorways Apophyllite, Green; Calcite, Stellar Beam; Herkimer Quartz 'Diamond'; Quartz, Portal; Quartz, Time Link; Stilbite
direction Quartz, Scepter
discernment Jade, Purple; K2; Sapphire, White; Tiger Eye
discipline Jasper, Fancy; Lazulite; Onyx; Blue Sapphire; Vanadinite
discrimination Heliodore; Jade, Blue; Sphalerite
disorientation Jasper, Picture; Magnetite
distress, emotional Kammererite; Rose Quartz
Divine Benevolence Agate, Purple Sage
Divine bliss, see *ananda*
Divine blueprint Agate, Dendritic; Agate, Fire; Agate, Moss; Clinochlore; Flint; Transmutite
Divine co-creation Imperial Gold Quartz
Divine communication Ajoite; Chalcedony, Blue; Covellite; Crocoite
Divine connection Alexandrite; Amethyst; Grape Agate; Lilac Lepidolite
Divine creation Wulfenite
Divine Father Gold (Metal)
Divine Feminine Aquamarine; Cuprite; Girasol Quartz; Larimar; Lemurian Jade; Lemurian Seed Crystals; Seraphinite
Divine guidance Ajoite; Ametrine
Divine intention Rutile
Divine inspiration Dumortierite; Lapis Lazuli
Divine knowledge Quartz, Initiation Crystal (Channeling); Sapphire, Star
Divine Love Alexandrite; Calcite, Green; Clinochlore; Elestial Quartz; Kunzite; Lepidocrocite; Morganite; Smithsonite; Tugtupite
Divine mind Alexandrite; Dumortierite
Divine purpose Beryllonite; Cryolite; Heliodore
Divine source Danburite
Divine, union with Rose Quartz
Divine Will Ametrine; Apatite, Golden; Calcite, Stellar Beam; Heliodore; Libyan Gold Tektite; Obsidian, Gold Sheen; Opal, Common; Prasiolite; Spirit Quartz; Topaz, White; Topaz, Golden; Tourmaline, Golden
divorce Dioptase
DNA Quartz, Raised Record Keeper
doubt Jade, Black; Yellow Sapphire
downloading of spiritual information Celestine
dowsing Diopside; Infinite; Vanadinite
dream enhancement Dream Quartz
dream state Hemimorphite; Moldavite
dream stone Albite; Apatite, Blue
dream time Sphene
dreamwork Angel Phanton Quartz; Herkimer Quartz 'Diamond'; Jade, Green; Jasper, Picture; Lazulite; Rhodonite
dreams Aqua Lemuria; Bustamite; Girasol Quartz; Goshenite; Herkimer Quartz 'Diamond'; Heulandite; Jade, Purple; Moonstone; Quartz; Smoky Quartz; Stilbite; Sugilite
dysfunctional relationships Hemimorphite

earth changes Faden Quartz
earth consciousness Jasper, Picure; Lemurian Jade
earth connection Diopside; Wulfenite
earth energies Jasper, Mook; Jet; Vanadinite
earth evolution Apophyllite
Earth Goddess Cuprite
earth healing Apophyllite, Green; Jasper, Rainforest; Obsidian, Gold Sheen
Earth Mother Ajoite; Chrysoprase; Moonstone; *see also* feminine, Goddess, High Priestess
Earth's love Jasper, Rainforest
ecstasy Opal, Fire
efficiency Sodalite
electromagnetic energy Astrophyllite; Hematite Magnets
elemental beings Apache Tears
elemental forces Merlinite; Nuummite
eloquence Gem Silica
emotional abuse Calcite, Honey; Dioptase; Pink Amethyst
emotional amplifier Opal, White Precious
emotional attachments, release Agate, Holly Blue
emotional baggage, release of Aquamarine
emotional balance Adularia; Calcite, Green; Jasper, Red; Malachite; Rainbow Moonstone; Thulite
emotional body Ajoite; Andalusite; Apache Tears; Aqua Aura Quartz; Azeztulite, Black Tourmaline; Azeztulite, Blue-Green; Girasol Quartz; Golden Aura Quartz; Grape Agate; Kammererite; Merlinite-Amethyst; Oogulite; Smithsonite; Topaz, Blue
emotional exhaustion Seriphos Green Quartz
emotional healing Amegreen; Apache Tears; Aragonite Star Clusters; Aragonite, Blue; Aventurine, Green; Calcite, Pink, Transparent; Dravite; Eudialyte; Gaia Stone; Gaspeite; Girasol Quartz; Hemimorphite; Heulandite; Kunzite; Lepidopcrocite; Lepidolite; Ocean Jasper; Oogulite; Opal, Common, Pink; Rhodocrosite; Rhodolite Garnet; Rose Quartz; Rubellite; Tourmaline, Pink; Trulite Silica; Variscite
emotional paralysis Staurolite
emotional patterns, destructive Epidote
emotional perception Aragonite, Blue; Turquoise
emotional polarities Ajoite
emotional protection Opal, Common, Black and Brown
emotional resilience Imperial Gold Quartz
emotional soothing Cataclosite Impact Stone; Cavansite
emotional stability Pallasite Meteorite
emotional trauma Obsidian, Mahogany; Pink Amethyst
emotional turmoil Calcite, Pink, Opaque
empathy Azeztulite, Lemurian Gold; Calcite, Pink, Opaque; Hemimorphite; Kyanite; Lemurian Mist Crystals; Lepidocrocite; Thulite
endurance Agate, Moss; Spinel; Vanadinite
energetic alignment Barite
energetic overload Blizzard Stone
energetic patterns Infinite
energy Aegirine; Ruby; Spider Jasper; Tiger Iron
energy, male, archetypal Gold (Metal)
energy, command of Crocoite
energy, creative Jasper, Red
energy drain Andalusite
energy, elemental Merlinite; Strombolite
energy, feminine, archetypal Silver (Metal)
energy fields Amethyst; Aragonite Star Clusters; Faden Quartz; Fluorite
energy infusion Elestial Quartz
energy, loving Rhodochrosite
energy, lunar Silver (Metal)
energy, magnification Rhodizite
energy, male Pyrite; Sunstone
energy, negative Apache Tears
energy overload Hematite Magnets
energy, regenerative Seriphos Green Quartz; Spinel
energy transmission Quartz, Double-Terminated
energy vortex Azeztulite, Sedona

enlightenment Angel Aura Quartz; Crocoite; Herderite; Nirvana Quartz; Platinum (Metal); Pietersite; Quartz, Temple Heart Crystal (Dow)
enthusiasm Adamite, Ruby; Ammonite, Rainbow; Auralite, Emerald; Brucite, Golden; Heartenite; Russian Red Quartz; Strontianite; Titanium Quartz; Vesuvianite; Wulfenite
entity attachment Muscovite; Opal, Common
entity removal Astrophyllite; Quartz (Clear)
envy Jade, Black
ESP Apophyllite, Clear; Lazulite
etheric attachments Angel Wing Blue Anhydrite
etheric bandage Faden Quartz
etheric blueprint Calcite, Stellar Beam; Faden Quartz; Rutilated Quartz
etheric body Agate, Moss; Faden Quartz; Infinite
etheric 'bodyguard' Jade, Black
etheric chakras Selenite
etheric entity Niobium (metal)
etheric guide Brookite
etheric parasites Proustite
Ets Astrophyllite; Brookite; Chrysoberyl, Cat's Eye; Libyan Gold Tektite; (Metal): Niobium; Chondrite Meteorite; Natrolite; Prehnite; Stibnite; Tektite
euphoria Brucite, Golden; Lithium Quartz
'Eureka!' moment Albite; Crocodile Rock
evolution, personal Cerussite; Fulgurite; Moldavite; Nirvana Quartz
exorcism Astrophyllite
expansiveness Agate, Ellensburg Blue
experimentation Sunstone
extrasensory perception Blue Sapphire
extraterrestrial communication Condrite Meteorite
extraterrestrial entities Calcite, Stellar Beam; Covellite; Ulexite; Zircon
exuberance Goethite, Rainbow

'facing the shadow self' Jade, Black
faery Apache Tears; Diopside; Fairy Stones; *see also* fairy
faith Beryllonite
fairy Chlorite Phantom Crystals; Faden Quartz; Fairy Stones; Infinite; Oogulite; Pallasite Meteorite; Peridot; Prasiolite; Prehnite; Smoky Quartz; Staurolite; Ulexite
fatigue Spinel
fear Agate, Blue Lace; Ajoite; Andalusite; Angel Phanton Quartz; Aragonite; Barite; Danburite; Spinel; Gel Lithium Silica; Jade, Red; Larimar; Lepidocrocite; Moldavite; Opal, Common; Opal, Owyhee Blue; Yellow Sapphire; Scapolite; Serpentine; Spirit Quartz;; Staurolite; Tourmaline, Golden
fear of confrontation Black Phantom Quartz
fear of death Shaman Stone; Tourmaline, Blue
fear of falling Apatite, Blue
fear of flying Pallasite Meteorite
fear of heights Apatite, Blue
fear of pain Shaman Stone
fear of the unknown Gaia Stone; Iolite
fear of using personal power Black Phantom Quartz
feeling at home on the Earth Siberian Blue Quartz
female energy Ajoite
feminine Moonstone, see also Goddess, Great Mother; High Priestess
feminine power Larimar; Moonstone
flight Angel Wing Blue Anhydrite
forgiveness Ajoite; Angel Wing Blue Anhydrite; Astrophyllite; Calcite, Clear; Chrysoprase; Dioptase; Sapphire, Pink; Stichtite; Turquoise
freedom Purpurite; Sunstone
frequencies, attunement Stibnite
friendliness Strombolite
fulfillment Nebula Stone; Rhodonite
future, key to Quartz, Trigonic Quartz
future lives Quartz, Portal Quartz (Time Link)
future time stream Cryolite; Muscovite

gemstone healing layouts Topaz, Blue
generosity Rhodonite; Thulite
gentleness Girasol Quartz; Rose Quartz; Trulite Silica; Vivianite
geomancy Diopside; Infinite; Vanadinite
ghosts Smoky Quartz
Goddess Aquamarine; Lemurian Seed Crystals; Moldavite; Moonstone; Quartz, Manifest Spirit Crystal (Isis); *see also* feminite, High Priestess, Great Mother
Goddess energy Chrysocolla; Gaia Stone; Gem Silica; Jasper, Picture; Larimar
Goddess stone, *see* stone of the Goddess
Golden Void Herderite
good fortune Chrysanthemum Stone
good luck Aventurine, Green; Gaia Stone; Tektite
gratitude Apatite, Green; Hiddenite
Great Central Sun Agni Gold Danburite; Golden Labradorite; Pallasite Meteorite; Obsidian, Gold Sheen; Satyaloka Quartz; Sunstone
Great Mother Gem Silica; Jasper, Rainforest; Lemurian Seed Crystals; Moonstone; Nebula Stone; Prehnite; Rose Quartz
Green Tara Gaia Stone
grief Alexandrite; Apache Tears; Aquamarine; Azeztulite, New Zealand White; Cavansite; Danburite; Datolite; Gel Lithium Silica; Lepidocrocite; Pink Amethyst; Rainbow Moonstone; Morganite; Stilbite; Strombolite; Dravite; Tugutpite; Zoisite
grounding Agate, Moss; Andalusite; Apache Tears; Black Obsidian; Blizzard Stone; Chrysanthemum Stone; Crocoite; Dolomite; Black Andradite Garnet; Healer's Gold; Hematite; Specular Hematite; Jet; Magnetite; Copper (Metal); Proustite; Ruby; Smoky Quartz; Sphalerite; Staurolite; Tiger Iron; Tourmaline, Black; Vanadinite; Zircon
grounding the Light Prophecy stone
grounding the spiritual in the physical Celestial Quartz; Flint
growth Agate, Dendritic; Aventurine, Green; Buddstone; Chrysoprase; Petrified Wood
guardian angels Agate, Purple Sage; Angelite
guilt, overcoming Agate, Dendritic

hall of records Calcite, Merkabite; Celestial Quartz
happiness Auralite, Emerald; Brucite, Golden; Papagoite; Protector Quartz
harmful vibrations Astrophyllite
harmony Amazonite; Aragonite, Blue; Healer's Gold; Moonstone, Polarity; Rainbow Moonstone; Spirit Quartz
hatred Black Jade
healing Agate, Purple Sage; Amber; Blizzard Stone; Charoite; Clinochlore; Crocoite; Cuprite; Diopside; Emerald; Healer's Gold; Iolite; Jasper, Fancy; Jasper, Unakite; Lemurian Jade; Lemurian Seed Crystals; Quartz, Self-Healed; Quartz, Temple Heart Crystal (Dow); Seriphos Green Quartz; Tourmaline, Green; Ziosite
healing a damaged root chakra Proustite
healing and love, broadcast Quartz
healing energy Nebula Stone
healing from grief Goethite
healing, genetic Jasper, Mook
healing herbs Seriphos Green Quartz

healing, physical Blizzard Stone; Faden Quartz
healing words Aragonite, Blue
health Calcite, Pink, Opaque; Chrysoprase; Clinochlore; Grossular; Jade, Green; Jade, Red; Jasper, Red; Spider Jasper
healthy habits Staurolite; Thulite
heart alignment Green Heulandite
heart, awakening Rasiolite; Colecite
heart awareness Scheelite
heart chakra, expansion Datolite
heart connection Calcite, Green
heart, courageous Rhodochrosite; Stichtite
heart frequency Quartz (Clear)
heart healing Hiddenite; Malachite; Rose Quartz; Rubellite; Tourmaline, Watermelon
heart intelligence Azeztulite, Green-Fire; Heartenite
heart, kindling Vivianite
heart knowledge Apatite, Green; Kunzite; Lepidocrocite; Moldavite; Muscovite
heart, loving Hiddenite
heart of the Earth Rubellite
heart opening Diopside; Eudialyte; Lemurian Seed Crystals; Tugtupite
heart, Universal Rubellite; Tugtupite
heart wisdom Crocoite; Cryolite; Magnesite
heartbeat of the Earth Chlorite Phantom Crystals; Gaia Stone
hidden talent Rhodonite
high heart Datolite; Dioptase; Emerald
High Priestess Cuprite; Silver (Metal); Moonstone
high will Datolite
higher brain Herderite; Natrolite
higher-chakra awakening Brookite
higher consciousness Natrolite; Tourmaline, Blue
higher dimensions Celestite; Papagoite
higher guidance Adularia; Gem Silica; Jade, Lavendar; Labradorite; Opal, Owyhee Blue
higher knowledge Calcite, Stellar Beam; Calcite, Merkabite; Magnesite; Blue Sapphire; Tremolite
higher mind Aragonite Star Clusters; Lemurian Jade; Titanium (Metal); Rutile; Scolecite; Tremolite
higher purpose Fulgurite
higher realms Agate, Ellensburg Blue; Apophyllite; Datolite; Jasper, Unakite; Petalite; Phenacite
Higher self Agate, Moss; Amegreen; Angel Phantom Quartz; Apophyllite, Clear; Auralite, Emerald; Barite; Chalcedony, Purple; Clinochlore; Elestial Quartz; Hollandite Quartz; Lithium Quartz; Natrolite; Prasiolite; Sapphire, White; Scapolite; Selenite; Spirit Quartz
higher vibrations Copper (Metal)
'holy fire' Opal, White Precious
Holy Grail Moldavite
honesty Flint
hope Alexandrite; Beryllonite; Spinel
hope, rebirth Rose Quartz
hopelessness Datolite
humiliation Obsidian, Mahogany
humility Dolomite
humor Brucite, Golden; Goethite, Rainbow; Jade, Purple; Kammererite; Oogulite; Strombolite; Titanium Quartz
hyperactivity Gel Lithium Silica
hypnosis Blue Sapphire
hysteria Aquamarine; Staurolite; Rubellite

I AM Cavansite; Satyaloka Quartz
imagination Citrine; Opal, Oregon; Ulexite
implants Quartz (Clear)
increase Peridot; Indicolite, *see* Tourmaline, Blue 'Indigos' Tourmaline, Pink
initiation Lemurian Jade; Phenacite; Purpurite
indecision Calcite, Orange; Datolite;
infusion with Light Astrophyllite
initiation Bustamite; Cataclosite Impact Stone
inner bridge Kyanite
inner child Brucite, Golden; Bustamite; Lepidocrocite; Pink Amethyst
inner exploration Albite; Diaspore
inner guidance Adularia; Agate, Purple Sage; Cathedral Quartz; Dumortierite
inner journey Jasper, Picture
inner king Adularia; Diamond; Lapis Lazuli; Libyan Gold Tektite
inner knowledge Phenacite
inner peace Angel Phantom Quartz; Cavansite; Celestite, Ohio; Fairy Wand Quartz; Lithium Quartz; Petrified Wood; Prehnite; Scolecite; Stilbite; Variscite; Vivianite
inner queen Diamond; Lapis Lazuli; Libyan Gold Tektite
'inner radar' Shaman Stone
inner release Obsidian Mahogany
inner sight Quartz, Initiation Crystal (Channeling)
inner silence Agate, Blue Lace; Agnite Gold Danburite; Nirvana Quartz; Vivianite
inner strength Aventurine, Blue; Nuummite; Onyx; Tourmaline, Golden
inner truth Ajoite; Gem Silica
inner vision Ajoite; Angel Wing Blue Anhydrite; Barite; Blizzard Stone; Calcite, Blue; Covellite; Diamond; Goshenite; Iolite; Lapis Lazuli; Lithium Quartz; Magnesite; Catseye Moonstone; Phenacite; Ulexite; Willemite
inner work Agate, Dendritic
innocence Tangerine Quartz
insight Apache Gold; Aragonite; Blue; Calcite, Clear; Calcite, Honey; Cinnabar; Lazulite; Moonstone; Obsidian, Snowflake; Pietersite; Purpurite; Rutile; Blue Sapphire; Scapolite; Siberian Blue Quartz; Sodalite
inspiration Iolite-Sunstone; Muscovite; Protector Quartz; Rutile; Spinel; Tangerine Quartz; Vivianite
inspired writing Iolite-Sunstone
instinct Jasper, Mook
integrity Crocoite; Gold (Metal)
intellectual power Calcite, Honey; Cinnabar
integration Hematite
integration of opposites Moonstone, Polarity
integrity Amazonite; Euclase
intensity Diamond
intention Topaz, Golden
interdimensional awareness Apophyllite, Clear; Roswellite;
interdimensional beings Brookite; Stibnite
interdimensional communication Aqua Aura Quartz; Astrophyllite; Brookite; Platinum (Metal); Chondrite Meteorite; Roswellite; Siberian Blue Quartz
interdimensional gates Cassiterite; Phenacite; Roswellite
interdimensional travel Barite; Calcite, Stellar Beam; Calcite, Merkabite; Cavansite; Danburite; Dream Quartz; Fairy Wand Quartz; Heulandite; Natrolite; Pallasite Meteorite; Phenacite; Pietersite; Quartz (Clear); Rhodizite; Roswellite; Rutilated Quartz; Scheelite; Scolecite; Sphene; Willemite
interdimensional world Apache Tears
introversion Gold (Metal)
intuition Agate, Holly Blue; Alexandrite; Amegreen; Aragonite, Blue; Azeztulite, New Zealand White; Benitoite; Euclase; Iolite-Sunstone; Jade, Lavender; Merlinite; Moonstone; Muscovite; Nuummite; Papagoite;

Phenacite; Pietersite; Prehnite; Pyromorphite; Shaman Stone; Shattuckite; Sodalite; Sphene; Tektite; Ulexite; Zoisite
invincibility Cinnabar; (Metal): Titanium
inward journeys Adularia; (Metal): Silver
isolation Andalusite;

joy Adamite; Alexandrite; Angel Phantom Quartz; Apatite, Green; Azeztulite, New Zealand White; Azeztulite, Sedona; Beryllonite; Bustamite; Calcite, Pink, Transparent; Dioptase; Gem Silica; Goethite, Rainbow; Hemimorphite; Jasper, Rainforest; Merlinite-Amethyst; Ocean Jasper; Oogulite; Opal, Oregon; Pink Amethyst; Rose Quartz; Smithsonite; Stilbite; Thulite; Tourmaline, Pink; Tourmaline, Watermelon; Tugtupite

karmic patterns Dioptase
karmic understanding Aegirine; Euclase
kindness Devalite; Thulite; Tourmaline, Pink
kinesiology Infinite
Kingdom of Heaven Quartz, Trigonic; Tremolite
Knights Templar Iolite
Knowledge, access Apatite, Blue; Cavansite; Black Andradite Garnet; Sunstone
knowledge fields Pallasite Meteorite
knowledge, higher Satyaloka Quartz
Kundalini Brookite; Cinnabar; Crocoite; Cuprite; Fulgurite; Almandine Garnet; Black Andradite Garnet; Infinite; Jasper, Red; Moldavite; Moonstone; Nebula Stone; Nickel-Iron Meteorite; Opal, Fire; Ruby; Russian Red Quartz; Seraphinite; Serpentine; Shiva Lingam; Stichtite; Strontianite; Tangerine Quartz
Kwan Yin Calcite, Pink, Transparent; Jade, Lavender; Quartz, Temple Heart Crystal (Dow); Smithsonite

language of Light Chalcedony, Blue
latent capacities, activation Herderite
leadership Heliodore; Iolite-Sunstone; Malachite; Strombolite; Sunstone
learning Apatite, Golden; Diopside; Dumortierite; Fluorite; Herderite; Rutile; Sphene; Ulexite
legal situations Azez Lemuria; Cathedral Quartz; Lemurian Seed Crystals; Quartz (Clear)
Lemuria Aqua Lemuria; Azeztulite, Lemurian Gold; Lemurian Mist Crystals; White Phantom Quartz
letting go Sapphire, Pink
ley lines Diopside; Infinite; Jasper, Picture
liberation Cryolite; Scapolite
life, enjoyment Ocean Jasper; Seriphos Green Quartz; Zoisite
life force Amber; Andalusite; Cuprite; Eudialyte; Jasper, Mook; Marcasite; Ruby; Russian Red Quartz; Sphalerite; Spider Jasper; Titanium Quartz; Zincite; Zircon; Zoisite; *see also* prana, chi
light Amber; Amethyst; Apophyllite, Clear; Hollandite Quartz; Satyaloka Quartz
light activation Hemimorphite
Light body Ammonite, Rainbow; Apache Gold; Herderite; Phenacite
Light body activation Brucite, Golden
Light embodiment Star Ruby
light frequencies Aegirine
light in darkness Beryllonite
lightheartedness Brucite, Golden; Crocodile Rock; Gem Silica
liminal threshold Cassiterite
linking higher and lower self Prasiolite
linking mind and heart Tanzanite; Thulite
loneliness Andalusite
longevity Amber; Rose Quartz
loss Cavansite
lost information, retrieval Datolite
lost objects Staurolite
love Adamite; Bixbite; Clinochlore; Crocoite; Emerald; Gaia Stone; Goethite, Rainbow; Lemurian Jade; Lepidocrocite; Lilac Lepidolite; Rhodonite; Rose Quartz; Sapphire, Pink; Smithsonite; Stilbite; Tourmaline, Pink; Tugtupite
love and will, blending Pyromorphite
love attractor Chrysoprase
love for the Earth Tugtupite
love, interpersonal Hiddenite
love, physical Almandine Garnet
love relationship Bixbitre; Almandine Garnet
love, unconditional Calcite, Pink, Transparent; Charoite; Scapolite; Tiger Eye
Love, Universal Smithsonite
lovingkindness Jade, Green; Trulite Silica
lucid dreaming Agate, Holly Blue; Albite; Angel Phantom Quartz; Covellite; Dream Quartz; Goshenite; Kyanite; Lazulite; Obsidian, Peacock; Rhodizite; Blue Sapphire; Scolecite; Sodalite; Staurolite; Sugilite
loyalty Goshenite;

magic Cerussite; Cinnabar; Jet; Labradorite; Merlinite; Nuummite; Onyx; Opal, Black Precious; Opal, Owyhee Blue; Pietersite; Spider Jasper; Strombolite
magic, benevolent Pyromorphite
Magic Presence Chalcedony, Purple; Stichtite
Magician Cuprite
Magician archetype Cinnabar
magnetic therapy Magnetite
magnifier of intentions Amazonite; Gray Moonstone
manifestation Apache Gold; Apatite, Golden; Brazilianite; Calcite, Clear; Cinnabar; Citrine; Gaspeite; Heliodore; Hematite; Imperial Gold Quartz; Spessartine; Uvarovite Garnet; Lemurian Jade; Libyan Gold Tektite; Obsidian, Gold Sheen; Opal, Black Precious; Petalite; Pyrite; Pyromorphite; Star Ruby; Rutilated Quartz; Rutile; Yellow Sapphire; Smoky Quartz; Tiger Iron; Topaz, Golden; Wulfenite, Zincite
manifestation and destruction Carnelian
marriage Moldavite
martial arts Jade, Red
mathematics Benitoite; Datolite; Goshenite
meditation Amethyst; Apophyllite, Clear; Aragonite, Blue; Brookite; Calcite, Green; Danburite; Diamond; Diaspore; Dioptase; Dream Quartz; Gel Lithium Silica; Gem Silica; Grape Agate; Halite; Healer's Gold; Herderite; Lilac Lepidolite; Lithium Quartz; Merlinite; Moonstone; Natrolite; Obsidian, Peacock; Opal, Common; Opal, Black Precious; Petalite; Phenacite; Prophecy Stone; Proustite; Quartz (Clear); Quartz, Initiation Crystal (Channeling); Rhodizite; Russian Red Quartz; Rutilated Quartz; Blue Sapphire; Scolecite; Sodalite; Sphene; Staurolite; Stibnite; Tibetan Black Quartz; Tiger Eye; Tourmaline, Blue; Tremolite; Vivianite
mediumship, *see* clairvoyance
memory Albite; Dumortierite; Herderite; Jasper, Red; Lazulite; Quartz (Clear); Sphene
memory, genetic Goethite
memorization Datolite
memory recovery Rhodochrosite
mental ability Albite; Cinnabar; Datolite; Blue Sapphire; Titanium Quartz; Ulexite
mental body Albite
mental clarity Adamite; Albite; Citrine; Siberian Blue Quartz; Sphene; Topaz, White

mental discipline Dumortierite
mental discomfort Papagoite
mental energy Jasper, Fancy, Kammererite
mental enhancement Diaspore; Fluorite; Sodalite
mental focus Ametrine; Lazulite; Libyan Gold Tektite
meridians Magnetite; Moldavite
Merkabah Vehicle of Light Papagoite
mind Calcite, Pink, Opaque; Heliodor; Topaz, Blue
mind/heart integration Amegreen
moderation Dolomite
morphogenic fields Pallasite Meteorite
mood swings Agate, Moss; Obsidian, Rainbow
morphic fields of knowledge Tremolite; White Phantom Quartz
multi-level awareness Agate, Holly Blue; Calcite, Clear; Cathedral Quartz
multidimensional self Astrophyllite
music of the spheres Danburite; Elestial Quartz; Fairy Wand Quartz; Golden Labradorite
musicians, *see* creative people
mystery Silver (Metal); Moonstone

namaste Prasiolite
Nameless Light Satyaloka Quartz
nature connection Devalite; Jasper, Rainforest; K2; Lyanite; Prasiolite; Serpentine
nature, heart of Serpentine
Nature spirits Agate, Moss; Apache Tears; Apatite, Green; Apophyllite, Green; Brookite; Chlorite Phantom Crystals; Devalite; Gaia Stone; Hemimorphite; Jasper, Rainforest; Oogulite; Tourmaline, Green; Tourmaline, Watermelon
negative attachments Lithium Quartz; Merlinite-Amethyst; Vesuvianite
negative energies Agate, Holly Blue; Aqua Aura Quartz; Azeztulite, Blue-Green; Jet; Merlinite-Amethyst; Obsidian, Gold Sheen; Pyromorphite; Smoky Quartz
negative entities, protection against Aegirine; Merlinite-Amethyst; Quartz (Clear); Trigonic Quartz;
negative influences Agate, Purple Sage; Tourmalined Quartz
negative psychic 'implants' Merlinite-Amethyst; Obsidian, Mahogany
negative thought patterns Citrine, Heat Treated; Jade, Purple; Pyromorphite; Thulite
negativity, internalized Charoite
negativity, purging Charoite; Jade, Black; Obsidian, Black; Ocean Jasper
negativity, transformation Euclase
new directions Calcite, Honey
new paradigm Rose Quartz
newborns Cassiterite
night terror Angel Phantom Quartz
nightmares Angel, Aura Quartz; Charoite; Dream Quartz; Gaia Stone; Tibetan Black Quartz
nobility Heliodore

objectivity Albite
observation Sodalite
OM Tibetan Black Quartz
oneness with the All Shiva Lingam
opening the heart Halite
opportunity Willemite
optimism Agate, Ellensburg Blue; Angel Aura Quartz; Aventurine, Green; Citrine, Heat Treated; Crocodile Rock Natrolite; Moonstone, Rainbow; Obsidian Rainbow; Opal, Fire; Ruby; Sugilite
oracles Pietersite; Shattuckite; Sodalite
order Fluorite
organization Smoky Quartz
orgone generator Rhodizite
originality Wulfenite
out-of-body experience Astrophyllite; Calcite, Stellar Beam; Papagoite; Rhodizite; Scapolite; Sphene

pain, release Aragonite Star Clusters
panic Chalcedony, Blue; Larimar;
paradox Muscovite Azeztulite, Green-Fire;
paranormal abilities Benitoite; Diamond
paranormal activity Agate, Holly Blue;
passion Agate, Fire; Azeztulite, Green-Fire; Bixbite; Crocoite; Jade, Red; Kammererite; Gold (Metal); Opal, Fire; Ruby; Sapphire, Pink; Tangerine Quartz; Tugtupite; Zincite
passive aggressive behavior Calcite, Pink, Opaque
past civilizations Cathedral Quartz; Heulandite
past life Amber; Angelite; Apatite; Blue; Azeztulite, Black Tourmaline; Black Shadow Quartz; Covellite; Dream Quartz; Elestial Quartz; Iolite; Jet; Lazulite; Nuummite; Obsidian, Snowflake; Opal, Common; Opal, Oregon; Papagoite; Quartz (Clear); Portal Quartz (Time Link); Scapolite; Sichuan Quartz; Sphene
past-life learning Almandine Garnet
past-life memories Apache Gold; Dioptase; Goethite; K2; Kyanite; Labradorite; Merlinite; Petrified Wood; Quartz (Clear); Quartz, Raised Record Keeper; White Phantom Quartz
patience Dolomite; Petrified Wood
path of service Charoite
pattern recognition Sodalite
peace Adularia; Agate, Moss; Angel Aura Quartz; Aqua Aura Quartz; Azeztulite, New Zealand White; Dioptase; Gem Silica; Grape Agate; Heartenite; Lilac Lepidolite; Moonstone Polarity; Opal, Common; Pink Amethyst; Smithsonite; Spirit Quartz; Sugilite; Turquoise
peacemaker Amazonite
perception Opal, Owyhee Blue; Smithsonite
perseverance Adamite; Jasper, Fancy; Obsidian, Black; Obsidian, Snowflake; Onyx; Zincite
persistence Agate, Moss; Auralite, Emerald; Calcite, Honey; Goshenite; Jasper, Unakite; Pyrite; Scapolite; Dravite; Vanadinite
personal power Petalite; Protector Quartz; Onyx; Zincite
personal will Citrine
perspective Stibnite
phobias Larimar
physical disruption, protection Faden Quartz
physical life, spiritualization Herkimer Quartz 'Diamond'
planetary consciousness Satyaloka Quartz
planetary healing Jasper, Rainforest
playfulness Calcite, Orange; Kammererite; Oogulite; Opal, Fire; Sapphire, Padparadscha; Tangerine Quartz; Vanadinite
pleasure Ammonite, Rainbow; Thulite
poets, *see* creative people
polarities, balancing Agate, Denritic; Hematite Magnets; Shaman Stone
poltergeists Pyromorphite
positive outlook Agate, Denritic; Apache Tears; Calcite, Blue; Healer's Gold; Strontianite
positive patterns Epidote
potential, personal Libyan Gold Tektite
poverty consciousness, overcoming Uvarovite Garnet
power Amblygonite; Golden Labradorite; Heliodore; Titanium (Metal); Purpurite; Rhodizite; Stibnite
power of the underworld Stibnite
practicality Flint; Strontianite
prana Calcite, Red; Cuprite; Flint; Healer's Gold; Jade, Red;

Shiva Lingam; Tiger Iron; Rubellite; Tremolite
prana yama Aragonite, Blue
prayer Fulgurite; Gel Lithium Silica; Gem Silica; Goshenite
pre-brith state Calcite, Stella Beam
precognition Pietersite
prescience Chalcedony, Purple
prefrontal lobes Lazurlite; Phenacite
probable futures Elestial Quartz; Nebula Stone; Prophecy Stone
problem solving Muscovite
procrastination Amblygonite; Ametrine; Calcite, Honey; Spirit Quartz
programmability Quartz (Clear)
prophecy Celestite; Chalcedony, Purple; Siberian Blue Quartz; Tourmaline, Blue
prophetic vision Apophyllite, Clear; Chrysoberyl; Dumortierite; Phenacite; Prophecy Stone
prosperity Apache Gold; Cassiterite; Chrysanthemum Stone; Chrysoprase; Dioptase; Emerald; Grossular; Uvarovite Garnet; Jade, Green; Jade, Red; Pallasite Meteorite; Peridot; Quartz (Clear); Ruby; Yellow Sapphire; Stibnite; Sunstone; Tourmaline, Golden; Variscite
protection Aegirine; Agate, Purple Sage; Amber; Amethyst; Andalusite; Apache Tears; Charoite; Black Andradite Garnet; Jade, Black; Jet; Labradorite; Malachite; Moldavite; Ruby; Smoky Quartz; Spirit Quartz; Stichtite; Tourmaline, Black
psychic activation Apatite, Blue; K2;
psychic abilities Agate, Ellensburg Blue; Agate, Holly Blue; Agate, Purple Sage; Albite; Amegreen; Amethyst; Aragonite, Blue; Benitoite; Calcite, Blue; Chalcedony, Purple; Chrysoberyl, Cat's Eye; Cinnabar; Covellite; Crocoite; Dream Quartz; Dumortierite; Flint; Fluorite; Halite; Herderite; Jade, Purple; Jade, Blue; Kammererite; Kunzite; Kyanite; Lazulite; Silver (Metal); Natrolite; Nuummite; Papagonite; Phenacite; Rhodizite; Rutilated Quartz; Rutile; Blue Sapphire; Scapolite; Siberian Blue Quartz; Sichuan Quartz; Tektite; Topaz, Blue; Tugtupite; Zircon
psychic attachments Protector Quartz
psychic attack Andalusite; Aqua Aura Quartz; Dream Quartz; Muscovite; Obsidian, Mahogany; Opal, Common; Opal, Owyhee Blue; Scapolite
psychic attunement Angelite; Apache Tears; Aventurine, Blue; Iolite; Jade, Lavender; Merlinite
psychic awakening Benitoite; Rhodizite; Siberian Blue Quartz
psychic awareness Lemurian Mist Crystals
psychic centers of the brain Agate, Holly Blue
psychic clearing Halite
psychic communication Brookite; Sichuan Quartz
psychic entitites Marcasite
psychic gifts Iolite; Sapphire, White; Topaz, White; Tourmaline, Blue
psychic healers Adamite
Psychic implants Azeztulite, New Zealand White; Protector Quartz
Psychic perception Agate, Ellensburg Blue; Angel Wing Blue Anhydrite; Aqua Lemuria; Eudialyte; Magnesite; Natrolite; Rainbow Moonstone; White Moonstone
psychic powers Nebula Stone; Petalite; Rutile
psychic protection Agate, Purple Sage; Andalusite; Apache Tears; Aqua Aura Quartz; Benitoite; Almandine Garnet; Golden Aura Quartz; Labradorite; Lepidocrocite; Libyan Gold Tektite; Obsidian, Black; Obsidian, Peacock; Purpurite; Shaman Stone; Tourmaline, Black; Tourmalined Quartz
psychic reading Albite; Labradorite; Prehnite
psychic surgery Calcite, Stellar Beam
psychic vampirism Adamite; Infinite; Proustite
psychic vision Calcite, Clear; Pietersite; Quartz (Clear); Blue Sapphire; Sodalite
psychics Covellite; Niobium (Metal)
psychokinesis Cavansite; Dumortierite; Lazulite; Phenacite; Siberian Blue Quartz
psychometry Cavansite; Chalcedony, Purple; Dumortierite
purification Amethyst; Bloodstone; Cacozenite; Chalcedony, Purple; Fulgurite; Grape Agate; Hanksite; Herkimer Quartz 'Diamond'; Jade, Black; Jet; Lepidolite; Opal, Common, Pink; Opal, White Precious; Protector Quartz; Purpurite; Selenite; Spirit Quartz; Sugilite; Tibetan Black Quartz; Tourmaline, Black; Tourmalined Quartz
purification, aura Jade, Purple
purification, energy field Agate, Dendritic
purifications, spiritual Agate, Ellensburg Blue; Agate, Purple Sage
purpose Agate, Fire; Golden Labradorite

qi gong Jade, Red
quickness Sphene

radiance Diamond
Rainbow Body Niobium (Metal); Rainbow Moonstone; Titanium Quartz
rapport Stombolite; Thulite
rapture Clinochlore; Purpurite; Sapphire, Padparadscha; Tourmaline, Blue; Tremolite; Tugtupite; Zoisite
reason Onyx
rebirth of hope, rebirthing Obsidian, Mahogany; Shaman Stone; Shiva Lingam
receptivity Girasol Quartz; Kunzite
recovery of knowledge Benitoite
regeneration of the body Cacoxenite; Chlorite Phantom Crystals; Hollandite Quartz; Seraphinite
reiki Danburite; Healer's Gold; Infinite
relationships Clinochlore; Gaia Stone; Hiddenite; Lithium Quartz
relaxation Agate, Ellensburg Blue; Apatite, Green; Aqua Aura Quartz; Calcite, Green; Dream Quartz; Fairy Wand Quartz; Gel Lithium Silica; Healer's Gold; Lepidolite; Ocean Jasper; Scolecite; Strombolite; Titanium Quartz; Tourmaline, Pink
release of anger Calcite, Pink, Opaque
release of negativity Epidote
release of stress Dream Quartz; Trulite Silica
relief Agate, Ellensburg Blue
remote viewing Ablite; Apophyllite, Clear; Benitoite; Covellite; Diamond; Lazulite; Phenacite; Ulexite
resentment Angel Wing Blue Anhydrite; Danburite
resilience Sapphire, Pink; Stichite
revitalization Apatite, Green; Spinel
retrieval of lost (ancient) information Andalusite
retrieval of lost soul parts Quartz, Trigonic Quartz
'return to paradise' Lemurian Seed Crystals
revelation Cavansite
revitalization Rhodizite
risk taking Agate, Fire
romance Strontianite; Thulite
royal virtue Labradorite

sacred expression Aqua Lemuria; Chrysocolla
samadhi Angel Aura Quartz
scrying Merlinite; Obsidian, Black; Onyx
'seat of the soul' Tourmaline, Watermelon

security Almandine Garnet
self-acceptance Angel wing Blue Anhydrite; Astrophyllite; Nirvana Quartz; Dravite;
self-confidence Heliodore; Protector Quartz; Ruby; Spider Jasper
self-discipline Aventurine, Blue; Flint; Iolite-Sunstone; Lazulite; Scapolite; Sodalite
self-discovery Astrophyllite; Transmutite
self-doubt Eudialyte
self-esteem Bixbite; Golden Labradorite; Opal, Oregon; Tanzanite
self-healing Chlorite Phantom Crystals; Lepidocrocite; Moldavite; Seraphinite; Spider Jasper; Tiger Iron; Dravite
self-knowledge Amazonite; Astrophyllite; Stilbite; Transmutite; Turquoise
self-judgment Black Phantom Quartz
self-love Eudialyte; Pink Halite; Rhodochrosite; Thulite; Dravite
self-mastery Nuummite; Onyx; Strontianite
self, positive Ocean Jasper
self-sabotage Apatite, Golden
self transformation Pietersite; Scapolite
self-worth Apatite, Golden; Rhodolite Garnet; Mahogany Obsidian; Protector Quartz; Spirit Quartz; Strontianite
sensory awareness Calcite, Red
sensual pleasure Ruby
Seraphim Lemurian Seed Crystals; Seraphinite
serenity Angel aura Quartz; Angelite; Azeztulite, Sedona; Celestite; Gel Lithium Silica; Girasol Quartz; Jade, Lavender; Lepidolite; Lilac Lepidolite; Scolecite; Seriphos Green Quartz; Variscite
'serpent power' Serpentine
service to the world Quartz (Clear): Trigonic Quartz
sexual abuse Calcite, Orange; Calcite, Honey
sexual energy Jade, Red; Jasper, Red; Kammererite; Marcasite; Ruby; Sapphire, Padparadscha; Vanadinite; Willemite
sexuality Adamite; Agate, Fire; Bustamite; Calcite, Orange; Carnelian; Spessartine; Marcasite; Gold (Metal); Opal, Fire; Russian Red Quartz; Sapphire, Padparadscha; Strontianite; Sunstone; Wulfenite
shadow Covellite; Proustite
shadow material Black Phantom Quartz
shadow, reclaiming Proustite
shakti Jet
shamanic journey Amber; Blizzard Stone; Iolite; Jade, Purple; Jade, Black; Merlinite-Amethyst; Obsidian, Peacock; Opal, Common; Opal, Owyhee Blue; Prophecy Stone; Shaman Stone; Sodalite; Sphene; Spider Jasper
shamanic practice Adamite; Cataclosite Impact Stone; Jasper, Fancy; Opal, Black Precious; Prophecy Stone
shaman Gray Moonstone; Quartz (Clear); Trigonic Quartz
shame Obsidian, Mahogany; Thulite
shape-shifting Cinnabar
shield of Light Sugilite
shyness Calcite, Orange
Sirius Calcite, Stellar Beam
social phobias Calcite, Green
solar energy Amber; Heliodore
soothing Aquamarine; Gel Lithium Silica; Larimar
soothing the emotional body Calcite, Blue; Lilac Lepidolite; Smithsonite; Topaz, Blue
sorrow, release Alexandrite
sorrow, transmutation Papagoite
soul energy Crocoite;
soul life Goethite
soul mate Chalcedony, Purple; Morganite
soul of the earth Gaia Stone
Soul of the World Azeztulite, Green-Fire, Heartenite;
soul potential Cathedral Quartz
soul purpose Chrysanthemum Stone
soul retrieval Iolite; Jade, Black; Lepidocrocite; Nuummite; Pink Amethyst; Shaman Stone
sound healers Aragonite, Blue
sovereignty Diamond; Imperial Gold Quartz; Purpurite
speaking in tongues Chalcedony, Blue; Speculite Hematite, *see* Hematite; Spessartine, *see* Garnet
spirit communication Merlinite; Merlinite-Amethyst; Obsidian, Snowflake; Obsidian, Peacock; Pink Amethyst; Shattuckite
spirit guides Dream Quartz; Hemimorphite; Platinum (Metal); Opal, Owyhee Blue; Selenite; Smoky Quartz; White Phantom Quartz
spiritual activation Selenite
spiritual assistance Goshenite
spiritual awareness Quartz (Clear); Strontianite; Tanzanite
spiritual blueprint Phenacite
spiritual commitment Euclase
spiritual connection Amegreen
spiritual courage Agni Gold Danburite; Phenacite
spiritual destiny Diamond
spiritual energy Quartz, Integration Crystal (Transmitter)
spiritual enlightenment Apophyllite; Cavansite; Datolite; K2; Moldavite; Satyaloka Quartz; Vivianite
spiritual evolution, rapid Moldavite; Spirit Quartz
spiritual expression Gaspeite
spiritual growth Ametrine; Azeztulite, Black Tourmaline; Blizzard Stone; Scheelite; Turquoise
spiritual guides Agate, Holly Blue; Agate, Purple Sage; Angel Wing Blue Anhydrite; Apophyllite, Clear; Calcite, Stellar Beam; Covellite; Lepidocrocite; Pink Amethyst;
spiritual healing Angelite
spiritual history Serpentine
spiritual information Cathedral Quartz
spiritual initiation Kammererite; Willemite
spiritual insight Angelite; Apophyllite, Clear; Gaspeite; Herderite; Hollandite Quartz; Jade, Green; Jade, Blue; Jet; K2; Quartz, Integration Crystal (Transmitter); Sapphire, White
spiritual light Azeztulite, Black Tourmaline; Azeztulite, Blue-Green; Azeztulite, New Zealand White; Nebula Stone
spiritual path Rhodolite Garnet
spiritual protection Golden Aura Quartz; Protector Quartz; Tibetan Black Quartz
spiritual strength Sapphire, White; Sugilite
spiritual transformation Fulgurite; Shiva Lingam
spiritual truth Cryolite
spiritual twin Agate, Moss; Chalcedony, Purple
spiritual warrior Bloodstone
spirituality Marcasite; Topaz, White
spontaneity Oogulite;
stability Agate, Moss; Aragonite, Blue; Gel Lithium Silica
stagnation, release Calcite, Clear; Sichuan Quartz
'stairway to heaven' Lemurian Seed Crystals
stamina Bixbite; Pyrite; Tiger Iron; Tourmaline, Green; Vanadinite
Star Seed Chondrite Meteorite; Quartz, Sunken Record Keeper
state of grace Papagoite; Stibnite
stimulant, mental Goshenite; Muscovite
stone energies Copper (Metal)
stone of Avalon Adularia
stone of eternal youth Agate, Fire

stone of miracles Benitoite
stone of Shambhala Moldavite; Tektite
stone of the Goddess Adularia; Chrysocolla
stone of the Grail Moldavite
stone of the muses Ametrine; Iolite
stone of truth Hanksite
strength Aragonite Star Clusters; Bloodstone; Almandine Garnet; Heliodore; Hematite; Jade, Red; Petrified Wood; Ruby; Sphalerite; Strontianite; Sunstone; Tiger Eye; Tiger Iron
stress Amblygonite; Apatite, Green; Fairy Wand Quartz; Opal, Common; Tremolite
stress, release of Calcite, Green; Danburite; Lepidolite; Lilac Lepidolite; Lithium Quartz; Ocean Jasper; Rose Quartz; Smithsonite; Staurolite; Tourmaline, Pink
structure, creating Flint; Sodalite
stubbornness Black Phantom Quartz
study Fluorite
subconscious Sodalite
subtle bodies Aegirine
subtle energies Infinite
subtle perception Diopside
subtle vision Datolite
'supramental force' Prophecy Stone
surrender Ajoite; Cryolite
synchronicity Benitoite; Charoite; Chrysanthemum Stone; Euclase; Eudialyte; Malachite; Merlinite; Moldavite; Natrolite; Nuummite; Obsidian, Snowflake; Opal, Common; Quartz (Clear); Ruby; Willemite
Synergy Twelve stones Azeztulite; Brookite; Danburite; Herderite; Moldavite; Natrolite; Petalite; Phenacite; Satyaloka Quartz; Scolecite; Tanzanite; Tibetan Tektite
Synergy, heart-brain Nirvana Quartz
synesthesia Shattuckite
synthesis Dumortierite; Titanium (Metal); Sodalite

tai chi Jade, Red
tantric love-making Crocoite
tantric practice Calcite, Red; Star Ruby
tarot Creedite; Dumortierite; Herderite; Iolite; Pietersite
teaching stone Chrysocolla
telekinesis Natrolite; Onyx
telepathy Apophyllite, Green; Calcite, Blue; Chalcedony, Blue; Diamond; Gaia Stone; Hemimorphite; K2; Kyanite; Labradorite; Lazulite; Mucovite; Natrolite; Petalite; Phenacite; Pietersite; Quartz; Rhodizite; Rutilated Quartz; Scapolite; Tektite; Ulexite
therapy Chalcedony, Blue
third-eye chakra Phenacite
third eye stimulation Angel Wing Blue Anhydrite; Phenacite
'thousand-petaled lotus' Magnesite
thrift Strontianite
time stream of the future Nirvana Quartz
time travel Benitoite; Herkimer Quartz 'Diamond'; Sphene
total union, *see* samadhi
toxins, clearing Hanksite
tranquility Adularia; Angel Aura Quartz; Angelite; Petalite; Scolecite
trance states Sodalite
transformation Cataclosite Impact Stone; Cerussite; Covellite; (Metal): Platinum; Moldavite; Quartz (Clear); Tugtupite
transition Lemurian Jade
trauma, emotional Cuprite; Lepidolite
trickster Stibnite
trust Nirvana Quartz
truth Agni Gold Danburite; Ajoite; Aquamarine; Devalite; Jasper, Red; Purpurite; Tanzanite; Turquoise
truth of the heart Kyanite

UFOs Sichuan Quartz; Smoky Quartz
unconscious Silver (Metal)
union of heart and will Prehnite; Vesuvianite
unworthiness Rhodolite Garnet; Hiddenite

verbal communication Shattuckite
vertical dimension Agate, Holly Blue
vibrational level Tektite
victory Spinel
viewing, distance Rhodizite
Violet Flame Sugilite
visionary ability Dumortierite; Iolite; Iolite-Sunstone; Jade, Lavender; Rhodizite
visionary experience Beryllonite; Danburite; Dream Quartz; Herkimer Quartz 'Diamond'; Heulandite; Natrolite
vitality Agate, Fire; Amber; Adventurine, Green; Bixbite; Bustamite; Calcite, Red; Carnelian; Clinochlore; Eudialyte; Golden Labradorite; Iolite-Sunstone; Jade, Red; Marcasite; Gold (Metal); Titanium (Metal); Pyrite; Ruby; Sphalerite; Strontianite; Tiger Eye; Tiger Iron; Titanium Quartz; Tourmaline, Green; Turquoise
Void of Potential Spider Jasper
vulnerability Sapphire, Pink; Stilbite; Tourmaline, Pink

walk-ins Astrophyllite; Goethite; Platinum (Metal); Pallasite Meteorite
warmth Amber; Peridot
wealth Agate, Moss; Alexandrite; Cinnabar; Emerald; Rutile; Yellow Sapphire
well-being Apatite, Green; Calcite, Pink, Opaque; Goethite, Rainbow; Healer's Gold; Peridot; Spider Jasper; Staurolite
White Light Phenacite; Satyaloka Quartz
white magic Black Andradite Garnet
wholeness Calcite, Pink, Opaque; Seraphinite; Tanzanite; Tourmaline, Green; Trulite Silica; Turquoise
will Agate, Fire; Amblygonite; Apache Gold; Golden Labradorite; Heliodore; Opal, Owyhee Blue; Pietersite; Yellow Sapphire; Sphene; Tiger Iron; Topaz, Golden; Tourmaline, Golden
willpower Marcasite; Onyx; Pyrite; Scapolite
wisdom Agate, Dendritic; Alexandrite; Jade, Red; Sphene; Sunstone; Tanzanite; Turquoise
Wisdom Eye Natrolite
work Vanadinite
worry Agate, Purple Sage; Almandine Garnet; Gel Lithium Silica; Lepidolite; Opal, Common; Tourmaline, Pink
wound, emotional Moonstone, Rainbow; Obsidian, Mahogany
writer's block Rutile

Yang polarity Malachite
Yin energy Gel Lithium Silica

zest for living Agate, Fire; Sapphire, Padparadscha

RECOMMENDED READING

Love and the Soul, by Robert Sardello. North Atlantic Books, ISBN 10 1556437536

Silence: The Mystery of Wholeness, by Robert Sardello. North Atlantic Books, ISBN 10 1556437935

Jung and the Alchemical Imagination, by Jeffrey Raff. Hays (Nicolas) Ltd, ISBN 10 0892540451

The Wedding of Sophia: The Divine Feminine in Psychoidal Alchemy, by Jeffrey Raff. Hays (Nicolas) Ltd, ISBN 10 0892540664

The Practice of Ally Work: Meeting and Partnering with Your Spirit guide in the Imaginal World, by Jeffrey Raff. Hays (Nicolas) Ltd, ISBN 10 0892541210

Alchemical Active Imagination, by Marie-Louise von Franz. Shambhala Publications Inc., ISBN 10 0877735891

Jung on Alchemy, by C. G. Jung, Nathan Schwartz-Salant (Editor). Taylor & Francis Ltd.; ISBN 10 0415089697

Psychology and Alchemy, by C.G. Jung. Taylor & Francis Ltd.; ISBN 10 0415034523

Memories, Dreams, Reflections, by C.G. Jung. Random House Inc.; ISBN 10 0679723951

Sophia–Goddess of Wisdom, by Caitlain Matthews. HarperCollins Publishers, ISBN 10 0044405898

Indra's Net: Alchemy and Chaos theory as Models for Transformation, by Robin Robertson. Quest Books, ISBN 10 083560862X

The Emerald Tablet, by Dennis Hauck. J.P. Tarcher/Perigee Bks., ISBN 10 0140195718

The Winged Energy of Delight: Selected Translations, by Robert Bly. Harper Perrenial; ISBN 10 0060575867

The Other Within: The Genius of Deformity in Myth, Culture and Psyche, by Daniel Deardorff. North Atlantic Books,U.S.; ISBN 10 1556437609

The Biology of Transcendence: A Blueprint for the Human Spirit, by Joseph Chilton Pearce. Inner Traditions Bear and Company; ISBN 10 0892819901

Jump Girl: The Initiation of a Spirit Speaker, by Salicrow. North Atlantic Books, ISBN 10 162317192X

The Book of Stones: Who They Are and What They Teach, by Robert Simmons and Naisha Ahsian. North Atlantic Books, ISBN 10 1583949089

Stones of the New Consciousness, by Robert Simmons. North Atlantic Books, ISBN 10 1556438117

Earthfire: A Tale of Transformation, by Robert Simmons. Heaven & Earth Books; ISBN 10 0962191027

The Pocket Book of Stones, by Robert Simmons. North Atlantic Books, ISBN 10 158394317X

Moldavite: Starborn Stone of Transformation, by Robert Simmons and Kathy Helen Warner. Heaven & Earth Books; ISBN 10 0962191000

RESOURCES

Robert Simmons continues to write about newly emerging stones and their spiritual qualities. Readers who wish to keep up on these new writings are encouraged to request the Heaven and Earth catalog and newsletter, which is published and distributed free of charge twice a year. Heaven and Earth also sends out regular email updates. To request a printed catalog, and/or to sign up for the email list, call 802 476 4775 or send an email with your information to: heavenandearth@earthlink.net

The Heaven and Earth catalog and website offer thousands of high-energy stone and jewelry items, including all the stones discussed in *The Alchemy of Stones.* To visit the website, go to www.heavenandearthjewelry.com

YouTube: To view Robert Simmons' videos about working with stones and their metaphysical energies, visit the Heaven and Earth YouTube Channel: heavenearthone

Robert Simmons offers Stone Workshops and Intensives in the USA, Japan, New Zealand, Australia and other countries. To receive notifications about these events, or to inquire about sponsoring an event with Robert, send an email to: heavenandearth@earthlink.net

Heaven and Earth offers video recordings of Robert's Intensive Workshops. To purchase these, visit the Heaven and Earth website, or call 802 476 4775.

Robert Simmons' other books include: *The Book of Stones: Who They Are and What They Teach* (with Naisha Ahsian), *Stones of the New Consciousness, The Pocket Book of Stones, Moldavite: Starborn Stone of Transformation* (with Kathy Helen Warner), and *Earthfire: A Tale of Transformation.* All of these books are available through the Heaven and Earth website, www.heavenandearthjewelry.com. Phone orders: 802 476 4775

Kathy Helen Warner works with an intuitive inner process to create visionary collage pieces that she calls Spirit Art. Her Spirit Art Cards are available through Heaven and Earth's USA website: www.heavenandearthjewelry.com. Larger prints of her pieces are available in the Heaven and Earth gallery in Tairua, New Zealand. To view some of Kathy's work, and to read about her visionary process, visit her website: www.womansway.com.

Consultations with Psychic Medium Salicrow*: For those who wish to explore to possibility of communicating with departed loved ones, or who are seeking psychic counseling, Robert recommends contacting Salicrow, a gifted medium in Vermont. Sali sees clients in person, and via online video sessions. For information, visit her website: salicrow.com

*__NOTE:__ This recommendation is based on Robert's personal experiences as a client, and assumes no responsibility for the experiences of other clients who consult Salicrow.

ABOUT THE AUTHOR

Robert Simmons has been a student and investigator of many spiritual paths since a spontaneous mystical experience during his first year at Yale changed the course of his life. Fifteen years later, his encounter with Moldavite activated his latent capacity for perceiving stone energies. This shifted and expanded his horizons yet again. In 1986, he married Kathy Helen Warner, and together they established their company, Heaven and Earth, which began as a crystal shop specializing in Moldavite, and expanded into a mail order company offering thousands of stone, gem and jewelry items to both individuals and store owners all over the world. Kathy and Robert are the co-authors of *Moldavite: Starborn Stone of Transformation.*

In 2013, Robert and Kathy moved to New Zealand's Coromandel Peninsula, and in 2016 they opened a Heaven and Earth crystal, stone and jewelry shop in Tairua, New Zealand. Both the USA and New Zealand companies continue to provide a huge array of minerals, gemstones and crystals for people who appreciate their energies and their beauty.

Robert has been writing and teaching about the metaphysical qualities of stones for over thirty years. In 2014, he began his exploration of spiritual alchemy. He soon realized that the work he and others had been doing with crystals and minerals had much in common with the ideas, aspirations and practices of the spiritual alchemists of past centuries. Further, he understood that the alchemical worldview has the capacity to greatly enrich and expand the experiences of healing and awakening that he and many others were seeking in their work with stones. He also recognized that envisioning the stones as Beings in their own right was a key to unlocking the spiritual secrets they offer. These insights led to the research that resulted in the writing of *The Alchemy of Stones.*

Robert is the author of several books, including *The Book of Stones, Stones of the New Consciousness, The Pocket Book of Stones,* and the award-winning visionary novel, *Earthfire: A Tale of Transformation.* He collects stories of individuals who have undergone profound spiritual experiences with Moldavite, Azeztulite, Phenacite, Rosophia, with other crystals and minerals, or with no stones at all. He believes that there is a great potential for worldwide transformation and enlightenment, and that engaging spiritually with the Stone Beings and the Soul of the World offers us a golden opportunity to actualize this possibility.

Robert offers Workshops and Intensives in the USA, Japan, Australia, New Zealand and other countries. Contact Heaven and Earth to find out about his schedule, or to discuss sponsoring an event with Robert.

To receive notifications about Robert's upcoming teaching events and new publications, or to share your stone story of healing and/or spiritual awakening, send an email request to heavenandearth@earthlink.net.